Encyclopedia of

JEWISH HISTORY

"Safed in the Galilee Mountains," painting by Reuben Rubin (1936). A spectacular primeval aspect and the holy and mysterious atmosphere surrounding its historic sites have given Safed, city of the *Kabbalah*, its special atmosphere.

Encyclopedia of JEWISH HISTORY

EVENTS AND ERAS OF THE JEWISH PEOPLE

Facts on File Publications
New York, New York • Oxford, England

Encyclopedia of JEWISH HISTORY

General Editors: Ilana Shamir, Shlomo Shavit

Editor of the English Edition: Joseph Alpher

Assistant Editors: Zehava Canaan, Bruria Ben-Baruch, Yaffa Gavish, Ruth Neugarten

Picture Editor: Naama Cifrony

Design and Production: Aryeh Ben-David, Doreet Scharfstein

Graphics: Ruthy Rosenblum, Eitan Ben-Tovim, Charles Goldin, Shlomo Mellul, Roma Annenburg

Maps and Diagrams: Dalia and Menahem Egozi, Ehud Oren, Carta

Translators: Haya Amir, Haya Galay, Sally Jacoby, Sara Kitai, Michal Moneta, Rachel Rowen, Riva Rubin, Shirley Shapira

Proofreaders: Ruth Lidor, Moshe Shalvi

Color Separations: Reprocolor Ltd.

Library of Congress Cataloging-in-Publication Data
Main entry under title:

Encyclopedia of Jewish history.

Includes index.
1. Jews-History-Dictionaries. I. Alpher, Joseph.
DS114.E53 1986 909'.04924'0321 85-23941
ISBN 0-8160-1220-2

Printed in Israel by Peli Printing Works Ltd.

10 9 8 7 6 5 4 3 2 1

Encyclopedia of JEWISH HISTORY

Writers: Dr. Ada Aharoni
Dr. Yom-Tov Assis
Eli Avrahami
Dr. Israel Bartal
Dr. Itzhak Bezalel
Shlomo Bunimovitz
Edna Elazari
Yossef Eshkol
Prof. Shmuel Ettinger
Dr. Giza Frankel
Dr. Isaiah Gafni
Dr. Abraham Gross
Prof. Avraham Grossman
David Hacham
Dr. Itzhak Handelsman
Prof. Simon Herman
Ida Huberman
Hava Katz
Dr. Yael Katzir
Dr. Dan Michman
Dr. Menachem Mor
Aviva Muller-Lancet
Prof. Yehuda Nini
Ruth Peleg
Dr. Dan Ronen
Israel Ronen
Dr. Shlomo Shavit
Ittai Tamari
Dr. Raphael Vago
Nissim Yosha

Advisors: Prof. Moshe Barash
Prof. Yoav Gelber
Prof. Binyamin Ze'ev Kadar
Prof. Charles Liebman
Prof. Hanoch Raviv

Contents

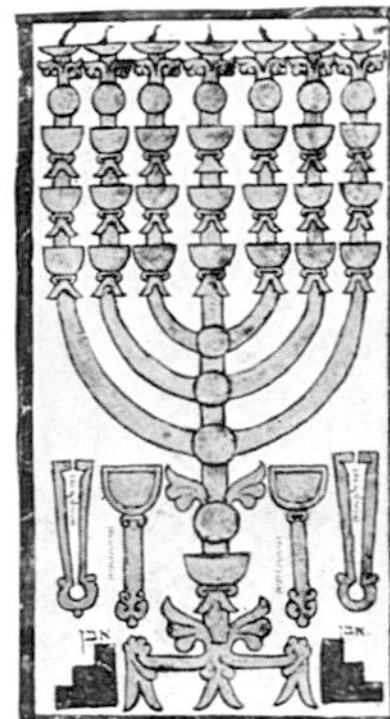

לא תרצח:
לא תנאף:
לא תגנב:
לא תענה:
אנכי לא תרצח
לא יהיה לך לא תנאף
לא תשא לא תגנב
לא תענה
כבד את לא תחמוד

Preface

The ENCYCLOPEDIA OF JEWISH HISTORY offers concise information about events, eras, and key figures in the annals of the Jewish people, from the dawn of its history until modern times: Ereẓ Israel during the period of the Bible, the Second Temple period, the time of the *Mishnah* and the *Talmud* in Ereẓ Israel and in the Diaspora, Jewish communities in Europe and in the East, the rise of Zionism, renewal of Jewish settlement in Ereẓ Israel, the Holocaust of European Jewry, the State of Israel, and the Jewish people today.

Israeli scholars, writers, and educators have joined together in writing this Encyclopedia, basing their contributions on the most recent studies and research. It includes 100 historical entries, and a dozen appendices on culture and ethnography. Each entry comprises a central article of around 800 words and some ten additional integrated feature items, including illustrations, photographs, maps, and diagrams. The feature items with their captions form an integral part of each subject and should be read along with the main article in order to obtain a full picture. The Encyclopedia is organized to be of use to the systematic reader as well as to the browser, or the reader who wishes to delve into isolated topics of special interest.

The **key**, an illustration appearing in the upper right hand corner of every entry, serves a double purpose. It provides a visual summary of the entry, and alludes to the body of facts related to the subject. **Connections**, appearing on each pair of pages, direct the reader to related chapters in the book. At the back of the book, a synchronic chart presents key events in the history of the Jewish people, against major events in general world history. The appendices on the development of the Hebrew letter and of Hebrew script provide the background for appreciating the developmental chronology of the manuscripts illustrated in this work. The

Moses on Mount Sinai, where the People of Israel undertook to follow God's commandments. Bible illumination from the Regensburg Manuscript, 14th century (facing page).

Ketuba from Afghanistan, 1859 (detail). Community and family customs ensured continuity of the traditions, precepts and beliefs of Judaism.

appendices on symbols in Jewish art and on Jewish costumes and paper-cuts add an ethnographic and cultural dimension. The last appendix is a glossary of the Hebrew and other foreign terms used in the Encyclopedia, which are generally transcribed and printed in italic face in the text. The glossary defines these terms, explains the concepts involved, and provides further elaboration. An index completes the book.

Much assistance has been given us in preparing the ENCYCLOPEDIA OF JEWISH HISTORY — from individuals, archives, museums, public institutions and enterprises. Their specific contributions are acknowledged in the list of credits. We wish to thank them all.

We hope that this book will bring the reader hours of enrichment and pleasure.

The Editors

The Structure of an Entry

A typical entry — A main article integrated with illustrative material, to present a general and comprehensive picture of the subject.

The main article — around 800 words long, presenting the subject of the entry.

Illustrations — photographs, drawings, and diagrams, which enrich the main article with valuable visual information.

Captions to illustrations — provide more detailed and informative descriptions.

The key — a single illustration that portrays or comprehensively sums up the subject discussed in the entry.

Connections — a list of cross references to entries in this and other volumes, related to the subject of this entry.

Markers — letters or numbers which identify parts of an illustration or which relate to descriptions in the text accompanying them.

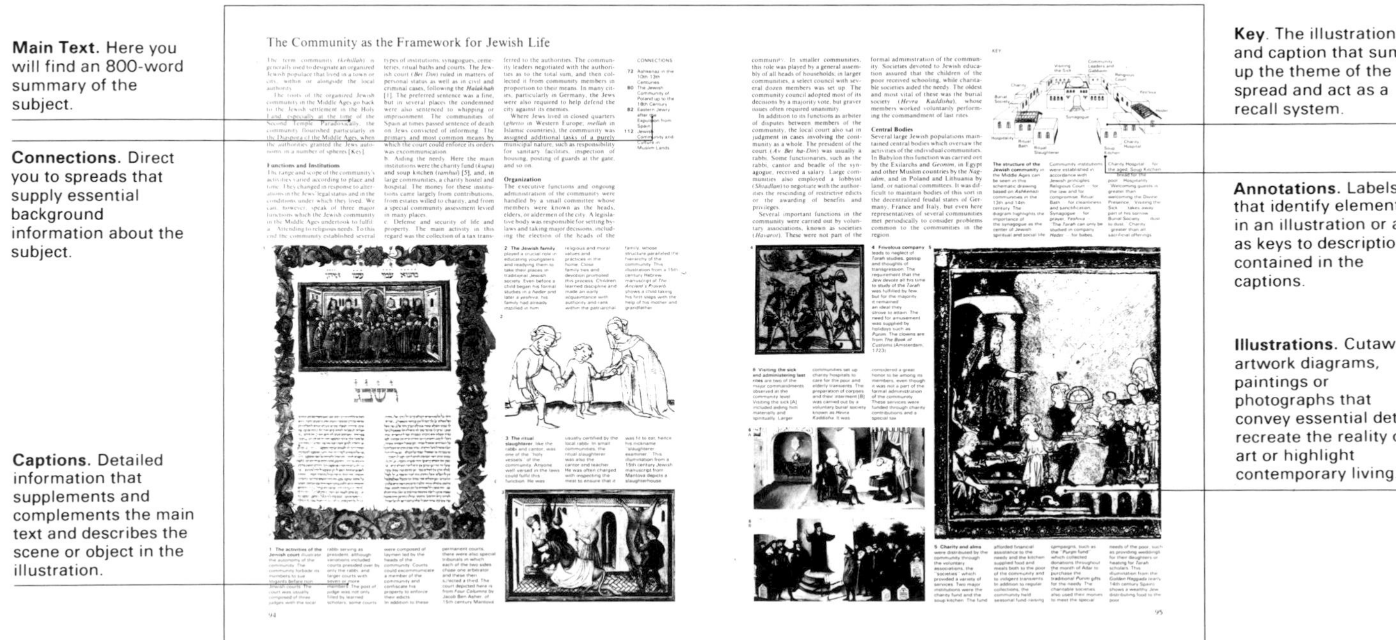
Main Text. Here you will find an 800-word summary of the subject.
Connections. Direct you to spreads that supply essential background information about the subject.
Captions. Detailed information that supplements and complements the main text and describes the scene or object in the illustration.
The Community as the Framework for Jewish Life
Key. The illustration and caption that sum up the theme of the spread and act as a recall system.
Annotations. Labels that identify elements in an illustration or act as keys to descriptions contained in the captions.
Illustrations. Cutaway artwork diagrams, paintings or photographs that convey essential detail, recreate the reality of art or highlight contemporary living.

Major Themes in the History of the Jewish People

Shmuel Ettinger

Professor of Jewish History, Hebrew University, Jerusalem

Every nation, just as every individual, has an image and a fate of its own. But the distinctiveness of a nation's history does not nullify the many things which all nations have in common. These find expression in power struggles, in victories and defeats, in systems of government and society, in religion and culture. Nevertheless, it is generally agreed by all that the special fate of the Jewish people sets it apart from the European, Asiatic, or African peoples with whom it has come into contact over the course of its long history. Its fate has made it a category unto itself.

The Jewish people is special not only because it has existed for so long — with its distinctive consciousness, its sense of sharing a common origin and fate, its unique religion and cultural heritage. It is unique also because of the conditions under which it has survived. From their very beginnings the Jews came into close contact with other peoples, and were even dominated by great nations and civilizations — Egypt, Assyria-Babylonia, Persia, Greece, Rome, the Arab-Muslim world, and Christian Europe; yet they preserved their own identity. The Jews did not shut themselves off from the influence of these other cultures; in their religious, cultural, linguistic, and social creativity one may find important elements taken from others. Yet the continuity of their intense and special creativity remained unbroken.

For most of its history the Jewish people was but a small minority in its political, religious, and cultural environment. Yet it did not deteriorate into a marginal group under the impact of these great civilizations. Rather, it faced the challenge they posed, revolted, and defended itself. As a result, it not only preserved its existence and uniqueness, but many peoples in Europe, Asia and Africa in fact adopted elements of its heritage, some of which even came to occupy a central place in their consciousness.

The Jews' Historical Uniqueness

For generations Jews and non-Jews have speculated on the reasons for the historical uniqueness of the Jewish people. Some have seen it as expressing election by Providence, while others have regarded it as testifying to rejection and curse; some have claimed it reflects the "will to survive" and the creativity and adaptability with which the Jews were graced, while others have asserted that this uniqueness is the fruit of a parasitic life — an ability to maintain one's existence at other nations' expense, while continuing to live among them. Some have suggested that the prolonged survival of the Jewish people under conditions of repression and persecution stemmed from its nomadic origins and the role which the Jews played in the commercial life of other peoples throughout the generations. Others, again, have attributed the existence of the Jews, with their different customs and practices, to the attitude of hatred, contempt and rejection which surrounded them.

All these explanations have one theme in common: consciously or unconsciously, they all derive from theological or ideological suppositions, from psychological stereotypes or from wishful thinking, and not from careful analysis of historical processes. Yet even scholars and historians have not been able to reach a general consensus regarding the cause of Jewish historical uniqueness. Hence, we must limit ourselves to an attempt to isolate several main themes that characterize the history of the people — the principal trends that may be assumed to have impacted most significantly on the Jews' image and fate.

The Concept of a Chosen People

The earliest traditions preserved in the history of the Children of Israel relate to their self-image as a people chosen by its God to obey Him alone and to keep His commandments. In exchange, the people's patriarchs were promised divine blessing and rule over the promised land — the Land of Israel. This election found expression in the Covenant which God made with the patriarchs, an idea to which no parallel has thus far been found in the history of ancient peoples. Despite the many testimonies to the existence of pagan cults among the Israelite tribes during the biblical period, the notions of divine election and monotheism struck deep roots in the national consciousness. In the course of time the people came to accept the demand that ritual observances and social behavior follow the "Law of the Lord," i.e. the *Torah* of Moses — the leader who forged the nation in accordance with a Covenant with the God of Israel, and led it to its promised land. This *Torah* also included demands for social justice, such as defense of the weak, and displayed sympathy and tolerance toward the stranger and outsider. Besides kings David and Solomon, the nation also recorded in its collective memory of great leaders the prophets Elijah and Elisha, Amos and Micah, Isaiah and Jeremiah, who chastised the kings for their frivolous ways, and placed great moral and spiritual demands upon the people. During the Second Temple Period there emerged the notion of the people of Israel bearing a religious mission; later, at the end of this era, the idea of mission was disseminated among the nations, and led to a mass movement of proselytism. Even after the schism with Christianity, and the polemics which Christians carried on against Judaism — the former claiming now to be the "True Israel" — the notion of divine election and mission remained central in the life of the Jewish people.

Traditional Jewish wedding in Frankfurt. Painting from 1861 by Moritz Daniel Oppenheim (facing page).

The Messianic Future

Another important element in the historical consciousness of the Jewish people was an awareness of its initial inferior, lowly status. Unlike traditions which glorify the origins of a tribe or people, and which describe the founding fathers as gods or hero-kings, in the historical consciousness of the Jewish people its patriarchs were nomads, forced to leave their homeland: the site of the formation of the people was the "house of bondage" in Egypt; and the first great act, symbolizing the beginning of its way as a people and personifying the figure of its leader and lawgiver, Moses, was the exodus from bondage to freedom. Hence a central place in the national consciousness came to be occupied by the concept that the "Golden Age" of the people lay not in any heroic past, but rather in its future — in the "End of Days" or the coming of the Messiah from the House of David, who would reign according to the principles set forth by the prophets. At that time a new era would come about, not only for the People of Israel, but for all the nations.

The unique combination of a people bearing a mission, with the idea of the "Golden Age" occurring in the future, deeply affected various groups among the Jewish people, and left its mark in subsequent generations both on the consciousness of nations and on ideological and religious persuasions. From it stem several widespread sociopolitical concepts: the refusal to accept a "reign of tyranny" which rules by virtue of power rather than merit; the righteousness of rebellion by "the few against the many," by "the weak against the strong;" and the idea of martyrdom, or the sacrifice of life and property for the sake of upholding lofty religious and spiritual ideas. During the revolt of the Maccabees such notions came to reflect the aspirations of the majority of the people, and therefore this successful rebellion against the Seleucid kingdom became a landmark in the history of both the Jewish people and the entire ancient world.

Amulet to ward off the evil eye, shaped like a house, with the *menorah* symbol, from the 5th century (left).

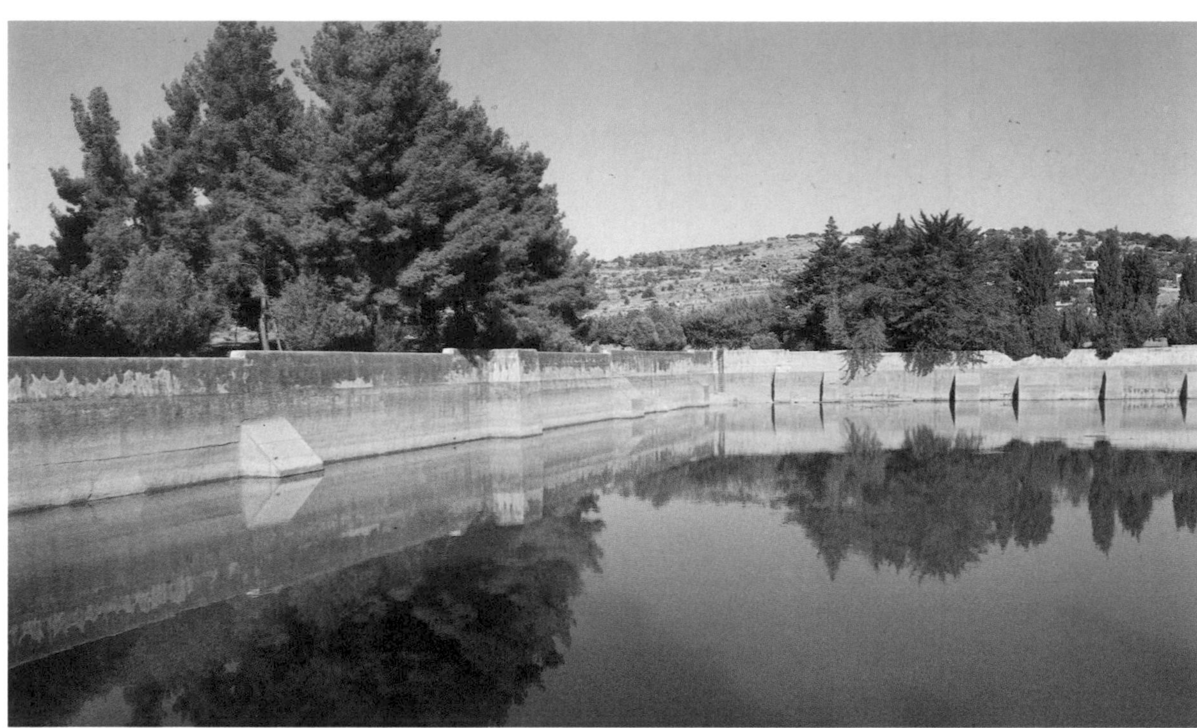

Pools of Solomon collect rainwater and drain springs near Bethlehem. For hundreds of years they supplied water to Jerusalem.

The Promised Land

Another fundamental notion is that of the "promised land" which stands at the center of the people's hopes and aspirations. This, according to tradition, is not the land of origin of the nation's founding fathers; not the land where the nation was forged; nor the place where it received its laws, its *Torah*. Rather, it is the land of the future, where the nation's spiritual and religious mission shall be realized, which is the focal point of the collective consciousness. Hence, expulsion from the land is the severest punishment which can be visited upon the nation, imposed for failing to fulfill its mission and to live according to its own law.

However, even after being exiled, while in foreign lands, the people did not forget the Holy Land and Jerusalem, and their centrality could not be obscured. During the many generations when the Jewish presence in Ereẓ Israel was small and impoverished, and the roads to it fraught with trouble and danger, the yearning for this land, the search for political and national revival on its soil, remained alive deep in the national consciousness. Messianic hopes became bound up with the land, and pilgrimages to it were born of longings for "Redemption." Indeed, the themes of divine selection, of messianic hopes and of return to the promised land, became united through the notion of "Redemption," and formed a powerful force in the life of the nation.

Here we must ask whether stressing these ideological and spiritual foundations in the life of the Jewish people does not somewhat distort our view of historical events as they truly occurred. Are we not sliding into a world of idealization and wishful thinking? After all, throughout the generations there have always been elements among the Jewish people — like in other nations — who worshiped "other gods," sought dominion and gain, and "built houses and planted vineyards" in foreign lands. However, as against such people many others have proven, time and again, through concrete action, their devotion to the hallowed ideals: Jews who refused to adopt the religion and way of life of the rulers of the land, who did not take recourse to the "courts of the gentiles," and who, in times of persecution, preferred exile, or chose a martyr's death that would "sanctify the Name." And even among those who gave in, who abandoned their faith and accepted the way of life of the victors, more than a few returned to their original religion and to the society from which they had come, as soon as such a move became possible. In the people's consciousness, throughout the generations, those who have "sanctified the Name" have been the greatest heroes.

The Community: Diversity and Creativity

Traditional values left a deep impression on the life of Israel in the Diaspora. With the Arab conquests the number of Jews remaining in Ereẓ Israel dwindled. The vast majority of the people lived elsewhere, beyond Ereẓ Israel's borders. Despite the halakhic and spiritual authority which continued for a long time to be held by the Sages of the *Sanhedrin* in Ereẓ Israel and the Exilarchs and Heads of Talmudic Academies in Babylonia, every Jewish community in the Diaspora gradually became an autonomous entity, managing its affairs on its own. Matters of religious worship, as well as social or judicial affairs, were settled within the context of the community, and local *minhag*, or religious practice, prevailed.

Nevertheless, a certain basic unity in *halakhah*, judicial procedure, faith, and religious practice was preserved throughout the Diaspora. In the struggle between the two great universal religions, Christianity and Islam, the dispersed Jewish communities preserved their religious independence, carried on their spiritual creativity, and waged lively religious polemics against these two religions, at times even rising up against them. For despite its political weakness, the Jewish people had entered the Middle Ages as a nation possessing long and rich historical experience. This found expression in the people's religious conception, laws of society and mode of economic life, and gave the Jews the ability to adapt to new circumstances.

In the early Middle Ages the foundations of the Jews' economic activity in their lands of dispersion changed radically. The Jews were deprived of the right to ownership of land — the basis of the economy during that period — and this greatly weakened their status in society. In the Islamic world they yet retained their position in commerce and crafts, although there, too, the Jews suffered sorely during periods of religious ferment and tension. In Christian Europe the crusades, the missionary activities of monastic orders, and the growth of cities all led to oppression of the Jews. They were shunted off to the fringe of society, both physically and economically. They were expelled from cities and even from entire states. They were forbidden to engage in most commerce and crafts, in some places only leaving open to them the occupation of moneylending, which was proscribed to the Christians by their religion. In those cities which tolerated their presence, they were isolated in special neighborhoods and ghettos. Europe was saturated with hostile propaganda by the clergy, with blood libels, and with accusations that the Jews were defiling the Eucharist bread, allied to satanic forces, poisoning the wells, and conspiring against the countries in which they dwelled. Hence it adopted a radical, negative stereotype of the Jews as deicides, bloodsuckers, and traitors.

After the Reformation and the Counter-Reformation of the 16th century essentially no Jewish communities remained except in Poland-Lithuania, the Ottoman Empire, the *Maghreb*, Yemen, and certain parts of Germany, Italy, and Persia. Nevertheless, the thread of creativity in *halakhah*, philosophy, *Kabbalah* and liturgical poetry remained unbroken. Modes of self-rule were further developed, and attempts were even made to establish supra-communal organizations, such as the Council of the Four Lands in Poland.

Paving the Way to Modernization

The turning-point occurred in the 17th century, when communities of exiles from Spain and Portugal, and *Anusim* who had fled those countries, became established in Western and Central Europe. Those few who adopted the culture and thought patterns of the enlightened Europeans, yet also contended with them and influenced them, were the ones who wrought changes in the Jews' economic life and in the structure of their society. While the vast majority of Jews in Eastern Europe and the Islamic world remained tied to the homestead economy, to petty urban commerce, and to crafts, and spiritually were strongly affected by Lurianic *Kabbalah*, one could yet feel the impact of this handful of enlightened Jews. The road had been paved for modernization of Jewish society, for its adaptation to the conditions prevailing in the advanced countries of Europe — England, Holland, France and, in the course of time, several of the Germanic states.

The efforts of the communal leaders and great Talmudic scholars (and, later, the leaders of Hassidism) helped ensure that, in many places, the vast majority of the Jewish public continued to adhere to variations of the traditional Jewish way of life. However, this could not halt the process by which many Jews became integrated into the economic, and subsequently also the cultural and even political life, of the societies around them. Jewish dialects were gradually abandoned as many Jews adopted the language of the state in which they lived. In the 19th century, gradual emancipation of the Jews increased their integration into their surroundings. In western countries special organizations were established to fight for the rights of Jews in countries where they suffered discrimination, and to spread the culture of Western Europe among them.

Ultimately, as a consequence of these developments, a deep internal rift emerged among the Jewish people in all its dispersion — between those faithful to the traditions shaped in the past by the heads of the Jewish community and its rabbis, and the advocates of integration into the surrounding society — which with time was leading to a loss of unique Jewish characteristics in the spheres of language, culture, and social structure. However, only a small minority of Jews reached a conscious severance from the historical continuity of the people and from Jewish society. The vast majority of the advocates of integration sought a compromise between preserving some form of Jewish tradition and integrating into modern life.

The Negative Stereotype and the Awakening National Consciousness

The Jews' acculturation to the Europeans' way of life, and their active participation in the life of the countries of Europe in which they lived, produced a negative reaction among broad circles there. The demonic stereotype of the Jew as it had emerged in the course of the generations continued to exist in the consciousness of many people; and even though relatively few Europeans actively participated in anti-Semitic parties and organizations, the ideas disseminated by such groups nevertheless found a response among wide circles of society in the countries of Europe. Henceforth, anti-Semitism became an important and significant component of the political, social and cultural life of the peoples of Europe.

Patterned after the nationalist movements which arose in Europe and Asia in the 19th century, and, to no small extent, as a reaction to the Jews' rejection by their gentile surroundings, "nationalist" circles also began to emerge within the Jewish people. During the 1880s the *Hibbat Zion* (Love of Zion) movement emerged. It proclaimed its aspiration to work for the "revival of the Jewish people in Ereẓ Israel," through establishing agricultural settlements and reviving Hebrew language and culture. This, however, was a minority movement. The vast majority of the Jews were at that time entering European society, and still championed the cause of equal civil rights for the Jews as their paramount objective. Since many circles in the non-Jewish environment adhered to the negative stereotype of the Jew, a relatively large number of Jews were active in the parties of the liberal, radical, and socialist trends, out of a conviction that changes in the structure of society would make complete equality for Jews possible. Anti-Semitism and economic discrimination in Eastern Europe increased the desire among the general Jewish public there to emigrate, especially to the United States, where, after World War I, the largest concentration of Jews in the world came into existence.

"And ye shall caste off to the depths of the sea all your sins...." On the banks of a river in Germany, 19th century lithograph by Karl Felshenhardt.

Zionism, the Holocaust, and the State of Israel

The emergence of Theodor Herzl as the leader of the Jewish people and champion of the idea of creating a Jewish state, and the rise of Zionism as a Jewish liberation movement, expressed a nationalist trend among the people. The notion of a "right to self-determination" spread rapidly during the time of World War I, just as the Jews were being rejected by the national states that emerged in Eastern and Central Europe. These parallel trends increased both the influence of the Zionists and the tide of emigration across the ocean. As the countries absorbing Jewish migrants gradually closed their gates, during the 20s and 30s of the 20th century, Ereẓ Israel remained for many people the only hope for a life of security and self-respect. The period between the two world wars witnessed the laying of the foundations for independent national existence in the *Yishuv* of Ereẓ Israel in terms of internal organization, economics, education, culture, and defense. And the rebirth of Hebrew as a language of daily use and of modern culture became a living fact.

Meanwhile, the Nazi rise to power turned anti-Semitism into a tool of international policy: Germany's legal and social discrimination against the Jews became a model for other states; and when the Nazis embarked on the systematic extermination of the Jews in the territories under their control, many nationalities in Europe collaborated with them. The Holocaust became a decisive landmark in the consciousness of the vast majority of the Jews, and of many of the world's peoples. Many came to share a recognition of the Jewish people's need for an independent existence in Ereẓ Israel, and this found expression in the United Nations decision to establish the State of Israel, on November 29, 1947. A heroic battle by the *Yishuv* led to the realization of the idea and to the rebirth of the State of Israel.

Ostensibly, establishment of the State of Israel made the Jewish people like the rest of the nations of the world. But its historical uniqueness persists — partially because of the existence of a Jewish community in the Diaspora, larger than that in Ereẓ Israel, and due to Israel's close ties with that Diaspora. Another important manifestation of Jewish distinctiveness continues to be the Jewish consciousness: the recognition of a common fate which characterizes the important world Jewish communities, despite their growing integration into their non-Jewish environment.

Erez̦ Israel in Prehistoric Times

The prehistoric era, which lasted for some two million years, is known as the Stone Age, for stone was the primary material from which man produced his tools. The transition between the prehistoric and historic eras was marked by the Chalcolithic Age which took place, in Erez̦ Israel, around the fifth millennium BCE [9].

The Paleolithic Period

The Stone Age in the ancient Middle East is divided into three periods: the early Stone Age or Paleolithic period (from Greek "paleo" meaning ancient and "lithos," stone), the Epi-paleolithic (i.e., the period directly following the Paleolithic), and the Neolithic or new Stone Age.

Climatic and geological changes caused some of the major features of the Israeli landscape to be formed during the Paleolithic period, including the coastal plain, the Jordan Valley and the Negev. The oldest human remains in Erez̦ Israel were found in Ubeidiya in the central Jordan Valley and at Nahal Amud.

Other remains of *Homo sapiens* were uncovered in caves on Mt. Carmel and are known as *Homo carmelitas.* These men lived as hunters and food gatherers in small groups. Remains of their sites and implements have been found throughout Erez̦ Israel [1].

Toward the end of the early Stone Age and in the Epi-paleolithic period, the region saw climatic and social changes that gave rise to agricultural societies. This new social organization was typical of the Natufian culture, named after Nahal Natuf in the Samarian Hills where it was first uncovered. It was characterized by large, highly developed sites, the relative sophistication of its dwellings, its graves, the production of objects from bone [6], and by barter in seashells. Although they continued to live as hunters and food gatherers, the wide use these men made of sickles and grinding implements attests to their extensive use of wild grains.

The Neolithic Period

The most outstanding feature of the Neolithic period was the shift from nomadic hunting and food gathering to the inhabitation of permanent sites. During this epoch pre-ceramic cultures followed those that used and fashioned implements of clay. Permanent Neolithic settlements have been found in Nahal Oren, in the Jordan Valley, on the edges of the Judean Desert, in the Negev and in Transjordan. These sites cover a broad area and actual villages can be distinguished. The structures were built of field stones and mud bricks and their floors were sometimes plastered. Findings in Jericho point to large-scale public building [2].

The burnt seeds, sickle blades and animal bones excavated on the sites of this period clearly indicate that the systematic planting of wheat, barley and pulses formed one of the foundations of the Neolithic economy, along with herding and hunting.

A major innovation at this time was

CONNECTIONS

22 Pre-Israelite Canaan

1

1 At M'arat ha-Yonim in the Western Galilee, a Natufian cemetery was found. Beneath it were artifacts from the Epi-paleolithic and the middle Paleolithic period. The Natufian settlement occupied the platform in front of the cave.

2

2 The Tower of Jericho from the eighth millennium BCE attests to public construction in the pre-ceramic Neolithic period. It stands about 8.5 meters (28 feet) high and contains an internal stairway running from the base to the top. An impressive stone wall was uncovered beside the tower. The function of the wall and tower is still unclear. They may have served to protect the city, which extended over a constructed area of about 10 acres. The buildings reflect the technical and organizational skills of their inhabitants.

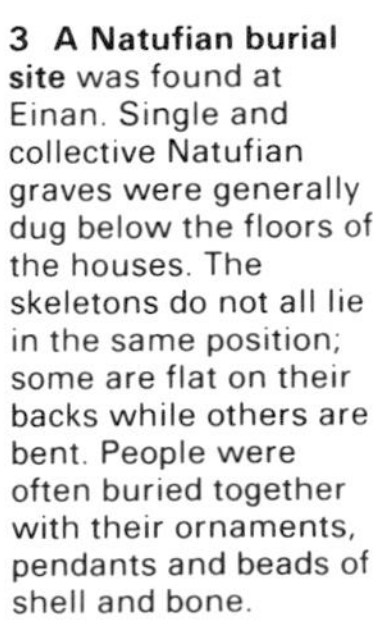

3 A Natufian burial site was found at Einan. Single and collective Natufian graves were generally dug below the floors of the houses. The skeletons do not all lie in the same position; some are flat on their backs while others are bent. People were often buried together with their ornaments, pendants and beads of shell and bone.

3

4

4 This clay figure from the ceramic Neolithic period was found at Hurvat Mincha some 15 kilometers (over 9 miles) south of the Sea of Galilee. Figures of this kind were made by shaping each part of the body separately and then joining them together. Examples of Neolithic art in Erez Israel include animal figures and schematic human forms etched into pebbles, as well as figures like this. Archaeologists tend to view these as seated female forms, wrapped in cloaks and wearing masks and caps. They apparently represent the mother goddess and are associated with fertility rites. Similar clay figures found at contemporary sites outside of Erez Israel, point to inter-cultural links. Besides such works the inhabitants of Hurvat Mincha produced clay vessels which they fired into ceramic.

5

5 Man-made tools in the early Paleolithic period were sometimes made from basalt, but primarily from flint. Implements of bone and probably of wood and skins were also used, but have not survived. The stones shown here have been chipped on both sides, and probably served as handaxes. At a later stage of the Stone Age man learned to produce scraping and grating tools, points and awls from natural flint.

the use of clay to produce vessels for storage and cooking. From this point on, the basic forms of pottery — bowl, jar, cooking pot, cup — become a prominent feature of material human culture. Inhabitants of the region bartered in obsidian (volcanic glass) from Anatolia, stone vessels and implements, turquoise from Sinai, bitumen from the Dead Sea, and seashells from the Red Sea and the Mediterranean.

The Chalcolithic Period

In the late Chalcolithic period (from Greek "chalco" meaning copper), copper was first extracted and the use of copper tools spread rapidly [Key].

During the first part of this era, agricultural cultures existed throughout the country and were similar to those in Lebanon, Syria and Northern Mesopotamia. In the second part, primarily in the first half of the fourth millennium BCE, the Ghassulian culture flourished. Named for the site at Teleilat Ghassul, northeast of the Dead Sea, where it was first uncovered, this culture achieved impressive accomplishments. The unwalled Ghassulian village contained groups of square houses with yards and silos. Most of the structures were built of mud bricks dried in the sun, and some of the walls were plastered and decorated with colorful frescoes. Great stress was laid on livestock and milk production. In their search for grazing land, the Ghassulians reached as far as the northern Negev and Beersheba Valley. In sites along the Beersheba river bed, at Hirbet Batar, Beer Matar and Beer Tsefed, living quarters were found in underground tunnels. These had been gradually replaced by permanent dwellings aboveground. An extensive copper industry was uncovered at Beer Matar, while nearby Beer Tsefed excelled in ivory carvings of ritual figures [7].

The reasons for the disappearance of the Ghassulian culture late in the fourth millennium BCE are still unclear. It seems to have been a protracted process marking the end of the prehistoric era.

KEY

This stylized mace head was uncovered in the "Treasure Cave" discovered in Nahal Mishmar. Among the hundreds of copper artifacts in the cave were also tools, and particularly ritualistic objects produced by a sophisticated process of metal casting. The items may have belonged to the Chalcolithic temple excavated at En Gedi. Conceivably, they were hidden in the cave for safekeeping.

6

6 The top of this Natufian sickle handle is carved in the form of an animal. It was found in one of the Carmel caves. Flint blades fixed in the bone handle and glued in place with resin or natural asphalt served as sickles. Similar handles have been found at other Natufian sites where they were used to cut wild grains, grass or reeds.

7 A

7 These ivory Chalcolithic figures were found at Beer Tsefed on the banks of the Beersheba River. The inhabitants of this site were experts at carving ivory for cult uses. An ivory workshop containing figures in various stages of production was discovered in one of the underground houses. Materials such as ivory, bone, limestone and slate were also used to make decorative figures. Basalt dishes found at the site were evidently imported from afar.

7 B

8 Clay chests (ossuaries) hold the bones in a Chalcolithic burial cave in Azor. This secondary form of burial was particularly prevalent along the coastal plain: at Ben Shemen, B'nei Brak and Hadera. The ossuaries are shaped in the form of houses or huts that attest to the use of wood for building. The molded decorations reveal the spiritual world of Chalcolithic society. Clay jars were also used for this form of burial.

8

9

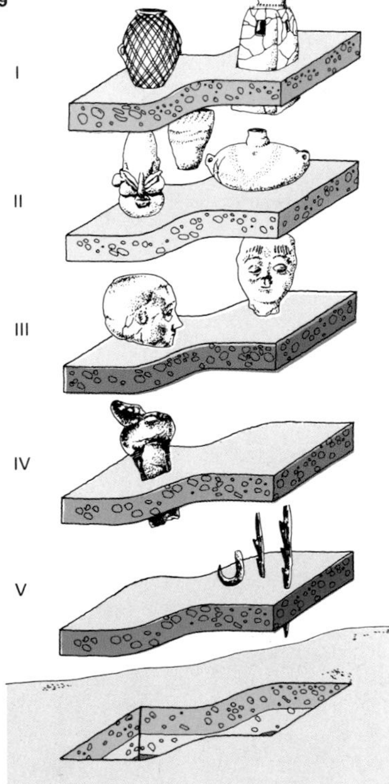

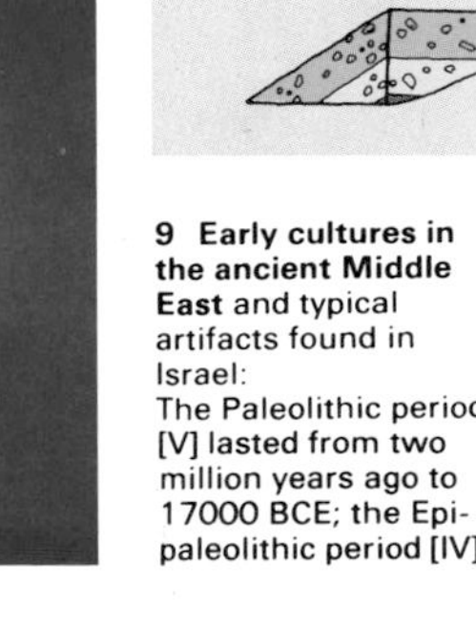

9 Early cultures in the ancient Middle East and typical artifacts found in Israel:
The Paleolithic period [V] lasted from two million years ago to 17000 BCE; the Epipaleolithic period [IV] from 17000-8000 BCE; the Neolithic period [III] from 8000-5000 BCE; the Chalcolithic period [II] from 5000-3300 BCE; the early Bronze Age [I], which corresponds with the early Canaanite period, from 3300-2200 BCE.

Pre-Israelite Canaan

Archaeologists refer to the period which begins with the end of the Chalcolithic period and ends with the Israelites' settlement (3300-1200 BCE), as the Bronze Age. Bronze was the principal metal from which man fashioned his tools at that time. During this age, many changes began to take place in Canaan — its settlements, its economy, and its social fabric.

The Early and Middle Bronze Ages

In the Early Bronze Age (approximately 3300-2200 BCE) the first urban society began to develop in Canaan. Relatively large, fortified settlements (from 10 to 60 acres), with public buildings, temples, residential quarters, and workshops [2] could be found throughout the country; unwalled settlements adjoined them and provided agricultural support. Farming was based on vineyards and olive groves, with grain and bean crops cultivated by plow and oxen. Strong commercial ties existed between Egypt and Ereẓ Israel: pottery from Canaan which once probably held agricultural produce has been discovered in Egyptian cemeteries, while a great deal of Egyptian pottery has been found at different sites in Israel.

In the 24th century BCE, the fortified cities were abandoned, and the urban and farming culture died out. The reasons for this are not clear: some attribute it to climate and environment; others claim that it was due to military campaigns of the Fifth Dynasty Egyptian kings. During Middle Bronze Age I — 22nd and 21st centuries BCE — a new type of culture began to converge upon Canaan, apparently originating in eastern Transjordan and southern Syria. The country was settled by bands of farmers, shepherds, and hunters, who used large, unwalled groups of round buildings as dwellings and for livestock. Unlike the communal burials found in caves typical of the Early Bronze Ages, vast Middle Bronze Age I cemeteries have been uncovered, with single burials in shaft tombs or *dolmen* (large, table-shaped constructions made of stone), or beneath stone mounds known as *tumuli*.

In the Middle Bronze Age II (approximately 20th-16th centuries BCE), urban and rural settlements began to reappear along the coastline, in the valleys, and in the inland regions. The country was divided into city-states, and these were surrounded by walls which had plastered ramparts and large, impressive entrance gates leading to impressive urban structures.

There is evidence of considerable contact between Canaan and Egypt during the Middle Bronze Age [1]. In the latter half of this period, the Hyksos — Asiatics who had infiltrated down to the Delta region through Canaan — took control over Egypt and raised a dynasty of their own. Extensive commercial and diplomatic ties were also maintained between Hazor and Laish (Dan) — two city-states in the northern part of Canaan — and the Syrian and Mesopotamian Kingdoms.

CONNECTIONS
20 Erez Israel in Prehistoric Times
24 From the Patriarchs to the Exodus

1 Evidence of the ties maintained between Egypt and Canaan during the Middle Bronze Age is revealed in documents found in Egypt as well as in Egyptian-made objects found in Israel. These Egyptian seals were discovered in Israel, as were "The Execration Texts," a group of clay bowls and figurines from Egypt (19th and 20th centuries BCE) inscribed with curses against persons and population groups throughout Canaan.

2 Typical urban dwelling in the early Bronze Age discovered in Arad. Houses of this kind included one main room, one side room, and a yard. The main room was wide — its entrance was on one of the longer walls; to the left of the entrance was a stone door socket. The room was entered by descending 2-3 steps from street level. Along all or most walls, stone benches were built. A stone base supporting a wooden beam stood in the center of the room; this supported the ceiling. The room would often contain a stone mortar permanently set into the floor, a pair of grindstones, clay storage containers, and a cooking stove. Groups of houses like this one, separated by streets and alleyways, are typical of residential quarters in Early Bronze Age cities in Canaan. Public buildings and workshops were located in different quarters of the city.

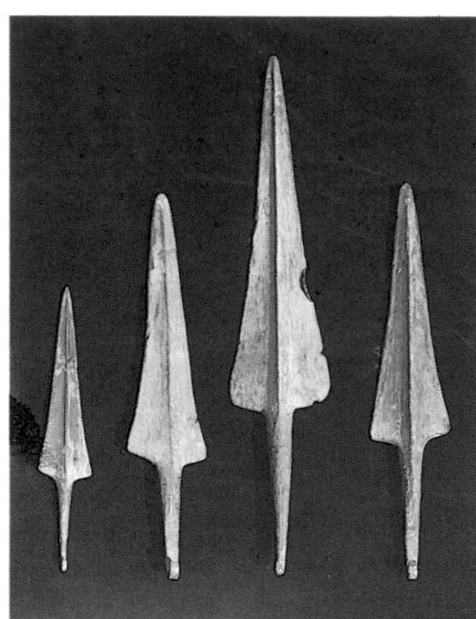

3 Copper spearheads from the Early Bronze Age, found in a cache in Kefar Monash. The cache was discovered by accident, in the midst of plowing; it contained 35 worktools and weapons, such as adzes, axes, chisels, a saw, spears, and daggers. The transition to tools made from bronze (an alloy of copper and tin) was made in Canaan relatively late, during the Middle Bronze Age. Tin was imported from afar; it arrived in Canaan via Mesopotamia and Syria, by means of a wide network of commercial and diplomatic ties.

4 An archive of royal letters was discovered at el-Amarna in Egypt. During the reign of Pharaoh Amenhotep IV (Akhenaton) this city served as the Egyptian capital for a short time. The archive contains letters exchanged during the first half of the 14th century BCE between Egyptian rulers and other major powers, and with Egypt's vassal kings in Canaan. The letters are written in Akkadian, and they reveal that the Egyptians maintained a permanent government in Canaan, including a military presence, administration, and tax collection; the local kings also took part in Egyptian military campaigns, and their city-states were charged with protection of Egypt's governing cities. The el-Amarna letters disclose internal power struggles among Canaanite city-states.

5 An ivory plate discovered in the basement of a Canaanite palace in Megiddo. The ritual scene shows the king's chariot returning from battle, with prisoners marching before it. The king of Megiddo headed a large alliance of monarchs that revolted against Egypt, encouraged by the Mitanni, and were defeated by Pharaoh Thutmose III. The Egyptians left intact the political arrangement which divided Canaan into separate city-states. But a series of new governing cities was established at key sites, such as Gaza, Jaffa, and Beth Shean, managed and administered by the Egyptians. Egyptian military activity in Canaan continued during the time of Thutmose III's successors.

The Late Bronze Age

After Egypt freed itself from the yoke of Hyksos rule, it conquered Canaan and retained it throughout the Late Bronze Age (1550-1200 BCE). Egypt was involved at this time in power struggles with the Mitanni Kingdom — which had risen in northern Mesopotamia, extending over Syria — and, later, with the Hittites in Anatolia, who inherited Mitanni hegemony. These power struggles affected events in Canaan. Many of the campaigns launched by the 18th and 19th Dynasty Egyptian pharaohs on their way northward passed through Canaan, and some were intended to suppress revolts that arose there. The journey of Thutmose III to Meggido (1482 BCE) was of special importance because it was during this time that the foundations of Egyptian administration were laid in Canaan [4].

The population of Canaan was largely western Semitic, with a minority of Hurrian origin. During this period, the number of settlements in the land was considerably reduced, and the central mountain region remained sparsely populated. City-states like Lachish, Gezer, Megiddo, and Hazor attempted to expand the areas in their control. The kings used *'apiru* — refugees who formed into bands, becoming robbers and mercenaries.

According to the findings at Lachish, Hazor, and Beth Shean, the Canaanite cities in the period continued to be fortified; they comprised public buildings, such as palaces, in which treasures of ivory and jewelry [5] were found, as well as elaborate temples with ritual and sacrificial objects [6]. Commerce expanded, too, during this time [7].

In the 13th and 12th centuries BCE, Egypt's military presence in Canaan increased, and new governing cities, such as Aphek, were annexed. The Egyptians appear to have begun their withdrawal from Canaan around the middle of the 12th century BCE, leaving behind a void which was soon filled by the Philistines and the Israelites.

KEY

Bronze figurine of a Canaanite warrior god from the Late Bronze Age, found at Megiddo. Metal idols became popular in the region during the Middle Bronze Age. Idols were usually made of cast bronze, covered with silver and gold leaves. Within the region governed by Egypt, the statue of the warrior god appears in typical Egyptian costume, and his consort — the goddess of love — appears naked. The warrior god is often identified with Ba'al, and his consort with the goddess Anat. Additional figurines found in Erez Israel describe a ruling god and a regally-dressed goddess, and these are identified with El and Asherah, parents of the gods of the Canaanite pantheon.

6

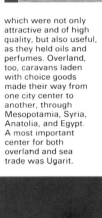

6 The Mazzeboth (stelae) Temple from the 14th and 13th centuries was discovered on the inner slope of the rampart surrounding the lower city of Hazor. It is a small sanctuary, with a ritual alcove at one end; inside are a row of basalt upright stones, one with two hands raised toward a lunar symbol — a crescent and a circle. Benches for ritual offerings were also found in the sanctuary. Next to the temple were artisans' shops where ritual vessels were apparently made. In another part of the lower city, four elaborate temples, one atop another, contained a wealth of cult objects and implements for offerings. The influence of northern Syrian culture is evident in the style of the temples' construction.

7

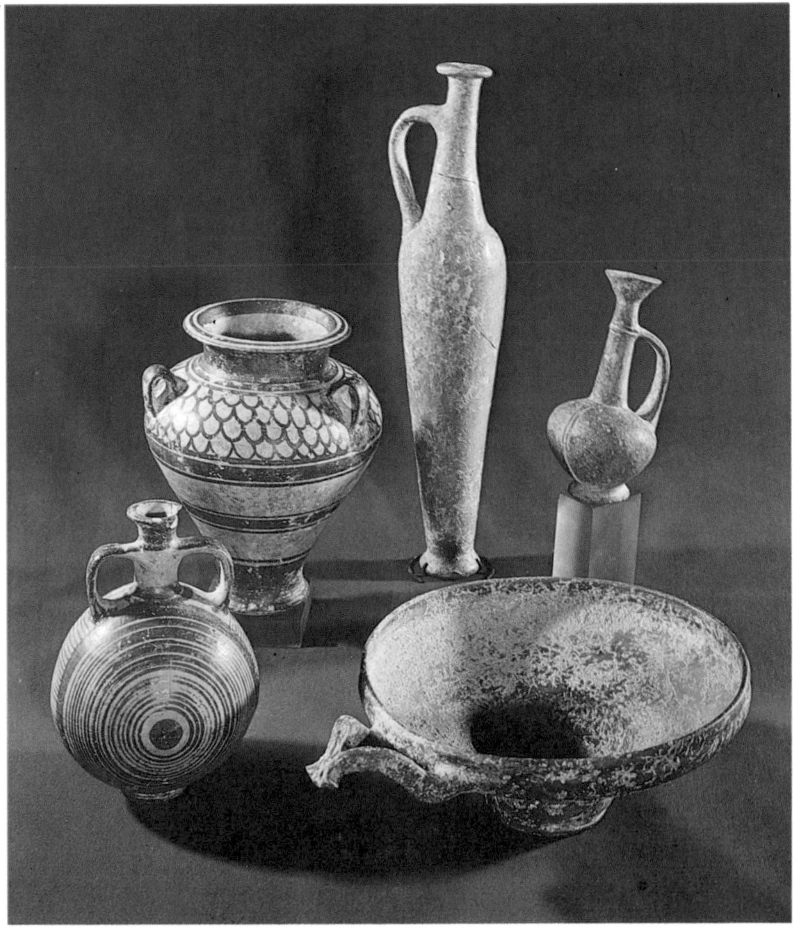

7 Pottery, imported from Mycenae, in Greece, and from Cyprus. Heightened commerce in the Late Bronze Age was evidenced by sea trade in pottery and various raw materials among Canaan, Cyprus, and the countries along the Aegean coast. The Canaanite market was flooded with the excellent wares of Mycenae and Cyprus, which were not only attractive and of high quality, but also useful, as they held oils and perfumes. Overland, too, caravans laden with choice goods made their way from one city center to another, through Mesopotamia, Syria, Anatolia, and Egypt. A most important center for both overland and sea trade was Ugarit, on the coast of Syria. Archives discovered there and documents from el-Amarna in Egypt and from Hattusa (the Hittite capital) reveal how extensive international commerce in the Mediterranean Basin was: they deal with arrangements for border crossing, trade rights and use of ports, payment of taxes and levies, and protection of traders and their goods. Each power was responsible for protecting all caravans passing through its own territory. Routes passing through Canaan — especially the *Via Maris* going the entire length of the land — were part of these complex commercial arrangements, as were port cities like Acre and Ashkelon.

8

8 Fish-shaped pottery, from Tell Poleg, in the Middle Bronze Age. This is typical of the type of pottery originally found at the Egyptian site for which all of this style of work is named: "Tell el-Yahudiyeh Ware." These small oil or perfume flasks were decorated with dotted geometric designs. Apparently this type of pottery was originally designed in Canaan, and distributed from there to the coastal cities of Syria, Cyprus, and Egypt. Later, these countries began to copy the design and produce their own.

From the Patriarchs to the Exodus

The Book of Genesis describes in detail the deeds and way of life of the Patriarchs — Abraham, Isaac, and Jacob. These descriptions provide a wealth of information on the land — its people, its society, legal system, customs, and life styles — in what is known as "The Patriarchal Period."

Opinions vary as to the reliability of these writings. Many of the stories about the Patriarchs reflect realities in Canaan on the eve of the Monarchy's establishment. Hence some historians maintain that they should be considered a collection of traditions from the periods of settlement and of the Judges, gathered during the period of the united monarchy in order to relate the ancient history of the People of Israel. Another vein of biblical research seeks to rely on the study of additional ancient peoples to compare and understand biblical writings.

The Patriarchs' spiritual, social, and material worlds show an affinity to ancient Semitic elements, typical of the inhabitants of the area west of the Euphrates River. These were a semi-nomadic people, who eventually took over the Mesopotamian kingdoms, establishing kingdoms of their own. In the first half of the second millennium BCE, they spread to Syria and Canaan. This affinity is manifest in genealogy records and in the similarity of the proper nouns and terms used to describe life styles, organizations, and culture found in documents both at Mari, on the Euphrates, and in the Bible [2].

The Patriarchs in Canaan

In the Bible, the Patriarchs are described as semi-nomadic herders of sheep, cattle, and camels, who lived on the outskirts of the desert and wandered short distances. They also engaged in farming; the bible describes the wells they dug in the Negev, often the cause of disagreements with the sedentary local inhabitants. In times of drought they had to wander great distances in their search for water and pastures [3]. The Patriarchs' families were clan-like in structure. The family constituted an independent economic and social unit of considerable wealth, which made its livelihood from livestock, home-based occupations, and bartering.

The Exodus from Egypt

Some researchers hold that the families of the sons of Jacob resided in the Land of Goshen in Egypt during the 18th and 17th centuries BCE — when western Semitic elements (the Hyksos) infiltrated and gained control over Egypt [5]. The episode of the enslavement inflicted upon the Israelites, which led to their exodus from Egypt, is not mentioned in Egyptian sources. However, a historical point of reference likely to support the biblical version is the construction of the city of Ramses by the Pharaoh Ramses (1290-1224 BCE).

Biblical historiography has invested the stories of the Israelites' journey through the desert with a national character: Exodus from Egypt, wandering

CONNECTIONS

22 Pre-Israelite Canaan

58 The Egyptian Jewish Community in Ancient Times

1 **Temple to the Egyptian Goddess Hathor** — goddess of the heavens and of love, of music and beauty — built at Serabit el-Khadim in Sinai. The goddess protected travelers in the desert who were journeying to foreign lands on trading expeditions or to mine copper and precious stones. During the Middle and New Kingdoms (20th-12th centuries BCE) the Egyptians mined turquoise here with the help of Canaanite workers.

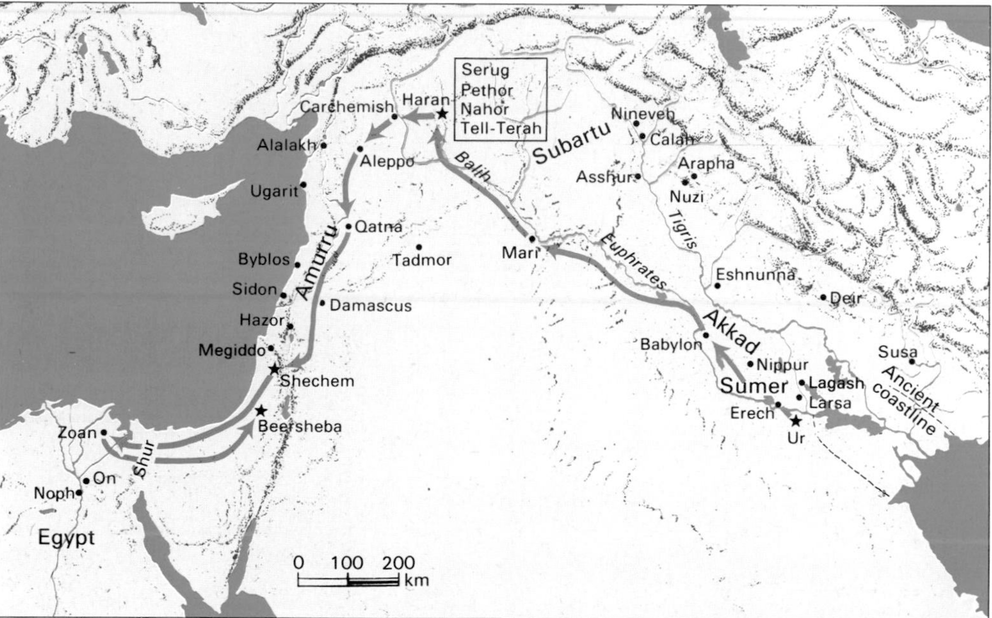

2 **The story of the wanderings of the Patriarchs**, as told in the Bible, mentions names of places which are known to have been in the Ancient Near East. Abraham's origins have been connected with Ur, an important city-state in the land of Sumer, in the southeastern part of the Fertile Crescent, which reached its zenith at the end of the 3rd millennium BCE. The biblical phrase "Ur of the Chaldeans" is from the 11th century BCE. Terah, Nahor, Serug, and Haran — the names used in the Bible for Abraham's relatives — are listed in outside sources as the names of well-known cities situated in northern Mesopotamia, near the Balih River. The stories of the Patriarchs in Canaan take place in the forested, sparsely populated central hill country, from Shechem to Hebron, in the Beersheba Valley, and in the central part of the Gilead region. The stories make reference to important urban centers located in these areas. Some were already in existence during the Middle Bronze Age, and others were established during the Iron Age.

3 **A caravan on its way to Egypt:** wall painting from the tomb of Khnum-hotep at Beni Hasan in Middle Egypt, 19th century BCE. The caravan included 37 western Semitic-looking men, women, and children, whose dress, work tools, and weapons are typical of the inhabitants of Syria and Canaan at that time. At the head of the group — which was carrying perfumes from the land of Shutu — stood Avsar, "The Ruler of the Foreign Land." These scenes indicate that there was Canaanite immigration to Egypt, just as the Patriarchs had gone with their herds and worldly goods in search of grazing pastures. During the time of the Middle Kingdom — in the Middle Bronze Age — Asiatics did in fact arrive in Egypt, taking over the eastern Delta region. This was to have a major influence upon the establishment of future dynasties of Canaanite rulers, the Hyksos, in Egypt.

under the aegis of a national leader, conquering of Canaan — all were described as the activities of a cohesive people. These descriptions are inconsistent with many biblical stories of isolated incidents, and with the description of Israelite tribal organization at the time. However it is logical to assume that the period of extensive wandering served to crystallize the tribal framework, and that the conditions prevailing during the Israelites' journey determined the size of the tribal units and their organizational framework.

The narrative of the Exodus has been embellished by legends of miraculous events expressing more than one traditional outlook. This is why certain historians postulate that the Israelites did not all wander together as a single group. There are differences of opinion on the date of the Exodus, and on the composition of the groups, and there are also three different biblical versions of the path their journey took [4]. Thus it has proven very difficult to identify the stops along the way — aside from the first phase of the journey, which included sites that have been found within Egyptian territory, and which are identifiable from Egyptian sources [6]. Even two key locations — the Red Sea and Mount Sinai — have not been identified positively [Key].

These uncertainties, however, do not undermine the importance of the Revelation at Sinai in the history of the People of Israel. Many traditions persist with respect to this event, at which a covenant was entered into between God and the Israelites; it is here that they were presented with the *Torah* — The Book of the Covenant — making them the "chosen people." Moses, whom the Bible presents as the people's leader and "The Lord of the Prophets," and whose historical image remains a puzzle to historians — Moses is the one who bequeathed to his people the concept of monotheism and thereby caused them to be unique among all the peoples of the Ancient Near East.

KEY

In the Bible, Mount Sinai is called alternately Mount Horeb, Mount Paran, and the Mountain of God. It has proven difficult to identify the mountain positively, because the Bible does not specify its exact location, which may even have been forgotten by the monarchial period. Since the Roman-Byzantine Period, the mountain has been identified with Jebel Musa (Mount Moses, known also as Mount Sinai, pictured here) which is in the southern portion of the Sinai Peninsula.

4 "And it came to pass, when Pharaoh had let the people go, that God led them not by the way of the land of the Philistines" (Exodus 13:17). The route passes along the northern coast of the Sinai Peninsula, connecting Egypt and Philistia. In the Late Bronze Age (16th-12th centuries BCE) the Egyptians built fortresses and water cisterns, and turned this into a military route for use on their way to and from Canaan. A detailed list of the stations established along the route — called "The Way of Horus" — appears on a wall relief of the Pharaoh Seti I (1304-1291 BCE) and on papyrus from the time of his successor, Ramses (1290-1224 BCE). Many locations have been verified by excavations. An Egyptian military presence along the coast of Sinai has even been alluded to in the Bible.

4

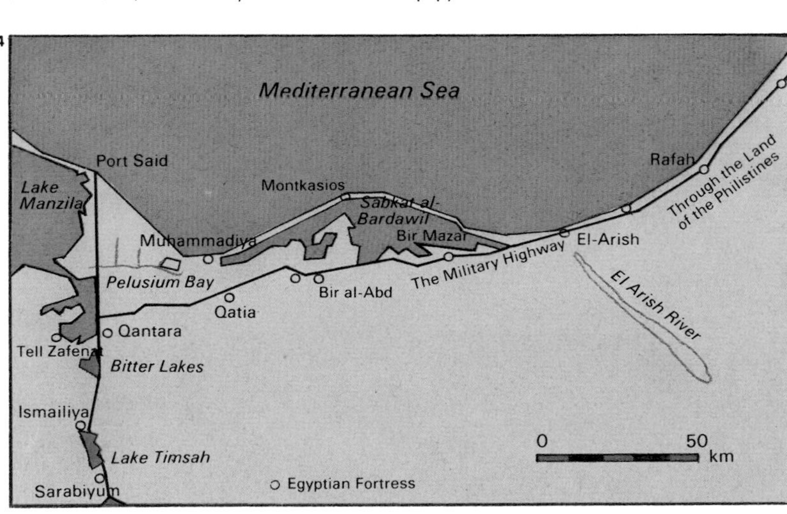

5

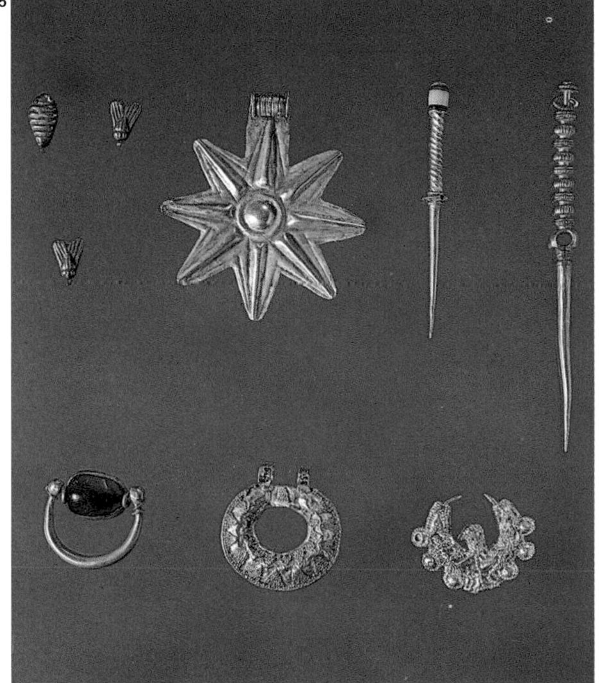

6 Tell el-Qudayrat — the largest oasis in the northern part of the Sinai Peninsula. The *tell* has been identified with Kadesh Barnea, in which, according to biblical tradition, the Israelites camped for a long time; and it was here that they created their first national and religious center, around which all of the tribes became united under the leadership of Moses, before entering the Land of Canaan. It was from Kadesh Barnea that scouts were sent to spy out the land; it was here that the incident of the waters of strife took place; and it was from here that the people set out on their journey eastward to Transjordan. Excavations at the site have revealed the remains of a settlement and royal fortresses dating back to the time of Solomon and ending with the Return to Zion *(Shivat Zion)*. The earliest fortress is elliptically-shaped; its rooms are of varying lengths and it is surrounded by a casemate wall. During the time of King Uzziah (8th century BCE), a rectangular fortress was built on top of the earlier one, consisting of a broad solid wall with eight protruding towers. The last fortress to be built at Kadesh Barnea was during the time of King Josiah.

6

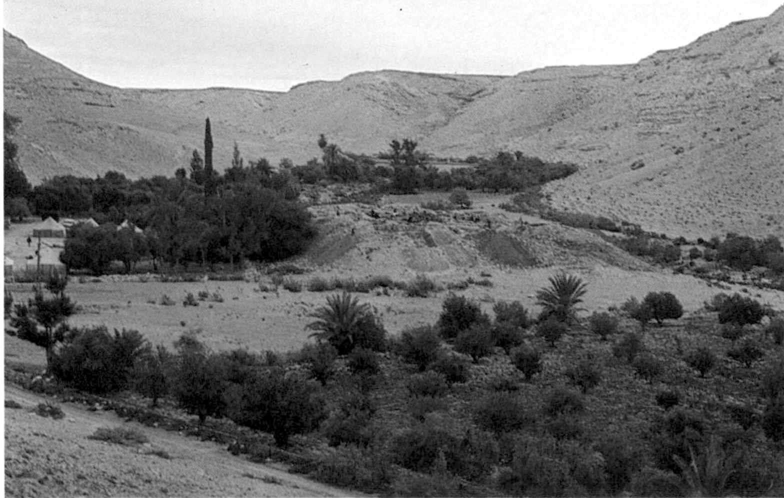

5 Gold jewelry, discovered at Tell el-Ajjul, at the mouth of the Brook of Besor near Gaza. This *tell*, located at the starting point of the route connecting Egypt with Erez Israel via northern Sinai, was the richest and most important of all sites in the Negev during the Middle Bronze Age. It appears to have been the Hyksos center, Sharuhen, which was conquered by the Pharaoh Ahmose, founder of the 18th dynasty in Egypt (16th century BCE), after a three-year siege. The conquest reflected the Egyptians' attempt to drive out the Hyksos (literally "Rulers of the Foreign Lands").

The Period of Settlement and of the Judges

The Israelites and the Philistines began to settle in Canaan at the time of the 19th and 20th dynasties in Egypt (end 13th to beginning 12th centuries BCE). During the 12th century BCE the Egyptians abandoned the region, and these two other nations began to expand their territory. Before long, serious conflicts arose between them — conflicts which were to have a crucial influence on the national and political unification of the twelve tribes of Israel.

The Bible describes the conquest of Israel as a campaign in which all twelve tribes took part — conquering portions of land one after another, in a well-organized military operation, and then dividing up the land among themselves. On the basis of accounts of other conquests not mentioned in the Book of Joshua, some scholars believe that the descriptions in the Bible were written at a later time, when it was thought desirable to create a common history for the newly-formed tribal union. In this view, nomadic Israelite families filtered in from border regions to the sparsely-populated hilly areas, where they eventually settled. Here they were far from the Canaanite population as well as from the Philistines in the southern coastal region [2]. The settlement process was long and slow, and thus the Israelite families evolved into tribal units, each with its own specific territory. As the Canaanite city-states were divided and politically isolated, the tribes were able to conquer several of them.

Archaeologists have, in fact, discovered that many of the Canaanite cities described in the Bible were destroyed during the late 13th and early 12th centuries BCE [1, 3].

The Philistines in Canaan

The Philistines are one of a group of peoples mentioned in Egyptian documents, and described as the "Sea Peoples." In the Late Bronze Age they invaded the coasts of Syria, Israel, and Egypt, eventually settling on the Syrian and Israeli coast. In the 14th-12th centuries BCE several groups of Sea Peoples are mentioned as having raided the coasts of Egypt and Cyprus; others were mercenaries in the pay of the Egyptians and Hittites in their conflicts. At the end of the 13th century BCE, with the collapse of Hittite control over the southern and western coasts of Anatolia and the dissolution of the Mycenaean Kingdom that ruled Greece and the Aegean Islands, a west-east migration began [4, 7]. Egypt is known to have faced a serious threat of invasion by Sea Peoples [6], while such great and important cities as Ugarit succumbed to them. Ramses III, however, succeeded in subjugating them, whereupon he installed them as mercenaries in the fortresses he had erected throughout Canaan.

When Egypt abandoned control over Canaan, the Philistines remained and began to expand. Their main area of settlement extended the entire length of the southern coast — from Gaza to the Yarkon River, and was called Philistia.

CONNECTIONS

24 From the Patriarchs to the Exodus

28 The Kingdom: United and Divided

1 A typical Israelite house of the Settlement Period. The reconstruction evokes the Four-Room type houses discovered in various parts of Israel. It has a central open courtyard used for livestock; on both sides are rectangular areas, and the roofs are supported by rows of pillars. Living and guest quarters are in the back, in two-story rooms extending the width of the building. Buildings of this kind were arranged in a circle, for protection.

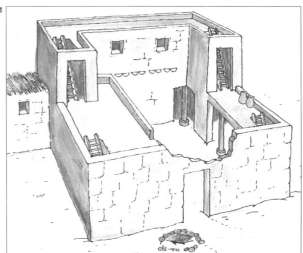

1

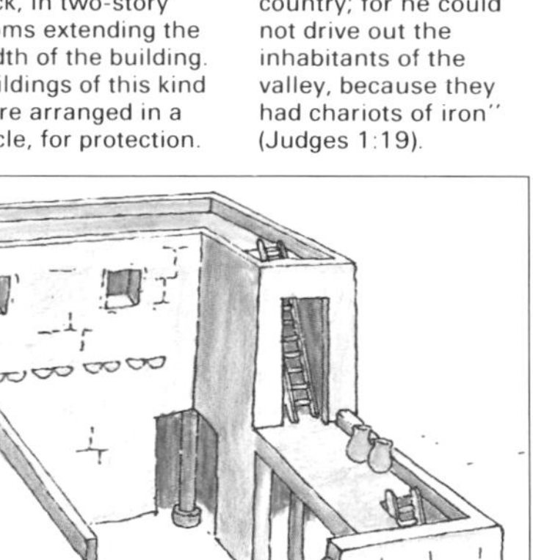

2 Areas of settlement: "And the Lord was with Judah; and he drove out the inhabitants of the hill-country; for he could not drive out the inhabitants of the valley, because they had chariots of iron" (Judges 1:19).

2

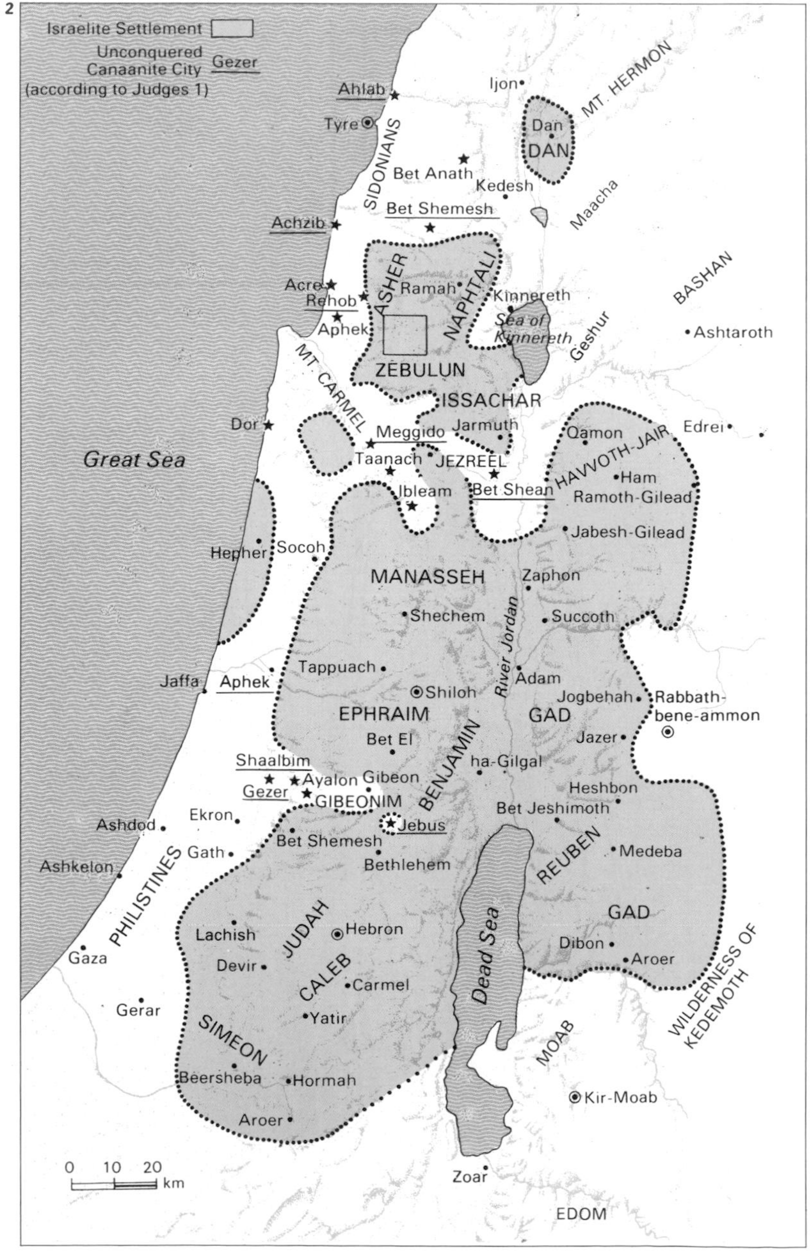

3

3 Israelite village in the Settlement Period (12th century BCE) discovered at the 'Izbet Sartah excavations near Rosh ha-Ayin. A large building of the Four-Room type was discovered at the center of the site. We learn from the dozens of grain silos in the vicinity that this was an agricultural settlement. Pottery found inside one of the silos has the ancient Hebrew alphabet engraved upon it several times over.

The only source of information on the political and social organization of the Philistines in Erez Israel at this time is the Bible. It describes the Philistine Pentapolis — a covenant of the five city-states Gaza, Ashdod, Ashkelon, Gath, and Ekron — established within Philistia, each with its own *seren* (leader). Thanks to strong military organization and tools and weapons made of iron [5], they enjoyed the advantage in their conflicts with the tribes of Israel.

National Consolidation

The Bible differentiates between the conquest and settlement period, on the one hand, and that of the Judges, on the other. It would appear, however, that these two periods were in fact interlocking, and that the Judges led the tribes of Israel all through the conquest and settlement. The Book of Judges describes the difficulties of the time: tribal division and fragmentation, territorial discontinuity, family and clan instability, social and economic transitions, and pressure from neighboring peoples.

The Judges were typical of the leadership during the Settlement period. Some of the Judges — Othniel, Ehud, Deborah, Gideon, Jephtah, and Samson — were courageous, heroic, and charismatic. In addition to these "deliverers," there were apparently other Judges — leaders in peacetime.

As early as the days of Gideon the People of Israel began to aspire to some centralized form of government, and this was evidenced by the attempt of Abimelech, the son of Gideon, to establish a monarchy in Shechem. It was the Philistine threat, however, which provided the stimulus to unite the tribes into one cohesive power. The Israelites' defeat in the battle against the Philistines at Eben Ezer, the Philistine penetration into the heart of the central hill region, their destruction of the religious center at Shiloh [Key] and capture of the Ark of the Covenant — all contributed to a crisis in the wake of which the people demanded to anoint a king.

KEY

Jars used for oil and wine were found at Tel Shiloh inside a public building dating back to the Period of Settlement and the Judges. Shiloh, in the central hill region, was the hallowed meeting place of the tribes of Israel at this time. The *Mishkan*, which contained the Ark of the Covenant, was kept at Shiloh for a long time; here Eli the Priest and the young Prophet Samuel served. In the 11th century BCE the Israelites were defeated by the Philistines in the Eben Ezer battle, Shiloh was destroyed, and the Ark of the Covenant was captured. Abundant pottery and traces of a great fire indicate that the inhabitants fled in haste to escape the invading Philistines.

4

4 Philistine jug from Tell 'Aitun in the *Shephelah*. The vessel is covered in white slip, upon which designs have been drawn in red and black. Philistine pottery reflects different influences and styles acquired by the artisans on their way to Canaan. The vessels bear a striking similarity to Mycenaean pottery from Rhodes, Cyprus, and the southern coast of Turkey, dating back to the Late Bronze Age. This similarity could be an indication of the Philistines' origins. The names of the groups which composed the Philistine people help substantiate this hypothesis.

5

5 Very few iron tools were found at archaeological sites dating back to the Settlement Period; during this time bronze was still the main metal in use. Apparently difficulties in tin and copper trade at the end of the Late Bronze Age, combined with the collapse of regional political systems, resulted in widespread use of iron, and in the 10th and 9th centuries BCE the technology for producing iron spread rapidly.

6

6 Part of the land battle between the warriors of the Pharaoh, Ramses III, and the "Sea Peoples," among them Philistines. This reproduction is a detail from a temple wall relief. The Philistines are shown wearing feathered headdresses. Square, solid-wheeled wagons drawn by four oxen hold their families (who accompanied the Sea Peoples in their wanderings and battles) and provisions. The chariots used in battle are drawn by a pair of horses, and have spoked wheels.

7

7 Clay figurine of a seated goddess, from the Philistine city discovered at Tel Ashdod. The figure, "Ashdoda," is very similar to the Mycenaean figurines of goddesses from the Late Bronze Age, possibly indicating that the Philistines were of Aegean origin. This is the first archaeological evidence that the Philistines had gods of their own; those that are mentioned in the Bible — Dagon, Baal-Zebub, and Ashtoret — are all of Canaanite origin. Just as their pottery and burial customs imitated the local Canaanites, the Philistines evidently modeled their gods, as well, on those adopted from the Canaanites. At Tell-Qasila, in Ramat Aviv, Philistine temples were discovered, containing a wealth of cult objects. The findings here also indicate that the Philistines tended to adopt or integrate the local culture into their own: temple structures and shapes of objects found had already been familiar to this area before their arrival.

The Kingdom: United and Divided

Saul's reign (1025-1004 BCE) served as the transition period between the time of the Judges and the Monarchy. Throughout his lifetime Saul was forced to deal with the Philistine threat, though it took him only a few years to establish an independent kingdom which covered the central and southern regions and the Gilead. To manage his wars, Saul established a standing army. The seat of royalty was his birthplace, Gibeah; members of his tribe, Benjamin, helped him rule the kingdom. Saul encountered resistance from the other tribes, who sought independence. This, together with his break with the prophet Samuel and David's budding strength, all combined to weaken his newly-established monarchy.

Military and Economic Strength

When David ascended the throne (1004-965 BCE), he moved the seat of government to Judah. David succeeded in uniting all the tribes under a stable government; he also built up a strong army, reinforced by mercenaries. He annexed Canaanite enclaves, pushing the Philistines back to the southern *Shephelah*, and subdued the kings of Aram. His conquests extended eastward to Transjordan and northward to the Lebanese Beka'a.

By the beginning of the first millennium BCE the political balance of power in the Near East favored Israel. Egypt was weak, the Hittite Kingdom was destroyed, and no new strong kingdoms had been established yet in the north. David and his son Solomon (965-928 BCE) after him controlled the principal commercial routes, the *Via Maris* and the "King's Highway," as well as Mediterranean and Red Sea ports. The government's close ties with Tyre led to cooperation in shipping and trade [3], and the Israelites took advantage of Tyre's skilled craftsmen and builders. Trade ships departed from Mediterranean ports bound for Cyprus, to load copper, or for Asia Minor, to buy iron. The ships sailed as far as the western Mediterranean in search of raw materials. A new commercial route was established between Ezion-Geber on the Red Sea coastline, and Ophir, on Africa's eastern coast. Careful attention was paid to the planning of cities [1, 8]. Various cities had administrative buildings and grain storehouses. Cities were able to billet entire armies, with their equipment and horses [6].

Administrative Reform, and Schism

The Kingdom of Solomon was divided into twelve districts, to enable royal officials to supervise taxation. Thus an upper echelon of ministers and bureaucrats was created. There were two principal forms of taxation: a property tax, and a corvée, or seasonal draft of forced labor for major building projects.

Jerusalem, captured by David from the Jebusites, was chosen as capital and administrative and cultural center, both because it was elevated, and therefore easy to defend, and because it was outside the territory of any of the tribes.

CONNECTIONS

26 The Period of Settlement and of the Judges
30 The Kingdom of Israel
32 The Kingdom of Judah

1 The Protoaeolic capital is typical of Israelite ashlar buildings found in royal centers such as Megiddo, Hazor, Samaria, and Jerusalem, from the 10th century BCE on. The motif on this capital was apparently designed to resemble a palm tree — the ritual symbol of the "tree of life" — but it may be the Egyptian lotus.

2 The Gibeon Pool provided water for the city under siege. Its waters came from a subterranean spring outside the city. The pool was hewn in stone. Spiral steps carved into its wall lead to a tunnel and the water level.

3 An Assyrian relief engraving, depicting ships loaded with wood. Hiram, King of Tyre, shipped cedars and cypresses to the port at Jaffa for the building of Solomon's Temple in Jerusalem.

6 BCE	8 BCE	9 BCE	10 BCE	13 BCE	15 BCE	
						א
						ב
						ג
						ד
						ה
						ו
						ז
						ח
						ט
						י
						כ
						ל
						מ
						נ
						ס
						ע
						פ
						צ
						ק
						ר
						ש
						ת

4 Alphabetic script — in which a symbol is used to represent only one consonant, and there are a limited number of symbols. It turned reading and writing into a simple skill, compared to the syllabic scripts of the Ancient Near East, such as Mesopotamian cuneiform or Egyptian hieroglyphics. It derives from picture writing in the Late Bronze Age, called Proto-Sinaitic or Proto-Canaanite script, which later became linear. Independent Hebrew writing crystallized in the middle of the 9th century BCE.

David strengthened the city's fortifications, and Solomon doubled its size and erected many public buildings. By building the Temple on Mount Moriah [Key], Solomon imparted great religious importance to the city of Jerusalem for all the nation. He transferred the Tent of Congregation and the Ark of the Covenant to the Temple, held a ceremony to sanctify the house of worship, and, by these acts, succeeded in binding the priesthood and the Levites to the service of the monarchy.

The administrative changes introduced by David and Solomon ultimately fomented division. An abortive rebellion by Absalom, David's son, was an early expression of the divisive tendencies rife among the people. During the revolt of Sheba son of Bichri of the tribe of Benjamin, the rebels circulated the slogan: "We have no portion in David, neither have we inheritance in the son of Jesse" (Samuel II 20:1). There were also economic reasons for these tendencies: the tax imposed by Solomon — at a time when great wealth was being amassed by the kingdom's treasury — became a heavy burden, and the corvée was the worst hardship of all. Agitation began toward the end of Solomon's reign when Jeroboam ben Nebat, of the tribe of Ephraim, incited an abortive rebellion.

Insurgence erupted in full force when Rehoboam, Solomon's son, ascended the throne (928 BCE). Rehoboam arrived in Shechem, where "all Israel were come to make him King" (Kings I 12:1). There he negotiated with representatives of the people on easing the economic burden — their condition for accepting his monarchy. His advisors suggested that he comply for the time being, but Rehoboam refused. His refusal was used to incite the people against the Davidic dynasty, and resulted in schism. The monarchy, which had been united for approximately one hundred years, was now divided into two separate sister kingdoms — Israel and Judah [5].

KEY

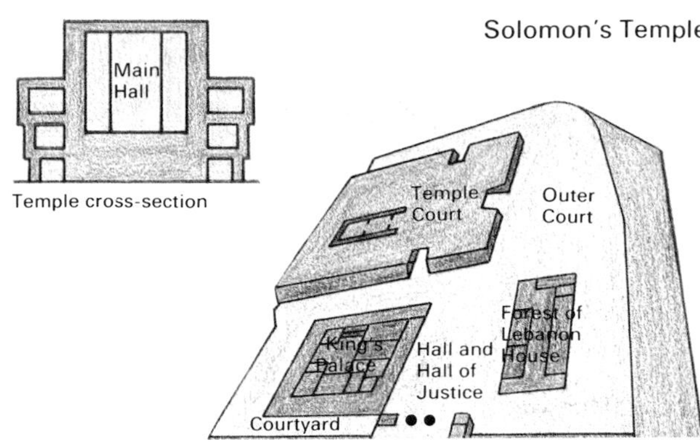

Solomon's Temple, the pinnacle of Israeli architecture in the 10th century BCE, was described in detail in the Bible (Kings I, chapters 6 and 7). It was situated near the king's palace. It was oblong, 20 cubits wide and 70 cubits long (the cubit is an ancient Egyptian measure, approximately 55 cm., or 21"); the Temple was divided into three parts: the eastern entrance hall or vestibule; the room for divine service; and the sanctuary — the Holy of Holies — on the west. Two ornamental pillars, Jachin and Boaz, stood at the entrance. The main ritual objects were the incense altars, and the Ark of the Covenant inside the sanctuary.

5

5 Division of the Kingdom resulted in changes in the political map. Benjamin's tribe joined Judah and the House of David, the Transjordanian tribes joined the Kingdom of Israel, and most other peoples living within the boundaries of the Monarchy threw off the yoke of Israelite rule. Revolts had already begun in Solomon's time in Damascus and Edom, while Ammon and Moab broke free after his death. As ritual centers Jeroboam chose Bet El and Dan, associated with ancient cult traditions.

6

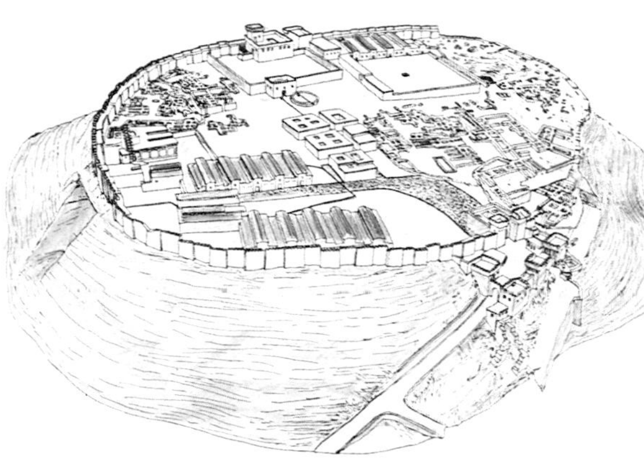

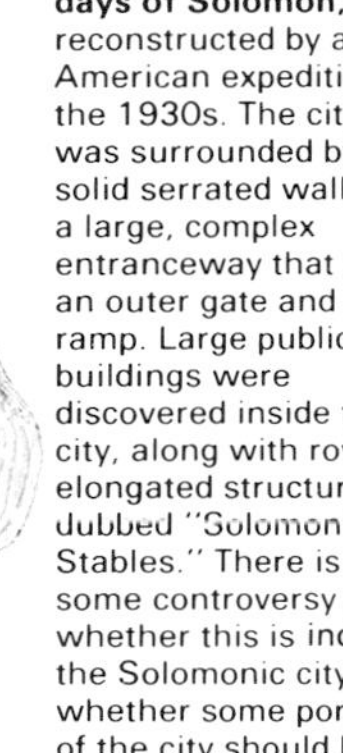

6 Megiddo in the days of Solomon, reconstructed by an American expedition in the 1930s. The city was surrounded by a solid serrated wall with a large, complex entranceway that had an outer gate and ramp. Large public buildings were discovered inside the city, along with rows of elongated structures dubbed "Solomon's Stables." There is some controversy as to whether this is indeed the Solomonic city, or whether some portions of the city should be attributed to Ahab.

7 Figure of the goddess Astarte from the Monarchy Period. Often called "pillar figurines" because of their shape, clay figurines of this type were found at many sites throughout Israel. Traditionally, these naked female figures with their prominent sexual parts have been associated with Astarte, the fertility goddess, and have been considered fertility idols.

7

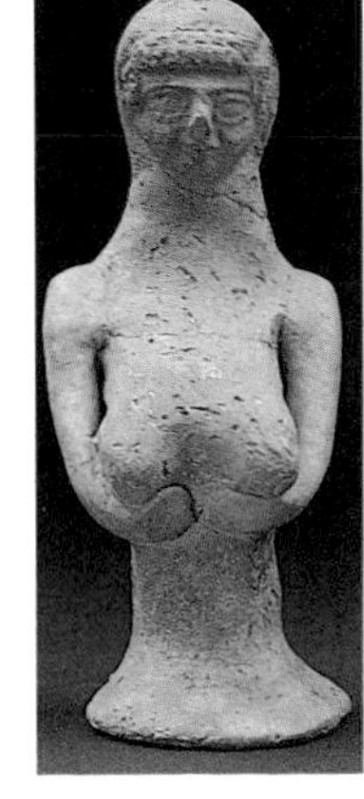

8

8 The gate at Gezer during Solomon's reign. The large gate in the southern part of the city was built of ashlar stones; it had six chambers and two towers. The first "Solomonic gate" was discovered at Megiddo. Some time later a gate of similar plan and proportions was discovered at the Solomonic city in Hazor. Archaeologist Yigael Yadin then surmised that there must be a similar gate at Gezer. He based his supposition on the biblical passage which stated that Solomon's architectural achievements included "Hazor and Megiddo and Gezer" (Kings I 9:15). Yadin managed to identify the western portion of the gate in the "Maccabean Castle" Plan discovered by Macalister, who had dug at the site at the beginning of the 20th century. And, in the course of a new dig at Gezer in the 1960s, the entire gate was in fact uncovered. Solomon had received the city from the king of Egypt upon marrying his daughter.

The Kingdom of Israel

The Kingdom of Israel, established in 928 BCE by Jeroboam ben Nebat and destroyed in 720 BCE by Assyria, did not enjoy stability for any extended period of time. Its dynasties changed many times, usually because of insurrections following military losses, or due to interference by foreign powers.

During its first fifty years, the Kingdom of Israel was constantly at war with the Kingdom of Judah [2]. When Omri acceded to the throne (882-872 BCE), establishing a new dynasty, he brought some degree of stability to the kingdom. Omri established an alliance with Judah, later strengthened by the marriage of Jehoram son of Jehoshaphat to Athaliah, a descendant of Omri. During this peaceful period, both Judah and Israel were able to strengthen their kingdoms politically as well as economically. Omri expanded his territory to Transjordan, defeating Moab. He also concluded treaties with Tyre and Sidon, enhanced by a royal marriage between his son, Ahab, and Jezebel, daughter of Ethbaal, Sidon's king. Omri's ties with the Phoenicians opened up new commercial and maritime opportunities, as in Solomon's time. Omri tried to create a broad economic and administrative infrastructure which would assure his control. The capital he built at Samaria was surrounded by a massive network of fortifications. Ahab (reigned 871-852 BCE) continued his father's political policies and building projects [4].

Foreign Cults and Cultures

Economic prosperity and ties with Phoenicia and Cyprus introduced a materialistic culture from the north. Thus pottery from this period [8] is of high technical quality, as are the ivory engravings discovered in the elegant palaces built by Ahab [Key]. The Bible describes how foreign customs were adopted, weakening Israelite religious tradition. Jezebel brought with her to Samaria the Baal and Ashera cults with all their trappings: priests from Tyre and the prophets of Baal, who served as court prophets and were paid from the king's treasury. The House of Ahab sought to adopt the tyrannical ways of government of the Sidon monarchy, and the foreign culture began to gain a foothold among the upper classes.

Led by Elijah, the prophets of Israel fought the Baal prophets, and were responsible for their massacre on Mount Carmel. Then they in turn were persecuted and killed, and even Elijah was forced to flee. But mass popular support for Elisha, Elijah's successor, gave him courage to revolt. He ordered Jehu, the minister of war, to murder Jehoram, Ahab's son, and all his family, in revenge for the blood of the prophets.

After Ahab's death, the Kingdom was debilitated. The Moabites revolted, while the Arameans chose this time to attack. This led to agitation and insurrection among the ranks of the Israelite army, which resulted in the crowning of Jehu ben Jehoshaphat ben Nimshi.

Archaeological findings indicate that during the time of Omri and Ahab, and

CONNECTIONS

28 The Kingdom: United and Divided

32 The Kingdom of Judah

1 A memorial stela erected by the Moabite king, Mesha, in honor of his god, Chemosh, in his city of Dibon in eastern Transjordan, north of the Arnon River. The stela was discovered by accident in 1868, and was shattered by local Beduin. Its inscription was deciphered after it was pieced back together. Carved of basalt, the stela was written in the Moabite language, in Hebrew script. It praises King Mesha who freed Moab from the yoke of bondage to King Omri of Israel, expanded his country's territory, and organized building projects. The inscription apparently concludes by citing the fall of both Jehoram, King of Israel, and Jehoshaphat, King of Judah, to Moab. According to this event, historians have dated the stela at approximately 850 BCE.

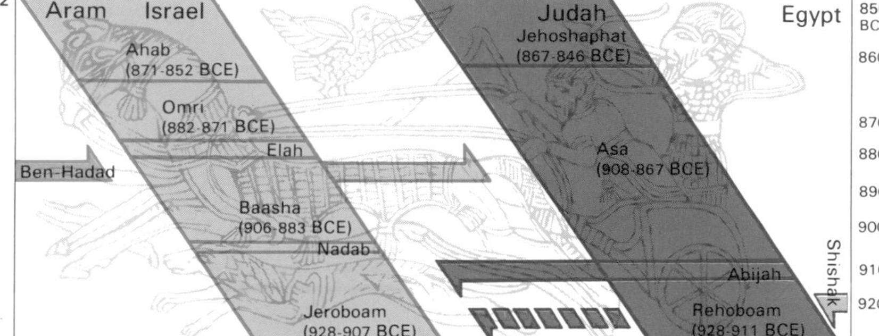

2 The wars between Israel and Judah after division of the kingdom (indicated by arrows).

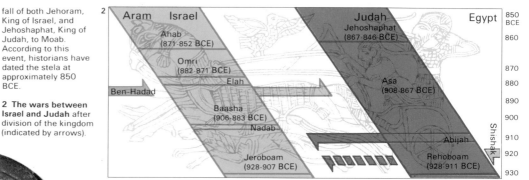

3 Seal of "Shema, the Servant of Jeroboam", found during the 1904 Megiddo excavations, and sent to the Ottoman Sultan in Istanbul, where it disappeared. One of the most elaborate ever to have been discovered, this seal belonged to a high official who served Jeroboam II, King of Israel. Many seals bearing the title "Servant of the King" or "Servant" and the name of the king, date back to the kingdoms of Israel and Judah.

4 A pillared building from Ahab's time, discovered at Hazor. Apparently used as a royal storehouse, it is located in the center of the city. During Ahab's reign (871-852 BCE) Hazor was at its zenith; it was twice as large as in Solomon's day, and was completely enclosed by a wall. A citadel erected at the southwesterly corner of the city protected it. An underground water system provided water during time of siege. Ahab followed his father, Omri, in initiating large-scale building projects.

for several years thereafter in the reign of Jeroboam II (784-748 BCE) [3] there was economic prosperity in Israel [6]; but it was limited to a few specific classes. The killing of Naboth of Jezreel and the expropriation of his vineyards because he refused to sell his lands to the king (Kings I 21), are an example of the king's attempts, on his wife Jezebel's advice, to place himself above the law. The prophets struggled against this moral deterioration and defended social justice.

The Last Days of the Kingdom of Israel
During the reigns of Jeroboam II and of Uzziah (middle 8th century BCE), Israel and Judah both expanded their borders, enjoying a temporary sense of security and well-being. Soon, however, dynastic changes and social upheaval were to weaken the kingdom. The Arameans took advantage of Israel's isolation to attack repeatedly. Only when they themselves were threatened by Assyrian onslaught did the two nations join forces to combat the Assyrian threat. But Tiglath Pileser III, king of Assyria (744-722 BCE), defeated both and annexed them as Assyrian provinces; he deported some of the Israelites to remote provinces and settled foreigners in their stead. On his campaigns through the country (734-732 BCE), he first laid waste to the large cities — Hazor and Megiddo — and then proceeded to sever the Galilee, the coastal plain, and Transjordan from the kingdom, turning each into a separate administrative unit. All that was left of the Kingdom of Israel was the Mount Ephraim region, and Hoshea son of Elah was appointed puppet king.

Hoshea was not reconciled to foreign rule, and he took advantage of an interregnum in Assyria, and an Egyptian promise of aid, to cease paying tribute. The result, however, was total conquest by the Assyrians, who proceeded to destroy the Kingdom of Israel, establish an Assyrian province in its place, and exile the remaining Israelites.

KEY

Winged sphinx made of ivory. The pieces present a wide variety of shapes, decorations, and crafting. They have been attributed to Phoenician art, but bear the influence of both Syrian and Egyptian styles. Most of the motifs have been taken from Egyptian mythology. Kings of the Ancient Near East used ivory to decorate their palaces and furniture, and even the Bible tells of the "ivory house" built by King Ahab and of the ivory objects used by the kings of Israel and Judah.

5

5 Part of the "Black Obelisk" of the Assyrian king, Shalmaneser III (858-824 BCE). The king is shown accepting tribute from "Jehu the son of Omri" who kneels before him. Behind Jehu stand Assyrian officials who carry the Israelite tribute. A marginal inscription notes that the tribute included silver, gold, a golden bowl, golden goblets and buckets, tin, a royal staff, and weapons. Additional inscriptions on the obelisk concern tribute from other countries that had also succumbed to the Assyrian king.

6 Inscription etched on a bowl fragment from Samaria, end 8th century BCE. Apparently this letter concerned barley distribution. In storehouses belonging to the Israelite monarchy discovered at Samaria — capital of the Kingdom of Israel until its destruction — over sixty ostraca written in Hebrew were discovered. They served as delivery notes for wine and oil shipments — apparently, tribute paid by the various Samarian settlements.

7 Fragment of an Assyrian memorial stela from Samaria, end 8th century BCE. The fragment is a remnant of a memorial stela erected in Samaria, apparently by Sargon II, the Assyrian king who conquered the city during his campaign to suppress revolt in the west. Sargon deported many Israelites, then made the city capital of the province of Samaria. The Bible attributes this conquest to Shalmaneser. The writing is Accadian cuneiform script.

6

7

8 A

8 B

8 Clay figurines of musicians [A], and various cult objects were discovered in the Phoenician burial grounds at Achziv. The graves are from the 10th century BCE to the end of the Iron Age, and are of special interest due to their wide variety of shapes. Clay model of a temple [B] whose facade is decorated in typical Phoenician style, was found in Transjordan. The columns at either side of the entrance have Protoaeolic capitals, typical of the architecture of Erez Israel and Phoenicia in the Iron Age, from the 12th to 6th centuries BCE.

The Kingdom of Judah

The Kingdom of Judah was neither as large nor as wealthy as the Kingdom of Israel. Judah was far from the main highways which passed through the region, and its monarchy was continually in the hands of the House of David.

Judah began to prosper during the time of King Asa (908-867 BCE), when commercial ties with Tyre and the cities of Philistia were renewed. These ties introduced pagan influences and led, in turn, to a struggle between priesthood and monarchy, which resulted in eradication of the foreign cults from Jerusalem. Jehoshaphat ben Asa (867-846 BCE) signed a peace treaty with Ahab and Omri, kings of Israel, and the royal marriage between Jehoram, son of Jehoshaphat, and Athaliah, Ahab's daughter, was a positive turning point in relations between Judah and Israel.

Judah's influence extended southward as far as Eilat. Metal production was increased, and commercial traffic via the Red Sea resumed. In order to make tax collection more effective, Jehoshaphat divided the kingdom into twelve districts. He strengthened and reorganized the army, improved fortifications, and built storehouses [Key]. Like his father, Jehoshaphat strove to limit cult worship. One of his most important projects was the establishment of a supreme court in Jerusalem, making the city the kingdom's legal and judicial focus.

Judah's status was consolidated primarily during the reign of Uzziah (769-733 BCE), who controlled the commercial routes along the coast and through the Negev [1], thereby increasing Judah's income from international trade. Uzziah also encouraged agricultural development, especially in the Negev region; he expanded settlements to Transjordan, and constructed extensive fortifications. Supported by the prophet Isaiah, Uzziah's grandson Ahaz (733-727 BCE) rebuffed an anti-Assyrian alliance, then survived an attempt to depose him. But Tiglath-Pileser III, King of Assyria (744-722 BCE), who was responsible for the fall of the Kingdom of Israel, did force Judah to pay a tribute, though failing to conquer it. Ahaz became an Assyrian vassal and was compelled to erect Assyrian cultic centers in Jerusalem.

Kings and Prophets

The first kings to reign in Judah after the Kingdom of Israel had been destroyed sent tribute to Assyria. But when Judah strove to break free from the Assyrian yoke, the prophets decried the fact that religious and moral standards were being lowered in favor of military strength. The prophets made their attitudes known, even if these were contrary to popular opinion and royal favor. They avoided condemning the monarchical institution itself, and many supported the kings of the House of David; however, they refused to condone despotism, severely criticized acts which led to social and economic stress, and supported religious and moral reform. The most important of these

CONNECTIONS

28 The Kingdom: United and Divided
30 The Kingdom of Israel
34 Destruction and Exile
58 The Egyptian Jewish Community in Ancient Times

1

1 Storehouses were discovered in Beersheba, near the city gates, extending over an area of 600 square meters (about one-quarter of an acre), and divided into three main sections. One of these is reproduced here. It in turn was divided into three long halls by means of two rows of square pillars that supported the ceiling. The side halls were found to contain fragments of hundreds of different types of pottery, while the empty center hall was apparently a corridor for donkey caravans. Supporting this theory are the troughs that were installed between the pillars, and holes for tying animals. The storehouse was used by administrative officials and army units.

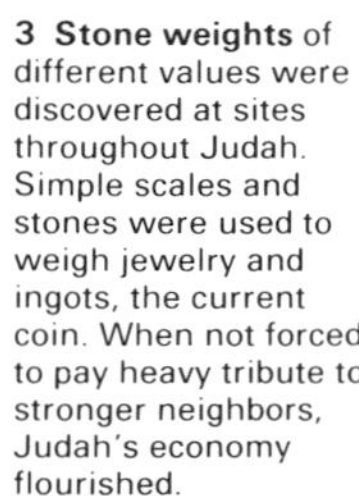

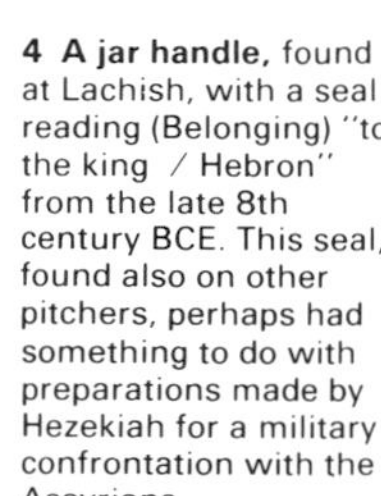

3

3 Stone weights of different values were discovered at sites throughout Judah. Simple scales and stones were used to weigh jewelry and ingots, the current coin. When not forced to pay heavy tribute to stronger neighbors, Judah's economy flourished.

4

4 A jar handle, found at Lachish, with a seal reading (Belonging) "to the king / Hebron" from the late 8th century BCE. This seal, found also on other pitchers, perhaps had something to do with preparations made by Hezekiah for a military confrontation with the Assyrians.

2

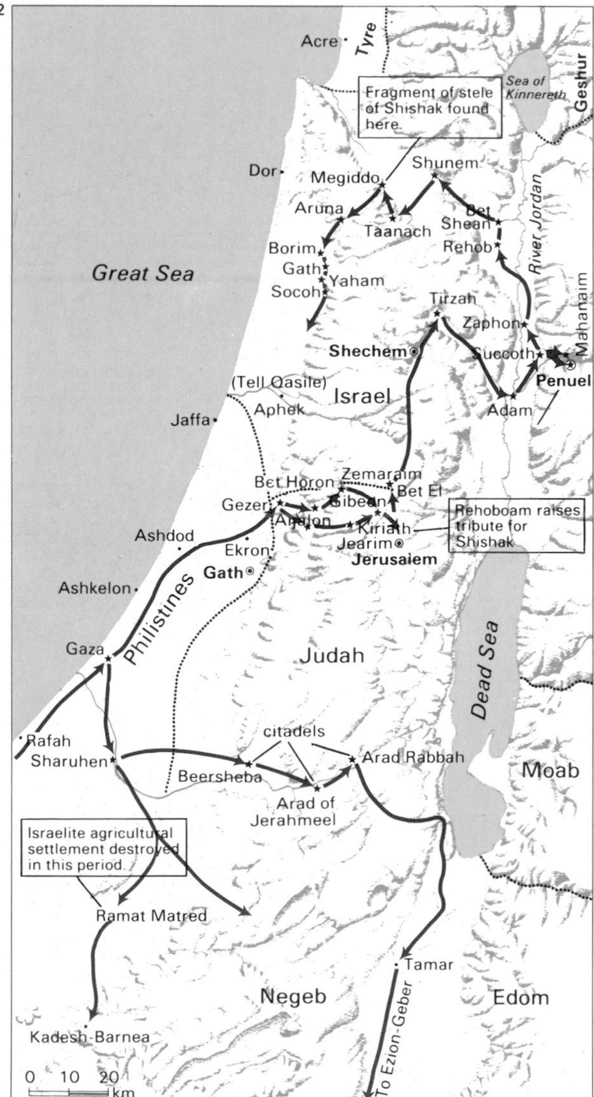

2 The campaign by Shishak, King of Egypt (924 BCE) was further explained when historians found a relevant inscription in Egypt. It confirms the biblical account that Shishak did, in fact, make for Jerusalem, but — apparently after receiving heavy tribute — he turned northward to the Kingdom of Israel. Later he assaulted locations in the Negev. The inscription includes a list of the cities in Erez Israel which he conquered.

reforms took place during the reigns of Hezekiah and Josiah. As the Assyrian king, Sargon, was more moderate than his predecessors, King Hezekiah (727-698 BCE) was able to minimize foreign idol worship. His attempt to rebel against Assyria, however, proved costly. He did succeed in fortifying Jerusalem, and in setting up emergency stores [4] and water reserves for the city [7]. However, he was not strong enough to stand up to Sennacherib and his armies. Many of Judah's settlements were destroyed [5], and its treasury drained — but Jerusalem itself was not conquered (701 BCE).

Approximately one hundred years later, during the final quarter of the 7th century BCE, Josiah took advantage of Assyria's weakened position (the fall of Nineveh, 612 BCE) and annexed Ephraim and Sumeria to Judah. Judah's ambitions for national and religious reawakening — expressed by the repair of the Holy Temple and the concentration of ritual in Jerusalem once again — represented a final effort to preserve the national and religious independence of the People of Israel.

The End of the Kingdom

Egypt and Babylonia vied between them in carving up the Assyrian Empire, and after Josiah's death, controversy among the people between those fávoring Egypt and those supporting Babylonia created serious tension. The prophets saw the Babylonians as the tribe of the Lord's wrath, through whom He sought to punish the different peoples. Nebuchadnezzar's siege of Jerusalem (598 BCE) and the exile of Jehoiachin were seen as proof of this prophecy.

In 589 BCE Judah again rebelled against Babylonia. Nebuchadnezzar invaded, Egyptian support arrived too late, and in 586 BCE, Nebuchadnezzar conquered Jerusalem, laid waste to its walls and luxurious houses, burned the Temple, and deported the vast majority of the Jewish people. The Kingdom of Judah was destroyed.

KEY

An Israelite administrative city from the period of the monarchy was excavated at Tell Beersheba. The extensively excavated city's small size (less than three acres) renders its overall plan easily distinguishable. A wall with an impressive gate surrounded the city, and several roads ran around its perimeter. Beneath the road surfaces, a system for rainwater drainage was found. The city comprised some 75 dwellings and administrative buildings — e.g., storerooms, governor's residence, temple, water system. Its small dimensions and the obvious effort invested in the administrative buildings, indicate that it was inhabited by a small group of royal officials and administrators.

5 A

5 B

5 The Assyrian conquest of Lachish in 701 BCE is described in detail on a stone relief discovered inside the palace of Sennacherib, King of Assyria, at Nineveh. In that year Sennacherib made for Phoenicia and Erez Israel to crush rebellions against his government led by Hezekiah, King of Judah. Many of Judah's fortified cities fell and their citizens were deported to the Assyrian kingdom. Excavations at Lachish have uncovered the Assyrian siege ramp, as well as arrowheads and slingstones. The city was destroyed by fire.

6

6 A group of pottery vessels typical of the Kingdom of Judah. In living quarters found at various sites, many complete sets of household pottery were discovered, including cooking pots, jugs, juglets, bowls, flasks, and lamps. These vessels give us a greater understanding of daily life in Judah at that time.

7

7 The Siloam inscription from Jerusalem describes the last moments of work as the tunnel was being dug. It was inscribed on the rock near the exit of the tunnel, which was designed to take the waters of the Gihon to the city. The winding tunnel (500 m. long) was hewn from both ends. The project has been attributed to Hezekiah.

8

8 A stone parapet, 7th century BCE, from the royal palace discovered at the elaborate citadel of the kings of Judah at Ramat Rahel. Its design — a row of columns with protoaeolic capitals — has been found on many ivory carvings excavated in Erez Israel, Syria and Assyria. The design represents the head of a woman etched on a window frame, leaning on a parapet with three or four balustrades having capitals similar to those found at Ramat Rahel. The "Woman at the Window" motif is common in the Bible and in Phoenician art, where the story is usually about a princess looking through a palace window.

Destruction and Exile

The Babylonians turned Jerusalem into a heap of ruins. The King's palace and the luxurious buildings of Judah were burned down [1, 5], and the destruction of the Holy Temple on the 9th day of Av has been commemorated in every generation since as a national day of mourning. Judah became a Babylonian *pashalik* — the regional administrative unit of the Babylonian kingdom — with limited autonomy, and a member of a noble Judean family was appointed commissioner. The center of government was removed to Mizpeh [4]. The first commissioner, Gedaliah ben Ahikam, was murdered shortly after his appointment, by conspirators who considered him representative of Babylonian rule. This act aroused great fear, and the last vestiges of the Judean population fled to Egypt. The country was emptied of Jewish inhabitants.

Like the Assyrians before them, the Babylonians exiled peoples from their conquered lands to prevent them from reorganizing, either militarily or politically, as well as to break their spirit and diminish their feelings of national identity [6]. Nevertheless, even in Babylonia the exiles from Judah retained their unique national character. Before the destruction of the Temple, the Prophet Jeremiah had sent a message to the first exiles in Babylonia — those deported together with King Jehoiachin (596 BCE) — in which he foretold that their exile would be a long one [2].

According to the Book of Ezekiel, most of the exiles were settled near the Chebar River — a large canal near the city of Nippur, between Assyria and Babylonia. This region had been destroyed and most of its native population apparently deported. Here most of the Judean exiles were farmers, while some engaged in commerce, as evidenced by the Murashu family documents discovered in the region. It would appear that the Babylonian exiles were free to organize as an ethnic community. Later lists of repatriates to Ereẓ Israel indicate that their communal organization was based on division into families and paternal households, and that the Elders were the leaders in exile, as they had been in Ereẓ Israel.

The Prophets of Exile

During the extensive period of their exile, the captives from Judah adapted to their new surroundings, becoming economically well-established. Captivity and the destruction of the Temple however had left them bitter and humiliated. They believed that they were being punished for the sins of their fathers, and that in order to be worthy of returning once more to their own land they would have to mend their ways. But with the passing of time they saw no end to their state of exile, and some began to assimilate. The prophets among the Jews in Babylonia saw it as their duty to preserve the moral and spiritual values of their people in captivity [Key].

The prophets Ezekiel and Isaiah ("The Second Isaiah") sought to console

CONNECTIONS

32 The Kingdom of Judah
36 The Return to Zion
58 The Egyptian Jewish Community in Ancient Times
60 The Jewish Community in Babylonia

1

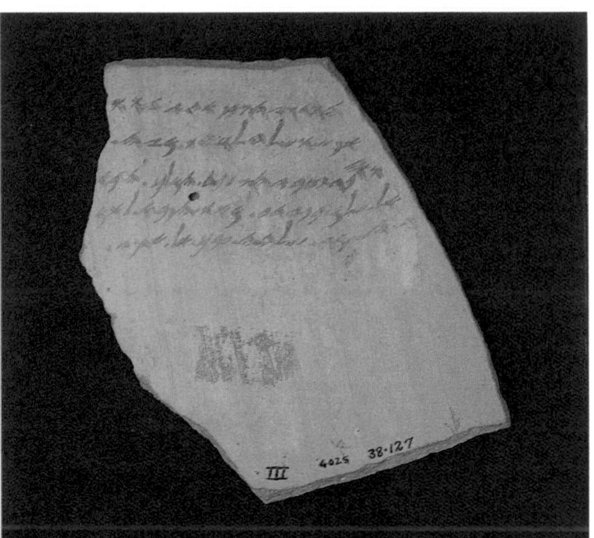

1 The Lachish Letters were discovered in the ruins of a small room in the outer entrance gate of the city wall. Lachish was conquered by the Babylonians in 587/6 BCE. The eighteen ostraca were written with black ink on shards in cursive Hebrew. Most deal with the fate of one of the prophets, whose name has not come down to us, and are written to Ya'ush, apparently the commander there.

2

2 Jeremiah lamenting the Destruction in a painting by Rembrandt (1606-1669). Jeremiah saw the Babylonians as the expression of God's wrath, and tried to influence the people to surrender to Nebuchadnezzar. After Jehoiachin was delivered into captivity and the Temple destroyed, he began to foretell Redemption for the Israelites after they had become purified of their sins through suffering.

3

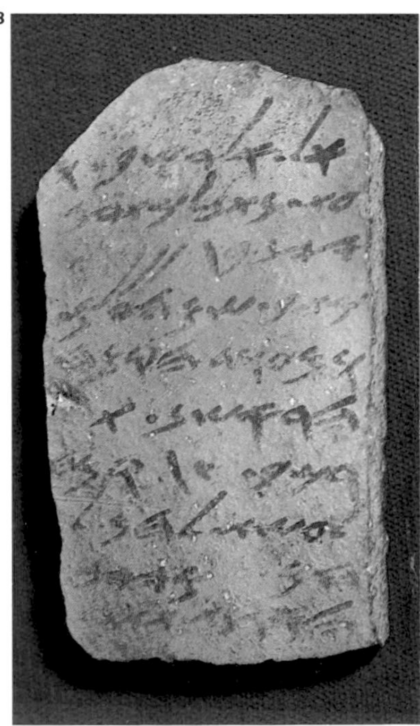

3 This Ostracon is one of dozens of Hebrew ostraca discovered at the royal citadel at Arad. This fortress, which included dwellings, workshops, a warehouse, and a temple, existed until the end of the First Temple Period. The collection of ostraca from the last Israelite level there includes mainly documents in Hebrew cursive, in the biblical style. The documents include instructions on how much wine, bread, and oil was to be given to those who delivered them. Eliashib preserved these in his archives as vouchers. They provide us with information on how border fortresses in the Negev were administered during the period of the Kingdom of Judah, and shed light on the Edomite threat to Judah's security.

the people. Ezekiel ben Buzi prophesied a return to Zion. He developed the theory of individual retribution, according to which the individual is responsible for his own actions, and children do not bear the burden of their fathers' sins. In "The Vision of the Dry Bones" (Chapter 37) Ezekiel prophesied a bright future for his people: like dry bones which become covered with sinews and flesh once again, so would the exiles rise up to national rebirth, and return to their own land. Never again would the people divide into two separate kingdoms, and the Holy Temple would be rebuilt in Jerusalem.

The prophet known as "The Second Isaiah" began to preach when Cyrus, king of Persia, first took the throne. Isaiah's words of salvation and redemption gave renewed hope to the people. God's universal plan, he said, would use Cyrus — the alien and idol-worshiping king — to overthrow the Babylonians, redeem the people of Israel, and rebuild Jerusalem and the Holy Temple.

Waiting for Deliverance

The exiles, allowed to lead their private lives freely, were able to nurture symbols and expectations — such as Renewal of the Kingdom of the House of David, and Rebuilding of the Temple — that strengthened their national and religious consciousness. The priests maintained ritual observances — involving purification and sacrifices at the Holy Temple — so that they would be able to serve in the Temple once again when it was rebuilt. In the "end of day" prophecies, the House of David was to play a major role in rebuilding the united kingdom. Jehoiachin, a descendant of the House of David, continued to be thought of as King of Judah, and remained the leader of the people even in captivity. Although imprisoned, his royal position was recognized, and he and his sons were even guests at the table of the Babylonian king. Thus, the view that the royal House of David, chosen by God, was eternal, became even more deeply rooted.

KEY

A figure of The Prophet, by the German artist, Emil Nolde (1867-1956). The prophets who counseled on the eve of the Assyrian and Babylonian conquests addressed dramatic events. Isaiah was the first to integrate the fate of Israel and that of other peoples: their histories were connected with that of Israel — which stood in the center of the world's history — and were dictated by a divine universal plan. The prophets of destruction, especially Jeremiah and Ezekiel, display feelings of indignation alternated with compassion. Ezekiel was forced to face the futility of his prophetic chastisement and to realize man's inability to affect the course of history.

4

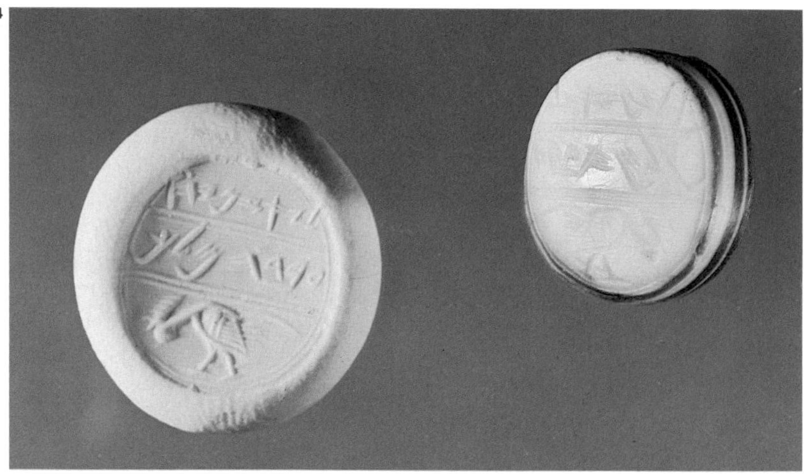

4 Seal "Of Iazniahu, Servant of the King" from the 7th century BCE, at the end of the period of monarchy in Judah. The seal was found at the site of Mizpeh, eight miles north of Jerusalem, which served as Judah's last administrative center after the destruction of Jerusalem by the Babylonians. The upper part of the seal shows the name and title of its owner. The lower part shows a cock in fighting stance — perhaps the family's emblem. This type of seal was given to high officials.

5

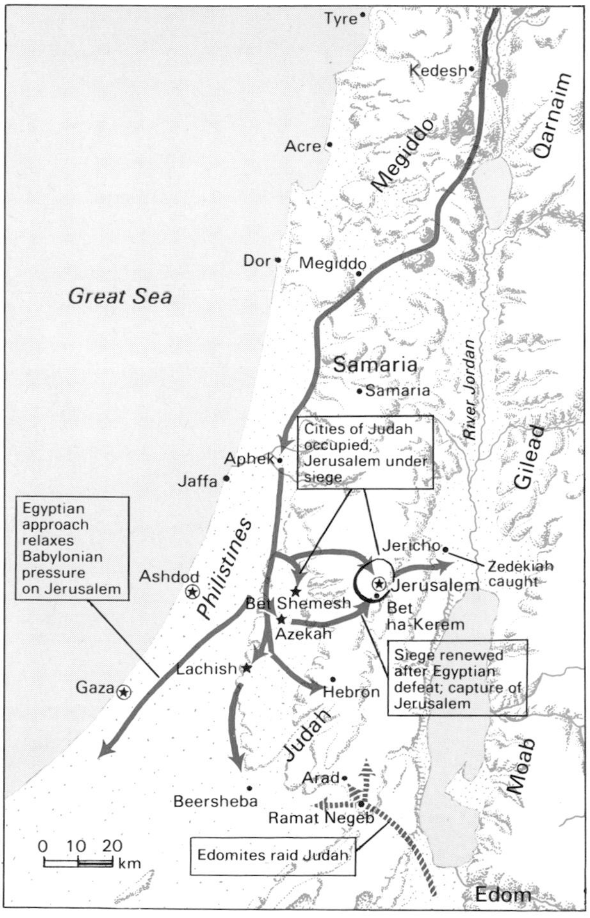

6

6 Exiles on their way to Mesopotamia are shown in this Assyrian relief engraving. The Assyrians would uproot a conquered people and settle exiles from other countries in their stead. By depriving the conquered of their national identity, the Assyrians reinforced their control. The Babylonians, in contrast, did not bring exiles to Erez Israel.

5 A campaign by King Nebuchadnezzar of Babylonia to punish Judah after the rebellion of Zedekiah, took place between 588 and 586 BCE. Excavations show that the Kingdom of Judah was totally destroyed. Erez Israel was annexed to the Babylonian Empire, and the people of Judah — aside from the very poor, the vinegrowers, farmers, and field laborers who were left in their villages — were exiled to Babylonia. Upon their return during the time of Persian rule, the repatriates met former neighbors who had appropriated their land. As the lands belonging to the tribe of Benjamin had not been destroyed, Mizpeh was established as the capital by Gedaliah ben Ahikam.

The Return to Zion

The fall of Babylonia and the victory of Cyrus, King of Persia (in 539 BCE), awakened high expectations among the Babylonian exiles. Cyrus issued a declaration permitting the Jews of Babylonia to go to Jerusalem, there to rebuild their ravaged Temple [Key]. The Jews remaining in Babylonia were allowed to send financial aid for the task of rebuilding the Temple. Many Jews, led by Sheshbazzar, of the House of David, left Babylonia for Judah [1]. The Books of Ezra and Nehemiah list some fifty thousand repatriates — apparently including all those who returned from the time of Cyrus' declaration until the return of Nehemiah (445 BCE).

Construction of the Temple

In describing the return of the exiles Scripture says simply that they "came again unto Jerusalem and Judah, every one unto his city" (Ezra 2:1). About half a year later a festive ceremony was held in Jerusalem to mark the beginning of reconstruction of the Temple. However work on the Temple was soon halted, for the inhabitants of Mount Ephraim (later known as the Samaritans) also requested to take part, claiming that they, too, worshiped the God of Israel [2]. Their request was denied on the grounds that the permit to build the Temple applied only to the repatriates; yet it seems that the real reason for denying the request was the suspicion that the Samaritans worshiped other gods as well. Through threats, harassment, and denunciations, the Samaritans managed to halt construction of the Temple until 520 BCE [8].

In 522 BCE Darius I ascended the throne of Persia (he ruled until 486 BCE). For the first two years of his reign the repatriates received encouragement from the prophets, Haggai and Zechariah, and resumed the work of rebuilding the Temple, under the leadership of Zerubbabel, son of Shealtiel, of the House of David. In the month of Adar (March-April) of 516 BCE the Temple was dedicated, thus symbolizing the hope that the kingdom of the House of David would be renewed (Ezra 6:16-18).

During the next sixty years (516-458 BCE) the Jews apparently began to draw closer to the local population, whom they had at first rejected, and some Jews even assimilated [7].

Ezra and Nehemiah

In the seventh regnal year of Artaxerxes I (458 BCE) Ezra arrived in Jerusalem, heading a group of several thousand repatriates. The King of Persia evidently encouraged renewed immigration to Erez Israel in the wake of serious uprisings which had broken out against him in Egypt; he presumably hoped in this way to win the allegiance of the inhabitants of nearby Judah. Ezra convened a gathering of the entire people, in which the *Torah* was read aloud, accompanied by explanation and interpretation (Nehemiah 8). Ezra's separatist approach was not well accepted by the general public, and his endeavors were not a complete success.

CONNECTIONS

34 Destruction and Exile

38 Erez Israel in the Fourth and Third Centuries BCE

1

1 The Land of Israel was part of the *satrapy* of *Abar-nahara* which extended from the Euphrates to Egypt. The Persian Empire was divided into administrative districts called *satrapies*, which were subdivided in turn, according to the nationalities inhabiting them, into districts also called *satrapies*, or states. Each *satrapy* was governed by a *satrap*, appointed by the king. Sometimes a Jew was appointed to this office, as in the case of Nehemiah. The *satrap* had a military force at his disposal, and his main duty was to collect taxes and forward them to the royal treasury.

2 Samaria was one of the provinces included in Erez Israel. Sanballat and his descendants governed Samaria until the conquest of Erez Israel by Alexander the Great (332 BCE). The Samaritans, who viewed themselves as the heirs of the ten exiled tribes, were considered gentiles by the repatriates, and were called "ignorant natives" (*Am ha-Aretz*).

2

3

3 Greek pottery appeared in Erez Israel as far back as the late 7th century BCE. These vessels were primarily imported from Corinth and Rhodes, but in the 6th and 5th centuries the vast majority of the pottery came from Athens. The pottery apparently reached the coastal cities via Greek traders, and was brought inland by Phoenician and Arab merchants. Greek material culture penetrated the area long before its conquest by Alexander the Great in the 4th century BCE.

4

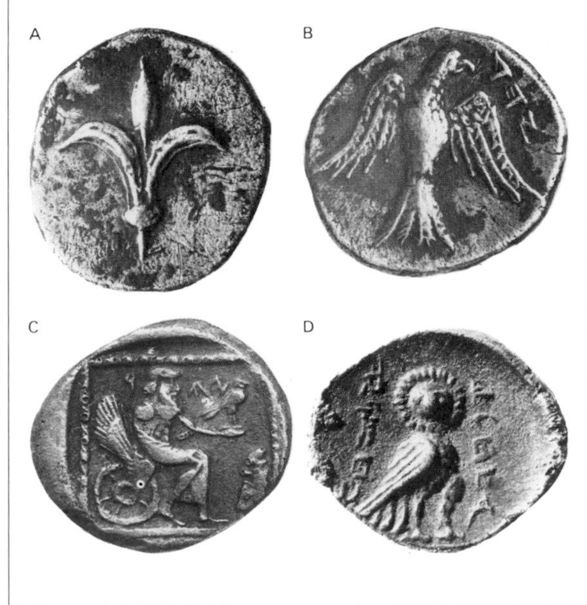

4 The coins in currency in Erez Israel during the Persian period were of several kinds: Greek coins, primarily from Athens; Phoenician coins; royal Persian coins; and local coins. A large number of coins from the late 5th and the 4th centuries, BCE have been discovered, bearing the Aramaic name of the province of Judah — Yehud. These coins bear a number of different impressions, including: a lily [A], a falcon spreading its wings [B], a demigod on a chariot [C], an owl [D],and the inscriptions *YHD* or *YHUD* (varying forms of "Yehud"). Scholars believe that coins bearing the name of the *satrapy* of Judah were minted both by the autonomous Jewish authority and by the Persian government.

In Artaxerxes' 20th regnal year (445 BCE) Nehemiah, who had been the cupbearer of the King of Persia, was appointed *satrap* of Judah, and received permission to rebuild Jerusalem. His first undertaking was to repair the destroyed city wall. The task was performed by groups of volunteers, and was completed in 52 days. His next step was to increase Jerusalem's population by edict, compelling one out of every ten inhabitants of the towns of Judah to move to Jerusalem. Nehemiah also carried out a social-agrarian reform which won him broad popular support, and helped him fight the opposition which emerged among the nobility. Now Nehemiah could set about putting Temple worship in order and carrying on the policy of segregation from the gentiles, initiated by Ezra. The "covenant" which he made with the people included a pledge to maintain Jewish separatism from the local inhabitants and to refrain from intermarriage; to observe the Sabbath and not engage in commerce on that day; to keep the commandments of the sabbatical year; and to see to the Temple worship.

After twelve years in Jerusalem Nehemiah returned to Persia. He served in the king's court for an unspecified period of time, and then returned to Jerusalem for an additional term of service as governor of Judah. Some of the legislation he had enacted had not been kept during his absence, so upon his return he took forceful action against the infractors (Nehemiah 13).

The foundations which were to shape the religious, cultural, national and social character of the Jewish people for generations to come were laid during the period of the Return to Zion. The *Torah* was established as the fundamental law guiding the life of the people, and autonomous Jewish existence under the aegis of a foreign sovereign power took root. Not all of the exiles returned. Thus was born the concept of a center and a diaspora, which has characterized the history of the Jews ever since.

KEY

"Cyrus' Declaration" was part of Cyrus' general policy toward the various nationalities annexed to the Persian Empire. A clay cylinder, written in cuneiform (the lingua franca of the time), discovered in 1890, publicized Cyrus' policy declaration regarding the nationalities residing in the areas he conquered. This inscription testifies to Cyrus' tolerance of various religious rites and his concern to rebuild temples which had been destroyed by the previous (Babylonian) government and to restore idols to their places: "... and as far as Ashur and Susa, Agade and Eshnunna... I returned to these sacred cities, the sanctuaries of which have been ruins for a long time, the images which used to live therein and established for them permanent sanctuaries. I (also) gathered all their (former) inhabitants and returned (to them) their habitations...."

5 Persian-Achaemenid jewelry has been assigned by scholars to the style of animal ornamentation. Pictured is the end of a gold earring, in the form of an animal head, discovered in Ashdod. The jewelry was either brought to the country by Persian soldiers or officials serving in the local government, or was made by local jewelers imitating the Achaemenid style. A pair of silver bracelets, with ends shaped like the heads of does or ibexes, was discovered at Gezer. Bracelets of this sort are widespread throughout the entire ancient East.

6 Seal impressions from the Persian period (6-5th centuries BCE) have been discovered on pottery jars. Most of them bear Aramaic or Hebrew inscriptions, including the Aramaic name of the *satrapy* of Judah, in its various forms: *YHUD, YHD, YH H*. These jars apparently contained the levies for the *satrap*, and perhaps even contributions to the Temple. A private name may appear on another kind of seal, with or without the office of *satrap*. Pictured is a clay seal impression discovered in a cavern in Wadi Daliya.

5

6

7

7 Metalware and cosmetic pallets from the beginning of the Persian period have been discovered in great numbers at sites in Israel and neighboring countries. Bowls found in Israel resemble ones found in Persia itself. Some may have been imported from manufacturing centers in Persia, but most were doubtlessly manufactured by local Phoenician craftsmen. These craftsmen apparently copied contemporary Persian models, which replaced Assyrian or Egyptian ones. Pictured is a bowl with characteristic ornamentation and a silver spoon with a handle shaped in the image of a woman, both discovered in a tomb from the Persian period at Tel al-Farah.

8 A

8 B

8 Friction between Jews and Samaritans existed throughout the entire Persian period, and was set off by repatriates' refusal to let the Samaritans join them in rebuilding the Temple. Ezra and Nehemiah concentrated on opposing marriages with gentile women, making Sanballat, governor of Samaria, one of their chief foes. Together with other leaders who opposed Nehemiah's way, Sanballat tried to foil part of his plans, but without great success. In contrast, Nehemiah succeeded in causing the high priest, who had married Sanballat's daughter, to flee from Jerusalem. The struggle intensified toward the end of the Persian period. King Darius III of Persia again appointed a Sanballat descendant *satrap* of Samaria, and the latter married off his daughter, Nikaso, to Manasseh, brother of the high priest in Jerusalem. This led to Manasseh's expulsion from Jerusalem. When Alexander the Great came to the region the Samaritans supported him in exchange for permission to build their own temple on Mount Gerizim [A, B]. But, when a Macedonian official was appointed governor of Samaria, the Samaritans revolted and burned him to death. As a result, the Jews were granted new privileges.

Ereẓ Israel in the Fourth and Third Centuries BCE

Alexander the Great's decisive victory over the Persian army at the battle of Issus (333 BCE) opened the way for him to Syria, Ereẓ Israel, and Egypt [Key]. The fate of the Jews of Ereẓ Israel after Alexander's conquest is mentioned in several Jewish sources. Josephus tells of a meeting between Alexander and the high priest, and of Alexander visiting Jerusalem; and a similar story is recounted in works of the Sages. Both stories share a certain bias: they seek to show the greatness of the God of Israel, whom even Alexander, the renowned conqueror, acknowledged and paid respect to; and to emphasize Alexander's support for the Jews and punishment of the Samaritans.

The legendary and possibly tendentious nature of these stories has led some scholars to challenge their historical validity; yet since Alexander is known to have followed a policy of tolerance toward the peoples he conquered it is reasonable to surmise that he did meet with Jewish officials and ratify the autonomy which the Jews had enjoyed under Persian rule, at least within similar territorial boundaries.

The Wars of the Diadochi

Alexander died in 323 BCE, and his senior generals, the *Diadochi* (Greek for successors), began to struggle for the crown. This was a period of great turbulence for Ereẓ Israel. Situated between Egypt and Syria, it was in the path of Alexander's warring successors: Perdiccas and Antigonus (Cyclops), based in Syria, fought Ptolemy I [3], whose stronghold was in Egypt. Ereẓ Israel was the scene of two battles in which Perdiccas and Antigonus attempted to attack Ptolemy, and of four invasions by Ptolemy. In the course of these wars cities were destroyed, and many inhabitants were sold into slavery or fled, primarily to Egypt. Josephus Flavius wrote that in 312 BCE, after a battle for Gaza, a group of Jews led by Hezekiah the "Great Priest" moved to Egypt. In the span of about 20 years (323-301 BCE) Ereẓ Israel underwent five changes of ruler.

The Ptolemies in Ereẓ Israel

In 301 BCE Ereẓ Israel passed into the hands of the Ptolemies for the fourth time. For most of the 3rd century BCE the Ptolemies ruled Ereẓ Israel on both sides of the Jordan River; the Mediterranean basin as far as Tripoli; and the Lebanon Valley as far as Baalbek. A commissioner (*strategos*), the supreme military and civilian authority in the region, headed the Ptolemaic regime in "Syria and Phoenicia," together with a senior treasury official (*dioiketes*), who was appointed over the revenues of the region.

The Papyri of Zeno, discovered at Faiyum, Egypt, shed light on Ptolemaic administrative practices [6, 7]. Ereẓ Israel was divided into small administrative districts, which continued to exist throughout the entire Second Temple period. They were populated by Samaritans and Edomites as well as

CONNECTIONS

40 Seleucid Rule and the Edicts of Antiochus
58 The Egyptian Jewish Community in Ancient Times

1 Qasr al-'Abd (Fortress of the Servant), apparently built by Hyrcanus son of Tobiah, at the beginning of the 2nd century BCE. The building is ornamented in Ptolemaic style, with sculptures and animal reliefs such as this lioness. They testify to the affluence of the Tobiads, and to their Hellenization. The Tobiads were among the leading families in Jerusalem to advocate Hellenistic culture.

2 A silver coin bearing the name of Alexander the Great. The coin was minted in Acre, apparently in 312 BCE. After the conquest of Tyre, Acre grew in importance, and a mint was set up there. The coin portrays Zeus, seated on his throne and holding an eagle in one hand and a scepter in the other. To his right is a Greek inscription, "Coin of Alexander." Beneath the eagle is the Phoenician inscription, "Acre 34," giving the city and year the coin was minted (by an unknown reckoning). Alexander appears on the reverse side of the coin.

3 Ptolemy I son of Lagus, was appointed ruler of Egypt after the death of Alexander. Here he appears on a coin from 300 BCE. On the reverse side is an eagle, emblem of the Ptolemies.

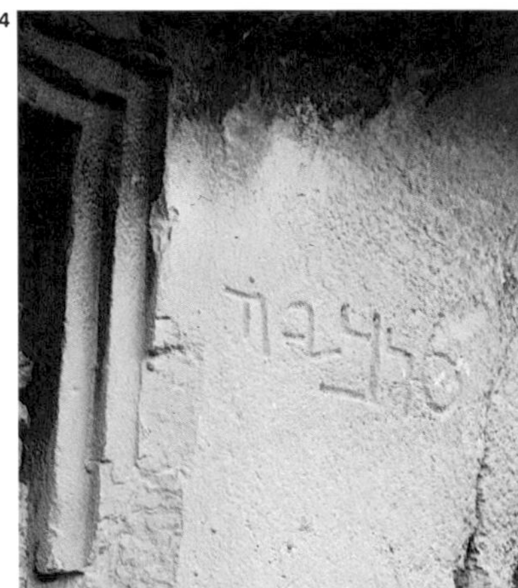

4 The name "Tobiah" is inscribed in a rock at al-Amir, in Transjordan, in southern Gilead. After the death of Joseph son of Tobiah his son, Hyrcanus, fought with his brothers over the powerful and lucrative office of tax farmer. Hyrcanus availed himself of the strength of the Ptolemies, while his brothers were more inclined toward the Seleucids. In the end Hyrcanus was forced to leave Jerusalem for Transjordan.

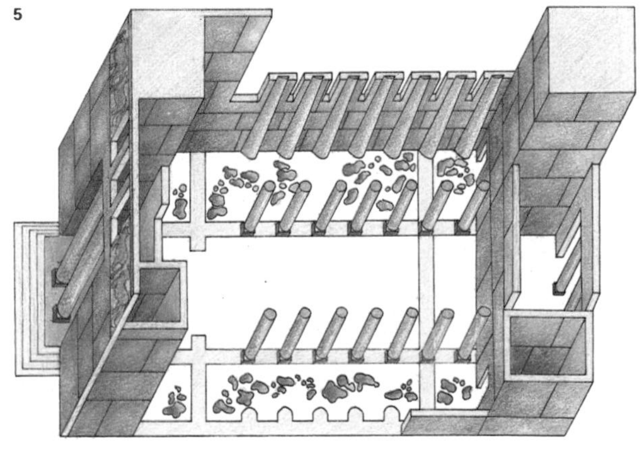

5 The Tobiads, an aristocratic family descended of the priesthood, were influential as early as the Babylonian exile. A man called Tobiah, designated "the Ammonite Servant," is mentioned in the Book of Nehemiah as a member of the opposition to Nehemiah's policy of separatism, and as a person having connections with the Judean nobility and with Eliashib the high priest. Under Ptolemy II Tobiah headed a military colony in Transjordan. Land in the colony was allocated to Jewish, Greek, and Macedonian horsemen who had fought in Ptolemy's army. The family attained greatest influence during the time of Joseph son of Tobiah, appointed by the authorities as tax farmer of Syria and Phoenicia. Pictured is a reconstruction of the palace known as Qasr al-'Abd, discovered in Transjordan, near 'Iraq al-Amir. This site is identified with "the *birta* of Ammon" and Tyros, mentioned by Zeno and Josephus as the center of Tobiah's colony.

Jews, and the Ptolemies allowed them a degree of autonomy. Two fundamental problems occupied the Ptolemaic administration: regularizing tax collection, and assuring security against the persistent Seleucid threat. The former task was entrusted to tax farmers, for the most part from distinguished families, who pledged in advance to forward to the treasury a fixed sum of money. The tax farmers were interested in collecting the highest possible sum of taxes, since they themselves pocketed the difference between what they collected and what they had pledged the treasury. Thus there emerged a class of the very wealthy, who worked in cooperation with the government and, when necessary, availed themselves of the army stationed in the land.

The Ptolemies maintained a mercenary force in the country's fortresses and key cities, as well as military colonies, some of which had been founded during the time of Alexander and the *Diadochi*. In exchange for pledging to serve in the army upon request, those who settled in these colonies received land from the king, and were responsible for the day-to-day security of their region. Such a colony in Transjordan was headed by Tobiah [1, 4, 5].

Little is known to us about the history of the Jews under Ptolemaic rule. Some information is provided by the Third Book of Maccabees, written by an Alexandrian Jew. It tells of Ptolemy IV breaking into the Temple, after defeating the Seleucids at the Battle of Rafah, in 217 BCE.

Both gentile and Jewish sources mention a Jewish population explosion. Judah and southern Samaria, the Jewish regions, could not accommodate their large populations [6].

Ptolemaic rule in Erez Israel had a great impact on cultural and social life; during this period Hellenistic culture spread throughout the country [9]. Jewish society was no exception in its inability to prevent the penetration of these foreign influences.

KEY

Alexander the Great crushed the Persian Empire in three decisive battles — at Granicus (334 BCE), Issus (333 BCE), and Gaugamela (331 BCE). By the end of his short life he ruled over Macedonia, the Persian Empire, and the greater part of the Greek world. His conquests and plans to fuse East and West greatly changed the face of the Greek world. Pictured is a section of a mosaic discovered at Pompeii. Alexander appears astride his horse, apparently at the battle of Issus, fought against Darius III, King of Persia.

6

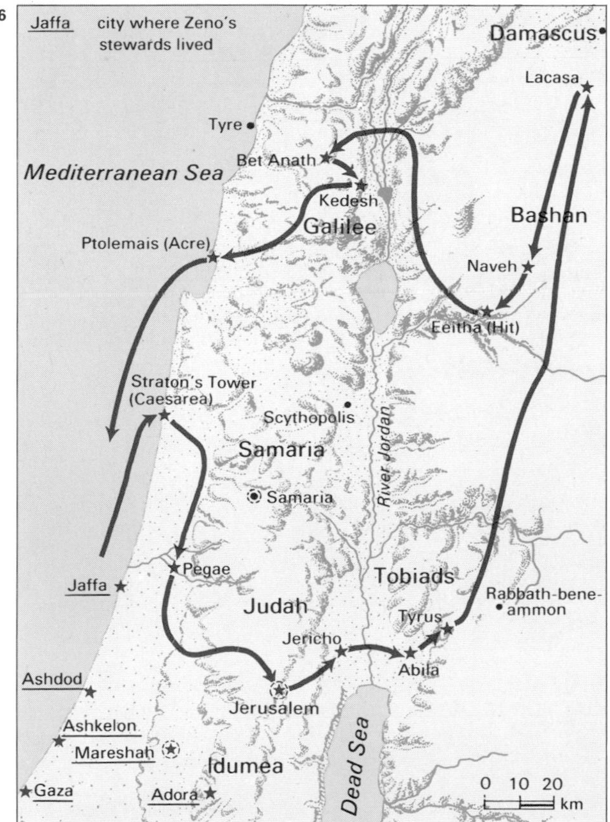

6 Zeno's expeditions in Erez Israel date to 259-258 BCE. Zeno son of Agreophontos was a Greek from Asia Minor who moved to Egypt, and served Apollonius, finance minister in the government of Ptolemy II (Philadelphus) (285-246 BCE). Under the Ptolemies Erez Israel, and particularly its coastal cities, benefited from the growth of trade with the countries of the western Mediterranean basin, the Aegean Sea, and southern Arabia. It specialized in two products — balsam (persimmons) from En Gedi and Jericho, and bitumen from the Dead Sea. It also exported and imported wine and olive oil. During this period the land could not contain its large population, Jewish and gentile. Overcrowding, repeated wars, and hardship compelled many to emigrate. The vast majority chose to settle in Egypt because of its flourishing economy under the Ptolemies.

7 Bill of sale for a maidservant — a papyrus from the Zeno archives. The contract was made between the seller, a military settler from the "Land of Tobiah," and Zeno Appolonius, finance minister of Egypt. The maidservant, a girl of seven from Sidon, was sold for 50 drachmas. Under the Ptolemies a seaborne slave trade flourished in Erez Israel. This and other papyri written by Zeno provide us with much information about daily life and the Ptolemaic administration. They illustrate such phenomena as an overblown bureaucracy, lax government officials who cultivated lucrative sideline occupations, and the important place enjoyed by Erez Israel in the Ptolemaic economy, due to its ports and its location at a strategic crossroads.

7

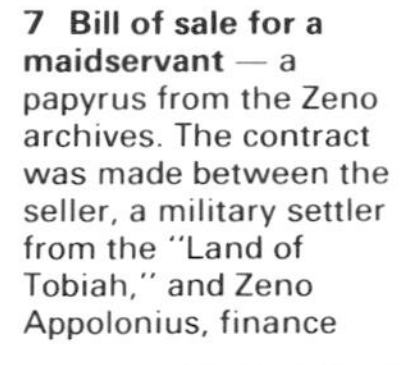

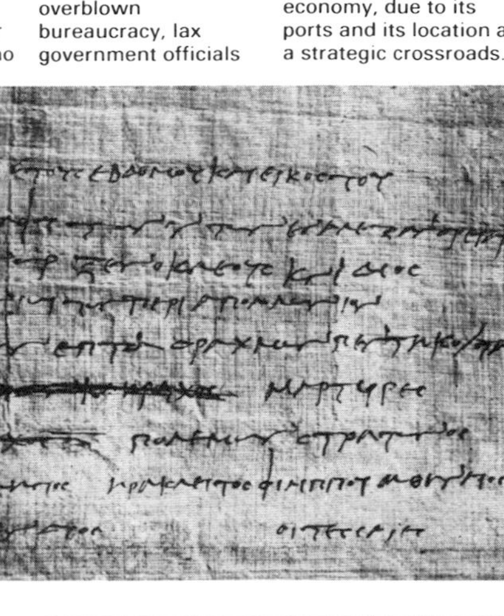

8 A three-pointed cast bronze beak-head, from the 4th-3rd centuries BCE, discovered in the sea near Atlit. War-galleys used beakheads to ram enemy ships. Ptolemaic control over the eastern Mediterranean assured prosperous trade routes by sea.

9 The cult of Aphrodite, the Greek goddess of love and fertility, was widespread throughout the classical world. The picture shows a Hellenistic style clay figurine of Aphrodite, apparently from the end of the 4th century BCE, found near the Mount Carmel caves.

8

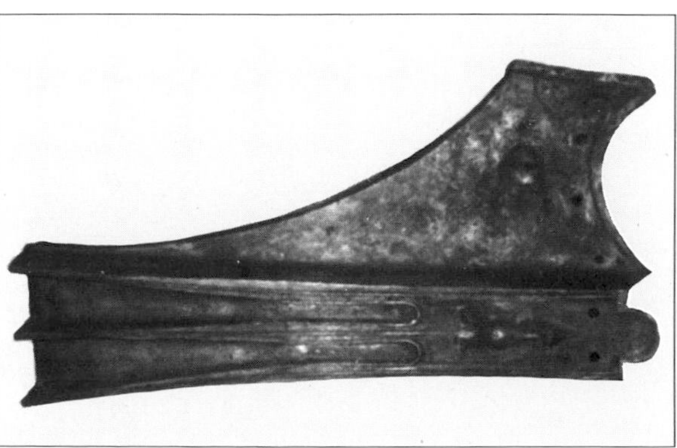

9

Seleucid Rule and the Edicts of Antiochus

In 201 BCE the Seleucid king, Antiochus III, invaded Erez Israel. A year later he routed the Ptolemaic army in a battle at the Banias (Panias). As a result of this victory all of Ptolemaic "Syria and Phoenicia" gradually passed into Seleucid hands. The official Seleucid designation for this region was *Coele* (Bastion of) Syria and Phoenicia, and its ruler continued to be a commissioner (*strategos*), appointed by the king [6].

Judah under Seleucid Rule

Jerusalem was split over the issue of whether to support the Ptolemies or the Seleucids, but the pro-Seleucid faction, headed by the high priest, Simon the Just, prevailed. In return Antiochus III granted them a charter of rights permitting them to live according to the law of their forefathers. This charter also exempted the priests and scribes from taxes, and authorized reconstruction of the city, which had suffered from the war.

Antiochus III was killed during an attempt to plunder a temple at Eilam, at the eastern end of his kingdom (187 BCE). His son, Antiochus IV (Ephiphanes) [7], inherited the throne, as well as the debt to Rome. At that time Onias III was high priest in Jerusalem. During his tenure a struggle for control of the city broke out. Simeon, a priest from the family of Bilga (one of the divisions of priests that ministered in turn), demanded that Onias appoint him *agoranomos* — official in charge of the city's market — a position of great economic importance. Onias refused, and Simeon retaliated by reporting to the Seleucid commissioner about the existence of Temple treasures, whose value far exceeded that needed to maintain Temple worship. This information was passed on to the king, who sent Heliodorus, one of his chief ministers, to Jerusalem to confiscate the treasures. When Onias refused to turn them over Heliodorus attempted to break in to the Temple, but was unsuccessful. Onias, suspected of disloyalty, was compelled to go to Antioch to defend himself.

During Onias' absence a coup took place in Jerusalem. Jason, brother of Onias, purchased the office of high priest from Antiochus IV (175 BCE), thus breaking the tradition of the high priesthood passing from father to son, and making of it an office acquired for money from the foreign ruler. Jason used the priesthood to institute extensive political and cultural reforms. He transformed Jerusalem into a Hellenistic *polis*, establishing in it traditional Greek institutions of education, culture, and sports — a gymnasium and an *ephebeion* [2, 4]. Those supporting this reform were called Hellenists, and those opposing it Hassideans.

Jason held the high priesthood for three years, until he was displaced by Menelaus, brother of Simeon of the Bilga family, who had outbid him for the office. With Menelaus' appointment the prestigious office was removed from the traditional high priestly family of Onias, a family which belonged to the

CONNECTIONS

38 Erez Israel in the Fourth and Third Centuries BCE
42 The Hasmonean Revolt and Political Independence

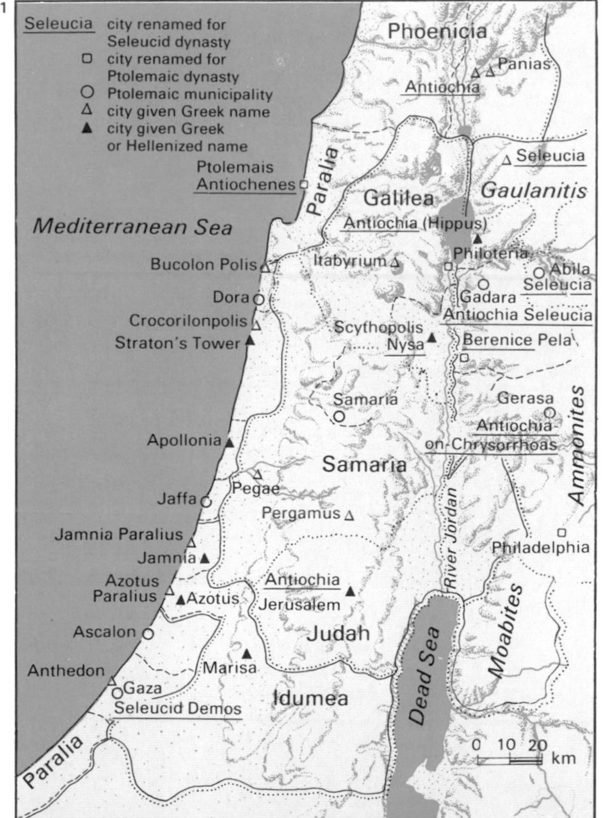

1 Some thirty cities in Erez Israel achieved the status of *polis*, or city-state, and adopted Hellenistic characteristics under Ptolemaic rule. Most were ancient cities; only a few were new. Greek emigrés and Macedonians comprised the bulk of these cities' population, and it was they who determined the cities' cultural and administrative character. These residents enjoyed special privileges vis-à-vis the native inhabitants, whose civil status suffered.

2 Cultivation of the body was a marked characteristic of Hellenistic civilization. Cultural and athletic activities were held in the gymnasium, a very widespread institution in the Hellenistic cities of the Middle East. In some of these cities education in the gymnasium was a precondition for receiving citizenship. The picture shows a detail of two wrestlers, from a painting on a vase discovered in Attica, Greece.

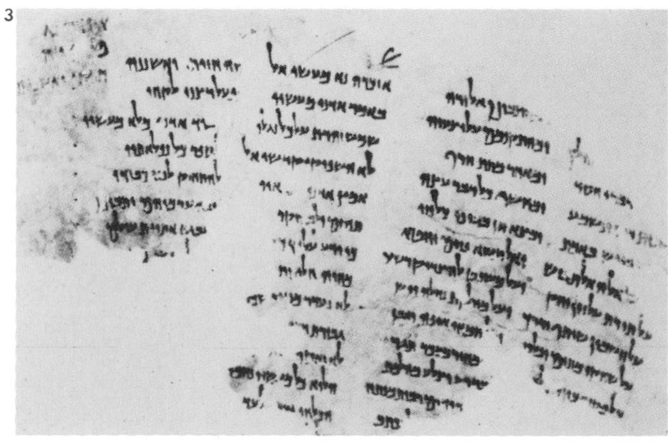

3 The Wisdom of Ben Sira deals with wisdom and morals. It was written by Simeon ben Jesus Ben Sira, of Jerusalem, 2nd century BCE. The book is in Hebrew, and consists of poetic maxims, in the form of the Book of Proverbs. Bearing the mark of its times, the book reflects the conflict between the Hassideans and the Hellenizers of Jerusalem society. In the picture is a fragment of an early version, discovered at Masada.

4 The Greek theater originated in the cult of Dionysus, the Greek god of wine and fertility, considered the patron of the Greek chorus and drama. An element of pagan worship attached to the dramatic activities, hence the intense opposition to these theaters by the adherents of Jewish tradition. The Hellenization of Erez Israel was manifest not only in the introduction of Greek religion and the spread of the Greek language, but also in the participation of the residents of the Hellenistic cities in Hellenistic cultural activities. The picture shows the theater in Epidaurus, Greece, end of the 4th century BCE.

line of Zadok and had held the priesthood since the time of King Solomon. Jason fled to Transjordan, and Onias was assassinated in Antioch, at Menelaus' behest.

The Edicts of Antiochus

Antiochus IV embarked on a series of military campaigns against Egypt from 169-168 BCE. His first campaign had to be curtailed because of riots erupting in Syria. Later he had to give up his aspirations to take Egypt due to pressure from Rome like that which had been brought to bear against his father, Antiochus III. On his return from his first campaign Antiochus IV entered Jerusalem and, with the cooperation of Menelaus, plundered the Temple treasury. During his second campaign false rumors of his death reached Jerusalem, and riots broke out in the city. Jason emerged from hiding, overcame Menelaus, and seized control. However, shortly thereafter he fled the city in the wake of a popular uprising. Antiochus rushed to Jerusalem to suppress the riots. A fortress, the Acra, was built south of the Temple Mount, and a Seleucid garrison was stationed there.

Continuing his radical measures against the rebels, Antiochus passed several edicts against the people: a statue of Zeus and an altar for pagan worship were placed in the Temple, and the Jews were forbidden to keep the commandments of the *Torah*, particularly observance of the Sabbath and circumcision; throughout Judah shrines were built to Greek gods, *Torah* scrolls were burned, and anyone violating the king's edicts was liable to be put to death [6].

Persecution of the Jews led to passive resistance — which usually took the form of martyrdom — on the one hand [5], and to growth of active opposition to Seleucid rule, on the other. Fugitives fleeing the cities to the Judean desert established a popular religious movement of rebellion, headed by the Hassideans.

KEY

Samaria, the city of the Samaritans, was captured by the Macedonian army in the wake of its revolt against Alexander the Great. Its inhabitants were expelled from the land and forced to resettle in Shechem. A military colony, called Samaria, comprised of discharged Macedonian soldiers, was set up on the site, and in the course of time may have attained the status of a *polis*. During the wars among Alexander's successors Samaria changed hands several times, and was destroyed and rebuilt in turn. Excavations there have revealed impressive remains of fortifications, the city wall, and round towers. These were apparently built during the beginning of the Hellenistic period, and are typical of fortifications of the time.

5

5 The edicts of Antiochus led to the emergence of martyrdom. In this liturgical poem for *Hanukkah*, from a 15th century Hamburg manuscript, miniatures illustrate the edicts.

7 The Hefzi-bah inscription, discovered accidentally in the Jezreel Valley, in 1960, comprises the correspondence of Antiochus III with several of his officials, the commissioner of Syria and Phoenicia, and the high priest, Ptolemy. According to Hellenistic practice, government orders were inscribed on stones and placed in central locations. These documents shed light on the state of administration and agriculture in Erez Israel at the beginning of Seleucid rule (202-195 BCE).

8

8 Mareshah (Marissa), a city in Idumea, illustrates the Hellenization of the upper echelons of society in the inland cities of Erez Israel. Excavations there revealed tombs ornamented by colored wall paintings — such as that pictured here — and inscriptions from the third century BCE. Stylistically the paintings resemble those current in Alexandria, Egypt, during the same period. The inscriptions are in Greek, and for the most part mention only the names of the deceased. Phoenicians, Idumeans, and Greeks all dwelled in Marissa together. Here it was the Idumeans and Phoenicians who appear to have been the champions of Hellenism.

7 A

6 A coin of Antiochus IV Epiphanes (ruled 175-163 BCE), with the king's head on one side, and Antiochus portrayed as Zeus on the reverse side. Repressive edicts against the Jews were the exception during his rule, and were apparently motivated primarily by political considerations.

6

7 B

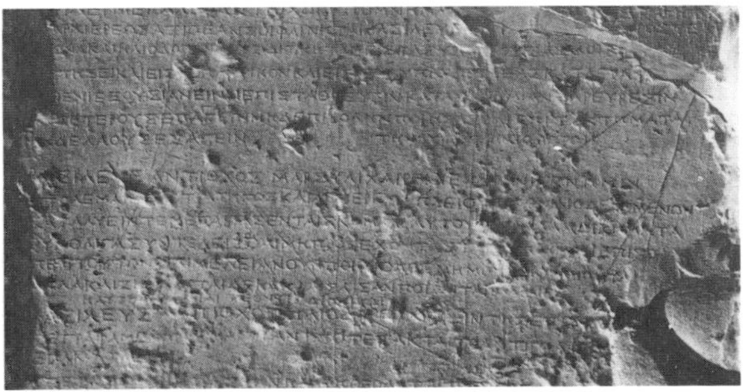

The Hasmonean Revolt and Political Independence

The Hasmonean family raised the banner of revolt, after Seleucid authorities attempted to enforce anti-Jewish edicts in Modi'in, the home of the Hasmoneans [3]. Mattathias and his sons struck out at the king's men, fled to the mountains around Gophna (north of Ramallah), and began to organize an army. The rebels initiated guerrilla tactics against the Seleucid authorities, and took reprisals against collaborators.

Judah Maccabee Leads the Revolt

Shortly after the outbreak of the revolt Mattathias died, and leadership of the revolt passed to his son, Judah Maccabee. The rebels began by cutting off the Hellenizers and the Seleucid garrison that was stationed in Jerusalem's Acra fortress from the major centers of Seleucid control in the lowlands or *Shephelah* (Gezer) and along the coast (Jaffa and Acre). Apollonius, the governor of Samaria, was ambushed and killed while trying to approach Jerusalem from the north. Seron, commander of the forces of Coele-Syria, tried to bring his army to Jerusalem from the direction of the *Shephelah*, but Judah successfully attacked him along the way, at Bet Horon (165 BCE).

Lysias, who had been appointed governor over the western part of the kingdom, dispatched a large military force to Judah, headed by three of his senior generals, including Gorgias. The Seleucid army reached Emmaus, on the western border of the Judean mountains, and set up camp there. Gorgias set out from Emmaus, leading a select unit, to attack Judah Maccabee in his camp at Mizpeh. However, Judah and his men abandoned camp as if in a panic and, while the Seleucid army was searching for them in the mountains, quickly marched down to the *Shephelah*. At dawn they attacked the Seleucid camp and set it aflame [1].

The defeat at Emmaus caused Lysias to embark on a military campaign of his own against Judah (164 BCE). Following a defeat at Bet Zur, Lysias learned that conditions at home required his return; as soon as Lysias and his army left the country Judah took control of Jerusalem and laid siege to the garrison and the Hellenizers in the Acra. The rebels also cleansed the Temple and renewed holy worship there. This took place on the 25th of Kislev, 164 BCE, and is commemorated in the holiday of *Hanukkah* [6].

Meanwhile Antiochus IV died, and the crown duly passed to his young son, Antiochus V, with Lysias effectively regent. Lysias renewed his attack from the south, this time taking Bet Zur. Judah met him in battle at Bet Zacharia [4], but was forced to retreat. Lysias reached Jerusalem, and laid siege to the Temple Mount; however intrigue at home again called him back to Antioch. The sides reached an accord, and Antiochus V announced recision of the edicts and return of control of the Temple to the rebels.

The fight against the Hellenizers continued, and they turned to the authori-

CONNECTIONS

40 Seleucid Rule and the Edicts of Antiochus

44 The Hasmonean State

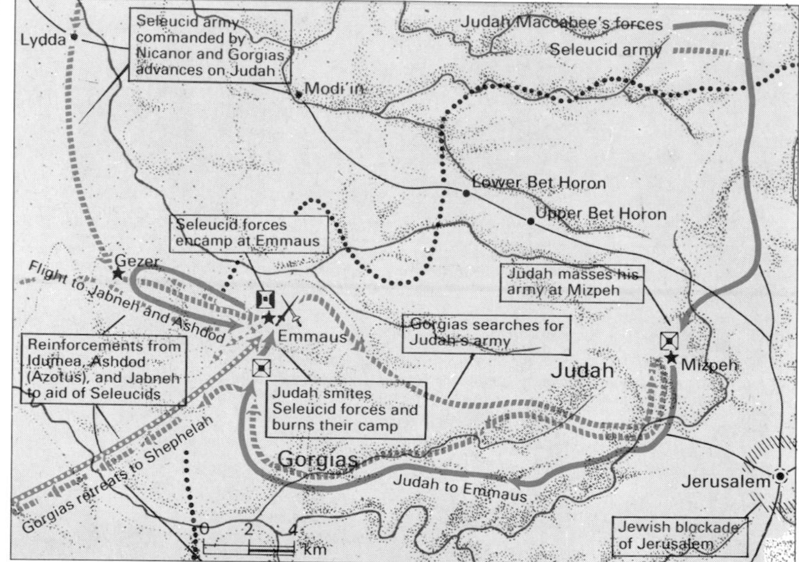

1 **The battle of Emmaus** (165 BCE). Reconstruction of the battle according to the account in the First Book of Maccabees indicates that Judah Maccabee had an intelligence network that informed him of Gorgias' departure from the camp at Emmaus and of the exact location of the Seleucid camp. In this instance Judah had to use a plan of deception. His impressive victory at Emmaus raised Judah Maccabee's stature as a commander and leader of the people, and brought his camp much booty and munitions. As a result many who previously had hesitated or opposed him were now prepared to join his camp.

2

ΑΙΗΜΕΡΑΙΜΑΤΤΑ
ΘΙΟΥΑΠΟΘΑΝΙΝ
ΚΑΙΕΙΠΕΝΤΟΙΣΥΙΟΙ·
ΑΥΤΟΥΝΥΝΕΣΤΗ
ΡΙΣΘΗΥΠΕΡΗΦΑΝΙ
ΑΚΑΙΕΛΕΓΜΟΣΚΑΙ
ΚΑΙΡΟΣΚΑΤΑΣΤΡΟ·
ΦΗΣΚΑΙΟΡΓΗΘΥ
ΜΟΥΝΥΝΤΕΚΝΑ
ΖΗΛΩΣΑΤΕΤΩΝ·
ΜΩΚΑΙΔΟΤΕΤΑ

2 **Of the four Books of Maccabees** only two deal directly with the history of the Hasmonean revolt. Only the first was written originally in Hebrew, probably during the reign of John Hyrcanus, and was translated into Greek before the 1st century CE. Its author was a close associate of the Hasmonean house. This passage from the Book of Maccabees was preserved in the *Codex Sinaiticus*, one of the manuscripts of the Septuagint found in St. Catherine's Monastery in Sinai.

3 **The "Tombs of the Hasmoneans"** are a series of rock hewn sepulchers near the Arab village of Al-Midya, identified as Modi'in. The tombs' Arabic name is *qibur al yehud* or "tombs of the Jews." The First Book of Maccabees states that Simeon established a burial ground in Modi'in.

4 **The wars of the Hasmoneans** in an etching from a German manuscript. The elephant in the picture may indicate that the illustration is of the battle at Bet Zacharia, in which Lysias deployed dozens of elephants and a large army to overcome Judah's men. In this battle Mattathias's son, Eleazar, was crushed to death by an elephant. The Jewish army was forced to retreat to Jerusalem. Meanwhile a threat to Lysias' office in Antioch forced him to a compromise which left control in the hands of Judah Maccabee and rescinded the anti-Jewish edicts.

ties for help. The Seleucids responded to their plea, and dispatched Nicanor. Judah Maccabee routed him twice. He also won an impressive political achievement: a delegation he sent to Rome made a treaty with the Roman republic. These accomplishments impelled the new Seleucid king, Demetrius I, to make a further attempt at suppressing the revolt. Judah Maccabee was forced to stand battle on the open plain, at the foot of Mount Ba'al Hazor, where he was slain (160 BCE).

Political Independence

With the death of Judah Maccabee the rebels' power began to wane. Leadership of the revolt passed to Judah's brother, Jonathan. Lysias was forced to come to an accommodation with Jonathan, according to which Jerusalem remained in the hands of the Hellenizers and Jonathan was permitted to dwell in Michmas. But a struggle for the throne in Antioch was beneficial to Jonathan, since both contenders for the Seleucid crown wooed his support. Jonathan became high priest in 152 BCE, and governor of Judah in 150 BCE. The three districts of Ephraim, Lydda, and Ramatayim were annexed to his territory, as well as Jewish areas of Transjordan. Jonathan renewed the alliance with Rome, in addition to entering political relations with Sparta.

Meanwhile Tryphon, one of the contenders for the throne, attained the upper hand over his opponent in Antioch, and then set out for Erez Israel. Apprehensive of Jonathan's growing power, Tryphon succeeded in capturing him by a ruse, and put him to death. The leadership was then assumed by Simeon, Mattathias' last surviving son. Simeon succeeded in taking the Acra, the only remaining Seleucid stronghold in Judah, and made a treaty with Demetrius II, the Seleucid ruler who opposed the rebel Tryphon. In exchange for Simeon's support Judah was exempted from taxes (142 BCE) and attained full independence.

Elephants were used in warfare as deterrents, conveyances, and means of destruction. The elephant's large height and appearance frightened horses, and his enormous weight could crush dense phalanxes of infantry. Elephants were even trained to catch enemy soldiers in their trunks and impale them on their tusks. Behind the elephant-driver (*mahout*) was a small tower providing cover for four bowmen or spearmen. This silver coin was minted to commemorate Alexander the Great's campaign to Punjab, India, and his victory over the Indian king. Alexander, mounted on horseback, is seen attacking the Indian king, fighting atop an elephant.

5 A

6 The Festival of Hanukkah commemorates the Hasmoneans' victory over the Seleucid army. The festival has been observed, in Israel and the Diaspora, sometimes even at the risk of life. In 164 BCE the Temple altar was rededicated by Judah and his men. A detailed description appears in the Book of Maccabees: "They arose early on the 25th day of the ninth month, the month of Kislev, in the year one hundred and forty-eight (of the Seleucid Era), and offered a sacrifice according to the Torah on the new sacrificial altar which they had made." Pictured are a French *menorah* from the 14th century [A] and clay lamps from the 1st and 2nd centuries BCE [B].

6 A

6 B

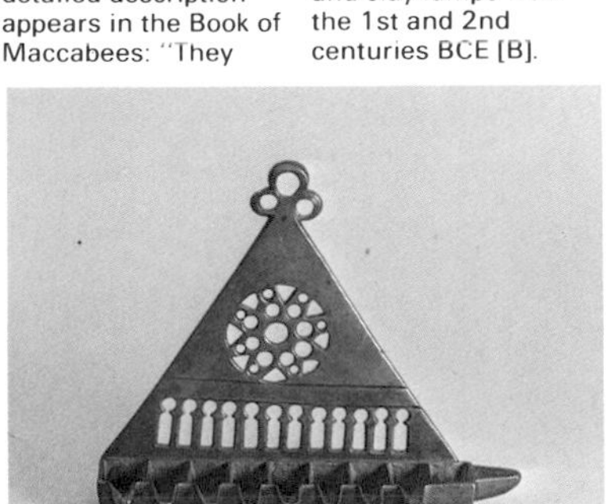

5 B

5 Jason's Tomb, discovered in Jerusalem, dates to the latter part of the 1st century BCE. The tomb is ascribed to Jason because his name is mentioned in an inscription carved on one of the walls. On another is a picture of a maritime battle. The pyramid above the tomb has been reconstructed, and was designed to serve as a monument, marking the site of the tomb from afar [A]. Large niches housing ossuaries, where the bones of the deceased were deposited a year after death, were hewn into the tomb. This custom is apparently related to a growth in the belief in the resurrection of the dead. Other objects for daily use were also found in the tomb [B].

7 The Hasmoneans
(167-37 BCE)

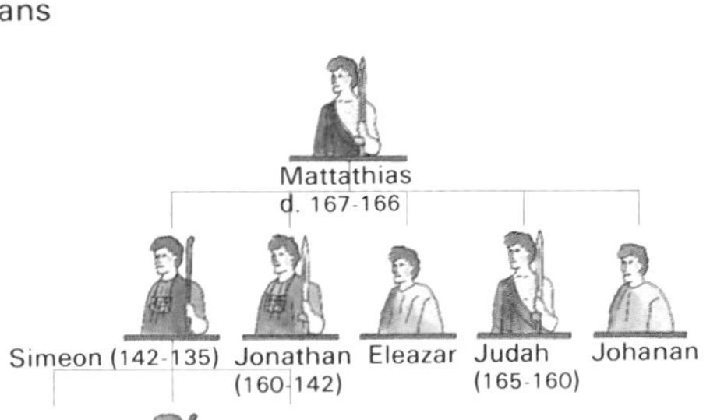

KEY

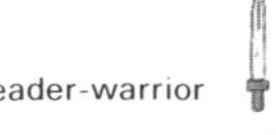

Leader-warrior

Ethnarch

High Priest

King

The Hasmonean State

An assembly of the people convened in Jerusalem in 140 BCE and empowered Simeon and his descendants to serve as ethnarch, high priest, and commander of the army. This provided the legal foundation for the rule of the Hasmonean dynasty. Simeon annexed the regions of Gezer [2] and Jaffa to Judah, thus strengthening the kingdom's western border and providing a close outlet to the sea. He also renewed the alliance with Rome and the link with Sparta, and sought to consolidate the government of the new state.

Territorial Expansion

In the meantime a new Seleucid king, Antiochus VII Sidetes (ruled 138-129 BCE), having overthrown the rebel, Tryphon, ascended the throne in Antioch. The king demanded that Simeon vacate the Acra, Gezer, and Jaffa, and pay war indemnities. Simeon rejected these demands. The Jewish army repulsed a Seleucid attack, and peace returned to the Hasmonean state for a short while. However, misfortune struck Simeon at home. He and two of his sons were murdered by his son-in-law (134 BCE), who then sought to seize power. But the army and the people supported John Hyrcanus, Simeon's third son, as heir to the throne.

Early in Hyrcanus' reign the Seleucid king, accompanied by a large army, embarked on a military campaign against Judah. A difficult and prolonged siege of Jerusalem ensued, and, neither side clearly prevailing, an accommodation was finally reached. The Seleucids acknowledged Hyrcanus' status as ethnarch and ruler of Judah; but Hyrcanus had to recognize the suzerainty of the Seleucid king, to pay indemnities for the areas conquered by the Hasmoneans, and to send an army to aid the Seleucids in their war against the Parthians.

With the death of Antiochus VII (129 BCE) the Seleucid kingdom continued to disintegrate, and thus Hyrcanus was able to enlarge Judah's borders. His main objective was to annex the Hellenistic cities throughout Ereẓ Israel, together with their rural surroundings. Hyrcanus destroyed the Samaritan temple on Mt. Gerizim, and conquered Idumea, giving the Idumeans the choice either to embrace Judaism or be expelled from their land (most chose to convert). Hyrcanus' foreign policy was based on ties with Rome (thrice during his reign he renewed this alliance), and, simultaneously, on strengthening relations with the Ptolemaic rulers in Egypt. He was succeeded by his son, Judah Aristobulus (ruled 104-103 BCE), who carried on his father's policies, completed the conquest of the Galilee, and converted its non-Jewish inhabitants.

Alexander Yannai, who deposed his brother, Judah Aristobulus, waged a series of wars, with only short respites between them. Primarily he attacked the Hellenistic cities situated along the coast of Ereẓ Israel (with the exception of Ascalon) and in Transjordan. He also fought against the Nabateans [6] to gain

CONNECTIONS

42 The Hasmonean Revolt and Political Independence

46 Herod and his Successors

48 Leadership in Hasmonean and Roman Times

1

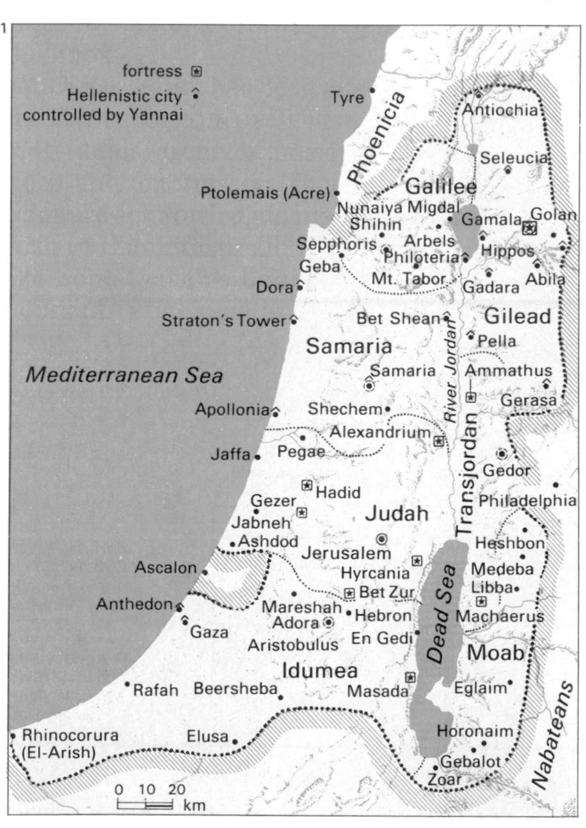

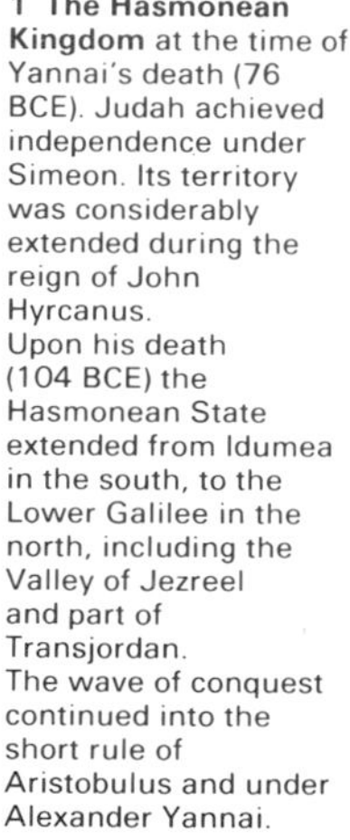

1 The Hasmonean Kingdom at the time of Yannai's death (76 BCE). Judah achieved independence under Simeon. Its territory was considerably extended during the reign of John Hyrcanus. Upon his death (104 BCE) the Hasmonean State extended from Idumea in the south, to the Lower Galilee in the north, including the Valley of Jezreel and part of Transjordan. The wave of conquest continued into the short rule of Aristobulus and under Alexander Yannai.

2

2 Gezer commanded the western approach to Judah. Until the time of Simeon a Seleucid garrison was stationed there. After Simeon captured Gezer, he turned it into a Jewish city. He restored the city's fortifications, then erected a palace there. Gezer remained an important Jewish settlement throughout the remainder of the Hasmonean period. This inscription is one of seven discovered hewn into rock in the area. The Hebrew is *THM GZR* (the boundary of Gezer), and the Greek *Alcios* presumably denotes the name of the ruler. These inscriptions may have been intended to mark the city limits of Gezer, or the boundary of a large estate in the area.

3

3 A silver coin minted in Ascalon in 105 BCE. Due to Ascalon's relations with Ptolemaic Egypt, the city was not attacked by the Hasmoneans. Rather, it remained an enclave in the Jewish state, and became the most important of the Hellenistic cities along the coast. The autonomous coins manifest the city's independence.

4

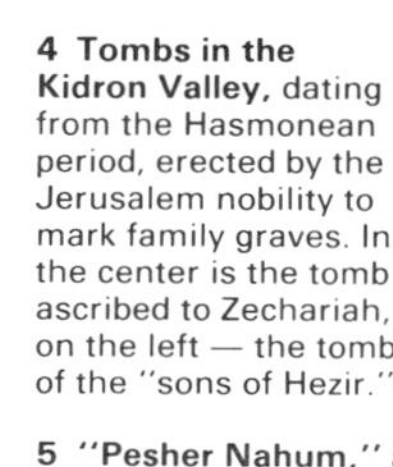

4 Tombs in the Kidron Valley, dating from the Hasmonean period, erected by the Jerusalem nobility to mark family graves. In the center is the tomb ascribed to Zechariah, on the left — the tomb of the "sons of Hezir."

5 "Pesher Nahum," a biblical commentary comprising part of the Dead Sea Scroll literature discovered at Qumran. Some scholars find parallels between this work and the writings of Josephus on the civil war during the time of Yannai (88 BCE).

5

control of the trade routes passing through the southern part of Ereẓ Israel and Transjordan. The Jewish state reached its greatest territorial expansion [1] during his reign.

Yannai adopted the title of king, thus abrogating the decision taken by the Great Assembly during the time of Simeon to deny the ruler legislative authority. Yannai's Hellenization of the regime aroused opposition on the part of some of the Jewish populace, led by the Pharisees, and ultimately led to the outbreak of an abortive revolt against him (89-84 BCE) [5]. In 76 BCE Yannai died. His wife, Salome Alexandra, took the reins of government, and his eldest son, Hyrcanus, was appointed high priest. Salome cooperated with the Pharisees and won their support. Her nine-year rule has been described by the Sages as the golden age of the Hasmonean kingdom.

Roman Conquest

Immediately after Salome's death war broke out between two of her sons. Aristobulus, supported by most of the army, prevailed over Hyrcanus and forced him to give up the crown and pledge to intervene no more in affairs of state. Hyrcanus, however, fled together with his adviser, Antipater the Idumean, and took refuge with Aretas, King of Nabatea, from whom he sought aid. Aristobulus was beaten, retreated to Jerusalem, and took up a position on the Temple Mount.

While Hyrcanus and the Nabateans were laying siege to Aristobulus and his men, the Roman commander, Pompey, reached Damascus at the head of a large army. Both sides sent delegations to recruit his support. Pompey opted to support Hyrcanus; Aristobulus attempted to oppose the decision and was captured by Pompey, who then laid siege to Jerusalem, and took it by force in 63 BCE. The territory of the state was reduced; Hyrcanus was appointed high priest and ethnarch, and the monarchy was abolished.

KEY

The Hasmonean fortress, Alexandrium, is identified with the remains of the fortress discovered on the peak of Mount Sartaba, overlooking the Jordan Valley. It is believed to have been built by Alexander Yannai, and named in honor of himself, or his wife. Some scholars even believe Hyrcania, a fortress in the Judean Desert, to have been built by Yannai and named in honor of his father. Masada too was built by a Hasmonean ruler. In *The Jewish Wars* (VII 8:3) Josephus writes, "On this high plateau the high priest Jonathan first erected a fortress and called it Masada." It is not clear whether he meant Jonathan, son of Mattathias, or Yannai, whose full Hebrew name was Jonathan.

6 A

7 A

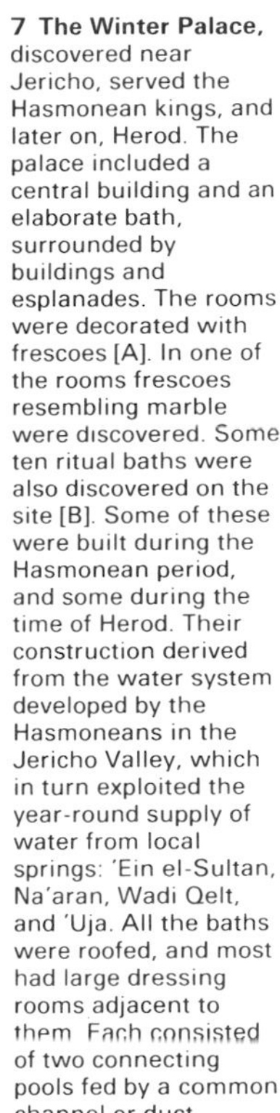

7 The Winter Palace, discovered near Jericho, served the Hasmonean kings, and later on, Herod. The palace included a central building and an elaborate bath, surrounded by buildings and esplanades. The rooms were decorated with frescoes [A]. In one of the rooms frescoes resembling marble were discovered. Some ten ritual baths were also discovered on the site [B]. Some of these were built during the Hasmonean period, and some during the time of Herod. Their construction derived from the water system developed by the Hasmoneans in the Jericho Valley, which in turn exploited the year-round supply of water from local springs: 'Ein el-Sultan, Na'aran, Wadi Qelt, and 'Uja. All the baths were roofed, and most had large dressing rooms adjacent to them. Each consisted of two connecting pools fed by a common channel or duct.

6 B

6 The Nabateans were semi-nomadic tribes living in the southern part of Erez Israel during the 3rd century BCE. Trade in spices and medicinal plants, and possibly even piracy in the Red Sea, were their primary occupations. During the 2nd century BCE they began to expand northward, and encountered Yannai. After a period of wars they made a peace treaty with him. This porticoed shrine [A] was hewn into the rock at Petra, the capital of the Nabatean kingdom; 'Avdat [B] was one of the Nabatean cities in the Negev.

7 B

Herod and his Successors

While the Hasmonean brothers, Hyrcanus and Aristobulus, were still fighting among themselves, the Romans conquered Ereẓ Israel (63 BCE). The commander of the Roman legion, Pompey, stripped Judah of most of the territory conquered by the Hasmoneans, leaving in the hands of Hyrcanus II only those areas inhabited by Jews. Judah lost its political independence, and the title of king was taken away from Hyrcanus who, by virtue of being high priest, became ethnarch. However, in actual fact, the ruler was now Antipater, son of an Idumean family which had converted while under Hasmonean rule. He was appointed *apotropos*, or "director of the affairs of the state," by Julius Caesar. One of Antipater's sons, Phasael, was appointed governor of Jerusalem, while another, Herod, was appointed governor of the Galilee (47 BCE).

Supported by the Parthians, who invaded Syria and Ereẓ Israel in their wars against the Romans (40 BCE), Mattathias Antigonus, son of Aristobolus ben Yannai (who ruled from 40-37 BCE), seized control of the government of Judah. Herod fled to Rome [2], and upon the recommendation of the consuls, Mark Antony and Octavian, the Roman Senate appointed him King of Judah as a reward for his loyalty. Following his coronation, Herod set out for Ereẓ Israel at the head of a mercenary army. After a three year war (40-37 BCE), he seized control of the government in Jerusalem, and Antigonus was executed.

Herod's Kingdom

Herod enjoyed little support among the Jews. Most of them viewed him as an "Idumean servant" who had seized power illegitimately. It was these circumstances which to a large extent shaped the character of Herod's rule. The first few years in particular were marked by the task of suppressing rivals. Dozens of people, including many members of the Hasmonean family, were executed, and their property expropriated. Herod aspired to transform his kingdom into part of the Roman Empire, and therefore strengthened Hellenistic and other foreign elements within it. These aims were particularly evident in his administrative apparatus and in the military, which primarily employed gentiles, in large-scale construction of new cities [6, 7], and in the Hellenistic cultural institutions which he established in his cities.

Herod encroached in various ways upon Jewish traditions and institutions. He usurped the authority to appoint and dismiss the high priest. He removed the sphere of criminal law from the jurisdiction of the traditional Jewish courts, through the many executions which he ordered arbitrarily. He also enacted the "Law of Robbers" which stipulated that thieves be sold into slavery to foreign countries, a provision contravening the laws of the *Torah*.

All this, in addition to the heavy taxes he imposed [9], aroused displeasure with Herod's rule among the people.

CONNECTIONS

44 The Hasmonean State
48 Leadership in Hasmonean and Roman Times

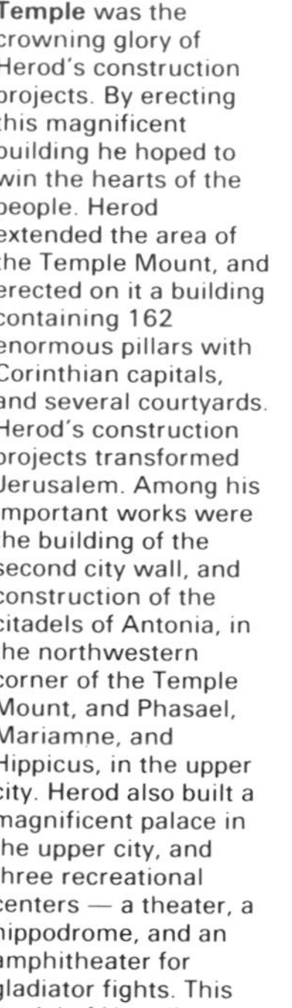

1 Renovating the Temple was the crowning glory of Herod's construction projects. By erecting this magnificent building he hoped to win the hearts of the people. Herod extended the area of the Temple Mount, and erected on it a building containing 162 enormous pillars with Corinthian capitals, and several courtyards. Herod's construction projects transformed Jerusalem. Among his important works were the building of the second city wall, and construction of the citadels of Antonia, in the northwestern corner of the Temple Mount, and Phasael, Mariamne, and Hippicus, in the upper city. Herod also built a magnificent palace in the upper city, and three recreational centers — a theater, a hippodrome, and an amphitheater for gladiator fights. This model of Herod's Temple is on display in Jerusalem.

2 Mattathias Antigonus, son of Aristobulus, conquered Jerusalem, disqualified Hyrcanus from serving as high priest by crippling him, caused the suicide of Phasael, Herod's brother, and compelled Herod to flee. As a descendant of the Hasmoneans, Antigonus received broad support from the Jewish people. His coins bear a Greek inscription, "of King Antigonus," and a Hebrew one, "Mattathias the High Priest and *Hever ha-Yehudim.*"

3 The building over the Cave of the Machpelah, in Hebron. Due to the style of construction of its exterior walls and in view of its monumental character, this structure too, is attributed to Herod.

4 "To the site of the horn blast for announcing" — an inscription revealed on a broken piece of rock, discovered in the southwestern corner of the Temple Mount. It marks the place where the priest would announce the beginning and end of the Sabbath and festivals. According to Josephus, "the first call was to tell the people to cease doing all work, and the second call was to return to work."

5 A ritual bath — discovered in excavations of the upper city in Jerusalem. The site was the residential area of the city's upper class and nobility. All the houses were equipped with facilities for water, apparently serving as ritual baths and testifying to the presence in the area of a high concentration of priests, who were required to immerse themselves daily, prior to eating the priestly offering.

Nevertheless, the construction projects which he initiated supplied the Jews with work, and the large cities provided a market for their produce. New roads and aqueducts were built, as well as a series of fortresses to guard against nomadic incursions [Key]. Foremost of these undertakings was the enormous project of building the Temple and extending the area of the Temple Mount [1], which was executed with scrupulous observance of ritual law. Toward the end of his days Herod placed a golden eagle on the facade of the Temple as a sign of his allegiance to Rome. This act aroused popular fury. Pharisee Sages destroyed the image, and Herod, in one of his last acts before his death, had them executed.

Judah as a Roman Province

In his will Herod divided the kingdom among his three sons, Archelaus, Antipas, and Philip, and his sister, Salome. After his death Augustus Caesar confirmed the partitioning, and appointed Archelaus to rule over Judah. Archelaus (ruled from 4 BCE to 6 CE) continued his father's construction and renovation projects, especially around the Jericho Valley. However, his cruelty caused the people to despise him. Frequent complaints to Augustus eventually led to his being removed and Judah being made into a Roman province (6 CE), henceforth known as Judea.

Administration of the province was entrusted to procurators from the privileged cavalry class (*Equites*), who were subject to the Roman legate in Syria. The procurators ruled Judea from 6 to 66 CE. The most extreme of these was Pontius Pilate (ruled from 26-36) [8], who tried to introduce images of Caesar, attached to the standards of the legions, into Jerusalem, and to use the Temple's treasury to build an aqueduct to Jerusalem. The rule of the procurators prepared the ground for the emergence of opposition to Rome, which erupted in full force at the time of the Great Revolt.

KEY

The fortress of Herodium was built by Herod atop a mountain near Bethlehem. The fortress also served as a palace, and after suppression of the Great Revolt (70 CE), provided refuge for the rebels who managed to flee Jerusalem. The fortress has a double wall and circular towers protruding at its four corners. According to Josephus (*Antiquities of the Jews* XV 324), "This fortress, which is some sixty stades (*c.* 7 miles) distant from Jerusalem, is naturally strong and very suitable for such a (fortified) structure." Herod is believed to have been buried there.

6

6 A colonnade in the city of Sebaste. The city was built in 27 BCE on the site of Samaria, as Herod's first large public construction project. Because of its location, Herod transformed it into a garrison town, surrounded it with a wall, and trained its inhabitants to serve him as soldiers.

7

7 Caesarea was built on the site of Straton's Tower [pictured here]. Herod spent a fortune building the city and its port. The city was constructed according to the plan of a Roman city, including fortifications, palaces, market places, an amphitheater, a hippodrome, a forum, and bath houses. Its large port was entirely man-made.

8

8 The rule of Pontius Pilate, the fifth procurator of Judea, marks a turning point in relations between Judea and Rome. Pontius Pilate's approach set the pattern for the behavior of subsequent procurators. His lack of consideration for the religious and cultural sentiments of his subjects led to great tension and violence. At the very beginning of his reign he deviated from the accepted Roman practice by bringing standards of the legions bearing graven images into Jerusalem. This inscription, found in the Roman theater in Caesarea, bears a dedication in Latin: "The Praefectus of Judea, Pontius Pilate, erected this building — Tiberium — in honor of the Caesar, Tiberius."

9

9 Herod's large income derived from the heavy taxes which he imposed on the people, from customs, from Hasmonean properties which came under his dominion, from Nabatean and maritime trade, and from his copper mines in Cyprus. With this money he financed his ostentatious construction projects, the bribes and generous gifts which he bestowed upon powerful Romans, and the grants which he made to the Olympic games and to various cities, in the form of land, produce, and money. These coins are from the period of Herod and the Roman procurators.

Leadership in Hasmonean and Roman Times

After the Return to Zion the high priesthood became the most important position of leadership in Judah, filling a religious and political function. Under Judah Maccabee the two offices were separated. Even after driving out the Seleucid army and restoring Temple worship, Judah contented himself with his status as political leader, and did not try to assume the office of high priest as well, though he belonged to a priestly family. Jonathan, who inherited the mantle of leadership from his brother Judah, attained office on his merits, and not because of his family connections. However, he wrought far-reaching changes when Alexander Balas, the Seleucid contender for the crown, appointed him high priest (152 BCE), and later also ruler of Judah.

Leadership in the Hasmonean Period

Simeon's double appointment, on the other hand, was endorsed by the sovereign will of the people of Judah, as expressed at the Great Assembly, a convocation of all the people held in Jerusalem in 140 BCE. The assembly, whose decision essentially constituted the legal foundation for the Hasmonean state, appointed Simeon to the offices of political leader, commander of the army, and high priest — positions which were to pass by inheritance to his sons after him. Thus the Hasmoneans' status as the family of the high priesthood attained legitimacy, displacing the family of Zadok, which had held the high priesthood from the time of the First Temple to the Hellenistic period. The assembly also established the trappings of sovereignty: "(Therefore) the Jews and the priests saw fit that Simeon should be their leader and high priest for ever, until a true prophet should arise. And he shall be their commander, and shall care for the Temple, and all shall obey him; and all contracts in the land shall be written in his name, and he shall don purple and carry gold" (*First Book of Maccabees* 44:41-43).

The form of government established in Judah renewed the independence of the Jewish people in its land. According to the concepts of the time and the accepted practice in neighboring Hellenistic states, the king presided over the legal system and the courts of his country, and served as sole legislator. Simeon and his heirs, however, were not given legislative or judicial authority, and therefore were not granted the title of king. They held the title of ethnarch, an office bearing the right of leadership solely in political and military affairs. The courts remained autonomous, and the Hasmonean ruler, just as any other Jew, was subject to the ancestral law of the Jews.

After Simeon's assassination his son, John Hyrcanus, took power. Coins minted during his rule specify his title, "Johanan High Priest Head of *Hever ha-Yehudim*," or "Johanan the High Priest and *Hever ha-Yehudim*." From these inscriptions we may infer that alongside the Hasmonean ruler, who was ethnarch and high priest, there was

CONNECTIONS

44 The Hasmonean State
46 Herod and his Successors

1 The Zugot were pairs of scholars whom their contemporaries viewed as the link that connected the men of the Great Assembly with the *tannaim* in the chain of transmission of the Oral Law. The chain began with Moses receiving the *Torah* at Sinai, passing it to the elders, and the elders to the men of the Great Assembly. The *zug* headed the *Sanhedrin* in Jerusalem. During the time of Alexander Yannai and Queen Salome the leading pair was Judah ben Tabbai and Simeon ben Shetah. Under Herod the pair was Shemaiah and Avtalyon. They advocated cooperation with the authorities, which won them Herod's respect and appreciation. The first pair of the *zugot* enjoyed absolute authority, whereas subsequent pairs had to share authority with the Hasmonean kings.

2 A divorce certificate discovered in Wadi Murabba'at. The document, in Aramaic, is dated "On the first of Marheshvan, in the sixth year, at Masada,..." Accordingly, scholars have placed it in 71-72 CE, on the assumption that the residents of Masada reckoned years from the beginning of the war against Rome.

1

[Moses received] the Law from Sinai and handed it down

Yose ben Johanan of Jerusalem	Yose ben Joezer of Zeredah
Joshua ben Perahiah	Nittai the Arbelite
Judah ben Tabbai	Simeon ben Shetah
Shemaiah	Avtalyon
Hillel	Shammai

2

3 Adherence to Jewish tradition, together with clear Hellenistic influence, was apparent in the spiritual and material culture of the Herodian period. A total ban on human or animal images was imposed. This representation of the Temple *menorah* was carved in stone, and predates the destruction of the Temple.

3

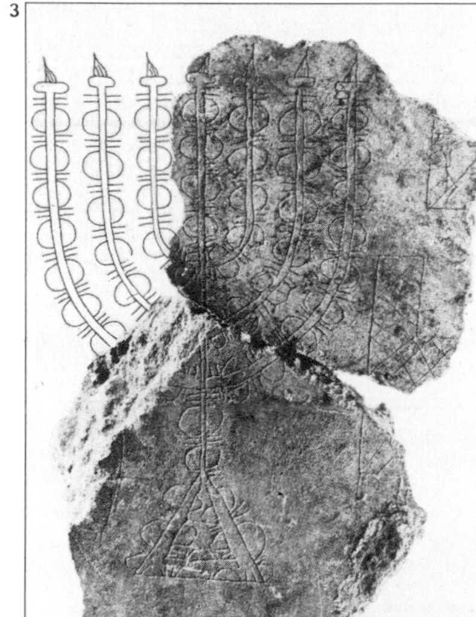

4

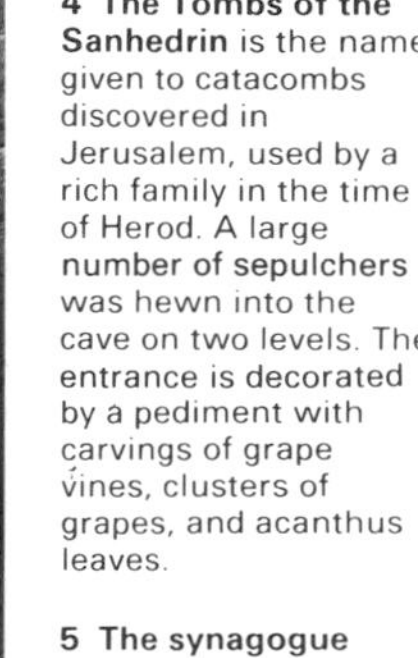

4 The Tombs of the Sanhedrin is the name given to catacombs discovered in Jerusalem, used by a rich family in the time of Herod. A large number of sepulchers was hewn into the cave on two levels. The entrance is decorated by a pediment with carvings of grape vines, clusters of grapes, and acanthus leaves.

5

5 The synagogue began to play a central role in the life of the Jewish community, side by side with the Temple, during the first century CE. Early synagogues have been discovered at Masada [pictured], Herodium and Gamala.

another, representative ruling body called *Hever ha-Yehudim* [Key].

Alexander Yannai, son of John Hyrcanus, acted against the popular will and assumed the title of king in addition to the office of high priest. His wife, Salome, who ruled after him, appointed her son, Hyrcanus, as high priest. From then on, throughout the entire period of Roman rule, the separation between these two institutions was maintained.

As far as we can tell, the religious-legal system operated during this period autonomously, and dealt with interpreting the ancestral laws, extending them to cover day to day requirements (The Oral Law). This took place in courts of the Sages or councils of the Pharisees, which served as institutions of study, instruction, and justice, and were headed by Sages referred to in the *Mishnah* as *zugot* or "pairs" [1].

Leadership under Roman Rule

Under Roman rule political and religious leadership diverged further still. The Romans refrained from intervening in religious matters, leaving them in the hands of the high priest and the Pharisee Sages. The high priest was in charge of the Temple and its worship, while the Pharisee Sages, working through the *Sanhedrin* and the courts, passed the laws and regulations governing holy worship, including the rites of the high priest on the Day of Atonement. Thus Ereẓ Israel had three types of leadership operating side by side: the Roman procurators; the high priests, who leaned primarily on the Sadducees, the representatives of the wealthy families of Judea ("Sadducee" is derived from the Zadok family name); and the Pharisee (Hebrew: *Perushim*) Sages, who continued to develop the Oral Law while carrying on ideological and religious polemics with the Sadducees. The emergence of a social class of Sages and their disciples laid the foundation for the leadership of the nation in the period following the fall of Jerusalem and the destruction of the Temple.

KEY

The high priesthood and Hever ha-Yehudim were the two governmental authorities granted to John Hyrcanus (134-104 BCE), the first of the Hasmonean rulers to mint his own coins. Coins like those pictured bore the inscription, "Johanan the High Priest and *Hever ha-Yehudim*," or, "Johanan High Priest — Head of *Hever ha-Yehudim*." These inscriptions indicate the importance of the Hasmonean ruler's status as high priest, and point to the existence of another ruling body, *Hever ha-Yehudim*. This sovereign assembly was viewed as embodying the will of the people. The "Head of *Hever ha-Yehudim*" was the ethnarch, who wielded political and military authority. Thus, the two inscriptions mention the bodies established by the Great Assembly during the time c ' Simeon.

6A

7

7 The Sadduce s, the Pharisees, and t e Essenes were th ee Jewish groups. According to Jos phus they emerged du ing the time of John Hyrcanus (mid 2 d century BCE). Th Dead Sea Scroll [pictured here], discovered stow d in caves in the Juc an Desert, were wr ten by the members of a Judean desert s ct identified with t e Essenes. The scrolls deal with laws and customs encompassing all walks of life.

6B

8

9

6 Secondary burial was customary during the time of Herod. About one year after death the bones were transferred to a stone ossuary. Over two thousand ossuaries have been discovered in Jerusalem. Some of them are decorated with geometric designs, such as rosettes [A]; others resemble facades of buildings [B]; and yet others bear the name of the deceased, as on ossuary [C], upon which is inscribed "Simon, builder of the Sanctuary."

6C

8 Khirbat Qumran. Excavations on the site revealed a large building containing halls, rooms, a kitchen, storerooms, and baths. Remains of tables and ink wells, which apparently served the members of this Judean sect for copying the scrolls, were also discovered there. The building served as the sect's central meeting house. The Essenes had gone to the desert to escape the sins of society and in order to realize a life of abstinence and purity.

9 The Dead Sea Scrolls were found in clay jars [pictured here], and include the *Manual of Discipline*, which spells out the laws of the society; the *Rule of the Congregation*, laying down regulations for the end of days; and *Blessings*, which presents prayers for the apocalypse. The *Damascus Covenant* deals with the laws of the sect. The *War Scroll* describes the ultimate struggle at the end of days between the Sons of Light (the members of the sect) and the Sons of Darkness (everyone else). The *Thanksgiving Psalms* praises the Almighty for his salvation.

The Great Revolt

Ever since the Roman conquest the people of Judea had never ceased hoping for political independence. With autonomy revoked and direct Roman rule by the procurators established (6 CE), the religious freedom and everyday life of the Jews suffered. In Judea there emerged a movement for revolt.

The Revolt Spreads

Jewish zealotry became extreme under the procuratorship of Antonius Felix (52-60 CE). The *sicarii* (from the Latin *sica* or curved dagger which they used) did not even hesitate to attack Jews whom they suspected of collaborating with the Romans. Relations with the Roman regime were further aggravated by the persistent struggle between the Jewish population and the local Hellenistic population that practiced pagan worship, particularly in cities where both lived side by side, as in Caesarea, where violence broke out in 6 CE.

On Passover of that year, when many Jews were in Jerusalem to celebrate the festival, tension peaked. Roman soldiers burst into the city, pillaged and murdered, and ransacked the Temple treasures. The Jews put up active resistance, and the soldiers of the procurator, Gessius Florus (64-66 CE), took many lives. The rebellion turned into an open declaration of war when priests who supported the revolt, headed by Eleazar ben Ananias, decided to do away with the Temple sacrifice in honor of the Caesar. The rebels seized control of the area of the Temple, conquered the Antonia fortress and wiped out the Roman garrison stationed there.

As this was happening in Jerusalem, the Jewish and gentile residents of the mixed cities were slaughtering each other, and the Roman forces were proving unsuccessful at containing the revolt. The Roman procurator in Syria, Cestius Gallus, set out for Judea at the head of a legion, but was repulsed at Bet Horon by a superior Jewish force, which included many who had come to celebrate the festival of *Succoth.*

The victory over Gallus drew many people from more moderate circles into the turmoil of rebellion. An assembly of the people that convened in Jerusalem selected a rebel government [Key]. Among its more prominent leaders were Joseph ben Gorion and the high priest, Anan ben Anan. Commanders were appointed for the regions of Idumea and the Galilee.

When Caesar Nero learned of Gallus' defeat, he delegated Vespasian, his best general, to crush the revolt [2]. Vespasian gathered an army of some 60,000 men, including three Roman legions, and set out for the Galilee. Sepphoris surrendered without giving fight, and became the forward base of operations from which Vespasian launched his attack. In the course of battle Yodfat fell, and Josephus, commander of the Galilee, who had fortified himself there, surrendered to the Romans [7]. Tiberias capitulated, and its warriors fled to Migdal Nunaiya (Taricheae), where a fierce battle was waged. Gamala [1],

CONNECTIONS

46 Herod and his Successors
52 The Nation Rallies after the Destruction
58 The Egyptian Jewish Community in Ancient Times
60 The Jewish Community in Babylonia

1

1 Gamala's strategic location in the lower Golan and its strong fortifications enabled its Jewish defenders to valiantly withstand the attack of three Roman legions for a month's time. After fierce battles Gamala was conquered in 67, and most of its inhabitants were slaughtered. The synagogue at Gamala, pictured here, is from the period of the Great Revolt.

2

2 Titus Flavius Vespasian, an experienced military commander, was called to quash the revolt in Judea. Together with his son, Titus, and other commanders, he conquered the rebel stronghold in the Galilee, took the remaining regions of the land and isolated Jerusalem.

3

3 This coin of "Judea taken captive" testifies to the great importance the Romans attached to quelling the revolt in Judea and capturing Jerusalem. The powerful empire commemorated its victory with vast numbers of coins bearing inscriptions like "Judea vanquished." Such coins were minted in various denominations, in gold, silver, and bronze. For propaganda purposes the coins also bore symbols of Judea's degradation, such as a captive Jewess seated at the foot of a palm tree, with an armed Roman soldier standing by her.

4

4 Many refugees fled to Jerusalem in the wake of the conquest of the Galilee and Judea. Various factions gathered in the city, and during breaks in hostilities, which were imposed by the frequent changes of Caesar, they fought among themselves for control of Jerusalem. This internal strife and destruction reduced the rebels' military effectiveness. Ultimately the Roman army, under Titus, captured the Temple Mount, burned the Temple, and carried off all its vessels to Rome, in the spring of 70. These captives bearing the *menorah* and vessels of the Temple are sculpted in the triumphal arch at Rome commemorating Titus' victory.

too, resisted valiantly, but fell to the Romans after a hard siege. Next the Romans took control of the coastal plain, Transjordan, Mount Ephraim, and large areas of Idumea. Only then did they turn to Jerusalem.

Destruction of the Temple

In Jerusalem at that time dissension reigned among the besieged forces. Simeon Bar Giora and John of Giscala, the two zealot leaders, fought each other for control of the city, and both were opposed by a third group of Jerusalem zealots, under the leadership of Eleazar ben Simeon. In the course of this civil war the rival factions themselves burned the city's stores of food [4].

Vespasian, who in the meantime had become Caesar, delegated his son, Titus, to put an end to the war in Judea. In 70 CE the Romans began their offensive. The city's fortified walls made conquest of Jerusalem difficult, but after fifteen days Roman battering rams breached the "Third Wall," and the Romans entered the city and took control of its outlying districts. At the beginning of the month of Av the Romans conquered the Temple Mount, broke into the Temple, and set it aflame. Many fighters retreated to the Upper City and took up fortified positions until eventually they, too, fell to the Romans.

The defeat had dire consequences [3, 6]. Thousands died on the battlefield, while many others, including the rebel leaders John and Simeon, fell captive. Even after the conquest of Jerusalem and destruction of the Temple, groups of zealots continued to fight from the three strongholds which remained in their hands — Herodium, Machaerus, and Masada. Herodium and Machaerus fell to Bassus [8], and Masada, where the *sicarii* had taken up their stand under the command of Eleazar ben Yair, was captured after a lengthy siege. Its defenders preferred to take their own lives rather than fall into the hands of the Romans [5].

KEY

Coins from the Great Revolt manifest the nature of the rebel government and its aims. During the revolt (66-70) the rebels minted silver and bronze coins with the inscriptions "Jerusalem the Holy", "Freedom of Zion", or "For the Redemption of Zion" on one side, and on the other side such symbols as a chalice (on a shekel and half-shekel coin, in the picture), pomegranates, an amphora (wine jug), grape vines, and palm branches. The inscriptions stress the holiness of Jerusalem and the nationalist-messianic aspirations of the people.

5
A

6 "The burnt house" is a portion of a private residential building discovered in the Upper City, in Jerusalem. The walls of the house were found destroyed, its roof and furniture burned, and its floor covered with ashes. Household implements, shown here, remained. Coins discovered on the site date the building to the time of the Great Revolt. The destruction of Jerusalem was described by Josephus: "So Caesar now ordered them to raze the whole City and Sanctuary to the ground, leaving the towers that overtopped the others, Phasael, Hippicus, and Mariamne, and the stretch of wall enclosing the City on the west" (*The Jewish War*, VII 1:1).

6

5 Masada is located in the Judean desert, on a precipitous cliff overlooking the Dead Sea [A]. With the fall of Herodium and Machaerus, Masada remained the last stronghold of the Jewish rebels. After the fall of Jerusalem the remaining zealots, led by Eleazar ben Yair, took refuge in Masada. In the year 73, Flavius Silva was appointed procurator of Judea, and laid siege to Masada. The besieged forces were well stocked with supplies [B, store rooms] and held out for about one year. But the Romans built a ramp some 200 meters long on the western side of the mountain, deployed a battering ram on it, and breached the first wall. Then they set fire to a second wall. When the besieged forces realized they stood no chance they committed mass suicide.

5
B

7

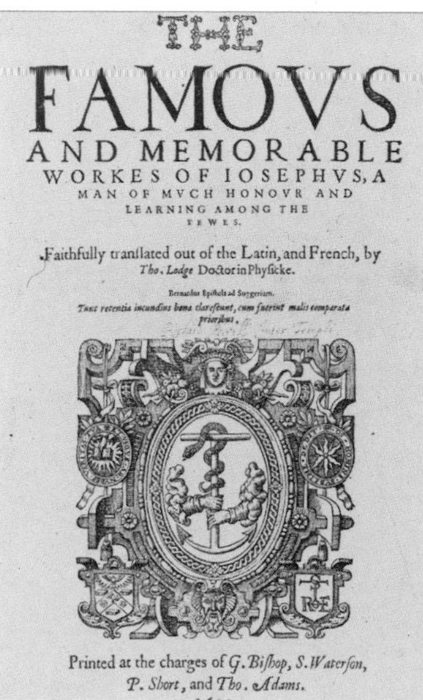

THE
FAMOVS
AND MEMORABLE
WORKES OF IOSEPHVS, A
MAN OF MVCH HONOVR AND
LEARNING AMONG THE
IEWES.

Faithfully translated out of the Latin, and French, by
Tho. Lodge Doctor in Physicke.

Printed at the charges of G. Bishop, S. Waterson,
P. Short, and Tho. Adams.
1602.

7 The writings of Josephus are our primary source of information on the Great Revolt. Captured by the Romans, he became the protégé of Vespasian. Thus Joseph ben Mattathias became Josephus Flavius. In Rome he documented his activities during the Great Revolt in his works, *The Jewish War* and *Life*, and wrote *Antiquities of the Jews* and *Against Apion*.

8 Herodium, Machaerus and Masada served as retreats for the rebels after the fall of Jerusalem. The fortress of Herodium, built by Herod near Bethlehem, was captured by Bassus with ease. Machaerus, built by Alexander Yannai and strongly fortified by Herod, proved harder to take. The besieged military force was freed by the Romans, but the inhabitants of Machaerus were put to death. The stones pictured were hurled by *ballistae*, from Herodium.

8

The Nation Rallies after the Destruction

Following the Great Revolt a Roman of senatorial rank was sent to Erez Israel to serve as *praetor* or magistrate. The tenth legion, permanently stationed in Jerusalem, was placed at his disposal [3]. Roman law viewed conquered territory as the property of the Emperor. Hence many agricultural lands were expropriated, and their owners became heavily-taxed tenant farmers.

Rabban Johanan ben Zakkai at Jabneh

The fall of Jerusalem and the destruction of the Temple eliminated the focal point of Jewish religious and spiritual life. Some of the nation's leaders had perished in the revolt, others were forced into hiding. One of the few who could act openly was Rabban Johanan ben Zakkai, a moderate who had expressed reservations about the revolt.

R. Johanan ben Zakkai, of priestly descent, served as deputy to the head of the *Sanhedrin* before the fall of Jerusalem. In the last stages of the siege he escaped clandestinely. According to the Talmudic account he turned himself over to Emperor Vespasian (ruled 69-79), and requested that he be given "Jabneh with its sages" and "the dynasty of Rabban Gamaliel." After suppression of the revolt a group of sages gathered in Jabneh, and together with Rabban Johanan ben Zakkai they reestablished the *Sanhedrin* [5]. Henceforth the *Bet Din* (court) in Jabneh determined the time of the new moon and the festivals and the intercalation of the year. The *takkanot*, or regulations, established at Jabneh were designed to enable proper Jewish life to continue. R. Johanan ben Zakkai changed several customs which had been integrally connected with the Temple, and refashioned them to suit the new reality.

Similar steps were taken with regard to proselytes. In the time of the Temple proselytes had had to fulfill three obligations: circumcision, ritual immersion, and sacrifice. After destruction of the Temple the obligation of sacrifice could no longer be fulfilled, hence proselytes were bid to set aside a quarter *dinar*, to be kept for the sacrifice until such time as the Temple were rebuilt. R. Johanan ben Zakkai repealed this payment as well, lest the money set aside be used for profane purposes. This *takkanah* was instrumental in assuring the continuation of proselytism.

The activity of the sages of Jabneh focused solely around rehabilitating spiritual life and religious ritual. This limited scope may be accounted for by restrictions imposed by the Roman authorities, as well as by the refusal of many sages to collaborate with R. Johanan ben Zakkai. The latter's escape from the beleaguered city of Jerusalem won him many opponents, and these eventually caused him to step down from the patriarchate.

Rabban Gamaliel and Jabneh's Sages

R. Johanan ben Zakkai moved to Beror Hayil, where he established a *bet midrash*, or house of study. The reins of leadership at Jabneh passed into the

CONNECTIONS

48 Leadership in Hasmonean and Roman Times
50 The Great Revolt
58 The Egyptian Jewish Community in Ancient Times

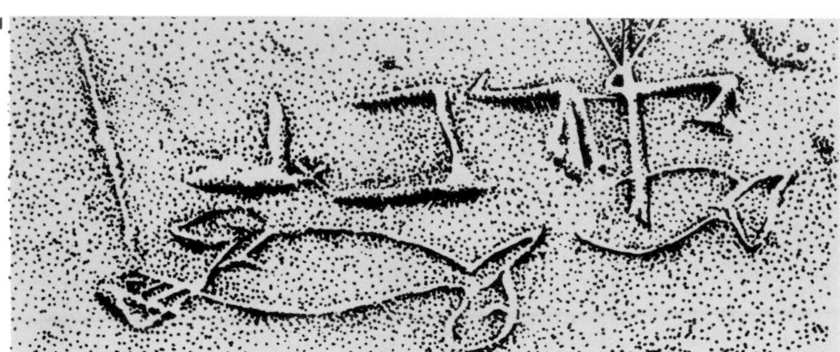

1 **This inscription,** *qrbn* (sacrifice), was found on a potsherd in excavations near the Temple Mount, Jerusalem. The ritual of sacrifice ceased in Erez Israel with the destruction of the Temple. The sages tried to come to terms with the new reality. Prayer and charity now took primacy. "For I desire mercy and not sacrifice" (Hos. 6:6). "For thus we find concerning Daniel, that greatly beloved man,... He used to outfit the bride and make her rejoice, accompany the dead, give a *perutah* to the poor, and pray three times a day — and his prayer was received with favor" (*The Fathers According to Rabbi Nathan*, version A, chapter 4).

2 **Ties with the Diaspora** were cultivated by the sages of Jabneh under Rabban Gamaliel. We know that R. Akiva traveled extensively both eastward and westward. En route to Nehardea, in Babylonia, he stopped in Tadmor, where there was a Jewish community in the 2nd century. Inscriptions bearing the names of Jews from Tadmor, which were discovered in Jerusalem and Bet She'arim, testify to the close ties of the Jews of Tadmor to Erez Israel. Some 200 Jews from Tadmor were buried in the catacombs discovered at Bet She'arim. This Roman theater in Tadmor dates from the 2nd century.

3 **The tenth Roman legion** took part in quashing the Great Revolt in the Galilee, Transjordan, and Jerusalem. The legion camped in Jerusalem, leaving evidence of its stay particularly in seal impressions, ashlars, and roof tiles discovered in great abundance in excavations at Sheikh Badr, in Jerusalem. This tombstone over the grave of Tiberius Claudius Fatalis, a soldier in the tenth legion, dates from the late first century. It was discovered in Jerusalem and bears an inscription in Latin, telling of the soldier's death at the age of 42, after 23 years of military service, and specifying his ranks and the legions in which he served.

4 **Nabatean clay lamp** displaying figures of gladiators. Thousands of Jews taken captive in the Great Revolt were forced to fight against beasts of prey or against their fellow Jews. Josephus describes Titus moving with his troops from Caesarea to Caesarea Philippi, where he exhibited "all kinds of spectacles. Here many of the prisoners perished..." (*Jewish War* VII 2:1).

hands of Rabban Gamaliel [6], son of Simeon ben Gamaliel, one of the leaders of the revolt. During his term of office (96-115) the patriarchate and the *Sanhedrin* gained greater legislative and judicial authority. Unlike his predecessor, Rabban Gamaliel enjoyed the broad support of the Jewish public in Erez Israel and the Diaspora, such that the law for all the Jewish people began to emanate from the center at Jabneh. Ties with the Diaspora were reinforced, and the institution of Jewish emissaries was renewed [2]. The emissaries were of importance organizationally, in terms of establishing communal institutions for education and financial assistance, and economically, as they collected contributions for the "center" in Erez Israel.

Rabban Gamaliel was also concerned with enacting regulations to help maintain religious customs under the new circumstance of life without a Temple. One of his well-known *takkanot* was that a *seder* be held on the eve of Passover, without sacrifice. The emphasis at Passover was shifted to the national and historical by means of the *Haggadah*, which elevated national freedom to a paramount value. Another innovation gave the Day of Atonement a new character by introducing the notion of repentance to atone for one's sin [1], as a substitute for sacrifice. Under Rabban Gamaliel the rite of prayer in the synagogue was formulated and regularized. Regulations governing fast days and pilgrimage to Jerusalem were also established, in commemoration of the destruction of the Temple. The leaders at Jabneh proscribed the sale of land to gentiles and encouraged redemption of land under gentile ownership.

During the patriarchate of Rabban Gamaliel centers for the study of *Torah* arose in Lydda, Bene Berak, Gimzo, and elsewhere. The leadership at Jabneh was now composed of *Torah* scholars who had been ordained and given the title of Rabbi, rather than survivors of the social elite from before the Destruction.

KEY

A coin of Nerva, from 97, issued in Rome on the occasion of plans to abolish the *Fiscus Judaicus*. This tax was imposed on all the Jews in the empire, replacing the half-shekel which the Jews formerly had donated to the Temple. It was added to existing taxes: a poll-tax, an *arnona* or annual crop tax, and the *angaria* — forced labor. Since Roman Law viewed conquered territory as the Emperor's property, farmers who formerly owned their land were now forced to pay heavy taxes for the right to work it. Flanking the figure of a palm tree are the letters *S(enatus)* and *C(onsulto)*, designating a decision of the Senate, and surrounding it is the inscription, *fisci Judaici calumnia sublata* or "The calumny of the Jewish tax is removed." The actual abolition of the tax did not occur until the 4th century.

5

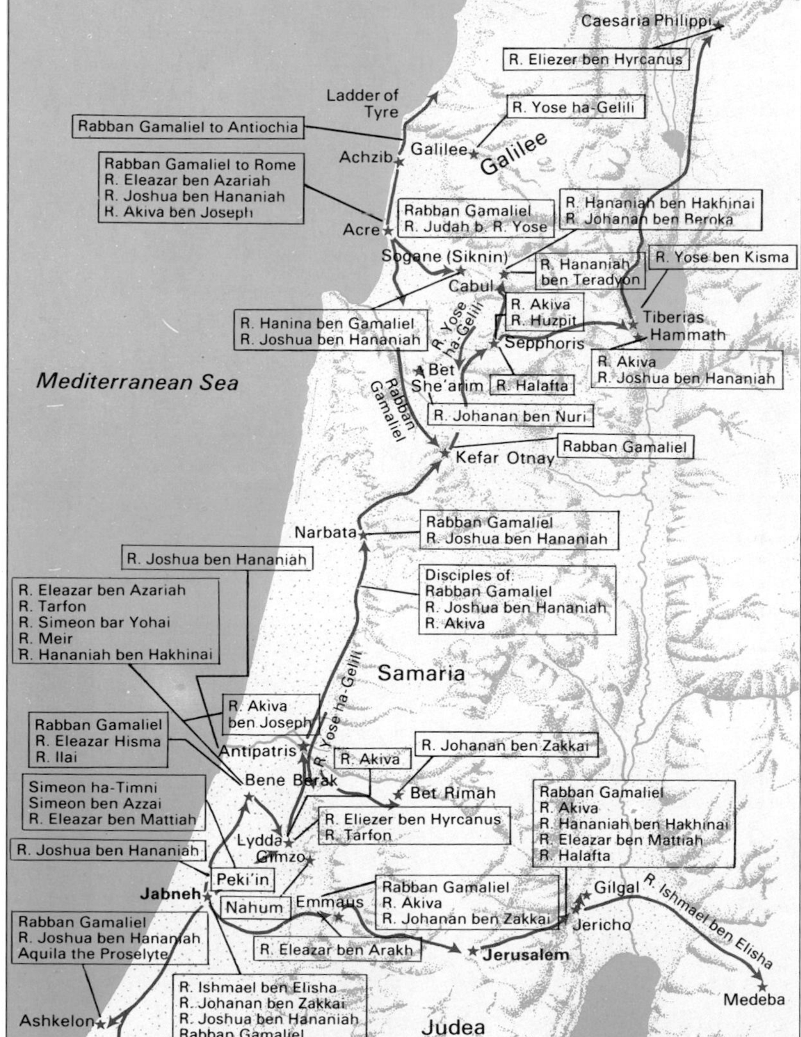

6 A

6 Rabban Gamaliel sought to unify the Jewish people in their dispersion by establishing a single body of *Halakhah*, or Jewish law. Jewish internal autonomy was strengthened by his work in developing these legal foundations. Together with R. Eleazar ben Azariah, R. Joshua and R. Akiva, he went to Rome to lobby the authorities to repeal a particularly stringent decree. He was removed from office for insulting R. Joshua, and was succeeded by R. Eleazar, known for his wisdom, his distinguished lineage, his mild manner and his exceptional wealth. Here Rabban Gamaliel [A] and R. Eleazar ben Azariah [B], are portrayed in a Greek *Haggadah*, probably from Crete, 1583.

5 Jabneh and its Sages. During the period of Jabneh a new leadership body arose, comprising the successors of the Pharisees. This group led the Jewish people until the 5th century. The sages of Jabneh began formulating the *Halakhah* through rulings which were binding on everyone. This trend was solidified by the pronouncement, "the law invariably follows the opinion of the House of Hillel" (*Tosefta Eduyot* 2:3), which ran contrary to what had been the case until then: "Whoever wishes to follow the opinion of the House of Shammai, may do so; and whoever wishes to follow the House of Hillel, may do so."

6 B

The Bar Kokhba Revolt

Suppression of the Great Revolt wrought devastation and destruction, which in turn gave birth to new tides. The leadership tried to bring the people to come to terms with Roman sovereignty, and thus to assure the nation's existence. But many of the people continued to hope for the defeat of Rome and the coming of the Messiah, which would bring political redemption and the rebuilding of the Temple [Key].

The Hadrianic Decrees

During the reign of Emperor Hadrian [3] tensions rose once more in Ereẓ Israel. Even before becoming Emperor, Hadrian had helped suppress a rebellion in the Diaspora that had ended in the destruction of Jewish communities in Egypt, Cyrene (Libya) and Cyprus. One of Hadrian's first acts in Ereẓ Israel was to reinforce the garrison permanently stationed there with a second legion, stationed in the north of the country. The Jewish population perceived this act as further intended to tighten the Romans' grip on the country.

Messianic expectations and the hope that Rome would be defeated were also nurtured by the socio-economic conditions of the Jews of Ereẓ Israel. After the Destruction many Jewish farmers became tenant farmers on their own lands, which passed into the hands of the Roman military, the nobility, and Jewish collaborators.

Unrest against Rome reached its peak in 130, during a visit by Hadrian to the region. Two acts of his struck at the very heart of Judaism: he forbade the Jews to practice circumcision (as part of a general prohibition against castration and mutilation); and he commenced the reconstruction of Jerusalem as a Roman city, with a temple to Zeus planned in its center, and changed its name to Aelia Capitolina [1]. The Jews viewed these acts as extreme violations of holy precept.

Revolt and Defeat

The revolt broke out in the summer of 132, after Hadrian had left Ereẓ Israel, and lasted until 135. It was led by Simeon ben Kosiba, who proclaimed a general conscription in Judea. Simeon received recognition and backing from some of the Sages, first among them being R. Akiva, who pronounced him the "King Messiah." This without doubt encouraged broad popular support for the revolt. It is said that R. Akiva applied to Simeon ben Kosiba a homiletical interpretation of the verse, "There shall come a star (*kokhav*) out of Jacob;" hence the name Bar Kokhba, or Son of a Star.

Little is known about the figure of Bar Kokhba, and even his name is somewhat of a mystery. Christian sources present him in a most negative light, as cruel and deceitful. In contrast, the Sages offer praise and admiration for the man, his strength and his forceful character. The communications which he sent to the commanders of his force paint a picture of a responsible leader and excellent organizer [4, 7]. His

CONNECTIONS

50 The Great Revolt
52 The Nation Rallies after the Destruction
56 Judah ha-Nasi and his Era
58 The Egyptian Jewish Community in Ancient Times

1 A coin of Aelia Capitolina, issued for the founding of Jerusalem as a pagan Roman city, was inscribed, "Colony of Aelia Capitolina founded," and portrayed an ancient Roman ceremony marking the founding of a city. The Emperor appears plowing with a bull and a cow, with the furrow marking the future boundaries of the city. Hadrian's plan to rebuild Jerusalem as a Hellenistic city, named after himself, was one of the primary causes for the outbreak of the Bar Kokhba rebellion. Hadrian sought a peaceful arrangement with the Jews, but he encountered stubborn resistance to his plans for Jerusalem and to such acts as banning circumcision.

2 Military reinforcements were called to the province of Judea when the revolt broke out. The tenth legion, permanently garrisoned in Jerusalem, and the sixth legion, stationed at Legio (Kefar Otnay), failed to overcome the rebels. Additional legions were summoned from Syria, Arabia and Egypt. This helmet of a Roman horseman during the time of Hadrian was discovered in Israel.

3 Hadrian Publius Aelius (ruled 117-138) was proclaimed Emperor upon the death of Trajan. Hadrian's objective was to restore the *Pax Romana* to his empire, and to concentrate on reconstruction and development. To this end he traveled extensively throughout his empire, in 129-130 visiting the province of Judea. The picture shows a bust of Hadrian, part of a monumental bronze statue discovered northwest of Tell Shalem. The statue may have been erected in the camp of the Roman legion in honor of Hadrian's visit.

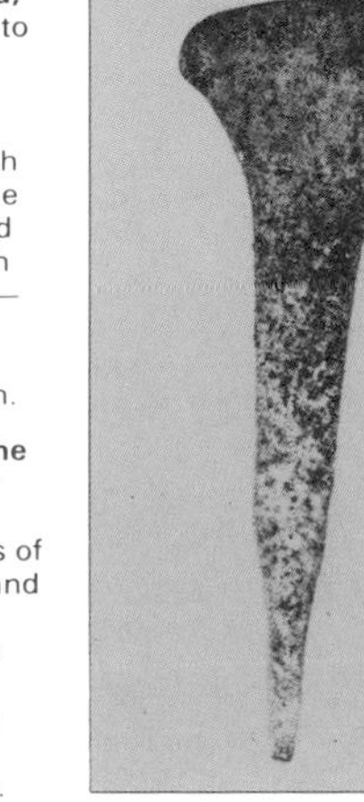

4 A letter from Simeon Bar Kokhba, leader of the revolt, to one of the commanders of his army, Joshua ben Galgula. It deals with arrangements for the supply of wheat, and concludes "Dispatch after the Sabbath" — testimony to the author's concern to observe the Sabbath.

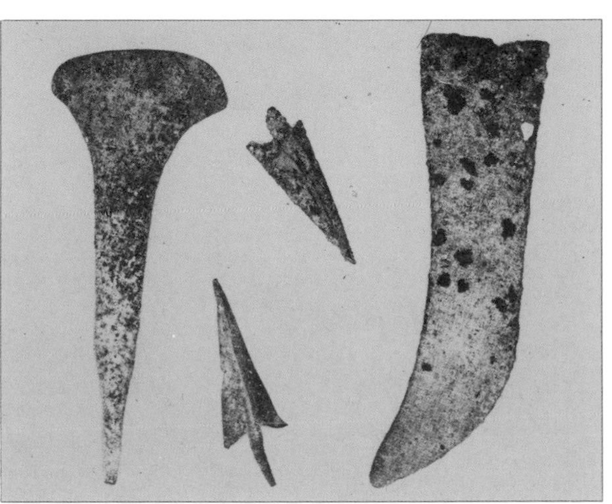

5 Refugees from the rebellion, with their wives and children, took shelter in caves of the Judean Desert and in underground fortifications, where they had stocked supplies. These iron implements were found in such caves.

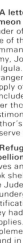

devoutness and strict observance of the commandments in his camp apparently made possible his close ties with the Sages and the *Sanhedrin* [8].

When the Bar Kokhba revolt broke out, it did so suddenly and with great force, and the Romans were caught completely off guard. The governor, Tinneius Rufus, failed to overcome Bar Kokhba's guerrilla tactics, and called for reinforcements from Syria and Egypt [2]. However, Bar Kokhba overcame these, too. The defeated Rufus removed his forces from Jerusalem, and the city evidently passed into rebel hands.

The pressure on the Roman garrison in Judea during the first stages of the revolt elicited a vigorous reaction from Hadrian. He called in his senior commander, the governor of Britain, Julius Severus, put a large military force at his disposal, and delegated him to run the war. Severus divided his forces and isolated the rebel strongholds and villages until, one by one, they were captured.

The remaining rebels retreated to Bethar, where, because of a strategic location and strong fortifications, they were able to withstand siege for a long time until Bethar fell as well. The few surviving rebels took refuge in caves in the Judean desert, but even there the Romans caught up with them [5].

The revolt had bitter consequences. Hundreds of thousands perished in battle, from hunger, or from disease, and tens of thousands were sold into slavery [6]. Judea was almost completely divested of its Jewish inhabitants. The Romans changed the name of the province to Syria-Palestina, and Jerusalem, now a Roman colony, was settled with gentiles. Jews were forbidden even to enter the city, and decrees of religious persecution were passed against them by the Romans.

The center of Jewish life shifted from Judea to the Galilee, which had not suffered in the revolt. There the leadership of the Sages again set about rebuilding the ruins of Jewish life.

KEY

Silver coins from the time of the Bar Kokhba revolt (134-135). The inscriptions read, "For the Freedom of Jerusalem," and "For the Redemption of Israel." They bear the names and titles of the leaders of the revolt — "Simeon *Nasi* of Israel," and "Eleazar the Priest." Their motifs, including vessels used in the Temple worship, all reflected the rebels' hopes and aspirations for political and religious independence, accompanied by a tone of messianism.

6

7 A

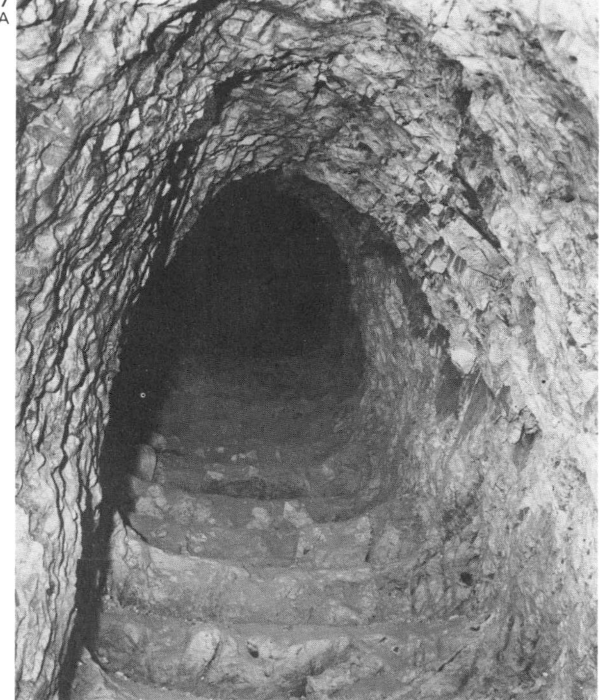

6 Many of the rebels died in caves. The absence of signs of physical injury testifies to their natural death. The Romans besieged them for an extended time, leaving them without food or water. Those who survived and were captured were sold into slavery. The picture shows copper housewares found in the Cave of Letters in Nahal Hever.

8 The synagogue at Herodium served the rebels during the revolt. The rebel army, like its leader, Bar Kokhba, was very strict in observing all the commandments.

8

7 B

7 The Jews' preparations for the revolt are described by the Roman historian, Dio Cassius (2nd-3rd century): "They seized the well situated locations in the country, and fortified them with trenches and walls, to serve them as places of refuge in time of trouble, and also to enable them to move about clandestinely. They bored openings into the underground passages to let in air and light" (*History of Rome* LXIX 12-15). The tunnel [A] was dug by rebels at Herodium; the cave entrances pocketing the cliff face [B] are in the Judean Desert.

Judah ha-Nasi and his Era

The gradual recovery of the Jewish community in Ereẓ Israel after the Bar Kokhba revolt was accompanied by significant demographic and political changes. The main area to suffer from the war had been Judea, leaving the Galilee with the largest Jewish population [Key], and the seat of two primary institutions of Jewish leadership — the Patriarchate and the *Sanhedrin*. The rehabilitation process was somewhat similar to that in Jabneh during the difficult years following the Great Revolt (70 CE).

At first R. Akiva's surviving disciples gathered in the Galilee [3] and, lacking a functioning Patriarchate, were themselves forced to assume the more pressing tasks of leadership. Later the city of Usha became the seat of the renewed Jewish leadership, which issued a call to the elders in the Galilee: "Whoever is learned, let him come and teach; and whoever is not learned, let him come and study." Little by little a new framework for the leadership of the Sages emerged. Some time later Rabban Simeon ben Gamaliel arrived in Usha and became *Nasi* of the Patriarchate. It appears that reestablishing the Patriarchate in Usha evoked some opposition among the Sages, just as had happened earlier in Jabneh to Rabban Gamaliel, father of Rabban Simeon.

The Sages of Usha worked to restore the Jewish community. For the first time they explicitly forbade Jews to leave the land, and a body of laws (*Sikarikon*) was formulated to encourage redemption of land from non-Jews. The Patriarchate and the Sages worked together to preserve the subordinate position of the Diaspora, particularly Babylonia, to Ereẓ Israel in the matter of declaring the new moon and intercalating the year; thus they retained Ereẓ Israel's primacy of place, and prevented a schism in the people. *Nesi'im* appointed and dismissed Diaspora community leaders as well, and Diaspora Jews sent contributions to support the Patriarchate.

New Attitudes to Roman Authority

Failure of the Bar Kokhba revolt made it necessary for the people to reexamine their attitude to Roman rule in Ereẓ Israel. From the time of Usha on, there is no evidence of any attempts at abolishing "the wicked government" (Rome) by force of arms. This change stemmed partly from a development in the Jewish notion of messianism, which came to be portrayed more as a gradual, spiritual trend than as an active military manifestation, such as in the Great Revolt or the Bar Kokhba revolt. The Sages too influenced this change by seeking to remove the threat posed by apocalyptic thinkers to the Jewish people. Now it was asserted that the redemption of Israel would resemble the morning star, whose light appears "at first little by little, gradually growing stronger and stronger." Such an approach made possible a certain degree of understanding, and even a cordial system of relations between the Roman government and the Jewish leadership in Ereẓ Israel. It

CONNECTIONS

52 The Nation Rallies after the Destruction
54 The Bar Kokhba Revolt
60 The Jewish Community in Babylonia

1 Emperor Caracalla Marcus Aurelius Antoninus (reigned 211-217) was remarkable for his good treatment of the Jews. Scholars believe Caracalla to have been the friend of Judah ha-Nasi who appears in Jewish sources under the name of Antoninus. The rulers of the Severus dynasty evinced understanding for the feelings of the Jews and their culture. More enlightened governors were appointed over Judea, many familiar with Erez Israel from a prior tour of duty. The Jews were granted extensive autonomy in the sphere of religion, the courts, and ownership of property.

2 Bet Shean, then known as Scythopolis or Nissa, was a mixed town. This Roman theater was built in Severus' time.

3 "This is the Bet Midrash of Rabbi Eleazer ha-Kappar" is inscribed in Hebrew on a basalt lintel discovered in the Golan. The lintel and the script are ornamented in the style used in 3rd century synagogues in the Galilee. Rabbi Eleazar ha-Kappar, a *tanna* of the late 2nd century said that "the synagogues and houses of learning in Babylonia will in time to come be planted in Erez Israel" (*Babylonian Talmud*, Tractate *Megillah* 29a). It appears that he moved from Lydda to the north of Erez Israel, where after the Bar Kokhba revolt many sages gathered in Safed, Tiberias, Sepphoris, and Acre. Usha, in the Lower Galilee, was the residence of Rabban Simeon ben Gamaliel and R. Isaac Nappaha ("the Smith").

4 The Mishnah is an anthology of the laws, *halakhot*, of the Oral *Torah*, arranged in six "Orders," according to broad topics: *Zeraim*, containing laws bearing on agriculture; *Moed*, laws governing the Sabbath and other holy days; *Nezikin*, civil and criminal law; *Nashim*, family law; *Kodashim*, sacrificial rites; and *Tohorah*, ritual purity. In the early 3rd century Rabbi Judah ha-Nasi gathered the religious laws and redacted them into the *Mishnah*. The principle used in organizing the material was not uniform; it appears to be related to the nature of the *Halakhah* and the currency it had gained among the Sages. This column of text is from the Kaufmann Codex, a manuscript of the *Mishnah* discovered in Budapest.

reached its peak during the reign of the Severus dynasty (193-235) [1, 2].

Judah ha-Nasi

Judah ha-Nasi (known as "Rabbi"), son of Rabban Simeon ben Gamaliel, served as *Nasi* from some time around 185 until about 220 CE. The sources present him as a political leader and a sage: "*Torah* and greatness in a single place." During his time the Patriarchate took on the trappings of local royalty, and emphasis was placed on the roots of the *Nesi'im* in the House of David. Judah ha-Nasi had the sole authority to confer the title of Rabbi — an ordainment of significant authority in the judicial system — and communal leaders were appointed on his behalf throughout Erez Israel.

The crowning glory of Rabbi's activities was his great undertaking to bring together all the traditions of the Oral *Torah* in the book of the *Mishnah* [4]. Early rabbis and scholars alike are of divided opinion concerning Rabbi's special role in this undertaking. Did he intend to create a legal codex which would be binding on all the Jewish people? Or did his *Mishnah*, i.e. the body of *halakhot* which he taught his disciples, simply become the most important book on the Oral Law, displacing the *mishnayot* of other sages of his day, due to Rabbi's forceful personality. Either way, Rabbi's *Mishnah* served as the axis of two additional great works — the *Babylonian Talmud* and the *Jerusalem Talmud*.

The death of Rabbi Judah ha-Nasi, like his life, had a great impact on his contemporaries. His death, and last will and testament, were described at length in the *Talmud* and the *Midrash*, and were viewed as sealing a chapter in Jewish history. "From the time Rabbi died, tribulations were multiplied two-fold." He was buried in the estate of the Patriarchate in Bet She'arim [7]. From then on Bet She'arim became a necropolis not only for the Jews of Erez Israel, but also for Jews from the Diaspora [5].

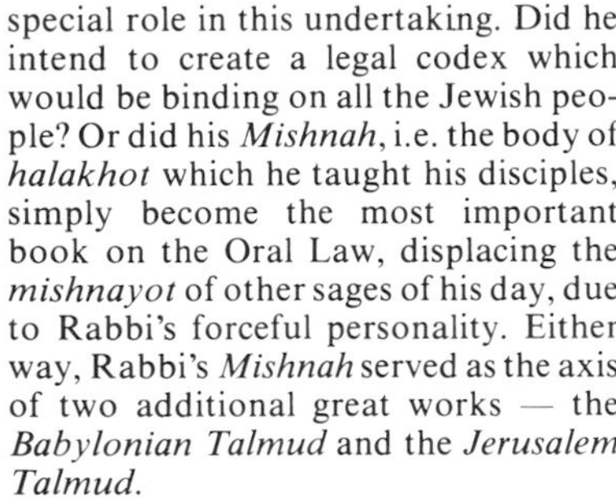

KEY

About a dozen ancient synagogues have been discovered in the Galilee. Their style of architecture and their Hebrew inscriptions help date them to the 2nd-3rd centuries CE. Two synagogues were uncovered in Kefar Baram, the site of a flourishing Jewish community near what is today the Lebanese border. The larger one was very ornate, and its well preserved facade and portico illustrate the monumental style of architecture characteristic of the Galilee synagogues. The facade has an arched door and two other openings. The inscription, "Built by Eleazar bar Judan," was found in the eastern window.

5

5 A serious economic crisis struck Erez Israel in the wake of upheaval in the Roman government, and undermined the institution of the Patriarchate. During this period many Jews emigrated, primarily to Babylonia, which had a thriving economy. Nevertheless, many Jews from the Diaspora still sought to be buried in Erez Israel. This tombstone from Bet She'arim was erected by a daughter, Zenobia, for her mother, Karteria, a member of the nobility. It is ornamented with a *menorah*, flanked on either side by a *lulav*, *etrog*, and *shofar*. The Greek inscription on it stresses its importance in preserving the memory of the deceased, and the language used clearly shows the influence of the Greek epic. Bet She'arim served at this time as principal burial ground both for the Patriarchate and for wealthy Diaspora Jews.

6 A console decorated by a palm tree [A], and a chariot carved in the form of a temple, with a holy ark [B], from the synagogue at Capernaum. Dating from the 3rd century, it is considered the most elaborate of the ancient synagogues discovered in the Galilee. According to the New Testament, a synagogue was built there by a Roman general. Its remains indicate that it was built of ashlars, with its capitals, lintels, and doorposts ornamented by stone carvings.

6 A

6 B

7 A

7 B

7 Bet She'arim was established in Hasmonean times, but flourished especially during the time of Judah ha-Nasi. Catacombs from the 2nd-4th centuries CE have been discovered there, mostly of the general public. They bear many decorations and inscriptions in Hebrew, Greek, and in the languages of Tadmor and of Himyar. The decorations, Jewish symbols and ritual objects, are done in reliefs, etchings, and murals in the style of Jewish folk art which was common during the Roman period. Illustration [A] shows one of the catacombs, and [B] shows the elaborate facade of the tombs.

The Egyptian Jewish Community in Ancient Times

Jews first migrated from the Holy Land to Egypt toward the end of the First Temple period (586 BCE), mainly for political reasons. The majority lived in the Faiyum district, in Migdol, Daphna, and Nof (Memphis) in Lower Egypt, and Petrus in Upper Egypt. Aramaic papyruses found at Yeb, on Egypt's southern border, attest to the existence of a colony of Jewish mercenaries there in the 5th century BCE. When the country was under Persian rule [1, 2], Darius II (ruled 424-404 BCE) reaffirmed the right of the Jewish garrison to worship their own God.

The Hellenic Period

In the wake of Alexander the Great's conquests in the East (332 BCE), Jews settled in Alexandria, the new city he had constructed [3]. Under the Ptolemaic dynasty which united Egypt and Erez Israel into one country (332-201 BCE), the Jewish community in Egypt expanded. Jews taken prisoner in Judah by the Ptolemaic armies were exiled to Egypt; many others migrated there freely throughout the period, even after Judah came under Seleucid rule. The political situation in Erez Israel — and particularly the Hellenizing decrees of Antiochus IV Epiphanes (167 BCE) and the resultant Hasmonean uprising — intensified emigration. Ptolemaic monarchs generally permitted the Jews to practice their religion freely. The Onias Temple, established at Leontopolis by the descendants of the Sadducees with the approval of Ptolemy IV (222-204 BCE), attests to this.

From papyruses and Talmudic sources we know of the heterogeneity of the Jewish socio-economic structure in Egypt. Jews were farmers, merchants, artisans, tax collectors, ship owners, ship captains and sailors. Under the Ptolemies, Alexandria's Jews were an autonomous community (*politeuma*), as regards jurisdiction and tax collection. They were headed by a governor — *ethnarch* — who supervised the judicial system and acted as supreme judge. A council of elders — *gerosia* — ruled on community affairs.

In the 1st century CE the Jews constituted 40% of the million-strong population of Alexandria. The preservation of their religious separatism, appointment to high government positions, economic prosperity and pride — aroused the hostility of both Greeks and Egyptians from the Ptolemaic era onward. This was particularly evident in Alexandria, whose Jews aspired to equal citizenship status, like the Greeks. The status of the Jews remained unchanged when Egypt became a Roman province (30 BCE); but their support for Julius Caesar (47 CE) aroused hostility against them. The Greeks came to regard the Jews as an alien element, which enjoyed Roman support.

Hostility took overt form in 38 CE, when Agrippas I came from Rome to Alexandria en route to the Holy Land, and was accorded a royal welcome by the Jews. Riots broke out, encouraged

CONNECTIONS
24 From the Patriarchs to the Exodus
34 Destruction and Exile
38 Erez Israel in the Fourth and Third Centuries BCE
60 The Jewish Community in Babylonia

1

1 Yeb was situated on an island opposite Aswan. As a frontier fortress it defended Egypt's southern approaches. The garrison consisted of numerous nationalities, including Jews. This picture of Yeb is by David Roberts (19th century).

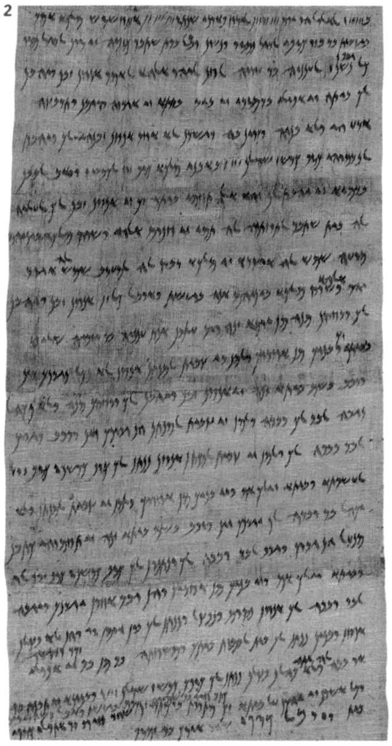

2 The "Jewish force" at Yeb was organized in "banners" — battalions bearing Persian or Babylonian names (apparently after their non-Jewish commanding officers). Jewish civilians also resided in the colony. Jewish settlement in Yeb can be traced to the 5th century BCE. Community life focused on a temple, destroyed in 411 BCE. Jews were permitted to purchase land, inherit it, and trade with gentiles. This Aramaic papyrus was a contract for the purchase of a house by Anania Ben Azaria from a gentile, in 437 BCE.

3 Alexandria, built in 332 BCE, flourished and became the greatest city of the Hellenistic world, and a major commercial center. The Jews contributed greatly to the city's glory from the 1st century BCE to the 1st century CE. Several became extremely wealthy from commerce. The Ptolemies made it a center of commerce and of culture, and granted a large measure of autonomy to the 400,000 Jews of Alexandria. Eventually Jewish separatism and prosperity aroused the enmity of Alexandria's Greeks and Egyptians. The various Christian sects which settled there battled one another too and, together, fought against pagan cultures. Jewish-Christian disputes led to the expulsion of Alexandria's Jews in 415. The city was packed with unrest, and its decline was completed by the Persian occupation in 616 and the Arab conquest of 642. The picture shows Alexandrian Jewish occupations in the Hellenistic era (reconstruction from sources).

3

4 This clay lamp from Egypt, decorated with figures of David and Goliath, is from the 4th century CE. Jewish cultural and community life revived in Egypt during the 3rd and 4th centuries CE, as Hellenistic influence waned.

4

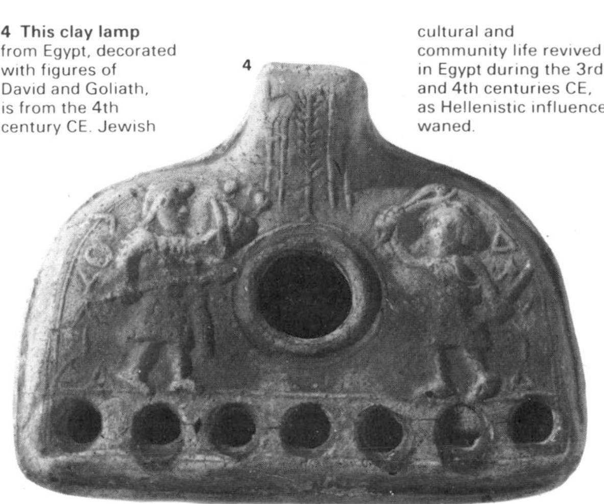

by the Roman prefect, Valerius Flaccus; synagogues were burned and shops looted; many Jews were murdered, and the remainder were forced into one quarter — in effect, the first ghetto. After the death of Caligula (41 CE), his successor, Claudius, confirmed the Jewish right to reside in Alexandria.

Jewish culture flourished in Alexandria throughout this period. Under Ptolemy II (285-247 BCE) the Bible was translated into Greek [Key], and thus brought to the knowledge of the non-Jewish world. Papyruses and documents in the Cairo *Genizah* tell of writers, poets and philosophers among Egyptian Jewry in the Ptolemaic era. They included Yehezkel the Tragedian, who wrote a drama entitled *The Exodus from Egypt*; Philo Epikon, who wrote the poem *Jerusalem* in Homeric style, and the historian Dimitrius, who dated biblical events. The outstanding Jewish philosopher and writer was Philo of Alexandria (20 BCE-40 CE), who, like other Hellenistic Jewish writers, sought to mediate between Judaism and Greek philosophy.

The Decline of the Community

When the Great Revolt broke out in Ereẓ Israel (66 CE), the situation of the Egyptian Jewish community rapidly deteriorated. Concomitantly, the Jews of Alexandria rebelled against the Romans; riots broke out and thousands of Jews died. After the destruction of the Temple, many Judean refugees fled to Egypt, and tried to incite the local Jews to rebel against the Romans. The Jewish leadership refused, however, and even handed over some of the Judean rebels to the Romans. Tension between Egypt's Jews and the Roman authorities did not ease, however, and while the Roman legions were occupied in the East, Jewish uprisings took place throughout the Empire — at Cyrene, Egypt and Cyprus. These were suppressed by Trajanus in 117 CE [5, 6, 8]. As a consequence, Babylonia became the foremost Jewish community [4, 7].

KEY

The Septuagint was the first translation of the Old Testament from the original Hebrew into another language. The translation project was accomplished mainly by the Egyptian community to satisfy the needs of Greek-speaking Jews. Translation of the Pentateuch was apparently completed by the 3rd century BCE, and was disseminated from Egypt throughout the Hellenistic world and Erez Israel. Within the next two centuries the translation encompassed the entire Old Testament. It was faithful to the form, content and grammatical structure of the Hebrew. This page from *Codex Sinaiticus*, a manuscript of the Septuagint, was found in the mid-19th century at the Santa Catherina Monastery.

5

6

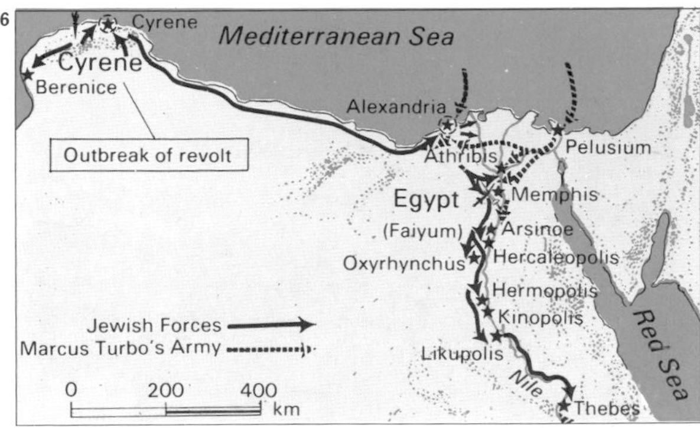

6 The revolt of Diaspora Jews against Trajanus was born of disputes between Jews and Greeks in Alexandria and Cyrene. It spread to the whole of Egypt, Cyprus and Mesopotamia. The revolt developed into a national liberation struggle against the Romans, with messianic overtones. It spread destruction throughout the contemporary Diaspora, and its impact was felt long afterwards.

5 The papyrus Annals of Alexandria's Martyrs records the attitude displayed by Marcus Ulpius Trajanus (53-117) toward the Jews. Though he had preferred the Jews to the Greeks, Trajanus eventually crushed their revolt mercilessly, together with Jewish uprisings in Libya and Cyprus. Of the decimation of Alexandrian Jewry the Sages said: "the light of Israel has been cut off, nor will it return until the coming of the Son of David." The destruction of the central Alexandrian synagogue is attributed to Trajanus himself.

7 A

7 B

7 Egyptian Jewish community life began to recover at the end of the 3rd century CE. Jewish institutions were restored in provincial towns, and Alexandria's Jews began to play an important economic role, which again came to an end with their expulsion in 415. There is considerable evidence that in the 3rd and 4th centuries Egyptian Jews used Hebrew names without the Greek endings customary in the Hellenic-Roman period, possibly indicating the waning lure of Hellenistic culture. In the pictures — two 4th century Egyptian lamps — [A] made of bronze, [B] made of clay.

8

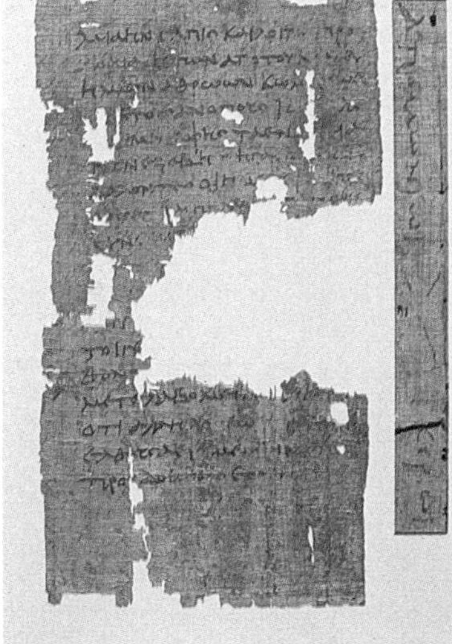

8 Jewish victories at Hermopolis in 116-117 CE are recorded in this papyrus. The Roman prefect in Egypt, Lupus, was unable to restore order using local forces, and had to summon reinforcements. Since Trajanus was away fighting the Parthians, the Romans were forced to recruit civilian officials to fill the role of army officers. The local Greeks, too, came to the aid of the Roman army, although Egyptian villagers generally sided with the Jews. Though the Jews inflicted heavy blows on their adversaries and checked their expansion eastward, they were ultimately to suffer a fatal defeat.

The Jewish Community in Babylonia

The Jewish community of Babylonia was one of the largest and oldest of the Second Temple period. Its beginnings date to the exile of the tribes of Israel and Judah, at the end of the First Temple period; yet, the history of this community during the Second Temple period is shrouded in mystery. Josephus, the historian of that era, noted only that the number of Jews in Babylonia was "countless tens of thousands, the exact number of which we cannot know" (*Jewish Antiquities*, 11:133). Like the other ethnic groups living east of the Euphrates, the Jews, too, were subject in various eras to the rule of Babylonia, Persia, the Hellenistic Seleucids, and the Parthians [2].

The Period of the Tannaim

The governmental structure and culture of the Parthian empire (2nd century BCE-3rd century CE) contributed greatly to the flourishing of the Jewish community in Babylonia [6, Key]. The Parthian kings could generally count on the Jews' support in the internal struggles which erupted in their empire, in exchange for which they granted the Jews both autonomy and power. In addition, Babylonia was the only Jewish community of the Diaspora, including the central community of Ereẓ Israel, which lay beyond the direct sphere of influence of Graeco-Roman culture. Free from foreign influence, the Babylonian Jewish community's spiritual vitality increased, winning it special status in the eyes of the Jews of Ereẓ Israel. Indeed, at the outset of the Great Revolt, in 66, the rebels looked to their brethren across the Euphrates for succor, and even hoped, in vain, for the Parthian empire to join in the war on its foe, Rome.

The Babylonian community's importance during the Second Temple period is eminently manifest by the place it occupied in talmudic literature. The *Mishnah* describes the line of beacons used to inform Jews in the Diaspora of the beginning of a new month with specific reference to its arrival at the community in Babylonia. The despatches sent to inform Jews of the intercalation of the year referred pointedly to "our brethren, the exiles of Babylonia and the exiles of Media." After the destruction of the Temple (70 CE) and the Bar Kokhba revolt (132-135), for the first time the Babylonian community challenged the hegemony of Ereẓ Israel.

The Period of the Amoraim

In about 226 CE, the Parthian empire fell to rebel forces from within, and the government passed into the hands of the Persian Sassanid dynasty [4], which ruled Babylonia until its conquest by Islam in the early 7th century. The Sassanids sought to set up a strong centralized government, and to restore the Zoroastrian cult. Attempts were made to restrict the Jewish community, but its leaders were wise enough to recognize the new regime and accept the law of the land; as the *amora* Samuel put it, "The law of the state is the law."

1

1 Aramaic was the vernacular of the Jews of Babylonia and Erez Israel in the first few centuries CE. The Jews of Erez Israel spoke a western Aramaic dialect, while the Jews of Babylonia spoke an eastern Aramaic dialect. The latter is the language of the *Babylonian Talmud*, which also has many Persian words in it, whereas the *Jerusalem Talmud* has many Greek words. This bowl from Nippur (6th century), bears Aramaic invocations.

2 A

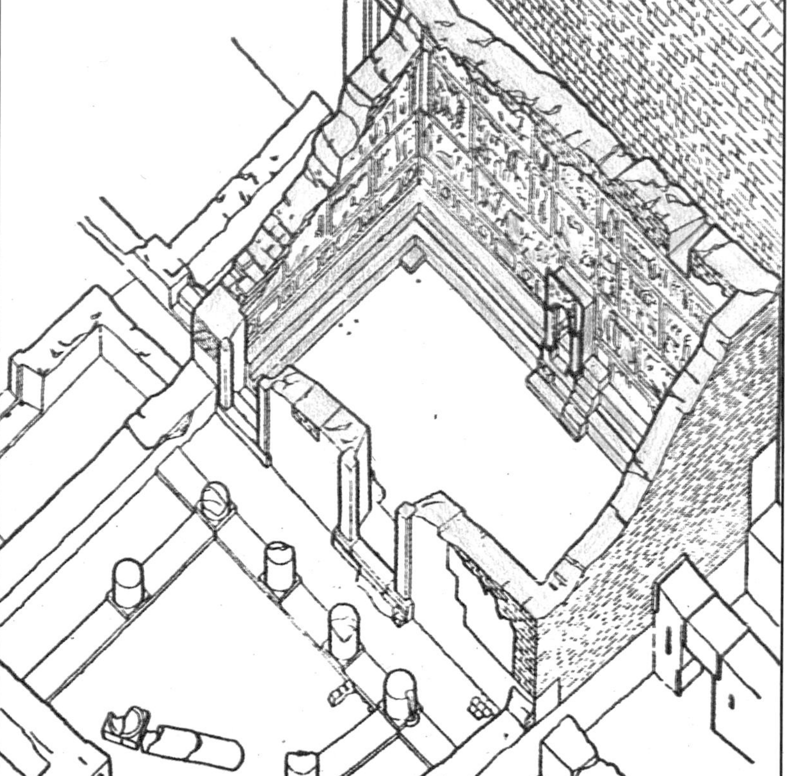

3

3 Shapur I (reigned 241-247), the Sassanian king referred to in the *Talmud* as *Shabur*, recognized the economic and political importance of the Jews of Babylonia, and put an end to their persecution. According to a tradition of the *Talmud*, he conversed with Samuel, the head of the Nehardea academy, on a variety of topics. The picture shows the Roman Emperor Valerianus bowing before Shapur I (in a 3rd century relief from Persepolis).

4

4 "Two people contending over one garment" is one of the questions discussed in the *Talmud*, concerning problems from daily life. This question introduces Tractate *Bava Mezia*, which deals with the law on things lost and found, fraud, usury, leasing, and promissory notes.

2 B

2 In Dura Europos, a city on the Euphrates, the remains of a synagogue have been discovered [A]. Its walls are covered with frescoes portraying figures and events from the Bible, the Temple sanctuary and its vessels [B]. The city was built by the Seleucids, and was conquered by the Parthians in 141 BCE, after which Jews resided in it. It was in Roman hands from 162 on, with the Persians capturing it several times in the 3rd century.

At least from the end of the 2nd century the Jews of Babylonia were represented before the authorities by a *Resh Galuta* (Exilarch), of Davidic lineage. During the period of the *geonim* attempts were made to trace the genealogy of the Exilarchs back as far as the time of Jehoiachin, King of Judah, in order to prove the pre-eminence of the Jewish leadership in Babylonia. One landmark in this prolonged struggle was the return in 219 of the sage Rav (Abba Arikha) to the land of his birth, after a prolonged stay with R. Judah ha-Nasi in Erez Israel.

Rav (d. 247) established a new center of study in the city of Sura, and became its head, while his colleague and adversary, Samuel (d. 254), headed the older, established Jewish center in Nehardea. Over the years, the two most eminent institutions of Babylonian Jewry gradually took shape in these two cities — the Academies of Sura and Nehardea. In 259 Nehardea was destroyed, and the academy moved between several cities until it was finally reestablished in the city of Pumbedita. At the beginning of the 4th century it was headed by Rabbah and R. Joseph b. Hiyya; then predominance passed to the Academy of Mahoza, near the Sassanian capital of Ctesiphon, headed by a different sage called Rabbah. Toward the end of that century and the beginning of the 5th century, Sura again became the most important academy. It was headed by Rav Ashi (died *c.* 425), to whom is attributed an important role in redacting the *Babylonian Talmud* [3, 7].

In the second half of the 5th century, fanatic Persian religious figures attained the upper hand, and the Jews were sorely persecuted. An obscure report tells of Mar Zutra, one of the Exilarchs, rebelling and establishing an independent Jewish state that lasted seven years on the soil of Babylonia. But recovery of the Babylonian community was not long in coming. The era of the *geonim* begins a new and brilliant chapter in the history of Babylonian Jewry.

KEY

Agriculture provided the source of livelihood for many of the Jews of Babylonia. An abundance of water made intensive cultivation of the soil possible. Generally, Jews were tenant farmers who received a fraction of the yield in exchange for their labor. Other common occupations were commerce, and crafts such as pottery-making, tanning and tailoring. Even fishing was a widespread occupation. This illustration of fish being gathered from a flooded field is from the Museum of the Diaspora, where it was reconstructed according to the style of the frescoes in the Dura Europos Synagogue.

5

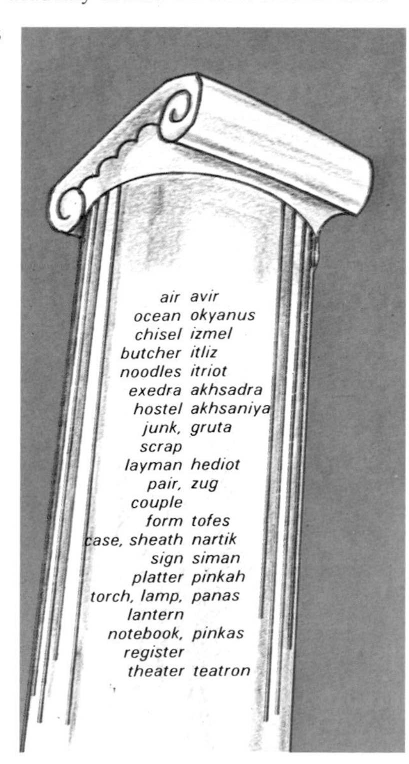

air avir
ocean okyanus
chisel izmel
butcher itliz
noodles itriot
exedra akhsadra
hostel akhsaniya
junk, gruta
scrap
layman hediot
pair, zug
couple
form tofes
ase, sheath nartik
sign siman
platter pinkah
torch, lamp, panas
lantern
notebook, pinkas
register
theater teatron

5 Hundreds of Greek words, some Hebraicized, found their way into the *Mishnah*, the *Talmud*, and the *Midrash*. Many designate objects or concepts from Hellenistic culture.

6 The Jewish community of Babylonia, during the period of the *Mishnah* and the *Talmud*, extended from the Tigris to the Euphrates. The Jews of Babylonia considered themselves genealogically pure if they lived in *Bavel le-yuhasin* (pedigreed Babylonia). The sages of Erez Israel and Babylonia also dealt with the definition of geographical Erez Israel, in order to ensure burial in Erez Israel, which was considered an issue of importance. In the 3rd century the *amoraim* of Babylonia sanctioned burial west of the Euphrates, basing their decision on the promised borders of Erez Israel.

6

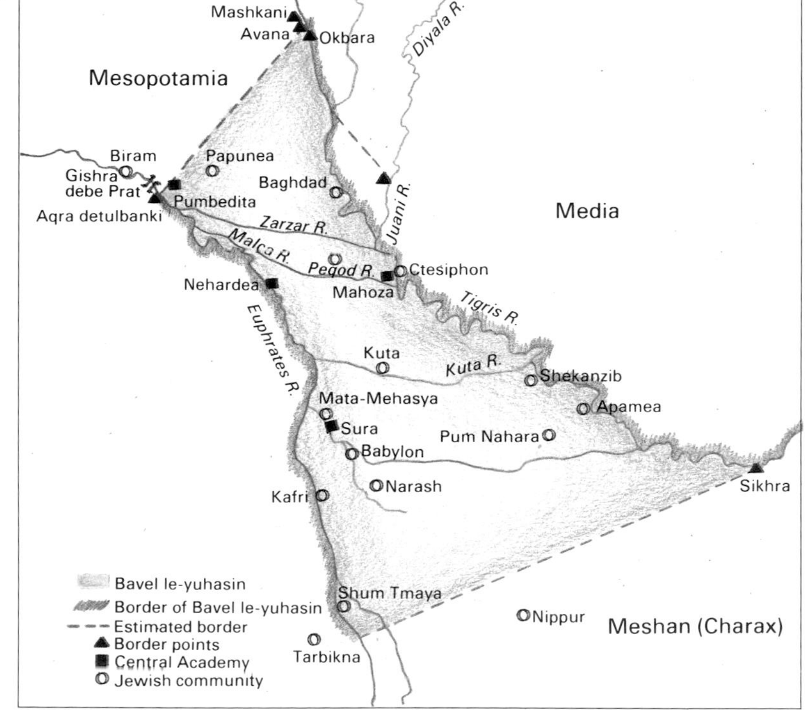

7 The Babylonian Talmud, a commentary on the Oral Law, contains homilies and commentaries on Scripture, legends, morals and aphorisms, traditions of *Halakhah* court rulings, and historical material. It was redacted over the course of some 300 years, and finalized sometime around the beginning of the 6th century, although even after that date many sayings were still added to it. This page is from the *Babylonian Talmud* printed by Daniel Bomberg, Venice, 1520-1527. This edition determined the accepted format for all later editions.

7

8

8 Interpretation of the Talmud was carried on in the academies of the Babylonian *geonim*. When centers for the study of the *Torah* arose in other communities of the Diaspora, exegesis through independent deliberations gained momentum. Rashi, the greatest of the commentators on the *Talmud*, incorporated the interpretations of the *geonim* and of the scholars of Ashkenaz. This commentary on Tractate *Yevamot* (14th century *Ashkenaz*) is by R. Asher ben Jehiel (1250?-1327) who summarized the rulings of *posekim* and commentators.

Ereẓ Israel under Byzantine Rule

The Christianization of the Roman Empire, which began during the time of Constantine the Great (reigned 306-337), wrought far-reaching changes in the status of the Jewish people throughout the empire [4], as well as in the character and demography of Ereẓ Israel. Until then the Roman emperors had recognized the Jewish religion as one of the legal national religions in the spectrum of ethnic groups under their rule.

Christianity Takes Over

In 324 the newly-converted Constantine vanquished his foe in the East, Emperor Licinius (reigned 308-324), thus becoming the first Christian ruler of Ereẓ Israel. He enacted laws to reduce Jewish proselytism and protect converts from Judaism to Christianity. Under the inspiration of Constantine and his mother, Helena, large churches were constructed throughout the land, among them the Church of the Holy Sepulcher, the Church of the Nativity, in Bethlehem, and the churches on the Mount of Olives and in Hebron. These churches attracted Christian pilgrims from all over the world, who in turn built additional churches [6, 7], particularly in those regions where the Jewish population was relatively sparse, such as in Judea and around Jerusalem.

The Impact on the Jews

Around 351-352, a Jewish uprising broke out in the Sepphoris region, and apparently spread to Tiberias, Lydda, and other centers of Jewish population. Ten years later, Emperor Julian, who was known as "the Apostate" because he opposed making Christianity the official religion of the empire, and himself adhered to the pagan religion of the ancient world, ascended the throne. Before embarking on a military campaign against Persia, Julian sought to win the Jews' support, hence he promised the Jews of Ereẓ Israel that he would restore Jerusalem and the Temple. Julian fell in battle against Persia, in 363, and the construction project in Jerusalem never came to fruition.

Toward the end of the 4th century anti-Jewish legislation was renewed, and during the reign of Theodosius II (408-450) the Church sought to undermine the status of the Patriarchate and the synagogues in Ereẓ Israel. For generations the Patriarchate had served to unify the Jews throughout the empire. The *Nesi'im* (Patriarchs) continued to exert influence in the Diaspora, by virtue of their authority to appoint local leaders through emissaries whom they sent from Ereẓ Israel. Their authority was also bolstered due to their lineage, traced to the House of David. All this increased the desire of the Church to weaken their power. Indeed, from approximately 425, the Patriarchate appeared no longer to be fulfilling its role, and thus dawned the end of the dynasty which had headed the Jewish nation for at least 350 years.

The ruling authorities also forbade construction of new synagogues, and in various ways encouraged the abandon-

CONNECTIONS

56 Judah ha-Nasi and his Era

64 Erez Israel under Arab Rule

1

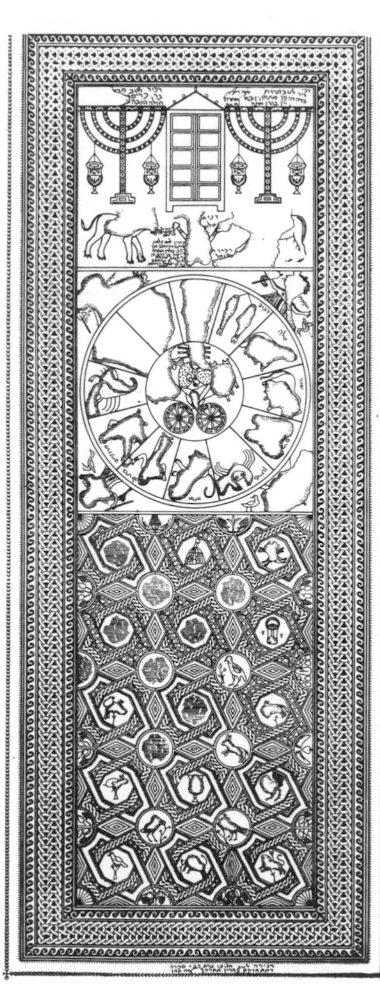

1 During the Roman period Naaran, in the Jordan Valley, was a Jewish village, unlike the neighboring town of Jericho, which was inhabited by gentiles. The *Midrash* (*Lamentations Rabbah* 40:71) refers to hostility between the two towns. Remains of a synagogue were accidentally discovered there in 1918. It had an atrium and a nave, divided into three sections by colonnades. Its mosaic floor, seen here, portrays two candelabra and the zodiac wheel (most of its signs defaced) and symbols of the four seasons.

2

2 This 6th century mosaic floor of the En Gedi synagogue is noted for its four Hebrew and Aramaic inscriptions, and for the names of the zodiac signs, appearing without the signs themselves (unlike other synagogues of the same period).

3

3 The ancient synagogue at Bet Alpha is one of the later synagogues built in Erez Israel, in the 5th-7th centuries. Unlike the earlier synagogues of the Galilee, these were built on a much smaller scale, and of unhewn stone, covered with plaster. Their typical features included division into an atrium (center court), a narthex (porticoed vestibule leading to the nave) and a nave, and especially an apse for the ark, and colorful mosaic floors. This is the central section of the mosaic floor discovered in the synagogue at Bet Alpha. The motifs of the mosaic, preserved in its entirety, include the signs of the zodiac. The inscription dates to the 6th century.

4

4 The status of the Jews in the Diaspora was affected by the Church's attitude. We know of a blood libel against the Jews of northern Syria in 414, and of the synagogue of Constantinople being turned into a church in 442. The status of the Jews of Italy deteriorated with the adoption of Christianity as the official state religion. This Byzantine period plate from Italy is from the 4th century.

ment of existing synagogues and their delivery into the hands of the Church. Nevertheless, archaeological findings indicate that precisely during this period there was increased activity in building and renovating synagogues throughout Erez Israel [1, 2, 3].

Notwithstanding the Jews' stubborn resistance to the pressures of the Church, the country's Jewish population dwindled throughout the Byzantine period. Meanwhile many pagans (and a few Jews) converted to Christianity, and many Christian pilgrims stayed in the country and joined the population already there, until, in the 6th century, the Christians became a majority in the country. Beginning in the 4th century monastic life became widespread, and many monks settled in and around Jerusalem, around Tekoa, and in Gaza. Even fundamentally Jewish cities, such as Tiberias and Sepphoris, absorbed Christian influence. The Samaritans suffered from Christian rule even more than the Jews. While the latter at least formally enjoyed the protection of the authorities, the Samaritan community was never even officially recognized by the Empire. This treatment roused them to frequent rebellion.

Despite the repressive conditions under which they lived throughout the Byzantine period, the Jews of Erez Israel nevertheless produced some of the outstanding literature of the Sages. About the time the Patriarchate was abolished, the editing of the *Jerusalem Talmud* was completed; and in the 5th and 6th centuries the famous *Midrashim* of Erez Israel, such as *Genesis Rabbah* and *Leviticus Rabbah*, were compiled. Toward the end of the Byzantine period well known *paytanim* (liturgical poets), such as Yose ben Yose, Yannai, and Eleazar ha-Kallir, were active in Erez Israel. Entire sections of post-Talmudic literature on the *Halakhah* were discovered in the Cairo *Genizah*. All this, in addition to the construction of synagogues, presents a picture of a vital community.

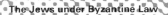

KEY

The Jews under Byzantine Law

Jews were forbidden:

to live in Jerusalem, or visit there (except for the 9th of Av);

to convert gentiles;

to own slaves, particularly Christians;

to receive appointments in government service;

to marry Christians;

to build new synagogues;

to renovate old synagogues unless they were on the verge of collapse.

Jews were permitted:

to observe their religion and assemble in synagogues;

to adjudicate their affairs in Jewish courts;

heads of synagogues were exempt from paying taxes;

the *Nasi* of the *Sanhedrin* was recognized as the leader of the Jews.

5

5 The beginnings of the community of Shivtah date to the Nabatean period. The city reached the zenith of its development in the 6th — early 7th century, when the Byzantines maintained a flourishing agricultural life there. A Byzantine cemetery and three churches have been discovered at the site. This baptistery, hewn out of a single rock and shaped like a cross, was found in the southern church.

7 St. Catherine's Monastery, in the Sinai, bears the name of Catherine of Alexandria, who died a martyr's death in the early 4th century as a result of her protests against persecution of the Christians under Emperor Maximanius. The monastery has served as a focus of pilgrimage since its founding in 527.

7

6 The synagogues and churches in Erez Israel during the time of the Christian emperors. Church construction throughout Erez Israel was begun during the reign of Emperor Constantine, primarily in regions with sparse Jewish populations. In the Galilee, the center of the Jewish community in that era, many synagogues were built, their architecture influenced by the basilical style of the churches. In front of the churches and synagogues was generally a large rectangular court. The main hall would be divided into a central nave flanked by two side aisles. In the churches the apse served the senior clergy, and in the synagogues it served as a place for the ark. Both synagogues and churches had colored mosaic floors.

6

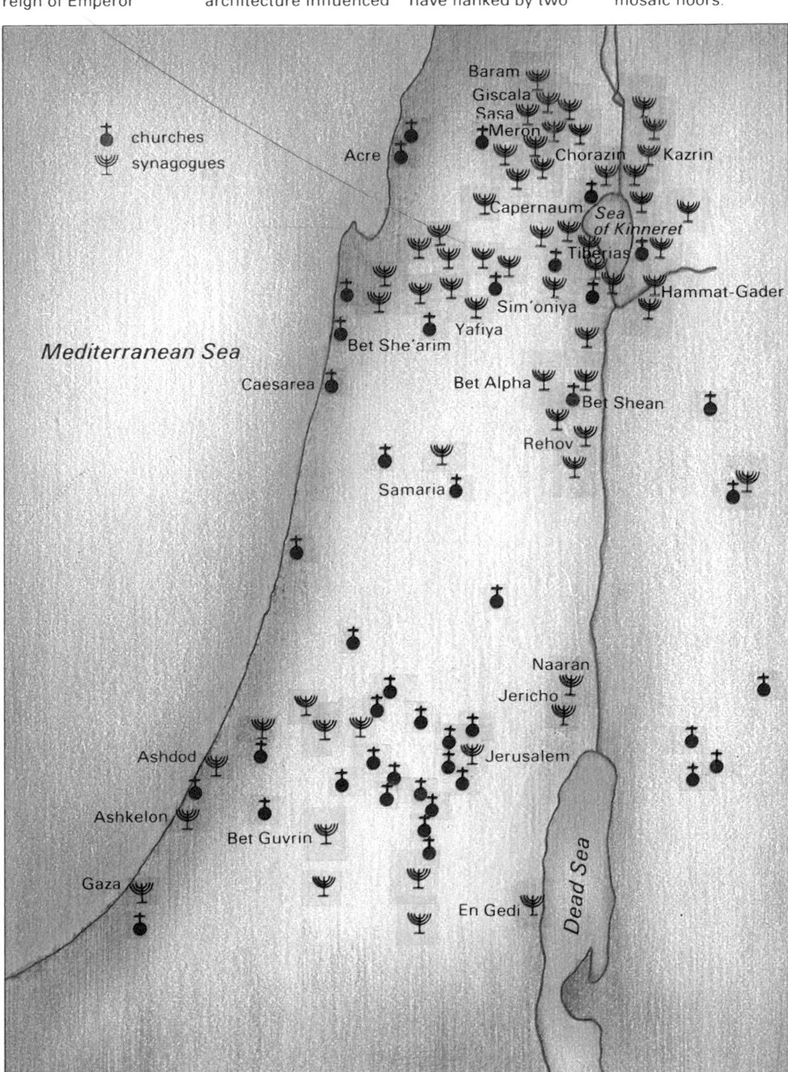

Ereẓ Israel under Arab Rule

In 640 Ereẓ Israel, its conquest by the Arabs complete, became part of the Umayyad Caliphate. The Muslim conquerors granted their Jewish and Christian subjects, adherents of monotheistic religions, special status as *dhimmi* (protected peoples). This gave them physical security and economic and religious freedom, but it also restricted and degraded them. The Jews, like the rest of the inhabitants of the land, had to pay a special head tax; they were banned from public administration; and they were forbidden to build new synagogues or to employ Muslim laborers or hold Muslim slaves.

The Umayyad Era

The Muslim conquest brought a large proportion of the Jewish people under one rule. Significant changes now took place in the structure of the Jewish community in Ereẓ Israel. The importance of Jerusalem as a religious and economic center was diminished, but Caliph Omar ibn al-Khattab permitted seventy Jewish families to settle in Jerusalem, for the first time since the defeat of Bar Kokhba in 135. Jewish settlement in Hebron was also renewed. A new urban community attracting many Jews was Ramlah [4].

With the transfer of the Academy (*Yeshiva*) of Ereẓ Israel to Tiberias, that city became a religious and cultural center. It was known for its *paytanim* (liturgical poets), Masoretes, and developers of the Hebrew vocalization system [3]. The Academy was considered the legal and halakhic heir of the *Sanhedrin*, and the *gaon*, or head of the Academy, calculated the months and holidays and intercalated the year for the entire world Jewish community.

Next to the *gaon* stood his deputy, the *Av Bet Din* (presiding judge), a group of 70 sages (the Great *Sanhedrin*) and one of 23 sages (the Small *Sanhedrin*). The *geonim* of Ereẓ Israel also decided economic matters and interceded between the Jewish community and the authorities. Due to many controversies over the office of *gaon*, its prestige in Ereẓ Israel declined in the mid-9th century. Its primacy of place was taken by the *gaon* in Babylonia, who became the source of halakhic authority for the Jews of the Muslim world.

The Abbasid and Fatimid Eras

The Umayyad Caliphate, which was centered in Damascus, viewed Ereẓ Israel as a strategically and economically important province. Therefore the country, and especially the Galilee, enjoyed reasonable security, and its merchants prospered [6]. The Abbasids, on the other hand, viewed themselves as the heirs of the Sassanid Persian Empire, and, with their rise to power in 750, made Baghdad their capital. From then on the focus turned to developing the eastern provinces of the empire, and Syria and Ereẓ Israel were neglected.

The Abbasid rulers granted the Babylonian Exilarch far-reaching authority over all the Jews in the Arab empire, from Persia in the East to Spain

CONNECTIONS
62 Erez Israel under Byzantine Rule
66 Babylonia as a National Center
74 Jews and Crusaders in Erez Israel

1 The Cairo Genizah was discovered in the attic of the "Synagogue of Ezra" in Fostat (ancient Cairo). The Jews were accustomed to deposit in this attic any written material which was no longer in use, including documentary material on the history of the Jews in Erez Israel during the period of the Arab conquest. The illustration shows part of a letter from the *Genizah*, dealing with the beginnings of Jewish settlement in Jerusalem after the Arab conquest.

2 Tower of the White Mosque, Ramlah. Construction of the mosque began during the Ummayad Caliphates, and continued until the early 15th century. The tower was completed in 1318 by the Mameluke Sultan Suleyman Bin Qalaun.

3 The Masorah is a body of notes on Scripture, determining exactly how the Bible is to be transmitted. Through general principles of reading, writing, vocalization, and cantillation, the Masoretes tried to establish a uniform and correct version of Scripture. Most of the undertaking was accomplished from the 8th to the 10th centuries, with the firm establishment of the text of Scripture by the Masoretes of Tiberias. The Tiberians dealt also with vocalization and cantillation of the text. Their notes fall into the categories of *Masorah Ketannah* and *Masorah Gedolah*. The former is written in great abbreviation, in the side margins of the page. The latter is much more detailed, and is found on the top and bottom of the page. This page is from a 10th century manuscript of the *Torah*, according to the Tiberias tradition.

4 Ramlah was the only city founded by the Arabs in Erez Israel. It was built on the sand (*raml* is Arabic for sand), along the coastal *Via Maris*, and from the outset was planned as a trading, industrial, and administrative city. Caliph Suleiman and his successors put great energy into developing the city, building a magnificent palace and mosque, water reservoirs, and apparently even a surrounding wall. Building lots were offered to potential settlers in the city. The Jewish community of Ramlah was extremely prosperous, and sometimes even overshadowed Jerusalem. In 1067 Ramlah, and its Jewish community, were destroyed by an earthquake. The illustration shows the Pool of St. Helena, built by Harun al-Rashid in Ramlah toward the end of the 8th century.

in the West. Alongside the Exilarch were the heads of the great Babylonian academies, who bore the title of *gaon.*

The Abbasid dynasty's decline began in the 9th century, as bands of Karamanians, members of the Shi'ite sect, overran Syria and Erez Israel [7]. Under the rule of the Fatimids (969-1099), a Shi'ite dynasty which came to power in Egypt and made Cairo its capital, the Jews of Erez Israel generally received preferential treatment, and filled government offices.

During this period the Academy of Erez Israel was returned to Jerusalem. Sources from the Cairo *Genizah* indicate that the population of Jerusalem now increased considerably [1]. Jewish Rabbanites, Karaites, and pilgrims extended the limits of Jewish residence to the northeast; and the Jews, together with the Christians, constituted a majority of the city's population. We know of strife between these two groups, going so far as Jews and Muslims burning Christian churches. We also know of power struggles and controversies between Jewish Rabbanites and Karaites. The economic condition of the Jews of Jerusalem continued to be difficult. Their main sources of livelihood were contributions from the Diaspora, the copying of books, and some trade, centering in Ramlah. Large Jewish populations still remained in Tiberias, Hebron, and several coastal cities. Because of the heavy land taxes imposed on non-Muslims, rural Jewish settlements were rather limited.

Due to the weakness of the Fatimid government in the 10th-11th centuries, various tribes, including Bedouins and Seljuks, took control of parts of Erez Israel and attacked the inhabitants. The Jewish population of Jerusalem declined, pilgrims were deterred from coming, and with that the influx of contributions also ceased. The Academy of Erez Israel was forced to move to Tyre, where it remained until the time of the Crusades. By then only a few thousand Jews remained in Erez Israel.

KEY

An inscription on a mosaic floor in the Susiyya synagogue, south of Hebron. The inscription details the circumstances in which Rav Assi donated the mosaic. The floor is decorated with geometric shapes, pictures of a hunt, Daniel in the lion's den, birds, and several inscriptions. The type of language in the inscription, rich in honorific epithets, is characteristic of the period of the *geonim.* The synagogue was built in the 6th century, the time of the *geonim,* and survived into the 10th century.

5 A carpet page, with the Tabernacle and its implements, ornamented in micrography, from the First Leningrad Bible. This manuscript was written in 929 by Solomon ben Buya'a, apparently in Tiberias. Vocalization and masoretic notes were added later by his brother. The earliest manuscript of the Bible known today, which was prepared according to the *Masorah,* is the Leningrad manuscript which was written in 846-847. In the 10th century several manuscripts were made according to the *Masorah* of Tiberias, the best known of which is the *Keter Aram Zova.* Many scholars view it as an important specimen of the Tiberian *Masorah,* since there is evidence that it was vocalized by Aaron ben Asher.

6 The Ummayad dynasty established an extensive Muslim empire, in which Erez Israel, close to the Ummayad capital of Damascus, received preferential treatment. It was ruled by members of the Caliph's family, who undertook construction and development projects such as rehabilitating the coastal cities and building up the Temple Mount. The best known of the palaces erected then is Khirbat al-Mafjar, on the north side of Jericho, also known as Hisham's Palace. This is a complex of magnificent buildings, apparently built during the time of Caliph Walid II (743-744). Illustration [A] shows stone carved pillars; [B] — a mosaic from a *divan* (council-chamber) wall.

6 A

6 B

5

7 With the disintegration of Abbasid rule, the increased anarchy in the land, and the rise in brigandage by bands of Shi'ites, many Jews left Erez Israel for Egypt. At that time Egypt had a large and prosperous Jewish community, which received many Jews from Babylonia and Syria, as well. The Jews from Erez Israel established communities of their own in Egypt, and recognized the authority of the *geonim* of Erez Israel. The Shi'ite dynasty ruling from Cairo treated the Jews generally well, at times preferring their services to those of Sunni Muslims. The illustration shows an illuminated manuscript of the scriptural portion, *Shelah lekhah.* The masoretic notes can be seen in the margins. (Egypt, 1106-7).

7

Babylonia as a National Center

During the period of the *geonim* (the 7th-11th centuries), the largest single concentration of Jews in the world — about 70% of the entire Jewish population of the time — lived in Babylonia. The leadership of the Jews there comprised four main bodies: the Exilarch; the heads of the talmudic academies (the *geonim*); the rich Jews of the community — the court Jews; and the local communal leaders. The governmental authority enjoyed by the Exilarchs and *geonim* and the great power and influence which they wielded endured for centuries, throughout the Islamic world, and even beyond it.

The Office of Exilarch

According to several traditions the institution of the Exilarch began with the descendants of Jehoiachin, King of Judah, who was exiled to Babylonia. During the period of the *Mishnah* and the *Talmud* the Exilarchs in Babylonia acquired far-reaching authority. They retained and even broadened their power after the Muslim conquest in 637.

The Exilarchs filled many and diverse roles in the political, social, judicial, and religious spheres. They represented the Jewish minority before the Muslim Caliph, participated in public disputations on religion, appointed the heads of the academies and the judges, saw to the punishment of lawbreakers, served as arbitrators in disputes which erupted between Jewish communities, and were in charge of public charity funds. In addition, they assessed taxes in order to supply their own personal needs and the needs of the community. Occasionally the scope of their authority reached even beyond the borders of Babylonia. Thus, for example, the early traveler Benjamin of Tudela writes that on his journeys (in the '60s of the 12th century) he visited distant communities, from Yemen to India, which were subject to the authority of the Exilarch.

The Jews, like other minority groups under Muslim rule, enjoyed great autonomy. However, as the Muslim population on the eastern borders of the caliphate increased, with many Persians converting to Islam, the rights of the leaders of the minorities were gradually curtailed, and in 825 Caliph al-Ma'mun ordered the Jews to abolish the office of Exilarch altogether. Nevertheless the Jews continued to view the Exilarch as their leader, and left many of his former powers in his hands [Key].

Several factors contributed to the gradual decline and ultimate disappearance of the Exilarchate: the disintegration and decline of the Muslim caliphate; the rise of religious fanaticism in Islam; the rise of new centers of power in Jewish society; the disputes between the Exilarchs and the *geonim*, and the internal controversies within the family of the Exilarchs. Nevertheless, the Exilarchate continued to serve as a symbol of Jewish resurgence in exile, for centuries after its decline.

The Talmudic Academies

The two large academies of Babylonia

CONNECTIONS

60 The Jewish Community in Babylonia
64 Erez Israel under Arab Rule
68 The Encounter with Islam in Spain

1

1 The response of Rav Hai (998-1038), *Gaon* of Pumbedita, to a letter sent him from Fostat (Cairo), Egypt, the home of two Jewish communities, one originating from Babylonia, the other from Erez Israel. The rivalry between the *geonim* of Babylonia and those of Erez Israel is especially evident in this letter. In his response Rav Hai called his Babylonian academy "The *Bet Din Gadol* (High Court) of all Israel."

2

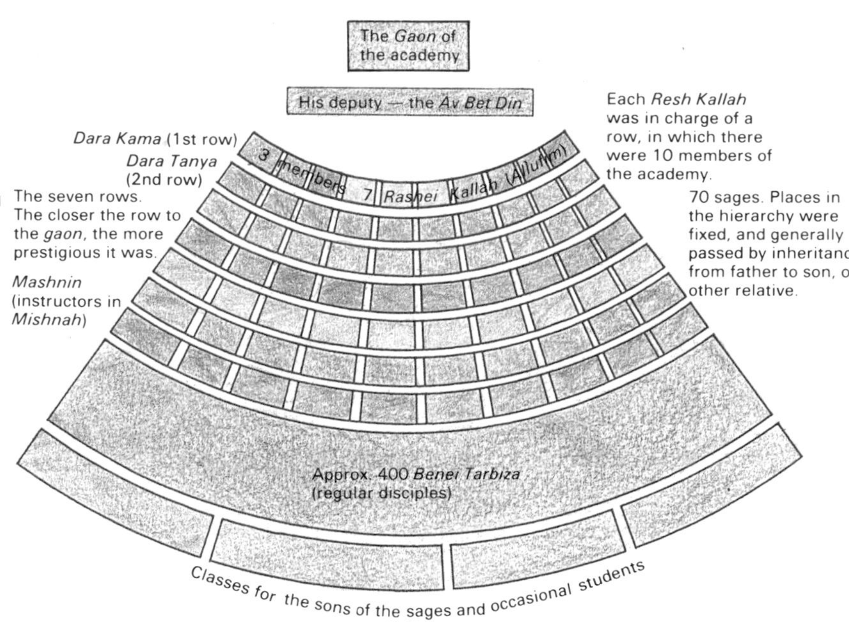

2 The academies, whose structure is described here, were recognized by the Muslim authorities as the institutions of leadership of the Jews as early as the mid-7th century. They were crucial in shaping the spiritual life of all Jews in the Middle Ages, and their rulings on Jewish law were recognized by all generations.

3

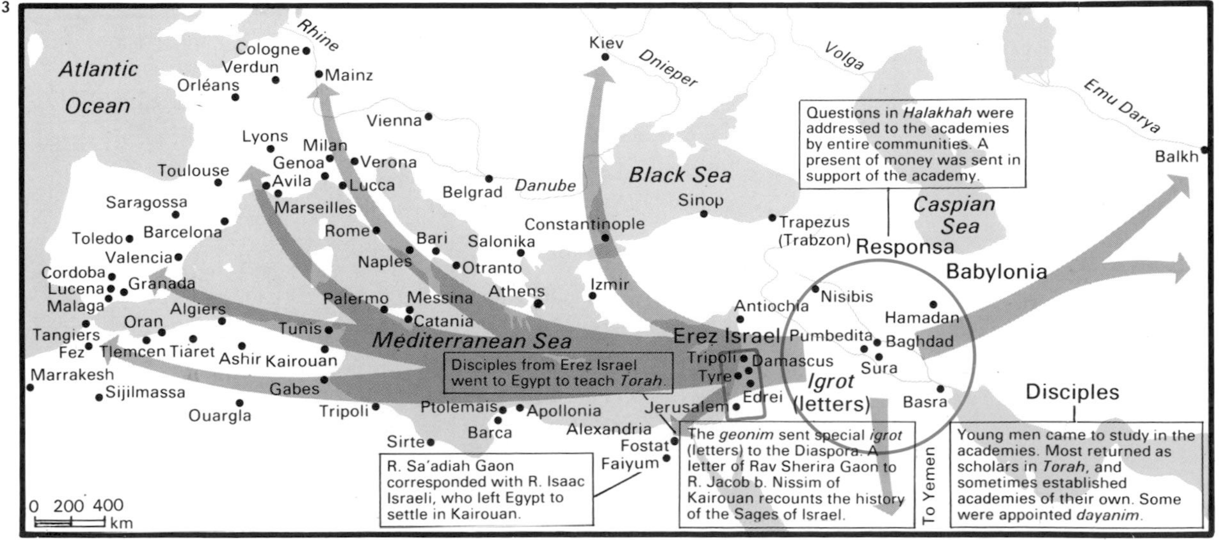

3 The Babylonian talmudic academies during the time of the geonim carried on the tradition that produced the *Babylonian Talmud*. The sages of Erez Israel fought against this development, and asserted their right to ascendancy. However, the Babylonian academies gradually prevailed. The Babylonian academies maintained especially close ties with the Jewish communities of North Africa and Spain, and it is there that most of the *responsa* of the *geonim* were sent. The *responsa* literature deals primarily with questions of *Halakhah*, commentary, and religious outlook.

— Sura and Pumbedita — drew on the ancient tradition of the famous Babylonian academies of the era of the *amoraim* [2]. The main role of the *geonim* was to serve as the spiritual pastors of the Babylonian Jewish community and, indeed, of almost all the world Jewish community [3]. Thus, for example, in the 11th century several great scholars from the Jewish communities in Italy came to study *Torah* under Rav Hai Gaon. The works on *Halakhah* and the prayer books which emanated from Babylonia governed most Jewish communities, especially within the Islamic world. Their commentaries made the *Talmud* into a codex of Jewish law.

Throughout this entire period the center in Ereẓ Israel and the one in Babylonia competed for influence over the Jewish communities of the Diaspora and for financial support from them. Ereẓ Israel held strong sway over Egypt [1], Italy, and Germany, while Babylonia was influential in the lands of the Muslim caliphate (aside from Egypt). Gradually the academies of Babylonia attained the upper hand, and by the 10th century they enjoyed clear priority in all the world Jewish communities.

However, the 10th century also marks the beginning of the gradual decline of these academies. The rulers of the new Muslim kingdoms did not view the spiritual and political ties of their Jewish subjects to their Abbasid rivals in Iraq with favor. Gradually the academies turned into closed professional institutions, where ceremonial trappings, family lineage, and institutional hierarchy were all closely safeguarded. Young children inherited their parent's place in the academy, even if they did not merit it. All this enhanced the fame and status of the academy, and increased support for it; yet it also impeded academic growth and development. During the 11th century new, and more vital centers of *Torah* study emerged in other parts of the world Jewish community, and ties with the Babylonian academies grew weaker.

KEY

The Exilarchs viewed themselves as descendants of the House of David, giving them the legal right to rule over the Jewish people in the custom of kings. Even their inaugurations followed biblical descriptions. The Jews of Babylonia willingly accepted their suzerainty, because their elevated status symbolized the resurgence of the Jewish people in exile and their hope of redemption. It also enhanced their status in the eyes of their Muslim neighbors. The illustration shows a 20th century model of the Exilarch in his court, according to ancient sources.

4 The Karaite sect was founded in Babylonia, toward the end of the 8th century, by Anan ben David. The Karaites, also known as the *Benei Mikra* (Sons of Scripture), denied the authority of the Oral Law and the *Talmud*, relying solely on Scripture. Initially they were based in Babylonia and Persia, but they spread rapidly to other Jewish centers. In the 10th-11th centuries, the Golden Age of Karaism, this sect encompassed almost all the lands of the Muslim caliphate, and Christian Byzantium. Karaites were appointed to important posts in the Muslim administration. The spread of the Karaites heightened the polemics between them and the Rabbanites. A Karaite community emerged in Erez Israel, as well, centered around Jerusalem and Ramlah. Of special fame were the Karaite *Avelei Zion* (Mourners of Ẓion), who lived a life of self-mortification, mourning over the destruction of the Temple. In the 12th-16th centuries the Karaite centers in the Islamic world, especially in Spain, grew weaker. However, in Byzantium, where power was gradually shifting from the Christians to the Ottoman Turks, the Karaite center grew even stronger, making Constantinople the most important Karaite center of that period. In the 14th century the first Karaite centers in the Balkans were established. During this period the bitter controversy between Rabbanites and Karaites eased, and the Karaites made some concessions in their rulings and no longer summarily rejected all the rabbinic rules.

4

Baltic Sea · Birzai · Nowe Miasto · Troki (Trakai) · Vilna · Lutsk · Derazhno · Kukizow · (Krasny Ostrow) · Halicz (Galich) · Dniester · Dnieper · Volga · Ural · Odessa · Eupatoria (Yevpatoriya) · Solkhat (Stary Krym) · Sevastopol · Feodosiya · Bakhchisarai · Danube · Black Sea · Caspian Sea · Adrianople · Constantinople · Nicomedia (Ismit) · Tigris · Euphrates · Nehavend · Isfahan · Qumis · Cyprus · Baghdad · Damascus · Ramlah · Ashdod · Ofakim · Jerusalem · Mazli'ah · Basra · Persian Gulf · Cairo (Fostat) · Nile · Red Sea

Main centers of settlement
7th - 11th century
12th - 16th century
17th - 18th century
19th - 20th century

Main Karaite Centers
7th - 11th century
12th - 16th century
17th - 18th century
19th - 20th century

5

שדי
ספר המבחר
וטוב המסחר
СЕФЕРЪ ГАМИВХАРЪ
גוזלוו
ЭВПАТОРІЯ.

5 The written Torah was the ostensible foundation of the religious law and practice of the Karaites. Initially they set their calendar by the moon, and were extremely strict in their Sabbath laws. Beginning in the 11th century, they relaxed their laws somewhat. This is the title page of *Sefer ha-Mivhar ve-Tov ha-Miskhar*, a Karaite commentary on the Pentateuch, by Aaron ben Joseph ha-Rofe (completed 1293, published 1839).

6 Controversies between the Exilarchs and the geonim over the right of leadership sometimes compelled the Muslim authorities to intervene. This 20th century model portrays the Caliph mediating the dispute between Rav Sa'adiah Gaon and the Exilarch, David ben Zakkai.

6

The Encounter with Islam in Spain

CONNECTIONS

76 The Jews in Christian Spain

Before the advent of the Muslims in Spain in 711 the Jews were persecuted by the country's rulers, the Visigoths, and either fled or had to convert. Needing capable, friendly people to help them administer their newly acquired territories, the Muslim conquerers allotted the Jews special quarters in many cities and even trusted them to guard fortresses. The new rulers taxed both Jews and Christians heavily, but their religious tolerance, together with political circumstances, permitted the Spanish Jewish communities to flourish. Arab geographers of the 10th and 12th centuries have referred to Lucena, Granada [2] and Tarragona as "Jewish cities."

The "Golden Age"

Following the establishment of an independent Umayyad kingdom with Córdoba [6] as its capital, Arab and Jewish cultures intermingled to create a cultural flowering that reached its peak in the 11th and 12th centuries — known in Jewish history as the "Golden Age" [1].

This culture was characterized above all by its diversity, exceptional receptivity, and admixture of sacred and profane. Jewry of Muslim Spain had ties with the Jewish center in Babylonia through which it absorbed the Talmudic tradition and the culture of the *geonim*. This did not prevent it, however, from creating an independent Jewish cultural center that had a marked influence on other Jewish communities. Under the patronage of Jewish courtiers, Jewish poets, grammarians, linguists, philosophers, scientists and translators produced works in Hebrew and Arabic that in the aggregate form a unique chapter of cultural achievement.

Hisdai ibn Shaprut, responsible for the foreign trade of the Córdoba Caliphate and influential in molding its foreign policy during the reign of 'Abd al-Rahman III (912-961), was one of the Jews who helped create a political climate conducive to this flowering. Hisdai's efforts included active support for Jewish intellectuals like Dunash ben Labrat and Menahem ibn Saruq, both important Hebrew grammarians. His endeavors were carried on by R. Hanokh ben Moses, Joseph ibn Abitur, the geographer Ibrahim ben Jacob and the linguist Hayyuj.

Early in the 11th century Andalusia was split into small states ruled by Arabs, Berbers and Swabians. Their political-military rivalry brought about accelerated cultural development, and Jewish culture flourished in their capitals. Jewish courtiers who rose to importance at the time considered themselves the ambassadors of their communities and, like their Muslim colleagues, became the benefactors of poets and philosophers whose works are still a major source of information about their patrons.

The most renowned Jewish courtier was Samuel ibn Nagrela (993-1056), called *Ha-Nagid*. For 30 years Samuel ha-Nagid, philologist and poet, well-versed in the *Torah* and *Halakhah*,

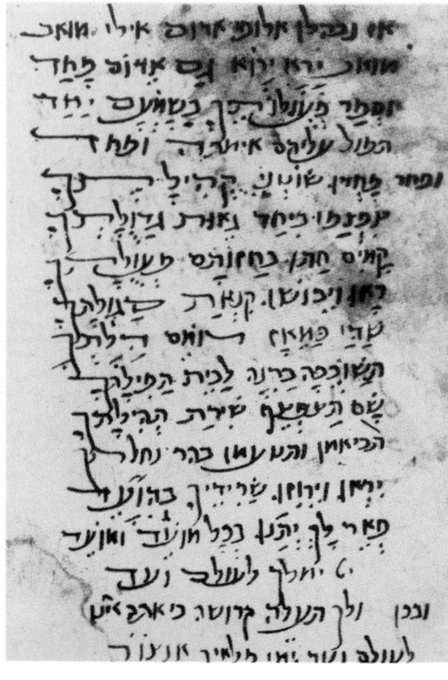

1 Hebrew literature unique in content and form was written in Spain under Muslim rule. Like their Muslim counterparts, the Jewish poets wrote on widely varied themes: love and passion for both sexes, praising patrons, wine songs and odes for pleasure, poems of Zion, and liturgical poems. The writing is rich in images, biblical references and allusions. This is the original manuscript of the liturgical poem "Then the rulers of Edom took fright" by Joseph ibn Abitur (10th-11th century). Ibn Abitur's work is characteristic of the Jewish cultural flowering of the Golden Age of Umayyad Spain.

2 At the beginning of the 11th century, with the decline of the Muslim Caliphate and the growth of many small principalities, Granada became a large, independent city, which the Berber Zirid dynasty made its capital. Samuel ha-Nagid and then his son, Joseph, managed affairs of state, while the Berber rulers engaged in frequent battles with the rival city, Seville. Due to the elevated rank of those powerful men, many Jews settled in Granada and loyally supported the monarchy. This incensed the masses both within and outside of the city and in 1090 its Jewish community was destroyed.

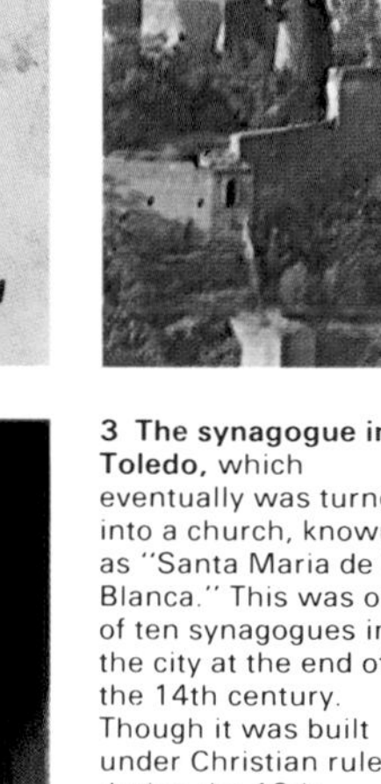

3 The synagogue in Toledo, which eventually was turned into a church, known as "Santa Maria de la Blanca." This was one of ten synagogues in the city at the end of the 14th century. Though it was built under Christian rule during the 13th century, its architectural style is typically Muslim.

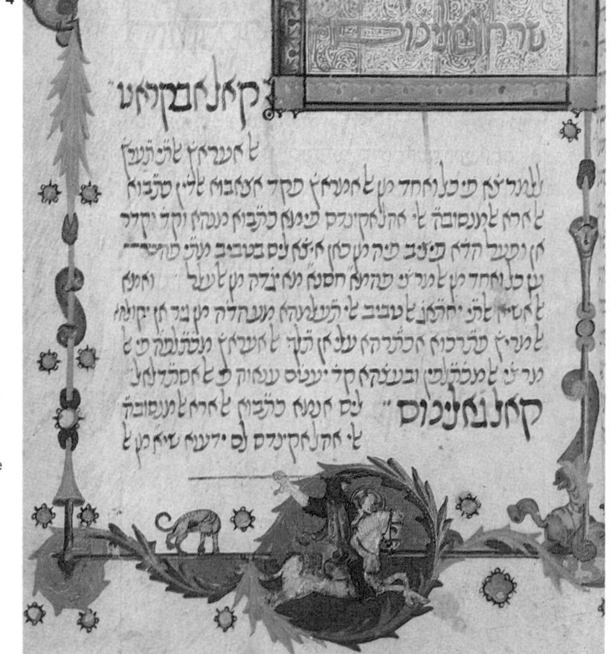

4 Jewish physicians served with great distinction at the courts of many Spanish kings and enjoyed special status. The Christian population too respected their knowledge. The picture shows the title page of Hippocrates' medical book with a commentary by Galinus, using the Arabic language in Hebrew script. The book was copied in Spain in about the 14th century.

served King Habbus and his son Badis, conducted Granada's internal and foreign policy and fought in its wars. Identifying completely with Granada's royal family, he nevertheless dreamed of Zion and viewed the events of his time in the light of their affect on his own people.

Jewish courtiers served other rulers as well [4], behaving much like the Muslim courtiers. But the high status enjoyed by the Jews aroused the enmity of their Muslim counterparts and sometimes ended in tragedy. A case in point was Joseph, son of Samuel ha-Nagid who inherited his father's post and in 1066 was murdered in his palace. On the whole, though, the Jews of Spain lived peacefully and struck roots in the society around them. This gave them a character distinct from that of other Jewish communities, particularly those in Christian countries: occupationally, they engaged in agriculture, crafts and industry; culturally, the difference was conspicuous primarily among the Andalusian Jews, who pursued scientific and other secular branches of knowledge.

Changes after the Reconquest

The Christians' reconquest of Spain began in the 11th century and lasted 400 years [5]. At the same time religious fanaticism grew among the Muslims and increasingly threatened the Jews, particularly during the invasions of the Almoravids and Almohads. When the latter invaded, for example, Maimonides (R. Moses ben Maimon, 1138-1204) had to flee Spain. Some Jews chose to migrate from Muslim Spain to the Christian north, where they were received willingly. With the extensive experience the Jewish courtiers had acquired in the Muslim principalities and with their cultural and social involvement, they were equipped to play important roles in the courts of the Christian rulers. Thus, at a time when the Andalusian Jewish community came into decline, the Jews in the Christian north began to rise.

KEY

The Córdoba synagogue was built in 1314-1315 by Isaac Mahab ben Ephraim. Though constructed some 80 years after the Christian conquest of the city, Islamic influence is paramount in its architecture — hailing back to the Golden Age of Spanish Jewry, when Jewish achievements reached unparalleled heights. This influence pervaded other walks of life as well, such as the practices and organization of the Jewish community, and the language and culture of its members. Numerous inscriptions, usually in red on a blue backdrop, decorate the synagogue. This Hebrew inscription, a metered and rhymed poem, records the identity of the builder and links the construction of the synagogue to the ultimate rebuilding of Jerusalem.

5 Jewish communities in Spain and the Reconquest (13th and 14th centuries). In the course of these centuries the kingdoms of Castile and Aragon crystallized and attitudes toward the Jews evolved. King James I renewed the Reconquest and called upon the Jews of Marseilles and North Africa to settle in his kingdom. They were given high administrative positions and acquired great influence. But the end of the Reconquest at the close of the 13th century also impaired the Jews' status. The first blood libel in Spain took place at the time of James I. The Inquisition was established in Aragon, and the Jews were forced to wear a mark of disgrace. The king vacillated between drawing the Jews close to the seat of power and clamping restrictions upon them. By the 14th century they were the victims of edicts and pogroms.

6

5

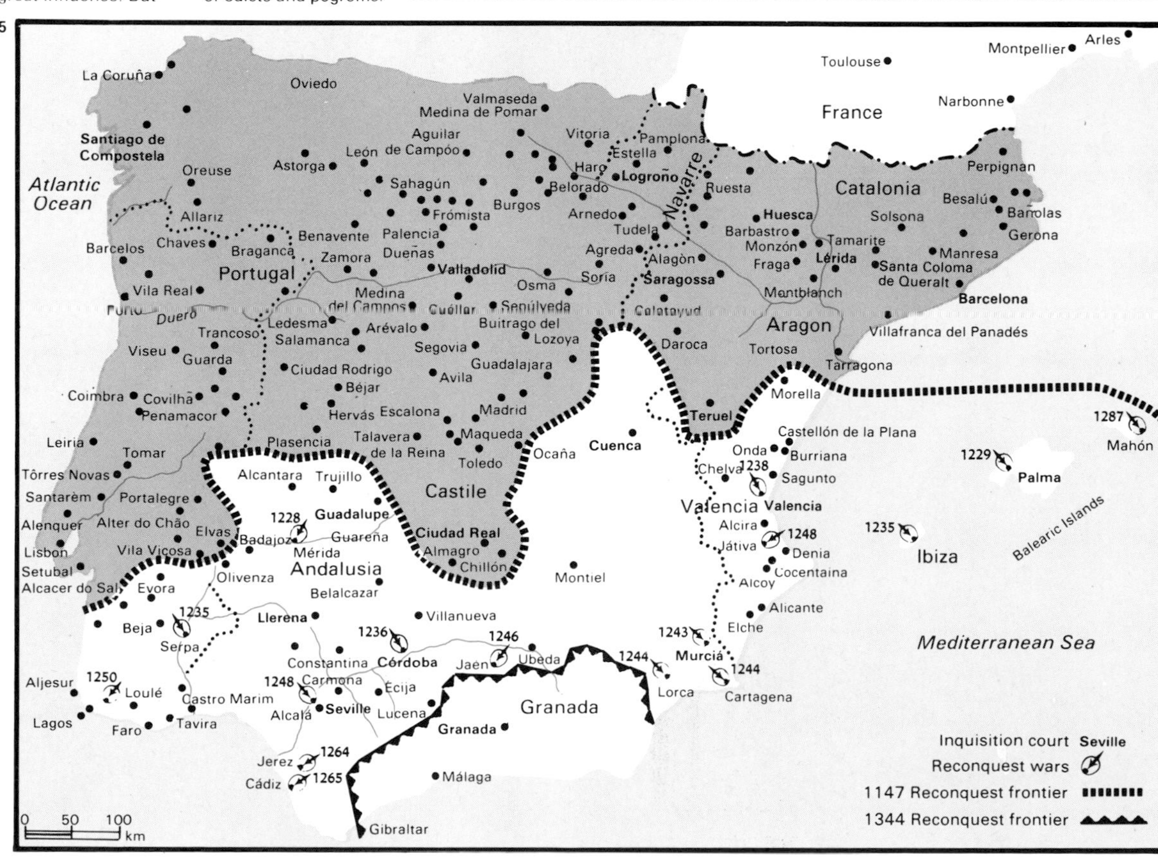

6 Córdoba attained its highest development as capital of the Ummayad Caliphate (755-1031), when it was a political, commercial-industrial and cultural center. Following the Berber conquest in 1013 the city was destroyed and many of its residents fled. It continued to decline under the rule of the Christians, who conquered it in 1236. During the Ummayad reign the Jews participated in the intense cultural life of the city, primarily at the encouragement of Hisdai ibn Shaprut, who served at the court of 'Abd al-Rahman III, where he managed the Caliphate's foreign trade and influenced foreign policy. Illustrious Jews such as Samuel ha-Nagid and Moses ben Maimon were born in Córdoba. The Jewish neighborhood in the southwest section of the city still exists, but a Jewish quarter built in the north as the community expanded was destroyed by the Berbers. One synagogue has remained.

Medieval European Attitudes to the Jews

In the seventh century, Christianity became the dominant religion of Western Europe. The Christian attitude to the Jews during the Middle Ages can be viewed from three aspects: the Catholic Church, the monarchy, and the people.

The Catholic Church and the Jews
For the Catholic Church in the Middle Ages, the Jews were proof of the truth of Christianity. They had been the Chosen People before Jesus, but because of their refusal to accept him and his disciples, their special status had been transferred to the Christians, the true spiritual heirs of the Israelites. The Jews' depressed state in Christian countries was a punishment for their intransigence and malice, and proof of the supremacy of Christianity [1].

The Catholic Church considered the conversion of the Jews as crucial confirmation of its superiority. To persuade them to convert, the Church tempted the Jews with material wealth and forced them to listen to the sermons of priests and monks and to participate in public debates in which they were required to defend their faith [6, 7]. The Church was, however, opposed to compulsory conversion for, if the Jews were completely eliminated, they could not fulfil their function as perceived by Christian theology. Nevertheless, it was also opposed to the return to Judaism of converts baptized by force, since baptism was a sacrament and its nullification was viewed as sacrilege.

From the end of the twelfth century, nearly every new pope issued a bull in defense of the Jews in which Christians were warned against harming them. In the thirteenth century, the popes issued strong denouncements of the blood libels prevalent at that time [2].

While the Church sought to absorb the Jews, it also feared their influence. Considerable evidence points to the conversion to Judaism of Christians from all walks of life, including priests. To forestall this, the Church attempted to reduce all contact between Christians and Jews. It opposed the appointment of Jews to public or government posts, and issued injunctions against personal or social contacts and against the employment of Christian servants by Jews. In the early thirteenth century, Jews were ordered to differentiate themselves from Christians by the use of external signs [4], and towards the end of the Middle Ages they were frequently required to live in separate or isolated neighborhoods.

The Monarchy and the Jews
As subjects of the realm, the Jews were entitled to its protection, and an attack on them was illegal. They were also afforded official sanctuary because of their central function in the economy of the state, in commerce and in the various trades. In the twelfth and thirteenth centuries, when more and more Jews in Western Europe turned to the business of lending money on interest — from which Christians were barred by the Church — high taxes were imposed on

CONNECTIONS

72 Ashkenaz in the 10th-13th Centuries
76 The Jews in Christian Spain
78 The Expulsion of the Jews from Western Europe

1 A

1 B

1 C

1 Ecclesia and Synagoga, female figures representing Christianity and Judaism, were common subjects in Medieval Christian art. They symbolize the supremacy of *Ecclesia* (the Church) over *Synagoga*; the triumph of Christianity and humbling of Judaism. [A] These statues stand in a thirteenth century church in Trier, Germany. Unlike the proud figure of Ecclesia, *Synagoga's* eyes are covered and the Tablets of the Law she holds are upside down, symbolizing the blindness which prevents her from understanding the true meaning of the Old Testament. [B] The disciples bury the sinful *Synagoga*, still holding the inverted Tablets of the Law. Behind them, proud and erect, the crowned *Ecclesia* watches the scene (from a fifteenth century French manuscript). [C] The serpent covering *Synagoga's* eyes replaces the blindfold in a twelfth century French manuscript).

2

2 Jews are accused of desecrating the sacrificial bread in order to repeat the torture of the body of Christ. Perpetrators are executed or exiled and the synagogue becomes a church (Germany, fifteenth century).

3

3 In the Christian court of law, Jews are required to take the "Jewish vow" which includes violent curses, intended to prevent them from giving false evidence (Germany, early sixteenth century).

them, making the Jews a major source of income for the royal treasury. As a result, in many places Jews were afforded special protection by monarchs and local rulers and were at times even considered the property of kings or servants of their treasury, so that an assault on them would be tantamount to an attack on royal property. This special status was embodied in deeds of privilege awarded the Jews by the rulers to ensure their life and property and the undisturbed conduct of their business. These deeds also accorded freedom of worship and autonomy in internal affairs. However, pressure from the Church, power struggles among the rulers, greed, and in particular the desire of the monarchs to unite their subjects, often engendered harsh policies in regard to the Jews, at times even in opposition to the Church.

The People and the Jews

It is difficult to speak of a single and consistent attitude to the Jews on the part of farmers, townspeople and nobles in Western Europe throughout the Middle Ages. Clearly the Christian faith that they all practiced had considerable bearing on their conduct. In the 7th to 11th centuries, relations between Jews and non-Jews were quite close, as evidenced by the repeated warnings of the Church against such contacts. These relations worsened at a later stage, particularly due to economic factors: the rise of a local merchant class which saw the Jewish tradesmen as competitors, the interest extracted for loans, and the desire to cancel debts to Jewish moneylenders [5]. In addition, Church propaganda which accused the Jews of responsibility for the death of Christ began to have a cumulative effect. Both the Church and the monarchy usually sought to restrain the dissemination of libels against the Jews, but when religious fervor grew and the power of the central government began to wane violence spread, leaving in its wake thousands of victims.

KEY

A deer is chased by a hunter and a pack of dogs in a painting from the *Darmstat Haggadah* from Germany (fifteenth century). The deer trapped within the circle apparently symbolizes Jewry persecuted by the Christians. One of the explanations for the Jews' status was the Christian hatred of them for having been chosen by God. The Diaspora was conceived of by the Jews as a temporary condition only, and as a penance and preparation for redemption. This view prepared the ground for mystical and messianic movements, which arose from time to time throughout the Middle Ages and until the early days of the modern era.

4 Pope Innocent III (1198-1216) was opposed to the persecution of the Jews, yet he persuaded the Fourth Lateran Council to require the Jews to wear a mark of disgrace.

4

6

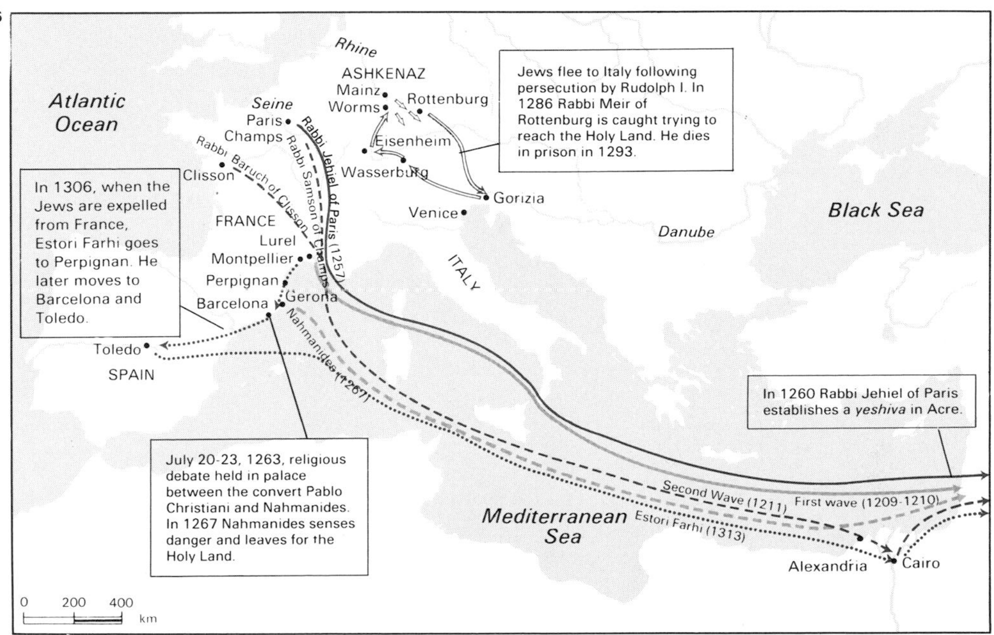

Rhine
ASHKENAZ
Mainz
Worms
Rottenburg
Jews flee to Italy following persecution by Rudolph I. In 1286 Rabbi Meir of Rottenburg is caught trying to reach the Holy Land. He dies in prison in 1293.
Atlantic Ocean
Seine
Paris
Champs
Eisenheim
Wasserburg
Rabbi Baruch of Clisson
Rabbi Samson of Champs
Rabbi Jehiel of Paris (1257)
Clisson
In 1306, when the Jews are expelled from France, Estori Farhi goes to Perpignan. He later moves to Barcelona and Toledo.
FRANCE
Lurel
Montpellier
Perpignan
Gerona
Barcelona
Gorizia
Venice
Danube
Black Sea
ITALY
Toledo
SPAIN
Nahmanides (1267)
In 1260 Rabbi Jehiel of Paris establishes a *yeshiva* in Acre.
July 20-23, 1263, religious debate held in palace between the convert Pablo Christiani and Nahmanides. In 1267 Nahmanides senses danger and leaves for the Holy Land.
Second Wave (1211)
First wave (1209-1210)
Estori Farhi (1313)
Mediterranean Sea
Alexandria
Cairo
0 200 400
km

6 Immigration to the Holy Land during the Middle Ages was partially motivated by the public debates imposed on the Jews. The debaters' lives became hard and dangerous. Some of them escaped to Erez Israel and settled in Acre, Tiberias and Jerusalem, where they studied the *Talmud*.

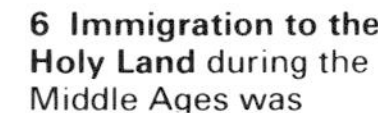

5

5 Judas Iscariot became, in Christian tradition, a synonym for treachery and greed. In this fifteenth century painting from southern Austria, he appears as a money-changer with a sack of coins on his back. His facial characteristics are those traditionally attributed to Jews by anti-Semites.

7

8

7 In religious debates Christians, often well versed converts, sought to prove the truth of their belief in Jesus as the savior with the aid of quotations from the Scriptures and the *Talmud*. In this early 13th century German manuscript the Old Testament is a sleeping figure.

8 Satan binds the eyes of a Jew and together they try to corrupt pious Christians (fourteenth century treatise from France).

Ashkenaz in the 10th-13th Centuries

The name *Ashkenaz* has several meanings in medieval Jewish sources. In its narrowest sense it refers primarily to Germany. In a wider interpretation it encompasses the Jews of northern France and Bohemia as well, since, in their way of life and religious activity, they formed part of a single cultural entity together with the Jews of Germany. In the broadest sense, *Ashkenazi* Jewry also includes the Jewish compounds in Poland and Russia, established largely by emigrants from Germany. The most outstanding hallmark of *Ashkenazi* Jewry is Yiddish, a language derived from German and used by German Jews in the Middle Ages. It remained their tongue in the various countries to which they immigrated.

The Early Jewish Community

There is evidence that Jewish settlement existed in Germany even in Roman times (fourth century CE). The first mention of a permanent Jewish settlement is from the tenth century, and at least some of these Jews appear to have reached Germany from Italy and France.

The first communities arose on the trade routes along the Rhine (at Mainz, Worms, Köln and Speyer), the Danube (at Regensburg) and the Elbe (at Magdeburg). The Jews at this time made their living mainly from commerce. In contemporary non-Jewish sources, the word "Jew" is used virtually as a synonym for "merchant" [4]. Jewish merchants traded with countries as distant as the Near and Far East, as well as with the neighboring Slavic lands, such as Poland and Russia.

The legal status of Jews was generally embodied in deeds of privilege granted by their local rulers. These assured them substantial freedom in conducting their business as well as freedom of worship and autonomy [Key].

Upheavals after the First Crusade

During the First Crusade (1096) bands of Crusaders destroyed many Jewish communities. Those worst hit were in the towns along the Rhine. The raiders demanded that the Jews convert, but detailed accounts of the events clearly demonstrate that the large majority of Jews preferred to die for their faith [1, 6]. Only a small number became Christians, and even these did so in name alone. The emperor later permitted them to resume their Judaism despite the opposition of the Church.

Events at the time of the First Crusade brought about major changes in the life of *Ashkenazi* Jewry, most significantly in their legal and social status. Ties between the Jews of Germany and the emperor became increasingly close. This was expressed, on the one hand, in the emperor's greater commitment to protect the Jews, considered "servants of the treasury," and on the other, in the levying of higher taxes from the Jews for the royal treasury. The Jews' social status was thus weakened, and they came to be thought of as property that could be sold or leased for profit; their free-

CONNECTIONS

70 Medieval European Attitudes to the Jews
78 The Expulsion of the Jews from Western Europe
94 The Community as the Framework for Jewish Life

1

1 "Jews at the Stake" is an illumination from a 14th century Belgian manuscript. At times of social or religious unrest, the view of the Jews as alien, together with the contention of the Church that God had condemned the Jews to slavery and humiliation, led to the shedding of much Jewish blood. During the Crusades of the 11th and 12th centuries, bands of Crusaders going off to free the Holy Land from the Muslim yoke sought first to rid themselves of the Jews amongst them, whom they saw as heathens. Blood libels which accused the Jews of desecrating the sacrificial bread or murdering a Christian child for the Passover ritual, incited other rampages against the Jews. During the bubonic plague — the "Black Death" that raged through Europe in 1348 — the Jews were accused of poisoning the wells and rivers, and this led to more bloody attacks that wiped out entire communities throughout Germany. Pope Clement VI published a bull in which he defended the Jews, admitting that they were equally hurt by the plague.

2 The name "Tosafist" (author of additions) is applied to the *Ashkenazi* rabbis of France and Germany, who added new commentaries or reservations to Rashi's exegesis of the Babylonian *Talmud*. Today Rashi's commentary appears in the inner margins of a page of the *Talmud* while the "additions" appear in the outer margins to the left and right.

2

Leading Ashkenazi Tosafists (12th-13th centuries)

Solomon Bar Isaac — known as Rashi — Troyes (1040-1105)	**Eliezer Ben Joel ha-Levi** — known as Ravia — Bonn (1140-1225)
Samuel Ben Meir — known as Rashbam — Ramerupt (*c.* 1080-1160)	**Isaac Ben Samuel ha-Zaken** — known as Ri — Dampierre (12th century)
Eliezer Ben Nathan — known as Raban — Mainz (*c.*1090-1170)	**Isaac Ben Moses** — Isaac Or Zarua — Vienna (late 12th-mid 13th centuries)
Isaac Ben Asher ha-Levi — known as Riba — Speyer (died before 1133)	**Jehiel Ben Joseph** — Paris (13th century)
Jacob Ben Meir — known as Rabbenu Tam — Ramerupt (1100?-1171)	**Mordechai Ben Hillel ha-Cohen** — Nuremberg (1240?-1298)

3 The conditions that prevailed from the 12th century on made lending on interest and the sale of pledges the major source of income for the Jews. The growth of cities and the evolution of a local class of merchants forced the Jews out of commerce. A Jewish money-changer in a sixteenth-century German engraving is seen demanding a pledge from a Christian in exchange for a loan, thus ensuring the capital and the interest. The scarcity of legal tender and insecurity involved in granting loans caused a sharp rise in the interest rate. As a result, the Jews were accused of "sucking the blood of Christians." Christian kings exploited the situation to collect heavy taxes from the Jews.

3

4

4 Coins for a horse, a drawing from the *Saxonspiegel*, depicts trade between a Jew and a farmer. The actual nature of the transaction is unclear. The Jew may be buying the horse or lending the money to the farmer with the horse as security. The rulers of the growing cities granted the Jews wide privileges in commerce, thus enhancing urban development.

5 "And he was tortured, as it is said." This illumination from a Passover *Haggadah* from Mainz (1427?) depicts the buildings of a typical medieval town. As a rule, Jews lived in separate quarters, at times surrounded by walls to cut them off from the rest of the town. In several German towns even today, a "Jew's Wall" or "Jew's Gate" survives, indicating the section of the wall built by Jews, or the part they were obliged to defend. *Geto nuovo* was the name of the first Jewish quarter (Venice, 1516), from which the term "ghetto" was derived.

5

dom of movement was restricted and they could not bear arms.

The Crusades hastened the withdrawal of Jews from trade, and they now worked primarily as money-changers or lenders [3].

Religious Activities

The foremost activities of *Ashkenazi* rabbis centered around the *Halakhah*, or Jewish law, and was based largely on the *Talmud*. The outstanding figure in this field before the First Crusade was Rabbi Gershom, known as the "Light of the Diaspora" (960-1028). He headed the *yeshiva* of Mainz and wrote both commentaries on the *Talmud* and answers to questions of *Halakhah*. He is known especially for his directives aimed at establishing order in family life, financial affairs and the life of the community of *Ashkenaz*. His most famous directive is his injunction against polygamy, known as "Rabbi Gershom's Ban."

The most prominent Talmudic commentator was Rashi, Rabbi Solomon Bar Isaac (1040-1105). Although he lived and worked in Troyes in France, he studied mainly at *yeshivot* in Germany. His commentary on the *Talmud* overshadowed all of the previous interpretations prepared by *Ashkenazi* rabbis. Rashi's most famous work is his commentary on the first five books of the Old Testament [10].

In addition to their concern with *Halakhah*, most of the early *Ashkenazi* rabbis wrote liturgical hymns and lamentations, some of which appear in *Ashkenazi* prayer books. Other rabbis, particularly "The *Hassidim* of *Ashkenaz*," propounded an occult philosophy thought to have been authored by Samuel Ben Kalonymus he-Hassid of Speyer (of the twelfth century) and his son Judah (1150?-1217) [7]. The movement was characterized by the stringent moral demands it made and its stress on the preparation of the individual and the nation for the possibility that they may be called upon to sacrifice themselves for their faith.

KEY

The special status awarded the Jews of Germany in the Middle Ages was expressed in the protection provided them by the emperor. Like most of the Jews of Western Europe, they were not integrated into the Christian social and political system. Because of their crucial role in the economy of the empire they were protected by law and their status was legally defined as "servants of the treasury" (*Servi Camerae*). In this illustration from the thirteenth century legal code from Saxony (the *Saxonspiegel*) a king decapitates a man who has killed a Jew. The Jew can be identified in paintings of this period by the bell-shaped cap he wears or the mark of disgrace fastened to his garments — both introduced to set Jews apart from Christians.

6

7

7 A banquet of the righteous in Paradise is an illustration from the Ambrosiani Bible from southern Germany of the mid-thirteenth century. The figures all have the heads of animals or birds, apparently to avoid depicting the human face. This custom may have arisen from the ban imposed by the *Hassidim* of *Ashkenaz*, led by Samuel and his son Judah he-Hassid, against the use of illumination in manuscripts, following the Bible (Exod. 20:4).

6 Martyrdom, dating from the reign of Antiochus Epiphanes in the second century BCE, became a symbol for the sacrifice of physical life for spiritual faith. These illuminations of a prayer recited at *Hanukkah*, which appear on a manuscript from Mainz (1427?), depict the killing of women for circumcising their sons; the murder of Elazar for refusing to eat pork; and Hannah being burned at the stake after her sons had been killed for their refusal to bow down before the emperor. Acts of collective martyrdom recurred during the Crusades. The Hebrew acronym of the phrase "God will avenge their blood" was added after the martyrs' names.

8

8 A poised lion drawn in micrographic letters appears on the frontispiece of the traditional annotation of *The Book of Ezekiel* in a thirteenth century German manuscript. Illustrations of this sort are common on both eastern and western manuscripts. The lion, mentioned in *The Book of Ezekiel* as one of the bearers of the chariot, became a popular symbol in Jewish tradition as a result of Jacob's blessing which identifies the lion cub with the tribe of Judah. The lion was later identified with the House of David.

9

9 "When a man first brings his son to school he writes the letters for him on a slate and washes him and clothes him in clean garments and bakes him bread with honey ... and brings him apples and fruits ... and reads him out the letters ...." (*Mahzor Vitry*, 1148)

10

10 Rashi script evolved from Hebrew cursive writing in Spain. The fact that this style of type was attributed to Rashi attests to the vast circulation of his works. His commentary on the *Torah* was the first Hebrew book ever printed (Italy, 1475).

Jews and Crusaders in Ereẓ Israel

The First Crusade set out from Europe for the Holy Land in 1096, with the aim of liberating the Holy Sepulcher of Jesus from the hands of the "Muslim infidels" [1]. Along their way the Crusaders massacred Jews in France, Germany, and Bohemia (known as the Massacres of 1096). Word of their deeds cast fear into the hearts of the inhabitants of the Holy Land, Muslims and Jews alike, and when the Crusaders entered Ramlạh and Jaffa, in June 1099, they found these cities deserted. Their forces and supplies depleted, the Crusaders reached Jerusalem and laid siege to the city [5]. On July 15 they breached the wall, penetrated the city, and slaughtered most of its residents. The Crusaders then forbade non-Christians to live in Jerusalem.

The Crusaders continued their campaign of conquest [2], and from 1100 to 1110 captured the coastal cities of the Holy Land, as well as Jericho, Bet Shean, and Tiberias on the Jordan Valley — Sea of Galilee axis.

First Crusader Kingdom (1099-1187)

Beginning in 1110, the Crusaders changed their policy toward the local population. They permitted the residents of the conquered cities and towns to remain, thus assuring continued habitation and economic life in the areas conquered. This change stemmed from the Crusaders' dependence on the inhabitants of the land, who supplied them a work force and revenues. In Sidon, Tyre, Ashkelon, and other cities conquered after 1110, the Jewish communities remained.

Indeed, the Jews and other ethnic groups were permitted to live according to their own customs and to settle disputes in their own courts. But "*Yeshivat* Ereẓ Israel," the supreme institution of Jewish leadership, which ruled on matters of *Halakhah* and custom, and whose authority was recognized throughout the Fatimid Muslim empire, had moved from Jerusalem to Tyre after the Seljuk conquest in 1087, and with the arrival of the Crusaders it moved to Damascus. In the 1160s the Jews of Ereẓ Israel sought guidance in *Halakhah* from Maimonides, at that time living in Egypt. In the course of time the Jews were permitted to resettle in any of the cities of Ereẓ Israel, save for Jerusalem, where they could only visit. Later on, the King of Jerusalem leased the monopoly on fabric dyeing to the Jews, a few of whom may have settled in the city. Yet, most Jewish settlement during the First Crusader Kingdom (1099-1187) was concentrated in the coastal cities [4].

Second Crusader Kingdom: 1191-1291

Jerusalem's conquest by Saladin in 1187, and the conquest of the entire country following the decisive battle at the Horns of Hittin, led to the renewal of Jewish settlement in Ereẓ Israel and Jerusalem [6]. However, economic and security conditions in Jerusalem, which in the 13th century was an unwalled city, impeded attempts at settling there. In 1229 part of the city was retaken by the Crusaders. In 1244 it was attacked by a

CONNECTIONS

72 Ashkenaz in the 10th-13th Centuries
76 The Jews in Christian Spain
78 The Expulsion of the Jews from Western Europe

1

1 A battle between the Crusaders and the Muslims — an illustration from *The History of Godfrey of Bouillon* (a 14th century French manuscript). Godfrey of Bouillon is described by the Jews as a "heroic and cruel warrior" and a man of destruction.

2 After conquering Jerusalem the Crusaders proceeded to take the coastal cities of the Holy Land and further north: Arsuf, Caesarea, Acre, Beirut, and Sidon were conquered, and their inhabitants slaughtered. After a siege which lasted about a month, Haifa was taken (1100) by a combined attack from land and sea. Jews and Muslims fought valiantly to defend the city, and "threw boiling hot oil and tar, and refuse" on the enemy, but in the end the defenders were massacred by the Crusaders.

2

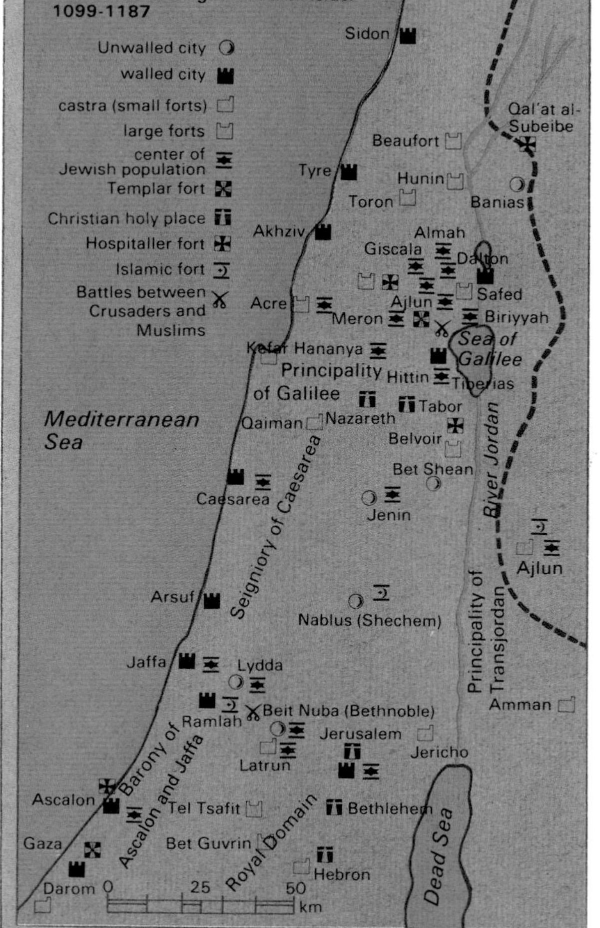

3 The extensive construction by the Crusaders in Erez Israel, which focused primarily on military and religious needs, reflects the character of their kingdom. Remains of Crusader churches, cities, castles and forts can be found throughout the country, especially in the coastal plain and in elevated places. The construction and ornamentation show the influence of the Romanesque style which was predominant in the Crusaders' countries of origin, particularly France and Italy, and some influence of the Gothic style of the late 12th and 13th century. This capital is from the Church of the Annunciation, in Nazareth, from the 13th century.

3

new group of invaders, the Hwarizmians, who came from the East; and in 1260 the city was besieged by the Mongols. Nahmanides [7], upon arriving in Jerusalem in 1267, wrote to his son: "Israel is gone from the city, save for two brothers who bought a dyeing concession from the ruler, and who are joined by a *minyan* to hold prayers in their house on the Sabbath". Nahmanides established a synagogue and brought *Torah* scrolls back into the city; yet he did not succeed in renewing a real Jewish community there.

During the 13th century the Jewish community of Acre, the capital of the Crusader kingdom from 1191 to 1291, grew considerably. In 1258, R. Yehiel of Paris settled there, and in 1267 Nahmanides moved there.

In the second half of the 13th century the Jews of Ashkenaz became eager to move to Erez Israel. This immigration changed the composition of the Jewish community there. In the 12th century, it had been composed of Arabic speaking, "Eastern" Jews. In the 13th century, the number of Jews of European origin, whose written language was Hebrew, increased. Most of the newcomers settled in the cities. Tension and controversy arose, in Jerusalem, Tyre and Acre, between Jews from different countries, leading to mutual declarations of bans.

In May 1291, the Mamelukes conquered Acre, and Crusader rule in the country came to its end. The Mameluke Sultan, Al Malik al-Ashraf Khalil (ruled 1290-1293), who headed the conquering forces, ordered a massacre to avenge the Crusader massacre in the conquest of Jerusalem. Many Jews were among the new victims. In order to prevent another invasion from Europe the Mamelukes destroyed all the coastal cities, and their inhabitants were forced to resettle further inland. With the end of the Crusader Kingdom, the Jewish community in Erez Israel reached a new ebb. Many years were to pass before it would recover.

KEY

The Crusader Fortress, Montfort, served as the headquarters of the Teutonic Knights. It stands in an isolated spot, on the spur of a mountain range, commanding the surrounding countryside, and is only a short distance from Acre, the capital of the Second Crusader Kingdom. The local topography dictated the structure of the fortress — a spur-castle, or long, narrow fortress, built on many levels. The constant Muslim threat to the Crusaders, their desire to rule large expanses of territory, and their continued shortage of manpower motivated them to build extensive fortifications.

4

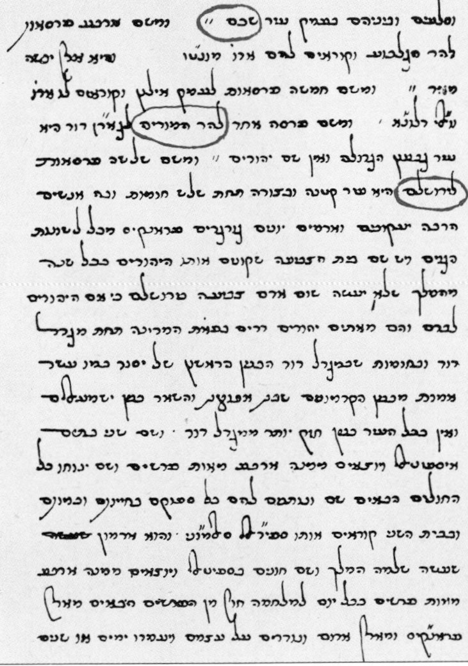

4 Benjamin of Tudela visited Erez Israel around the year 1170, and recorded his impressions in his *Itinerary* [section shown here]. According to him, there were relatively large Jewish communities in the coastal cities. Tyre had 500 Jews, who were engaged in the manufacture of glass; Acre and Caesarea each had 200; and Ashkelon, an important commercial center, had 200 Rabbanite Jews, 40 Karaites, and 300 Samaritans. The inland towns had only a few Jews, who earned a living from dyeing, and were apparently itinerant.

5

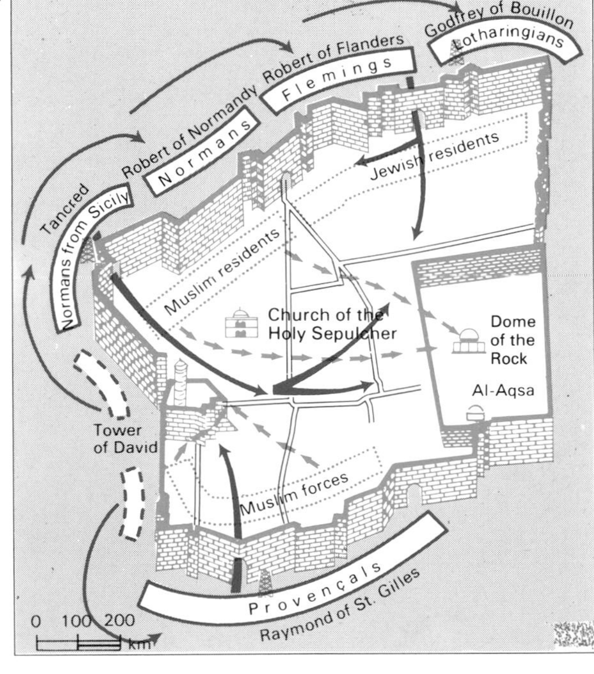

5 In the Crusader siege of Jerusalem the Jews defended the section of the wall near their quarter of the city. It was this section which the Crusaders breached.

6 Saladin (1137-1193), the Crusaders' arch-foe, conquered Jerusalem in 1187, and took over most of the Crusader Kingdom. In the Third Crusade (1189-1192) the Crusaders succeeded in winning Acre from him, after a prolonged siege. After taking Jerusalem, Saladin summoned the Jews to resettle there; and, indeed, many Jews of Ashkelon responded to his call, along with Jews from North Africa, France, and England. In 1192 he negotiated the "Treaty of Jaffa" with Richard the Lion-Hearted, according to which a truce was proclaimed, and Christian pilgrims were allowed access to Jerusalem.

6

7 The seal of Nahmanides (1194-1270), discovered near Acre. In 1263 the King of Spain forced Nahmanides to enter a debate on religion with the apostate Jew Pablo Christiani. This disputation ended in Nahmanides' victory, as a result of which he was accused of slandering Christianity and was forced to flee Spain.

7

The Jews in Christian Spain

Jews living in Christian areas were affected by the Christian-Muslim struggle for dominance over the Iberian Peninsula. In the 11th century Christian kings of the north began to reconquer Spain from the Muslims. To ward off their advance, during the 11th-12th centuries, Berber tribes (Almoravids and Almohads) invaded Spanish border settlements from the south. This gravely endangered the Jews and many of them left for the Christian principalities of the north.

The Reconquest and the Jews

The Reconquest went on until the end of the 13th century. During the entire period the Christian kings made use of their Jewish subjects, whose acquaintance with Muslim mores, knowledge of languages, ties with Jews in other parts of the peninsula, neutral status and lack of political aspirations — as well as the resources they could invest in settling and administering the newly-conquered territories — made them invaluable to the rulers. The kings conferred a special status on the Jews: their communities were tax-exempt, houses and lands were allocated to them, and they were granted other favors bestowed on servants of the crown [1].

Among the better-known Jews was Judah ibn Ezra, tax-collector for Alfonso VII of Aragon (1126-1157); in 1147 ibn Ezra was responsible for the Christian garrison in the Calatrava stronghold. R. Moses ben Nahman (Ramban, or Nahmanides, 1194-1270) also served a Spanish Christian king — James I. Jews from Muslim areas brought with them traditions that had governed much of their community life in Muslim Spain [2], including the name by which the Jewish communities were known — *aljama* — and the title given to leading figures — *muqaddamin*.

A Jewish community emerged in each of the Christian kingdoms that formed in the north of the Iberian peninsula, i.e., Castile-León, Aragon-Catalonia, Navarre, and Portugal. The Jewish communities were largely autonomous, although subject to the *Fueros* — a compilation of local laws. They were organized on a regional basis. Thus, the community in Catalonia, the *collecta*, encompassed a large center and villages in its vicinity.

"Seven of the city's best" — and sometimes more than seven — headed the community and were assisted by the communal institutions and the wealthy families. The Rabbis were very important in the Spanish Jewish communities: they and the *dayyanim* established independent judicial systems that were even authorized to try criminal cases. Other unique features of these communities were the "regulations" — *takkanot* — that fixed the individual's responsibilities to the group, including even financial arrangements in marriages.

Intellectual life

Spanish Jewry reached a zenith of economic, cultural [3] and social development in the 11th and 12th centuries.

CONNECTIONS

68 The Encounter with Islam in Spain
70 Medieval European Attitudes to the Jews
78 The Expulsion of the Jews from Western Europe
86 *Anusim* and Iberian Jews in the West

1

1 The Jews in Christian Spain enjoyed broad autonomy. Authority to deal with all spheres of life was vested in their leaders and law courts. The leadership was first drawn from an affluent strata and from among the scholars; they led the Jewish public with a firm hand. A class struggle took place in the 13th century, following which the lower classes in many Jewish communities — primarily in Aragon — achieved representation in the leadership. The picture shows a *Kashrut* seal and its impression from the vicinity of Tarragona, 13th-14th centuries.

2

2 Both western-Christian and eastern-Muslim influences manifested themselves in the art of illustrating Bibles in Christian Spain. The western influence, apparently emanating from Provence, was expressed mainly in the choice and blending of colors. But Islamic decorative art, which had been adopted by the Jews during the "Golden Age," was the more decisive influence. In the second half of the 13th century a new school of combined styles developed in Castile, which the "Crown of Damascus" [*Keter Damascus*, pictured here] exemplifies. The manuscript was copied in Burgos, Spain in 1260 by Menahem ibn Malik, after a biblical manuscript kept in a Damascus synagogue. The centerpiece "tapestry" is typical of Muslim manuscripts. It is adorned with micrographic letters and features traditional annotation of the scriptural text (an innovation introduced in Christian Spain). The colors however are western in style.

3

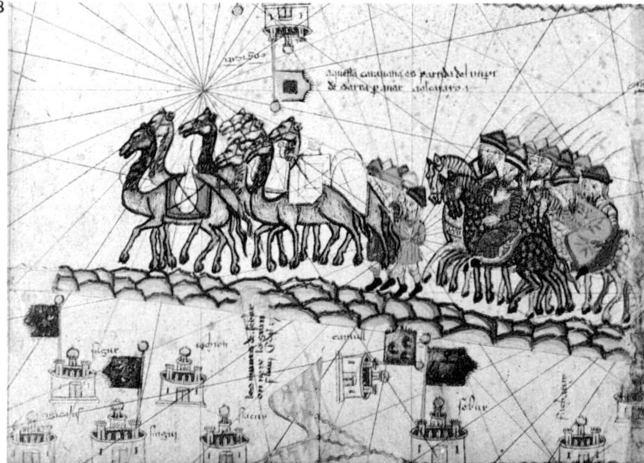

3 The Jews played a significant role in the lively cultural life of Christian Spain. With their knowledge of languages, and close acquaintance with Muslim customs and intellectual tradition, translation was one outstanding field of contribution. Alfonso X (the "Wise"), King of Castile and León (1252-1282), wanted to merge the Christian culture of his realm with eastern culture. He initiated the translation to Castilian of works on astronomy, astrology, belles lettres and the Bible, using Jewish translators and scientists. The forecasts of two Jewish astronomers were the basis for the calculation of the "Alfonso Tables." In the picture: A map depicting the silk-traders' route, from the Atlas compiled in accordance with the method devised by the Catalan Jewish cartographer Abraham Cresques (died in 1387) and his son Judah for the Crown Prince Don Juan.

After the 13th century its diversified culture was a bridge between Jews in the Islamic countries and those in Christian Europe [Key]. The Jewish communities retained their strength despite weighty intellectual developments that generated dissidence. Nahmanides' halakhic undertakings, based on his teachings of the system of the French tosafists, changed learning patterns in the Spanish *yeshivot*. Regarding learning as sufficient unto itself, Nahmanides strengthened rabbinic and academic circles. He looked for incontrovertible proof of the tosafists' theories which they themselves could not adduce, as they worked from secondary sources. Among his many disciples were Solomon ben Adret and Aharon Halevi of Barcelona. He made his strongest mark on the Rabbinical literature produced in Spain, such as the novellae of the Rashba and the commentary on Alfasi's Code.

In philosophy too, changes occurred in the 13th and early 14th century, centering around R. Moses Ben Maimon — Maimonides (1138-1204), and the debate engendered by his books *Mishneh Torah* and *Guide of the Perplexed* [6]. Maimonides tended to replace literal and allegorical interpretations with an intellectual-rationalistic approach. This antagonized moderates and kabbalists, who feared lest it lead to alien beliefs and apostasy. (In the 13th century a parallel struggle ensued between rationalism and absolute faith in both Islam and Christianity.)

At that time the *Kabbalah* began to make inroads into the intellectual world of Spanish Jewry. The largest part of the *Zohar*, the main book of the *Kabbalah* attributed to Moses de Leon (1240-1305), was completed in Guadalajara in 1286. De Leon consorted with a group of kabbalists in Castile and with the Gerona circle, having been particularly close to the kabbalists Tordos Abulafia and Joseph Gikatila. The *Kabbalah*, however, made its greatest impact in the 16th century, after the expulsion from Spain.

KEY

The war between Christians and Muslims for control over large parts of Spain went on for hundreds of years. The concurrent cultural struggle for ascendancy resulted in a richly variegated cultural life. On this fertile soil a unique, highly diversified Jewish culture flourished, different from that of all other centers of Jewish dispersion. It was a blend of sacred and profane, *Kabbalah* and rationalism, science and literature, linguistics and medicine. Construction of the Toledo synagogue, pictured here, was financed by Samuel Halevi Abulafia. Planned and decorated in the Mudejar style, the synagogue became the El Transito church.

4 Jewish quarters in Spanish cities generally came into existence because the Jews wanted to live together, rather than as a consequence of persecution. Both Muslim and Christian rulers allowed the Jews to reside in the center of cities, sometimes near the palace or the local stronghold. During the Reconquest the Christians gave Jews houses that had been Jewish property under Muslim rule, and even permitted them to expand their quarters. As attacks on Jews increased, many communities began to close their quarters — or were requested to do so. The gates of some Jewish quarters were locked at night and at Easter the Jews were forbidden to leave their houses. The rulers occasionally quarantined the quarters until the residents paid their debts. Here we see the house of Don Samuel Halevi Abulafia, Finance Minister to Pedro I, King of Castile [A], and a house in the Jewish quarter of Seville [B].

4 A

4 B

5

5 The Inquisition, law court of the Christian Church, began to function in Spain in 1480. As a result of its intensive activities, by the 16th century almost all Spanish *anusim* were ferreted out. This 19th century engraving depicts the process of interrogation by torture in the basement of the Inquisition chambers. It is by S.P. Jacobs after a drawing by B. Picart.

6

6 Maimonides set forth his philosophy in his *Guide of the Perplexed*. This was a recondite book that roused sharp controversy between the rationalistic circles — who claimed it supported their concepts and exegetic approach — and the moderates, who feared lest Maimonides' teachings encourage alien beliefs and weaken the faith. Pictured here is the Copenhagen manuscript of *Guide of the Perplexed* (Barcelona, 1348), with glossary prepared by Samuel b. Judah ibn Tibbon.

The Expulsion of the Jews from Western Europe

In the late 13th century, some half million Jews, or 30-50% of the world's Jewish population, were living in Western Europe (including Germany). By around 1500, the Jewish population of this region was no more than 150,000. There were a number of reasons for this demographic decline: riots, plagues (the Black Death of 1347-1352), and principally expulsions. Between the end of the 13th century and the middle of the 16th, the Jews were expelled from most of the countries of Western Europe and were forced to seek new havens [3].

England and France

The first country to banish its Jews was England. In fact, in no other country of Western Europe were the Jews considered so uncompromisingly as "servants of the treasury" as they were in England. The great majority of the Jews who had arrived in the British Isles in the second half of the 11th century now made their living as moneylenders and in financial transactions. While they loaned money to people from all walks of life, their primary economic function was to supply funds to the king, both through the heavy taxes levied on them, and through loans they made available to the monarch [1]. For example, King Henry II (reigned 1154-1189) owed the Jewish banker Aaron of Lincoln nearly £100,000, a figure equivalent to a year's revenues from taxes to the royal treasury.

The kings viewed the Jews and their business as the crown's personal property and thus protected them and their capital. During the 13th century, however, the kings increasingly extorted funds from the Jews, and the Jewish population declined. The Jews' role of royal banker was gradually taken over by Christian financiers who reached England from the European continent. In 1275 King Edward I (reigned 1272-1307) issued the Jewish Affairs Bill which forbade the Jews of England to loan money on interest, thus removing their only source of income. They were, however, to be allowed to support themselves as tradesmen or farmers for a short trial period. But in point of fact, they could not do this since they were ineligible for membership in the tradesmen's guilds, and as farmers they lacked security of tenure.

The Jews were left penniless, and the king could not collect his taxes. He thus reached the decision, on the basis of the situation he himself had created, to issue the expulsion order of July 1290. During the following three months, all of the Jews of England, some 4,000 people, left the country, most for France or Germany.

A similar process led to the expulsion of the Jews from France. In the Melun edicts of 1230, King Louis IX (reigned 1226-1270) forbade Jews to lend money on interest on religious grounds: "In order to save my soul and to save the soul of my predecessor." In 1253, the king ordered the expulsion of any Jew who did not undertake a more productive occupation [Key, 4].

CONNECTIONS

70 Medieval European Attitudes to the Jews
76 The Jews in Christian Spain
82 Eastern Jewry after the Expulsion from Spain
86 Anusim in the West

1

1 This cartoon of English Jews comes from the English treasury records of 1233. The figure with three faces is Isaac of Norwich, a moneylender considered at the time the richest Jew in England. The crown he sports represents his great influence. The scales held by the Jew on the left were apparently used to weigh coins, and symbolize the principal occupation of the Jews — loaning money on interest. The figures are arranged as if in a play with the demons, led by Satan, preparing to drag them down to Hell.

2

2 Clifford Tower was the scene of a mass martyrdom. Situated in the center of the city of York in northern England, it served as a refuge for the Jews of the city during the rioting that broke out there in 1190, at the time of the Third Crusades. For several days the Jews struggled to fend off the mob surrounding them, but on March 16, when it was clear they could no longer hold the tower, they set fire to all of their property. The men slew their wives and children and then took their own lives.

3

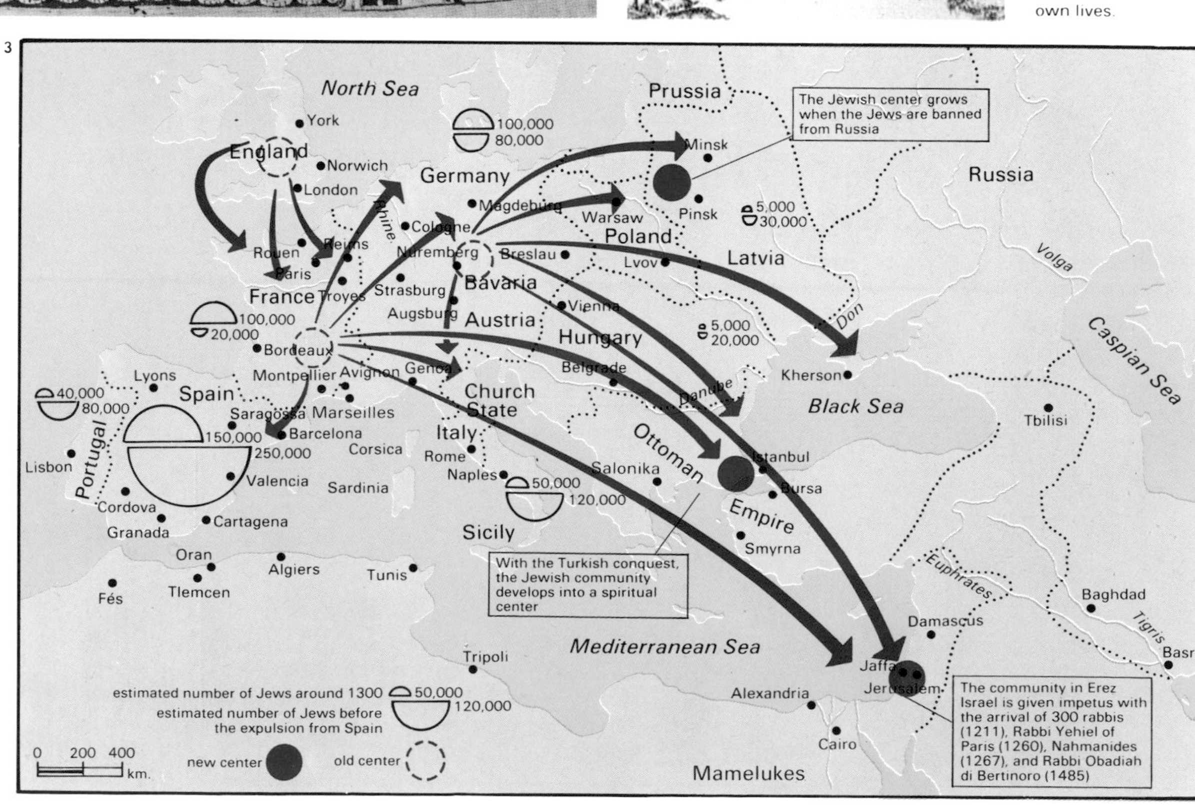

3 The Jewish population in the Middle Ages was severely diminished by rioting, expulsion and plagues, which at times affected entire communities. Expulsions were erratic, as in France in the early 14th century, when Jews were alternately expelled and allowed to return. Exact statistics are unavailable, but one can get an idea of the size and nature of the population from the lists of taxpayers and martyrs. They indicate that the Jews lived largely in cities and had a wide range of occupations.

MAJOR EXPULSIONS OF JEWS

1290 — England
1306, 1322 — France
1367 — Hungary
1381 — Strasburg
1394 — France
1421 — Austria
1426 — Cologne
1439 — Augsburg
1453 — Breslau
1467 — Tlemcen

The Jews Become Expendable

The most sweeping expulsion was from Spain and Portugal. The Jewish community of Spain was the oldest and largest of any in Western Europe. Jews lived there continuously from Roman times until they were banished in 1492. For hundreds of years they played a prominent role in Spanish life. Their importance stemmed from their large number, as well as from their cultural contribution and their extensive experience in commerce, the trades, financial affairs, and administration.

The Jews' status was also affected by the prolonged struggle between the Christians and the Muslims in Spain. From the 11th century, the Christian kingdoms in the north of the Iberian peninsula waged constant war to wrest control of all of Spain from the Muslims holding the south. In these *reconquista* (reconquest) wars, each side tried to barter for the Jews' support by granting them "privileges" that ensured broad freedoms in regard to legal, economic and religious affairs and autonomy. The Christian kings of Castile and Aragon made use of the Jews to resettle areas abandoned by the Muslims. They also sought the aid of the Jews for their financial and administrative experience and appointed rich Jews to various posts in their courts, ignoring Church protests.

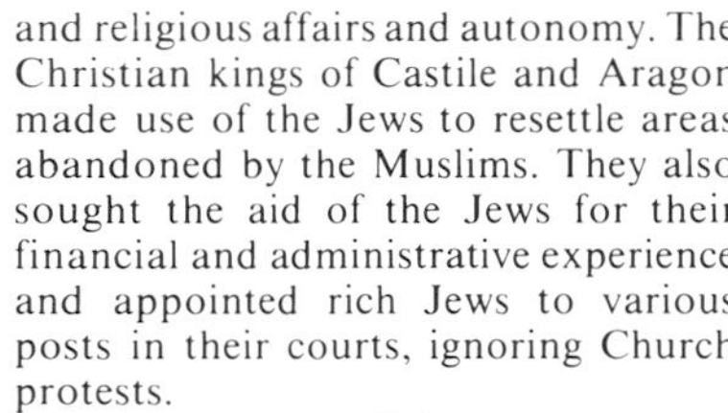

This state of affairs underwent a change when victory over the Muslims was assured. The Jews were no longer needed and the Christian kings now showed a greater readiness to accede to the demands of the Church and the townspeople that the Jews convert and assimilate into Spanish society.

On March 31, 1492 — shortly after Granada, the last Muslim stronghold in Spain, was conquered by the Christians — the monarchs of Spain issued an order requiring all of the Jews to convert within three months, or leave the country. The Christians' victory over the Muslims had spelled the doom of the Jewish community of Spain [6].

KEY

Prejudice and economic considerations induced the King of France, Philip Augustus (reigned 1180-1223) to order the expulsion of the Jews from his territory in 1182. All their property was confiscated and Christians' debts to them were cancelled with the payment of one-fifth of their value to the treasury. In 1198 the Jews were allowed to return. This painting from 1321 shows Philip Augustus ordering the Jews, marked with yellow circles, to leave. In reality, French Jews were not required to wear the special badge until the 13th century. Because of decentralized rule in medieval France, not all of the Jews were expelled at once.

4

4 Figures of French Jews appear on a 15th century alabaster plaque in the Museum of Carcassonne. From the late 13th century, conditions for French Jews began to worsen. In 1283 they were prohibited from living in the countryside and in 1294 they were restricted to special quarters of the cities.

5 In Italy and Germany it was impossible to banish all of the Jews since these countries were highly decentralized. In this picture, a detail from "The Madonna of Victory" by the 15th century Italian painter Andrea Mantegna, we see the family of the banker Daniel da Norsa of Mantova, who was given special permission by the Church to remove a painting of the Madonna from a house he had purchased from a Christian. In 1495 the ruler of Mantova confiscated the house in retribution and turned it into a church of the Madonna.

5

6 A

7

7 "Conditional Residents" was the term applied to the Jews in German towns when they were received back after the Black Death (1347-52). Expulsion was seen as merely the rescinding of the right of residence granted in the agreement. This illumination of a *Haggada* from 1427, most probably from Mainz, uses the expulsion of a Jewish family from a German town to illustrate the verse "Thy father went down into Egypt with threescore and ten persons" (Deut. 10:22).

6 The expulsion decree against the Jews of Spain [A] was issued in March 1492 by Ferdinand and Isabella [B], shortly after the conquest of Granada and the total *reconquista* of all of Spain from the Muslims. Ferdinand was king of Aragon and Isabella queen of Castile, and following their marriage in 1464 the two kingdoms were united and the Christian Kingdom of Spain established, creating one national Christian state.

6 B

The Jewish Community of Poland up to the 18th Century

The first Jews reached Poland from the Byzantine Empire, the Khazar Empire, and Kievan Russia, but by the Middle Ages most of the Jews in Poland were emigrés from Bohemia and Germany [2]. It was they who had the greatest impact on the way of life and intellectual activities of Polish Jewry.

The mass immigration of Jews from *Ashkenaz* into Poland was the consequence of two developments: the worsening of living conditions in Germany, with its wave of pogroms and expulsions; and the wide range of opportunities made available to the Jews in Poland. The Polish rulers, seeking to develop their urban economy, welcomed Jewish and other townspeople from Western Europe, in particular from Germany, and granted them various privileges.

The earliest documented *privilegium* (deed of rights) was granted by Boleslaw the Pious, Duke of Kalisz (1264). It guaranteed the Jews protection, freedom of worship, legal autonomy in internal matters, and freedom of movement, thus facilitating their economic activities.

At first the major occupation of the Jews who came from Germany was that which they brought with them — moneylending. However, Poland's expanding economy offered them new opportunities, and many Jews turned to commerce, the trades and leasing transactions (*arenda*) [Key].

The Jews and the Poles

In Poland, as in the countries of Western and Central Europe, opposition to the Jews emanated largely from the Catholic priesthood and the townspeople. The Church, fearing the Jews' "harmful" influence, demanded that restrictions be placed upon them to segregate them from the Christians. The townspeople, fearing competition, fought to restrict the Jews' economic activities and to expel them from the cities, while the lesser nobility competed with them in the leasing business. Nevertheless, neither the king nor the higher nobility were willing to forego the benefit they were able to glean from the Jews.

Several towns banned Jews from living within their jurisdiction, but this did not prevent the settlement of special Jewish quarters beyond the city limits in which the Jews continued to conduct their business [4]. In many instances the Jews left the royal cities and moved to "private" towns set up by nobles on their estates. As Poland expanded eastward during the 16th century, densely populated Jewish settlements sprung up in the Ukraine and Byelorussia, mostly on nobles' estates, where the Jews dealt in leasing.

Religious and Social Life

Polish Jewry's link to *Ashkenaz* was reflected in its language — Yiddish — and in the way in which it organized its public and religious affairs. The education Polish Jews provided their youngsters centered around the *Talmud*, Rashi and the Tosafists. Until the 15th

CONNECTIONS

78 The Expulsion of the Jews from Western Europe
92 Shabbateanism
94 The Community as the Framework for Jewish Life
96 The Insular Community and Jewish Art
106 Russian Jewry and the Pale of Settlement: 1772-1881

1 **A page from the official minute book of the Council of Four Lands** shows the by-laws, decisions and some of the judgements issued by the Council. The Council of Lithuania kept similar records.

2 **Jews lived in Poland** as early as 1098. According to the reports of Cosmas of Prague, Jews moved from Bohemia into Poland following Crusader raids. These 12th century coins found in Poland bear Hebrew inscriptions. One reads "Abraham bar Isaac Nagid," probably the name of the Jewish coiner. These coins are imprinted with the word *bracha* (blessing). Others bore the words *Kraka* (the name of the former Polish capital Krakow) and *Meshko Karl Polski* (Mishko King of Poland).

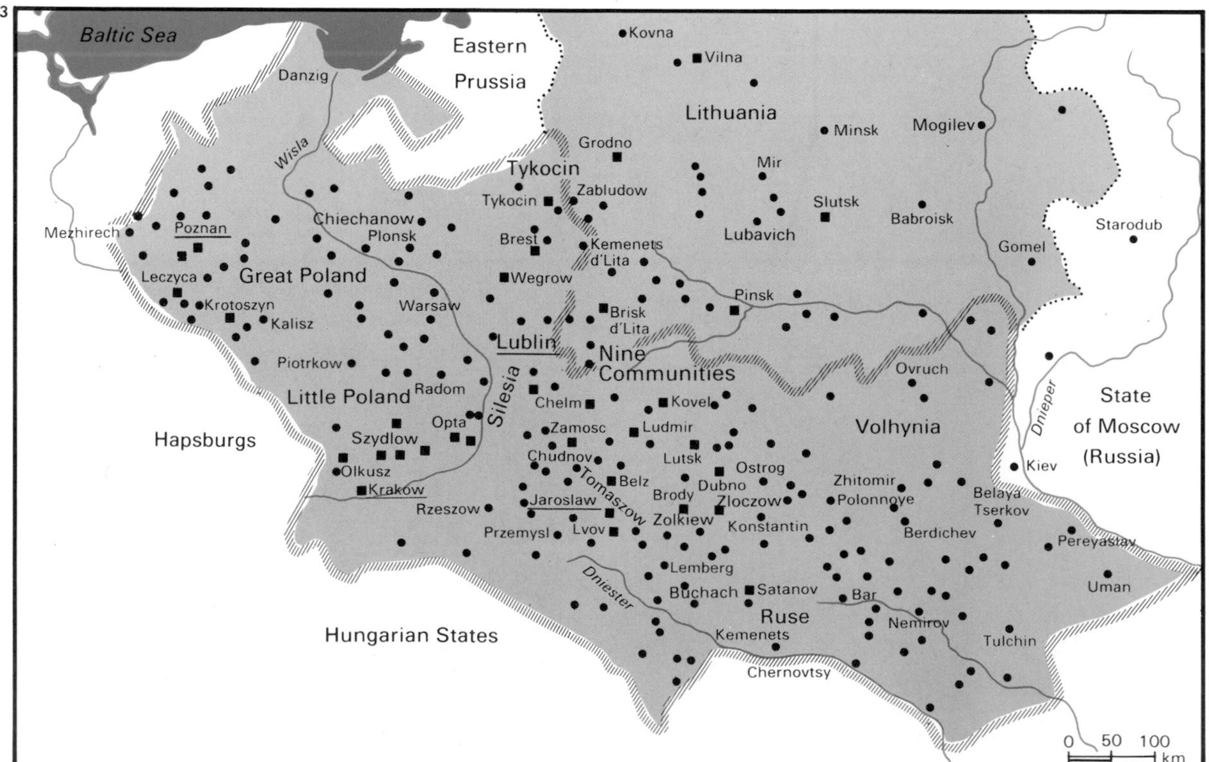

3 **The Council of Four Lands** was composed of representatives of the leading communities and the provinces of Poland — except for Lithuania, which even before 1623 had an independent council. The major provinces sending representatives to the Council included Great Poland (its foremost community was in Poznan), Little Poland (with its leading community in Krakow), the Lvov States, and Volhynia. Other provinces included Lublin, Podolia, Podlesia and the "Nine Communities."

Jewish Community •
urban center ■
border of the Four Lands
Four Land Center Krakow

century, boys from Poland went to Germany to study in the *yeshivot* there, and German scholars were invited to serve as the rabbis of Polish communities. In the 16th century, the focus of educational activities and religious scholarship moved eastward.

The first of the new generation of rabbinical authorities in Poland was Rabbi Jacob Pollak (1460-1511), head of a *yeshiva* in Krakow, the Polish capital at the time. He is considered the father of the "divisions" system (*pilpul*), a method of Talmudic reasoning later adopted by most of the *yeshivot* of Poland. Outside Krakow, other major *yeshivot* were established in Lublin, Poznan and Ostrog.

The public life of the Jewish communities of Poland was characterized by two elements: self-government with very broad authority, and super-communal bodies. The latter took the form of the Council of Four Lands [3] which was the organizational framework for all Jews living in Poland and operated from the mid-16th century to 1764.

The primary function of the Council of Four Lands was to negotiate with the Polish authorities in regard to the rate of taxes imposed on the Jews and to distribute these monies among the different communities. It also negotiated for new privileges for the Jews or for the removal of restrictions. In addition, the Council organized Jewish domestic life, and the rulings it handed down were binding on the whole of the Jewish public [1]. Affiliated with the Council of Four Lands was a superior court for all of Poland's Jews.

The disturbances of 1648-1649, in which Cossacks led by Bogdan Chmelnickij ravaged many communities, and the Russian and Swedish invasions that followed, struck a severe blow at the Jews of Poland, and destroyed the prosperity and sense of security that had typified their life. They also altered the direction of Jewish immigration: to Western Europe and, later, the United States, rather than eastward.

KEY

This arenda (rental in Polish) jug from the 17th century was used for alcoholic beverages and shaped in the figure of a Jewish tavern keeper. It bears phrases mocking the Jewish leasing business. This was a very common occupation of Polish Jews at the end of the Middle Ages and had variations: the leasing of sources of income from the state — taxes, customs, coins and salt mines, and the leasing of estates. Estate leasing was particularly common in Byelorussia and the Ukraine. Payment was made in advance in consideration for the income from the estate. Sub-leaseholders also operated on the estate, administering inns, flour mills, forests, etc.

4

4 The Old Synagogue (Alte Schul) was built in the mid-14th century in Kazimierz, near Krakow. In the 16th century, the Jews of Krakow enjoyed a "golden age," due to the support of the Polish kings, a liberal and humanistic policy, excellent rabbis and court doctors who were members of the community, and the establishment of autonomous Jewish bodies.

5 The roof of the wooden synagogue of Chodorow was built in 1651. The arched roof was decorated with a myriad of colorful paintings with motifs of flora and fauna, the zodiac and Biblical verse.

5

6 A Polish Jew is dressed in the manner typical of the late 17th and early 18th centuries in this woodcut. Special Jewish apparel started to evolve at the beginning of the 13th century in the wake of the decision of the Fourth Lateran Council that Jews be distinguishable from Christians.

6

7

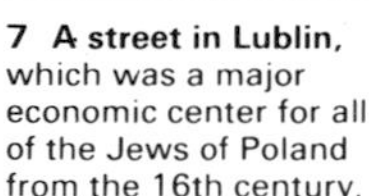

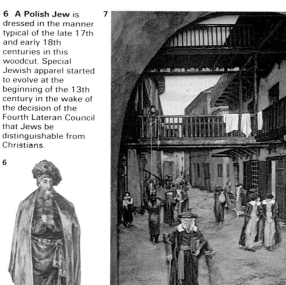

7 A street in Lublin, which was a major economic center for all of the Jews of Poland from the 16th century. Lublin also became a center for the study of the *Torah*, and was nicknamed "Jerusalem of Poland."

8

חמשה חומשי תורה

צאנה וראנה

באסיליאה

8 Ze'enah U-Re'enah, first published in Prague in 1608, was written by Rabbi Jacob Ben Isaac Ashkenazi. It is a free translation of the Pentateuch into Yiddish, together with stories, homiletics and the commentaries of Rashi, Nahmanides, Rabbenu Bahya, and others. The book answered the needs of the Jewish woman who, unlike the men, did not study *Torah* and *Talmud*.

9 The fortified synagogue of Lutsk was erected in 1626 with the permission of Zygmunt III. Fortified synagogues were erected outside the city walls as defence posts in case of enemy attack. The building permit stipulated that the Jews must purchase a "proper cannon" at their own expense and that members of the community be posted to defend the city as required.

9

Eastern Jewry after the Expulsion from Spain

The expulsion of the Jews from Spain and Portugal was crucial in molding the demographic, social and cultural character of most of the Jewish communities in the Islamic countries. Almost all of those countries — in North Africa, along the Mediterranean coastline, in the Middle East and the Arabian Peninsula — were under the aegis of the Ottoman Empire. Many of their Jewish communities anteceded the emergence of Islam: Jewish settlements in Egypt, Babylonia and Persia are mentioned in the Bible; Jews are known to have been in North Africa since the time of the 2nd Temple, and there is historical evidence of Jewish settlement in Yemen from the 1st century CE.

During the Middle Ages Jewish communities in North Africa lived in relative peace under Islamic rule [2]. Led by Maimonides (1135-1204), Egypt's Jewry flourished. Although little is known about the Jews of Yemen before the 16th century — or those of the Middle Eastern countries after the era of the *geonim* — their communities probably existed continuously.

Waves of Immigration

After the expulsion from Spain and Portugal [3] tens of thousands of Jews came to countries within the Ottoman Empire: North Africa, Egypt, Christian Balkan countries — Greece, Yugoslavia and Bulgaria [1] — as well as Turkey, Syria [5] and Ereẓ Israel. The Ottoman Sultans who expanded the empire during the 16th century, entrenching their economic and administrative systems, encouraged the Jews to settle and make their talents available to the rulers. Several thousand found their way to western and northern Europe, and some even reached the New World.

Emigration from Spain actually began in 1391, following the disturbances in Aragon and Castile, where Jewish communities were destroyed. Thus a century before the expulsion from Spain, the city of Algiers became an important Jewish center led by Isaac ben Sheshet (1326-1408). The expulsion of 1492 brought additional waves of exiles to North Africa and points further east. In the 17-18th centuries emigration was renewed when many *conversos* ("new Christians") left Portugal and joined Jewish communities in the cities of the Mediterranean and in Amsterdam. Many traversed Leghorn, Italy, to disperse in cities throughout the Ottoman Empire. They appeared in Tunis as well as in Izmir, Salonika and Aleppo, where they were known as *Frankos* — Europeans.

Intercommunal Frictions

Jewish communities that had existed since the days of the Roman Empire and Byzantium — known as *Romaniots* — were affected by the arrival of the Spanish exiles (*Sephardim*). The latter brought different customs, language — Judeo-Spanish, or *Ladino* — dress, prayers and communal regulations (*Takkanot*). For several generations there was friction between the old established

CONNECTIONS

70 Medieval European Attitudes to the Jews
88 16th Century Erez Israel
108 The Legal Status of Jews in Muslim Lands
110 Jewish Economic Life in Muslim Lands
112 Jewish Community and Culture in Muslim Lands

1

1 Jewish communities of Bulgaria, which was part of the Ottoman Empire from 1396 to 1908, comprised the long-established *Romaniots*, the Spanish exiles and the *Ashkenazim* from Germany and Bavaria. All adopted *Ladino*, the *Sephardi* prayerbook, and the rabbinical legal system brought from Spain. The picture shows a Scroll of Esther from Bulgaria, 19th century.

3 Exiles from Spain and Portugal (1492-1497) spread along the Mediterranean coast. Some reached northwestern Europe and even the New World.

2

2 The Home of Maimonides in Fez, a mountain city of Morocco, was adorned with 13 water clocks symbolizing his 13 Principles of Faith. Tradition has it that he dwelt in this house from 1160 to 1165. There were Jews in Fez from the time it was founded in 789. Although they suffered severe persecution, thousands more came after the expulsion from Spain, intensifying the intellectual and economic life of the Jewish community. The situation improved after 1912, when French rule began, but most Jews of Fez moved on after 1956 to Israel or France.

3

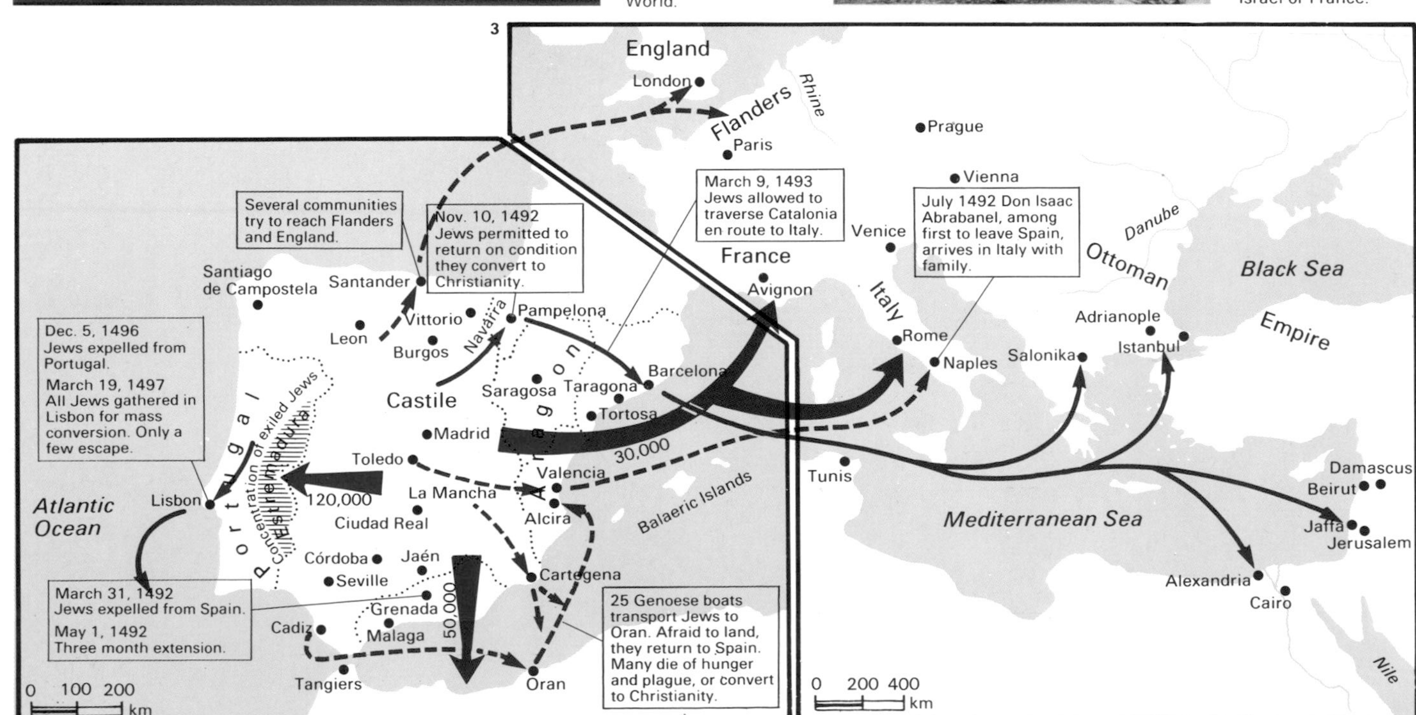

settlers and the new arrivals, particularly in Istanbul and Salonika. There the Spanish exiles organized separate congregations, usually according to place of origin in Spain and Portugal or place of settlement in Italy after the expulsion [4]. Their skills developed the weaving, armament and metal industries; they brought great progress to medicine and crafts. Gradually, the *Romaniots* adopted Sephardic customs, prayerbook and language.

Led by scholars such as R. Samuel de-Medina (1506-1589) and R. Moses Almosnino (1516-1580) [8] in Salonika, R. David ben Zimra in Egypt (1480-1574), and R. Joseph ben Lev in Istanbul (1500-1586), the congregations were all subject to a single central authority — that of the religious court and its leaders — and all were bound by the same "agreements" and a united educational system. R. Samuel de-Medina, a leader of the "Lisbon" and "Portugal" congregations in Salonika, was called upon to settle jurisdictional disputes and matters of taxation affecting the different Salonika congregations. These and other congregations eventually united within an overall framework that was officially recognized in the 18th-19th centuries when Ottoman non-Muslims — Jews, Greek Orthodox and Armenians — were defined as religious sects — *millet*. The influence of the Spanish exiles was apparent in the North African countries as well [6].

Many Spanish exiles reached Erez Israel when it was part of the Ottoman Empire and reinforced the Jewish communities in Jerusalem [7], Tiberias, Gaza, Hebron and particularly Safed. In the 16th century Safed became an intellectual and economic center; great scholars of the *Halakhah* and *Kabbalah*, and eminent liturgical versifiers concentrated there. The *Sephardi* prayerbook, liturgical poems and the *Halakhah* as compiled in the *Shulhan Arukh* by R. Joseph Caro (1488-1575) were adopted by all the Jewish communities in the Islamic countries [Key].

KEY

The Kabbalah of R. Isaac Luria (ha-Ari) that evolved in the 16th century in Safed. It increased eastern Jewry's affinity for mysticism and exacerbated the messianic tension that prevailed. Luria's *Kavvanot*, *Tikkunim* and *Yihudim* were incorporated into the *Sephardi* prayerbook used by Jews in the Islamic countries. The liturgical poetry renewed in Safed by R. Israel Najara and R. Solomon Alkabez, full of intense messianic fervor, also found its way into the *Sephardi* version of the prayers. In the picture: ha-Ari prayerbook (Morocco, 1791).

4 In the 17th century Salonika had more than 30 Jewish congregations — *kehalim*. Some were founded by exiles from Spain and Portugal, others by the *Romaniots* who had settled there even before the expulsion from Spain — or by *Ashkenazim*. Istanbul had as many as 44 *kehalim*, each of which introduced its own regulations, collected taxes and maintained separate institutions, following the customs of the city of origin. Contemporary leaders recognized the grave difficulties caused by this organizational separatism and diversity of traditions, but did not press for change as they were aware that pressure would not hasten integration. In later generations, most of the congregations indeed united.

4

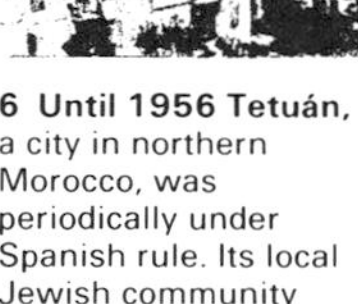

5

5 The Jews of Syria, which was conquered by the Ottomans in 1516 along with Lebanon and Erez Israel, were concentrated mainly in the cities of Damascus, Aleppo and Kamishli. Lebanon featured a large community in Beirut. The *Frankos* — exiles from Italy via Spain and Portugal — became part of the established communities. The most important community arose in Aleppo, a thriving city along the trade route between Persia and Europe. This wine jug, inscribed in Hebrew, is from Syria, 18th century.

6 Until 1956 Tetuán, a city in northern Morocco, was periodically under Spanish rule. Its local Jewish community was augmented by Spanish and Portuguese exiles, and *conversos* from both countries. In the 18th century Portuguese *conversos* returned to Judaism and were absorbed by the Jewish community. This gravestone is from the old Jewish cemetery in Tetuán. It is similar to gravestones found in cemeteries in Spain from the 12th to the 14th centuries.

6

7

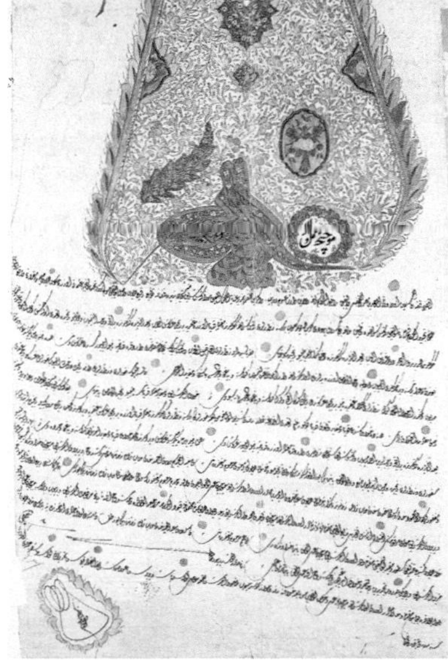

7 Jerusalem submitted to Ottoman rule in 1516-7. The main source of income of the Jewish community there was *Halukka* money, and the Jews were thus in difficult straits. The government taxed them exorbitantly. In the picture: a royal order — *firman* — issued in 1791 concerning taxes on the Jews of Jerusalem.

8

ספר הנהגת החיים

8 R. Moses Almosnino of Salonika headed a Jewish delegation to Istanbul to request tax concessions from the Sultan in 1568. The request was granted: A *firman* was issued, known as the "writ of freedoms." In the picture: a page from *Sefer Hanhagot ha-Haim*, a philosophic work written by Moses Almosnino.

The "Anusim"

The term *Anusim* (Hebrew for "forced ones") is applied to Jews who were forced to convert as a result of external pressures. To the eyes of the outside world they scrupulously practiced their new religion, but in secret they continued to observe at least some of the commandments and customs of Judaism. In the Islamic world, we meet them in Morocco during the reign of the Almohads (1160-1269); in Yemen in the second half of the 12th century; and in Persia at various periods. In 1839 all of the Jews in Mashhad, Persia were compelled to convert to Islam. Remnants of the community still living in the city lead a double life to this day.

The majority of *Anusim* lived in Christian countries, both because of the many edicts of forced conversion issued in these countries against the Jews, and due to the Church's persistent refusal to allow even the forced converts to return to Judaism [4].

A large number of *Anusim* lived in 7th century Visigoth Spain. In *Ashkenaz* we encounter them as early as the beginning of the 11th century. Other Jews were forced to convert to Christianity in the persecutions of 1096. Kaiser Heinrich IV (reigned from 1050 to 1106) later allowed them to resume their Jewish faith. In the late 13th century, forced conversion was decreed against the Jews of southern Italy. Thousands of *Anusim* (*Neofiti*) who preserved their unique way of life remained there until the 16th century.

The Marranos of Spain and Portugal

From the 14th century the Iberian peninsula was the home of the greatest number of *Anusim*. The riots of 1391 which began in Seville produced many *Anusim*, and these were joined by a large number of other forced converts during the religious debate in Tortosa, Aragon in 1404-1413. When the Jews were expelled from Spain in 1492, many preferred to convert, foremost among them the court rabbi and chief tax collector of the Spanish kings, Don Abraham Senior. The Jews of Portugal, whose community had been aggrandized with the arrival of Spanish Jewish exiles, were similarly compelled to worship clandestinely.

A certain proportion of the converts adopted their new religion out of an inner conviction, and became fervent spokesmen for conversion. The vast majority, however, led a double life. Outwardly they lived as Christians, yet clandestinely they continued to observe at least some of the Jewish commandments [3].

Documents from Spain and Portugal refer to these Jews as *conversos*, but the derogatory term in popular use was *Marranos* (pigs). They came from all walks of Jewish society. For the wealthier ones, conversion to Christianity meant new opportunities for advancement, particularly in public life. Nonetheless, Spanish society retained a deep-seated hostility toward the *Marranos*. Moreover, precisely because they were freed from the restrictions imposed

CONNECTIONS
70 Medieval European Attitudes to the Jews
72 Ashkenaz in the 10th-13th Centuries
82 Eastern Jewry after the Expulsion from Spain
86 Anusim in the West

1 **"Auto-da-fé"** (act of faith) is a painting by Pedro Berruqueta (1450-1503). Burning the condemned at the stake was designed to warn any who might question the faith. The tribunal of the Inquisition first declared a "grace period" in which anyone whose confession was accepted by the court would not be tried for heresy. Despite the assurance that the confidentiality of these confessions would be preserved, there was an atmosphere of fear. Many *Marranos* made haste to vindicate themselves lest they be informed on in someone else's confession. At first the Inquisition concentrated on the *Marranos'* leaders, condemning them whether they were its prisoners or had managed to escape. It next turned to those of a lower status and finally even put the deceased on trial.

2A

2B

2 **Barefoot and clothed in the "sanbenito,"** a yellow sack-like smock with black crosses on it [A], the penitents marched in the ritual of the *auto-da-fé*. Some *Marranos* were made to wear this garment for a year or more to make a public show of remorse for their deeds. Those condemned to death were also clothed in the *sanbenito* for their procession to the stake. Their smock was painted with demons and flames, symbols of Hell. Their heads were covered by a hood (*coraza*) [B]. *Marranos* whose confessions were received during the grace period or who were not sentenced to the stake or to imprisonment, were required to repent and were readmitted to the Church. Their property, however, was confiscated.

3 **A medallion in honor of the Spanish general** Amrogio di Spinola (1569-1630), most likely a *Marrano*, bears the Hebrew inscription "We beseech Thee, O Lord, to save us." Most of the children of the *Marranos* were apparently informed of their Judaism only when they reached the age of *Bar-Mitzvah*.

upon them as Jews, the *Marranos* now represented competition. Prejudice against them was voiced in the sermons of priests (among them many converts), in preachings and writings, and ultimately in riots which at times escalated into civil warfare between the Christians and the "New Christians."

The Inquisition

The Inquisition served as the court of law of the Catholic Church. Initially, heretics were tried by the bishops. From the 13th century special tribunals, charged with interrogating and passing judgement on anyone suspected of heresy against the Church, were utilized exclusively against Christian heretics. *Marranos*, seen by the Church as sinful Christians, were also brought before these courts [6].

The Spanish Inquisition was created in 1480 in response to a request made to the pope by the Spanish monarchs, Ferdinand and Isabella. In 1483 Tomás de Torquemada was made Inquisitor General [Key]. In Portugal, the Inquisition was established in 1536.

Marranos who had been informed on for observing Jewish practices were brought before the Inquisition and interrogated under extreme torture. Those who confessed their sins and promised to repair their ways were given a variety of sentences: mortification of the flesh, fasting, prayer, pilgrimages to holy sites, and even public whippings [2]. The more recalcitrant cases were sentenced to imprisonment for terms ranging from short periods to life.

Prisoners who refused to recant were turned over to the state authorities — the secular powers — who were charged with carrying out the death sentence by burning at the stake. These executions were held before a mass audience in the ceremony of the *auto-da-fé* [1]. Until it was abolished in 1834 in Spain and in 1821 in Portugal, the Inquisition tried and sentenced hundreds of thousands of victims. Tens of thousands of "heretics" were burned at the stake.

KEY

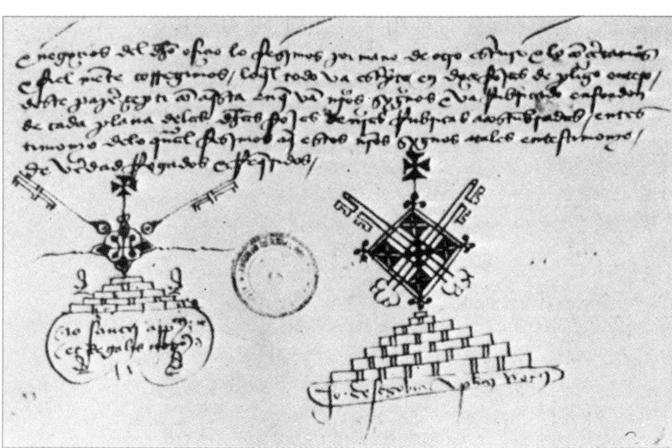

The Protocols of the Inquisition were scrupulously compiled during the interrogations and trials of the *Marranos* and serve as a major source of information as to their way of life and their fate. This picture shows the signing of the sentence of Maria Dias Serera, who managed to flee her town of Ciudad Real in Castile and was tried in her absence. Ultimately, only an effigy of her was burned at the stake. When the Jews of Ciudad Real openly resumed their Jewish faith, the situation was exploited as justification for the acts of the Inquisition. The tribunals rose systematically and gradually came to encompass all of Spain.

4

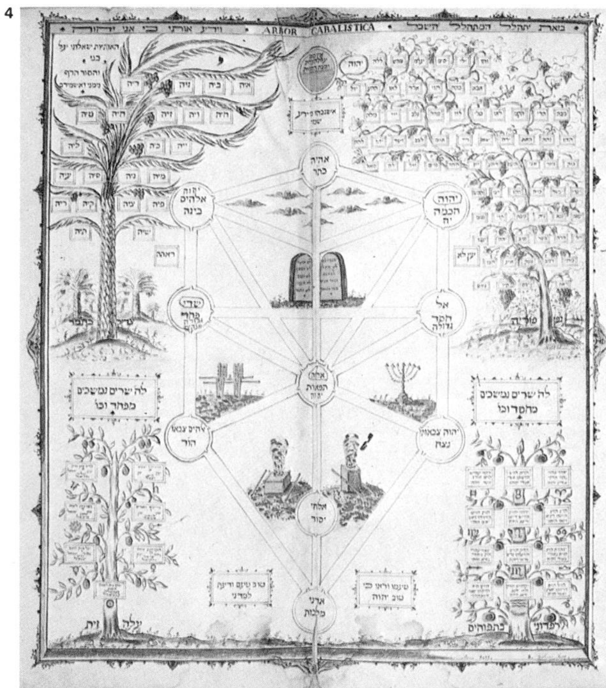

5A

BANDO DECHIARATIONE ET REVOCATIONE DEL Sereniss. Duca di Sauoia, contra li Marani Apostati.

EMANVEL FILIBERTO PER GRATIA DI DIO DVCA DI SAVOIA PRENCIPE DI PIEMONTE, ETC.

5B

PRIVILEGGIO CONCESSO PER IL SERENISSIMO DVCA DI SAVOIA.

Ad instantia di M. Vitale di Sacerdoti Hebreo, per tutta la natione Hebrea, e d'essa stirpe cosi Italiani, Todeschi, Spagnuoli, Portughesi, di Leuante, Barbaria, di Soria, per poter stare, negotiare nelli suoi stati: et per tutti i mercanti cosi Turchi, Mori, Persiani, Armeni, per mercantar nelli sui stati. Dat. in Turino alli IIII. di Settembre. 1572.

5 Because of their commercial contacts and experience, the *Marranos* were welcomed in many European countries. The strong family and personal ties linking their communities throughout Europe and the rest of the world furthered the development of international trade. In 1572 the Duke of Savoy granted "privileges to the *Marranos*" [A], but at the insistence of King Philip II of Spain, supported by the German emperor and the pope, the Duke issued a second edict [B] ordering the banishment of any *Marranos* who had openly resumed their Judaism.

4 The life story of the Marrano Alonso Nunez de Herrera, who became the Kabbalist Abraham ha-Cohen Ben David ha-Cohen de Herrera, illustrates the ordeal of a *Marrano* returning to Judaism. He is thought to have been born in Portugal but raised and educated in Italy. Abraham received a basic Jewish education which enabled him to read the Bible, philosophical works and Kabbalistic books in Hebrew. He traveled to Cadiz in southern Spain where he was taken prisoner by the English. He was released after the Sultan of Morocco intervened on his behalf. In 1602 the Grand Duke of Tuscany appointed Herrera his commercial agent in Rouen, France. At that time the Jews of Rouen were living as *Marranos* and we may assume that Herrera similarly kept his Judaism secret. He moved to Amsterdam when Jews there first began to practice their Judaism openly. There, he produced his two major works of Kabbalistic writings, *The House of God* and *The Gate of Heaven*. Recently, his influence on the Jewish philosopher of *Marrano* extraction, Baruch Spinoza, has come to light. This picture shows the "counting tree" according to Herrera.

6

6 "The Tribunal of the Inquisition" was painted by Francisco Goya (1746-1828). In 1267 Pope Clement IV instructed the Franciscans and Dominicans to conduct an "inquisition" against the "New Christians" who had reverted to Judaism. The Inquisition in Spain and Portugal also issued the *limpieza de sangre*, a document testifying to the Christian purity of the blood of its holder, since any Christian whose family was of Jewish or Muslim extraction was banned from holding public or ecclesiastical posts. Tribunals were even established in Latin America.

Anusim and Iberian Jews in the West

After the expulsion of the Spanish Jews (1492) and the forced conversion of Portuguese Jews (1497) only *Anusim* and apostates remained in Spain and Portugal. They were known as the "New Christians" or *Marranos* ("pigs"). But their Jewishness had not been rooted out. Persecution at the hands of Catholic society and the terrors of the Inquisition brought about the migration of many *Anusim* in the 16th and 17th centuries. In the East, they were received into communities already established by their brethren expelled from Spain; but in Christian western Europe and on the American continent they attempted to establish their own framework for a Jewish existence [1].

Anusim in South America

The end of Jewish life on the Iberian Peninsula was also the beginning of Jewish settlement in America. Indeed, there were *Anusim* among Columbus' contingent when he set out on his voyage of discovery in 1492 [2]. In the New World, the *Anusim* hoped they would be able to continue their lives in an "Iberian Society" while escaping the clutches of Inquisition, and would take advantage of new economic opportunities. For example, in 1502, a group of "New Christians" obtained a concession from the King of Portugal allowing them to trade in Brazil and to export wood to Portugal. With the conquest of Mexico by Cortés (1521), many *Anusim* migrated there, mainly to Mexico City.

When it became clear that many *Anusim* had succeeded in migrating illegally to Spanish settlements on the American continent, branches of the Spanish Inquisition were set up there. Inquisitional records from the 16th and 17th centuries depict a Jewish way of life that was somewhat richer than that of the *Anusim* of the Iberian Peninsula. Apparently they maintained firm contact with Jewish communities in Europe and the East. But by the beginning of the 19th century, after the annulment of the Inquisition, all that survived to remind following generations of *Marrano* origins were some personal religious articles, such as candelabras and Star of David ornaments, and a few customs.

When the Dutch conquered territories in Brazil, *Anusim* living there were able to return openly to Judaism. Indeed, Jews from Amsterdam served in the Dutch fighting ranks. By 1636 there was a synagogue in Recife and *Anusim* who had returned to their faith were part of the community established by Amsterdam Jews. At its zenith, the community's *minyan* (congregation for religious services) reached some 1,500 souls. But in 1654 the Portuguese reconquered Recife; the majority of its Jews returned to Amsterdam, while some went to Dutch Curacao, British-ruled Barbados, French Martinique, and other Caribbean islands. A group of 23 turned to New Amsterdam, as New York was then called.

Anusim and Jews in Western Europe

As a rule, *Anusim* who fled the Inquisi-

CONNECTIONS

84 The *Anusim*
128 Origins of the American Jewish Community

1 The synagogue named after Isaac Turo in Newport, Rhode Island, was inaugurated in 1763. Isaac Turo came to Newport from Amsterdam, in 1760. The community was founded by 20 immigrant families from the Barbados Islands. A hideaway in the center of the podium apparently recalls the way of life of the community's *Marrano* forefathers.

2 Joden Savannah — the Jewish Savannah — was the name given to a forested area on the banks of the Surinam River. The Jews cleared the forest and established a flourishing community. They called their capital "Jerusalem-on-the-River" and gave biblical names to their plantations of sugar, coffee and cotton. They enjoyed full autonomy. In the picture — Isaac Aaron Levy's store in the Joden Savannah, from a drawing by Benoit, in 1839.

3 Isaac Orobio De Castro (1620-1687), of the Portuguese *Anusim*, who returned to Judaism, wrote polemics against Spinoza's philosophical thought. This is the title page of his book: *A Philosophical Argument in Defense of Divine and Natural Truth* (1684).

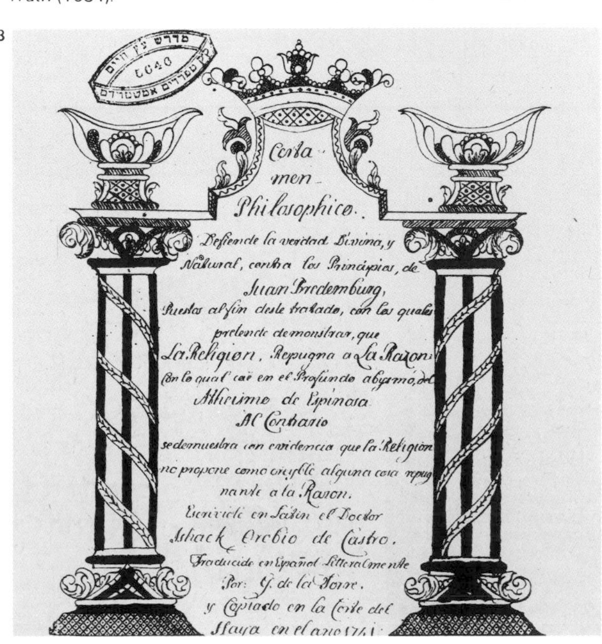

Certamen Philosophico.
Defiende la verdad Divina, y Natural, contra los Principios, de Juan Bredemburg, Puestos al fin deste tratado, con los quales pretende demonstrar, que La Religion, Repugna a La Razon: Con lo qual cae en el Profundo abysmo, del Atheismo de Espinosa
Al Contrario
se demuestra con evidencia que la Religion no propone como creyble alguna cosa repugnante a la Razon.
Escriviolo en Latin el Doctor Ishack Orobio de Castro.
Traducido en Español Litteralmente Por: G. de la Torre.
y Copiado en la Corte del Haya en el año 1741

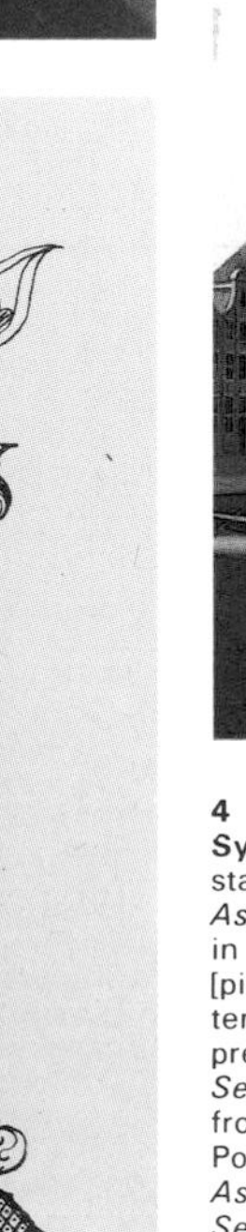

4 The "Portuguese Synagogue," which stands opposite the *Ashkenazi* Synagogue in Amsterdam [picture], actualizes the tense relationship that prevailed between the *Sephardim* — *Anusim* from Spain and Portugal — and the *Ashkenazim*. The *Sephardi* Jews arrived in Amsterdam in about 1600. As a result of the economic interests they shared with the Dutch traders, and thanks to the religious tolerance of the Dutch Protestants, they received many privileges which enabled them to return to their Jewish faith and establish a strong community, materially and spiritually. The *Ashkenazi* Jews — refugees from Polish riots and the Thirty Years War in Germany — came to Amsterdam in 1635. The great difference between them and the *Sephardi* community was evidenced in their economic pursuits and their cultural and social position, with the *Sephardim* generally more prosperous and more integrated intellectually. The *Sephardim* received the *Ashkenazim* with mixed feelings and were afraid lest their presence adversely affect *Sephardi* privileges.

tion to western Europe were forced to continue living under the guise of Catholicism. Such groups, known as "Portuguese," lived in France in cities like Bayonne and Bordeaux. Some *Anusim* who returned to Judaism lived in Italy, where the constant threat of exposure and detention hung over them. An unusual case is that of the Ancona *Marranos*, who were given the Pope's assurance that they would come to no harm. The promise was broken by his successor, and several of them died at the stake in 1555.

The most prominent of the *Sephardi* communities in West Europe was that in Protestant Amsterdam. From the beginning of the 17th century scores of *Anusim* arrived there every year, returning to Judaism after an estrangement that had lasted for generations [4]. This community produced an outstanding merchant stratum, whose international trade connections were aided by contacts maintained with relatives in settlements in South America, England and the Ottoman Empire [5]. A variety of books, which have survived to the present, bear witness to the community's extensive cultural activity [9, Key]. Local intellectual activity gained much from the *Marranos*' spiritual torment, also known as "Marranic Heresy." The world of rabbinical Judaism was foreign to them, and after having experienced Catholic religious coercion, the authority of Jewish religious institutions lay heavily on them [3]. For example, Uriel Da Costa (1585-1640), who rejected the Catholic faith despite his Jesuit education in Portugal, wrote a critique of Jewish Oral Law, which he considered to be in contradiction to the Bible. He was excommunicated and ended by taking his own life. Others daring to express rationalistic opinions which contained heresies were the physician Juan de Prado, and Baruch Spinoza [7]. Spinoza was the first Jew to leave Judaism without adopting another faith. His situation presaged the new era of secularity.

KEY

"Truth Springeth out of the Earth" — a figure grasping a wanderer's staff appears on the printer's banner of Manasseh Ben Israel. In 1626 Manasseh Ben Israel founded the first Hebrew printing house, in Amsterdam. In 1627, he published the first prayerbook printed in Hebrew. Thereafter, he published many treatises and books. The freedom of opinion and expression prevailing in Amsterdam attracted many intellectuals and scholars, such as Voltaire, Descartes and Locke. The Jews exploited this freedom by publishing a great many books — Bibles, religious laws and poetry — in Spanish, Portuguese, Hebrew and Yiddish.

5

5 Antonio (Isaac) Lopez Suasso, son of a Spanish banking family that established branches in Holland and England in the 17th and 18th centuries. A senior partner in the "Dutch West Indies Company," he was considered one of the wealthiest merchants in Holland.

6 Manasseh Ben Israel (1604-1657), son of a Spanish *Marrano* family, escaped to Amsterdam with his family when he was a child. In Holland he acquired a broad education in theology and secular subjects. He was regarded as one of the greatest Jewish scholars of his generation, and pioneered Hebrew printing. Ben Israel took an active part in the negotiations about allowing Jews to return to England, from which they had been expelled at the end of the 13th century. In 1655 he successfully petitioned Cromwell to allow Jews to settle in England, where *Anusim* had already been living for some 30 years. The petition emphasized the economic benefits which would come to the country, and argued that the Messiah would come only after the Jews reached all corners of the earth.

6

7

7 Baruch (Benedictus) Spinoza (1632-1677) was a Jewish philosopher, son of Portuguese *Anusim*, who escaped to Amsterdam. Spinoza cast doubt upon the religious principle of divine revelation, and criticized the Bible and tradition from a rationalist point of view. In many ways he pioneered modern secular philosophy. In 1656 he was excommunicated.

8 Rabbi Isaac Aboab Da Fonseca (1605-1693) of Portugal, arrived in Amsterdam via France, as a child, with his father. He received a Jewish education and, at the age of 21, was appointed *Hakham* of the Bet Israel synagogue. In 1641 he joined the Recife community, in Brazil — the first rabbi in America. With the Portuguese conquest he returned to Amsterdam and accepted the post of rabbi. Aboab was a member of the *Bet Din* (Court) which declared the excommunication of Spinoza in 1656. Like most members of the community, he supported Shabbetai Zevi.

8

9

9 "Divine Rule in the Harmony of the Universe" — a picture from the poem written by Daniel Levy (Miguel) Da Barios (1625-1701), one of the important poets of the Amsterdam community. He was born in Andalusia and served as a captain in the Spanish army. In 1659 he moved to Leghorn and openly returned to Judaism. Two years later he settled in Amsterdam.

16th Century Ereẓ Israel

The two centuries of Christian-Muslim struggle over Ereẓ Israel impoverished the Jews there. When the Mamelukes conquered the country in the 13th century they destroyed the coastal towns for security reasons. This severed the hinterland from international trade routes and an economic depression set in. Immigration of Jews from Europe and North Africa was too small to check the decline of the existing Jewish communities.

In 1516 the Ottomans conquered Ereẓ Israel, dividing the country into five districts. These were generally neglected by the Sublime Porte in Istanbul. In the 16th century, however, there was still a fairly efficient Ottoman government and the Jews, centered in Jerusalem [1], the Galilee area, Hebron and Gaza, enjoyed relative security, affluence [4] and an intellectual flowering. Unlike the Christians, they suffered no discrimination, some of them even filling government posts. The best known of these were Don Joseph Nasi (1524-1579), tax-farmer and advisor to the government, and Donna Gracia Nasi-Mendes (1510-1569) [3].

The Center in Safed

Imbued with the fervor of redemption, most of the new immigrants to the Holy Land settled in Safed [6, Key] which then had a thriving Jewish community estimated at about 15,000. Proximity to Damascus and Beirut enabled Safed's residents to trade with those cities in grains, cloth and small household wares, while the silk and wool fabrics they exported through Salonika port were renowned throughout Europe. Safed's Jews also engaged in peddling and agricultural trade with the surrounding villages. Illustrious halakhists, poets and Kabbalists gathered in Safed, transforming it into a center of teaching and learning that set the tone for all communities in Ereẓ Israel [7].

R. Jacob Berab, head of Safed's distinguished scholars, came to the town in 1524 and established a large *yeshiva*. He is associated with the attempt to renew ordination of rabbis in Ereẓ Israel (the practice had apparently been abolished in the middle of the 4th century). By reinstating ordination Berab hoped to bring about the formation of a rabbinical court of judgment authorized to mete out punishment and adjudicate controversies. He looked upon such a manifestation of independent political-organizational power as the beginning of redemption. He was opposed, however, by R. Levi ben-Habib, head of the Jerusalem rabbis, who feared that the issue might split the nation and anger the rulers. R. Berab had to flee, but before leaving for Syria he ordained four of his pupils and they in turn ordained a few pupils of their own.

Berab was replaced by one of his pupils, R. Joseph Caro (1488-1578), author of the *Shulhan Arukh*. This comprehensive compilation of laws and judgments is essentially an abstract of Caro's first book *Bet Yosef*, which discussed the *Arba'ah Turim* of R. Jacob

CONNECTIONS

74 Jews and Crusaders in Erez Israel
82 Eastern Jewry after the Expulsion from Spain
90 Messianism in Jewry
92 Shabbateanism
132 19th Century Erez Israel

1

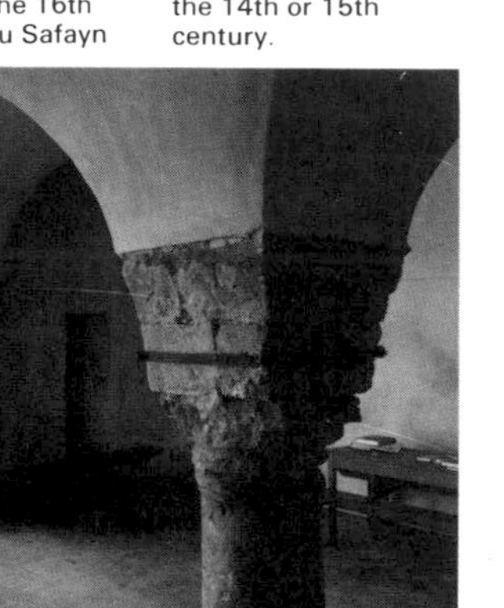

1 The Jewish community in Jerusalem, comprising *Musta'rabs*, Spanish exiles and immigrants from European countries, flourished culturally until the end of the 16th century — despite friction with the authorities over transit duties, the poll tax and the use of synagogues. Toward the end of the 16th century, Abu Safayn governed the city with a heavy hand and many Jews left. He even expropriated the Ramban Synagogue [pictured here], built in the 14th or 15th century.

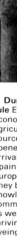

2

2 After the Mameluke conquest many Muslims from Persia, Iraq and Syria fled to Erez Israel in fear of the Mongols. Among them were ascetics and hermits from all the Islamic countries, some of whom came as pilgrims, others with the intention of settling in Jerusalem or in the Sidni Ali mosque, the Nabi Rubin mosque or the Nabi Musa hospice near Jericho [pictured here]. Ordinary pilgrims too visited this hospice built by Sultan Baybars (ruled 1260-1279). Muslims comprised the majority of Erez Israel's population, and the country took on a Muslim character. Christians and Jews were small minorities.

3

3 Donna Gracia Nasi-Mendes, daughter of *anusim* from Portugal, engaged in commerce and in smuggling of *anusim*. She was also known for her generosity and for the charitable projects she established. In 1558 she and her nephew, Don Joseph Nasi, received the Sultan's permission to lease Tiberias. They wanted to restore the city and turn it into a haven for exiles from Spain. In 1564 they surrounded the city with a wall and construction started, but although a small Jewish nucleus was formed, the resettlement plan failed. A few Jews settled there again in the 18th and 19th centuries, supported by *halukka* money.

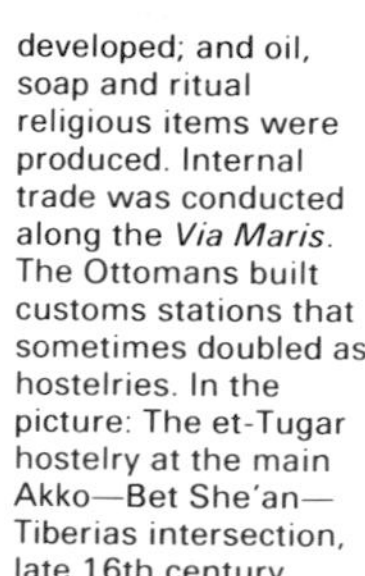

4 During Ottoman rule Erez Israel's economy was based on agriculture. Additional sources of livelihood opened up with the arrival of Jews from Spain and other European countries. They brought knowledge of commerce and crafts as well as capital; a thriving weaving and dyeing industry developed; and oil, soap and ritual religious items were produced. Internal trade was conducted along the *Via Maris*. The Ottomans built customs stations that sometimes doubled as hostelries. In the picture: The et-Tugar hostelry at the main Akko—Bet She'an—Tiberias intersection, late 16th century.

4

5

5 The Mamelukes engaged in construction projects in Erez Israel primarily for religious or security purposes. Although they destroyed the coastal cities to prevent invasion from the sea, they rehabilitated the interior of the country. To block possible Mongol invasion from the north and to facilitate supervision of Syria from Cairo — the seat of government — the Mamelukes developed a network of roads and bridges, border posts and strongholds. They also built many mosques, hospices, and inns for pilgrims; renovation of the Dome of the Rock was another important project. The lions adorning St. Stephen's Gate (Lion's Gate) in the wall of Jerusalem [pictured here] which Suleiman the Magnificent renovated (1538-9), were apparently taken from a structure that had been built by Baybars.

ben Asher. The *Shulhan Arukh* at first elicited sharp criticism in both the East and the West, but all of Israel eventually accepted it and R. Moses Isserles adapted it for European Jewry.

After the expulsion from Spain there was a burgeoning of mystic-Kabbalistic tendencies in Jewry. Kabbalists from all parts of the Diaspora gathered in Safed, near Meron, where, according to tradition, R. Shimon bar Yohai wrote the *Zohar*. Outstanding creators of Kabbalistic systems in Safed were R. Moses Cordovero (1522-1570) and R. Isaac Luria Ashkenazi (*ha-Ari ha-Kadosh*). In his book *Pardes Rimmonim* Cordovero systematized Kabbalistic thinking. There and in his commentary on the *Zohar, Or Yekarot*, he expanded on his innovative concept of the *Sefirot* (emanations) through which the divine world is revealed to the mundane world. Luria, who was in Safed for only some three years, was profoundly influential [9]. At the end of the 16th century his pupils Israel Sarug and Moses Jonah disseminated his theories in Italy, Poland and Turkey — although R. Hayyim Vital, his outstanding student, had reservations. From the center in Safed new prayers, rites and rituals spread to all Jewish communities.

Decline of Erez Israel's Jewry

Toward the close of the 16th century Safed and the Galilee waned and the Jews who remained in Erez Israel gathered in Jerusalem [8], Hebron and Gaza. The decline of Jewry in Erez Israel resulted from Ottoman socio-economic policies and the decentralization of tax collection (local tax collectors were interested in extorting the highest rates possible so that they could pocket large profits). Many villagers therefore abandoned the land to nomads; the agricultural needs of the cities were unfulfilled, trade declined and population in urban centers fell sharply. Most of the Jews were supported by the *halukka* — money contributed by Jews abroad for Jews in Erez Israel.

KEY

Moses Galante, one of Safed's outstanding 16th century scholars who was ordained by R. Joseph Caro, wrote a kabbalistic commentary on *Ecclesiastes*. The book was printed in Safed in 1578, and was one of six books produced by the Safed printshop. In 1577, when the town was thriving intellectually, Abraham ben Isaac Ashkenazi established the printing press; five of the books printed there were written by scholars belonging to the town's community of halakhists, poets and kabbalists. The first published was *Lekach Tov*, Yom Tov Zahalon's commentary on the *Book of Esther*. In 1587, when Safed's economy as a whole was suffering, the press was closed.

6

6 In the 16th century Safed became a thriving intellectual and economic center. As Muslims and Christians had no claim to the town, Jews preferred it to Jerusalem, and it had the largest Jewish community in Erez Israel. Jews were also attracted by the proximity of the grave of Shimon bar Yohai at Meron and the graves of other great *Tannaim*. Guide books were prepared at that time, showing the holy sites in Erez Israel [in the picture]. The town declined during the 17-18th centuries and many Jews left. They began to come back in the second half of the 18th century, but the earthquake of 1837 destroyed the Jewish quarter and many perished. Not until the second half of the 19th century did the Jewish community begin to expand again.

7

7 The Kabbalists of Safed, like those of Provence and Spain, exhibited philosophical, mystical and anthropomorphic tendencies, together with their esoteric studies. They were characterized by intense devotion and a profound mystical sense. Their spiritual and intellectual makeup and way of life, the moral regulations and special rituals they established — such as taking walks in the countryside and prostrating themselves on the graves of *Zadikkim* — exercised widespread influence. This is the *Ashkenazi* ha-Ari Synagogue, in Safed.

8

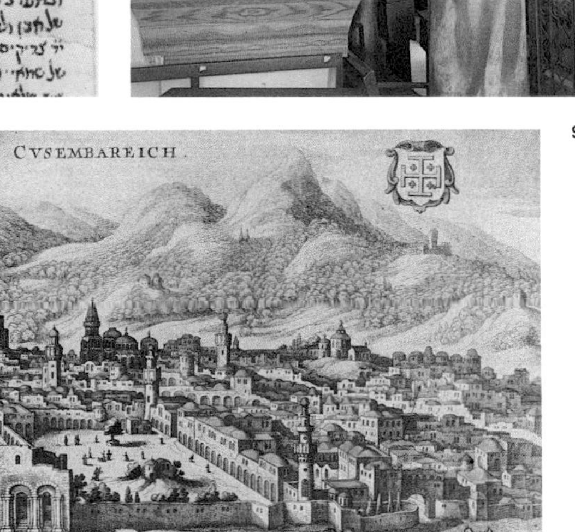

8 During the 17th century Jerusalem replaced Safed as an intellectual center. The Kabbalists there gathered at the schools of R. Isaac Gaon and R. Jacob Zemach, a *converso* and editor of the works of R. Hayyim Vital. In the middle of the century R. Jacob Hagiz (1620-1674) founded *Bet Yaakov*, an institution that became famous for its innovative organizational and educational methods. The city's sages opposed Shabbetai Zevi and instigated his banishment (1682). Led by R. Judah he-Hasid, hundreds came to Jerusalem from Europe in 1700. In the middle of the 18th century a group came from North Africa, led by Hayyim ben Attar. Despite these influxes of new *olim*, Jerusalem's Jewish community continued to suffer poverty. This copper engraving of Jerusalem is from Amsterdam, 1657.

9 Kabbalists who anteceded Ha-Ari

R. Joseph Caro

R. Solomon Halevi Alkabaz

R. Moses Cordovero

R. David ben Zimrah

R. Solomon Turiel

Ha-Ari

gurei ha-Ari

R. Joseph Arzin

R. Jonathan Sagis

R. Samuel ibn Tabul

R. Joseph di-Uzira

R. Hayyim Vital

9 Ha-Ari's Kabbalah was based on the philosophy of R. Moses Cordovero, but with his profound and far-reaching innovations, R. Luria (known as ha-Ari, meaning "the lion") created a new kabbalistic system. He stressed the role of the individual in repairing the divine breach (*tikkun* of the divine *shevira*). His teachings were recorded by his disciples, *gurei ha-ari* (the lion's cubs). To them he was the "Messiah, son of David." Ha-Ari's teachings roused messianic fervor and prepared the ground for the advent of Shabbetai Zevi.

Messianism in Jewry

Messianism, the vision of redemption and the reign of God, has engendered a rich and variegated literature. It deals with the time of the Messiah's arrival ("millenarial reckonings"), what he would be called, the miracles he would perform, and the "signs" foreshadowing his advent — Elijah the Prophet announcing the Messiah's arrival by blowing the ram's horn [Key], the ingathering of the exiles, the battle of Gog and Magog, Judgment Day [8], the resurrection of the dead [2], and the afterworld. Messianic hopes are first mentioned in the Bible and then recur in the *Talmud*, in the exegetical literature (*Midrashim*) and in mystic and later kabbalistic works. All these sources promise that the reign of God will be miraculously established and will bring about redemption of the Jews.

The first messianic movement arose in Ereẓ Israel during the Second Temple period when the people sought divine help to rid themselves of Rome's oppressive yoke. There were also messianic elements in the Great Revolt that ended in the year 70 with the destruction of the Temple and Jerusalem. Such elements were stronger in the revolt led by Bar Kokhba, who was described by Rabbi Akiva — to whom the messianic redemption and the national-earthly redemption were identical — as the "Messiah-king."

Messianic Movements in the East

In the 8th century a wave of messianism swept the eastern countries, largely because of oppression — which the Jews interpreted as "birth-pangs of Redemption." Isaac ben Jacob Abu'isa (known as Ovadiah) appeared in Isfahan, Persia and proclaimed himself the Messiah's prophet. A tailor turned writer, Abu'isa formed a popular sect, known as Isunis or Isfahanis, in Persia, Babylonia and Syria. He changed certain rituals, introduced seven daily prayers, prohibited divorce and forbade meat and wine. He mobilized an army and led it against the Muslims. He died in battle near Teheran, but his supporters believed he would be resurrected to continue prophesying.

During the 12th century David Alroy [3] headed a movement in Kurdistan that was quickly suppressed. He was killed in the mountains of Kurdistan on his way to "conquer Jerusalem." Moses Dar'i appeared in Fez, Morocco, in 1122 (or 1127). His adherents sold all their worldly possessions to follow the "Messiah" to Ereẓ Israel. "Messiahs" appeared in both Yemen and Persia during the 13th century.

During the Crusades and Inquisition

During the First Crusade (1096-1099) a leaderless messianic movement arose in Byzantium, heralded by appropriate signs and portents, and word spread that the Jews were to gather on their way to Ereẓ Israel. A "Messiah" with thousands of followers appeared in England in 1140. When the Mongols invaded the Ottoman Empire many believed them to be the ten lost tribes.

CONNECTIONS

50 The Great Revolt
54 The Bar Kokhba Revolt
70 Medieval European Attitudes to the Jews
78 The Expulsion of the Jews from Western Europe
88 16th Century Erez Israel
92 Shabbateanism

2 In his vision of redemption — the Vision of the Dry Bones — the Prophet Ezekiel describes such portents of salvation as the resurrection of the dead, the reunification of Israel and Judah, the battle of Gog and Magog, the redemption of the nation and the ensuing serenity and happiness. This illustration is a detail from a 3rd century fresco in the Dura Europos Synagogue on the Euphrates.

1 The Leviathan (from a late 13th century French manuscript), the *Behemoth* and a huge legendary bird are to take part in the redemption. The *Behemoth* will come from the land and the *Leviathan* from the sea, to sustain the survivors in Erez Israel. The meat of the *Leviathan* will be saved for the Just; its skin will be used to build a sanctuary.

3 Menahem ben-Solomon (Alroy) assumed the name David when he declared himself king of Israel and the Messiah-king. The miracles he claimed to have wrought brought him many followers in Syria and Persia. David Alroy made the *Magen David* the emblem of his movement; this helped transform it from a magical symbol to a national one. Here we see [A] an imprint of another seal with messianic manifestations (called the Seal of Solomon) from the 4th century BCE, found at Ramat Rachel; [B] *Magen David,* 4th century CE, from the synagogue at Eshtemoa.

4 The Mount of Olives has special significance in the vision of the "End of Days." Ezekiel prophesied that God would appear on the mountain east of Jerusalem and tradition has it that on the day of resurrection, the bodies of the Just from all countries of the dispersion will roll to the Mount of Olives. A recurring motif in the depiction of the Redemption is a low mountain with a single tree on its crest, as in this manuscript from Saragossa, Spain, 1404. This symbol reflects the prophecies of Zechariah where the figure of the Messiah-king is linked to a plant.

Messianic hopes intensified in France and Germany, reinforced by the fact that 1240 marked the end of the 5th millenium after the Creation.

The first messianic movement among Spanish Jews arose in about 1100. It was believed that Ibn Arieh from Andalusia, whom the community's leaders excommunicated, would appear as the Messiah. The kabbalist Abraham Abulafia (about 1240-1292), who instituted kabbalistic ecstasy, concluded that 1295 was the year of the Millennium. So convinced was he of his messianic mission that he traveled to Rome to convert the Pope to Judaism. The Pope ordered him burned at the stake — a fate he avoided by dying of other causes.

During the decade 1523-1532 David Reuveni [6] and Solomon Molcho [7] encouraged messianic hopes among the Jews of Italy, Portugal, Spain, Germany, Egypt and Ereẓ Israel. Announcing that he was minister of the army of the "Ten Tribes," Reuveni brought the Pope a plan for taking Jerusalem from the Ottomans. The Pope recommended that he be received by the King of Portugal. There, a young *converso* acting as the king's scribe decided to revert to Judaism, circumcised himself and assumed the name of Solomon Molcho. Molcho and Reuveni tried to convince the Emperor Charles V to support their plan, but he sentenced Molcho to death. Reuveni was arrested and apparently died in the Inquisition dungeons.

Some decades later, influenced by Isaac Luria (Ha-Ari) and Hayyim Vital, messianic hopes arose in Safed. Shabbetai Zevi's messianic movement during the 1660s — the largest and most completely documented — closes this period. Such movements continued to appear only in Yemen, where as late as 1861 a "Messiah" advocated penitence and tried to organize a Jewish regiment. The rulers had him executed. Seen in a positive light, the messianic movements may be said to have expressed Israel's deep longing for a renewal of independence in its own land.

KEY

The Messiah astride a donkey at the gates of Jerusalem (from an Italian *Hagaddah*, 1478). The scene illustrates the concept of individual redemption as expressed in the *Hagaddah*: "In every generation each individual is bound to regard himself as if he personally had gone forth from Egypt." As it tells the story of the deliverance from slavery in Egypt, the *Hagaddah* frequently alludes to hopes of redemption, thus giving expression to messianic ideas. From the 15th century on, the *Hagaddah* was often adorned with pictures of the Temple in Jerusalem and of the Messiah with his messenger, Elijah. Elijah was sometimes identified with the Messiah, which led to the custom of opening the door during the reading of the *Hagaddah*, in expectation of the prophet's arrival.

5 The Temple and Jerusalem have a special place in Jewish tradition in general, and in the messianic vision of the "End of Days" in particular. When the Millennium comes, Jerusalem will be rebuilt; it will stand forever as the spiritual center of the entire world, and knowledge, justice and peace will emanate from it. This view of the city of Jerusalem is from the *Hamburg Hagaddah* (Germany, 1768).

6 David Reuveni, whose origin and true identity are unknown, claimed to be the son of King Solomon and brother of Joseph, king of the tribe of Reuben that settled in the Khaybar desert in Arabia — whence his name, Reuveni. In a contradictory version of his origins, he claimed to be related to the House of David. Reuveni kept a journal in which he described apparently imaginary travels in the Orient and Erez Israel. He often held forth on the redemption of the Jews, and had his greatest success among the *anusim* in Portugal.
The map shows Reuveni's reputed travels in the East; these have never been confirmed by other sources. The sites in Europe indicated on the map are places where Reuveni's travels have actually been substantiated by documentary evidence.

6

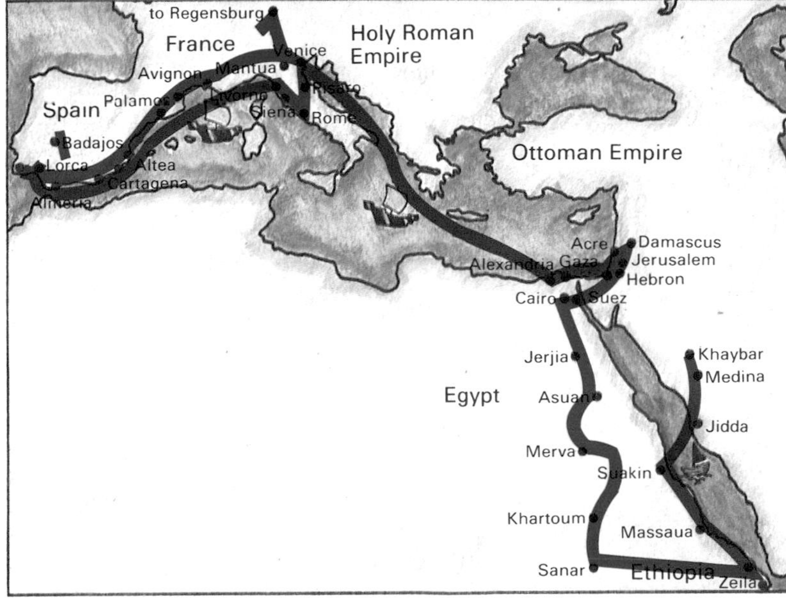

5

7 All his life Solomon Molcho (1500/1-1532) was obsessed by the need to cleanse himself of his Christian past. After studying *Kabbalah* in Salonika and meeting Joseph Caro, he presented himself in Rome as the Messiah. He predicted a flood in Rome and an earthquake in Portugal. When his predictions came true and Pope Clement VII granted him a writ of freedom (1530), belief in him grew, but more and more Jews also came to fear that he would undermine their position. Illustration: Molcho's signature.

8 On "Judgment Day" revenge would be taken on the gentiles who harassed the Jewish people. Then the redeemed Jews would gather from all corners of the world and settle in Erez Israel. The picture "Pour out thy wrath" is from the *Mantua Hagaddah*, 1568.

8

Shabbateanism

Shabbateanism, a messianic movement that started in Ereẓ Israel in 1665-66, eventually spread to most of the lands of the Diaspora. The Shabbateans incorporated messianism — with its supernatural signs and portents — into kabbalistic mysticism. Rites and rituals, fasts and mortification would all help "repair" flaws incurred during the Creation and would hasten the advent of the Messiah. The growth of the movement was related to social and political events such as the Chmielnicki massacres in Poland (1648-9), emigration from the Iberian peninsula of *anusim* who openly reverted to Judaism and sought penance for their past, and oppression of Jews in Morocco and Yemen.

Shabbateanism Spreads

Shabbetai Zevi was born in Izmir (Smyrna) on the 9th of Av, 1626. In his youth he studied *Kabbalah* and immersed himself in asceticism and rituals. He did not hesitate to pronounce the ineffable name of God (a practice forbidden to the religious Jew) and claimed that he himself was the Messiah. The Rabbis of Izmir banished him and for several years (1651-4) he wandered around the Jewish communities of the Balkans. In 1662 he arrived in Jerusalem where he lived for about a year, frequently visiting the holy places. Then he left to collect money for Jerusalem's Jews in Egypt, where he married Sarah, a refugee from the Chmielnicki massacres. On his way back to Jerusalem he stopped in Gaza to seek spiritual succor with R. Nathan, a young kabbalist "soul healer." In an ecstatic trance Nathan saw Shabbetai Zevi as the Messiah. He announced this publicly on the 17th of Sivan (31 May) 1665, launching the Shabbatean movement.

The messianic message began to spread from Ereẓ Israel to the dispersion, primarily through the letters of Nathan of Gaza [4], which wakened messianic hopes: people fasted, donated money and began to prepare for the redemption and for the return to Ereẓ Israel. The euphoria was accompanied by stories of signs and miracles and rumors about the appearance of the ten lost tribes in Africa, Mecca, or near Gaza. Declaring that the Redemption had begun, Shabbetai Zevi abolished the fasts commemorating the Destruction of the Temple [7]; traveling from place to place, he declared himself "your God Shabbetai Zevi" or "the Messiah of the God of Jacob." Some time in 1665 he returned to rouse the Jewry of Izmir [2]. On his way to Constantinople he was arrested and sent to the fortress of Gallipoli. His behavior during detention increased his prestige among the faithful, who called his prison *Migdal Oz* (Tower of Strength).

Those who believed in Shabbetai Zevi came from all circles and classes, from the leaders to the masses, and from all the dispersions of the East and the West — from Yemen to North Africa, from Poland and Russia to England. His great popularity evidently frightened the Turkish authorities, and in Sep-

CONNECTIONS

88 16th Century Erez Israel

90 Messianism in Jewry

1 "Shabbetai Zevi, the False Messiah," is the inscription on an 18th century copper engraving from Germany in which the "Messiah" is seen wearing a Muslim turban. His apostasy astounded his followers, and disillusioned most of them. A minority, nevertheless, sought a theological justification for his conversion.

2 Shabbetai Zevi returned to Izmir in 1665, after being banished from Jerusalem. At first he lived an extremely ascetic life, but he soon began to show a predilection for "strange and paradoxical actions" that conflicted with *Halakhah*. The rabbis of Izmir hesitated to interfere in view of the mass support he enjoyed. He assumed the title *Amirah* — an acronym for the Hebrew words "Our Lord and King, may his Majesty be exalted," introduced a prayer for his own health and abolished the fast of the 10th of Tevet. Here he is seen in Izmir, in an engraving from "Two Trips to Jerusalem" (London, 1685).

3 Jacob Sasportas (1610-1698), a halakhist from Amsterdam, strongly opposed Shabbetai Zevi. His book *Zizat Novel Zevi* (1673) discusses the history of the Shabbatean movement. He maintains that Shabbateanism conflicts with the Messianic concepts of traditional rabbinical Judaism and contains elements close to Christianity.

4 Nathan of Gaza (1643/4-1680), Shabbetai Zevi's prophet and standardbearer, was the ideologue, moving force and popularizer of the Shabbatean movement. After declaring Shabbetai Zevi the Messiah, Nathan urged the masses to perform penitential acts, and inundated Jewish communities with letters announcing the advent of the Messiah and telling of the miracles he performed. Nathan made innovative additions to the Lurianic *Kabbalah*, thus creating the Shabbatean *Kabbalah*. He introduced new prayers and established new laws and rituals. Even after Shabbetai Zevi's apostasy, the prophet clung to his Messiah, trying to justify his actions with mystical explanations which he elucidated in his "Book of the Creation" (1670) and *Zemir Aritzim*.

tember 1666 Shabbetai Zevi was tried by the royal council in Adrianopolis and given a choice of death or apostasy. He chose to convert to Islam [1]. Those of his followers who condoned this act maintained that temporarily the Messiah must bury himself in the heart of the infidel — as did Moses in Pharaoh's court — in order to save the "spark" of sanctity.

Shabbetai Zevi remained in Adrianopolis for six years, practicing Judaic and Islamic rituals and periodically calling upon his followers to accept Islam. In August 1672 he was again arrested, this time accused of betraying Islam and of lawlessness. He was sentenced to exile and detained in the Dulcigno fortress (now in Albania).

In his final years Shabbetai Zevi promulgated his version of the "Mystery of the True Faith" that had a profound influence on the continuation of Shabbateanism. On Yom Kippur of 1676 Shabbetai Zevi, the apostate Messiah, died.

Offshoots of Shabbateanism

After Shabbetai Zevi's death some Jews, primarily in Salonika and Italy, awaited his reappearance. While most of his followers remained Jews, the more extreme among them were convinced that his advent had abolished the old Judaism, and considered violation of its commandments commendable. After his conversion to Islam the rabbis forbade all discussion of Shabbetai Zevi's ideas and in 1725 they denounced him openly, banning his movement and asking that secret Shabbateans be reported [5].

Shabbateanism was a crossroads, so to speak, in Jewish history. It brought about renewal of *aliyah* to Erez Israel by groups like that of Judah he-Hasid that came in 1700; it generated separatist sects such as the *Dönme* — a sect in Salonika whose members appeared to accept Islam. Another offshoot of Shabbateanism was the Frankist movement, whose members eventually converted to Christianity [8].

KEY

Regal splendor was part of Shabbetai Zevi's attraction [here, in an engraving from Germany, 1666]. His handsome appearance, impressive voice and many-faceted nature held a magnetic appeal for the masses.

5 Jacob Emden (1697-1776) of Altona, Germany, an outstanding rabbi, bitterly opposed Shabbateanism and its offshoots. His most famous disputation was with Jonathan Eybeshutz (1690/5-1765), well known kabbalist and scholar, whom Emden suspected was a secret Shabbatean. The dispute split the *Ashkenazi* Jewish public into two camps. Suspicions concerning Eybeshutz increased when Shabbatean elements were discerned among his students and his son Wolf appeared as a Shabbatean prophet. The caricature depicts a Christian-Jewish Frankist from Emden's book: *Sefer Shimush* (Book of Use) (1758-62).

5

6

6 A letter sent by Nathan of Gaza to Aram-Tzova (Aleppo) indicates the size and power of the Shabbatean movement as well as its adherents' fears of the established religious authorities. The letter contains an announcement of the abolishment of the Fast of the 9th of Av and explains the reason therefore. It is from a collection copied in Hebron in the 17th century by supporters of Shabbateanism.

7

אנאיי אלהינו הצמיח

תקון

קריאה לכל לילה ויום

וישב אל יי וירחמהו

לראות עזו וכבודו

בבית ובמצות דוד

פה

אמשטרדם

7 Title page of Tikkun — readings for each night and day — a Shabbatean prayerbook printed in Amsterdam in 1666. According to the Shabbateans the mysterious changes that occurred in the entire Creation with the advent of the Messiah necessitated changes in customs, rites and rituals. Thus Shabbetai Zevi transformed fast days into festivals.

8 Shabbateanism's final metamorphosis was Jacob Frank (1726-1791) and his movement. Persecuted by the Rabbinate, the Frank movement finally found a haven in Christianity. Its members became part of the Polish and Austrian nobility, high officialdom and the military; many Frankists became Freemasons, combining mystic, Kabbalistic and revolutionary ideas with the concepts of Enlightenment. One of their number, Ephraim Joseph Hirschfeld, pictured here, was a member of the "Asian Brethren" — a new sort of Masonic order that adopted both Jewish-Kabbalistic and Christian elements. Another member of this order was Moses Dobroschka, who was known, after converting to Christianity in 1775, as Franz Thomas von Scheinfeld. He was executed in France in 1794 as a Jacobin.

8

9

9 "Our Lord, Shabbetai Zevi," written in the Hebrew acronym, in the center of a charm from 17th-18th century Europe. The charm is adorned with passages from the Bible. The passages and their sequence allude to Shabbetai Zevi as the Messiah.

The Community as the Framework for Jewish Life

The term community (*kehillah*) is generally used to designate an organized Jewish populace that lived in a town or city, within or alongside the local authority.

The roots of the organized Jewish community in the Middle Ages go back to the Jewish settlement in the Holy Land, especially at the time of the Second Temple. Paradoxically, the community flourished particularly in the Diaspora of the Middle Ages, when the authorities granted the Jews autonomy in a number of spheres [Key].

Functions and Institutions

The range and scope of the community's activities varied according to place and time. They changed in response to alterations in the Jews' legal status and in the conditions under which they lived. We can, however, speak of three major functions which the Jewish community in the Middle Ages undertook to fulfil:

a. Attending to religious needs. To this end the community established several types of institutions: synagogues, cemeteries, ritual baths and courts. The Jewish court (*Bet Din*) ruled in matters of personal status as well as in civil and criminal cases, following the *Halakhah* [1]. The preferred sentence was a fine, but in several places the condemned were also sentenced to whipping or imprisonment. The communities of Spain at times passed sentence of death on Jews convicted of informing. The primary and most common means by which the court could enforce its orders was excommunication.

b. Aiding the needy. Here the main institutions were the charity fund (*kupa*) and soup kitchen (*tamhui*) [5], and, in large communities, a charity hostel and hospital. The money for these institutions came largely from contributions, from estates willed to charity, and from a special community assessment levied in many places.

c. Defense and security of life and property. The main activity in this regard was the collection of a tax transferred to the authorities. The community leaders negotiated with the authorities as to the total sum, and then collected it from community members in proportion to their means. In many cities, particularly in Germany, the Jews were also required to help defend the city against its enemies.

Where Jews lived in closed quarters (*ghetto* in Western Europe; *mellah* in Islamic countries), the community was assigned additional tasks of a purely municipal nature, such as responsibility for sanitary facilities, inspection of housing, posting of guards at the gate, and so on.

Organization

The executive functions and ongoing administration of the community were handled by a small committee whose members were known as the heads, elders, or aldermen of the city. A legislative body was responsible for setting bylaws and taking major decisions, including the election of the heads of the

CONNECTIONS

72 Ashkenaz in the 10th-13th Centuries
80 The Jewish Community of Poland up to the 18th Century
82 Eastern Jewry after the Expulsion from Spain
112 Jewish Community and Culture in Muslim Lands

1 The activities of the Jewish court illustrate the autonomy of the community. The community forbade its members to sue litigants before non-Jewish courts. The court was usually composed of three judges with the local rabbi serving as president, although variations included courts presided over by only the rabbi, and larger courts with seven or more members. The post of judge was not only filled by learned scholars; some courts were composed of laymen led by the heads of the community. Courts could excommunicate a member of the community and confiscate his property to enforce their edicts. In addition to these permanent courts, there were also special tribunals in which each of the two sides chose one arbitrator and these then selected a third. The court depicted here is from *Four Columns* by Jacob Ben Asher, of 15th century Mantova.

2 The Jewish family played a crucial role in educating youngsters and readying them to take their places in traditional Jewish society. Even before a child began his formal studies in a *heder* and later a *yeshiva*, his family had already instilled in him religious and moral values and practices in the home. Close family ties and devotion promoted this process. Children learned discipline and made an early acquaintance with authority and rank within the patriarchal family, whose structure paralleled the hierarchy of the community. This illustration from a 15th century Hebrew manuscript of *The Ancient's Proverb* shows a child taking his first steps with the help of his mother and grandfather.

3 The ritual slaughterer, like the rabbi and cantor, was one of the "holy vessels" of the community. Anyone well-versed in the laws could fulfil this function. He was usually certified by the local rabbi. In small communities, the ritual slaughterer was also the cantor and teacher. He was often charged with inspecting the meat to ensure that it was fit to eat; hence his nickname "slaughterer-examiner." This illumination from a 15th century Jewish manuscript from Mantova depicts a slaughterhouse.

community. In smaller communities, this role was played by a general assembly of all heads of households; in larger communities, a select council with several dozen members was set up. The community council adopted most of its decisions by a majority vote, but graver issues often required unanimity.

In addition to its functions as arbiter of disputes between members of the community, the local court also sat in judgment in cases involving the community as a whole. The president of the court (*Av Bet ha-Din*) was usually a rabbi. Some functionaries, such as the rabbi, cantor and beadle of the synagogue, received a salary. Large communities also employed a lobbyist (*Shtadlan*) to negotiate with the authorities the rescinding of restrictive edicts or the awarding of benefits and privileges.

Several important functions in the community were carried out by voluntary associations, known as societies (*Havarot*). These were not part of the formal administration of the community. Societies devoted to Jewish education assured that the children of the poor received schooling, while charitable societies aided the needy. The oldest and most vital of these was the burial society (*Hevra Kaddisha*), whose members worked voluntarily performing the commandment of last rites.

Central Bodies

Several large Jewish populations maintained central bodies which oversaw the activities of the individual communities. In Babylon this function was carried out by the Exilarchs and *Geonim*, in Egypt and other Muslim countries by the *Nagidim*, and in Poland and Lithuania by land, or national committees. It was difficult to maintain bodies of this sort in the decentralized feudal states of Germany, France and Italy, but even here representatives of several communities met periodically to consider problems common to the communities in the region.

KEY

Visiting the Sick
Community Leaders and *Gabbaim*
Religious Court
Charity
Yeshiva
Burial Society
Heder
Synagogue
Hospitality
Ritual Bath
Ritual Slaughterer
Soup Kitchen
Charity Hospital

The structure of the Jewish community in the Middle Ages can be seen in this schematic drawing based on *Ashkenazi* communities in the 13th and 14th century. The diagram highlights the importance of the synagogue as the center of Jewish spiritual and social life. Community institutions were established in accordance with Jewish principles. Religious Court — for the law and for compromise; Ritual Bath — for cleanliness and sanctification; Synagogue — for prayer; *Yeshiva* — "The *Torah* can only be studied in company;" *Heder* — for babes; Charity Hospital — for the aged; Soup Kitchen — "bread for the poor;" Hospitality — "Welcoming guests is greater than welcoming the Divine Presence;" Visiting the Sick — "takes away part of his sorrow;" Burial Society — "dust to dust;" Charity — "greater than all sacrificial offerings."

4

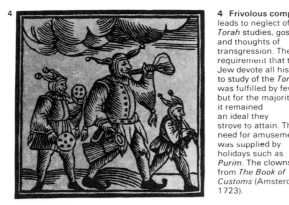

4 Frivolous company leads to neglect of *Torah* studies, gossip and thoughts of transgression. The requirement that the Jew devote all his time to study of the *Torah* was fulfilled by few, but for the majority, it remained an ideal they strove to attain. The need for amusement was supplied by holidays such as *Purim*. The clowns are from *The Book of Customs* (Amsterdam, 1723).

6 Visiting the sick and administering last rites are two of the major commandments observed at the community level. Visiting the sick [A] included aiding him materially and spiritually. Larger communities set up charity hospitals to care for the poor and elderly transients. The preparation of corpses and their interment [B] was carried out by a voluntary burial society known as *Hevra Kaddisha*. It was considered a great honor to be among its members, even though it was not a part of the formal administration of the community. These services were funded through charity contributions and a special tax.

6 A

6 B

5

5 Charity and alms were distributed by the community through the voluntary associations, the "societies" which provided a variety of services. Two major institutions were the charity fund and the soup kitchen. The fund afforded financial assistance to the needy and the kitchen supplied food and meals both to the poor of the community and to indigent transients. In addition to regular collections, the community held seasonal fund-raising campaigns, such as the "*Purim* fund" which collected donations throughout the month of Adar to purchase the traditional *Purim* gifts for the needy. The charitable societies also used their monies to meet the special needs of the poor, such as providing weddings for their daughters or heating for *Torah* scholars. This illumination from the *Golden Haggada* (early 14th century Spain) shows a wealthy Jew distributing food to the poor.

The Insular Community and Jewish Art

Medieval Jewish art took its subjects from religion, and from the holiday and family rituals associated with it. Its artists plied their trade building and decorating synagogues, producing ritual objects and illuminating Hebrew books for religious ceremonies.

Despite the apparent insularity of Jewish society in the Middle Ages, its art attests to the influence of aesthetic forms popular in the non-Jewish community. Even so, the topics and motifs borrowed from local art were subjected to a culling process whose criterion was their suitability to Judaism and Jewish thought. Medieval Jewish art did not develop a unique style; rather it served to satisfy man's natural need to express his emotions and faith.

Synagogue Design

The central function of the synagogue in the Jewish community was reflected in the site, size and structure of the building. It was generally built in the heart of a crowded Jewish quarter. Its size was limited on the basis of restrictions imposed by the church or local government. The design of the structure was considerably influenced by the style popular in the region: in *Ashkenaz*, Romanesque or Gothic arches and ceilings; in Spain, Moorish arches and ornamentation which shows the influence of Spanish Islamic art [3]. Nevertheless, small and narrow Jewish prayer halls, as in the modest synagogues of Worms, Regensburg and Prague, could not be mistaken for the large halls of Christian churches [Key].

The lectern, the focal point of the religious and social activities of the community, evolved throughout the 13th to 15th centuries and reached a pinnacle of artistic balance and beauty in the prayer halls of Eastern European synagogues in the 16th and 17th centuries. These contained a central space in which four pillars stood, the lectern rising between them. These structures displayed an impressive aesthetic balance between the major elements of the hall, the lectern, and the Ark of the Law, all of which were profusely ornamented.

Synagogues of a very special design were erected in the small towns of Eastern Europe. They were built of wood with sloping roofs, requiring highly sophisticated building techniques and were adorned with decorative woodcarvings [4]. The walls and ceilings were often graced with colorful paintings.

In Spain, as in the countries of *Ashkenaz*, the synagogues were not large. The lectern was placed near the entrance — as in the Portuguese Synagogue built in Amsterdam in the 17th century [2]. In Italian synagogues of the 16th and 17th centuries, most of which were of modest proportions, the Ark of the Law and the lectern were situated opposite each other on the eastern and western walls, with the congregation seated along the northern and southern walls and rituals celebrated in the center.

In Islamic countries as well, synagogues reflected the influence of local architecture. Thus, in the synagogue of

CONNECTIONS

94 The Community as the Framework for Jewish Life

102 Jewish Art and the Emancipation

1 This headstone, showing the friendship of David and Jonathan, is from a Jewish cemetery in the town of Ouderkerk near Amsterdam. The cemetery served the "new Jews" from the first days of their settlement in the area. One of the plots contains costly marble headstones attesting to a unique convergence of cultures that took place when the *Anusim* discarded Catholicism and resumed their Judaism. The motifs and style are characteristic of the Catholic tradition and are both alien to the spirit of Judaism and unlike that of the Dutch Protestant.

2 The Portuguese Synagogue of Amsterdam was built between 1671 and 1675 by a community whose origins were in Portugal. Protestant Holland welcomed the Spanish and Portuguese *Anusim*, offering them freedom of religion. Once established in Holland, these forced converts resumed their Jewish faith and in the 17th century theirs was the largest and richest Jewish community in Western Europe. Their prosperity enabled them to commission a noted architect to design their lavish synagogue in the style of the Protestant churches of Holland. The synagogue served as an object of imitation for many Jewish communities throughout the world, particularly *Sephardi* communities, and its influence reached as far as Curaçao in the Caribbean. This picture, from an engraving by Picart, depicts the grand dedication ceremony of the building.

3 The Synagogue of Toledo, part of whose interior wall can be seen here, was built in 1356 by Samuel Halevy Abulafia, who served as treasurer in the court of King Pedro I of Spain. After the expulsion of the Jews from Spain, the Catholics turned the synagogue into a church they called El Tránsito. The synagogue was built in the Mudejar style which combines Muslim Moorish elements with the Christian Gothic style. Its external walls were adorned with delicate stucco work.

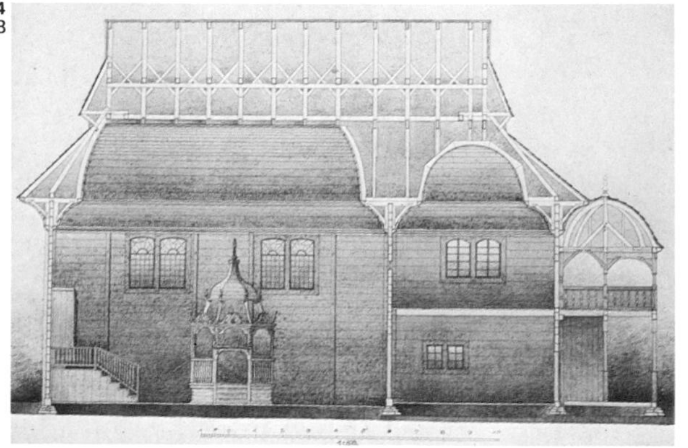

4 Many wooden synagogues were built in the towns of Eastern Europe in the 17th and 18th centuries. Most are characterized by a unique architectural design that exploits the properties of wood, the most plentiful building material in Poland. The interior was adorned with woodcarvings, with floral and faunal motifs carved on the lectern and the Ark of the Law.
[A] the synagogue of Zabludow.
[B] a drawing of the Zydaczow synagogue.

Aleppo, Syria, prayers were conducted in the inner courtyard in whose center stood the lectern.

The Illumination of Hebrew Books

The craft of producing books was viewed with awe and a sense of sanctity by Jewish society. A great deal of effort was invested in the faultless production of the square Hebrew letters. The *Sephardi* style of letter was formed with a stylus, highlighting its stability, grace and stateliness; the *Ashkenazi* letter was formed with a quill because of its greater flexibility.

Illuminated manuscripts from the 9th and 10th centuries have been found in the *Cairo Genizah*. Most of the surviving manuscripts, however, are from the 13th to 15th centuries. The Passover *Haggada* [6, 7] used by the entire family seems to have been awarded the greatest share of paintings and illuminations, but Bibles [5], prayer books, books of commentary, and in Italy even non-religious books such as medical volumes, were not ignored. The subjects of the illuminations were generally borrowed from biblical tales; but a contemporary element is also reflected in the depiction of the life of the figures or in their dress, in the structures, and, at times, even in symbolic or allegorical devices relating to current events.

In Spain the illumination of Hebrew manuscripts was influenced by Islamic and Christian traditions. Some show a fondness for abstract designs. The placing of illuminations on separate pages rather than alongside the written words is also typical of Spain [7]. *Ashkenazi* illuminators often worked in the margins of the written pages.

Many Jews in Islamic countries, particularly Yemen and the countries of North Africa, were skilled in ornate metalworking. This expertise may have influenced the style of illustration in Hebrew books in these countries, which comprised primarily geometric and floral motifs. Micrographic illustration was also widespread.

KEY

The synagogue of Regensburg appears in a copper engraving from the 16th century by the artist Albrecht Altdorfer. The long hall of the synagogue is divided by three pillars which support arches whose shape shows the early influence of the Gothic style. Note the size of the lectern and its central position in the hall. The Jews of Regensburg built the edifice in the 13th century and its elongated shape is characteristic of many synagogues built in Europe during the Middle Ages. The synagogue was destroyed after the expulsion of the Jews from the city. The inscription in the engraving reads: "The Jewish Synagogue in Regensburg, uprooted by God's justice in the year of the Lord 1519."

5

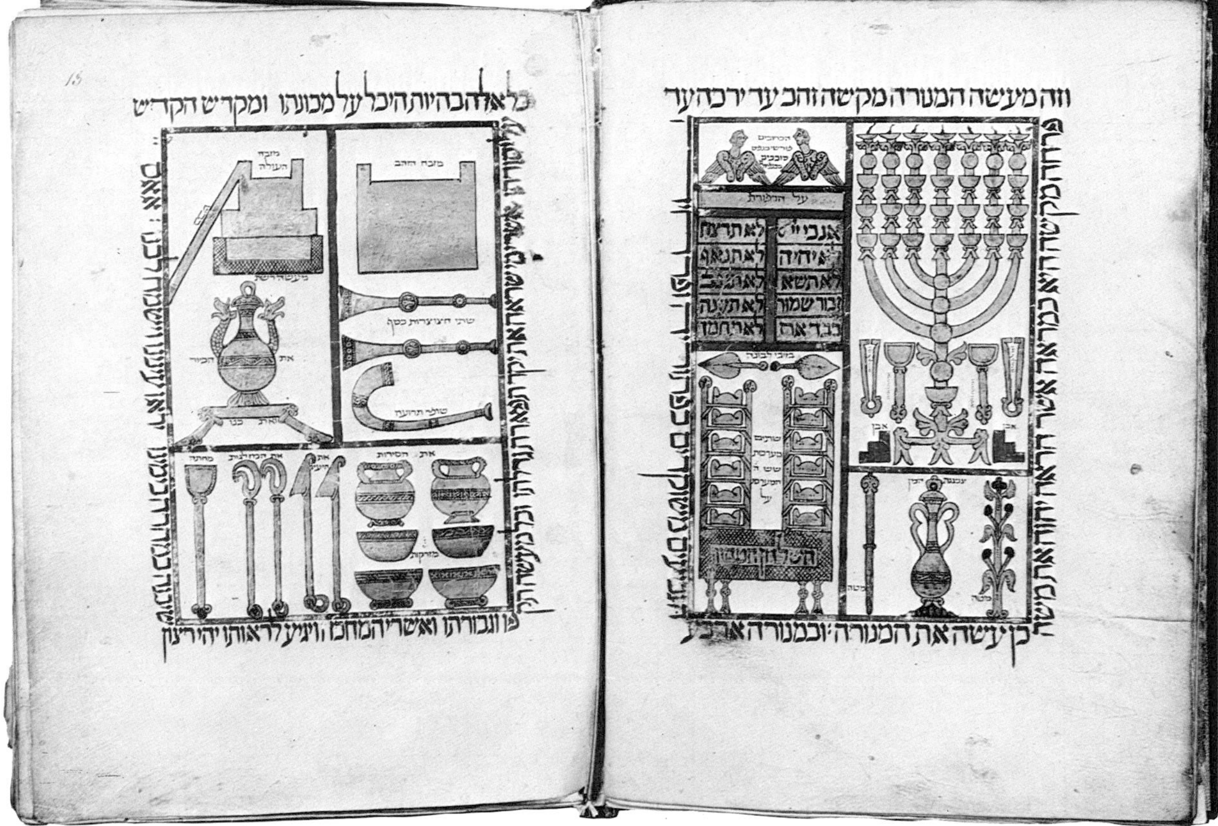

5 The Perpignan Bible was completed in the 13th century by the scribe Solomon Bar Raphael in the town of Perpignan in Provence (southern France near the Spanish border). A Jewish community prospered in this town in the 13th century and its golden days are reflected in Jewish manuscripts illuminated in a unique style that bears both *Ashkenazi* and *Sephardi* influence. These two pages from the Bible, written in Hebrew and illuminated in gold, are an example. In this, as in several other Jewish manuscripts from Provence, the ritual objects of the Temple are depicted. They are painted in detail, and the name of each object appears beside it in clear Hebrew script. The pages are framed by verses from the Bible. On the right-hand page the verses describe the seven-branched candelabra, on the left-hand page the anticipation of redemption and hope for the reconstruction of the Temple in Jerusalem is expressed.

6

6 The Prague Haggada from 1526 was one of the first printed, and became the prototype for many other illuminated *haggadoth*. The letters are formed with a flexibility and balance typical of the Hebrew letter printed in the *Ashkenazi* style. The margins of the text are adorned with figures and the first three pages of the *Haggada* are decorated with ornamental borders. All illustrations were done by woodcut and printing techniques.

7

7 The Sarajevo Haggada, discovered in the home of a Jewish family in the Yugoslav city of Sarajevo, was written and illuminated in Spain in the 14th century. The manuscript has the form typical of medieval Spanish Passover *haggadoth*: it is divided into pages of text written in imaginatively ornamented letters, and pages of biblical illuminations. This picture shows Jacob's ladder.

How to Merit the Status of Citizen

In the debates that raged in the late 18th — early 19th century concerning the granting of equal rights to Jews and their integration into European society, many argued that the Jews first had to be "reformed" and "made useful," while others saw "improvement" as a consequence of equality. The assumption that the Jews had to be improved was itself hardly questioned at all. In several countries measures were even taken to impose the anticipated "improvement," such as the Edict of Toleration decreed by Emperor Joseph II in the Hapsburg Empire (1781), Napoleon Bonaparte's "Infamous Decree" (1808), and the Law Concerning Jewish Education enacted by King William I in The Netherlands (1817).

The Jewish Enlightenment Movement

The Gentile view of the Jews influenced even the Jews themselves, particularly the enlightened intellectuals (*maskilim*) among them. They had been stimulated by the richness of European culture and ideas and looked upon their own Jewish world as inferior and inadequate. Hence they, too, adopted the concept of "reform." The call for self-improvement became part of the ideology of the Jewish emancipation movement, which came into being in the early 1760s [2].

The first "enlightened" school opened in Berlin in 1778. Within sixty years a virtual revolution took place in the Jewish educational system of Germany and other western European countries. Religious studies were considerably reduced while secular studies, including the spoken and written language of the country [4], were expanded.

Christian society accused the Jews of restricting themselves to such unproductive professions as peddling [1] and moneylending; the negative attributes associated by Christians with these professions — e.g., greed and dishonesty — were considered typical of Jews themselves. Some enlightened Jewish intellectuals called upon Jews — particularly the large population of poor Jews — to move to productive professions like the skilled trades and agriculture. The range of occupations held by Jews did indeed expand during the 19th century — though due less to emancipation than to the extensive economic development sweeping Europe as a whole. By the 19th century, too, most Jews had adopted the surrounding majority's style of dress [6].

The enlightened intellectuals were also vehemently opposed to the Yiddish language — the *lingua franca* of Jews that set them off from their Gentile neighbors. Through the schools they set up and the articles they published, the intellectuals encouraged Jews to learn the national tongue as well as biblical Hebrew, a language highly rated by Christians as well. By the middle of the 19th century, Yiddish was no longer the colloquial language of Jews in central and western Europe.

"The Entry Ticket to European Society"

The greatest difficulty arose concerning Judaism itself — an ethnically national

CONNECTIONS

100 "Liberté, Egalité, Fraternité" for Jews as well

132 19th century Erez Israel

1

1 The Jewish Peddler was viewed by enlightened Jews as a figure requiring reform and improvement. In 1781 the German historian C.W. Dohm (1751-1820) published his essay "Upon the Civil Amelioration of the Condition of the Jews" in which he called for granting them equal status. Dohm claimed that the Jews' evil nature was rooted in the oppressive laws they lived under and not in the Jewish faith itself. Their situation could be put right and the Jews turned into grateful and loyal citizens, by abolishing these laws and encouraging Jews to adopt the general culture.

2

2 Moses Mendelssohn (1729-1786), a philosopher and leader of the Jewish emancipation movement, won first prize for an essay on a metaphysical subject. In the same competition, Immanuel Kant received only an honorable mention. Following a debate with Lavater, a Lutheran minister, concerning the status of the Jewish people, Mendelssohn dedicated himself to the emancipation and enlightenment of the Jews. In this painting by M.D. Oppenheim, Mendelssohn is seen playing chess with Lavater while the German playwright, Lessing, looks on.

4

Die

Psalmen.

Uebersetzt

von

Moses Mendelssohn.

Mit allergnädigsten Freyheiten.

Berlin,

bey Friedrich Maurer, 1783.

4 Frontispiece of the Book of Psalms translated into German by Mendelssohn. In 1783 he also finished his German translation of the *Torah*, with an enlightened Hebrew "commentary." Mendelssohn hoped the translations would teach Jews the German language, improve their knowledge of Hebrew and impart the basic values of the enlightenment movement. He also helped set up the first Jewish school in Berlin.

3

3 The "Salon" of Henrietta Herz. Henrietta, daughter of a Jewish family from Portugal, married Marcus Herz, the physician and philosopher, and held a regular cultural "salon" in Berlin. It was through these "salons," organized by many such wealthy Jewish ladies in Germany, that the enlightened Jewish intellectuals tried to change the image of Jews. A general secular education, acting as a common basis for Jews and non-Jews, was meant to ease the integration of Jews into Gentile society.

religion whose rituals differentiate the Jew from his non-Jewish environment. The issue for the enlightened intellectuals was: how can one be a Jew as well as a regular citizen of a European nation state? A few despaired of ever finding a solution to this problem and converted to Christianity — thereby gaining what Heinrich Heine called an "entry ticket into European society" [Key]. Many others did indeed move away from a traditional Jewish way of life, hoping to integrate into the general society, but they were not willing to give up their Jewish identity entirely. "All this naturally led us," wrote David Friedländer, an enlightened Jew, in 1799, "to closely examine Mosaic Law, its spirit and aims, and to adapt it to our times, our customs, our climate and contemporary forms of government."

The enlightened intellectuals' solutions to the religious quandaries they confronted were many and varied, but they all shared two foundations: the view that the country in which Jews found themselves was their "homeland," rather than an "exile;" and an emphasis on the basic moral precepts of Judaism, especially the Ten Commandments and the teachings of the Prophets. This approach was called the "Mission of Israel," and its slogan was a Talmudic saying, "that the Almighty had shown great charity in scattering the Jewish People among the nations" so that they might spread the lofty and universal moral principles of Judaism. The Reform Movement, spearheaded by Abraham Geiger, and the Neo-Orthodox Movement, founded by Rabbi Samson Raphael Hirsch [5], balanced preservation of Jewish identity with acceptance of emancipation and integration into the general society.

There were also outward signs of adapting Judaism to contemporary life — in synagogue architecture and rabbis' dress and sermons. Thus was created the emancipated "German" or "French" Jew who was also a "member of the Mosaic faith" or an "Israelite."

KEY

Heinrich Heine (1797-1856), a German-Jewish poet and writer, converted to Christianity at age 28. His personality and his attitude toward Judaism embodied the problematic reality faced by an enlightened Jew in 19th-century Europe.

5

5 Rabbi Samson Raphael Hirsch (1808-1888) believed that Judaism should be modernized and the best of world culture adopted, but he rejected the approach of the enlightened intellectuals. In his essay "Nineteen Letters on Judaism" (1836), Hirsch outlined his ideal figure of the *Yisrael-Mensch* as an "enlightened Jew who observed traditional Jewish law." Hirsch claimed that it was not Judaism, with its principles of faith and observances, that needed reform, but the Jews themselves.

6

6 Dress was the most obvious stumbling block to Jewish integration into the general society. In this painting by K.J. Ackersberg (1818), the Nathanson family is depicted wearing their best Gentile-style festive attire. Mendel Levin Nathanson initiated the opening of Free Schools for girls and boys in Copenhagen and was also instrumental in the publishing of the royal decree (1814) that granted near equal civil status to the Jews of Denmark. Full equality was achieved in 1849.

7

7 Jews were granted Emancipation either through legislation or through gradual evolution. In certain countries no rights at all were granted during the 19th century.

8

8 The Spirit of the Romantic Movement is apparent in "The Two Marys Beside the Tomb of Jesus" by the Jewish painter Philip Veith (1793-1877). Romantic concepts like "nationality" and "people" influenced the perception of the emancipation as a movement to adopt the general culture while preserving Judaism.

Liberté, Egalité, Fraternité — for Jews as well

CONNECTIONS

98 How to Merit the Status of Citizen
102 Jewish Art and the Emancipation
118 Modern Anti-Semitism

During the 17th and 18th centuries, Jews in western and central European countries enjoyed a "protected" status: after Jews had requested to settle in a certain place, the ruler of the country weighed the request and decided the duration of their stay in terms of the economic benefit he expected they would bring to his realm. But a royal "charter of protection" did not confer regular civil rights. It also imposed severe restrictions on freedom of movement and on the kind of economic occupations a Jew could hold [2]. While the Jewish communities usually enjoyed extensive autonomy, the non-Jewish authorities often intervened in their internal affairs, and the threat of expulsion constantly hung over their heads. With economic development and the spread of secularism at the end of the 18th century, Jews were gradually permitted to enter the general walks of life of the countries in which they lived, but their legal status was not amended. Only on September 27, 1791, did revolutionary France grant equal rights to the Jews within its borders, becoming the first European country to do so.

Origins of Emancipation

The roots of the idea of emancipation go back to the general enlightenment movement. The core of its ideology was the notion that "reason" should be the fundamental criterion on which to base one's world view. According to this conception, society and the state were created after logical consideration of their usefulness. The supposition was that in the past human beings had been living in a "natural state," devoid of any obligatory framework, in which all were equal. Only when they had reached the conclusion that living together would improve their lot and provide them with security, it was believed, did they make a "Social Contract" which each individual could freely join or reject. From these assumptions the idea evolved that becoming a citizen was an act of joining society, and, since all Jews were human beings, each one of them could join the "Social Contract" — in other words, could become a citizen of his country with equal rights.

Beginning in the 1780s, public debates arose, mainly in France and Germany, about the possibility of Jews becoming citizens [6]. In the French Revolution, representatives of the French people who saw themselves as the renewers of the Social Contract in France, met in the National Assembly and published the "Declaration of the Rights of Man and of the Citizen" (1789). In the deliberations held on the floor of the National Assembly, those who opposed granting the Jews equal rights pointed to the competing national foundations of Judaism, and cited Jewish loyalty to another country (Erez Israel) and another king (Almighty God). They also noted Jewish particularistic observances and alleged negative attributes [4]. Some devout Christians stated that the Jews had to continue existing separately so they might fulfill

1

2

Hochfürstlich und Hochgräflich Oettingisch Gleit
Nördlinger Meß
auf fußgehende Juden.
15. Kr.
Den Ao. 17

1 Napoleon, the disseminator of the idea of equality, is seen in this 1802 engraving granting freedom of worship to members of different religions. Yet it was this same Napoleon who in 1808 issued the "Infamous Decree," once more restricting the rights of Jews.

2 Travel tolls, like these late-18th century German transit coupons, were collected from Jewish travelers before the emancipation. When the tolls were canceled in the Swiss canton of Aargau in 1856, however, they were quickly reinstated due to local opposition.

3

3 The Hapsburg Empire granted equal rights to Jews only in the 1860s. The delay was caused both by the political reaction that set in after the failure of the "Spring Revolutions" (1848-1849) and by the fact that among the prominent leaders of the Liberal movement in Vienna, which opposed the regime, were a number of Jews. This medallion was struck to commemorate the granting of the right to acquire land to Austrian Jews (1860).

4

4 The Jews of Alsace, who mostly engaged in moneylending and peddling, became the targets of economic and social criticism. The hatred directed toward them occasionally even led to violence. The book *The Alsatian Jews — Should They be Granted Equal Rights?* published in Alsace in 1790 (the frontispiece is pictured), called upon the Jews to abandon unproductive occupations and take up the skilled trades and agriculture.

the destiny that Providence had thrust upon them.

Those in favor of equality replied that Jews, as human beings, were entitled to the "natural right" of joining the society of French citizens on condition that they truly wished to do so and that they gave up their national distinctiveness [5]. "To the Jews as a nation nothing shall be granted; to the Jews as human beings — everything," was the argument of one of the deputies of the nobility in the States-General. Even Robespierre maintained that it was impossible to preserve the revolutionary principles of freedom and equality while denying them to certain people. After two years of postponements, Jewish emancipation was finally accepted and made part of French law.

Problems in Achieving Emancipation

Still, the French public did not immediately change its traditional negative attitude toward the Jews. Moreover, equality was given to the Jews as individuals, not as a group. In exchange, they were expected to abandon all their traditional customs and institutions as well as to surrender the long-standing autonomy enjoyed by the Jewish community — concessions which many Jews were loath to make.

During the 19th century, emancipation spread [1], mainly as a consequence of the French conquests during the Revolution and under Napoleon. A difficulty arose, however, when new views were disseminated throughout Europe after the fall of Napoleon, the most important and outstanding of which were romanticism and nationalism. Romanticism questioned the central role of reason in creating society and the state. It viewed nations as fundamental natural bodies, not the products of the human mind; thus an individual could not move from one nation to another even if he wished to. It followed then that Jews could not become part of a nation just because they were granted equal rights.

KEY

Daniel Mendoza (1764-1836), an English Jew, won a championship boxing match in 1780. His boxing method enabled him to defeat much heavier opponents. He always introduced himself as "Mendoza, the Jew" and was the first boxer to enjoy royal patronage. His contribution to the field of boxing and his special status brought about an improvement in the image of the Jews of England. With Mendoza as their example, Jews began using force against physical insult, and thereby gained new respect in the eyes of the surrounding society. Mendoza's case illustrates a change in attitude toward Jews not sparked by legislation or abstract ideology.

5 A

6

5 B

5 Emancipated Jews, seeking acceptance by the general society, expressed intense patriotism and a willingness to lay down their lives for their new homelands. In the painting [A] "The Return of the Jewish Volunteer from the War of Liberation to the Bosom of his Family, Still Living According to the Old Tradition," Moritz Daniel Oppenheim (1801-1882) sought to commemorate the part played by Jews in the German victory against Napoleon. However, in this cartoon [B] it is implied that Jews are not fit for army service because of their physical stature, their cowardice and a character not adapted to military discipline. The "Holy Alliance" (Russia, Prussia and Austria) saw in the triumph over Napoleon a victory of the "German spirit" over the "French spirit." The result was that the Germans forsook the ideology of the enlightenment movement for the ideas of nationalism and romanticism which clung to traditions of the past. It was these notions and the Congress of Vienna (1815) that brought about a resumption of propaganda against the Jews and abolition of their newly acquired rights.

6 Nathan the Wise, the drama written by the German playwright G.E. Lessing (1729-1781), and *The Jews*, an earlier Lessing play (1749), helped bring about the "emancipation debate." A staunch supporter of the enlightenment, Lessing expressed the idea that wisdom — not religious affiliation — was the source of morality. Lessing took for his model the personage of the enlightened Jewish intellectual and philosopher, Moses Mendelssohn. The emancipation debate in Germany lasted 100 years until equal rights for Jews were legislated in 1871.

Jewish Art and the Emancipation

Jewish art in Europe strongly felt the impact of the Emancipation. The synagogue, for example, which previously had been a rather modest structure, became a highly impressive showplace in the 19th century. Ritual objects also bent to the thrust of contemporary styles and began to embody motifs and symbols that had formerly been rare. The most significant change, however, affected Jewish artists, for whom there were now new opportunities to study at advanced institutes and academies.

The Role of the Synagogue

Moses Mendelssohn, the 18th century philosopher and one of the major voices of the Jewish Enlightenment, criticized the appearance of the old-fashioned synagogue as unsuited to the mentality and aesthetic taste of the times. And in fact, during the 19th century new synagogues incorporating contemporary styles were erected, first in Central and Western Europe and later throughout the world. Unlike the synagogues of the Middle Ages, which were built in closed Jewish quarters, these new structures sprung up all over the city. Their size, magnificence and style reflected the solidity of the Jewish community and its aspiration to take part in the social and cultural life around it.

The architectural fashion of the 19th century, which combined artistic motifs and styles from various periods of the past, also directed the design of synagogues. Their construction and ornamentation showed a "national" European or an oriental Jewish style, in line with the social thinking of the Jews during the Emancipation: a desire both to identify fully with the culture of the country in which they lived [6], and, in certain cases, to stress the particularity of Judaism with its roots in the east [5]. In the wake of changes in ritual and liturgy introduced by the Reform Movement, prayer halls were designed so that the religious ceremony centered around one focal point. The Ark of the Law and the lectern were placed side by side on the eastern wall with the seats in the hall and the galleries facing them. The plan of the synagogue thus came to resemble that of the church.

Motifs and Symbols

The symbols which became particularly popular during the Emancipation and are still considered representative of the Jewish people are the Star of David and the Tablets of the Law. Both forms had been used before, but much less widely than they were in the 19th century. They rose on rooftops and gables, on gates and synagogue facades, and served to decorate the central spaces around the Ark of the Law. Additional synagogue ornamentation was generally confined to repeated motifs based on geometric or floral shapes. The Star of David came to be accepted as a symbol that could be placed in synagogues where a cross would be hung in a church. Despite its wide use, however, European Jews preferred to assign the Tablets of the Law the central position on ritual items, usu-

CONNECTIONS

100 "Liberté, Egalité, Fraternité" — for Jews as well

1 Moritz Daniel Oppenheim learned in a *cheder* and *Talmud Torah* (religious schools) as a child. The Emancipation enabled him to study in art academies in Germany, France and Italy. Oppenheim was still a young man when he painted "The Jung Brothers and their Teacher," shown here. The simplicity of style indicates the influence of the Nazarener school of art, which took its inspiration from Italian Christian art and the paintings of the German Renaissance. In his final years most of his paintings were characterized by a spirit of idealism and by subjects drawn largely from Jewish life.

2 Maurycy Gottlieb, who died at the age of 23, was a talented and prolific artist. He grew up in the town of Drogobycz in Galicia, one of the centers of the Enlightenment. He studied in art academies in Krakow, Munich, Vienna and Lvov and was the protegé of the Polish artist Jan Matejko (1838-1895), noted for his historical paintings. Gottlieb favored Jewish subjects. The painting of a young girl shown here is a fine example of the sensitivity and psychological depth of his portraits.

3 This Star of David (*Magen David*) on a case for a Torah scroll is from 19th century North Africa. The Jewish communities in Islamic countries kept their scrolls in cases made usually of wood, which was sometimes metal-plated. The case shown here pictures traditional geometric and leaf-like patterns worked into the metal plate.

4 This plate for a Torah Scroll from the 19th century is decorated with the Tablets of the Law set between two lions. The lion as a symbol has retained its vitality since ancient times. The popularity of the Tablets is more recent. The plate was originally used as a mark separating the scrolls from each other, and later served to ornament them.

ally placing them, carried by animals such as lions, in the highest spot on the *Torah* plate or the *Menorah*.

The shape of the Tablets had been set in previous generations and had been seen as a symbol of the *Torah*. But the great weight given to questions of ethics and law in western society during the Emancipation promoted their acceptance as a prominent symbol at this time [4]. In Islamic countries, however, the Star of David was preferred as decoration for ritual objects [3], often appearing in a circle together with a compass rose or round cosmic shapes.

The Jewish Artist

The Emancipation might be said to have had the same impact on Jewish art that the Renaissance had on that of Europe in general. Talented young Jews could now study at art academies and serve as the architects of public buildings or as portraitists, making a name for themselves among the flourishing Jewish middle class or even the urban Christian communities. The Jewish bourgeoisie preferred to decorate their homes with pictures of Jewish subjects. Even non-Jews favored scenes with a Jewish flavor, which they regarded as romantic and exotic. Biblical themes were equally popular.

A number of Jewish artists became active in Germany, England, Holland, Austria and the United States. One of the most outstanding was Moritz Daniel Oppenheim (1801-1882) [1].

The Emancipation was even felt in the small towns of Eastern Europe. Their young artists journeyed to the cultural centers of Paris, Vienna and Berlin, where they studied and worked. Among these artists were Maurycy Gottlieb (1856-1879) [2] and the Hungarian-born Isidor Kaufmann (1854-1921). Kaufmann's paintings display minute detail, balanced composition and sensitive brushstrokes, and depict the life of the Jews in the towns of Galicia, Poland and the Ukraine with consummate realism and humor.

KEY

"Removing the Torah Scroll from the Ark" is the work of the German-Jewish artist Wilhelm Tielman. His lithographs depicting the interior of the synagogue in Kassel, Germany, were published in 1898 in a richly decorated edition. At that time lithographic printing methods were at the height of their development. In this picture we see the figures of the rabbi, the cantor and the beadle standing near the Ark as the scroll is removed. The figures in the hall are drawn realistically, emphasizing their gestures, clothing and facial expressions, making it possible to distinguish one from another.

5

5 This synagogue in Frankfurt, built in 1860, is one of many erected in Germany between 1850 and 1880. The prayer hall is divided by two rows of columns supporting the upper floor. The design of the interior was meant to enable the congregants to face the focal point of the ritual conducted by the eastern wall. Like the churches they resembled, synagogues became places where congregants went primarily for religious services.

6

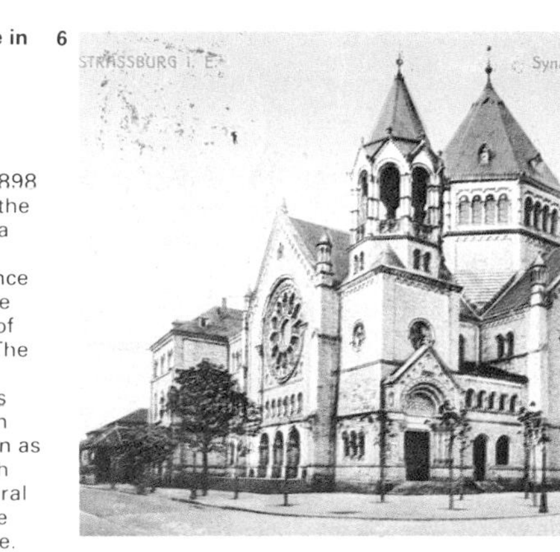

6 This synagogue in Strasbourg was designed by the Jewish architect Ludwig Levy. Outwardly the building, built in 1898 (and destroyed by the Nazis), resembles a church. Its design reflects the influence of the Romanesque and Gothic styles of the Middle Ages. The adoption of architectural forms based on European traditions was seen as proof of the Jewish community's cultural integration into the local social scheme.

7

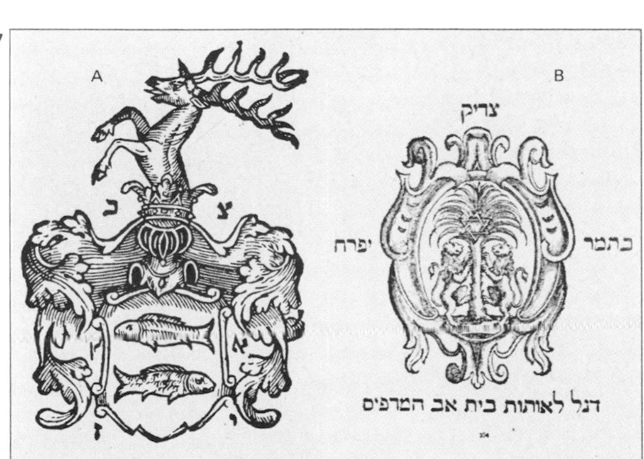

7 Printer's marks were the "trademarks" of families and firms involved in the printing and publishing of books. They became very common as a result of the widening demand for printed matter in Hebrew. Many of them were graced by traditional Jewish symbols, such as the tree of life. A highly imaginative depiction of the Temple appears on the mark of the 18th century Foa family of Venice [B]. Some of the marks were embellished with new forms, such as writing or printing tools or even well known towns. In many cases, among the ancient symbols there appeared the identifying mark of the head of a publishing house, like the deer (in Hebrew *zvi*) on the printer's flag of Zvi Ben Abraham Kalonimus Yaffe of 18th century Lublin [A]. Collaboration between Christians and Jews often led to cross-cultural influence that is reflected both in the illuminations of their books and in their printers' marks. New symbols became popular in Europe partly because of the desire of emancipated Jews to rid themselves of the mystical symbols of national-religious redemption popular in the Middle Ages.

8

8 This curtain for the Ark of the Law is from Germany (1725). In the tradition of *Ashkenazi* Jews, the curtain hangs over the outside of the Ark, whereas in the *Sephardi* tradition it hangs inside. It is made of velvet embroidered with gold thread and appliquéd. The lavish decorations include some of the most popular forms and motifs in Jewish art at the time, and they serve as a reminder of the original function of the curtain, to separate the Holy from the Holy of Holies in the Temple before its destruction. The traditional symbols include pillars, lions and eagles. The crown is given the highest position, symbolizing the crown of the *Torah*, the crown of the Kingdom and the crown of the Priesthood. In the second half of the 18th century and in the 19th, the choice and positioning of the motifs underwent a change and the Tablets of the Law were usually afforded the central position.

Hasidim and Mitnaggedim

Hasidism is a religious and social movement that spread throughout the Jewish communities of Eastern Europe in the mid-18th century. Immigrants then brought the movement with them to other Jewish centers, notably the United States and Israel.

Hasidism is based on four major principles: the importance of emotional experience in general, and prayer in particular, in the worship of God; the paramount significance of the individual's inner "intent" as he observes the commandments; joy, rather than fasting and abstinence, as the proper way to worship God; the *zaddik* (righteous man) or *"rebbe"* whose unique qualities enable him to come closer to God than ordinary people and thus qualify him to act as mediator between God and the believer.

The Beginning of Hasidism

The crisis that gripped the Jewish communities in the southeastern provinces of Poland (Volhynia and Podolia) following the attacks of 1648-1649, the raids of the Haidamack brigand bands in the first half of the 18th century, and the failure of Shabbateanism and its offshoots, paved the way for the activities of Rabbi Israel Ben Eliezer (the Ba'al Shem Tov; 1700-1760). He was born in Okop in the province of Podolia, the site of pogroms and not far from the centers of Shabbateanism in the Ottoman Empire. His childhood was unremarkable. Some years after marrying he worked in an inn run by his wife, and according to legend it was at this juncture that he formulated the basic precepts of Hasidism.

In his thirties he revealed himself. Initially he traveled from place to place as a *ba'al shem*, a miracle-worker who could cure the ills of the body and soul not only with the medicinal herbs with which he familiarized himself, but also by means of vows, amulets and prayer. He was known for his gracious manner and talent as a storyteller, and people seeking advice and guidance in all spheres of life congregated around him. From this nucleus he drew his circle of disciples, the *hasidim*. He instructed them in his philosophy by dialogues or short homilies spiced with stories and fables. His way of life and leadership strongly influenced his followers. They were particularly impressed by the way in which he prayed. He did so with such great fervor that he would faint, at which time he would have visions, among them the sight of his own soul rising to heaven, where he would intercede with the Messiah and the angels on behalf of the nation. In many respects, the Ba'al Shem Tov was the prototype of the Hasidic *zaddik* in generations to come.

The Spread of Hasidism

After the death of the Ba'al Shem Tov, his place as leader of the movement was filled by his disciple Rabbi Dov Baer of Mezhirech, known as the Maggid (1704-1773). Disciples streamed to his home in Mezhirech, and returned home with the

CONNECTIONS

80 The Jewish Community in Poland up to the 18th Century

92 Shabbateanism

106 The Jewish Community in Russia: 1772-1881

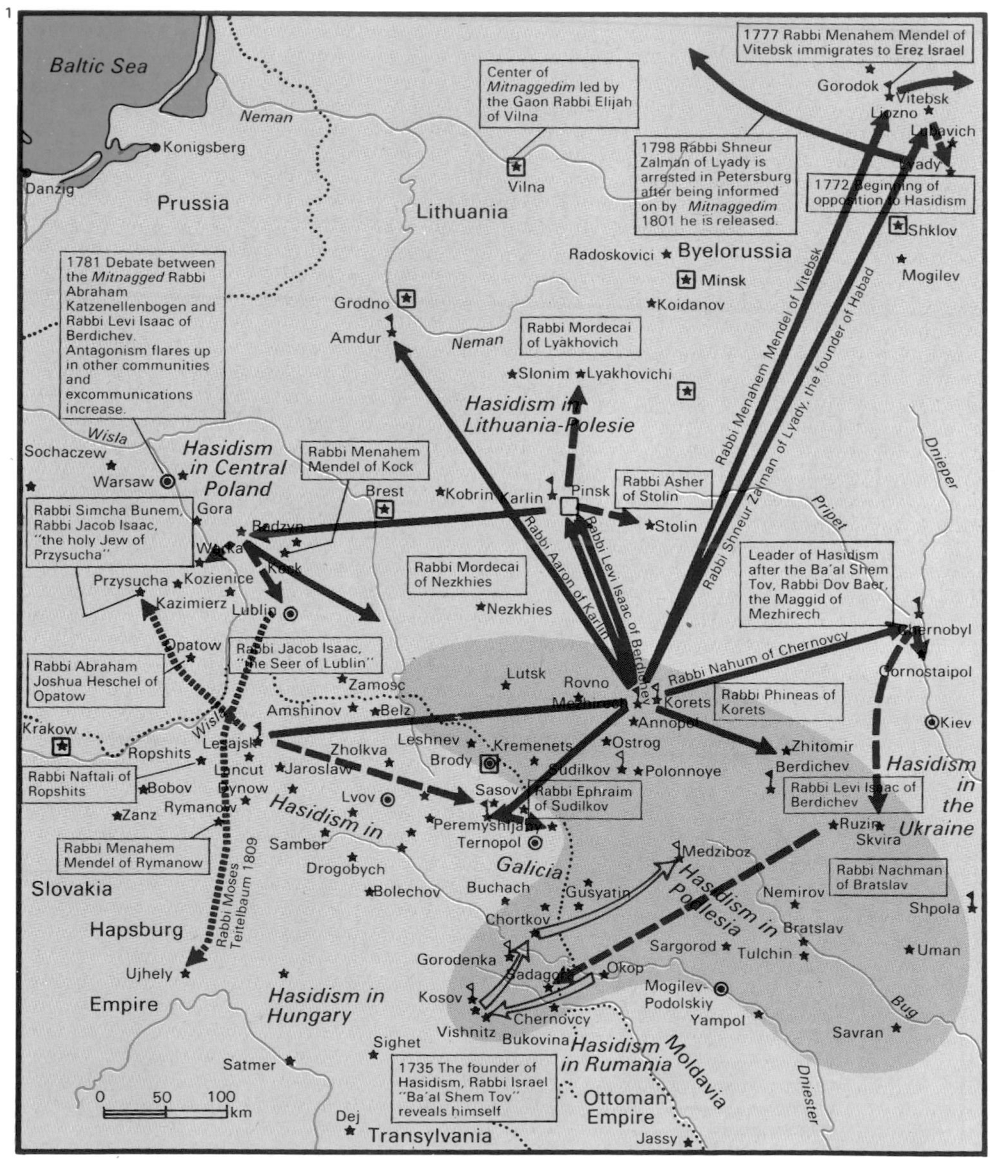

1 The spread of Hasidism after the death of its founder, Rabbi Israel Ben Eliezer (Ba'al Shem Tov) was promoted by the activities of the heir to his leadership, the Great Maggid, Rabbi Dov Baer of Mezhirech. The Maggid moved the center of the movement from Podolia to Volhynia and worked to disseminate its precepts. Rabbi Jacob Joseph of Polonnoye, his rival to take over for the Ba'al Shem Tov, held that the leadership should be in the hands of one *zaddik*. But the Maggid favored the transfer of leadership in different communities from rabbi to disciple. This tendency to decentralize authority fostered the spread of Hasidism. The Maggid's students, together with special emissaries he sent to the Ukraine, Galicia, Reissen (Byelorussia), Lithuania and Central Europe, founded secondary centers tied to that at Mezhirech, where the Maggid held court.

2 A hasid and his wife in typical attire. The principles and practices of Hasidism wrought changes in the *hasid*'s way of life, including a new conception of the place of the family, and particularly of the wife. The fact that the religious experience stressed devotion and fervor, and that everyone congregated around the figure of the *rebbe*, accompanied by strong emotional involvement, eroded the *hasid*'s emotional attachment to his wife and led to a lowering of her status. It is against this backdrop that several women particularly esteemed by Hasidism stand out. Hannah-Rachel (1805-1892), known as "the maid of Ludomir," was said to have observed all of the commandments prescribed for men until her marriage; she even attained a status near that of a *zaddik*. Toward the end of her life she immigrated to Erez Israel.

principles of Hasidism. The movement spread far beyond the borders of Podolia-Volhynia — to Galician Western Poland and Byelorussia [1].

After the death of the Maggid, the leadership split. There was no longer the one *rebbe*, but several in different places. Each was surrounded by those *hasidim* who saw him as their *zaddik* [5]. In many cases, the leadership was passed down from father to son, so that "courts" or "dynasties" of *zaddikim* came into being. Different groups, each with its own brand of Hasidism, evolved around the various dynasties: Lubavich *Habad* [4], Bratslav, Ruzhin, etc.

Hasidim and Mitnaggedim

The rapid spread of Hasidism met with severe opposition from wide circles known as *Mitnaggedim* ("opposers" in Hebrew). In the initial stage of the Hasidic movement, it was seen as an outgrowth of Shabbateanism, since both groups showed strong Kabbalistic inclinations. These suspicions were soon dispelled. The Ba'al Shem Tov and the *zaddikim* who followed him never claimed to be messiahs, and Hasidism did not pretend to bring immediate redemption to the Jewish people.

The *hasid*'s style of prayer, accompanied as it was by strange and exuberant movements, aroused the contempt of the *Mitnaggedim*, who considered it evidence of rowdiness and debauchery. The idea of worshipping God through joy was similarly thought to be frivolous. Opposition to Hasidism came largely from the provinces of Lithuania and Reissen (Byelorussia), the sites of large *yeshivot*. In the late 18th century, the *Mitnaggedim* united under the leadership of Rabbi Elijah Ben Solomon Zalman (1720-1797), the Gaon of Vilna.

Most of the fears of the *Mitnaggedim* never materialized. The new groups that grew up around the courts of the *zaddikim* existed side by side with the community establishment and did not replace it. And study of the *Torah* was not neglected.

KEY

Worshipping God through joy is one of the principles of Hasidism. Morbidity could lead a man into sin, while joy not only urges the individual to good deeds, but also leads to his devotion of his Maker. In order to banish sadness from his heart, the *hasid* makes a variety of movements during prayers and dances with wild exuberance. In this way he reaches a state in which he "divests himself of materiality" and "invalidates reality." The *Mitnaggedim* rejected these and similar unorthodox styles of worship.

3

3 A poor courtyard in the Jewish quarter of Kazimierz in Krakow can be seen in a painting by Alexander Kutzich (1830-1877). The political and economic disintegration of Poland, which had begun in the mid-17th century, paved the way for the rise of Hasidism. Difficult economic conditions and the widening of socio-economic gaps found the wealthy and many of the scholars at odds with the masses struggling to survive. The authority and credibility of the institutes of Jewish autonomy were seriously undermined. A heavy burden of taxes and duties impoverished the Jewish community and exposed it to pressure by the authorities.

4 A

5

5 The shmirot cup is from 18th or 19th century Poland. The *shmirot* were silver coins given by the *zaddik* to his disciples as amulets. Some were melted down and made into cups or plates. The *hasid* saw lofty intentions and sparks of the divine in every action of the *rebbe*, be it the most mundane, and from this evolved the practice of eating the scraps from the *zaddik*'s meal.

6

6 Small artisans, peddlers and other Jews found the religious experience in Hasidism that had been denied them in rabbinical Judaism. The photograph depicts a Polish-Jewish knife-sharpener.

4 B

4 The Habad movement (the name is an acronym of the Hebrew words for wisdom, understanding and knowledge) was founded by Rabbi Shneur Zalman of Lyady [A], and is distinguished for its stress on observation and reason as the way to God. The greatest opponent of Hasidism was the Gaon Rabbi Elijah of Vilna (1720-1797) [B].

The Jewish Community in Russia: 1772-1881

During the late 19th century, the Jews were acknowledged as equal citizens throughout most of Europe — but not in Russia or Rumania. At this time the majority of Polish Jews, as well as the Jewish communities of the Baltic States were also Russian subjects. Toward the end of the 19th century, Russia ruled over more than five million Jews — nearly half of the Jewish population of the world.

The Pale of Settlement

Jews were forbidden to reside in Russia until the mid-18th century. The country first held sway over large numbers of Jews following the annexation of territories conquered from the Ottoman Empire to the south and the partitions of Poland and subsequent annexation of most of its territory by Russia (1772, 1793, 1795) [2]. The tsars did not permit these Jews to move into the areas of old Russia, and restricted them to residence in a Pale of Settlement along the western border of Russia.

The Pale of Settlement encompassed about one million square kilometers, with the Jews accounting for some 11% of the population and constituting the majority in many small towns. Most were employed in a small number of occupations providing services for the non-Jewish population: commerce, brokerage, leasing, and the trades [4]. The opportunities for making a living were few and competition fierce, and the situation was worsened by financial burdens imposed by the authorities. Thus the towns in the Pale of Settlement were afflicted by appalling poverty.

"The Stick or the Carrot"

The tsars perceived the Jews as a foreign, unproductive element that was injurious to the economy of the country and impoverished its farmers [3]. Accordingly, the various tsars adopted one of two policies: some sought to coerce the Jews to "reform" and assimilate; others held that the Jews should be afforded rights and privileges as inducements to assimilation. Alexander I (reigned from 1801 to 1825) used both methods. On the one hand he made it illegal for a Jew to run a tavern or lease property in the villages. On the other hand, he encouraged the Jews to farm, even allocating government lands for Jewish settlement, particularly in southern Russia. These settlers were granted tax benefits and allowed to hire Christian laborers. The Tsar also admitted Jews into public schools. Toward the end of his reign, Alexander I partly reversed his liberal policy, withdrawing some of the privileges he had granted the Jews.

The reign of Tsar Nicholas I (1825-1855) is noted almost entirely for its harsh edicts and restrictions in regard to the Jews. The most hurtful was the Cantonist Act (1827) which required Jewish communities to supply quotas of boys aged twelve and over for military training. The training took place in Cantonist (inductee) camps under the auspices of Christian foster families. At the age

CONNECTIONS

80 The Jewish Community in Poland up to the 18th Century
104 Hasidim and Mitnaggedim
114 The Pogroms of Eastern Europe
122 Jewish Culture in Eastern Europe until World War II

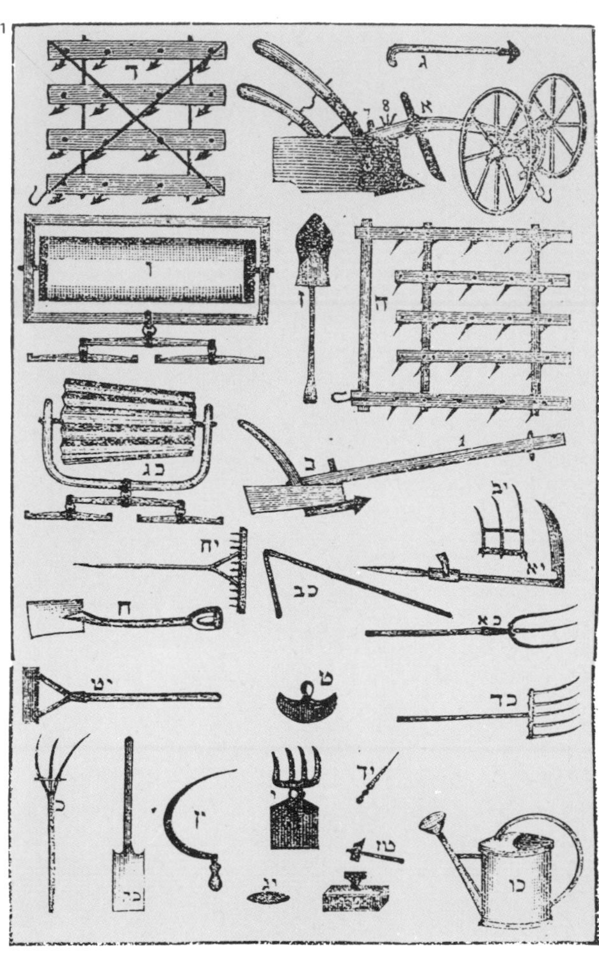

1 Guide to Farming and Gardening, a book by the agronomist H.S. Schneider, reflected the Jews' desire to do productive work and to return to the land. For this reason, exponents of the *Haskalah* supported the Russian authorities' program to settle Jews within the Pale of Settlement on farmland. They also saw this as a way to ease the severe poverty rampant among the Jews. ORT (known by its Russian initials, meaning The Society for the Dissemination of Artisan and Agricultural Work), was founded in Russia in 1880. It worked to bring vocational and agricultural training to the Jews, as did ICA (Jewish Colonization Association). The founder of this organization, Baron Maurice de Hirsch, first tried to provide agricultural training for the Jews in Russia. But in 1891 he began to organize Jewish farming settlements in Argentina. The *Am Olam* and *Hovevei Zion* societies were also active in attempts to settle Jews in an agricultural role on the land.

2 In the Pale of Settlement about half of the Jews lived in villages or small towns; the other half, in cities like Warsaw, Odessa, Lodz and Vilna. During the 19th century Jewish settlements were restricted even within the Pale of Settlement and Jews who were not farmers were required to leave the villages. Jews were banned from certain cities within the Pale, such as Kiev, Sevastopol and Nikolayev. In 1825 Jews who owned no land were forbidden to settle along Russia's western border on the pretext that they were smuggling. The lands of the Pale were taken over by Russia in the late 18th century by virtue of conquest and annexation.

more than 40,000 Jews ⊡
30-40,000 Jews ⊙
20-30,000 Jews •
10-20,000 Jews ○
city barred to Jews (by order of Nicholas I) ▲
Pale of Settlement ━━
Regional Border ──
Provincial Border ....
Jewish population in region **724,500**
percent of Jews in province (13.6%)
Jewish population in province 345,000

of eighteen, the boys began their military service, which lasted for 25 years. The law was designed to remove the youngsters from their families and Jewish way of life and at the same time to coerce them to convert.

Alexander II (reigned 1855-1881) tended to be more liberal; he rescinded or moderated some of the harsher laws, such as the Cantonist Act. A number of the restrictions relating to the Pale of Settlement were lifted for those Jews favored by the authorities, such as wealthy merchants, academics, artisans, and ex-army personnel, and these then established large communities in St. Petersburg and Moscow. The Tsar also granted special benefits to Jews who graduated from Russian high schools, and induced Jewish youngsters to attend these schools.

On the whole, the Russian tsars were unsuccessful in their attempts to "reform" the Jews. Only a small minority of the more educated supported the tsars on the theory that a change in the Jewish way of life would pave the way for emancipation. In contrast, many Jewish youngsters joined revolutionary movements that sought to change the regime in Russia [Key], though here too this was done partly in the hope of improving the Jews' lot. Many were arrested and exiled, and several were sentenced to death.

The Jewish *Haskalah* (Enlightenment) movement in Russia — unlike its more veteran counterpart in Germany — did not bring about widespread assimilation. Most educated Jews believed that a broad education could be compatible with the continued promotion of Jewish culture. They adopted the motto coined by Jehudah Leib Gordon: "Be a man abroad — and a Jew in your own tabernacle." In fact, the Jewish *Haskalah* movement in Russia produced authors and poets who are considered the fathers of modern Hebrew literature: Abraham Mapu, J.L. Gordon, Mendele Moykher Seforim, Feuerberg, and others.

KEY

A demonstration of the Bund in 1905, probably in Smorgon. The *Bund*, a Jewish socialist party, was founded in 1897. Most of its members were workers or young intellectuals. Like other socialist organizations with a large Jewish proletarian membership, the *Bund* was mainly concerned with improving the Jewish proletariat's working conditions and wages, as well as replacing the existing regime with a socialist government. To this end, it organized strikes and conducted courses to broaden Jewish workers' education and social consciousness. The *Bund* played a central role in organizing Jewish self-defense leagues in the wake of the pogroms.

3

3 Anti-Semitic Propaganda spread throughout Russia in the late 19th century. Unlike in Western Europe, in Russia it was openly encouraged by the authorities, reaching its peak during the reigns of Alexander III (1881-1894) and Nicholas II (1894-1917). One popular form of such provocation was the cartoon. Here a Jew is seen testifying before a judge. The cartoon mocks the backward and illiterate Jew who could only read and write "Jewish" and was a foreign element in the country. But the most blatant form of anti-Semitism remained the governmental restriction.

4

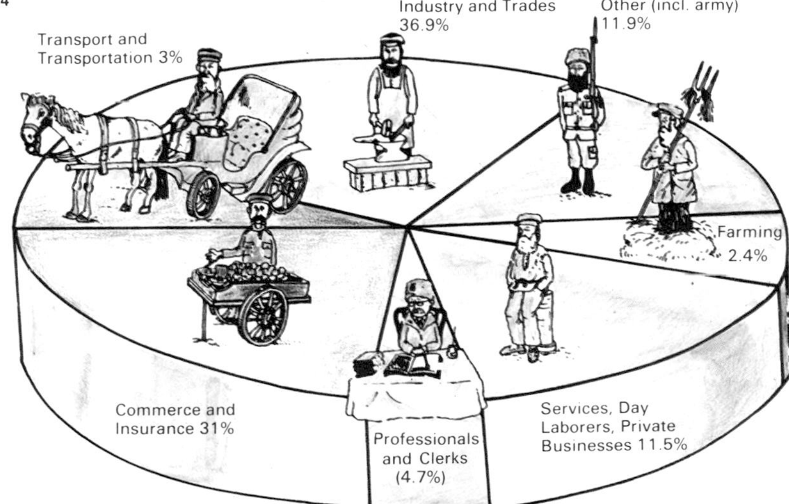

4 The sources of livelihood of Russian Jews at the end of the 19th century were considerably different from those at the beginning of the century. In particular, leasing transactions in the villages decreased, while there was a large increase in the trades and industry. Forced to leave the villages, many Russian Jews earned their living as tailors, shoemakers and furriers, or in the light industries. This trend contributed to Russian Jewish interest in socialist movements like the *Bund*.

5

5 Soldiers of the Jewish National Guard took part in the Polish rebellion against the Russian regime in 1830-31. Here they appear in a cartoon entitled "The March of the Jewish National Guard in Warsaw." Several circles within the Jewish community, largely of assimilated Jews, supported the uprising and were eager to join the Polish army, hoping in this way to save the Jews of Poland from the edicts of Nicholas I and to demonstrate their patriotism. Their offer was opposed by various Polish groups. Eventually, volunteers were admitted into the National Guard, but not the regular army. Those Jews unwilling to shave their beards served in special Jewish units.

6

6 This sign was hung in the Volpa synagogue in honor of Tsar Alexander III, who brought with him to the throne a new attitude toward the Jews — one of suspicion and animosity — which encouraged anti-Jewish pogroms.

The Legal Status of Jews in Muslim Lands

In the 15th-19th centuries, many communities of Jews lived under Muslim rule, mainly within the Ottoman Empire. A few large communities lived in other Muslim states — Morocco, Persia, Afghanistan and Yemen.

Protected Subjects

The Muslim attitude to non-Muslim residents was structured on Islamic religious principles that distinguished between "believers" — Muslims — and "unbelievers." Within this division, Jews and Christians belonged to *Ahl al-K'tab* — the People of the Book. Since their faith was anchored in the Old or New Testaments, their status was that of tolerated subjects (*dhimmi*); they were entitled to physical protection and to religious, social and legal freedoms (in contrast to pagans, who were to be converted to Islam). The Jews' payment of a poll tax (*jizya*) symbolized both the rulers' obligation to extend them protection and understanding, and their debased condition as "unbelievers" [2].

The Jews were also subject to a set of restrictions that had apparently crystallized in the 8th century under the reign of Caliph 'Umar II, and were known as the Pact of 'Umar: they were obliged to conduct their prayers in silence and their funerals unobtrusively; building of new synagogues was prohibited, though renovation of old ones was permitted [8]. They were compelled to wear special clothing of a distinctive color, and were prohibited from owning land, keeping slaves, building houses higher than those of Muslims, riding horses, and inducing Muslims to drink wine.

The Jews were trusted by the Ottoman regime. Hence, despite their *dhimmi* status, they received more favorable treatment than the Christians. However, their economic, political and legal status was frequently conditioned by arbitrary local rulers, who imposed heavy taxes and harsh decrees on them. These grew more severe at the turn of the 16th century when the Empire began to disintegrate.

Although Islam prohibits conversion of Jews, there were some instances of religious persecution, blood libels, and proselytizing — mainly in countries under the rule of Shi'ite zealots, or where the central government had weakened. Famous among these are the "Exile in Mawza" (1679) — in which all the Jews of San'a exiled themselves rather than become apostates, many meeting their death; the affair of the forced converts of Meshed in Persia (1839) [3]; and the Damascus Affair (1840), in which the Jews were accused of murdering a Capuchin monk and his Muslim servant in order to use their blood on Passover. Additional decrees plagued the Jews of Yemen in the 19th century: the "Crown Decree" — compelling them to go about with uncovered heads and tangled hair; the "Orphans Decree" — forcing Jewish orphans to convert to Islam; and the "Dung Collectors Decree" — obliging the Jews to perform humiliating sanitation jobs.

Generally, local rulers encouraged

CONNECTIONS

1 The philanthropist Sir Moses Montefiore (1784-1885) began his political activities in 1840 when he interceded with the Sultan to stop the Damascus blood libel. Thereafter he interceded for Jews in many places, and supported Jewish settlement in Erez Israel.

2

2 The legal and political status of Jews in Islamic countries was dictated, in theory, by the Koran. *Sura* 9:29 enjoins Muslims to "fight against those who do not believe... until they pay the *jizya* out of hand and have been humbled." In practice, popular attitudes were dictated by the interests of the various rulers.

3 A

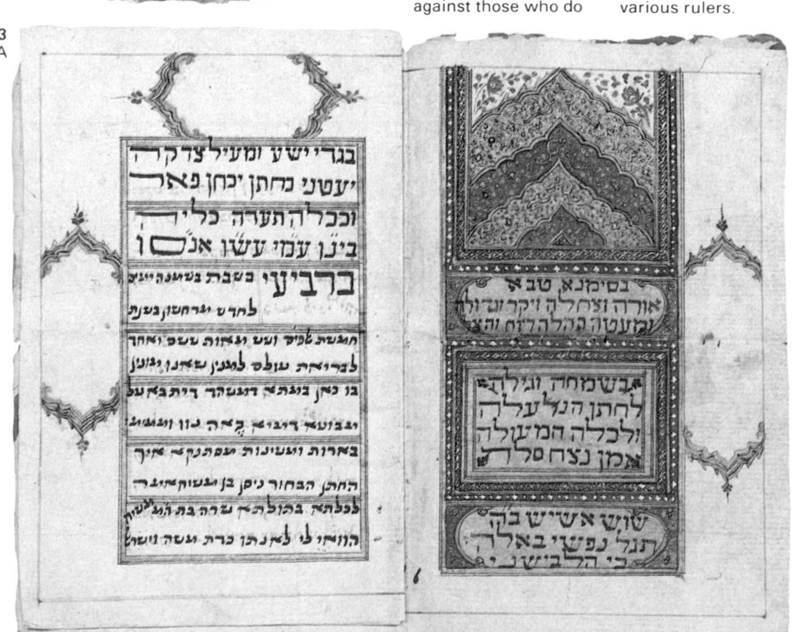

3 B

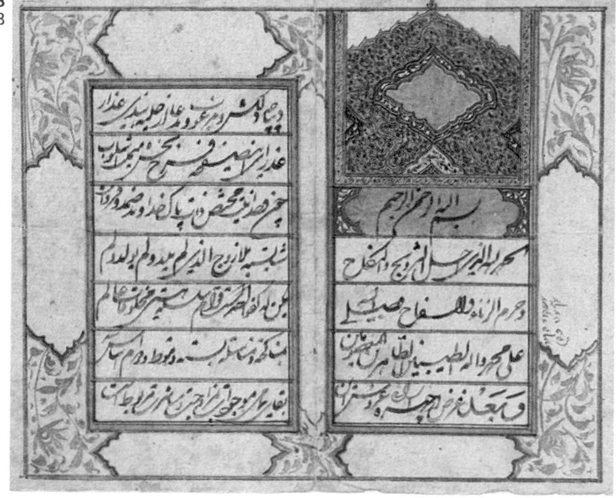

3 The affair of the forced converts of Meshed involved persecution of the Jews of Persia. During the rule of the Safavids (1507-1736) the Shi'ite faith was made the official religion of the country. Under the influence of extremist religious leaders, who saw in the Jews the "impurity of unbelievers," crippling new laws were passed. Finally, in the wake of a blood libel against the Jews in 1839, Muslims invaded the Jewish quarter, robbing and murdering many; survivors were caught and forced to convert. These converts, who were dubbed "New Muslims" (*Jedid al-Islam*) lived as *anusim*. This duality in their lives finds expression in a bridal contract (*k'tubbah*) written in Hebrew, dated 1901 [A]; and in a Muslim marriage certificate issued to one of the Meshed *anusim* in 1902 [B]. Many of the Meshed *Anusim* eventually fled, and some — disguised as pilgrims to Mecca — reached Jerusalem.

the establishment of a central leadership in the Jewish community. In the Ottoman capital and other large centers, this was the *hakham-bashi* — Chief Rabbi [Key]; in Moroccan communities it was the *nagid*; in Tunisia, the *qa'id*; and in Yemen it was the Central *Bet Din* (court). The rulers were aided by the Jewish leadership in tax collection and in conducting their affairs with the Jewish population. For its part the Jewish leadership was able to protect the communities against local persecution by making representations to the central government. In some instances Jews held senior positions at the ruler's court — as consultants, diplomatic agents, physicians [7], or interpreters [4].

Modern Trends

Improvement of the Jews' legal and political status in the Ottoman Empire began in 1839 with the publication of a *firman* (royal decree) canceling the poll tax. In mid-century, Jews' civil and legal status was made equal to that of the rest of the population. This process was hastened by the involvement of the western powers in the affairs of the Ottoman Empire.

The political activities of personalities like Sir Moses Montefiore [1] in England and Adolphe Crémieux [5] in France, and of organizations such as the French *Kol Yisrael Haverim* (*Alliance Israélite Universelle*) and the English *Agudat Ahim*, contributed as well to the granting of equal rights to Jews. In 1878 the *Alliance* interceded for the Balkan Jews at the Berlin Congress; in 1913 it assured the rights of Rumanian Jews; it also improved the legal situation of Moroccan Jews in 1880.

The rise of Arab nationalism, the strengthening of Zionist activities and the establishment of the State of Israel hastened the end of the Jewish communities in Islamic countries. After World War I many began to immigrate to western Europe, the USA and Latin America. But the bulk of the Jewish population immigrated to Israel.

KEY

The hakham-bashi (Chief Rabbi) of Istanbul was recognized, at the beginning of the 19th century, not only as the highest religious authority of Jews in the Ottoman Empire, but also as their representative to the sultan and his government. The institution of *hakham-bashi* extended to all important communities under Turkish rule. As was customary with religious leaders, the *hakham-bashi* was accompanied by an armed bodyguard (*kawas*), was honored with titles of distinction, and enjoyed the protection of the local governor. In the picture — the *hakham-bashi* of Salonika (1873), on the right, escorted by his bodyguard.

4 Interpreter for the British Consulate in Tangiers, the Jew Aaron Even Zur (in the picture — second from the left in the group at the center) is seen at a reception organized in Fez by the Sultan of Morocco, Muhammad ben Abd al-Rahman, in 1868, for a British delegation. Some of the Jews of Tangiers were descended from those expelled from Spain and Portugal, and most engaged in international trade. But some also served in foreign consulates as interpreters and diplomatic agents. One of the leaders of the community in the 19th century, Samuel ben Simbel, was an advisor to the king.

4

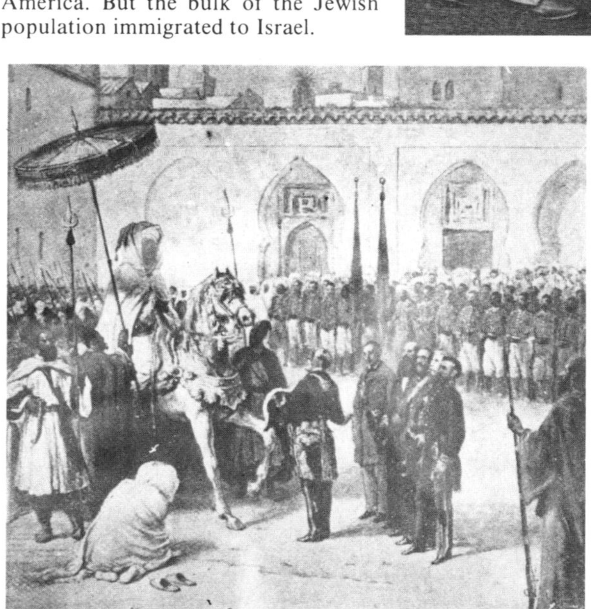

5 Isaac Adolphe Crémieux (1796-1880) worked with Montefiore against the Damascus Affair libel, and founded the *Kol Yisrael Haverim* society. In his capacity as minister of justice in the French government, he conferred French citizenship on Algerian Jews, in 1870.

5

6

6 The status of Jewish women in Muslim countries was dictated by Jewish religious law, rabbinical decree, and the influence of the local lifestyle. Eastern rabbis worked to ensure women's economic rights — such as the return of her dowry, *k'tubbah* and jewelry upon the husband's death. In Morocco, for example, the rabbis decreed that a daughter, even if unmarried, inherited her father's property as did a son. This 1589 engraving shows a Jewish girl from Adrianopol.

7

8

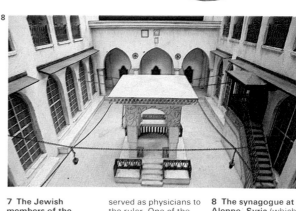

7 The Jewish members of the Ottoman royal court attained wealth and honor, but danger constantly hung over them, owing to intrigues and upheavals in government. Most engaged in finance and diplomacy, and some served as physicians to the ruler. One of the most famous court physicians was Tuvia Ben Moshe Hacohen (1652-1729). In the picture — a comparison of the human body with a house, from Hacohen's *Ma'aseh Tuvia* (Venice, 1708).

8 The synagogue at Aleppo, Syria (which the Jews called Aram Zova) was, according to tradition, built during the days of the Second Temple. It was renovated in the 15th century and in 1947 (a model is in the *Bet Hatefuzot* Museum, Tel Aviv).

Jewish Economic Life in Muslim Lands

The conditions under which Jews lived in Islamic countries determined the nature of their economic activities and the range of their occupations. Most of the Jews were concentrated in the large cities along the Mediterranean coast, living in separate neighborhoods [2]. But there were important communities, too, in cities situated along major trade routes in more remote districts, such as Samarkand and Bukhara in Central Asia, which were centers of the Chinese-European silk trade; in Basra, Iraq; in Shiraz and Isfahan in Persia (carpet exports); and in the Port of Hudeida, Yemen, which handled the coffee trade. More recently, the process of modernization and emancipation gave rise to a trend among a minority of the Jews to abandon their neighborhoods and settle in affluent districts populated by Europeans and Muslims — until the liquidation of the communities, in the mid-twentieth century.

In Morocco, Yemen, Kurdistan and Persia many Jews wandered inland, settling in provincial towns, remote rural areas and mountainous districts [1]. There they engaged in peddling and handicrafts, serving as conveyors of civilization by bringing innovations to the villagers far from the capital cities. Many engaged in agriculture [5], and some established farming partnerships with their Muslim neighbors.

Economic Constraints

The Jews' livelihood was determined by the necessity to observe religious injunctions as well as by place of residence. To facilitate observance of dietary laws, Jews concentrated on those branches of the economy concerned with processing agricultural produce: oil [8], cheese, meat products and, mainly, the wine and alcoholic beverages industry. The latter, prohibited under Muslim religious law, frequently caused tension between Muslims and Jews, who were accused of corrupting their neighbors' morals. With the growing process of emancipation at the close of the 19th century, Jews came to be integrated into public administration in North Africa, the Balkans, Iraq and Egypt. They began to work on the Sabbath, which aroused the ire of the communities' rabbis.

The uncertainties of their existence caused many Jewish breadwinners to turn to handicrafts or businesses in which investment in production facilities was low and tools easily transported. In Yemen, Persia, Syria and Morocco jewelry and precious metal crafts were characteristic Jewish occupations [6]. Many prosperous Jews in Muslim kingdoms also served as minters of coins. The weaving and dyeing industries in the Ottoman Empire were concentrated in the hands of Jews expelled from Spain, and the establishment of flourishing textile centers in Salonika, Safed and other cities from the 16th century onward was related to the Jews' expertise in this branch as well as to negative Muslim attitudes to these trades. In Persia, where Shi'ite Muslim

CONNECTIONS

82 Eastern Jewry after the Expulsion from Spain
108 The Legal Status of Jews in Muslim Lands
112 Jewish Community and Culture in Muslim Lands

1

1 Jews in the Atlas Mountains worked fields and plantations, all owned either privately or in partnership with Berber neighbors. In some instances irrigation was employed. The Jews also produced vegetable oils. This is the Jewish neighborhood in Ayat village, Wally, Atlas Mountains.

2

2 Jewish neighborhoods in the big cities were known as *Harat-al-Yahud, Juderia, Mahleh* or *Mellah*. They were created out of the Jewish desire to maintain a Jewish life-style, and out of a custom which had taken root in most Islamic countries — the concentration of different religious groups in separate quarters. The synagogue pictured here is on the island of Djerba, near Tunis.

3

3 In Kushta (Istanbul), capital of the Ottoman Empire, a large Jewish community arose in the 16th century. In the 18th and 19th centuries Jews acted as bankers and agents for European trading companies, as well as tax brokers, tax advisors and suppliers to the Empire's armies. In the picture — A Jewess against the background of the port of Kushta (engraving by la Chapelle, approx. 1650).

4

4 The craft of weaving — cloth as well as carpets — was renowned as a field of Jewish specialization. Home weaving expanded into an independent industry for women. They wove silk cloth — in Bukhara, mainly — and carpets — in Persia, where Jewish women frequently also engaged in carpet merchandizing. In Kurdistan, looms were to be found in almost every Jewish household, making mainly ark-curtains and carpets for synagogues. This woolen spread is from Kurdistan.

5

5 The Kurdish Jews lived in the mountainous districts of northern Iraq, part of Kurdistan. The range of their economic activity was extensive, but their major occupation was agriculture and the raising of sheep and cattle. Kurdish Jewish city dwellers engaged in commerce and handicrafts, and Jewish peddlers sold their wares in Muslim villages. In the picture — a farmer plowing in Kurdistan.

zealotry reigned, Jews were forced to refrain from any trade concerned with food, since the *ulama* claimed food was tainted by Jewish contact. Persian Jews were extensively involved in trading precious stones, jewelry and carpets [4], while the Jews of Afghanistan and Bukhara controlled trade in karakul furs with India and Europe.

Unrestricted Opportunities

The Ottoman rulers placed no economic restrictions on Jews; however, certain typically Jewish occupations developed as a result of the special conditions prevailing in the Empire. Jews served as tax brokers, even forming guilds to restrict entry into the profession. The most famous of these brokers were Don Joseph Nasi in the 16th century and Ezekiel Gabbai in the 19th century. Many Jews acted as suppliers to the rulers and to the Ottoman army — and provided everything from credit to food and clothing.

The concentration of Jews in port cities — mainly in Kushta [3], Salonika and Smyrna — produced new Jewish occupations, such as porters [Key], laborers and sailors; but, mainly, the Jews were engaged in international trade [7] and in small-scale business. Jews also attained high governmental posts in the courts of the rulers, serving as physicians, diplomats, etc.

With the opening of the Suez Canal (1869) and the expansion of western influence in Islamic countries, the process of urbanization was hastened. As living conditions of masses of Jews in the big cities improved, involvement in traditional Jewish occupations began to decline. Competition among European trading companies pushed Jews away from international trade and many turned to banking and finance. Simultaneously, small businessmen and craftsmen were edged out of their livelihood by Muslim and Christian competitors and a process of proletarization began to develop. Consequently, many uprooted themselves and emigrated.

KEY

Salonika served as an economic center until World War I, as its port was the outlet to the sea for all the Balkan countries. In the 16th and 17th centuries, Spanish-Jewish exiles established flourishing textile industries there. Its economic importance declined in the 18th century, but in the 19th century the tide turned in its favor again and the Jews of Salonika participated in all central branches of its economy — industry, commerce, banking, fishing, portering and stevedoring [pictured here]. Since Jews dominated Salonika's shipping trades, the port was shut on Sabbaths and Jewish festivals, as were other branches of commerce and banking which depended on trade.

6 Jewelrymaking was a thoroughly Jewish occupation in all Islamic countries, and Jewish jewelers attained the highest artistic levels. Jews may have viewed the craft as a means for securing their capital by converting it into precious metals and easily transportable tools. Moreover, jewelrymaking required little fixed investment in production facilities, thus making it doubly mobile. Jews also undoubtedly viewed jewelry in relation to moneychanging and coin minting activities — particularly in zealous Muslim countries such as Persia and Yemen. Jewish jewelrymaking also benefited from Jewish expertise in coppercraft, particularly beaten copper, which in Damascus attained the level of a fine art. In the picture — [A] Persian silver *Torah* ornaments; [B] jewelry from Bukhara.

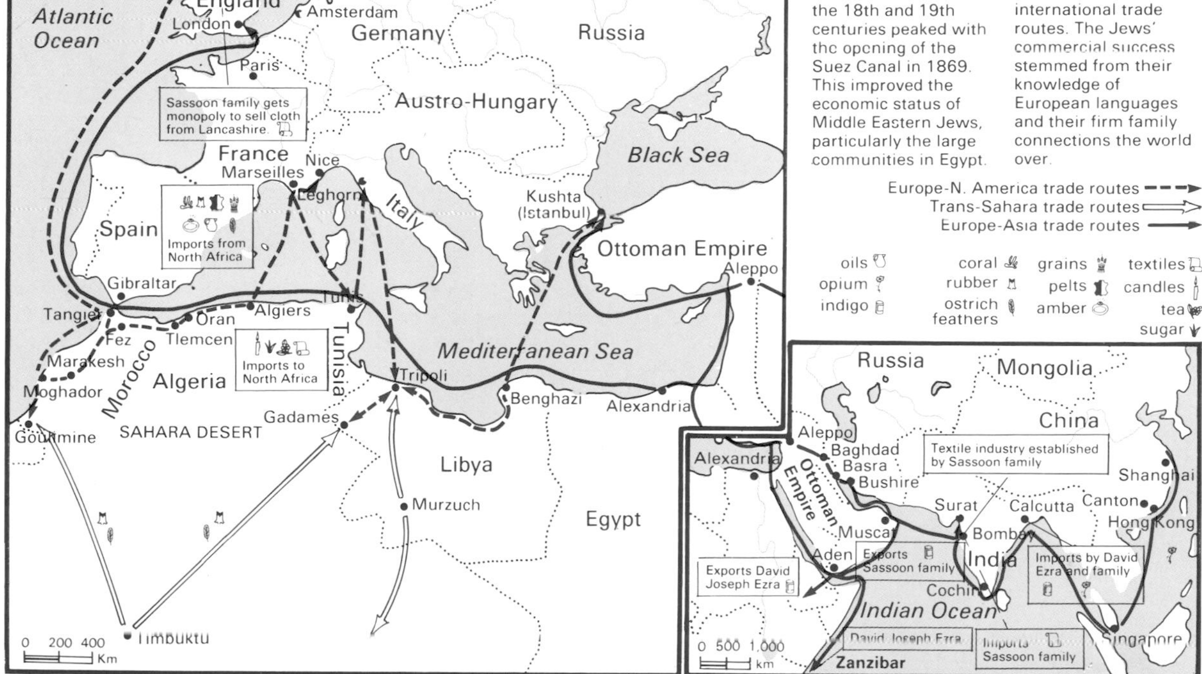

7 The rapid development of international trade in the 18th and 19th centuries peaked with the opening of the Suez Canal in 1869. This improved the economic status of Middle Eastern Jews, particularly the large communities in Egypt.

A few Jewish businessmen actually came to control certain international trade routes. The Jews' commercial success stemmed from their knowledge of European languages and their firm family connections the world over.

6 A

6 B

8 The Benei Israel, the Cochin Jews and Jews from Baghdad comprised the Jewish communities in India. Until the mid-18th century, the Benei Israel congregation lived in the villages near Bombay. Though totally cut off from centers of Jewry, they observed Jewish religious laws — such as the Sabbath, circumcision and dietary restrictions — while also adopting some local customs. Their main occupations were coconut oil extraction [pictured here, in Shool, a village in Conkan], agriculture, small-scale business and handicrafts.

8

Jewish Community and Culture in Muslim Lands

Throughout the Ottoman Empire — as well as in Islamic countries not within its sphere — Jewish communities (*Kehilot*) enjoyed wide autonomy. In the absence of a supreme cultural and judicial authority, the different communities established their own administrative, judicial and educational systems.

Structure and Education

Standing side by side at the head of community administration were the Sages (*Hakhamim*) — rabbis who functioned in the religious, legal and educational spheres — and the community leaders, who dealt with matters such as tax collection and liaison with the country's rulers. From the end of the 18th century, the rulers recognized the Chief Rabbi as the only representative of the community. Both the religious and the secular leaders were chosen by the *Ma'amad*, a board of community notables. The sages were usually elected for life and the secular leaders for periods ranging from one to three years.

The management of everyday affairs was conducted by committees. Prominent among these was the *Arikha*, which collected taxes. Additional bodies dealt with charity, welfare, and other functions that derived from specific religious injunctions. In the 18th and 19th centuries these institutions also functioned within the framework of trade organizations known as the Jewish Guilds.

Community rules and administration were determined jointly by the sages and the secular leaders by means of Articles (*takanot*) and Agreements (*haskamot*). The *haskamot* served as the local book of statutes, together with the halakhic rulings which applied to all Jewish communities [2]. Special status was conferred on the Learned Scholars: from their midst came the rabbis and judges who presided in the lower and higher courts, men of learning who disseminated the *Torah*, preachers, and the rabbinical decisors who ruled on everyday matters. They amassed power and status through the judicial and administrative authority invested in them and through their sound economic position.

Traditional Jewish education was the primary concern of the communities until the 19th century and was based on the *Talmud-Torah* (religious school) — known as the *Khutab* or the *Meldar* [1]. At the higher levels of education, "Sacred Vessels", "Sages" and "*Torah* Disseminators" trained through concentration on the study of the *Mishnah* and the *Talmud*. Besides the regular *yeshivot* (talmudic schools) — also known as *hesger* — esoteric doctrines and *Kabbalah* were studied at other, mystic *yeshivot* [4].

Spiritual Creativity and Organization

In the halakhic field, the communities of Spanish origin produced rabbinical decisors who established halakhic laws for all Jewry — such as Rabbi Joseph Caro of Safed (1488-1575), who wrote the *Shulhan Arukh* (Codification of Laws), and Rabbi Joseph Haim (1835-1909) of Baghdad, author of the *Ben Ish Hai*,

CONNECTIONS

82 Eastern Jewry after the Expulsion from Spain
100 "Liberté, Egalité, Fraternité" — for Jews as well
108 The Legal Status of Jews in Muslim Lands
110 Jewish Economic Life in Muslim Lands
124 Jewish Ethnic Communities
126 The Wandering Jew

1

1 Jewish education in the Yemen was conducted within traditional frameworks, which stressed erudition and memorizing. At three, the child was handed over to the *Mori*, who taught him Hebrew reading and writing, some arithmetic, prayers, reading the *Torah* with the Aramaic translation by Onkelos, *Mishnah*, *midrashim* and a little *Halakhah*. The high cost of manuscripts forced Yemenite Jews to commit many passages to memory, hence their erudite knowledge of source works. Schooling took place in a *Khutab* or *Heder* like this one.

2

2 The takanot of the community were read before the congregation and were recorded in the community ledgers. Infringement could provoke punishment. These rabbinical signatures appear on a collection of decrees by Moroccan rabbis of the 18th-19th centuries.

3 Jewish communities in Russian Georgia and in Afghanistan were distant from large centers of Jewry. Until the 19th century, the Georgian Jews kept up commercial and cultural contacts with the communities in Persia, Bukhara, Caucasia and the Crimea, and under their influence adopted the *Sephardi* prayerbook and rabbinical decrees. The Afghanistan Jews maintained contact via commerce between Persia and India. These skullcaps are embroidered in the style of Georgia [right] and Afghanistan [left].

4

זה השער לה׳

ספר הזהר

4 The Zohar — the principal book of *Kabbalah* — was sanctified among the eastern communities with its publication in Mantua (1558). Eastern Jews read it on occasions like the eve of ritual circumcision. Among the commentaries written on the *Zohar* were *Hesed le-Avraham*, by Rabbi Abraham Azulai of Morocco.

3

6 Kol Yisrael Haverim (*Alliance Israélite Universelle*) was founded in Paris in 1860. It strove to further the education and cultural achievement of Jews in Islamic countries, in order to improve their political status. In 1862 the first school was founded in Tetuán, Morocco. Here, its pupils are seen at the beginning of the 20th century.

5

5 The Baghdad community revived under Turkish rule in Iraq (1534-1623, 1638-1917) after it was destroyed by Tamerlane in 1393. As the rabbinical decisory center for Jewish communities in Persia and Bukhara, its influence reached Syria and Erez Israel. This is the ancient synagogue in Baghdad, restored several times in the 17th and 19th centuries.

6

which serves today as the binding halakhic text for the Jews of Iraq [5] and other communities of the East.

The literature of moral discourse was a central branch of the intellectual and spiritual creativity which developed in Islamic countries after the expulsion from Spain. Prominent among the known works was *Reshit Hokhma*, written in Safed by Rabbi Elija de Vidas (died *c.* 1588); *Shevet Musar* by Rabbi Elijah ha-Cohen ha-Itamari of Smyrna (died in 1729); *Me'am Loez* written in *Ladino* by Rabbi Jacob Khuli (1689-1732) of Kushta; and *Hemdat Yamim*, a composition of unknown authorship saturated with messianic yearning. This spiritual creativity also found expression in poetic verses known as *bakashot* (supplications) and in various folk compositions, particularly those handed down orally from generation to generation — such as Spanish-Jewish romance lyrics and ballads, folktales, proverbs and folksongs [7, 10].

The processes of emancipation and secularization which commenced in the second half of the 19th century influenced both the organization and the spiritual life of the communities. Many community-centered functions now passed to the state. The communities retained authority in their rabbinical courts, but this diminished to cover only material and family matters. The disintegration of the communities was prevented to a large extent by the expansion of voluntary activity in fields like welfare and education.

The increased influence of the western powers and of the European educational network, together with the activities of *Kol Yisrael Haverim* [6], also wrought changes: Jewish languages which had held sway beside Hebrew in the various communities were now pushed aside by French in North Africa and the Balkans, and by English in Egypt and Iraq; secular subjects were taught in the schools, and many Jews sent their children to European-style schools and universities.

KEY

The shadarim (abbreviation of the Aramaic *Sheluha de Rabnan*, or rabbinical emissaries) worked mainly in outlying communities, from the 16th century, collecting donations and "taxes" for Erez Israel and the *yeshivot*. Their activities contributed to the strengthening of ties both between Erez Israel and the Diaspora, and among the various communities. The *shadarim* brought instruction from Erez Israel on *Halakhah*, philosophy and commentary, and distributed Jewish literature written in the various communities. Some acquired positions of power when they settled in a community. This *shadar* script is from about 1900.

7

7 The Jews of Kurdistan belonged to the political and communal framework of Iraq (Babylonia), but fell under the often arbitrary control of local Kurdish rulers. In the picture — a book of religious readings and verse for *Shabbat ha-Gadol* (before Passover) and other festivals (1864).

8

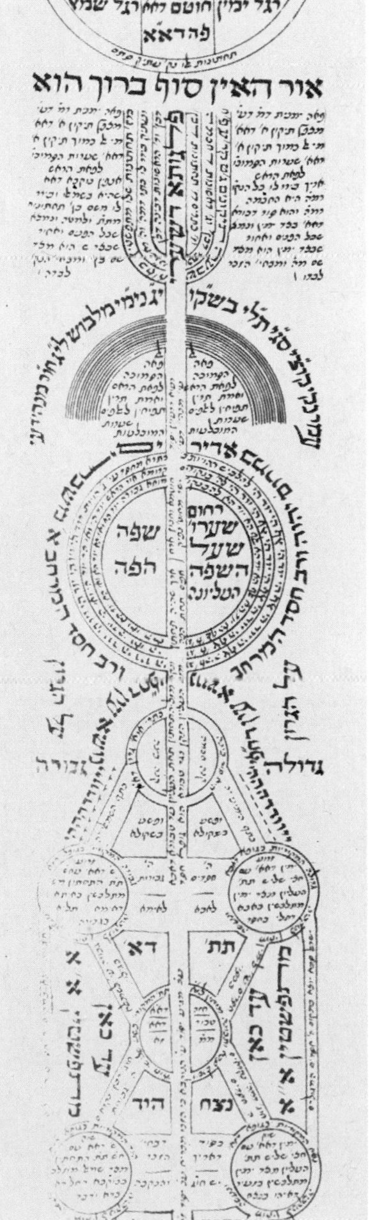

8 The Lurianic Kabbalah made a deep imprint on eastern Jewry and its mark is strongly evident in contemplative philosophy and liturgy, e.g., songs and readings for the seventh night of Passover. This 19th century talisman from the Middle East depicts the Tree of Life and the *Sephirot* according to the Lurianic *Kabbalah*.

9 R. Amram ben-Diwwan worked as a *shadar* from Erez Israel at the close of the 17th century. After his death and burial in Ouzan, Morocco, he was sanctified and his tomb, pictured here, became a pilgrims' site for Jews and Muslims. This shared belief reflects the peaceful coexistence that prevailed between Jew and Muslim in daily life.

9

10 Persian Jewry developed its individual spiritual creativity despite its dependence on the authority of mentors in Baghdad. In the 18th century, Persia attained a cultural flowering under Nadir Shah. He initiated the translation of Holy Scripture into Persian. In the 18th century, the Sage Simantov Melamed of Meshed was known for his essay *Azharot*, which was written in Judeo-Persian, Hebrew and Aramaic, and for his essay on Maimonides. Under the influence of the *shadarim* and the Baghdad community, the Persian Jews adopted the *Sephardi* prayerbook and decrees. The illustration shows a page from *Mussa Na'ame* (the Book of Moses, 1327), by the Persian-Jewish poet Shahin.

10

The Pogroms of Eastern Europe

The pogroms that erupted in Russia in the early 1880s represent a turning point in the history of the Jews of that country who had, until then, lived in relative security. The pogroms resulted both from growing and uncontrollable unrest, and from increasingly virulent anti-Semitism in Russia, which was fomented by the spread of anti-Semitism throughout Western and Central Europe.

"Storms in the South"

The first wave of pogroms (1881-1884), in which hundreds of Jews lost their lives, is known in Jewish history as the *Sufoth ba-Negev* ("storms in the South") because initially it was largely concentrated in southern Russia and the Ukraine; at later stages pogroms broke out elsewhere as well (in Warsaw and Novgorod) [2].

The immediate pretext for the pogroms was the assassination of Tsar Alexander II in 1881 by members of the revolutionary organization *Narodnya Volya* (Will of the People). Among those sentenced to death for the crime was a Jewess, Hessia Helfman. The Russian authorities tried to depict the pogroms as the people's spontaneous will to avenge their murdered king. There are, however, clear indications that the riots were initiated and directed by circles close to Tsar Alexander III (the murdered tsar's son and successor) with the aim of using the Jews as a scapegoat. Failure on the part of the police to intervene immediately to halt the killing and looting only lends support to this view. Moreover, during the pogroms, the government issued "temporary orders" (published in May 1882 and therefore known as the "May orders") designed to eliminate the causes of friction between Russians and Jews. These restricted Jewish domicile rights even further than previously, and reduced the professions that Jews were allowed to practice. These measures in turn served to confirm the contention that the Jews, through their behavior, had actually brought the pogroms on themselves.

The "storms in the South" badly shook the Jews of Europe. The reforms instituted during the reign of Alexander II had led many to hope that they would soon achieve emancipation as had Jewish communities in Western and Central Europe.

The Jewish Response

The Jews' first reaction was to leave Russia. Most emigrés headed west, through Central and Western Europe, to the New World [7]. Others, however, sought a radical solution to the problem of the homeless Jewish nation and so turned in the direction of Erez Israel [1, 3]. Their vanguard led the first *aliyah*, or wave of immigration, from Europe (1882-1903), and established the *Hovevei Zion* Zionist associations.

Some educated Jewish youth and workers in Russia continued to support the socialists. The Jewish contingent in this camp was impressive, both among

CONNECTIONS

106 The Jewish Community in Russia: 1772-1881
116 The Reawakening of Jewish Nationalism
126 The Wandering Jew
128 Origins of the American Jewish Community
134 Zionist Settlement in Erez Israel

1 Emigration became a central aspect of Jewish life in Eastern Europe in the late 19th and early 20th century. It was induced by sizable natural increase — the Jewish population doubled at this time — the Jews' loss of the right to farm land, and the fear of restrictive edicts and pogroms. Jewish emigration was unusual in two respects: its composition — entire families uprooted themselves, attesting to their intention never to return; and its purpose — the migrants were not seeking merely a safe haven, but freedom and independence as well.

2 "After the Pogrom" was painted by the Jewish artist from Warsaw Maurice Minkowsky (1881-1930). Hatred of the Jews was exploited by the authorities as a means of appealing to the masses or exerting pressure for political ends. In 1881 a pogrom broke out in Warsaw, which was within the Pale of Settlement. It was apparently designed to win over the Polish people, who were hostile to the Jews, to the Russian regime, as well as to prove that it was not only Russians who persecuted Jews. Polish public figures, however, protested these actions.

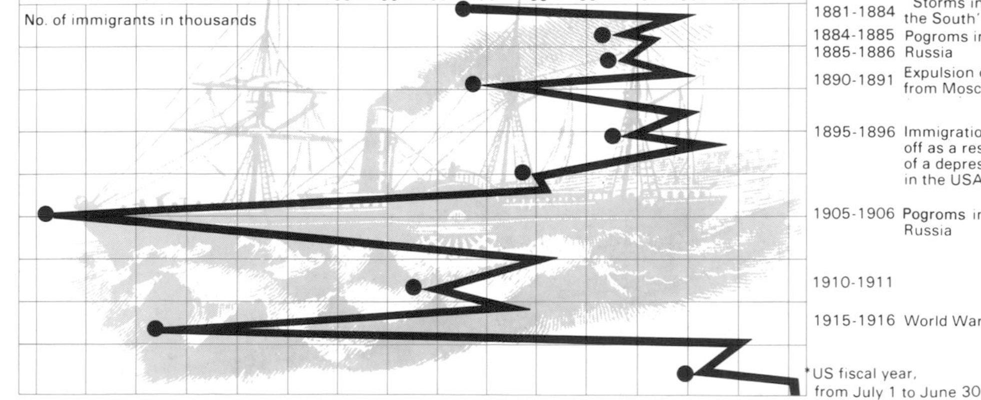

3 The waves of immigrants entering the United States were in direct proportion to the pogroms in Russia. As the graph indicates, the rise in the number of Jewish immigrants began immediately after the "storms in the South" (1881-1884) and gained impetus in 1891 when Jews were expelled from Moscow. 111,000 Jews entered the United States in that year, and 137,000 the following year. As pogroms increased throughout Russia, the number of immigrants in one year alone (1905-6) exceeded 200,000. Following the libelous Beilis trial (1913) and pogroms in the Ukraine after World War I, more immigrants again streamed in. Parallel waves of immigrants also arrived in Erez Israel. What is known as the First *Aliyah* to Erez Israel followed in the wake of the "storms in the South." The Second *Aliyah* began to arrive after the Kishinev pogroms (1903) and their aftermath. The third began after World War I.

the rank-and-file and the leadership. But many were also becoming aware of the special needs of the Jewish working class, and this led to the establishment of separate organizations for Jewish workers, among them the *Bund* party founded in 1897.

Self-Defense

The second wave of pogroms (1903-1906) broke out in conjunction with the unrest that led to the revolution in Russia in 1905. In an attempt to discredit the liberal and socialist parties, the authorities capitalized on the presence of Jews among their leadership to depict these organizations as lackeys of the Jews.

The first of these pogroms occurred in Kishinev in Bessarabia during Passover of 1903 [Key, 5]. Some 49 Jews were murdered, hundreds wounded, and around 1,500 Jewish homes and shops looted. Once again the security forces generally kept their distance, and once again the masses took up the cry: "Strike at the Jews and save Russia."

The extent of the killing, and especially the Jews' helplessness at the start of the pogroms, caused deep frustration. In response, "self-defense" societies were established. Those who joined these organizations were mostly young Zionists or socialists. Their weaponry was minimal: axes, sticks and stones. In the Gomel pogroms which erupted shortly after those in Kishinev, these primitively armed youngsters proved that it was possible to stop the rioters and defend their communities.

At Gomel and elsewhere, Jewish self-defense activities were obstructed by the police and the army who, instead of controlling the rioters, attacked the self-defense leagues and arrested their members. Some of those persecuted by the authorities at the time were among the first to reach Ereẓ Israel with the second wave of immigration (1904-1914). They formed the nucleus of the *Bar-Giora* and *HaShomer* groups that were founded later to guard and defend Jewish settlements.

KEY

Scrolls of the Law are interred after being desecrated at Kishinev. In the pogrom, which began on the last day of Passover 1903, 49 Jews were killed, hundreds were wounded, and considerable property was destroyed. The behavior of the rioters, who sadistically brutalized their victims, shook the Jewish community in Russia and throughout the world. Under the pressure of international public opinion, several rioters were brought to trial, but received only light sentences. In the wake of this incident, Jewish self-defense leagues sprang up and Jewish intellectuals who had been fervent socialists became disillusioned and again took up the Zionist ideal.

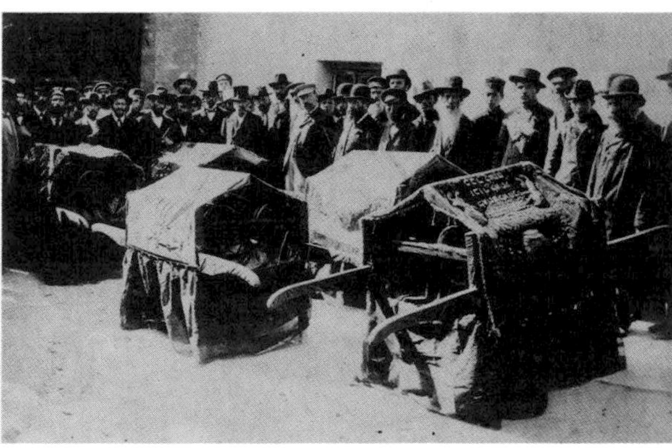

4 **The blood libel against Beilis** (1913), in which Menahem Mendel Beilis was charged with the murder of a young Christian boy in Kiev, focused attention on the "Jewish problem" in Russia. Beilis was eventually acquitted, and this was taken as a triumph of the liberal-revolutionary forces over the government.

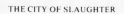

6 **Jewish refugees** after the pogrom in Poland (1915). Painting by William Wachtel (1875-1941).

5 **After the Kishinev pogroms** a commission headed by the historian Simon Dubnow was established in Odessa to investigate the incident. The poet Chaim Nahman Bialik, sent by the commission, proved that the pogroms had been contrived by the authorities in advance. Bialik gave literary form to his impressions from the atrocities in his poem "The City of Slaughter."

THE CITY OF SLAUGHTER

Arise and go now to the city of slaughter;
Into its courtyard wind thy way;
There with thine own hand touch, and with the eyes of thine head,
Behold on tree, on stone, on fence, on mural clay,
The spattered blood and dried brains of the dead.
Proceed thence to the ruins, the split walls reach,
Where wider grows the hollow, and greater grows the breach;
Pass over the shattered hearth, attain the broken wall
Whose burnt and barren brick, whose charred stones reveal
The open mouths of such wounds, that no mending
Shall ever mend, nor healing ever heal.
There will thy feet in feathers sink, and stumble
On wreckage doubly wrecked, scroll heaped on manuscript,
Fragments again fragmented —
Pause not upon this havoc; go thy way.
The perfumes will be wafted from the acacia bud
And half its blossoms will be feathers,
Whose smell is the smell of blood!
And, spiting thee, strange incense they will bring —
Banish thy loathing — all the beauty of the spring,
The thousand golden arrows of the sun,
Will flash upon thy malison;
The sevenfold rays of broken glass
Over thy sorrow joyously will pass,
For God called up the slaughter and the spring together,—
The slayer slew, the blossom burst, and it was sunny weather!

7 **Immigration to Argentina was** supported by Baron Maurice de Hirsch (1831-1896) who planned the gradual evacuation of millions of Jews from Russia. He founded the Jewish Colonization Association (JCA) to aid him in setting up autonomous Jewish settlements. In 1877 there were 25 JCA farming settlements in Argentina. This photograph shows the village of Moisésville, established by JCA.

The Reawakening of Jewish Nationalism

From the time of the Exile, the Jewish People cherished the hope of renewing national life in Ereẓ Israel. They never considered themselves a people without a land, but rather a nation dispossessed, and daily prayed for the Return. During the first half of the nineteenth century, when many European peoples achieved national independence, Jews, too, began to cultivate a desire for national fulfillment. The Jews' integration into European society during the latter part of that century, however, did not proceed as they had hoped. When it became clear that emancipation would not solve the Jewish problem, the notion of a physical "return to the land of our fathers" took hold. The idea of reestablishing Jewish sovereignty in Ereẓ Israel gained support even among Christians and a variety of European non-Jewish political circles [3].

Forerunners of Zionism

Both emancipated Jews and traditionally religious Jews were among those who first called upon their brethren to abandon the Diaspora and settle in Ereẓ Israel. Most notable were two rabbis, Zevi Hirsch Kalischer (1795-1874) and Judah Alkalai (1798-1888), together with Moses Hess (1812-1875), a philosopher and one of the founders of German socialism [10]. The Serbian-born Alkalai, who actually settled in Ereẓ Israel in 1871, and the Polish-born Kalischer, who spent most of his life as a rabbinical scholar in Germany, shared the belief that the Redemption could be hastened by human action. To this end, they not only preached and wrote, but also organized settlement societies. Part of their plan was to enlist the aid of wealthy Jews to finance the purchase of land in Ereẓ Israel, where towns and villages would be established for the absorption of the Jewish masses.

Hess, though not a religious Jew, believed that the Jews had no future in the Diaspora; they would be able to lead normal lives, socially and economically, only in a state of their own. Hess agreed that by returning to Ereẓ Israel and establishing a just society based on socialist principles, the Jewish people would be taking part in mankind's great historical movement toward human redemption.

The efforts of these proto-Zionists did not bear immediate fruit. It was only in the 1880s that the idea of Jewish national rebirth became a reality.

The Spread of Zionism

The pogroms of 1881 in Russia were of decisive importance in crystallizing Zionism as a national movement. The need to provide immediate physical sanctuary for Jews made the idea of settlement in Ereẓ Israel relevant. Numerous societies of *Hovevei Zion* (or *Hibbat Zion*) sprang up, independently, throughout Russia. Their members believed that immigration to Ereẓ Israel provided the only feasible solution to the Jewish problem [5]. One of the more important of these groups was the *Bilu* society, whose aim was "the politico-

CONNECTIONS
100 "Liberté, Egalité, Fraternité" — for Jews as well
114 The Pogroms of Eastern Europe
116 The Reawakening of Jewish Nationalism
118 Modern Anti-Semitism
132 19th Century Erez Israel
134 Foundations of Zionism in Erez Israel

1 Ahad ha-Am (Asher Ginsberg, 1856-1927) was a strong believer in the value of Jewish education in the Diaspora. Erez Israel was to be a spiritual center for the Jews in which Jewish and humanist morality would produce a just society.

2 Eliezer Ben-Yehuda (1858-1922; seen here with his wife Hemdah) settled in Erez Israel in 1881, founded the *Va'ad ha-Lashon* (eventually to become Israel's Academy of the Hebrew Language), published a number of journals in Hebrew and introduced hundreds of new words into the language. His major work was a dictionary of the Hebrew language.

3 Laurence Oliphant (1829-1888) was the most important Christian supporter of Zionism, and the most active. He went to Kushta with letters of recommendation to the Turkish authorities; while he impressed officials, he was unable to influence the Sultan. A second visit roused great hopes, but failed due to a dispute between Britain and Turkey. Oliphant settled in Haifa, lending assistance to the pioneers of the First *Aliyah* — the first wave of Zionist immigrants to Erez Israel.

4 Cover of the by-laws of The Bilu Society. *Bilu* was founded in Russia in 1882 by young Jewish intellectuals in reaction to the 1881 pogroms. *Bilu* tried to influence all Jews to join together for the settlement of Erez Israel. The name *Bilu* was an acronym for the biblical passage: "House of Jacob, come ye and let us go." The first *Bilu* group reached Jaffa in 1882.

5 Official Stamp of the "Committee for the Pioneers of Yesud ha-Ma'alah in the Holy Land," founded in Jaffa in 1882 by members of *Hovevei Zion* from Russia who had come to purchase land in Erez Israel. The motto describes the pioneers returning to their homeland, and appeals to others to join them in achieving the satisfaction of working the land.

ירושלם יום ה׳ כד תמוז | השקפה | אלף תתליה לחרבן

שנה חמישית | גליון מב

HASHKAFA V année № 42

עתון יוצא לאור פעמים בשבוע

ביום השלישי וביום הששי

בעלת הפירמן: חמדה בן־יהודה

העורך: א בן־יהודה

הגיע תלגרם

כי היום הוא יום הקבורה של דר׳ הרצל.

ראשי עדת הספרדים החליטו לעשות

מספד בצבור על מתנו הגדול

בבית הכנסת הגדול לרבן יוחנן בן זכאי בשעת הצהרים.

הרב דר׳ גרינהוט, ראש בית היתומים הפרנקפורטי הספיד את דר׳ הרצל לפני כל היתומים תמול יום ד׳ בשעה שבע וחצי בערב בבית הכנסת של בית היתומים. דר׳ גרינהוט דבר בהתלהבות גדולה, בדמעות בעיניו, ויתאר לפני היתומים את גדל הצרה הזאת, ויאמר כי לו היו נביאים עתה כי אז בודאי קבעו את היום הזה לתענית לעולם רבים מהנכחים הורידו דמעות.

גבאי בית הספרים לבני ישראל פרסמו מודעה זו:

אחב"י האספו היום (כד תמוז) יום קבורת מתתיהו הרצל לבית הספרים לבנ"י בשעה חמש וחצי אחה"צ (שעה י"א וחצי ערבית) לספוד ולבכותו.

ועד ביה"ס.

6 Hashkafah-Viewpoint (1900-1910), the journal published by Ben-Yehuda with the aim of turning Hebrew into an everyday language. In his articles, he introduced renewed words; a special column featured new words.

economic and national-spiritual revival of the Jewish people in Ereẓ Israel" [4].

A great impetus to the movement was given by the publication, in 1882, of a pamphlet entitled *Autoemancipation*, by Leon Pinsker (1821-1891), an Odessa physician [8]. Pinsker considered anti-Semitism an incurable disease and advocated Zionism as the only possible antidote, emphasizing that the Jews would have to be emancipated through their own efforts.

The founding of the *Zerubavel* society in Odessa in 1883 marked the real beginning of organized Zionism. *Zerubavel* was led by Moses Leib Lilienblum (1843-1910) and Pinsker, who issued a call to Zionist societies all over Russia to unite into one organization. Czarist limitations on political activity proved an obstacle, however, which was overcome only in 1884 when the centennial of the birth of Moses Montefiore provided legitimization for the first conference of all *Hibbat Zion* activists. This took place in Kattowitz, on November 6, 1884; it was decided there to unite the movement. In order to preclude interference from the hostile Russian authorities, the organization adopted a rather innocuous name — *Yesod Mazkeret Moshe be-Ereẓ ha-Kodesh* (Foundation to Commemorate Moses [Montefiore] in the Holy Land) — and a program which was ostensibly to provide charitable support for Jewish settlers in Erez Israel.

The organization was beset by enormous problems; financial difficulties, the struggle for leadership among the various branches, friction between religious and secular members, etc. The net result was that the movement failed in its major undertaking — a mass migration of Jews to Ereẓ Israel. It did succeed, however, in awakening the national consciousness of the Jewish people and intensifying interest in Hebrew culture [Key]. In this respect, *Hibbat Zion* provided the sturdy foundation upon which the World Zionist Organization would, not long after, rise.

KEY

One result of the national reawakening was the proliferation of Jewish newspapers and magazines. Some fifteen hundred Jewish journals were published during the course of the 19th century. *Ha-Melitz* (1860-1904) was one of the first and most influential Hebrew journals in Russia, with Y.L. Gordon, Bialik and Ahad ha-Am among its contributors. In Poland, the first Hebrew journal, *Ha-Zefirah*, appeared in 1862. Some time later it came out in support of political Zionism.

7

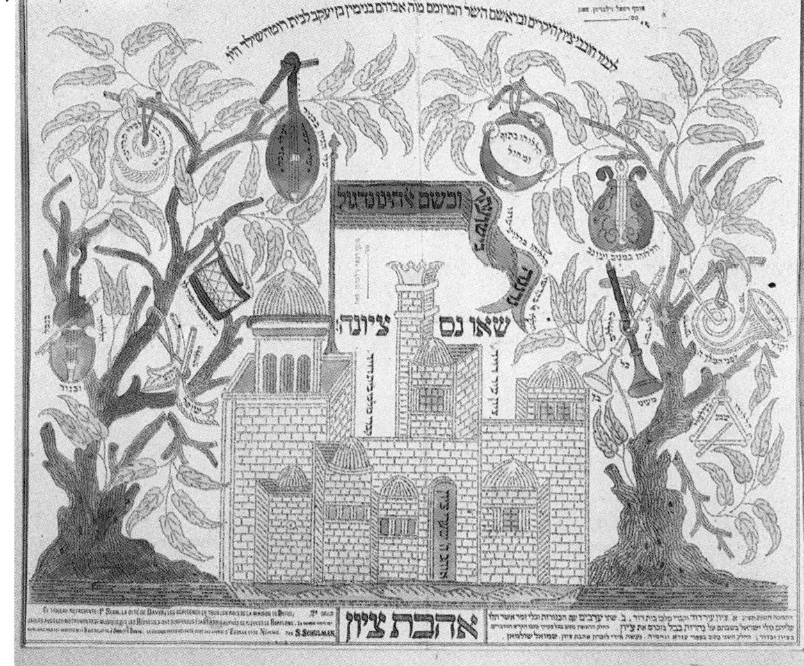

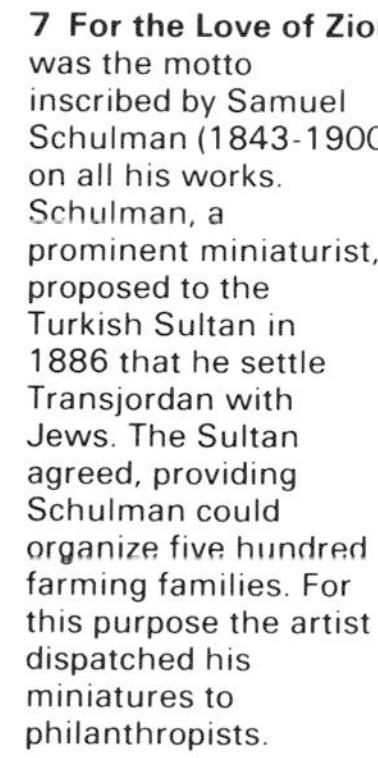

7 For the Love of Zion was the motto inscribed by Samuel Schulman (1843-1900) on all his works. Schulman, a prominent miniaturist, proposed to the Turkish Sultan in 1886 that he settle Transjordan with Jews. The Sultan agreed, providing Schulman could organize five hundred farming families. For this purpose the artist dispatched his miniatures to philanthropists.

8

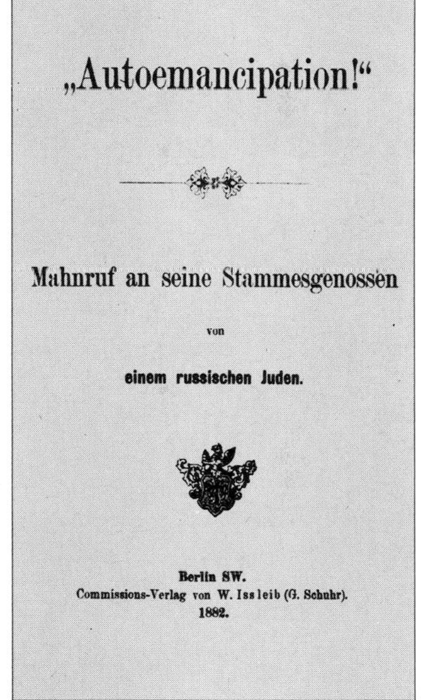

„Autoemancipation!"

Mahnruf an seine Stammesgenossen

von

einem russischen Juden.

Berlin SW.
Commissions-Verlag von W. Issleib (G. Schuhr).
1882.

8 Autoemancipation, Pinsker's appeal to the Jews to take their destiny in their own hands, was published as a response to the failure of European emancipation and the emergence of modern anti-Semitism. The pamphlet considerably encouraged the subsequent organization of the *Hovevei Zion* movement.

9

9 The lands of Petah Tiqwah, previously the Arab village Umm Lebis, were acquired by a group of Jerusalem Jews in 1878 for the purpose of settlement. Warned that the area was uninhabitable, they persisted nonetheless, claiming that they would make of "the valley of Achor... a *petah tiqwah*," or door of hope (Hosea 2:15), and even enjoyed some success. But their hopes were dashed when they were afflicted by malaria and constrained by the religious laws of *shemittah* — leaving the land fallow once every seven years — and they abandoned the village. It was resettled in 1882 by pioneers of the First *Aliyah*.

10

10 Moses Hess (1812-1875), one of the forerunners of socialist Zionism, believed that socialism would solve the moral and human problems of man rather than those of class. Hess, one of the founders of German socialism, first believed in assimilation for the Jews. The emergence of modern anti-Semitism, however, together with the new nationalist movements of Europe, brought him to change his mind. He published his views in *Rome and Jerusalem* (1868), a book which calls for the establishment of a Jewish state in Erez Israel, based on the social-democratic principles of Judaism.

Modern Anti-Semitism

Although secularism spread throughout European society during the 17th century, anti-Semitism remained. Prolonged Christian cultural predominance had managed to instill in Europeans of all nationalities a hatred of Jews that became part and parcel of their culture — in music, theater, literature, painting, sculpture, language [4] and even popular games [3]. Anti-Semitism in a new guise even surfaced in the enlightenment movement, in romanticism, in the new nationalism and in socialism.

Racism and Anti-Semitism

By the middle of the 19th century, a racial theory was taking hold in the European intellectual world, based on developments registered in technology and the natural sciences since the 17th century. In the mid-18th century, anthropology had divided mankind into races according to physical characteristics such as skin color and body measurements. In 1829 an English researcher put forward the notion of "historical races" to distinguish different races within one skin-color group. Scholars claimed that there was a connection between a man's race, his position on the "skull scale" they had developed, and his characteristics and abilities. Biology in the early 19th century promulgated the idea that nature had evolved over hundreds of thousands of years from a primitive and inferior state to more developed forms. The man who fashioned this theory was the Englishman, Charles Darwin, author of *Origin of the Species* (1859). His theory of evolution introduced to the world such concepts as "natural selection," "survival of the fittest" and "war of survival."

But viewing nature in this way had social implications. Darwin stated that the potential for evolution was limitless. This assessment led some to the idea that the processes of natural selection and evolution were still going on among human beings, and thus there were "better" — i.e., fitter — human beings and "worse" ones. In their search for differences that would prove this ongoing evolution of the human species, many held fast to the anthropological division of mankind into races and to the distinctions linguistics had made among language families and related cultures. Hatred of the Jews soon became based on this new branch of science, and modern anti-Semitism was the result.

Modern ("racial") anti-Semitism did not view confrontation with the Jews as a religious, economic or social conflict, but as a contest between competing races, a biological struggle for survival. The logic of such a position demanded extreme and uncompromising measures. As the Jewish people were intrinsically an inferior race, racial anti-Semites detested and feared Jews who had converted and assimilated even more than Jews who had retained their cultural identity. In time racial anti-Semitism led to an attitude that removed the Jews entirely from the realm of humanity. The Jew was finally

CONNECTIONS

100 "Liberté, Egalité, Fraternité" — for Jews as well
114 The Pogroms of Eastern Europe
116 The Reawakening of Jewish Nationalism
120 Zionism Becomes a Political Movement
146 Nazi Anti-Semitic Policy

1

1 "The wandering Jew," a caricature of an illustration by P.G. Doré (1852). The origin of "the wandering Jew" or "the eternal Jew" harks back to the Christian legend of a Jew named Ahasuerus or Cartaphilus who humiliated Jesus on his way to the crucifixion and was therefore doomed to eternal wandering. The legend appeared in Constantinople in the 4th century and reached the west in the 17th century via a German folk tale. Constantly readapted to suit changing times and places, the character became immortalized in dozens of works of art and literature. To Christians, the character embodied the Jews' existential state after the death of Jesus; anti-Semites especially emphasized its disturbing presence and reappearance generation after generation, in every corner of the world. To Jews, it was a symbol of their persecution and alienation.

2

2 "Suess the Jew" was Joseph Ben Issachar Suesskind Oppenheimer (1698-1738), a tax collector, who in 1733 became finance minister to the Duke of Wurtemberg. Suess substantially increased the state treasury and helped organize its administration, thus gaining wealth and candidacy for nobility. But immediately after the Duke's death, Suess was accused of embezzlement and adultery, was executed and his corpse displayed in an iron cage. The event was commemorated on a medallion. For anti-Semites, Suess was a symbol of pervasive Jewish influence.

3 "The Jew Game" — a gameboard from Alsace (circa 1750) with a picture of a Jew in the center. Anyone landing on the Jew had to pay a penalty. The Jews' limited range of occupations — trade and moneylending — fostered a negative image of them as evil-natured and physically feeble, with peculiar religious rituals. With emancipation, Jews began reaching high positions in society and accumulating wealth. Now their image underwent a change: they were seen as a tightly-knit group threatening the very existence of the country — a sort of exploitative "International Trading Company."

3

4

787. Lending – N. lending &c. *v.*; loan, advance, accommodation; mortgage &c. 771; investment.
pawnshop, spout, my uncle's.
lender, pawnbroker, money-lender, usurer, Jew, Shylock.
V. lend, advance, loan, accommodate with, lend on security; pawn &c.

819. Parsimony – N. parsimony; parsimoniousness, stinginess &c. *adj.*; stint; illiberality, avarice, tenacity, avidity, rapacity, extortion, venality, cupidity; selfishness &c. 943.
miser, niggard, churl, screw, tightwad, skinflint, crib, codger, money-grubber, lickpenny, curmudgeon, harpy, extortioner, Jew, usurer.

4 "Jew" as a concept with special connotations entered into various European languages. In the two entries here, taken from an English dictionary of synonyms published in 1957, the word "Jew" has meaning in two negative contexts: moneylending and greed. This is damning proof of the deeply rooted negative image ascribed to the Jew in European culture. In later editions, these definitions were removed.

characterized as the member of a disintegrating "anti-race," actually akin to a microbe (*Bacillus Judaicus*).

19th Century Anti-Semitism

Anti-Semitism in all its variations — religious, social and racial — spread rapidly in the latter half of the 19th century. Two catalysts made it an influential factor in European life. The first was the growing sense of alienation and socio-economic insecurity that swept through European society following the industrial revolution. Difficult living conditions rendered the middle class, and particularly the proletarian working class, open to the influence of ideas that promised deliverance from present suffering.

The second development was democratization, which extended voting and candidacy rights to all classes of citizens, while improvements in education brought literacy to the masses. Politics soon became an arena where the masses were courted with simplistic slogans that appealed to the basest instincts. The way was prepared, therefore, for the successful dissemination of an all-inclusive and extremist theory like anti-Semitism. European political movements adopted or even emphasized anti-Semitic positions in order to strengthen their bases of support. Examples include the Catholic People's Party in Hungary, the Protestant Anti-Revolutionary Party in the Netherlands and the socialist *Narodnya Volya* Party in Russia.

Anti-Semitism was also at the center of the stormiest political crisis in France at the turn of the 20th century — the Dreyfus Affair. Contrary to Jewish hopes that anti-Semitism would eventually fade as humanity progressed, it was soon obvious that the tides of contemporary modernization and nationalism had led to an anti-Semitism of new and different proportions. And this, in turn, led to the greatest disaster to befall the Jewish people in their entire history — the Nazi Holocaust.

KEY

That the Jews were scheming to take over the world was one of the central arguments used in anti-Semitic propaganda of the modern period, as depicted in this cartoon (Vienna, 1912). The claim was most vehemently articulated in *The Protocols of the Elders of Zion*, a libelous document most of whose editions included two parts: "The Rabbi's Sermon" (a chapter from an anti-Semitic novel) and 24 "protocols" meant to be reports of decisions taken at a secret Jewish gathering — but which were, in fact, forgeries of a real essay having nothing to do with Jews. The forgery was compiled by agents of the Russian secret police in the late 19th century.

5

WÄHLT
CHRISTLICHSOZIAL
DEUTSCHE
CHRISTEN
RETTET·ÖSTERREICH!

5 Anti-Semitism in Austria resulted partially from the bitterness felt by Austrians when their preferential status in the Austro-Hungarian Empire deteriorated. After the defeat in World War I these sentiments were even further reinforced. In this 1920 election poster for the Christian Social Party of Austria, the Jew is depicted as a deadly snake strangling the country. Numbers denoting sums of money are written on his body to symbolize Jewish capitalism, while beside him are the hammer and sickle, symbols of Jewish Bolshevism. The caption reads: "Save Austria!"

6

6 Paradoxes and contradictions have characterized anti-Semitic portrayals. Opposing traits clashing within the Jew, such as unbridled power vs. terrible cowardice, have underscored his alleged lack of humanity. In this English cartoon of 1799, an ugly, dirty Jewish peddler has seduced an innocent Christian maiden. Portrayals of this type became more frequent by the late 19th century, and culminated in the advent of Nazi anti-Semitism.

7

7 The Jewish personality was the theme of satirical plays and cartoons even after Jews were granted equal rights in European countries. In the atmosphere following the Congress of Vienna (1815), the Jew was denounced for being a "pseudo-intellectual" trying to hide every trace of his Jewish identity. This cartoon (Germany, 1820) satirizes the alleged greed and stinginess of Jews: a Jewish family administers castor oil to its son so he will excrete a coin he has swallowed.

8

8 Richard Wagner (1813-1883), the German composer, claimed in "The Jews in Music" (1850) that the Jews had ruined musical taste. In Wagner's opinion, since the Jews innately lacked artistic creative potential, the success enjoyed by Jewish composers such as Mendelssohn could only be due to Germany's weakness. Although the Jewish artist functioned within the general society, Wagner held that he could not be influenced by an alien folk culture: because the spirit and language of the German people were foreign to the Jew, he could create only superficial works.

Zionism Becomes a Political Movement

The *Hibbat Zion* movement in Eastern Europe was soon bogged down in everyday affairs. But during the last decade of the 19th century, it acquired a new sense of momentum from the countries of Western Europe which enabled it to reorganize within the World Zionist Organization.

It was precisely in those countries which had granted the Jews equal rights during the emancipation — France, Germany and Austria — that modern anti-Semitism emerged, and popular sentiment opposed Jewish penetration into the fabric of national life. Once again the Jewish problem surfaced. The Dreyfus Trial in 1894 — in which anti-Semitism manifested itself at the highest levels of French society — proved the catalyst [2]. Theodor Herzl (1860-1904), a Viennese Jewish journalist assigned to cover the trial, was astounded by the anti-Semitic outbursts it generated. In his diary he wrote: "I have the solution to the Jewish problem. Not *a* solution but *the* solution."

Herzl's Jewish State

Herzl argued that the Jews of Western Europe, even after receiving equal rights, had been unable to assimilate, and still comprised a "nation within a nation." In "The Jewish State" he defined the Jewish problem as a national problem rather than a social, religious or economic one, and the establishment of a Jewish state as the solution to it. Anti-Semitism, predicted Herzl, would prove catastrophic to the Jews and traumatic to the nation-states. Liberal regimes would be racked by inner dissension; the Jews would be pushed into the arms of the socialist revolution; and the stability of the present order would be severely undermined. It was therefore incumbent upon the states of Europe to assist in establishing a Jewish state and assuring it of international legitimation.

Jewish response to Herzl's program was not uniform. Numerous leaders of Western European Jewry opposed the idea altogether. The wealthy Jews to whom he appealed for support considered him somewhat deranged. Leading rabbis feared that his ideas would provoke a new wave of anti-Semitism; they denounced "The Jewish State" in pamphlets and at a special conference. They held that Jews were a religious community alone, with a mission among the nations.

The members of *Hovevei Zion*, on the other hand, were wildly enthusiastic. Herzl's program breathed new life into their stagnant affairs [8]. They mobilized around him, proffering all possible aid and insisting that he assume the mantle of leadership.

In the summer of 1897, the First Zionist Congress took place in Basle, Switzerland [Key], with delegates attending from all over the world. The Jewish problem was publicly debated and the solution to it defined in the Basle Program: "Zionism seeks to establish a home for the Jewish people in Erez Israel secured under public law." In pursuit of its goals, the Congress deter-

CONNECTIONS

1 Israel Zangwill (1864-1926; seen here with his wife) was active in the Zionist Society of London and among the founders of the Jewish Territorial Organization in 1905. The JTO sought any territory which would enable the Jews to settle productively and enjoy political or cultural autonomy. When the Balfour Declaration was issued in 1917, many JTO members joined the WZO. The Zionist Federation of Great Britain was oriented on "political" Zionism with an affinity to Britain.

2 Alfred Dreyfus (1859-1935), an assimilated Jew and officer in the French Army, was falsely accused in 1894 of betraying his country. He was brought to trial, found guilty, deprived of his rank and sentenced to life imprisonment on Devil's Island. During the trial there were manifestations of anti-Semitism, including a demand to abrogate the civil rights of the Jews of France. It took many years to prove his innocence. The affair caused many Jews to reconsider their orientation.

3 Nahum Sokolow (1859-1936), a writer and journalist, was covering the First Zionist Congress for his paper when he met Herzl and was transformed into an ardent Zionist. He initiated and maintained contact with a large number of European political leaders.

4 Menahem Ussishkin (1863-1941) was one of the foremost leaders of *Hibbat Zion* and one of the fathers of "practical" Zionism in the WZO. His differences with Herzl over the "political" Zionism that Herzl put forward became particularly acute at the time of the Uganda crisis. Ussishkin, who headed "the Zionists of Zion," published "Our Program" that year (1903), in which he laid down the principles of what came to be known as "synthetic" Zionism. He subsequently helped organize most of the public institutions of the *Yishuv* in Erez Israel.

5 Herzl's political activity was directed toward obtaining a charter for mass immigration of Jews into Erez Israel. His offer of economic aid to the Turkish Sultan (the Ottomans then ruled Palestine) did not produce results, nor did the pressure exerted on his behalf by Kaiser Wilhelm of Germany. In the wake of a meeting with the British Colonial Secretary, it was agreed to give the Jews the British-held Sinai Peninsula (the El-Arish Project), but this, too, came to nought. Herzl also met with Russian leaders as well as with the Pope. Here he is seen in Turkey in 1898.

mined to settle Ereẓ Israel with farmers and artisans; to strengthen Jewish national identity; and to lay the groundwork for obtaining the international agreement which was necessary for realizing Zionist goals. The World Zionist Organization was founded [9] and Herzl elected president, an office he held until his death.

The Uganda Crisis

The Zionist Congress functioned as an all-Jewish parliament. It established an infrastructure of institutions for the future Jewish state, including economic bodies. Among the latter were a Zionist bank — the Jewish Colonial Trust (1898) — and the Jewish National Fund (1901). Most of the early efforts of the movement focused on obtaining a charter for widespread Jewish settlement in a sovereign Jewish territory [5]. To this end appeals were made to the nations of the world to provide land. Herzl's efforts in this direction failed, but in 1903 new hope was raised by a British proposal that the Zionist Organization examine the possibility of settling Jews in East Africa ("The Uganda Scheme").

There were a number of serious crises facing the Jews at the time — pogroms in Russia, Algeria and Galicia, and the stalemate in Herzl's political contacts — and the discussion of Uganda at the 1903 Congress produced bitter divisions in Zionism. Those who opposed the scheme claimed that it was impossible to have Zionism without Zion [4]. Those who favored it saw Uganda as a temporary refuge for persecuted Jews, and an opportunity to prepare the Jewish people for building their national life. The Congress ultimately decided not to reject the British offer.

When Herzl died, in 1904, the position of the anti-Uganda faction was strengthened. The 1907 Zionist Congress rejected the idea of settlement outside of Ereẓ Israel. From that time forward all efforts were directed toward Jewish settlement in Ereẓ Israel.

KEY

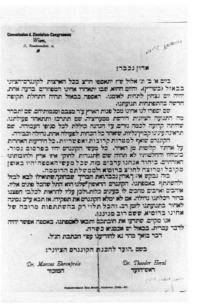

To organize the First Zionist Congress, invitations were sent to Jews from all over the world. The invitation enunciated the aims of the Congress and emphasized that everything would be done "above board" and in accordance with the position of the Russian authorities. This was done to facilitate the participation of Russian Jews who made up the large majority of the delegates, and to dispel suspicions regarding the Congress' objectives and Zionist aspirations. The Congress Hall was decorated with a blue and white flag — the eventual design of the flag of the State of Israel — and with the *Magen David* symbol.

6 Stages in the fulfillment of the Basle Program (till 1914)

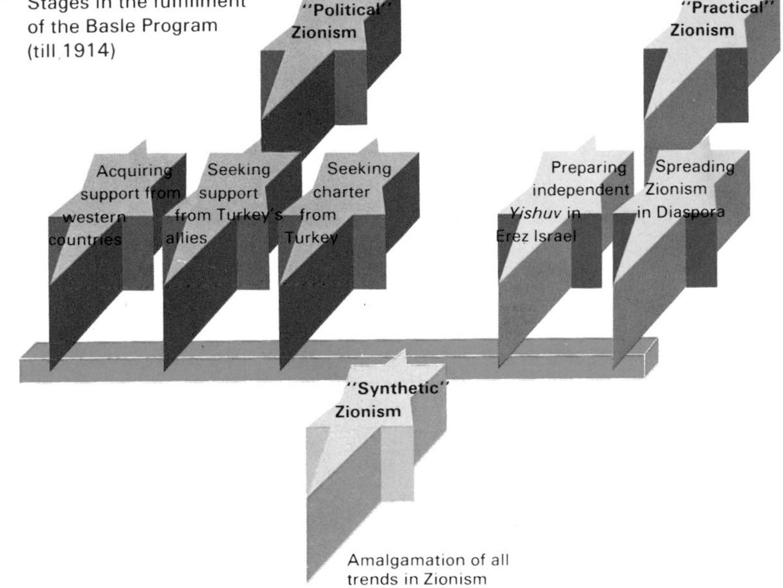

7 Zionist Congresses, 1897-1921

Date	Locale and President	Important Resolutions and Events
Aug. 29-31, 1897	Basle; Herzl	Founding of WZO and articulation of Basle Program.
Aug. 28-31, 1898	Basle; Herzl	Founding of Jewish Colonial Trust.
Aug. 15-18, 1899	Basle; Herzl	Ban on use of Zionist funds for activities outside Syria and Erez Israel.
Aug. 13-16, 1900	London; Herzl	Agreement to work for improvement of Jewish life in Diaspora.
Aug. 26-30, 1901	Basle; Herzl	Founding of Jewish National Fund.
Aug. 23-28, 1903	Basle; Herzl	"Uganda Scheme."
July 27-Aug. 2, 1905	Basle; Wolffsohn	Rejection of "Uganda Scheme" and secession of Territorialists.
Aug. 14-21, 1907	The Hague; Wolffsohn	Presentation of "synthetic" Zionism which stressed Erez Israel as only place where Zionism could be realized.
Aug. 26-30, 1909	Hamburg; Wolffsohn	Beginning of cooperative settlement in Erez Israel as proposed by Oppenheimer.
Aug. 9-15, 1911	Basle; Warburg	Victory for "synthetic" Zionism; expansion of practical work in Erez Israel.
Sept. 2-9, 1913	Vienna; Warburg	Decision to establish Hebrew University of Jerusalem and make *aliyah* obligatory.
Sept. 1-14, 1921	Karlsbad; Weizmann	Balfour Declaration and British Mandate accepted; appeal for agreement with Arabs.

8 The Tehiyya Society was one of the first youth groups of *Hovevei Zion* in Eastern Europe. It added a socialist dimension to Zionism and stressed the importance of physical labor. The many socialist-Zionist youth movements, such as *Ze'irei Zion* and *He-Halutz*, combined the ideas of national rebirth with those of socialist revolution. They hoped to establish a new society in Erez Israel based on the idea of economic and social cooperation. Their members laid the foundations for modern Israel's *kibbutz* and *kvutza* movements (collective agricultural settlements), labor political parties, and the General Federation of Labor (*Histadrut*).

8

9

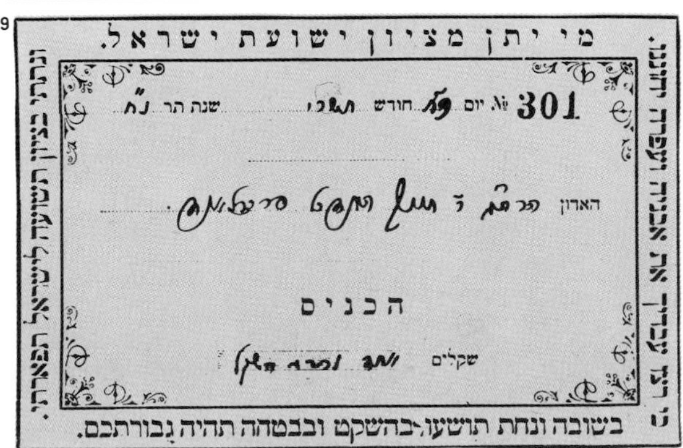

9 The Shekel was declared the unit of membership dues at the First World Zionist Organization Congress, held in Basle in August 1897. It conferred voting rights.

Jewish Culture in Eastern Europe until World War II

In the 19th and 20th centuries, Eastern Europe was the greatest center of Jewish culture in the world. Within only a few decades after the partition of Poland — whose Jews then became subjects of Prussia, Austria and Russia — literary activity in Hebrew, Yiddish and the local languages blossomed; the Jewish press flourished [1]; schools sprang up; and institutes of Jewish studies were founded. In the years before World War II, Jews were a vital part of the cultural scene in Russia, Poland and Germany.

From Haskalah to Nationalism

Modern Jewish culture began in Eastern Europe with the spread of the ideas of the German *Haskalah* (Enlightenment) movement, which preached the elimination of social and cultural barriers between Jews and local society, the study of local languages, and the adoption of European cultural values. The movement received active government support in Eastern Europe. In Galicia, public schools run by *Haskalah* proponent Hertz Homberg were established as early as the late 18th century. The Russian authorities followed a similar policy in the middle of the 19th century. In the early 20th century, champions of *Haskalah* such as Joseph Perl in Galicia and Isaac Baer Levinsohn in Volhynia wrote satires mocking the traditional Jewish way of life they sought to change. At the same time, they laid the foundations of modern Hebrew and Yiddish literature.

Nevertheless, *Haskalah* activities were neither widespread nor influential until the latter half of the 19th century, when Europe underwent social and economic upheaval: modern capitalism took shape, cities grew, and thousands of Jews flocked to the centers of economic activity in Warsaw, Kiev and Odessa. This accelerated the Jews' adoption of the local language and cultural values.

Many Jews, however, quickly became disillusioned by the hostile reaction of non-Jewish intellectuals to their attempts to join in local society, and sought to revise their positions. This led, by the 1880s, to works of a nationalistic Jewish nature. For example author Shalom Jacob Abramowitsch (pen name: Mendele Moykher Seforim; 1836-1917) was originally a *Haskalah* enthusiast highly critical of traditional Jewish society, but went on to become one of the fathers of modern Jewish literature in Hebrew and Yiddish. Isaac Leib Peretz (1852-1915), who first wrote in Polish, similarly altered his views and became a major author in Yiddish and Hebrew.

The image of traditional society that had emerged through the depiction of the Jewish hamlet (the *shtetl*), now underwent a change. The authors who, as proponents of the *Haskalah*, had mocked this society, now portrayed it with neo-romantic idealization, seeing the life of the *shtetl* as the fulcrum of national and social renewal for the next generation [2]. Having once accepted much of the aesthetics and ideology of

CONNECTIONS

1

№ 204 A

פרייז 20 גראשן

HAJNT

הײנט

מאניפעסט פון מלוכה-פרעזידענט

מארשאל שמיגלי-רידז העכסטער אנפירער פון דער ארמעע

און נאכפאלגער פון פרעזידענט

דער בעפעהל פון הויפט-אנפירער צו דער ארמעע

2

3

1 The Jewish press in Hebrew, Yiddish and Polish flourished between the two world wars. In the late 1930s, 200 Jewish journals were being published, 30 of them daily newspapers. The circulation of the Yiddish dailies was some 600,000. Efforts at cultural integration through modernization were generally encouraged by the authorities in Eastern Europe. Here we see the last issue of *Haynt* (Today), which was founded in 1908 by Samuel Jacob Yatzkan.

3 The modernization of Jewish society began in Germany and spread to Eastern Europe. In the 1860s a Temple [shown here] was erected in Krakow in Galicia. The grand structure shows the influence of Christian and eastern aesthetic traditions typical of the synagogues associated with the *Haskalah* movement in Central Europe.

2 Popular Jewish music thrived in Eastern Europe. Every city and town had its musicians — *kleyzmerim* — their profession passed on from father to son for generations. They performed at weddings, Jewish festivals, and balls held by the Polish nobility. Most of their music was composed by folk artists and was passed on from one generation to the next. Jewish musicians such as Joel Engel recorded and notated the tunes popular in Eastern Europe, and these inspired works by composers like Stutschewsky, Achron and Boskowitz. This picture shows a group of musicians in Rohatyn in Galicia in 1912 with their typical instruments: violin, contrabass, clarinet, flute and trumpet. The musician's life was a favorite subject of Jewish authors. Sholem Aleichem, for instance, wrote the novella "Playing the Fiddle" and dedicated his novel *Stempenu* (1888) to a famous musician who lived in the second half of the 19th century. The popular traditions of Eastern European music have been preserved and developed among the ultraorthodox Jews, primarily in the Williamsburg section of Brooklyn, and in Jerusalem.

4

4 YIVO — Yidisher Visenshaftlikher Institut (the Institute for Jewish Research), one of the foremost research centers in Poland between the two world wars, established its center in Vilna in 1925. Its fields of study included the linguistics of Yiddish, the history and sociology of the Jews in Eastern Europe, demography and economics. Photographed here are the heads of YIVO, the Yiddish specialist Max Weinreich; Zalman Rejzen, the author of a lexicon of Yiddish literature; and the literary scholar, Zelig Kalmanovitch. They are seen standing before the half-finished institute in Vilna (1929). Since 1940, the institute has continued to operate from New York.

contemporary Russian or Polish literature, they now expressed these ideas in Yiddish and Hebrew [Key]. Many had also been influenced by social radicalism and populist thinking — intellectual trends that characterized historical writing, and whose foremost proponent was historian Simon Dubnow (1860-1941). In the period preceding World War I, however, Jewish culture was still trilingual. Sholem Aleichem (1859-1916) for instance, wrote most of his work in Yiddish, but published at different times in Russian or Hebrew.

Pluralism Between the Wars

After World War I, Jewish culture again changed. In the Soviet Union, encouraged by the authorities, secular radical literature in Yiddish had its heyday, while Hebrew authors were no longer heard from, or left for Berlin, Warsaw, and Tel-Aviv. Simultaneously, Jewish writers continued to produce works in Russian. By the 1930s and 40s, however, Yiddish culture in the Soviet Union was being virtually wiped out in the Stalinist purges. In independent Poland, secular Zionist literature and modern Yiddish writing flourished side by side, and Warsaw and Vilna were the centers of Jewish culture in all languages. The abundant Jewish press gave voice in three languages to the different trends: from identification with Polish culture, through extreme nationalism — in Polish and a variety of Hebrew journals — to the *Bund* publications and communist press in Yiddish. A network of Hebrew (*Tarbut*) and Yiddish schools sprang up throughout Poland, while newly established research centers in Vilna [4] and Warsaw attracted the foremost scholars of Jewish studies, including the historians Meir Balaban, Emanuel Ringelblum, and Elias Tcherikower. During the Holocaust these authors and scholars continued their work despite near impossible conditions. Those who survived the Nazi genocide brought this legacy with them to Israel and the USA.

KEY

An-ski's The Dybbuk, a drama based on Eastern European Jewish folklore, won great popularity both in its original Yiddish version ("Between Two Worlds") and in its Hebrew translation by C.N. Bialik. An-ski, the pen name of Solomon Zainwil Rapaport (1863-1920) wrote in Russian and Yiddish. He was deeply interested in Jewish folklore and headed an ethnographic mission that collected folk material from the Jews of Volhynia and Podolia. The author is seen here reading from his play in a painting by Leonid O. Pasternak, whose portraits immortalized several of the greatest Jewish writers and statesmen of his time.

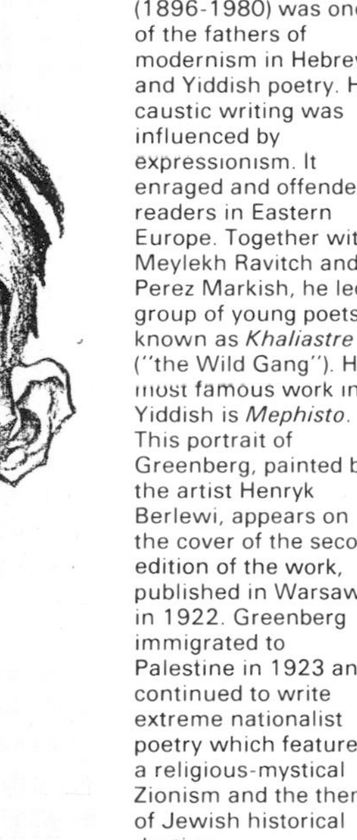

5 Uri Zvi Greenberg (1896-1980) was one of the fathers of modernism in Hebrew and Yiddish poetry. His caustic writing was influenced by expressionism. It enraged and offended readers in Eastern Europe. Together with Meylekh Ravitch and Perez Markish, he led a group of young poets known as *Khaliastre* ("the Wild Gang"). His most famous work in Yiddish is *Mephisto*. This portrait of Greenberg, painted by the artist Henryk Berlewi, appears on the cover of the second edition of the work, published in Warsaw in 1922. Greenberg immigrated to Palestine in 1923 and continued to write extreme nationalist poetry which featured a religious-mystical Zionism and the theme of Jewish historical destiny.

6 Chaim Nahman Bialik (1873-1934) [portrayed by L. Pasternak] was an outstanding figure in the great cultural rebirth of the Jewish communities in Eastern Europe. His nationalistic poetry became a source of inspiration and identification, while the monumental anthology he produced with Y.H. Rawnitzki, *Sefer ha-Agadah* ("The Book of Legends"), was an attempt to preserve Jewish traditional writings.

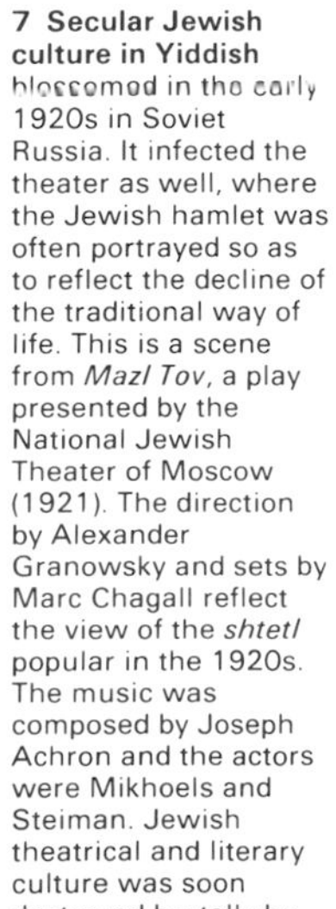

7 Secular Jewish culture in Yiddish blossomed in the early 1920s in Soviet Russia. It infected the theater as well, where the Jewish hamlet was often portrayed so as to reflect the decline of the traditional way of life. This is a scene from *Mazl Tov*, a play presented by the National Jewish Theater of Moscow (1921). The direction by Alexander Granowsky and sets by Marc Chagall reflect the view of the *shtetl* popular in the 1920s. The music was composed by Joseph Achron and the actors were Mikhoels and Steiman. Jewish theatrical and literary culture was soon destroyed brutally by Stalin.

8 Jacob (Jankel) Adler (1895-1949), a Jewish artist from Lodz, Poland, captured Jewish folk traditions in his paintings. In his depictions of Jewish soldiers he portrayed the experience of World War I, an event that threatened the very survival of traditional Jewish life.

Jewish Ethnic Communities

In everyday speech, in newspapers, literature, and in research, the Jewish people are often divided into groups: Eastern and Western, Asian-African, European-American, etc. Sometimes the groups are defined by a common region or country of origin: Yemenite Jews, Kurdish Jews, Hungarian Jews, Eastern European Jews, or North African Jews. All these categories are examples of a general tendency to distinguish Jews by their land or region of origin: hence the widespread use of the terms *Ashkenazi* and *Sephardi* [1].

Characteristics

The main distinguishing features of Jewish ethnic communities have been language, religious customs, traditions, life style, and creative arts. Different Jewish ethnic communities in the Diaspora spoke different languages. Sometimes the Jews of a country spoke a language different from the national language spoken there, like the Yiddish of Eastern Europe or the Ladino of Spain and the Balkans. In certain places the Jews created their own unique version of the local tongue [5]. Moreover, in their Hebrew — the language used by all of these ethnic communities — there were differences in several vowel and consonant pronunciations, as well as in accentuation.

Laws and customs, like the versions of the prayer texts, rules for ritual slaughtering, and family practices, differed from one ethnic community to another [Key]. Some claim that the most essential difference derives from the fact that the *Ashkenazi* Jews lived in Christian countries while the *Sephardi* and Eastern Jews -- in Muslim lands [4]. But this characteristic is not comprehensive: many *Sephardi* and Eastern communities lived in non-Muslim countries such as Greece, Italy [2], Yugoslavia, Russian Georgia, and India.

Still, the majority of *Sephardi* and Eastern Jews did live in Muslim or Muslim-ruled countries; Judeo-Arabic, Ladino, and Judeo-Persian were the popular languages in their communities; and they abided by Joseph Caro's *Shulhan Arukh* (Code of Jewish Law). Among *Ashkenazi* Jews, the vast majority of whom were from Eastern Europe, Yiddish dominated. Their religious code was also that of Joseph Caro, but with the addition of the *Mappah* glosses by Moses Isserles (the *Rema*).

Within *Ashkenazi* Jewry, after emancipation was granted to the Jews of Central and Western Europe, the differences between them and Eastern European Jews became increasingly pronounced. Among the Jews of Spain and the eastern countries, the differences between one local ethnic community and another were much more apparent, particularly in their spoken languages.

Formation

Jewish ethnic communities were created as a result of the Jewish people's dispersion throughout the Diaspora. But for centuries after the dispersion there were no differences among them at all. Jews

CONNECTIONS

78 The Expulsion of the Jews from Western Europe
82 Eastern Jewry after the Expulsion from Spain
94 The Community as the Framework of Jewish Life
126 The Wandering Jew

1 The name "Ashkenazim" at first referred only to the Jews of Germany and northern France. In the 13th and 14th centuries it was also used for Polish Jews, most of them from France and Germany. After the 17th century, increasing numbers of *Ashkenazi* Jews emigrated to Eastern and Western Europe. They spoke and wrote in Yiddish. Today, Yiddish books and newspapers are still being published, especially in the United States. On the right [A] The Erna Michael *Haggadah*, Germany, early 15th century; on the far right [B] Jewish children in the country, 19th century Poland.

1 A

1 B

2

2 In Italy's Jewish communities, people from many different cultures have been intermingling for hundreds of years. The first Jews came as early as the 2nd century BCE. After the failure of the Great Revolt and the destruction of the Second Temple in 70 CE, many Jews were deported to Italy. During the Middle Ages, despite the injustices meted out to them by Christian rulers, Jewish communities expanded. Refugees who fled the Spanish Inquisition settled in Italy in the 15th century; and in the 16th century *Anusim* came from Spain and Portugal. The Jews of Spain became integrated in the local communities, but also influenced the Italians, especially in the field of theological literature. Meanwhile, Italian Jews were attaining high posts as doctors and university lecturers, and their achievements in both religious and secular art were noteworthy. Pictured: a *Ketubah* (marriage contract) from Ancona, 1772.

3

3 The Jewish community of Morocco embodied a wide variety of cultures. This mother and child are in typical dress of the Dadès Valley, which borders on the Sahara. The woman wears a white shawl (*izar*), with an elaborate crown.

4

4 Differences among ethnic communities became increasingly pronounced as time went on. The Jews were influenced by the culture and language of their adopted countries. This is reflected in the *Ardashir Na'ame* [picture], by the Jewish poet Shahin, written in 1332 in the Judeo-Persian language, which uses Hebrew letters. The book is steeped in motifs from the epic poetry of the Persian poet, Firdusi — *Shaah-Na'ame* (The Book of the Kings) — and in popular legends.

lived in countries near Erez Israel or bordering the Mediterranean basin. Only around the 9th century did Jews begin to live in Christian European countries in any continuous fashion. The first such inhabitants settled in *Ashkenaz*, in the cities on the Rhine. In time they spread throughout Europe. At the same time, the Jewish community in Spain (*Sepharad*) — which alternated between Christian and Muslim rule — was becoming well-established. By the time of the Spanish Inquisition, the division into ethnic communities had crystallized [3].

The similarities among the different ethnic communities — religious beliefs, a common history, holidays, the anticipation of Redemption, and the coming of the Messiah — far outnumber their differences. In particular, Jews have shown their unity in times of crisis. All of the communities lent aid and support, for example, to the Polish refugees who fled the pogroms of 1648-9. The blood libel in Damascus (1840) aroused a strong Jewish protest in Central and Western Europe.

For long periods of time, contact among the various ethnic communities was intermittent, and ties were maintained chiefly by merchants, talmudic scholars, and emissaries from Erez Israel. Where the ties were stronger, this was usually the result of emigration and expulsion, as in Holland, England, and Italy — which absorbed the Spanish refugees; or in the United States — whose first immigrants were *Sephardi*, then came mainly from Germany, and finally, in the early 20th century, arrived from Eastern Europe.

The greatest contact among Jewish ethnic communities takes place in Israel today. For the first time since the Diaspora began, several million Jews from all over the world are together, and this has created certain pressures and problems. Probably the most significant indication of success in dealing with these differences is a steady increase in ethnic intermarriage.

KEY

Amulets have been popular among all the Jewish ethnic communities. They were used against evil powers. In the east, the *Hamsa* was popular; shaped like the palm of a hand, it wards off the evil eye (above right — 20th century *hamsa* from Morocco). God's name was said to have magical powers, and it appears in different forms on jewelry (above left — 19th century amulet from Germany), on parchment or paper amulets, and on *mezuzot* fixed to the doorposts of Jewish homes. Names, too, were said to have special powers: throughout the Diaspora names which mean "life" (*chaim*) are meant to ensure long life; hence, Vidal and Vidas, taken from the word *vita* ("life" in Latin), or Ochayon, Chaim, etc.

5

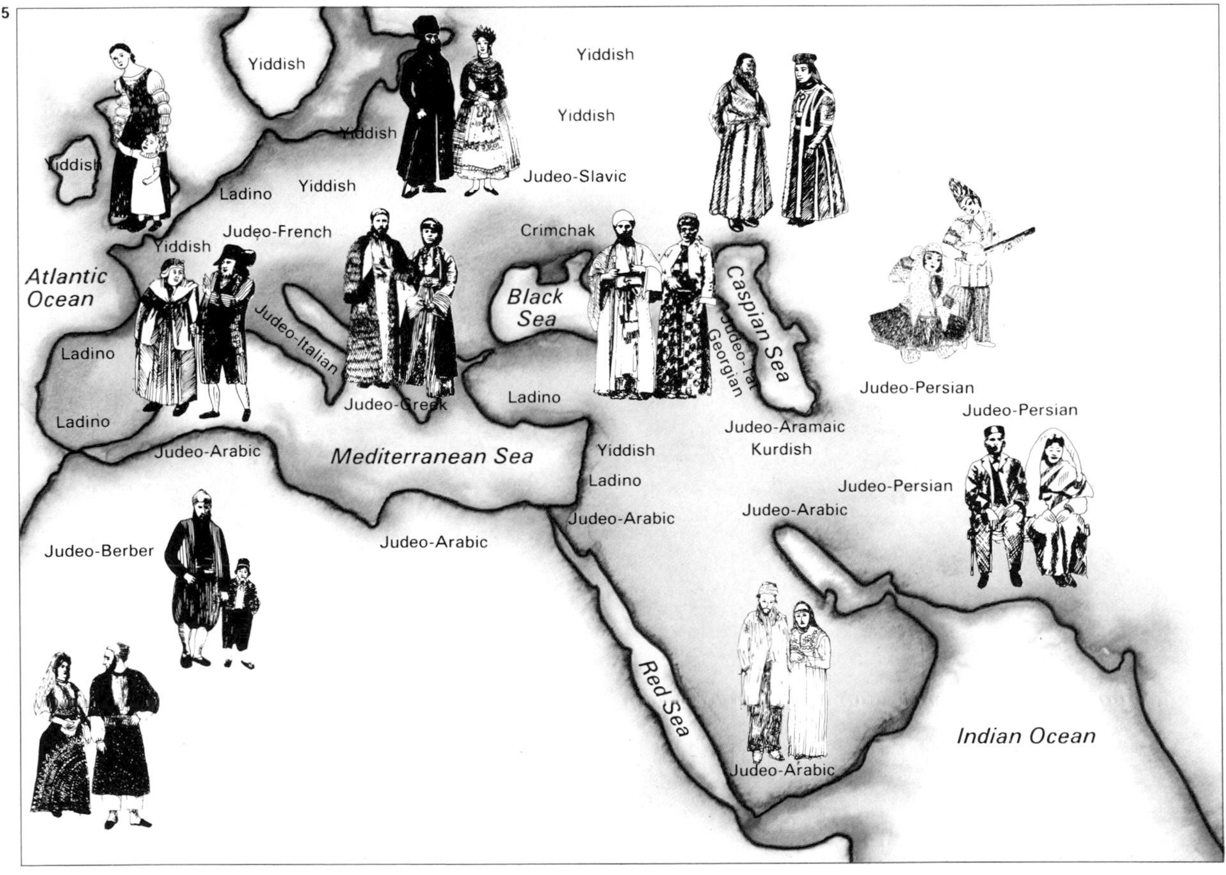

5 The spoken languages of the Jews usually developed through a process of Judaizing a local language — combining it with Hebrew and Aramaic, both of which the Jews brought with them to the Diaspora. After the end of the Second Temple Period, Hebrew was used less and less as a spoken language, because of the dispersion of the Jews. It continued, however, to be the language of prayer and creativity. All community matters were administered in Hebrew, and Jews learned to read and write it from an early age. The local languages spoken by the Jews were generally written in Hebrew script. Yiddish and Ladino did develop into spoken as well as written languages, and both are being used in cultural and creative efforts to this day. Modern national languages caused the other Jewish tongues to die out, but perhaps the survival of Yiddish and Ladino is due to the fact that they developed at the same time as Europe's other national languages.

6 Jewish communities maintained halachic, cultural, and commercial ties. This was initially limited to academic matters among sages and community leaders. The interpretations of Rashi and the Tosafists (who wrote the annotations to the *Talmud*) became known in Spain and influenced its Jewish population, while the writings of Maimonides deeply affected *Ashkenazi* Jews. After the expulsion from Spain, this influence was felt in all areas of life. The *Venetian Haggadah*, for example, was printed in 1609 in three languages: Ladino, Judeo-Italian [A], and Yiddish. It was especially popular in the Mediterranean countries. In 1848 the *Haggadah* was even published in Bombay, India [B] in the Marathic language.

6 A

6 B

The Wandering Jew

Wandering seems to have been a constant characteristic of the Jewish People [1]. In general, it derived from external pressures, e.g., the deportations after the destruction of the First and Second Temples and the failure of the Bar Kokhba Revolt, the expulsions in the Middle Ages from Christian European countries such as England (1290), France (1380), and Spain (1492); or from European cities like Mainz (1084), Prague (1542), Vienna (1670), and Moscow (1891).

Where the Jews were not expelled — generally the Muslim countries — there was relatively little need to wander, and in such places there was continuous Jewish settlement for 2,000 years and more. This was the case, for example, in Babylonia and in Persia, in Yemen, and in the North African countries. The direction in which the people wandered was likewise determined by external factors. Refugees were generally forced to resettle wherever the local government thought they would serve the most benefit. This is how the large Jewish centers were created in Muslim and Christian Spain in the 10th-12th centuries; in Poland, in the 13th to 15th centuries; and in the Ottoman Empire, in the 16th century.

Before World War II

During the past century, the phenomenon of wandering took on far greater dimensions than ever before. Between 1880 and 1920, over 2.5 million Jews left Eastern Europe, most of them from Russia [Key]. This mass emigration was due to the Russian government's restriction of Jews to the Pale of Settlement, as well as to economic hardship, rapid population growth, extreme poverty, and, most important — to the pogroms inflicted upon the Jews by masses encouraged and supported by their government.

Russian Jewish emigrants headed for the neighboring countries of Central and Western Europe. There, however, they were refused, for the most part, and were forced to continue their search. It was the United States that was willing to give them shelter, for the USA was then undergoing a period of heightened development, and accordingly opened its doors to all who wished to settle. Between 1900 and 1914, Jewish immigration constituted approximately 10% of the total immigration to the USA [6]. Most Jews settled in the large cities.

During the two decades following World War I, emigration from Europe continued. The Soviet Union prohibited Jews from leaving, while Poland and other East European countries which had grown intensely nationalistic encouraged Jewish emigration. With the rise of Nazism in Germany in 1933, approximately 250,000 Jews left there in just six years.

But where to? In 1921 the United States had begun limiting immigration; at the International Conference at Evian in 1938, called to consider the refugee problem, not one of the countries was willing to take in any signifi-

CONNECTIONS

1A

1B

1 Immigration and wandering were the lot of the People of Israel from their very origins, beginning with the Patriarch Abraham. According to the Bible, the People of Israel wandered in the desert for 40 years before arriving in Erez Israel. They settled in the Promised Land, but as a result of the destruction of the First Temple, they were exiled to Babylonia; then, fifty years later, many of them returned to Erez Israel. The destruction of the Second Temple and the failure of the Bar Kokhba Revolt caused the Jews to emigrate or be expelled once again, and since that time this has been the fate of generation upon generation of Jews. Pictured: Israelites leaving Egypt, from the *Nuremberg Haggadah* (mid-15th century) [A] and the *Hamburg Haggadah* (1768) [B].

2 The world Jewish population increased from 1750 to 1940 almost 17 fold. This growth took place largely among the Jews of Eastern Europe. In Muslim countries, growth was considerably slower, mainly because of the high infant mortality rate. During World War II, six million Jews were murdered in Europe. After the war, the natural rate of reproduction dropped, and the average number of children in Jewish families became one of the world's lowest, especially among those from European backgrounds. In addition, the ever-growing number of mixed marriages has caused the assimilation of hundreds of thousands of Jews. The only place where the natural reproduction rate is relatively high at the present time is in Israel. Should these trends continue, the Jews of Israel will comprise an increasing percentage of the Jewish people, who numbered 13 million in 1980.

2

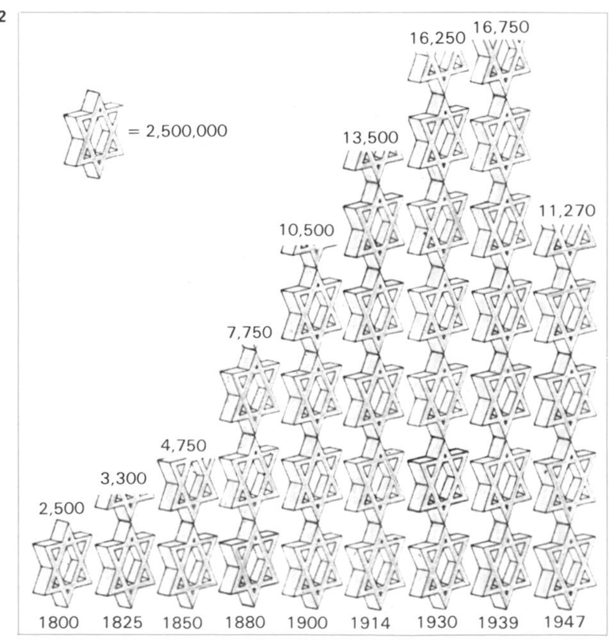

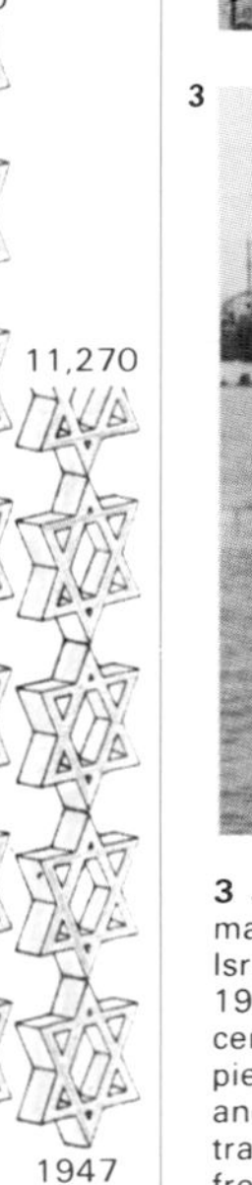

3

3 Jaffa served as the main gateway to Erez Israel all through the 19th and early 20th centuries. It had no pier, and passengers and luggage were transferred ashore from incoming ships in rowboats. Jaffa became even more important after completion of the railroad line connecting it to Jerusalem (1892). In the late 1800s, several Jewish neighborhoods were built on Jaffa's northern outskirts — Neve Zedek (1885) and Neve Shalom (1890). During the time of the Second *Aliyah* (1904-1914) Jaffa became the center of the *Yishuv* and provided the infrastructure for construction and development of the new city of Tel Aviv. Jaffa's function as principal port of entry to Erez Israel ended with the development of Haifa port.

cant number of Jewish refugees. Only the Jewish *Yishuv* in Ereẓ Israel asked for them. By the end of 1936, about 100,000 Jews had managed to obtain British mandatory government approval to immigrate to Ereẓ Israel. But in 1937 the British decided to limit this immigration, and in 1939 they stopped it almost completely. Thus thousands of Jews who could have been saved if the doors had not all been closed — were murdered during World War II.

Immigration after World War II

When World War II was over, a new period of mass Jewish migration began, mostly in the direction of Ereẓ Israel [4]. The survivors of the Holocaust in Europe saw Israel as their last refuge, and thousands made the journey, on dilapidated, overcrowded ships, braving a British naval blockade. Following the UN decision of November 29, 1947 to establish a Jewish State in Ereẓ Israel, approximately 300,000 Holocaust survivors came to Israel from Europe.

At the same time, heightened Arab nationalism and resistance to Israel's establishment combined with the ignominy of defeat at the hands of Israel to fan the flames of Arab antagonism toward the Jews. One after another the Jewish communities in Muslim countries were uprooted. More than 500,000 came to Ereẓ Israel, including entire communities from Yemen and Iraq, and tens of thousands from Syria, Egypt, and Libya. Many *Maghreb* Jews — especially those from Algeria, who were French citizens — preferred France.

The overall picture changed considerably as a result of these migratory movements. Only 100 years before, most of the Jews had been living in underdeveloped countries, under autocratic regimes, in Eastern Europe and the Muslim countries. Only 3.5% of all the Jewish people lived in the United States, and 0.5% in Ereẓ Israel. In 1984, 50% of all Jews lived in industrialized nations in the West, about 25% lived in Israel, and 20% in the USSR.

KEY

Jewish emigrants were generally refugees who had been forcibly uprooted from their homes, whereas other peoples have usually emigrated — in groups or as individuals — out of their own free will. In recent centuries Europeans have often left their countries of birth to seek their fortunes in other lands, whereas Jewish emigrants usually had to leave with their entire families, often without knowing where to turn. Pictured: Jews who fled Russia and emigrated by ship, after the Pogrom of 1881.

4 Since 1948 the majority of Jewish migration was directed to Israel. During the years 1948-1960 nearly a million Jews, or 75% of total emigrants, made *aliyah*. The rate dropped to about 55% during the 1960s, but rose again to nearly 73% during 1969-1974.

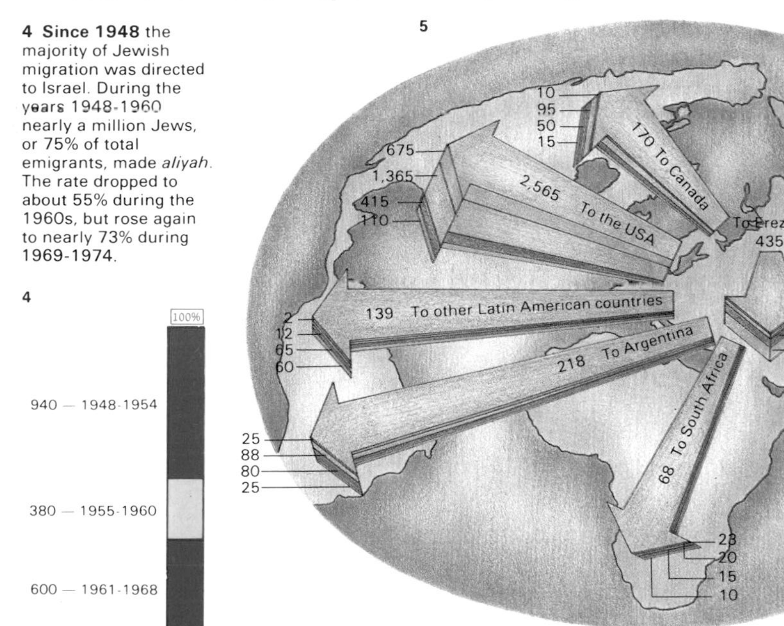

5 Between 1881 and 1939 3,715,000 Jews emigrated from Europe: 73% to North America, 10% to South America, 12% to Ereẓ Israel, and 5% to other countries.

6 Immigration restrictions such as quotas or health statutes were inflicted on those who arrived to the USA. Despite the difficulties, approximately two million Jews immigrated to the United States betweeen 1881 and 1914, mostly from Eastern Europe. The majority made their way to England and the USA via Germany and Austria. In the picture: a doctor examines Russian Jewish immigrants on the boat at Liverpool, England.

4

940 — 1948-1954
380 — 1955-1960
600 — 1961-1968
350 — 1968-1974

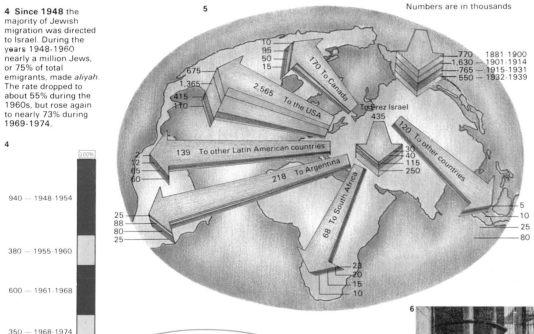

To Canada 95
To the USA 260
To W. Europe 285
To other countries 85
To Israel 1,545
From Rumania
From the Soviet Union
From Iran and Iraq
From North Africa
From South Africa
From Yemen

Main directions of migration
Mainly in the 1950s
Mainly in the 1960s and 1970s

Numbers are in thousands

Origins of the American Jewish Community

The history of Jewish immigration to America can be divided into three periods, according to the dominant immigrant element in each: 1654-1820, Spanish-Portuguese Jewry; 1820-1860, German Jewry; 1880-1924, East European Jewry.

Years of Growth

The *Anusim* who came to the Dutch colony of New Amsterdam in 1654 founded the American Jewish community. After 1664, when America's eastern seaboard was ruled by England, New Amsterdam became New York, and a Jewish community was reestablished there [2]. Additional communities were founded in Newport, Savannah, Charleston and Philadelphia.

When the colonies were declared independent in 1776 only about 2,000 Jews lived in them, mainly merchants who enjoyed a fairly good standing of living. The First Amendment to the Constitution passed in 1791 included the principle of separation of church and state and implied equal rights for Jews. Nevertheless, there were vestiges of legal discrimination until the beginning of the 19th century.

The 19th century witnessed a large wave of Jewish immigration from Central and Western Europe, that reached a peak in the mid-1800s. German Jewry emigrated because of disappointment with the Revolutionary Spring of 1848, the slow spread of emancipation, and persistent economic crisis. The immigrants from Germany increased American Jewry from 5,000 in 1826 to about 280,000 in 1880; they also influenced the American Jewish way of life.

During the period of German immigration, many new communities joined the Reform movement, which had its ideological roots in Germany. Reform Judaism accorded with the prevalent tendency of these immigrants to integrate into the mainstream of society. By 1880 there were some 200 Reform congregations in the United States [7], and only a few Orthodox ones.

Immigrants from Central and Western Europe started out as peddlers or small businessmen. As trade and travel moved westwards, Jews settled along the route, founding the large Jewish communities of Cleveland, Chicago, Detroit, Milwaukee, and Cincinnati — the largest Jewish community along the Mississippi. Gradually, they established themselves economically: the pushcart peddler bought a covered wagon and then a shop, which often grew into a chain of stores [1].

After the Civil War — in which some 10,000 Jews fought (7,000 with the North) — American Jewry achieved economic stability, and comprised many well-known bankers and famous commercial figures.

By the late 1920s American Jewry was the largest Jewish community in the world. From 1880 to 1929 it increased from 280 thousand to 4.5 million; some 8% of the newcomers to America were Jews. The large majority (94%) of the Jewish immigrants during this period

CONNECTIONS

86 Anusim and Iberian Jews in the West
114 The Pogroms of Eastern Europe
126 The Wandering Jew
130 Shaping the American Jewish Community

1

2 A

1 Peddling and retailing provided a livelihood for many Jews who came with the large wave of immigration. They were eventually supplanted by large companies. These were characteristic Jewish occupations in the large cities and on the American frontier. This sketch — apparently on a match box — is from the end of the 19th century.

3 Few immigrants chose to settle in agricultural communities. In 1882 members of the *Am Olam* society from Odessa established two villages in the Dakotas. These were managed cooperatively but soon became private farms and were abandoned a few years later. A fund was established by Baron Maurice De Hirsh (1831-1896; founded the Jewish Colonization Association in 1891) to create occupational opportunities for the Russian immigrants. It helped support the settlers, enabled the building of agricultural schools, and facilitated vocational training and the study of English. These efforts were instrumental in the early distribution of Jewish immigrants throughout Latin America.

2 The Franks family from England was among the immigrants to whom the British Crown offered economic privileges and letters of naturalization. Jacob (1688-1769), head of the American branch of the family, came to New York in 1708-9 with Moses Levi (1665-1768), father of his wife Abigail-Bilhah [A]. Through connections with the London branch of the family Jacob supplied the British army and also dealt in the slave trade. By the end of the 18th century not one member of the family remained Jewish. David Salisbury Franks (1743-1793) [B] was a colonel in the American Army, fought to free the colonies, and was a close associate of leaders of the Revolutionary War — which most Jews supported. Commercial connections enabled many Jews to supply both the army and the civilian population.

3

2 B

were from Russia, and this was known as the "Russian immigration."

Emigration from Europe was caused by dwindling sources of livelihood for a rapidly-increasing Jewish population, improved intercontinental transport, and reports of almost unlimited economic and social opportunities awaiting arrivals in the New World. Eastern European Jews had additional reasons to migrate: legal discrimination, government-sponsored anti-Semitism, the pogroms of 1881-1883, the 1903-05 expulsions from Moscow, and anti-Semitic economic policies.

Difficulties of Acclimatization

Most of the Jewish immigrants lived in the industrial and commercial cities of the east and mid-west, with New York City absorbing the greatest number. At first the immigrants congregated in cheap, crowded residential areas. These neighborhoods quickly acquired a Jewish coloration: Yiddish was the language spoken and most people lived some sort of traditional Jewish life, although very few were Orthodox. Manhattan's Lower East Side had some 350,000 Jews in an area of about 6 square kilometers (2.5 square miles) [Key]. Despite the crowding, the Jewish neighborhood gave its residents a sense of security and hope, and it encouraged a rich cultural life.

But it was not easy to eke out a livelihood. The more veteran settlers engaged in commerce, finance and even the academic professions. The newcomers, on the other hand, worked mainly in the garment industry under very poor conditions. They toiled 70 hours a week in dark, crowded sweat shops [4]. Many eventually attained economic independence. Others, Jewish activists, organized the workers to struggle for better conditions, creating institutions for mutual aid and community betterment. In so doing they contributed to the foundations of the American labor movement, and left their mark on American political life.

KEY

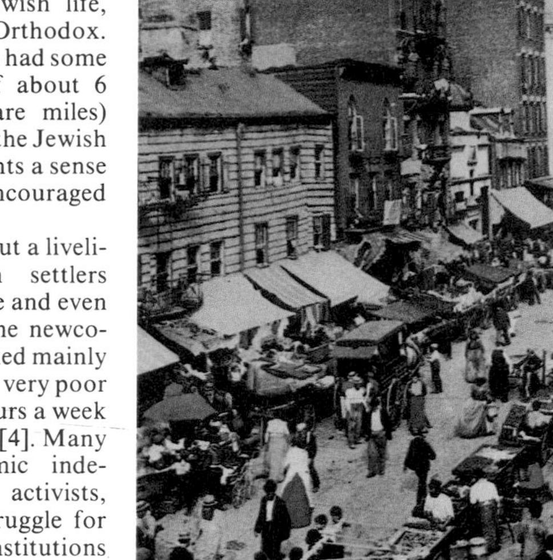

The Jewish market on New York's East Side at the beginning of the 20th century. Here, in the southern part of Manhattan, new immigrants came to join relatives or former neighbors from the hamlets of Russia and Poland. Here they found a congenial social atmosphere, and worked in shops run by Jews. From 73,000 in 1880, the number of Jews in New York reached 1.1 million (23% of the city's population) in 1910 and 1.65 million (29% of the city's population) in 1920. As their economic situation improved, they left the crowded neighborhoods. A generation later, Jews began leaving New York for other cities. Still, they remain a prominent element in New York.

4

4 The sweat shops were described in a poem by Morris Rosenfeld, who worked in a tailoring shop. Freely translated from the Yiddish the poem reads: "... and in the third floor above / a poor room where they slept, heaven help them, what sleep! / Never cleaned or aired, moldy and filthy; / they clung to one another there / there..., so overworked / but satisfied, so it seems, about thirty of them / all thin, the women too are thin, their spirits trampled, their bodies withered." The sweat shops spawned Jewish leadership of the garment industry and the garment labor unions.

5

5 Jewish immigrants from Russia, by Ben Shahn (1941), after a photograph taken in 1906, the high point of immigration. "America is being built on the ruins of Kasrilevka," wrote Sholem Aleichem in *Motel, Son of Peisy the Cantor*. Kasrilevka was a typical Eastern European Jewish town in Sholem Aleichem's stories.

6 A

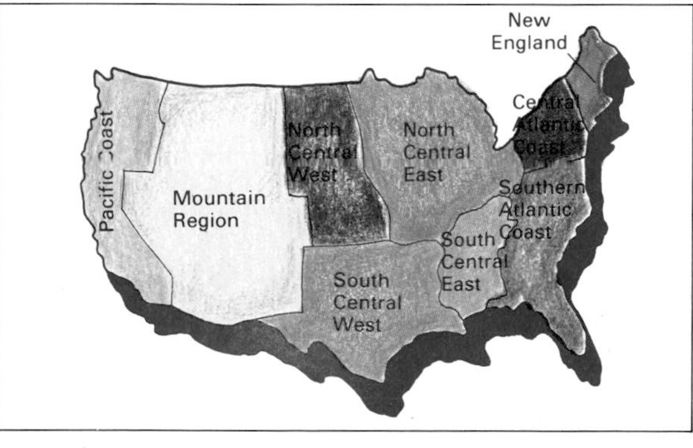

6 Since World War II the Jewish population of the United States has been characterized by geographic mobility, primarily in the direction of the Sun Belt in the south, the west and the southwest. Mobility is typical of college graduates and young families and among its hallmarks is the weakening of the extended family and the disintegration of long-established community frameworks.

Jewish Population in Various Areas of the USA (in thousands)

6 B

Year	New England	Central Atlantic Coast	Southern Atlantic Coast	North Central East	North Central West	South Central East	South Central West	Mountain Region	Pacific Coast (incl. Hawaii and Alaska)	Total
1878	11.8	104.3	21.9	36.4	10.1	11.7	12.3	2.0	19.7	230.2
1907	131.0	1,125.0	75.5	238.0	80.0	30.3	32.1	11.2	53.6	1,776.7
1927	355.4	2,534.2	177.2	672.6	166.6	61.3	79.7	30.1	151.1	4,228.2
1955	334.3	3,035.5	291.0	576.8	138.2	37.7	74.6	36.8	449.3	4,974.2
1980	372.1	2,886.1	779.4	532.9	130.0	38.8	94.5	97.2	759.0	5,690.0

7

7 Temple Emanuel, a Reform House of Prayer in New York, designed in Neo-Gothic style and built in 1868. According to Kaufmann Kohler, one of the founders of the Reform movement in the USA, the movement held that the legalism of *Halakhah* prevented the cultivation of Judaism's spiritual and moral elements. Reform Judaism attributed major importance to the idea that Jewry's mission was to spread religious and moral light. The movement instituted prayers in the language of the country of residence and refused to be bound by the demands of *Halakhah*.

Shaping the American Jewish Community

The large wave of immigrants that came to the United States between 1881 and 1924 was received by Jews who were already well established economically and integrated culturally. Charitable and mutual-aid enterprises were founded to hasten the "Americanization" of the new arrivals.

Economic and Social Organizations
The immigrants themselves created cultural and ideological frameworks that eased their absorption. The founders of the Jewish trade unions, influenced by East European socialist ideas, sought to improve the lot of the Jewish workers, but at the same time were creating the base for a general American labor movement. In 1888 some Jewish unions united to form the United Jewish Trade Union, and conducted a series of strikes that improved working conditions and groomed public opinion to recognize the function of labor organizations. In the early 1920s there were 250,000 organized Jewish workers [2].

Seeing their function as more than just increasing salaries, the labor leaders established health services and offices for economic assistance. The largest Jewish organization of workers was the Yiddish-speaking *Arbeiter Ring* (Workmen's Circle). There was a daily, weekly and monthly Yiddish press, literature and theater flourished, and extension courses, radio programs and films were available [1, 4].

Cultural activities and the workers' organizations helped keep the Jews together. Many were organized in "membership" societies or *Landsmannschaften* based on their East European countries of origin [3]. Very quickly, however, the encounter with the new environment, secular urban culture and new economic frameworks made its mark; many began to go to synagogue only on the Sabbath and holidays, and the second generation went even less frequently. Those more attached to traditional ways of life founded the Conservative movement, considering it preferable to the Orthodox — which began to seem obsolete and foreign to the American spirit — and to the Reform, which was considered too "gentile."

Total integration seemed the solution to the problems of the immigrant generation. The stress of getting settled, and possibly the fear that their status as loyal Americans would be questioned, kept many away from Zionism. Nevertheless, some had a sentimental attachment to the Zionist movement and it gradually found its place in America. However very few of those ascribing to socialism were attracted by Socialist-Zionism, which advocated establishment of a model socialist society in Ereẓ Israel.

Jewish expectations were reflected in the attitude to education. The veterans, who had adopted liberal values and extolled American society as a social model, sent their children to public schools. Most Jewish education was supported by the synagogues, and was

CONNECTIONS

128 Origins of the American Jewish Community
178 American Jewry's Political Activities

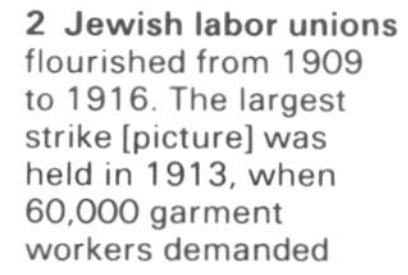

1 **Yisrulik in his own Land,** musical selections published in New York in 1912. References to the United States as the Homeland reflected successful integration.

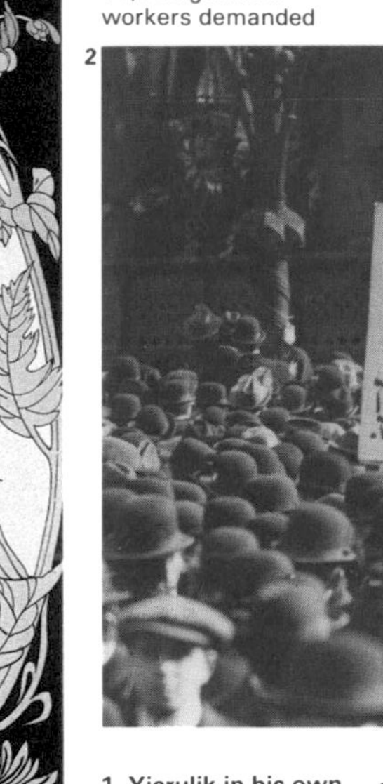

2 **Jewish labor unions** flourished from 1909 to 1916. The largest strike [picture] was held in 1913, when 60,000 garment workers demanded that their union be accorded the right to represent the workers. In the "permanent peace agreement" mediated by Judge Louis Dembitz Brandeis (1856-1941) a pattern was established for negotiations between workers and employers. The declining number of Jewish industrial and crafts workers gradually weakened the Jewish unions, but Jews went on to play a key role in union organizing in general.

3 **The Bialystoker Synagogue** was one of 534 societies formed by Jews hailing from the same places of origin that functioned in New York before World War I. The sense of fraternity created among members of these societies, the practical aid they extended and also the certainty of a *minyan* in the synagogue, made the acclimatization of the new immigrants easier. As the Jews integrated and left New York, many of these societies disappeared.

4 **The Yiddish theater** combined experiences in the new country with romantic memories of the countries of origin. By the turn of the century theatrical institutions had already been established in six cities, and itinerant companies traveled from community to community. Performances were based on song and dance and comic situations describing experiences in the new country. Melodramas were popular, but some of the finest works of the Jewish and general repertoires were also performed. The Yiddish theater began to decline after World War I, when speakers of Yiddish sought to leave the crowded Jewish neighborhoods.

usually limited to only a few hours of study a week. Many children had no formal Jewish education at all.

The World Wars and Depression

During World War I, the integration of American Jewry appeared to have reached a peak. There were some quarter of a million Jews in the army, and over 3,000 fell in battle. After the war, however, isolationism grew in America, and nationalistic tendencies were articulated by a core of Americans whose ancestors had come from England, Scandinavia, Germany and other Protestant countries of Europe. From 1921 to 1924 laws were enacted that drastically limited immigration from any but these north-European countries. The intention of this legislation — to limit the Jewish presence, hence Jewish influence, in America — was clear. Inevitably other, less subtle forms of anti-Semitism now reared their head [6]. Jews were discriminated against in social clubs and some of the universities — particularly in medical and engineering schools. These anti-Semitic tendencies were opposed by most of America's political leaders and almost all of its intellectuals, and although they caused the Jewish leaders great concern, they remained marginal.

Within Jewry changes were also taking place in the economic sphere, as many moved into wholesale and retail commerce, management, the law, teaching and social work [Key].

The economic crash of 1929, following years of prosperity and growth, hit the American Jewish community as well. Jewish institutions that depended on financial contributions were seriously affected. Anti-Semitic propaganda now singled out the Jews as responsible for the economic troubles. But all the difficulties notwithstanding, American Jewry united to help refugees who managed to leave Europe. And national sentiments were reinforced among the Jews by the threat of anti-Semitism both at home and abroad.

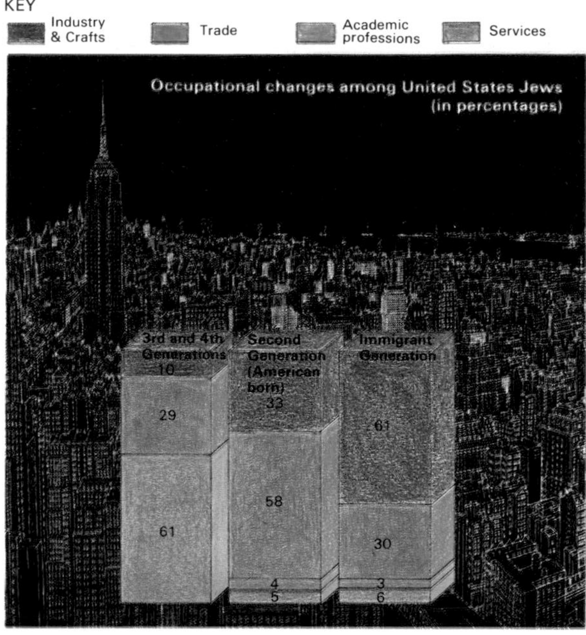

5 **Rabbinical and teacher training institutions** were the beginnings of higher Jewish education. In 1873 the Reform Movement founded Hebrew Union College in Cincinnati, Ohio [pictured]; the Orthodox established Yeshiva University in New York in 1897, and in 1902 the Conservatives created the Jewish Theological Seminary, also in New York. Brandeis University, the first Jewish-sponsored liberal arts institution, opened in the 1950s, and pioneered non-discriminatory admissions policies.

6

6 **Manifestations of anti-Semitism** in the United States were fanned by the severe economic depression. Some of the propaganda was on the Nazi model prevalent in Europe, which was altogether alien to the American spirit. The Jews were accused of communism and of forming a secret Jewish government. The Ku Klux Klan disseminated racist, anti-Semitic propaganda, declaring the Jews strangers in America and blaming them for the country's troubles.

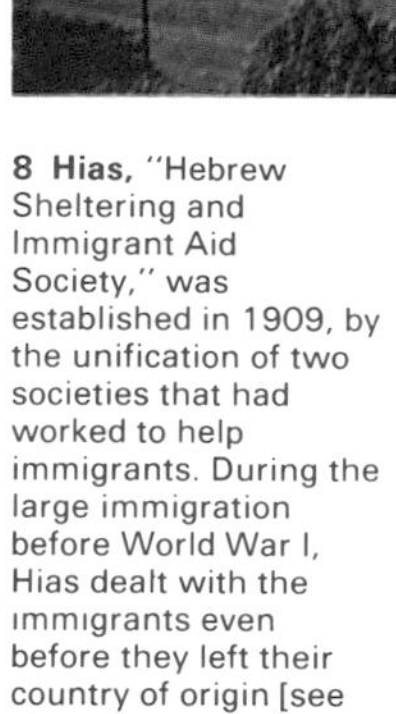

8 **Hias,** "Hebrew Sheltering and Immigrant Aid Society," was established in 1909, by the unification of two societies that had worked to help immigrants. During the large immigration before World War I, Hias dealt with the immigrants even before they left their country of origin [see picture], but primarily took care of them upon their arrival in the United States. It gave legal assistance to those who were not permitted to disembark; fought the restrictions placed on Jewish immigration after World War I; helped immigrants find housing and employment, and gave advice concerning naturalization procedures. The organization also helped those going to Erez Israel, particularly after World War II.

7

8

7 **Habad Hassidim** maintain independent educational institutions, from kindergarten through *Yeshiva* or teachers' training school. Various Jewish sects, advocates of Hebrew or Yiddish, Jewish communists and others also established independent educational institutions before World War I and during the 1920s. Most have ceased to exist. After World War II Jewish day schools were renewed.

9

9 **The Talmud Torah** was meant to supplement general studies in the public schools. These institutions, open in the afternoons, gave education a Jewish content. Most Jewish elementary school education still takes this form. Some 25% of the Jewish youth that receives Jewish education study in Jewish day schools. Most of these are Orthodox; the Reform and Conservative movements maintain extensive Sunday School facilities.

19th Century Ereẓ Israel

The end of the 16th century saw the decline of the center at Safed, and Jerusalem became the main focus of attention, but for a short time only. Heavy taxes imposed upon the Jerusalemites, coupled with persecution by the Ottoman authorities, made life there almost intolerable. In the late 1600s some 1,200 Jews were left in the city, while Jewish ethnic communities still remained in Gaza and Hebron. The 18th century saw some improvement, as a result of the arrival of Hassidic Jews from Poland and Russia (in 1774) and the financial support of the Jews of Istanbul.

The Middle East's altered international status in the second half of the 19th century resulted in many economic and social changes in Ereẓ Israel. The European powers, anticipating the dissolution of the ailing and backward Ottoman Empire [6, 7] were waiting for the opportunity to carve it up among them. The construction of the Suez Canal (1859-1869) and the competition for control over the Far East trade routes heightened the strategic importance of Ereẓ Israel; accordingly, the European powers took pains to secure military, political, and strategic outposts there. This they did under the guise of philanthropic and religious good works. A great deal of building activity took place — churches, missions, schools, and hospitals, all supported by the various Christian churches. The European powers opened consulates, encouraged missionary activity, and took advantage of the Capitulations — legal and financial immunity conceded by the Turks to European nationals. This heightened economic involvement also resulted in improved transportation and communications [1]. More Europeans also meant more economic assets in the land for the European Powers, heightened development, modernization, and an extrication from cultural and economic stagnation [3, 4]. Along with the economic and strategic interest exhibited by the Europeans, institutions and individuals engaged in geographic and archaeological research [2].

The Yishuv

In the first half of the 19th century, there were 8,700 Jews living in Ereẓ Israel, concentrated in the four holy cities. They eked out meager livings, dependent on the *halukkah* [8], and were burdened with heavy taxes. The second half of that century brought with it transition. Improved transportation, and the protection provided by the consulates for Jews with European nationality, led to new waves of *aliyah*. Whereas over the past three hundred years the Jewish settlement (the *Yishuv*) in Ereẓ Israel had been predominantly *Sephardi* or Eastern in character — indeed, in the first half of the 19th century most of the *olim* were still from Muslim and North African countries — it was *olim* from Europe who began to come after 1850. Within fifty years' time they accounted for more than half of the Jewish population in the *Yishuv*.

CONNECTIONS

88 16th Century Ereẓ Israel

120 Zionism becomes a Political Movement

134 Foundations of Zionism in Erez Israel

1

2

1 The German post office built in Jerusalem in 1905 provided telegraphic communications with Europe. Religious Germans - the Templars — established few agricultural colonies in Erez Israel, and founded educational and health institutions as well. Their structures, built in a rugged northern European style, survive to this day. When the British conquered the land during World War I, the Templers were deported.

2 Archaeologists, Bible lovers, military men, engineers and adventurers were all attracted to Ereẓ Israel — for religious or professional reasons, and out of curiosity to discover a land yet uncharted. Between 1800 and 1878, approximately 2,000 such travelers came and many set down their impressions in books, drawings and paintings. Famous among these was the painter David Roberts (1796-1864), whose *Jaffa Port* is shown here. Rabbi Yehoseph Schwarz (1804-1865), a German Jew, was among the first to study geography, history, and nature in Ereẓ Israel.

3

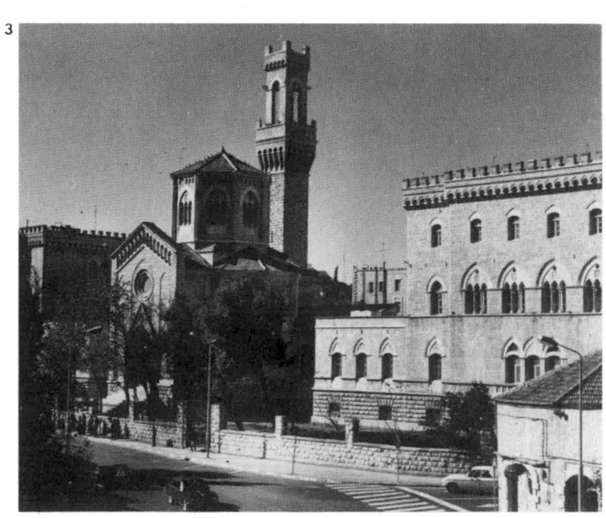

3 The Italian Hospital and adjacent church were built in Jerusalem in the early 20th century. Like many of the buildings constructed by European powers, their location was determined by strategic considerations. The architectural styles were typical of Europe in the second half of the 19th century, and sought to emphasize national motifs: the Italian Hospital was built in Renaissance style, typical of the Tuscany region. Next to the church was a tower modeled on the Palazzo Vecchio in Florence's main square.

4

4 In and around Jerusalem, the Russians established churches, monasteries, hospitals, and pilgrim hospices. They also established a network of educational institutions for the Greek Orthodox, for whom they served as patrons. Pictured: The Russian Compound in Jerusalem (completed 1864), including consulate, cathedral, Bishop's palace and religious mission, hospital and pharmacy, pilgrims' hospices, and living quarters.

These *olim* represented a new kind of society: along with the elderly who had traditionally come to be buried in Erez Israel, this new wave included family men, tradespeople, and artisans, who helped to lay the foundations for the economic and cultural changes to come.

Jerusalem in the 19th Century

Jerusalem had now become the largest Jewish center in Erez Israel [Key]. From 1840 to 1900 its Jewish population increased from 5,000 to 35,000, and comprised 62% of the city's total population. Jewish life in Jerusalem centered around the synagogues and *Yeshivot*, many of which were renovated.

The Jerusalem community comprised many different sects, that squabbled over the distribution of the *halukkah* monies. In 1866, the *Ashkenazi* community, in an attempt to overcome its own divisiveness, set up a General Committee, headed by Rabbi Samuel Salant (1816-1909) and Rabbi Meir Auerbach (1815-1878). The Jewish community's official representative before the Ottoman government remained the *Sephardi* Chief Rabbi, the *Hakham Bashi.*

The European countries' involvement in Erez Israel made it easier for Jewish philanthropists and charitable institutions to operate in the land. They were active in establishing secular schools for both boys and girls, such as the Evelina de Rothschild School, the Lämel School, and the Alliance Israélite Universelle School, all of which taught trades and general studies. With the help of Moses Montefiore, the first Jewish settlement outside the walls of the Old City was built in 1856 [5].

Hebrew journalism flourished in Jerusalem. Journalists rebuked the local leadership and the *halukkah* system, calling for education and creative activity. The atmosphere of change, combined with the interest awakened among Enlightenment circles, paved the way for the new ideas and life styles introduced by the *Hibbat Zion* Movement.

KEY

Jerusalem and its Holy Places. Part of an illustration from the second half of the 19th century, by an unknown artist. In the first half of the 19th century, Jerusalem served merely as a municipal center for the surrounding countryside. As it was holy to the three principal monotheistic religions, the Ottoman government attached religious importance to the city, but took no pains to develop it. Toward the end of the 19th century, the city's position changed, however. Its population and economy grew, and its political status in the imperial system was enhanced. Apartments and public and religious buildings were built, and transportation was improved to outlying areas as well as to Jaffa, Shechem (Nablus), Bethlehem and Hebron.

5 A

5 B

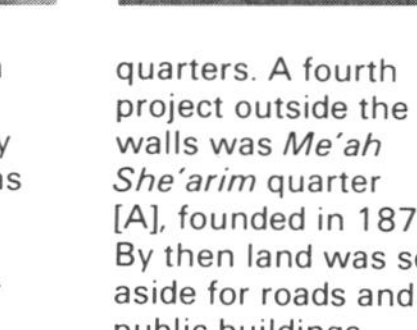

5 "Outside the Walls" of the Old City of Jerusalem, the foundations for the New City were begun in 1856, with construction of the *Mishkenot Sha'ananim* quarter [B] built by Moses Montefiore (1784-1885). For security reasons it was composed of long rows of buildings, and had iron gates. It was considered dangerous to live there, and in order to encourage settlement, tenancy was rent free. It was followed by the *Mahaneh Yisrael* (1867) and *Nahalat Shivah* (1869) quarters. A fourth project outside the walls was *Me'ah She'arim* quarter [A], founded in 1874. By then land was set aside for roads and public buildings.

6

6 The Ottoman rulers and provincial governors demanded heavy taxes, and the Turkish soldiers were both policemen and enforcers. The only way to avoid their cruel and brutal treatment was bribery. This painted glass picture of Turkish soldiers decorated the Scroll of the *Book of Esther*. Probably the work of Joseph Geiger of Safed, 1893.

7

7 The social and economic gap between *effendi* and *fellah* was very great. *Effendis* — the rich estate owners — extorted heavy taxes for themselves from their tenant farmers, the *fellahin*. Also as government tax collectors, they took advantage of their positions to line their own pockets. The thresher photographed here is supervised by an *effendi*.

8

8 A Sabbath tablecloth made by Hannah Rebecca Herman, of Jerusalem, presented to Rabbi Akiva Lehren, in hopes of increasing her family's share of the *halukkah* — charity collected abroad and distributed to the Jews in Erez Israel. This money provided the very barest subsistence for the families in Erez Israel. It was also used to maintain public institutions and to help pay taxes to the Ottoman government.

Foundations of Zionism in Ereẓ Israel

The year 1881 was a turning point in Jewish *aliyah* to Ereẓ Israel. Most of the *olim* who arrived after that time were members of the *Chovevei* or *Hibbat Zion* Movement, who believed that revitalization of national life in Ereẓ Israel would provide the solution for the plight of the Jewish people. Despite limitations and prohibitions imposed by the Ottoman government, the pioneers (*chalutzim*) continued to arrive, to buy land, establish settlements, and lay the foundation for an independent *Yishuv* in Ereẓ Israel.

The First Aliyah (1881-1903)

Seventy thousand *olim* came to Ereẓ Israel on the first wave of *aliyah*, but only half managed to withstand the difficult conditions facing them and to stay. Most of these made their way to the cities: Jaffa, Haifa, and the new suburbs of Jerusalem. Only a minority — including the members of the *Bilu* Movement, who were the symbol of the First *Aliyah* — associated the idea of the return to Ereẓ Israel with a return to agricultural activity, and proceeded to establish new settlements [8]. However, the limitations that were imposed on permanent settlement, land purchase, and construction by the Ottoman government — which was afraid of too great an influx of enemy subjects (from Russia and Rumania) — and the settlers' unfamiliarity with the country and with farming methods, all seemed to doom them to failure. They bought lands which were inappropriate for either settlement or agriculture, and they suffered from starvation, poverty and malaria.

Help came to the pioneers in the form of the Baron Edmond de Rothschild (1845-1934) [6]. Rothschild sent in agricultural experts who introduced dozens of new crops — such as tea, cotton, and tobacco — based farming in the *moshavot* on citrus groves, and improved work methods and management. The Baron also established factories to process the agricultural produce — wine cellars, tobacco plants, and textile factories. His financial investments were estimated to have been twenty times greater than all other outside investments combined. The Baron's support saved the Zionist settlement project in Ereẓ Israel, and laid the groundwork for additional settlements.

By the end of 1903, the Jews had purchased approximately 100,000 acres and founded 23 agricultural settlements. In the cities, the number of Jewish inhabitants doubled, and trade, banking, and artisan workshops expanded. Jaffa became the hub of Zionist, economic, and cultural activity. Eliezer Ben Yehuda's call to all Jews to revitalize the Hebrew language was met with great enthusiasm, and Hebrew-speaking schools were opened in the cities and towns. In 1903 the Teachers' Federation was established in Zichron Ya'akov, with the principal intent of intensifying national education and making Hebrew language and culture predominant [1].

CONNECTIONS

120 Zionism Becomes a Political Movement
126 The Wandering Jew
132 19th Century Erez Israel
140 Aliyah During the 1920s

1 The Technion, in Haifa, was intended as a university-level school for technical studies. Before its opening, in 1913, its founders — the *Ha-Ezra* Company — decided that studies would be in German, because Hebrew lacked sufficient scientific and technical vocabulary. Students and teachers alike, however, were sharply opposed to this decision, and a "War of Languages" ensued. The Technion's opening was delayed because of World War I, and studies began only in 1925.

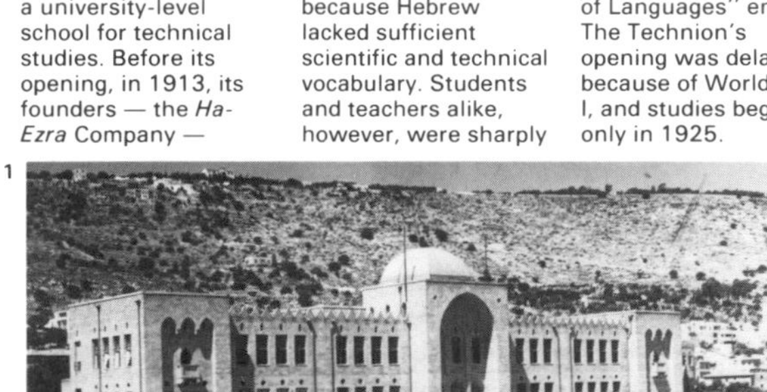

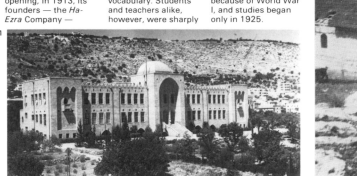

2 Sejera, the agricultural training farm founded by the Jewish Colonization Association (1899), was the workshop in which many Second *Aliyah* enterprises were forged. The pioneer group that conceived the idea of *Bar-Giora* — a small, secret society whose aim was to take charge of settlement defense — settled at Sejera in 1907. They undertook to handle all of the farming, and after much effort took charge of its security as well. As problems of security and defense became increasingly serious, *Bar Giora* decided to expand, and on Passover 1909 *Ha-Shomer* was founded at Sejera — "a corps of recruits prepared to go anywhere and perform any mission they are called upon to fulfill."

3 One of the Chovevei Zion groups living in Jaffa broke ground for Ahuzat Bayit on Passover, 1909. At first, it was intended as a "pretty Jewish suburb with gardens near Jaffa." Loan money was provided to the residents by the *Keren Kayemet* (Jewish National Fund) on the condition that all construction and development be done by Jewish laborers. The area developed quickly, and in 1914 boasted 1,000 inhabitants. Ahuzat Bayit was renamed Tel Aviv — the Hebrew words for the title of Theodor Herzl's book *Altneuland*. Within two decades Tel Aviv became the largest city in Erez Israel. Pictured — *Tel Aviv, small white houses amidst the sand dunes* (1923) by Reuven Rubin (1898-1980).

4 The editorial board of the newspaper Ha-Ahdut in 1911 (from right to left) Rachel Yannait Ben-Zvi, David Ben-Gurion, Jacob Zerubavel, and Itzhak Ben-Zvi. These and other pioneers of the Second *Aliyah* were among the founders of the labor parties and party press in Erez Israel. They held important positions in *Yishuv* leadership, and, later, in the government and sovereign institutions of the State of Israel. They were among the founders of the *kevutsah* and the *kibbutz*, the Labor Federation (*Histadrut*), *Ha-Shomer*, and *Kupat Holim*.

The Second Aliyah (1904-1914)

The Second *Aliyah* consisted, in the main, of immigrants who had left Russia after the pogroms of 1903 and 1905 and the abortive 1905 Socialist Revolution. Like their predecessors, most of this group turned to the cities, but a minority sought to create an ideal society in Erez Israel, one which would integrate the ideas of national rebirth and social revolution based on Zionist-Socialist principles.

The labor force working in the citrus groves at that time consisted mainly of hired Arab workers [5]. The Second *Aliyah* pioneers wanted to prove to the farmers that they were just as good as the Arab hands, and that the farmers should employ them instead — out of feelings of nationalist identification.

The Hebrew laborers received the support of the Zionist Federation, which accepted the principles of "Synthetic" Zionism. In 1908 it opened the Erez Israel Office in Jaffa to handle Zionist settlement activities. The office was headed by Arthur Ruppin (1876-1943), who believed that idealistic young people were "the Zionist Federation's most important asset" [7].

In 1909 three enterprises which were undertaken independent of each other made their mark on the era and influenced the character and development of the *Yishuv*: the establishment of Deganyah, first agricultural commune [Key]; founding of a Hebrew defense organization, *Ha-Shomer* [2]; and founding of Tel Aviv, the first all-Jewish city [3]. Since the first Zionist activities commenced in the second half of the 19th century, the number of Jews in Erez Israel had grown from 24,000 to 85,000 — including 12,000 living on new agricultural settlements. The cities continued to develop as well: Hebrew language and culture took root in the *Yishuv*, and welfare institutions and mutual aid societies developed. All of this activity and development came to a standstill, however, with the outbreak of World War I in 1914.

KEY

Early days at Deganyah, the first *kevutsah*. In December 1909 a group of laborers settled at Umm Juni, in the Jordan Valley. Poor conditions combined with a collective social philosophy to produce a new way of living — the *kevutsah*. By definition, this is a settlement on state property, based on the labor of its members, who live collectively. The *kevutsah* was the realization of Second *Aliyah* pioneer dreams: a way of life where Zionist principles — Jewish labor and socialism — were combined with cooperative living and social equality. The *kevutsah*, and later the *kibbutz*, became the symbol of the revolution in Zionist agricultural settlement in Erez Israel.

5

5 The Jewish laborer was in constant competition with the Arab laborer, who was preferred by farmers and industrialists because he was more experienced and settled for lower wages. In 1913 approximately 1,500 Jews were employed as laborers. Pictured — Jews working at the Rishon le Zion vineyards, 1910.

6 A

6 B

6 Baron Rothschild, "The Well-Known Benefactor" [B, on right, with clerks] gave his support to the *Yishuv*, but supervised all his projects very carefully. His autocratic overseers very often aroused deep antagonism and opposition, and even brought settlers close to revolt. In addition to support for existing settlements, he also bought lands in different areas of the country. He founded — in the south — Mazkeret Batyah (the ancient city of Ekron), named after his mother [A], and Be'er Toviyah (1887); in the central region — Bat Shlomo (1889) and Me'ir Shefeyah (1892); and, in the north, Metulla (1896). In 1891 he even bought land for Jewish settlement in the Golan. In 1900 he transferred these settlements to the Jewish Colonization Association, and conditions changed: settlers were allowed independence, but were required to plan their farms on an economic basis. In 1924 the Palestine Jewish Colonization Association was formed, headed by his son, James Armand de Rothschild (1878-1957).

7

7 A training farm for women workers was founded at the *moshavah* Kinneret (1911). Studies there centered on specific branches of agriculture, such as orchards, poultry, and dairy farming. Pictured are the poetess Rachel (1890-1931), seated at left, with members of the Kinneret farm.

8

8 Hadera in the northern Sharon Valley, was founded in 1890. Although more than half its population perished from malaria, the remaining settlers refused to abandon Hadera, and, with the help of Baron Rothschild, they drained the swamps. Hadera became a symbol of steadfast determination.

9

9 Keren Kayemet le-Israel (Jewish National Fund), the Zionist Federation's central fund for land purchase and development, settlement, and afforestation, was founded in 1901. Hermann Schapira (1840-1898) originated the idea of *Keren Kayemet*, because he believed that the lands of Erez Israel must be made the property of the people. The fund was financed by contributions and the lands were leased to the settlers. Pictured — The Golden Book, made by Meir Gur-Aryeh (1913). To be inscribed in this book was considered a great honor, and was bestowed on generous contributors.

Yemenite Jews and Erez Israel

Some sources link the arrival of Jews in Yemen to the tale of King Solomon and the Queen of Sheba [3], while others date the beginning of Jewish settlement in the country to the 7th century BCE, when trading colonies developed along the Spice Route extending from Damascus to the Indian Ocean. A Yemenite Jewish tradition claims that the first Jews arrived after the destruction of the First Temple (586 BCE). Josephus writes that King Herod sent Jewish battalions to conquer Yemen in the 1st century BCE, and that none of the troops returned; possibly some founded the Yemenite Jewish community. A Himyarite inscription on a burial cave at Bet Shearim attests to the existence of a Jewish community in the southern Arabian peninsula in the first centuries CE. Up to the 6th century a large influental community apparently existed under the Himyaritic Kingdom.

The Middle Ages

When the Muslims of the Hijaz occupied Yemen in the 7th century, the Jews became a 'protected' community. The Cairo *Genizah* contains evidence that, in the 10th century, they were in contact with the Babylonian academies. In the following centuries, as trade with India flourished and Yemen, and the port of Aden in particular, became an important trading station, numerous Jews from Babylonia, North Africa, Egypt and Persia settled there.

The late Middle Ages witnessed an upsurge of messianic fervor among Yemen's Jews, inspired, in part, by Muslim religious fanaticism. At the end of the 12th century Maimonides sent his *Epistle to Yemen* from Egypt, responding to news of the appearance of a false messiah there. In the 17th century, messianic movements abounded, most influential among them the Shabbatean movement, and the authorities reacted by imposing harsh anti-Jewish decrees, culminating in the expulsion of the entire community to Mauza in 1680. References to forced conversion and banishment appear in the works of the great Yemenite Jewish poet, R. Shalom Shabbazi (1619-*c.* 1680).

The Cairo *Genizah* refers to the presence of Yemenite Jews in Ashkelon and Jerusalem in the 12th century, but there is scant additional information on immigrants from Yemen before the end of the 19th century [Key]. R. Yeshua Adani immigrated with his family in 1571, and his son, Shelomo Adani, wrote a renowned commentary, *Melekhet Shelomo*, on the *Mishnah*. Rabbi Shalom Sharabi, who arrived in the first half of the 18th century, later headed the kabbalist Bet-El *Yeshiva*, as did his son after him. He wrote several books of kabbalist lore, including the famous *Rehovot ha-Nahar*.

The imamate regime (which replaced the Ottoman rulers in 1635) collapsed in the 19th century, and the Jews suffered greatly in the subsequent period of instability. After the British occupation of Aden in 1839, the community reestablished contact with fellow-Jews

CONNECTIONS

82 Eastern Jewry after the Expulsion from Spain

1

1 Carved wooden door of Jewish house in San'a, early 20th century. Yemenite Jews were carpenters and woodcarvers, as well as pursuing more characteristic crafts such as silversmithing, weaving, milling, tanning and pottery. Upon immigration to Israel, many were obliged to become farmers; others received training in new trades.

2

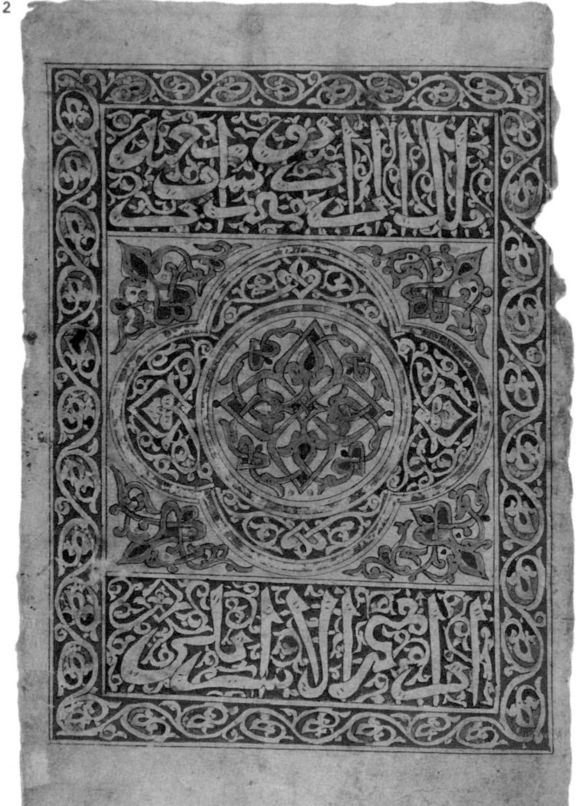

2 Last page of a Bible manuscript, San'a 1469, with arabesques and Muslim-style Arabic lettering. Print reached Yemen late, and biblical texts were copied by hand. Yemenite scholarship focused mainly on the *halakhah, midrashim* and *shira*. It was influenced initially by Babylon — particularly biblical and linguistic *masorot* — and subsequently, after renewal of contact with Egypt, by Maimonides. In the 16th century the influence of the Lurianic *Kabbalah* is evident in *midrashim* and *piyuttim*.

3

3 Sheban inscription from northeastern Yemen. The capital of Sheba, in eastern Yemen, is identified with modern Marib.

4

4 Street of the Jews in San'a, *circa* 1900. Internal division of rooms stemmed from the way of life and family structure. Larders and storerooms were on the ground floor, with open internal courtyards above. The interior was divided into different levels, and passageways connected houses.

abroad. After the Ottoman reoccupation in 1872, the country was opened to Jewish merchants. At that time some 80,000 Jews lived in Yemen.

The 19th century

The cultural isolation, economic plight and wide dispersal of Yemen's Jews [5] precluded intensive scholarly and literary creativity [2]. The few outstanding scholars included R. David Ben Amran, author of *Midrash ha-Gadol*; the aforementioned R. Shelomo Adani; R. Yihya Salih (1715-1805), author of *Peulat Tzadok*, a book of responsa; and R. Yihya Kafeh (1850-1932), a rare blend of scholar, innovator and critic. But, in general, the strength of Yemenite Jewry lay more in preservation of tradition than in innovation.

The community became known in the 19th century mainly through emissaries from Ereẓ Israel, such as Yaakov Sapir, author of *Hadrei Teman*, one of the most important travel books on the country, and researchers such as Prof. Joseph Halevi of the *Academie Française* and Edward Glazer, a Bohemian Jewish scholar. Ultimately, the motives for *aliyah* from Yemen were many and varied: Renewed contact with the Jewish world and with Ereẓ Israel; the corrupt practices of the Ottoman regime and its persecution of the Jewish religion; the undermining of traditional Jewish crafts — pottery, tinsmithery, weaving — as a result of import of ready-made goods; and wild rumors that Rothschild had purchased Ereẓ Israel and was handing out land to immigrants. One individual who spurred *aliyah* was Shmuel Yavnieli, a Palestine Office official who visited in 1911 and reached such remote spots as Habban and Hadhramaut. About one-third of the community immigrated between 1881 and 1948 [7].

In Operation "Magic Carpet" which ended in August 1950, some 50,000 Jews were flown from Yemen to Israel. About 2,000 Jews emigrated after this date. Today some 800 Jews remain in Yemen.

KEY

Until the end of the 19th century, links between the Jews of Yemen and the Holy Land were maintained through emissaries, who were despatched from Jerusalem, Safed, Hebron and Tiberias, and through individual immigrants. Various sources — an epistle from the Jerusalem community (1454), a work by Obadia of Bertinoro (1488), and the testimony of an Italian traveler (1553) — inform us that Yemenite Jews lived in Jerusalem and Safed. R. Israel Aryeh, an emissary from Safed, visited Yemen in 1689. Throughout the 18th and 19th centuries, emissaries collected money in Yemen for the Jews of the Holy Land. The picture shows a Yemenite Jew making his way on foot to Palestine (1907).

5

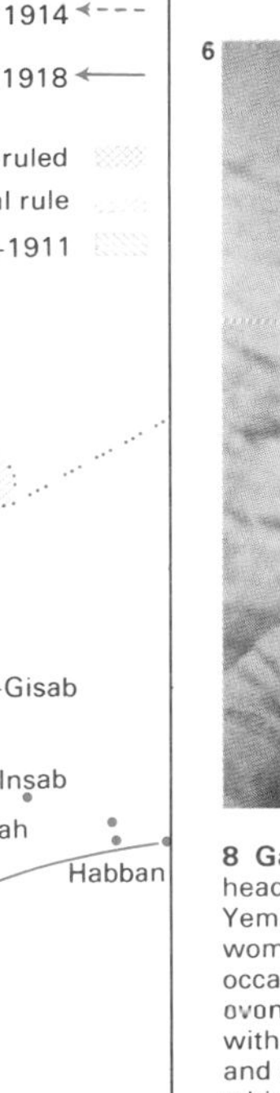

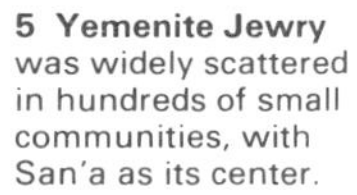

6 The Jewish woman in Yemen was responsible for running the household and educating the children in proper conduct. Often she pursued a craft that required highly intricate manual dexterity. The picture shows a Yemenite mother and son.

6

8

8 Gargush — headcovering of Yemenite Jewish women at ceremonial occasions and festive events, is decorated with the embroidery and silverwork in which the Jews specialized. Craftsmen used woven gold and silver thread, affixed to the cloth or interwoven in it by various methods.

5 Yemenite Jewry was widely scattered in hundreds of small communities, with San'a as its center.

7

7 Mass aliyah began in 1881, and continued on a wide scale from 1882 up to the turn of the century. Most immigrants settled in Jerusalem. Large groups came in the wake of the 1911 visit to Yemen of Shmuel Yavnieli. Early immigrants worked as farm laborers [here, in Rehovot, 1918].

The British Mandate and the Zionists

The Balfour Declaration (1917) signified recognition by Britain, the world's greatest power, of the aspirations of the Zionist Movement in Ereẓ Israel [6]. One of the main purposes of the Declaration was to ensure Allied support for British rule in Ereẓ Israel — a prize which Britain had coveted for over a century. France and Britain had been rivals over Middle East spheres of influence ever since the 19th century. The competition, both economic and political, was based largely on control of the India and Far East trade routes, and the railways built throughout the British Empire. When Turkey joined the war on Germany's side in 1914, Britain's position in the region became precarious, and it accordingly sought ways of ensuring its interests.

Some parties in England feared the ascendancy of France, which had entrenched itself near the Suez Canal. They believed that Ereẓ Israel could serve as a buffer zone between Egypt and the land to the north, Syria, which was destined for French domination. As early as 1915, Sir Herbert Samuel (1870-1963) attempted to persuade the British heads of government that if they would ease the conditions of Jewish settlement in Ereẓ Israel, the British would not only acquire the loyalty of the Jewish *Yishuv* [2], but also that of the World Zionist Movement. In 1915, however, British policymakers were still interested in other options.

The British proceeded to sign a number of agreements. One, the secret Sykes-Picot Agreement of 1916, provided for partition of the Middle East between Britain and France into separate spheres of influence and control, if and when the Turks were defeated, and envisioned an international administration for the central part of Ereẓ Israel, from the Lower Galilee to Beersheba. At the same time, Britain's high commissioner in Egypt, Sir Henry McMahon (1874-1919) promised Sherif Hussein of Mecca, of the Hashemite dynasty, that Britain would recognize an Arab kingdom under his rule. In return, Britain asked that the Arabs revolt against Turkey during the course of the war, and then recognize British interests at certain strategic points throughout the Middle East. This and similar British obligations to the Arabs would frequently redound against Zionist interests in the future.

Britain and Zionism

Ever since the 18th century, British Protestant reverence for the Bible had encouraged the belief that Ereẓ Israel had been promised to the Jewish people. English writers and romantics called for the Return to Zion and drew up plans for widespread Jewish settlement there. Only Great Britain, of all the Powers, showed any interest in the problems faced by the Zionist Movement. The British government had even proposed several solutions: it was prepared to allow Jewish settlement in the Sinai Peninsula in 1902, and in East Africa in 1903.

CONNECTIONS

120 Zionism Becomes a Political Movement
132 19th Century Erez Israel
140 Aliyah During the 1920s

1 Opposition to the pro-Zionist Balfour Declaration was expressed by many British. Prominent among them were assimilated Jews, including Samuel Edwin Montagu (1879-1924). Jews like Montagu believed that the demand for a National Home would raise doubts about the loyalty of Jews to their countries of origin, and thus could encourage anti-Semitism.

1

2A

2B

2 Aaron Aaronsohn (1876-1919) [A] world renowned scientist who first discovered wild emmer wheat, and founder in 1915 of the espionage ring, *NILI* (Hebrew acronym for "the Eternal One of Israel will not lie"), and his sister, Sarah (1890-1917) [B]. The Aaronsohns felt that Erez Israel's future as a Zionist homeland would be furthered by the British, and sought to help the British in the war against the Turks. From the experimental agricultural station set up by Aaronsohn at Atlit, information was relayed to Cairo and decoded by Aaronsohn, who served as a British Intelligence officer. In 1917 the Turks uncovered the network, and most of its members were executed.

3

3 During the course of World War I Jews who were not Ottoman subjects were expelled; property was confiscated and people died of hunger. In 1916 many *Yishuv* leaders were deported, and as the British advanced northwards through Sinai, the residents of Tel Aviv were expelled from the city (on Passover Eve, 1917). Turkey's antagonistic attitude encouraged many Jews to fight for the British. At the initiative of Joseph Trumpeldor (1880-1920) and Ze'ev Jabotinsky (1880-1940) the Zion Mule Corps and, later, the Jewish Legion, were formed; they were composed of volunteers from Erez Israel, Britain, the US, and Canada. This woodcut, *Soul Divided* by A Melnikoff, expresses the mixed feelings aroused by Jew's volunteering for the British side, which was seen as a rejection of Zionist settlement.

4

4 The British Army arrived at the gates of Jerusalem in December 1917. General Allenby, commander of the conquering troops, dismounted and marched into the city on foot. The British conquest of Erez Israel was completed in September 1918, and a British military government was established. In July 1920 the new League of Nations, in the course of dealing with those lands and colonies lost by Germany and the Ottomans, awarded a mandate over Palestine-Erez Israel to Britain, on the condition that it help to establish the Jewish National Home and work toward realization of the Balfour Declaration.

The Goal in Sight

The Zionist leaders in England during World War I who pinned their hopes on a British victory, felt that the war presented Zionism with a unique opportunity. Nahum Sokolow (1861-1936) and Chaim Weizmann (1874-1952) sought to establish ties with British leaders and persuade them that it would be to their advantage to support the Zionist cause [Key].

The British were anxious to have world Jewry on their side, believing that this would engender widespread Jewish support for British policies. In particular, Britain wished to persuade the United States to join the war, and Russia to remain a combatant after the Bolshevik Revolution. Many in Britain believed that a British pro-Zionist declaration would lead American and Russian Jewry to put pressure on their respective governments in favor of Great Britain. There were also rumors that Germany, as well, was about to offer to ensure Zionist rights in Erez Israel.

In December 1916 the British government changed hands, and many key positions — including that of prime minister — were now filled by individuals with whom Weizmann had been in contact. The new government did not approve of the Sykes-Picot Agreement; and it sought to speed up the conquest of Erez Israel in order to ensure British control there.

On October 31, 1917, the British War Cabinet convened to discuss Weizmann's proposal for the text of a sympathetic declaration. The final text, presented by Sir Mark Sykes to Weizmann, was not the wording for which the Zionists had been hoping — recognition of Erez Israel as the National Home of the Jewish People. It was, nevertheless, the international recognition which the Zionist Federation had been striving to achieve ever since the First Zionist Congress in 1897. Despite its cautious, ambiguous wording, the Balfour Declaration inspired new hope in the Jewish People [7, 8].

KEY

Chaim Weizmann (1874-1952), born in Belorussia, immigrated to Britain in 1904. Weizmann lectured in chemistry at the University of Manchester. Thanks to his scientific work, which contributed to the British war effort, he was appointed to a senior position in the Admiralty laboratories. He originated the idea of the Balfour Declaration, was active in efforts to establish the Hebrew University of Jerusalem, and founded the Daniel Sieff Institute of Science in Rehovot — today called the Weizmann Institute. He was president of the World Zionist Organization (1920-1931 and 1935-1946). When the State of Israel was established, he was elected its first president.

5

5 The Arab world expressed opposition to the Balfour Declaration. Since its publication on November 2, 1917, Arabs stage an annual anti-Zionist demonstration on this date. Pictured: a synagogue in Cairo, destroyed on November 2, 1945.

6

משרד לעניני חוץ ב׳ נובמבר 1917

לורד רוטשילד היקר

שמח אני מאד למסור לך בשם
ממשלת הוד מלכותו את הדקלרציה
של חבה לתנועה הציונית של היהודים
שנמסרה לקבינט ונתאשרה על ידו:

"הממשלה של הוד מלכותו מביטה ברצון על יסוד
"בית לאומי בארץ ישראל לעם ישראל
"והיא תשתמש בכל האמצעים הטובים לאפשר את השגת
"המטרה הזאת אך במובן הברור שלא יעשה שום דבר שיוכל
"לנגוע בזכיות האזרחיות והדתיות של קבוצות לא־יהודיות בא״י או
"בזכיות והעמדות הפוליטיות שהיהודים נהנים מהן באיזו ארץ אחרת".

אשמח מאד אם תביא את
הדקלרציה הזאת לפני
הפדרציה הציונית.

שלך במסירות
ארטור ימס בלפור

6 The Balfour Declaration was sent as a personal letter from Lord Arthur James Balfour (1848-1930) to Lionel Walter Rothschild (1868-1937), who played an important role in the political discussions preceding its presentation. The Declaration recognizes the right of the Jewish People to build their national home in Palestine, and supports the rights of the non-Jewish citizens residing there, as well as the rights and political status of Jews in other countries. It signaled a new stage in Zionism. Seen here: a commemorative Hebrew version.

7

7 The Moshava Balfouria, established in 1922, was an expression of the enthusiasm aroused by the Declaration among the Jewish people.

8

8 Balfour was greeted with much enthusiasm in every Jewish settlement he visited in mandatory Palestine. He was invited to participate in the inauguration ceremony for the Hebrew University in 1925. On his visit to Palestine he was given a picture depicting *The Modern Exodus* by Meir Gur Aryeh, of the Bezalel School of Art.

Aliyah During the 1920s

Between 1919 and 1929, the number of Jews in Palestine multiplied threefold. Institutions of Jewish self-government were established, more than sixty new settlements were founded, and the groundwork was laid for manufacturing and industry. The period is usually divided into the Third *Aliyah* and the Fourth *Aliyah*.

The Third Aliyah (1919-1923)

The collapse of the European empires after World War I, and the pogroms that accompanied the Russian Civil War (1918-1920) and the Russo-Polish War (1919-1920), led to a mass emigration of Jews. Approximately 37,000 came to Palestine. The right of self-determination which led to the establishment of nation-states in Europe, together with the Balfour Declaration, strengthened the belief among Jews that the Zionist solution could be viable. The new *olim* were a varied group, but most were members of the *he-Halutz* youth movement, which sought to establish a Zionist-Socialist national center in Ereẓ Israel. The movement imposed upon its members the duty of 'self-fulfillment,' and before *aliyah* many underwent agricultural training and learned Hebrew on farms and training collectives in Europe [2].

The *Yishuv* lacked the economic infrastructure for immigrant absorption, and the Zionist Federation, too, lacked funds for settlement and absorption. Unemployment threatened to destroy the little that had already been achieved. A partial solution was found when the mandatory administration provided public work in army camps, laying railroad tracks, and paving roads. The workers' parties organized as contractor, and assumed responsibility for this work. Between 1922 and 1923, 80% of all Jewish laborers in the cities were organized in these work brigades [1].

After World War I, the purchase of lands in the Jezreel Valley was completed by Yehoshua Hankin [4, 5]. In 1920, the Jewish Labor Federation (*Histadrut*) was founded. It embodied the Second *Aliyah* vision of a "model society" based on cooperation, equality, social justice and mutual aid. However, the years 1922 and 1923 were years of depression, due to heightened tension over security in the Jewish settlements after the 1921 riots, and because the mandatory government had ceased to provide jobs. *Aliyah* practically came to a standstill, while 4,000 people left the country.

The Fourth Aliyah (1924-1929)

Aliyah resumed in 1925. To the 93,000 Jews already living in Ereẓ Israel in 1923, another 48,000 were added in the space of 18 months. Half of this number were from Poland, where anti-Semitism and economic restrictions affected the Jewish middle class. Some 20% came from the Soviet Union, 10% from Rumania and Lithuania, and 12% from Yemen and Iraq.

The social makeup of this *aliyah* dif-

CONNECTIONS

138 The British Mandate and the Zionists
148 Immigration and Settlement in the 1930s
208 The Histadrut (General Federation of Labor)
210 The Kibbutz

1 **Third Aliyah halutzim** organized into work groups for practical as well as ideological reasons. Within the *kevutzah* ("group") the *halutzim* could acquire trades and prepare for lives as workers. The group evoked a special atmosphere of comradeship and provided for all the members' needs — food, lodging, work and cultural activities. The first *kevutzot* organized to pave roads, and later founded agricultural settlements or went to work in cities. In the cities, too, work cooperatives were established, like this *To'elet* cooperative for shoemaking and tailoring, one of many cooperatives operating in the 1920s.

2 **The he-Halutz Movement,** established from 1915 to 1917 at the initiative of Joseph Trumpeldor in Russia and David Ben-Gurion and Itzhak Ben-Zvi in the United States. *He-Halutz* members considered themselves soldiers, ready to fulfill any assignment. This *he-Halutz* training farm was in Memel, Lithuania (1932). In 1935 there were 600 *he-Halutz* cadres.

4 **The lands in the Jezreel Valley** — 1,200 acres of predominantly swampland — were purchased in 1921. Here, two new types of settlement were established, the *kibbutz* and the *moshav*, beginning with Kibbutz En Harod and Moshav Nahalal in 1921. By 1930, more than 20 new settlements had been established. The valley's reclamation became a symbol for Zionist settlement in Ereẓ Israel.

3 **The economic crisis** led to a rise in unemployment, which reached 8,440 in 1927. The situation strengthened the argument that carefully controlled and planned national construction should be favored in the *Yishuv*. Here unemployed workers are demonstrating in Hadera, late 1920s.

5 **"Redeemer of the Land", Yehoshua Hankin** (1864-1945) [pictured, with his wife, Olga], came to Ereẓ Israel in 1882 and began his reclamation project in 1890. Rehovot and Hadera were founded on lands he procured. He constantly pressed for greater acquisitions of land, fearing increasing difficulties with the *effendi* landowners. His initiative and influence were behind the purchase of the Jezreel and Hefer valleys. In 1932 he began buying lands in the Negev. Hankin is credited with having acquired during his lifetime a total of about 150,000 acres.

fered from the earlier ones. A minority were from pioneer youth movements, including religious *halutzim*. The great majority were members of the urban lower middle class. Approximately 83% headed for the cities, with Tel Aviv absorbing about 65% [6]. Tel Aviv's rapid expansion, and the high standard of living attained by its inhabitants, rested on shaky economic foundations. A severe economic crisis began in 1926; many factories failed, and construction — the backbone of the economy up to that time — came to a standstill [3]. Approximately 15,000 people left the country between 1926 and 1928. It was the Zionist Federation which came to the rescue, investing all its resources in public works financed by the Jewish National Fund and the *Keren Hayesod*.

This economic crisis was barely felt in the other cities and in the agricultural settlements. Jerusalem was the center of the British mandatory government, whose institutions provided work for many, while the Hebrew University attracted intellectuals and scholars [9]. Haifa absorbed many immigrants in the industries which began to develop in the Haifa Bay vicinity. Many technological experts were attracted there when the Technion opened its doors.

Seeking an agricultural way of life, many *olim* founded new towns like Magdiel and Herzlia, where middle class farmers invested private funds in orchards and groves. The citrus industry became one of the important branches of the country's economy.

The economic crisis, which hurt the wealthy capitalists, was responsible for a change in the composition of *aliyah*. In 1927 an increasing influx of pioneer movement members began. Many settled in *moshavim* and *kibbutzim*, or worked as farm laborers or in urban industry and construction. At the end of the twenties, while the western world was embroiled in a bitter economic crisis, the Jewish settlement in Palestine found itself benefiting from a period of recovery and prosperity.

KEY

"The Joseph Trumpeldor Labor Battalion" (Gedud ha-Avodah) was established shortly after the fall of Tel Hai (August 1920) by a group of *he-Halutz* members, headed by Yizhak Landsberg (Sadeh) (1890-1952). They sought to build the land by establishing a general commune of laborers, facilitating mass *aliyah* to Erez Israel, and organizing a Hebrew defense force. Battalion work squads accepted the principles of communal life, but opposed membership selectivity. Eventually dissension struck the *Gedud*, and it disbanded in 1929. Over the years it had encompassed more than 2,000 members. Pictured: A labor battalion paving roads, 1925.

6 A

6 B

6 In the twenties, Tel Aviv became a city. It was awarded the status of a municipal council, permitting it to set up its own police force. From a total population of 3,604 in 1921, Tel Aviv grew to 54,110 by 1931. It was the only city in the country that was entirely Jewish. Widespread construction began in 1925, and architects endeavored to give the city an "Erez Israeli" appearance. Levinsky Street and the streets branching off it were planned as a seven-branched *menora*. Two and three-story houses were uniquely styled to combine western functionalism with eastern ornamentation: arches, pillars, and the use of ceramic tiles decorated with biblical figures and events. [A] Granovsky House in Tel Aviv, planned by the architect Yehuda Megidovitz; [B] ceramic tiles from the workshop of Eisenberg at Lederberg House. As the population increased, small factories, restaurants, shops, grocery stores and kiosks were established alongside legitimate theater and silent movie halls. The Hebrew newspaper and publishing houses were also founded.

7

7 Chaim Arlosoroff (1898-1933), one of the leaders of the *Yishuv* and of the Labor Movement, cautioned against the "pseudo-prosperity" of 1924-5, warning that an economic crisis was inevitable. From 1931 on he served as director of the Jewish Agency's Political Department. In 1933 he was murdered. His violent death cast a shadow over relations between the Labor and Revisionist movements for many years, as the latter were accused of the murder — although their guilt was never proven in court.

8

8 Talpiot [pictured in 1925], a neighborhood established in 1922, is typical of building patterns in Jewish Jerusalem. The new part of the city was composed of a series of separate, isolated, distant neighborhoods. Between 1921 and 1931, 16 new Jewish neighborhoods were founded in Jerusalem, increasing its Jewish population from 33,971 in 1922 to 51,222 by 1931. Unlike Tel Aviv, Jerusalem was composed of many different suburbs bordered by parks. When British civil administration was introduced, it was decided that all public and private structures would be built of Jerusalem stone, and the city began to take on its unique character. When the *Yishuv*'s national institutions were transferred to Jerusalem and the Hebrew University opened its doors, the city became the center of political and academic activities.

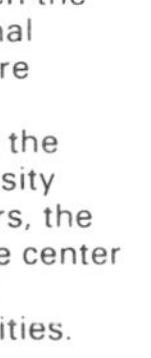

9

9 Opening ceremonies at the Hebrew University (1925) were described as "a national holiday." The idea of establishing a Jewish university which would "fulfill the ancient Hebrew spirit" had been proposed as early as 1897. Its founders wanted Erez Israel to become a cultural center which would attract Jewish men of letters and of science, and would provide higher education for Jewish youth.

Arab Nationalism

The impact of the European nationalist movements of the 19th century was felt by Arab intellectuals in the Middle East as well, so that at the same time that a national Jewish movement was gaining strength in Europe, Arab nationalism was growing in the East. Zionism saw its foothold in Palestine as a renewal of Jewish national life in the homeland that had been taken from it, while the Arab nationalists regarded Zionism as an alien concept impeding Arab unity.

Prior to World War I, two separate factions emerged in the Arab national movement. One faction favored self-determination within the Ottoman Empire, while the other sought an independent Arab nation. The few Palestinian Arabs who displayed an interest in Arab nationalism sided with the pro-Turkish faction.

The Movement in Palestine

World War I brought about a realignment of positions. The collapse of the Ottoman Empire and the British promise of Syria to Feisal, lent support to the champions of "Greater Syria." In 1919, the first congress of Arabs of Palestine convened and defined Palestine as "Southern Syria."

From the very first, the Arabs opposed the Zionist settlement project. In 1891, 100 Jerusalem dignitaries sent a petition to the Ottoman authorities demanding that Jews be barred from immigration to Palestine or the purchase of land in the country. Yet at that time, opposition was still limited to a small group of urban intellectuals.

The British conquest of Palestine and the adoption of the Balfour Declaration as basic British policy fanned Arab opposition. Zionism was now a real threat, and the Arab protests assumed a more aggressive and violent form. The British endeavored to mediate between the two national movements, and their efforts led to an agreement by Chaim Weizmann and Emir Feisal early in 1919 [2]. However in February a pan-Arab congress convened in Syria and demanded that all Zionist claims be rejected.

Fearing for his status among the Arabs, Feisal acceded to the congress' demand that he be proclaimed "King of All Syria." Arab forces in Syria-Lebanon simultaneously launched a campaign against the French army, during which they attacked Jewish settlements in the Galilee. The settlements were evacuated, and in a heroic battle on March 1, 1920, Tel Hai fell [4]. In April 1920 the San Remo Conference met to debate the peace accords signed after World War I and to divide the Ottoman Empire among the victors. As the conference deliberated the British Mandate in Palestine, Arab rioting resumed. A furious mob rampaged through the Jewish Quarter in Jerusalem. The mandate, including Britain's commitment to implement the Balfour Declaration, was approved, and the British appointed Sir Herbert Samuel, a Zionist Jew, High Commissioner. More Arab protests followed.

CONNECTIONS

138 The British Mandate and the Zionists
150 The Arab Uprising

1 A

2 The meeting between Weizmann and Feisal (1918) resulted in an agreement signed in January 1919 calling for close cooperation between Zionists and Arabs. In fact, this meant Arab recognition of the Balfour Declaration. But the agreement was soon rendered worthless by Arab opposition and Feisal's flight from Syria.

2

1 The Western Wall Commission was set up by the League of Nations in 1930 in the wake of the rioting that erupted in 1929 over the question of prayer privileges at the Wall. The commission [A] endorsed the Jews' right to pray at the Wall [B], but banned the presence of *Torah* scrolls and prayer benches, or the blowing of the *shofar* on the site. These prohibitions became a symbol of foreign rule, and there were constant attempts to disobey them. Jewish rights at the wall remained a source of international dispute until 1967.

1 B

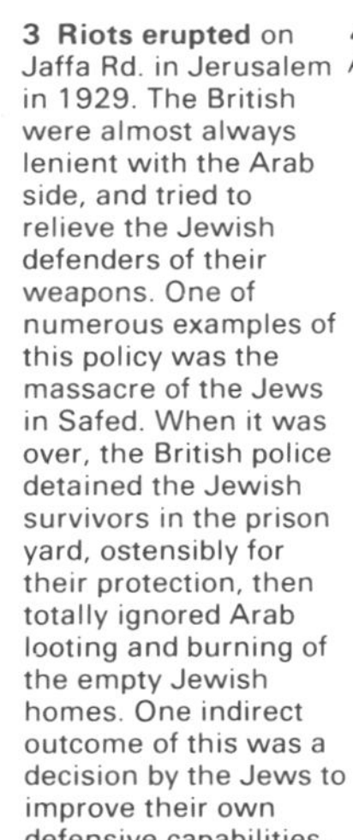

3 Riots erupted on Jaffa Rd. in Jerusalem in 1929. The British were almost always lenient with the Arab side, and tried to relieve the Jewish defenders of their weapons. One of numerous examples of this policy was the massacre of the Jews in Safed. When it was over, the British police detained the Jewish survivors in the prison yard, ostensibly for their protection, then totally ignored Arab looting and burning of the empty Jewish homes. One indirect outcome of this was a decision by the Jews to improve their own defensive capabilities.

4 A

4 Tel Hai was one of four settlements in the northern Galilee which were cut off in 1919 and attacked. Joseph Trumpeldor (1880-1920) was sent to organize the defense of the region. After resisting tenaciously for several months, the settlement fell in a final attack in which Trumpeldor and the seven other defenders were killed. [A] a memorial to Trumpeldor and his comrades; the motto engraved upon it is attributed to Trumpeldor and has become a hallmark of bravery — "It is good to die for one's country." [B] Tel Hai.

3

4 B

Violence in Palestine

The collapse of Feisal's regime in Damascus forced the Arab national movement to revise its policy. The concept of Palestine as "Southern Syria" was dropped. The local Arabs now began to define themselves as Palestinians, and turned their efforts to bringing about a repudiation of the Jewish national home and the establishment of a representative Palestinian Arab government. When the British rejected these demands, the May Day parade of 1921 in Jaffa served as the pretext for a new wave of violence [7]. These riots resulted in restrictions on Jewish immigration to Palestine, but did not achieve the main Arab goal — the abolition of the Jewish national home. The Arab leadership began to question the effectiveness of violence, and increasingly turned to political struggle.

Between 1922 and 1928, rifts widened among the factions in the Arab national movement, while development of the Zionist settlement slowed in response to economic recession. As a result, Arab opposition to the Jewish homeland ebbed. National consciousness typified only very narrow circles, and was no match for the rising standard of living enjoyed by broad sectors of the Arab population. But the quiet was deceptive. The Mufti, Haj Amin al-Husseini, the religious and political leader of the Palestinian Arabs, was working tirelessly to prepare an all-out attack on the Zionist settlement and British policy. He incited the populace by depicting Zionism as a threat to the Muslim holy sites on the Temple Mount, and exploited disputes over prayer privileges at the Western Wall [1].

In August 1929, bloody Arab riots swept through Jerusalem and soon spread throughout the country [3]. They were unprecedented in scope and in their brutality [Key]. They brought an end to mixed Jewish and Arab quarters, and in their wake the Jewish residents of Nablus (Shechem), Jenin, Gaza and Hebron fled their homes.

KEY

The massacre in Hebron took place in August 1929. Arabs from the city and outlying villages stormed Jewish homes and the large *yeshiva*, brutally slaughtering helpless people. Jews had lived in Hebron since the 14th century. Most were students in the *yeshiva* or religious schools, and lived in close contact with their Arab neighbors. Secure in their faith in their Arab friends, they refused the *Haganah*'s offers of assistance and protection. Only a very few Arabs, however, came to the aid of the beleaguered Jews. The massacre raged for two days, with police reinforcements slow to arrive. Only when it was over, were the wounded and the survivors transported to Jerusalem.

5

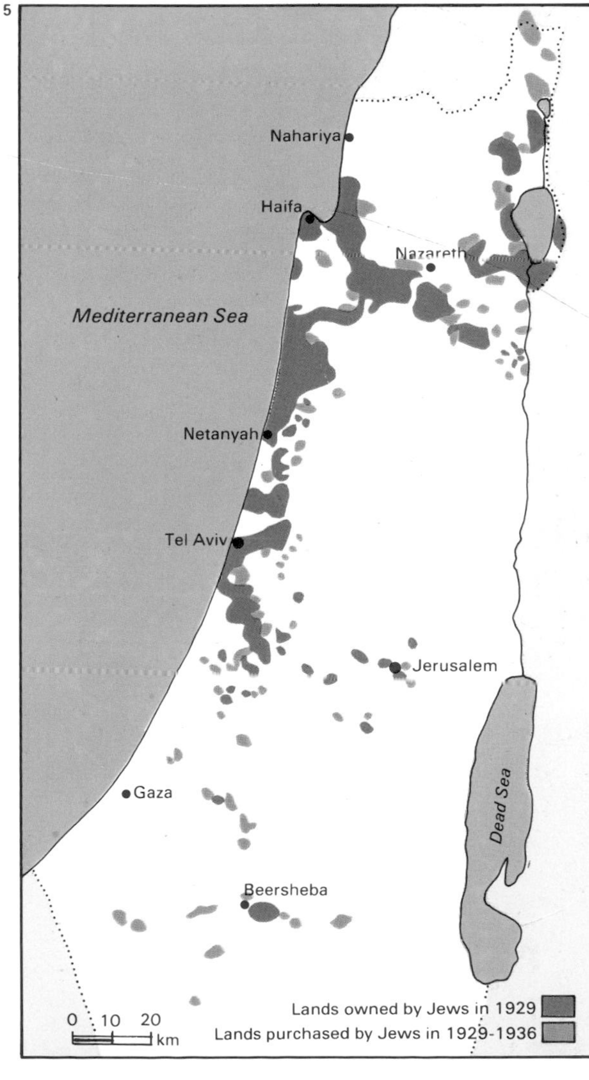

5 The purchase of land in Palestine by Jews was subject to mandatory restrictions, as well as to the settlement policy fixed by Zionist authorities, which changed in response to the political situation and in accordance with the availability of funds. Private capital was generally used to buy urban plots or small orchards along the coastal plain. Funds held by the Zionist authority were allocated to acquire large tracts, such as the Hefer and Jezreel Valleys, which were to be densely settled and thus serve to establish the borders of the *Yishuv*.

6

7

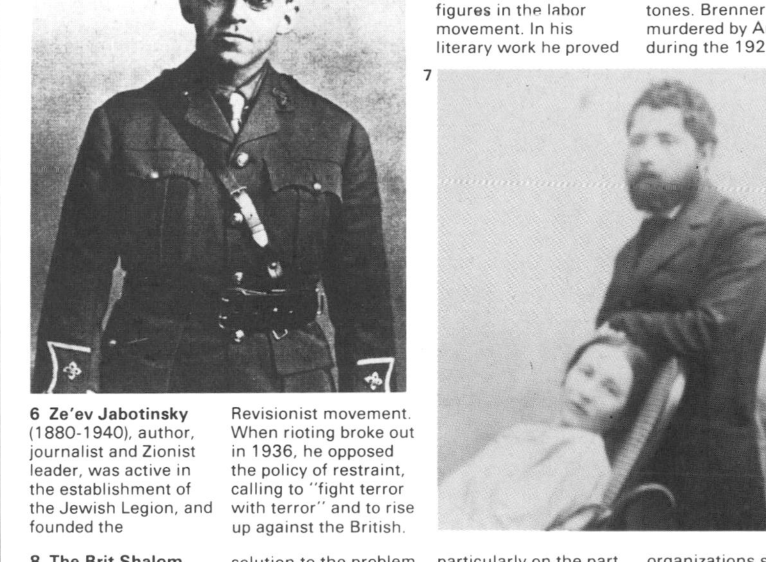

6 Ze'ev Jabotinsky (1880-1940), author, journalist and Zionist leader, was active in the establishment of the Jewish Legion, and founded the Revisionist movement. When rioting broke out in 1936, he opposed the policy of restraint, calling to "fight terror with terror" and to rise up against the British.

7 The author Joseph Chaim Brenner (with his wife) came from Russia in 1909 and was one of the central figures in the labor movement. In his literary work he proved a sharp social critic, depicting the intellectual and moral problems of the "New Jews" in somber tones. Brenner was murdered by Arabs during the 1921 riots.

8 The Brit Shalom Society was founded in the mid-1920s by intellectuals and public figures. Its aim was to promote amity between Jews and Arabs and to find a mutually satisfactory solution to the problem of Palestine. To this end the Society supported far-reaching compromises on the question of immigration. These proposals met with widespread opposition, particularly on the part of the Revisionists, and engendered dissent within the Society itself. *Brit Shalom* ceased its activities in the early 1930s. Similar aims were later adopted by organizations such as *Kedma Mizracha*, the League for Jewish-Arab Rapprochement, and Unity. The document reproduced here is *Brit Shalom*'s by-laws, in Hebrew and Arabic.

8

بريت شالوم

برنامج

جمعية عهد السلام (بريت شالوم)

اولاً = ان الجمعية تدعى باسم: «جمعية عهد السلام»

ثانياً = ان الجمعية في القدس. ولها ان تنشئ الفروع في كل مكان سواء في فلسطين او في الخارج.

(غايات ومقاصد الجمعية)

ثالثاً = ان غاية الجمعية تمهيد السبيل بين اليهود والعرب، بايجاد الطرق للحياة المشتركة في فلسطين، على قاعدة التعديل التام في حقوق الشعبين السياسية ذات السلطة الذاتية الواسعة، والبحث في كيفية اعمالها المشتركة في تقدم البلاد.

رابعاً = وللتوصل الى الغايات المتقدمة، تتخذ الاجراءات التالية: —

(١) — درس المسائل المتعلقة بحياة الشعبين المشتركة في

אגודת «ברית שלום»

תקנות

1. שם האגודה: „ברית־שלום״.

2. מקום מושבה: ירושלים. סניפים לה יכולים להוסד בכל מקום, הן בא״י והן בחו״ל.

3. תעודת האגודה: לסלול דרך הבנה בין עברים וערבים לצורות חיים משותפות בארץ־ישראל על יסוד שווי שלם בזכויותיהם הפוליטיות של שני לאומים בעלי אוטונומיה רחבה ולצורותיה של עבודתם המשותפת לטובת התפתחותה של הארץ.

4. בתור אמצעים להשגת המטרה הזאת ישמשו:

א. חקירת הפרובלימות הנובעות מתוך חייהם המשותפים של שני הלאומים בא״י ומתוך המנדט של חבר הלאומים.

Jewish Defense Organizations

Jewish defense began in 1908 with *ha-Shomer*, a secret organization whose limited membership combined work with guard duty. Its soldier-laborer formula was passed on to the *Haganah*, which had a broad popular. base and was subject to civilian authority [2].

The Need for Defense

When the British took over Palestine in 1917, many in the *Yishuv* felt that the government should be responsible for the safety of its residents. The 1920 riots and the fall of Tel Hai changed this attitude. The Zionist Federation authorized Ze'ev Jabotinsky to establish a Jewish Defense Force, but he was unable to persuade the British to agree to any legally-recognized force.

At the First *Histadrut* Convention (1920) the need to establish an organization to take responsibility for the security of the entire *Yishuv* was discussed. Although associated with the *Histadrut* and the Labor Movement, the *Haganah* declared that it "would be open to every Jew and Jewess who desires to join and has had the necessary training."

The 1921 riots — which broke out before the *Haganah* had actually begun to function — showed how serious security problems were, and caused heated controversy regarding the policy towards the Arabs. Jabotinsky claimed that only a Jewish Battalion, serving in the British Army, could provide a dependable force. On the other hand, David Ben-Gurion argued that only a force under the authority of the *Yishuv* could defend it. Meanwhile, *Haganah* members obtained weapons, which were smuggled into the country and hidden in caches [5]. However, this was discovered by the British, who made it difficult for *Haganah* members to obtain funds, and limited their activities. These were reduced to physical training, in the guise of sports lessons [8], and to defense preparations on days when Arab attacks were anticipated, such as the Balfour Declaration anniversary. Despite their importance, *Haganah* matters remained the preoccupation of only a small minority during 1921-1929. In the summer of 1929, the Arabs launched simultaneous attacks on settlements throughout Erez Israel. Smaller, more isolated settlements were abandoned; at Hebron and Safed Jews were slaughtered; and at a heroic battle at Huldah many were killed or wounded [6].

After the 1929 Riots

British inability to maintain order, and the political results that followed — the "White Paper" prohibiting sale of land to Jews and limiting *aliyah* — strengthened supporters of an independent Jewish defense force. The *Haganah* was now subordinated to the *Yishuv* authorities. A national headquarters was set up, headed by Israel Galili. Fifty percent of members were *Histadrut* representatives, the rest from civilian circles. Despite this seemingly "equal" division, it was the Labor Party and several key movement members who remained the

CONNECTIONS

134 Foundations of Zionism in Erez Israel
140 Aliyah During the 1920s
142 Arab Nationalism
148 Immigration and Settlement in the 1930s
150 The Arab Uprising
158 The Underground Movement

1

2
Members of ha-Shomer (photo)

1 The "Moving Guards" (*Manim*) were a special unit of about 400 police, all *Haganah* members. They secured the convoys and transportation lines. The *Manim* were a cover for illegal *Haganah* activities, and participated in arms smuggling and illegal immigration.

2 Members of ha-Shomer "would be given orders to either go out to work or to perform guard duty, because labor and guard duty were intertwined." They operated as "conquest units" whose task was to prevent lands purchased by *Keren Kayemet* from being tilled (thus establishing ownership rights) by Arab *fellahin*. Hence it was they who established the borders of Jewish settlement. They realized their dream of combining labor, defense, and settlement, by establishing *ha-Shomer* settlements — Moshav Tel Adashim and Kibbutz Kefar Giladi. In order to be accepted as a member of *ha-Shomer* one had to pass stringent tests, in which applicants had to prove their courage, resourcefulness and levelheadedness. Helping a friend in trouble — even if it involved risking one's own life — was an imperative, and use of weapons was permitted "only as a last resort." These values were bequeathed by *ha-Shomer* members to their comrades and to those who followed in their footsteps — the *Haganah*, the *Palmach* and the Israel Defense Forces. The Arab dress [photo] reflected these early settlers' search for authentic roots in the land.

3

3 Eliahu Golomb (1893-1945) who helped shape the *Haganah*, came to Erez Israel in 1909. Before the country was taken over by the British, Golomb was an initiator of the Jewish Legion volunteer movement. In 1921 he was a member of the *Haganah* Council. Golomb believed that the *Haganah* must represent the entire *Yishuv*, and not be a limited, elitist military group. He helped establish the field companies and the *Palmach*.

4A

4B

4 The Special Night Squads [A] were established by Charles Orde Wingate (1903-1944) [B], in order to fight Arab irregulars with bold tactics. Because of his ardent support for Zionism, Wingate was transferred from Palestine (1939). He died in World War II at the Burma Front. His dream of commanding a Jewish Army within the British Army went unfulfilled. Wingate was called "The Friend" and he won the admiration and appreciation of the entire *Yishuv*. Many *Haganah* commanders were pupils of his. They adopted his methods — the element of surprise, and unconventional fighting tactics. The "Night Squads," formed in 1937, were trained in his spirit.

determining factor within the organization. The key personality at headquarters was Eliahu Golomb [3].

While efforts were being made to embrace all of the *Yishuv*, quarrels broke out within the *Haganah*'s Jerusalem branch, concerning the organization's nature and connection to the *Histadrut*. In April 1931, a group led by Abraham Tehomi set up a parallel underground organization, *Irgun Bet*. In 1937 many of them returned to the *Haganah*, while the remainder renamed their faction *IZL — Irgun Zvai Leumi* (National Military Organization), linked to the Revisionist Movement.

Severe anti-Jewish riots took place between 1936 and 1939. When Arab hostilities also turned against the British, the mandatory government and the *Yishuv* agreed to collaborate. Jewish volunteers joined the British police force. While organized into *Plugot Notarim*, or constabularies [1, 7], they actually were *Haganah* members who took their orders from the *Yishuv*.

At the initiative of Yizhak Sadeh (1890-1952) [Key] the *Haganah*, now several thousand strong, decided to move from passive to active defense. The constabulary framework enabled the *Haganah* to train thousands of new recruits, move more freely, and control weaponry. Cooperation with the British reached its height with the establishment of the Special Night Squads [4]. Many who served in these companies eventually became commanders in the *Haganah, Palmach*, and, later, the IDF (Israel Defense Forces).

The *Haganah*, considering itself the army of the state-in-the-making, opposed individual terrorism or reprisal operations, and supported the establishment of field companies. Subsidiary organizations were established, such as *Shai* (Intelligence Service) and *Ta'as* (Military Industry) for the underground manufacture of hand grenades and explosives. By 1937, about 25,000 men and women were members of the *Haganah*.

KEY

Yizhak Sadeh [pictured with protegés Moshe Dayan and Yigal Allon] came to Erez Israel in 1920 from Russia. The bulk of his defense and security work began in 1936. He developed the "beyond the fence" approach to initiating operations, established a fighting squad in the Jerusalem hills (*ha-Nodedet*), and helped establish the *Palmach* in 1941. During the War of Independence he served as advisor to Ben-Gurion and commander of the IDF's first armored brigade.

5 Slicks were arms caches in which the *Haganah* hid their weapons. Arms were either manufactured in small workshops or smuggled into the country and stored in pits specially prepared for this purpose, or inside double walls. Until the beginning of the 1940s, the British were unsuccessful in discovering even one of the *slicks*, and there were no informants. Building and stocking a *slick* were extremely dangerous activities. Pictured — the *Sela* (rock) *slick*, Tel Mond.

6 "Eternal Memorial to the Defenders of the Homeland" — the inscription on a monument in memory of Ephraim Chizhik (1899-1929), the commander at Huldah, and to his sister, Sarah, who died in the defense of Tel Hai. During the 1929 riots, hundreds of Arabs attacked Huldah, and its 23 defenders waged a heroic battle. Due to British pressure, they were forced to abandon the site, and upon their return they found the settlement burned and looted.

5

6

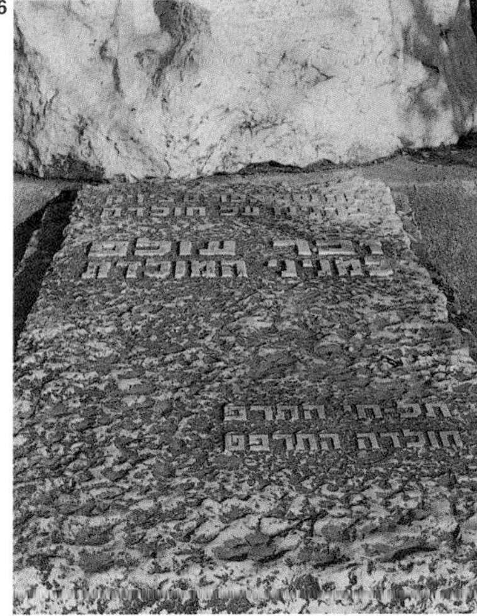

7

8 Close combat training was done with sticks instead of rifles. Following cooperation with the British in establishing the constabulary units and participating in Wingate's training projects, Jewish training exercises became more military in character. In 1941 a platoon commanders' school was set up at Juara and courses in intelligence, radio operation, and demolition were also given. In 1939 a training bureau was created in the *Haganah*. Here, manuals on weaponry and military tactics were published under various guises.

8

9

9 Since the earliest days of Zionist settlement, women worked toward full partnership in both labor and defense. One of the founders and initiators of *ha-Shomer* was Mania Shochat (1880-1961). The *Haganah* opened its ranks to women in 1925. Their main task was smuggling weapons. On the settlements, women handled guns, and labored side-by-side with the men. Pictured — settling Hanitah (1938).

7 After the 1936 riots the British agreed to organize a Jewish constabulary force, to help suppress disturbances and guard the Jewish settlements. The draftees, who were outfitted with English uniforms and rifles, were called *notarim* (constables) or *ghaffirs* in Arabic. By 1939, 22,000 residents of the *Yishuv* had joined the *ghaffirs*. They operated within the framework of a national unit which remained active until the end of the British Mandate. Having thousands of Jews legally in possession of arms very much improved the defense situation in the *Yishuv*.

Nazi Anti-Semitic Policy

CONNECTIONS

118 Modern Anti-Semitism
160 The Jews in the Trap of Nazi Rule

The reasons for the rise of the National Socialist German Workers' Party (NSDAP) date back to the mid-19th century: problems of rapid industrialization in a society which remained basically conservative; the shock of defeat in World War I and the harsh terms imposed on Germany in the Treaty of Versailles in 1919; the lack of deep democratic roots in the Weimar Republic; and severe economic crises in the early 1920s and early 1930s. Within this maze of traumatic difficulties, Hitler succeeded in captivating the masses with a new, more promising direction.

The Early Years

When Hitler was appointed Chancellor on January 30, 1933, the Nazi Party did not have a majority in parliament, it held only three out of eleven cabinet posts, and it did not yet control the government apparatus. Thus, Hitler's first objective was to establish his rule. His anti-Jewish policy had not yet taken full form. Yet, within party ranks, there emerged a demand that the "promises" of anti-Jewish action given by the party leaders be fulfilled post haste. Outbreaks of violence and attacks on the Jews increased after new elections on March 5, 1933, in which the Nazis won almost 44% of the vote, and their steady coalition partners 8%.

The first conspicuous act was to declare an economic boycott on the Jews, beginning April 1, 1933 [2]. In the wake of protests and demonstrations throughout the world, the boycott was curtailed to a single day, during the course of which it became clear that such questions as "Who is a Jew?" and "What is a Jewish enterprise?" had not yet been clearly answered. For the first time, members of the party became aware of the gap between sweeping anti-Semitic ideas and reality. A large number of departments and bureaus, designed to deal with the Jews, were set up in the offices of the government and the party. There were also "research institutes" which studied the Jewish problem, and all these bodies competed for primacy of place in drawing the blueprint of the policy of anti-Semitism.

Solving the "Jewish Problem"

Various approaches to solving the Jewish problem emerged. One focused on legislation to give the Jews a status of inferiority. Initially they were removed from civil service posts. In order to implement this law the concept "Jew" was defined for the first time as any person who had one Jewish grandparent. Discriminatory legislation reached its peak in the Nuremberg Laws (September 1935), which rooted the theory of racism in German law and stripped the Jews of citizenship [4].

Another approach stressed economic sanctions. Jews were dismissed from their jobs, and professionals, industrialists and merchants were affected. The policy of "Aryanization" transferred Jewish enterprises to Aryan hands. This trend was curtailed for a while due to the serious economic crisis facing Germany,

1 "Jewish" and "judaized" books were burned in Germany on May 10, 1933, under the direction of Josef Goebbels. A notice published at the University of Berlin at that time said: "The Jew is capable of thinking only in a Jewish manner. When he writes German he lies. German writing is intended only for Germans. The non-German spirit shall be removed from the public libraries." Official anti-Semitic propaganda was taught in the schools, in the form of the Nazi theory of racism. Ultimately legislation was passed to prohibit contact with Jews.

2 "Do not buy from Jews," a sign cautions residents of Berlin. Choosing an economic boycott as the first step against the Jews stemmed from the anti-Semitic perception that the Jews controlled the German economy, and that striking at the pocket of the Jew was the best way to hurt him.

3 "Come children, have some candy, but in return you must come with me" — a 1930s Nazi portrayal of the old anti-Semitic concept of the Jew who entices small children. Efforts were made to educate children from an early age to beware of the devious Jew.

4 A chart for implementing the Nuremberg laws. The 1935 definition differentiated between a Jew and an ethnically-mixed person. A Jew was defined as a person who had at least three Jewish grandparents, or who had two Jewish grandparents and was either married to a Jew or belonged to a Jewish community. Next came people of mixed extraction, who were divided into two categories: Class A — those who had two Jewish grandparents but did not belong to a Jewish congregation nor were married to a Jew; Class B — those who had one Jewish grandparent. The status of the mixed classes was considered superior to that of the Jews.

in which the important contribution of Jewish enterprises to the German economy was acknowledged.

Legislation and economic measures were accompanied by a psychological campaign of defamation and degradation, intended to imbue the entire German public with anti-Semitic consciousness, and to give vent to the anti-Semitic sentiments harbored by members of the party. This job was orchestrated by fanatic party men like Minister of Propaganda Josef Goebbels and Julius Streicher, editor of the anti-Semitic paper *Der Stuermer*.

Other Nazi organizations dealt with Jewish emigration from Germany [7]. In the mid-1930s, due to the efforts at economic recovery and the 1936 Olympics, emigration dropped. The volume of emigration from Germany was also tempered by German Jews' emotional ties to their homeland, and by severe restrictions placed by other countries on immigration of Jews to their shores.

In 1938 anti-Jewish policy became more extreme in all spheres. With Germany's annexation of Austria (the *Anschluss*) in March, pressure on Jews to emigrate was increased. In Vienna, Adolf Eichmann, head of the Jewish Section of the Gestapo in the SS, began to implement forced emigration. By the end of October some 17,000 Polish Jews had been expelled from Germany [5].

Violence against the Jews reached a peak on *Kristallnacht* (November 9-10, 1938), in which hundreds of synagogues throughout the country were set on fire or demolished [8], dozens of Jews were killed and thousands arrested and imprisoned in camps. Upon instructions from Hitler, coordination of actions against the Jews was placed in the hands of a special central body in the Ministry of Interior, established in January 1939, and called the "Reich Central Office for Jewish Emigration." It was headed by an SS man, Reinhard Heydrich, chief of the Reich Security Head Office. This marked the beginning of the phase which led to the "final solution."

KEY

"He steals the soul, sucks the blood — beware of the Jews" — anti-Semitic Nazi propaganda on a street sign. During the first few years of Nazi rule anti-Semitic awareness was heightened by such means, but toward the end of the 1930s the government published official instructions to minimize as far as possible any contact between the Jews and the German population. Thus, for example, public benches in the parks were labeled "Jews not wanted here," a notice which in 1938 became an explicit instruction: "Aryans only."

5

5 Herschel Grynszpan, born to a Jewish family expelled from Germany to Poland, assassinated a German diplomat, Ernst vom Rath, in Paris as an act of revenge. This served as the pretext for *Kristallnacht*, although the pogrom itself had been planned many weeks in advance. The Jews of Germany were also fined one billion marks.

7 The name "Israel" was added to the name of every Jew, and "Sarah" to the name of every Jewess, beginning in 1939. The Jews' passports or travel papers were marked with the letter J. After October 1941 Jews were no longer permitted to leave Germany.

6

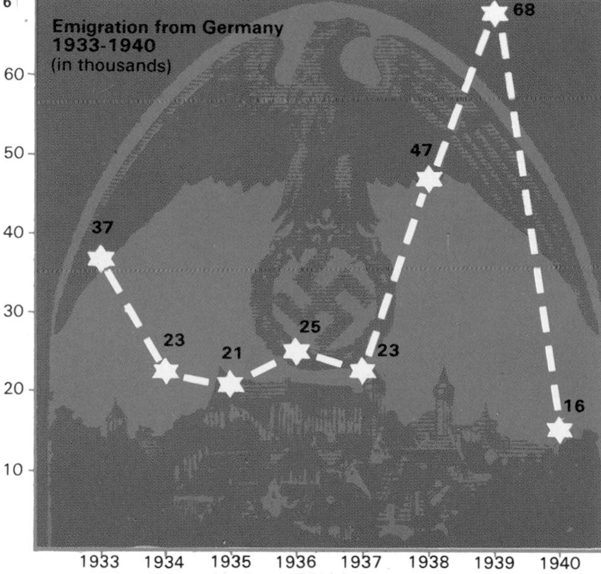

6 Around half a million Jews were living in Germany in 1933. By the end of 1937 about 130,000 of Germany's Jews had emigrated, and from the beginning of 1938 until 1941 another 130,000 were either expelled or had fled. Until 1939 the main countries to which the Jews immigrated were the US (63,000) and Palestine (55,000). Another 100,000 went to European countries, and 58,000 to South America (These figures include emigration from Germany and conquered territories. In the chart, figures relate only to Germany proper.) From 1939 all Jews' passports were so designated to make immigration more difficult.

7

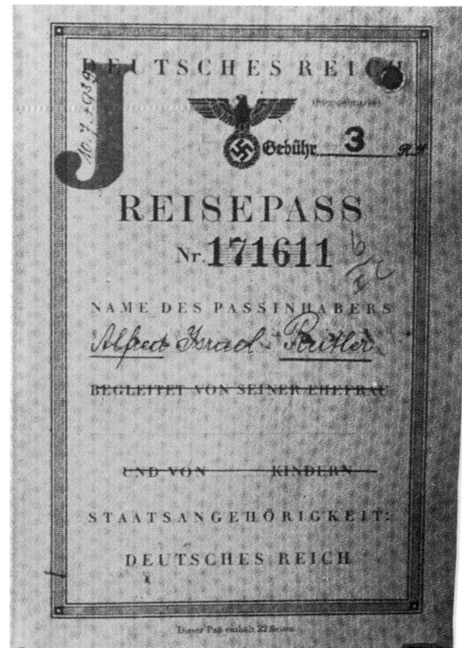

8

8 The gutted sanctuary of the Berlin synagogue in Fasanenstrasse after *Kristallnacht* (or 'night of broken glass', so named because of the many windows smashed in synagogues and Jewish businesses). An eye-witness related: "they smashed everything in their way, even the marble tablets in front of the Ark of the *Torah* were shattered. *Torah* scrolls... went up in flames." Jews who called the police that night were told that they could not be protected because of a shortage of manpower, and that they "must share their fate with the fate of others."

Immigration and Settlement in the 1930s

The period 1929 to 1939 marked great years of growth for the *Yishuv* in Palestine. This change followed two main developments: the Nazi rise to power in 1933, and the Arab revolt in 1936-1939. During this period, called the Fifth *Aliyah*, 230,000 immigrants arrived. The Jewish population grew from 175,000 in 1931, to 475,000 in 1939. By then the Jews comprised over one third the population of the land.

With the Nazi rise to power the socio-economic status of German Jewry was undermined, and over the succeeding six years its very physical survival became a pressing question. At that time the Soviet Union forbade Jews to leave, and in Poland and Rumania anti-Semitic policy prevailed. Many countries of Western Europe locked their gates to refugees and emigrés, and the US, South Africa and Australia enacted strict immigration laws. Thus, Palestine became almost the sole place of refuge. Over half of all the Jewish emigrés during that period came to Palestine, compared with a rate of 4% until then.

We may point to several distinct waves of immigration during this period: after the 1929 Arab riots, and until 1932, thousands of young men and women from Zionist-socialist youth movements came to Palestine, and joined rural labor movement settlements,, or found work in urban construction or industry. Then, from 1933 to 1936, the number of capitalists, middle class, adults with families, and professionals increased. From 1936 to 1939 the immigration became more varied. Thousands of "illegal" immigrants arrived, entering the country as tourists, athletes in the Maccabiah competitions, or by means of fictitious marriages. The Zionist movement was confronted with unprecedented problems of absorbing a new type of immigrant: men of capital, industrialists, and men of note in the humanities, the arts, and the sciences.

In the decade from 1929 to 1939 about 56% of the immigration was from Eastern European countries, especially Poland; 36% from Germany and Central Europe, 6% from Asia and Africa (of whom 3% from Yemen), and 2% from the Americas.

Absorption of German Jewry

The undertaking to rescue German Jewry was headed by Chaim Weizmann (1874-1952) and Arthur Ruppin (1876-1943). They established the Central Office for Settling the Jews of Germany, which saw to their absorption and to the transfer of their wealth to Palestine [4]. In Germany itself Zionist organizations became very active. One of the important institutions founded in that era was Youth Aliyah, initiated and run by Recha Freier and Henrietta Szold. Thousands of children arrived in Palestine during these years and were taken in by *kibbutzim, moshavim*, and educational institutions such as Ben Shemen and Ahavah. By the end of World War II some 15,000 children had been brought to Palestine by Youth Aliyah [Key].

CONNECTIONS

140 Aliyah During the 1920s
146 Nazi Anti-Semitic Policy
152 The Jewish Economy in Palestine until 1939
154 The Emergence of Hebrew Culture in Erez Israel

1 Stockade and tower settlements [painting by Zionah Tadjar] became a necessity following the Arab riots of 1936-1939. For fear of interference by the British, watchtowers prepared in advance were set up in the new settlements in surprise one-day operations. All settlement movements took part in these operations, assisted by hundreds of volunteers. Hanitah, a *kibbutz* near the Lebanese border (founded 1938), has come to epitomize the stockade and tower settlement.

1

2

Ma'yan Zvi 1938
Mishmarot 1933
Kefar Glickson 1939
En Iron 1934
Pardes Hannah 1929
Kefar Pines 1933
Gan Shomron 1934
Bet ha-Shitta 1935
Sede Nahum 1937
Hamadya 1939
Nir David 1936
Newe Etan
Maoz Hayyim 1937
Bet 1938
Mesilot 1938
Shean
Kefar Ruppin 1938
Jenin
Sede Eliyyahu 1939
Tirat Zvi 1937
Kefar ha-Ro'eh 1933
Hibbat Zion 1933
Kefar Vitkin 1933
Giv'at Hayyim 1932
Bet Yannai 1933
En ha-Horesh 1931
Bet Aharon 1936
Hogla 1933
Elyashiv 1933
Havazelet ha-Sharon 1935
Ma'abarot 1933
Kefar Hayyim 1933
Mishmar ha-Sharon 1933
Netanyah 1929
Yedidyah 1935
Ramat Tiomkin 1933
Kefar Yonah 1932
Tulkarm
Kefar Netter 1939
Ge'ulim 1936
Zur Moshe 1937
Qadimah 1933
Bet Yehoshua 1938
En Vered 1930
Kefar Jawitz 1932
Tel Yitzhaq 1938
Even Yehudah 1932
Tel Mond 1929
Herut 1930
Kefar Hess 1933
Nablus
Ramat ha-Kovesh 1932
Rishpon 1936
Shefayyim 1935
Zofit 1933
Sedeh Warburg 1938
Kefar Shemaryahu 1937
Gan Hayyim 1935
Ramot ha-Shavim 1933
Ganne'am 1934
Yarkonah 1932
Ramat Hadar 1938
Hadar 1929
Emek Hefer
Kefar Avraham 1932
Kefar Syrkin 1936
Tel Aviv
Jaffa
Kefar Azar 1932
Be-Hadragah (Ma'as) 1935
Holon 1933
Neta'im 1932
Bet Hanan 1930
Lod
Ramlah
Bet Oved 1933
Tirat Shalom 1931
Kefar Bilu 1932
Gibbeton 1933
Na'an 1930
Gan Yavne 1931
Kefar Marmoreq 1931
Jericho
Sha'ar ha-Negev 1937
Hulda 1930
Ma'ale ha-Hamisha 1938
Bizaron 1935
Yibneh
Bet ha-Arava 1939
Moza Ilit 1933
Jerusalem
Be'er Toviyya 1930
Kefar Menahem 1937
Kefar Warburg 1939
Bethlehem
0 5 10 km
Negba 1939

■ Jewish urban settlement
□ Arab urban settlement
◗ Mixed urban settlement
★ *Moshavah*
✱ *Moshav*
△ *Kibbutz* and *Kevutzah*
1935 Year of Founding

2 In the 1930s, some 140 new settlements were founded in Erez Israel. Many immigrants were received by existing settlements, including 3,525 young German Jews by the *kibbutzim*. Families of means were accepted by established *moshavot*. Great effort was invested in establishing new settlements in Emek Hefer [see map] — a new region of settlement joining the Northern and Southern Sharon. This filled an important link of contiguous settlement in the country. Settlements of the *moshav ovedim* type, *kibbutzim* based on a mixed economy, and private middle-class *moshavim*, which developed the sector of large farms based on orchards and citriculture, were established there. Settlement was also accelerated in the Jezreel Valley.

3 Pinhas Rutenberg (1879-1942) set about obtaining a concession to harness the power of the rivers of Erez Israel, in 1919, in cooperation with the Zionist Congress. Upon receiving the concession, in 1921, he began constructing power stations. In 1923 he established the Palestine Electric Corporation, and in 1928 the power station at Naharayim [pictured, in 1931]. The power stations helped develop modern industry, and expand settlement and agriculture.

3

Meanwhile, German *olim* established new, technologically advanced industries; German musicians were among the founders of Erez Israel's first orchestra; academics and doctors were taken into the hospitals, the university, and the Technion, where they had an impact on methods of instruction, research, and medicine [6]. Other German *olim* turned to agriculture, and founded Nahariya, Kefar Shemaryahu, Ramot ha-Shavim, and Shavei Zion. Many others, under the pressure of economic realities, were forced to learn new professions.

Stockade and Tower

The Arab disturbances of 1936-1939, which were intended to undermine the *Yishuv*, achieved the opposite result. The *Yishuv* united and summoned all its strength to secure its achievements. Despite the restrictions placed on immigration by the Mandatory government, about 86,000 *olim* reached Palestine.

The course of events, and the 1937 recommendations of the Peel Commission to partition Palestine between the Jews and the Arabs, brought about a change in the notion of settlement. Henceforth greater emphasis was placed on establishing Jewish settlements in regions of political and strategic importance: to prevent Arab infiltration, hold key strategic sites, create continuous blocs of Jewish settlement while dividing centers of Arab hostility from one another, and assure the inclusion of key areas within the borders of the Jewish state, should there indeed be a partitioning. Some 50 new stockade and tower settlements were established during this period [1].

All told, Palestine's rural Jewish population grew from 41,000 in 1931 to 138,000 in 1939 [2]. The population of Haifa grew from 16,000 in 1931 to 69,000 in 1939, and the population of Tel Aviv reached 177,000 [5]. The 1939 White Paper immigration restrictions and World War II put a check on this era of growth.

KEY

Henrietta Szold (1870-1945) became director of Youth Aliyah in 1933. She cultivated especially close ties with the youth [as illustrated], played a major role in easing their absorption into the country, and has been called the "mother of the *Yishuv*." During the war Youth Aliyah cared for the "Teheran children" (Polish Jewish refugees) and the orphans of Transnistria. Following the war, young Holocaust survivors from Eastern Europe were received by Youth Aliyah. The graduates of the first Youth Aliyah group, who were accepted by Kibbutz En Harod, established Kibbutz Alonim in 1938.

4

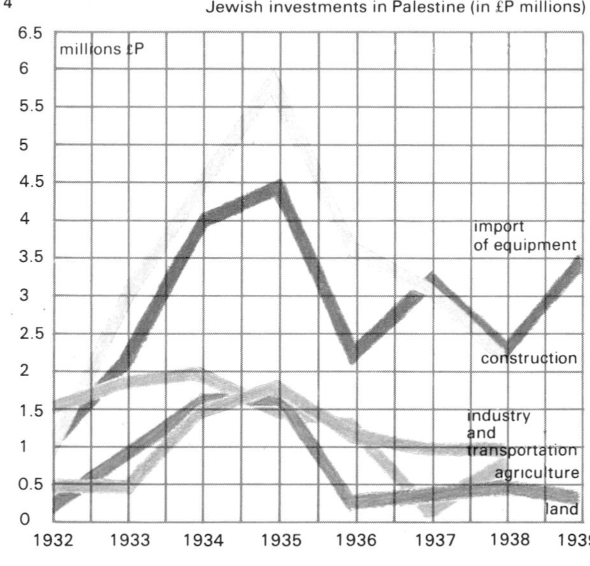

5

6

7

4 Enormous capital — 94 million marks — flowed from Germany to Palestine during the years 1933-1939. A transfer agreement, signed with the government of Germany in 1933, allowed those Jews who wished to leave Germany to exchange part of their wealth for machinery, manufactured goods, and raw materials. These were then exported to Palestine, where they served to set up modern industrial enterprises and to purchase lands. In exchange for their property these Jews received immigration permits under quotas for "capitalists," whose immigration was unrestricted. German Jewish industrial and technical expertise and experience constituted a vital adjunct to the funds they brought.

6 The Hadassah Hospital in Tel Aviv was erected (1924) by the Hadassah Organization. The many doctors who arrived from Germany during this period were absorbed by the medical services in the country, which they profoundly influenced. They introduced new diagnostic techniques, and the practice of specialization. The most developed sectors were surgery, roentgenology, psychiatry, and public health. This laid the foundation for modern Israel's vanguard role in medical research and treatment, with the world's highest number of doctors per capita. Hadassah Hospital in Jerusalem, where medical research was promoted by the German immigrants, today treats patients from all over the third world, including many Arab countries. German Jewish *olim* also contributed immensely to industry, academic life, art and agriculture.

5 On Purim, Tel Aviv's place as a cultural center for the *Yishuv* was particularly evident. The city held a midnight performance and an *Adloyada Purim* carnival procession was staged. *Purim* celebrations in this style became the practice throughout the *Yishuv*. Other Jewish holidays also received a specifically Erez Israel coloration, expressing the ties with the past while imparting a new, national-secular emphasis [*Purim* stage by N. Gutman].

7 Aliyah cigarettes — an advertisement by Franz Krauss. The 1930s immigrants brought new ways of life with them. Their impact was especially evident in Tel Aviv, which was transformed from a provincial town to a full-grown city.

The Arab Uprising

In 1936, the Arabs in Palestine launched a campaign of violence and terror against the *Yishuv* and the British authorities. Known as the Riots of 1936-1939, the uprisings reflected Arab aims to abolish the Zionist settlement in Palestine and establish an Arab nationalist government in Jerusalem.

Political developments made the time ripe for the Arabs to begin their fight. Britain's prestige was on the wane; and the Italian conquest of Ethiopia (1935) and the Rome-Berlin axis heightened the interest of Italy and Germany in the Middle East and shifted the balance of power in favor of the Arabs. The Arab national movement in Egypt and Syria gained strength as these countries achieved a measure of independence; in Iraq, Feisal assumed the throne in 1921. It seemed that only in Palestine was Arab nationalism suffering setbacks.

The many new immigrants to Palestine and the burgeoning prosperity and economic strength of the Jewish settlement fed Arab apprehensions. Their concern grew when the British Parliament declined to approve a bill that would have established a legislative council to determine administrative norms in Palestine through decree. This rejection of Arab demands persuaded them that the international Jewish community was influencing British policy in favor of Zionist objectives. In March 1935, an Iraqi delegation to Palestine urged the local Arabs to take steps to achieve their aims. The speaker of the Iraqi Parliament assured them of his country's aid in their struggle, and called on them to launch a holy war (*jihad*).

The Arab uprising took the form of acts of terror and murder and a general strike aimed at paralyzing the economy of Palestine. Hostilities began in Jaffa in April 1936 and spread throughout the country. Hundreds were killed and injured and thousands of acres of fields and orchards were destroyed. The Arabs even terrorized their own population in order to prevent any attempts at compromise; Arabs known to hold moderate views were assassinated. Paramilitary bands victimized regions throughout the country [3]. The newly-established Arab High Committee headed by Mufti Haj Amin al-Husseini [Key] declared a general strike, which lasted for 175 days.

The Yishuv's Response

To cope with the uprising, the *Yishuv* was compelled to reorganize itself politically, militarily and economically. When supplies of Arab agricultural produce were cut off and Arab workers stayed away from Jewish farming communities, Jewish workers were recruited, and a network for the marketing of agricultural produce was created [5]. Within a short time, work on the *moshavim* and in the markets was entirely in Jewish hands. With the Jaffa port paralyzed, a new port in Tel Aviv was built [1]. In response to the razing of isolated Jewish settlements, stockade and tower settlements were erected.

CONNECTIONS

142 Arab Nationalism
144 Jewish Defense Organizations
148 Immigration and Settlement in the 1930s
152 The Jewish Economy in Palestine until 1939
156 Britain Retreats from its Support for Zionism

1

1 Construction of the Tel Aviv port ended the *Yishuv*'s dependence on the port of Jaffa. May 1936, one month after the general strike was declared, saw the groundbreaking ceremony for the wooden quay of the port, and within a short time it was ready to handle passengers and freight. Jews in Palestine and abroad regarded the port with pride, and labeled it *The Gate of Zion*. The first bag of cement to be unloaded was placed in a museum.

2 The Arab population of Palestine doubled during the 30 years of the British Mandate. That was a result of improved living and sanitary conditions which brought infant mortality down, and rapid economic development which attracted more than 100,000 Arab migrants from lands as far away as the Sudan. Jewish settlement induced many Arabs to leave their mountain homes and stream to the cities and villages on the coastal plain where economic opportunities enabled them to achieve a higher standard of living.

2

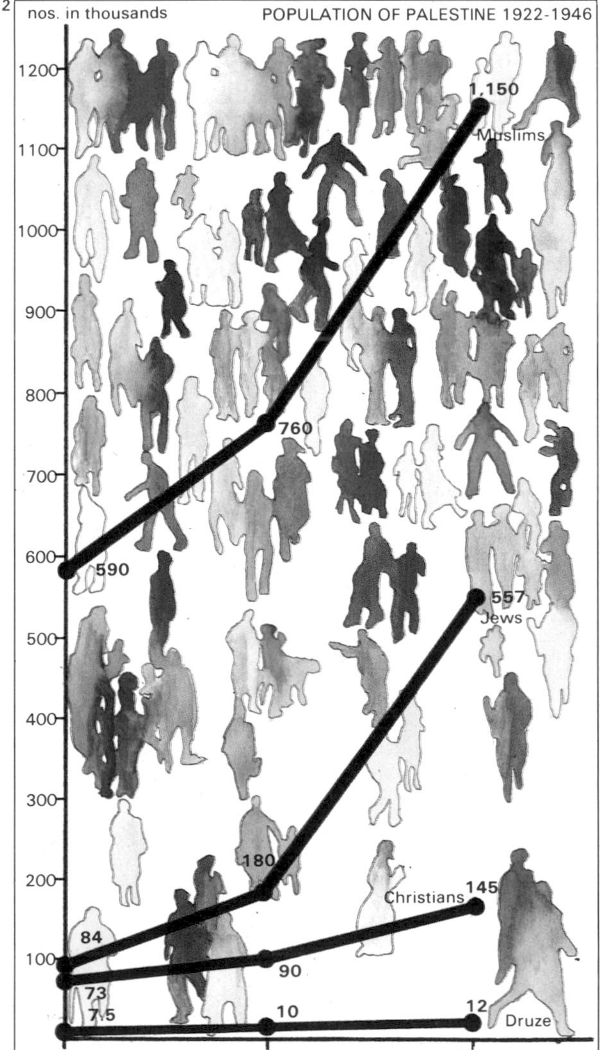

3 A

3 B

3 Arab bands [A] assembled to terrorize the Jewish settlements in 1936, and from 1937 moved against the British as well [B]. At first they organized randomly, in small gangs headed by local leaders. In time their organization improved, and a terrorist network was founded. Most of the members were simple farmers, although some were escaped convicts and wanted murderers. In the second phase, from August 1936, the organization of these bands underwent a change. Fawzi al-Kaukji, an ex-officer in the Syrian army, arrived in Palestine with some two hundred volunteers from Arab countries. These reinforcements were an expression of pan-Arab support. Kaukji organized a broad guerrilla movement in the Arab villages, which also attacked the British. With the tough British response that followed, most of the bands ceased to operate, and Kaukji was allowed to slip out of the country. He was to return at the head of an Arab army invading the Galilee in 1948.

The Jewish community faced two problems: dealing with Arab violence, and preventing the British from bowing to Arab pressure. The solution was a policy of active restraint [4]. *IZL* opposed this policy and determined to "fight terror with terror." But the large majority of the community united behind the *Haganah* decision which stated: "We shall stand up to those who rise against us, but do not wish our arms to be stained with innocent blood."

The British Response

The British sought initially to end the Arab violence through appeasement and reason, and requested the aid of the heads of Arab states. And, indeed, the acts of terror ceased and the strike was ended — ostensibly in response to an appeal by Arab leaders to the Arabs in Palestine to rely on the friendship of the British, but in fact because of the economic hardship generated by the self-imposed embargo. In August 1937 the Peel Commission was appointed in London to investigate the causes of the riots and recommend future measures. Its proposal to partition the country was rejected by the Arabs, and in September 1937, acts of terror were resumed with the assassination of the British district commissioner in Galilee.

The primary targets were now British soldiers and military installations, and the British response was harsh. The Arab High Committee was declared illegal, many of its members were arrested or deported, and the Mufti was deposed and fled the country. The British were now also ready to accept Jewish aid. The Jewish police was expanded, and a British officer, Orde Wingate, set about training special field companies to be used against Arab terrorism.

England, however, did not despair of finding a peaceful compromise, and Round Table Discussions convened in London resulted in the White Paper of 1939: Britain submitted to Arab pressure and backed down from its commitment to the Zionist movement.

KEY

Haj Amin al-Husseini belonged to one of the most prominent Muslim families in Palestine. In 1921, after being reprieved from a jail sentence for his role in the 1920 riots, he was appointed Mufti of Jerusalem and the following year was made president of the Supreme Muslim Council. Calling on the Muslims to defend the holy sites of Islam, he managed to draw many of them into the battle against Zionism. He played an active role in the riots of 1929, and directed those of 1936. In 1937 he was deposed by the British and fled to Germany. In Berlin he spread pro-Nazi propaganda among the Muslims, met with Hitler and actively participated in discussions of the "final solution."

4

4 Defense of the Jewish settlements depended on local forces and the arrival of reinforcements. Each settlement had a "sealed weapons box," opened only in case of attack. In remote settlements, the members were provided with "loyalist certificates" — special licenses to carry guns, which were issued only after the individual had sworn fealty to the King of England. Guards patrolled the homes and fields of each settlement 24 hours a day [photo: guard at En ha-Horesh, 1936]. The situation improved when the Mobile Guards patrolled roads and potential target areas of Arab attack.

5

ההסתדרות הכללית של העובדים העברים בארץ-ישראל

מועצת פועלי תל-אביב - ויפו

אל פועלי תל-אביב!

להתגיסות נמרצה

לחודש תוצרת הארץ!

לחודש החלב!

5 The Arab boycott compelled the Jewish community to speed up production and reorganize its marketing facilities. As a result, vegetable crops grew by 52%, chickens and eggs by 37%, and milk and cheese production by 34%. Various campaigns called on the Jews to buy only home-produced goods. "Milk Month" [announced in this poster] was declared following "Nine Butter Days" and the "Hebrew Vegetable" campaign. Within a short time, Ben-Gurion could declare: "The Arab strike does not threaten our economic survival. On the contrary, our economic independence has grown."

6

7

6 Contact between Arabs and Jews never ceased entirely, even with the atmosphere of terror. Commercial dealings, joint work and neighborly relations continued, particularly in the mixed cities. This painting by Nahum Gutman from 1935 shows an Arab shepherd in Sharona.

7 The Aviron Company, designed to promote aviation in Palestine, was the "air force" of the *Haganah* and later of the *Palmach*, and from it the Israel Air Force was born. The company was founded in 1936, although the idea had already been formulated by leaders of *ha-Shomer* in 1923. They conducted negotiations abroad regarding pilot training and acquisition of aircraft. The 1936 riots heightened the need for an expanded force to ensure contact with isolated settlements. The first flight course, with ten students, took place in Afikim (1937). These pilots played a vital role in transporting the wounded from remote settlements. From the summer of 1937 they maintained constant contact between the Dead Sea potash plant — which was virtually cut off from the *Yishuv* — and Tel Aviv and Jerusalem.

The Jewish Economy in Palestine until 1939

Prior to World War I, modernization and development of the Jewish economy in Erez Israel were extremely slow. With the British Mandate (1920), the economy began to develop more rapidly, and shifted to production for a larger market.

British Interests

Britain's military and strategic interests in the region required transportation arteries and a modern communications system. Yet British policy also led to flooding of local markets with cheap goods that competed with local production. Political considerations, and Britain's obligations toward the Arabs, often led it to take steps which contravened Zionist interests. Given this setting, the growth and development of the Jewish economy were viewed not merely as an economic undertaking, but also as furthering nationalist objectives.

From the beginning of Zionist settlement there were two rival views regarding economic development: One view supported private enterprise and capital investment; the other perceived of development as a national undertaking, to be accomplished by idealistic pioneers supported by national capital investments. From 1920 on, the vast majority of land was purchased with national capital, whereas most industrial enterprises were based on private investment.

Agriculture and Industry

Land purchase and agricultural development were given first priority in Zionist ideology. The agricultural settlements, above all, symbolized the "new Jew," returning to his land to till its soil [2]. In privately sponsored settlements emphasis was placed on citriculture [1], while in nationally sponsored settlements the emphasis was on mixed farming. Mechanization and technological advances in agriculture led to increased profitability, and systematic agricultural training led to improved strains and higher yields. The growing modern agricultural sector soon supplied about half the agricultural consumption of the *Yishuv*, and provided a base for agricultural processing industries [4].

Several stages may be discerned in the industrialization of the country: from the beginnings of Zionist settlement until 1923; 1924-1933; and from 1933 on. Until the mid-1920s there were few industrial plants in the country, both because the Zionist movement was putting most of its effort into agricultural settlement, and because the technological infrastructure was inadequate for developing modern industries.

The immigrants who came to Palestine in 1924-1925 were merchants and craftsmen. They brought with them capital amounting to £10 million (compared with existing national capital investments in the country at the time, which came to only £2 million). Many continued in their former occupations, and established dozens of small workshops. Among these immigrants were

CONNECTIONS

140 Aliyah During the 1920s
148 Immigration and Settlement in the 1930s
150 The Arab Uprising
172 Palestine During World War II
208 The Histadrut (General Federation of Labor)

1

2

2 Aharon David Gordon (1856-1922) was the spiritual mentor of the pioneers of the Second *Aliyah*. He was influenced by the 19th century utopian thinkers, but added a Jewish dimension. His "Religion of Labor" centered around the idea of labor, and tied redemption of Erez Israel as a country to the redemption of man and labor. "We are missing the central thing, we are missing labor.... By labor we were smitten, and by labor we shall be cured." At the age of 46 he immigrated to Palestine, and joined the laborers. He wandered among the *moshavot*, looking for work, and suffered from hunger and malaria. The last years of his life he spent in Deganyah.

1 The citrus industry became one of the important sectors of the economy in Palestine from the 1920s on. New strains were introduced, and techniques of cultivation and packing were improved. By the late 1930s over 30,000 Jews were employed in citriculture, and citrus fruits comprised about 75% of total exports. On the eve of World War II the country's citrus exports comprised 18% of the world total. Illustration — "The Orange Packers" by Zionah Tadjar, 1925.

3

3 The silicate brick factory was founded in Tel Aviv in 1922. [Pictured is a sketch advertisement for the factory.] This was one of the largest and most modern factories in the country.

4

4 The processing of agricultural produce became a necessity, due to Erez Israel's lack of natural resources on which to base alternative industrial development. In the late 19th century Baron Rothschild founded large wine cellars in Zichron Ya'akov and Rishon le-Zion [pictured — the machine room in the Rishon le-Zion winery]. In the 1920s and 1930s a number of factories for tobacco products and perfumes were founded, although food factories comprised most of the enterprises which processed agricultural produce. In the 1930s they numbered 392.

also investors who established sophisticated factories [8], thus laying the foundations for a modern industry.

The British government did not view the Jewish attempt to develop industry with favor. Britain's primary fear was that industrial growth would lead to greater economic absorptive capacity, and hence to increased Jewish immigration. This governmental opposition did not facilitate comprehensive planning and coordination, and therefore most enterprises were the result of private initiative. Nevertheless, Jewish industry marched forward, winning concessions for developing the natural resources of the country: Pinhas Rutenberg (1879-1942) obtained the concession for constructing the electric power plant in Naharayim (1928), and Moshe Novomeysky (1873-1961) for establishing the Dead Sea potash works (1930) [7].

The immigrants who arrived in Palestine from 1933 on brought with them large sums of capital, advanced technology, and professional skills. Aided by the Jewish Agency, working together with the Manufacturers Association and the Cooperative Center, industrial enterprises became more diversified. From 1925-1935 the number of people employed in industry and crafts increased to 30,000, and the number of factories grew from 550 to 4,050. About 55% of them were located in the Tel Aviv area, 17% in Haifa, and 15% in Jerusalem.

Along with the growth of industry and agriculture, the banking system also developed [6], and commercial services were improved. Industrial growth was further stimulated by World War II, as the British army stationed in the Near East generated increased demand. On the eve of World War II, exports by the Jewish sector of the economy constituted two thirds of Palestine's foreign trade. The Arab Revolt, 1936-1939, strengthened and consolidated the *Yishuv* by freeing it from dependence on Arab agriculture and creating marketing opportunities for Jewish produce.

KEY

The building industry symbolized the development of the country, and enjoyed a special status in the pioneering enterprise. Spin-off industries included quarrying, stonecutting, brickmaking, limestone and cement works, and transport. This industry employed more people, including many women, than any other sector in the entire economy. Most construction was private. In the 1920s laborers founded *Solel Boneh*, which became the building concern of the *Histadrut*. During the 1930s public housing companies were founded, such as *Shikun Ovdim* and *Rassco*. The illustration, from 1936, shows a cooperative for transporting sand to be used in making concrete for building.

5

6

6 The Anglo-Palestine Company was founded in 1902 as a subsidiary of the Jewish Colonial Trust. From the 1920s onward it was the guiding body in the Jewish economy. In 1939 there were 32 commercial banks and 89 cooperative credit unions in the country. Most of the capital was used for investment in building, industry, and development. In 1933 the market for securities began to develop, and in 1935 the Tel Aviv stock exchange was opened.

7 The Potash works were the largest and most sophisticated plants in the country during the 1920s and 1930s. Two sites were founded, the northern in 1930 and the southern in 1934. Their output, which reached tens of thousands of tons, made potash an important export industry. The difficult living conditions in Sodom made working there one of the important pioneering goals of the period.

7

5 The foreign and domestic trade of the Jewish economy expanded, and the import of capital in the 1920s and 1930s led to a growth in retail trade and in cooperative and private marketing. New department stores were founded, and the number of cooperative markets grew. Income from exports doubled from 1923 to 1933, and on the eve of World War II the Jewish economy produced two thirds of Palestine's total exports (although Palestinian Arabs still constituted the majority of the population). The growth of commerce and industry found expression in the Levant Fair — a gigantic display of products from all over the world. Fairs were held in Tel Aviv from 1925. Some Arab states participated as well. The main pavilion of the *Yishuv* at the fair featured "Products of Erez Israel." The fairs showed the country's economic potential, and symbolized its transformation from an agricultural land to an industrial country with modern technology.

8 A

8 B

8 The Lodzia factory [A] and the Shemen factory [B] were among the large plants founded in the country during this period. *Shemen* was established in Haifa to process olive oil, and eventually specialized in a variety of oils and oil products. The *Lodzia* textile mills were founded in Holon, and were named after the Polish textile city of Lodz, whence the founders of the enterprise had come. It exemplified the initiative of Polish immigrants and their integration into the life of the land.

The Emergence of a Hebrew Culture in Ereẓ Israel

The spread of the notion of national revival, and the feeling that Jewish culture in the Diaspora was in danger of demise, provided incentives to turn Ereẓ Israel into the center of a nationalist-Hebrew culture, closely tied to the nature and landscape of the country and to the history of the Jewish people in its own land.

Language and Education

Developing a Hebrew culture was dependent upon reviving Hebrew as the spoken language of the country. This involved a long struggle, in which many of the *Hovevei Zion* movement participated. They forced themselves to speak, write, and teach their children in a language which yet lacked many basic words and expressions. Indefatigable efforts were made by *Va'ad ha-Lashon*, founded in 1890, to adapt Hebrew to the needs of modern society. In the early settlements, founded during the period of the First *Aliyah*, Hebrew nursery and primary schools were established. The Hebrew secondary-school system was expanded during the period of the Second *Aliyah*: *Gymnasia Herzliah* was founded in Tel Aviv (1906), and *Ha-Gymnasia ha-Ivrit* in Jerusalem (1909). The teachers fought to provide a nationalist and general education, and drafted the curriculum and wrote the textbooks themselves.

During the Mandate period the Hebrew educational system received further stimulus when the legislative assembly enacted a mandatory elementary school education law. In 1919 the Hebrew educational system encompassed some 10,000 pupils. Over the next 30 years this figure grew to 100,000.

In the field of higher education the Technion in Haifa, opened in 1925, was established to train building, mechanical and chemical engineers. The Hebrew University was opened the same year, and the day of its inauguration was celebrated as a national and cultural holiday. Academic life which developed in Jerusalem provided an incentive for intellectual, political, and public activity, and helped to shape the national consciousness of the *Yishuv*.

During the Mandate the Hebrew press blossomed. Periodicals and newspapers, including literary supplements known for their high quality, contributed to the development of the language, and served as a forum for the best writers of the time. In the 1920s Ereẓ Israel began to attract the giants of Hebrew literature — Chaim Nahman Bialik [Key], Shmuel Yosef Agnon [3] (who returned after several years absence during the war), and Saul Tchernichowsky — known as the poet of "Beauty and Heroism" — whose works lent expression to the revival of the Hebrew language and to man's tie to nature. Hebrew poetry occupied a prominent place in the Hebrew literary revival. It bore the mark of the modern trends in world poetry, contributed to establishing nationalist values, and was greatly innovative, both in its content and form [2, 7].

CONNECTIONS

132 19th Century Erez Israel
134 Foundations of Zionism in Erez Israel
140 Aliyah During the 1920s
148 Immigration and Settlement in the 1930s

1

1 Ha-Ohel was a laborers theater, founded in 1926 by the *Histadrut* under the name Workers' Theater of Palestine. It began its cultural activities with "Peretz parties" (named for the Hebrew and Yiddish polemical short story writer I.L. Peretz), at which passages of literature were acted out. The main repertoire of the theater comprised plays based on the history of the Jewish people, or with a socialist message. The actors participated in the *Purim* and harvest festivities, too. In 1934 the theater toured Europe, where it enjoyed great success. The illustration shows a scene from the biblical play *Jacob and Rachel* by Krasnikov, adapted by Shlonsky. *Ha-Ohel* closed in 1969.

2 Uri Zvi Greenberg (1896-1981) wrote highly political and ideological poetry. He viewed poetry as a tool for expressing the practical aspect of the vision of redemption, and a mystical view of Zionism as fulfilling Judaism's historical destiny. He immigrated to Ereẓ Israel in 1924, and saw himself as the spokesman for the "proletarians on the Hebrew island." He left the Labor Movement for the Revisionist camp in the wake of the 1929 massacres. After the establishment of the State, he represented *Herut* in the First *Knesset*. This notice inviting the public to an evening of poetry reading by Greenberg is characteristic of *Yishuv* cultural activity during the 1920s and 1930s, when such cultural evenings constituted standard entertainment. Artists' exhibits and concerts also attracted large audiences.

2

3

3 Shmuel Yosef Agnon (1888-1970) [right] was one of the central figures in Hebrew literature. He wrote about life in the Jewish city in the Diaspora, and about life in Ereẓ Israel during the time of the Second *Aliyah*, creating a style all his own. In 1966 he was awarded the Nobel Prize for literature. The literary works of Joseph Chaim Brenner (1881-1921) [left] portrayed in somber colors the trials and tribulations of renewing Jewish life in Erez Israel. He was murdered in the 1921 riots. David Shimoni (Shimonovitz) (1886-1956) [second from right] and Alexander Siskind Rabinovitz (1854-1945) also gave expression to the life of the pioneers and the Zionist endeavor.

4

4 A group of young artists — Israel Paldi [pictured is his painting, *Landscape*, 1928], Reuven Rubin, Nahum Gutman, Menahem Shemi, Yossef Zaritsky, Pinhas Litvinovsky, and Zionah Tadjar, organized "exhibits of modern artists" from 1926-1928. They threw down the gauntlet at the Bezalel tradition, which laid the foundations for art in the *Yishuv*, and was built on the search for national roots in the experience of the Jewish people. In their works they attempted to combine Eastern exoticism with the pioneering experience. The strong, bright light of the country had a great impact on their style and usually played a central role in their paintings.

The Arts

The foundations for the Hebrew theater were also laid in the 1920s, with the founding of The Ereẓ Israel Theater and *Ha-Ohel*, a workers' theater which produced plays on social-realist themes [1]. A turning point in the life of the theater occurred in 1928, with the arrival of *Habimah*, which became a central artistic and cultural institution in the life of the *Yishuv* [8]. The theaters lent expression to Hebrew creativity, putting authentic Hebrew plays on the stage. In the course of time works from the world repertory of drama were also produced. Another theater to be founded was the satirical *Ha-Kumkum* (The Kettle), which later changed its name to *Ha-Matateh* (The Broom). It provided a stage for criticism aimed at various aspects of society and at the British regime.

One of the great achievements of the arts in Ereẓ Israel was in the sphere of music. By the 1920s there were many local choral groups and orchestras. Musical life received further impetus with the founding of the Ereẓ Israel Opera, in 1923; it began to flourish in the 1930s, with the arrival of the best of the Jewish instrumentalists and composers, who immigrated from Central Europe in the wake of the Nazi rise to power in Germany and the cultural repression there. Composers in Ereẓ Israel were influenced by Hassidic tunes, motifs from the liturgy, Yemenite singing, and the pioneering life. The climax was the establishment of the Ereẓ Israel Orchestra [9] (since 1948 the Israel Philharmonic Orchestra), by the violinist Bronislaw Huberman.

The predominant artistic approach during the 1920s was to search for roots and authenticity, embracing motifs from the Bible, and, especially, integrating Eastern motifs into artistic creativity. These trends found expression in music, dance, painting [4], sculpture [5], and architecture [6]. The dream of establishing a center of Hebrew culture in Ereẓ Israel became a reality.

KEY

Chaim Nahman Bialik (1873-1934) is considered the national poet of the Jewish people. In such works as *Metei Midbar* ("The Dead of the Desert"), *Ha-Matmid* ("The Talmud Student"), and *El ha-Zippor* ("To the Bird") he lent expression to the trials of his generation, and to their tribulations as Jews and Zionists. In order to further a new, nationalist education for young people, he compiled and edited Jewish classical and traditional works (cf. *Sefer ha-Agadah*, published together with Y.H. Rawnitsky). In March 1924 he immigrated to Erez Israel, where he was enthusiastically received by the public [picture]. He was a member of the Academy of the Hebrew Language, founded the literary periodical *Moznayim*, and was among the founders of the *Dvir* publishing house.

5 The sculpture "Nimrod," 1939, made in sandstone by Itzhak Danziger (1916-1977), is considered the best of his works, and the pinnacle of modern Israeli sculpture. Danziger was born in Germany, grew up in Tel Aviv, and studied in London and Paris. His works show the influence of sculptors working in the style of primitive peoples, and of the sculptors Z. Ben-Zvi and A. Melnikoff. Danziger had a great impact on Israeli sculpture. In the 1930s he headed a group of sculptors who were influenced by "Canaanite" culture. This group sought to find a more natural place in the cultural setting of the land, and advocated adopting pre-Israelite mythical elements in their works.

5

6

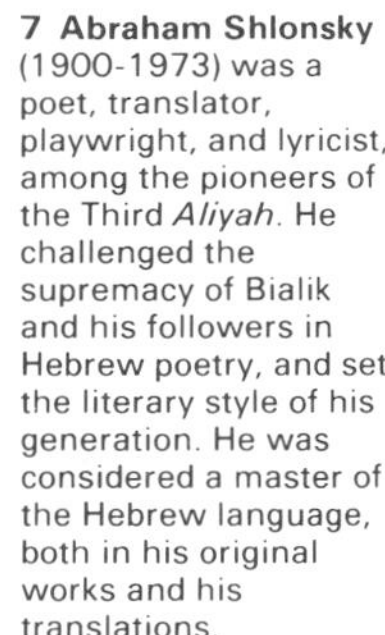

6 These workers housing units in Tel Aviv were built according to the modern Bauhaus school, taught at the Technion. The guiding principle was to adapt architecture to the climatic, economic, and demographic conditions of the *Yishuv*. Ornamental construction, with arches and pilasters, was set aside, and its place taken by straight-lined functional architecture.

7

7 Abraham Shlonsky (1900-1973) was a poet, translator, playwright, and lyricist, among the pioneers of the Third *Aliyah*. He challenged the supremacy of Bialik and his followers in Hebrew poetry, and set the literary style of his generation. He was considered a master of the Hebrew language, both in his original works and his translations.

8

8 The Habimah theater was founded in Moscow in 1918, and became a stronghold of Hebrew language and culture. Its founders were influenced by the Vakhtangov and Stanislavsky methods of directing. Various Jewish and Hebrew plays were produced in the theater. The photograph is from *Mikhal bat Sha'ul*, by Aharon Ashman, with actors Hanna Rovina and Aharon Meskin.

9

9 The great Italian conductor Arturo Toscanini (1867-1957) arrived in Palestine in the middle of the 1936 riots, in order to conduct the Erez Israel Orchestra. The founding of the orchestra was the crowning glory of the *Yishuv*'s extensive musical activity, and Toscanini's consent to conduct its premier performance was testimony to its high quality. The problems of the orchestra players reflected the difficulties of immigrant absorption: the musicians played according to different schools, and the orchestra only became a cohesive body after laborious rehearsing.

Britain Retreats from its Support for Zionism

When Britain received the mandate over Palestine, Zionists expected it to work toward implementing the Balfour Declaration. However, a change of government in Britain and the pressures of political circumstance led to a turn for the worse in Britain's relations with the Zionist movement. The decline reached a peak in 1939 [Key].

The first signs of rift emerged with the establishment of a British military government, headed by pro-Arab British generals who opposed the Balfour Declaration. Their attitude found expression in the 1920 disturbances, when they tried the Jewish defenders together with the Arabs who had attacked them. However, the establishment of the civilian administration in 1920, and the appointment of Sir Herbert Samuel to the office of high commissioner, seemed to prove that Britain intended to fulfill its commitments.

That same year, at the Cairo Conference, it was decided to establish an emirate of Transjordan, and to limit the borders of the Jewish national home to the western part of Palestine. The Zionist leadership agreed in the hope that Britain would fulfill all its remaining mandatory obligations. In 1921 the Arabs began a new wave of terrorist actions. The British reaction set a fixed pattern of behavior: The Arabs would try to achieve political gains, using acts of violence; the British government would decide on an immediate halt to Jewish immigration, and would establish a commission of inquiry into the causes of the violence; the commission would "understand" the Arab's apprehension and would publish its recommendations in a White Paper. Thus, the 1922 White Paper confirmed that the Jewish national home would be established in the western part of Palestine, and limited immigration to the *Yishuv*'s economic absorptive capacity.

The 1930 White Paper

The Labor Party came to power in Britain in 1928. Its anti-Zionist line found expression in a new White Paper, published in the wake of riots, that declared that Jewish immigration should be halted [6] and the sale of land prohibited. This policy statement, which made no mention of the Balfour Declaration, aroused a storm of protest even in the non-Jewish world. Pro-Zionist British statesmen spoke of "a blot upon Britain's honor;" Chaim Weizmann, president of the World Zionist Organization and the Jewish Agency, resigned in protest. After lengthy negotiations, British Prime Minister Ramsay MacDonald (1866-1937) abrogated the White Paper and stated that Britain's undertaking to foster the Jewish national home was a binding international obligation.

While spirits in the Zionist camp were assuaged, lack of trust in the Mandate government and its intentions continued to grow. In the wake of Britain's policy of appeasement, Arthur Wauchope was appointed high commissioner [3]. During his tenure (1931-

1 The idea of partitioning Palestine between two nations and of establishing two states in its territory, was first raised in 1937. The size of each state was to be determined according to the density of population and the concentration of settlements in a given region. Even though the proposal was rejected by both sides, Britain adopted the idea in its Palestine policy. The *Yishuv* embarked on extensive settlement activity, intended essentially to determine the borders of the future Jewish state. Proposals for partitioning the country were advanced in 1937, in 1938, and lastly on November 29, 1947, when the borders of the Jewish state were established by UN resolution.

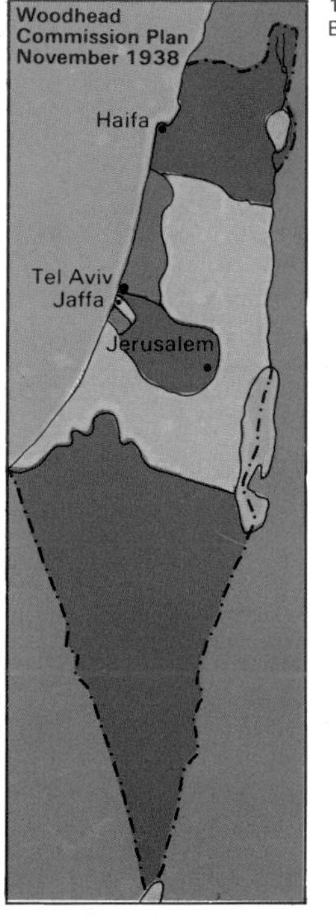

1 B Peel Partition Plan July 1937

Haifa

Tel Aviv

Jaffa

Jerusalem

British Territory

Arab Territory

Jewish Territory

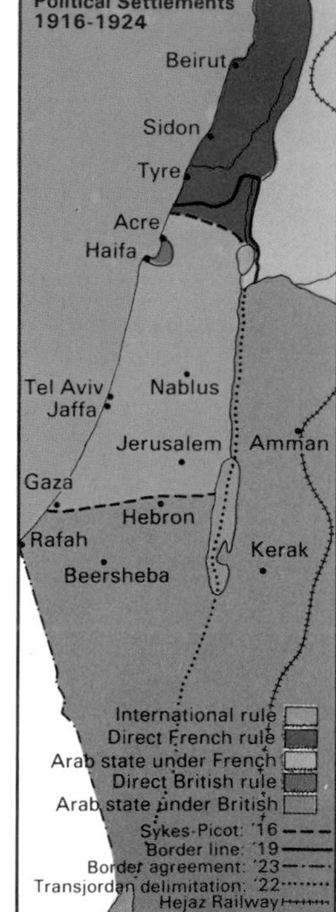

2 The Palestine Royal Commission spent around six weeks in Palestine in 1936. The Arab High Committee boycotted it, and only on the last day did Arab representatives appear to demand abrogation of the "Jewish national home." In contrast, dozens of Jews gave testimony, and expressed the desire of the Jewish people to live in peace with the Arabs. They also spoke of the Jews' inalienable right to build a national home in Erez Israel. The caricature by Aryeh Navon portrays the six members of the Commission, embarrassed and amazed by the contrasting testimonies.

3 High Commissioner Sir Arthur Wauchope (1874-1947) took a hard line toward the Arabs in the riots of 1933, and supported cooperation between the Jews and the British in the riots of 1936. According to Chaim Weizmann, Wauchope was impressed by the achievements of Jewish settlement work in Palestine, and particularly by the *kibbutz*, which he viewed as a boon to human society. Here Wauchope [center] is seen with actress Hanna Rovina and painter Reuven Rubin.

4 The S.S. Parita, a boat with illegal immigrants, landed on a shoal north of Tel Aviv in 1939. To prevent ships carrying illegal immigrants from reaching Palestine the British placed a blockade on the shores of the country, and developed search techniques throughout the Mediterranean. Nathan Alterman called the immigrant boats: "The battleships / Of our immortal fleet. / Its praise is not inscribed in bronze... Yet, is there, in all the world, another fleet which has withstood / Such desperate battles as ours?"

1938) the *Yishuv* flourished. The commissioner did not give in to Arab pressure; and, in view of the plight of European Jewry, he radically increased the number of immigration permits issued, more than doubling the size of the *Yishuv*. During the 1936-39 Arab Revolt, Wauchope saw to arming the *Yishuv* through the Constable Force.

But British policy began to change again in 1937, at which time immigration was again restricted [4], and one year later Wauchope was replaced by Sir Harold MacMichael. Fears lest the Palestine problem push the Arab-Muslim world to support Britain's foes in Europe led to the establishment of a Royal Commission of Inquiry [2]. It declared the Mandate unworkable, and proposed to partition the land into a Jewish and an Arab state. The principle of partition served as the foundation of British policy in Palestine.

Round Table Conference

Due to Arab opposition to the partition plan, representatives of the Jewish Agency and the Arab states were invited to a Round Table Conference in London in 1939. This was the first time the Arab states intervened in any official way in the problems of Palestine. The British expected that their representatives would be able to control Arab extremism in Palestine, and that the British would be able to steer the ever strengthening pan-Arab movement in accordance with their own interests.

In the course of the talks, which were held separately due to the Arabs' refusal to sit down with the Jews, British hopes were dashed. The Arab states adopted an extremist line, and Britain, on the verge of World War II, became increasingly inclined to give in to them. In the wake of the London talks another, more extreme White Paper was published in 1939. It aroused protests among world Jewry and among the friends of the Zionist movement in Britain and caused the *Yishuv* to begin open political and military struggle against Britain.

KEY

Restrictions on immigration and the locked gates of Palestine awaited Jewish refugees who fled Nazi Europe. The fight for the right of immigration became the paramount feature of the *Yishuv*'s struggle. In their battle against Jewish immigration the British sent armed forces against immigrant vessels, and used arms and tear gas against illegal immigrants. Such an attack on the illegal immigrants of *Knesset Israel* evoked great fury and protest [Illustration]. The younger illegal *olim* jumped into the water, but were captured by the British.

5

5 Enmity and suspicion characterized relations between the British police and the *Yishuv*. With the rise of tension in early 1947, the British decided to evacuate those British citizens whose presence was not essential. Those who remained were gathered in security districts, surrounded by barbed wire and guards. The *Bevingards* were considered a victory by the *Yishuv* over the British, who were compelled to live in virtual detention. [Pictured: the British police station in the Russian Compound, Jerusalem].

6

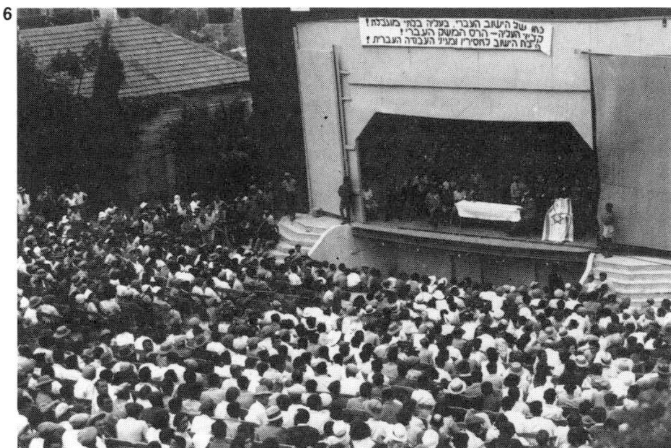

6 Protest demonstrations were employed by the *Yishuv* in its struggle against the Mandate government. The placards carried during the demonstrations—in condemnation of the British government and in support of the Zionist endeavor — brought out *Yishuv* solidarity in Palestine in such key matters as settlement and immigration. The demonstrations also served as a means of rousing world public opinion.

7

7 "But do you have a certificate?" the British officer asks the drowning illegal immigrant, in a 1939 caricature by Aryeh Navon in *Davar*. The Hebrew press was one of the tools with which the *Yishuv* fought against the Mandate government. From time to time papers which expressed open criticism or protest were closed on instructions from the authorities. The *Yishuv* made good use of these sanctions, protesting the denial of its freedom of expression. Criticism launched at the government also found expression in poems and political caricatures.

8

8 The Poppies, soldiers of the Sixth Airborne Division, whose red berets won them this nickname, were brought in as reinforcements to the British army and police forces in Palestine. At the end of World War II the British government stepped up its fight against the Zionist endeavor. Select army units helped suppress the *Yishuv* and pursue illegal immigrants. This scene was recreated in a recent Israeli film.

The Underground Movements

During the Mandate, a variety of underground movements, differing in organization and ideology, came into being in Palestine.

Haganah and Palmach
From its founding, the *Haganah* operated both underground and in the open. By 1937 its membership had grown to some 25,000 men and women. In the light of lessons learned from the 1936-1939 riots, the *Haganah* organized into two central forces: a local civil defense force and a field force for active defense, as well as a unit for special operations.

With the publication of the White Paper in 1939, the *Haganah*'s ideology was redefined to adapt to the supervision of *Yishuv* and Zionist institutions and to the struggle against the British [4]. With the outbreak of World War II that struggle was modified and with the collapse of the Western Front in Europe and the Germans' approach toward Ereẓ Israel, the *Haganah* joined forces with the British.

As the German armies drew closer, the *Haganah* High Command required a specialized military force, and founded the *Palmach*. In 1942, with the passing of the danger of a Nazi invasion, it went underground. The *Palmach* attracted the cream of Jewish youth. Its members underwent stringent training, and evolved an individual style of leadership [1] and a basic familiarity with Ereẓ Israel [Key].

IZL and Lehi
In the wake of the 1929 riots, a group broke away from the Jerusalem branch of the *Haganah* and founded Organization B, claiming that the *Yishuv* had to respond more aggressively and frequently to Arab attacks. After the 1936 riots it became clear that the members of the organization supported a policy of "terror against terror" [3], and their actions were aimed at revoking the policy of *Havlagah* (self-restraint) [8].

The nature of the organization's retaliatory actions caused Avraham Tehomi, its founder, to return to the *Haganah*, along with over half of the members. But members of *Betar* and followers of the Revisionist line — who had joined the organization during 1931-1936 — did not leave. Henceforward the organization bore the name *Irgun Zvai Leumi* (National Military Organization) — *IZL*. It was subject to the political leadership of the Revisionist movement, and served as its underground arm. Weak political control within *IZL* allowed extremist groups to carry out autonomous terrorist activities and robberies during which scores of people were harmed. On November 14, 1937, *IZL* embarked on a chain of retaliatory actions against Arab localities. The British responded with imprisonment and executions.

With the outbreak of World War II, *IZL* adopted the policy of the *Haganah*, but differences of opinion about cooperation with the British caused a new split in *IZL*. An extreme faction left to establish *Lohamei Herut Israel* (*Lehi*,

CONNECTIONS

156 Britain Retreats from its Support for Zionism
172 Palestine During World War II
176 The Yishuv Takes up the Struggle
180 Establishing the State of Israel

1 In Juarra, *Haganah* and *Palmach* commanders were trained. The intention was to produce officers able to "assess, consider, decide and execute." Besides military exercises, training included attendance at political and ideological lectures. The *Palmach* developed a unique image of the combat commander as one who held his position by virtue of strength of personality rather than rank. Graduates of the Juarra courses molded the image of the IDF and became its senior officers.

2 The Palmach took up the fight in November 1947, when Arab terrorist operations against the Jewish community erupted. With the establishment of the Israel Defense Forces (IDF), the *Palmach* was absorbed into the army. Most commanders of IDF battle units were drawn from the *Palmach*, and its brigades — *Yiftach*, *Harel*, and *ha-Negev* — played an important role in the victory. This print of fighters in the *Yiftah* brigade in the Naftali Mountains is by Shmuel Katz.

1

2

3

נפץ את כבלי העבדות
היה לאיש חפשי וגאה

כך רק

התנדב
למחתרת הלוחמת
המשחררת

3 Rak Kach (Only Thus). The *IZL* slogan and badge express the main tenets of the organization.

4

4 The Haganah's underground broadcasts, *Kol Israel* (Voice of Israel), began in 1939, when British military censorship, adapting to White Paper policies, assumed anti-Zionist overtones. The station operated mainly from Tel Aviv, with the transmitter moving from flat to flat to evade detection by the British. The anti-British tones of the broadcasts were modified upon the outbreak of World War II.

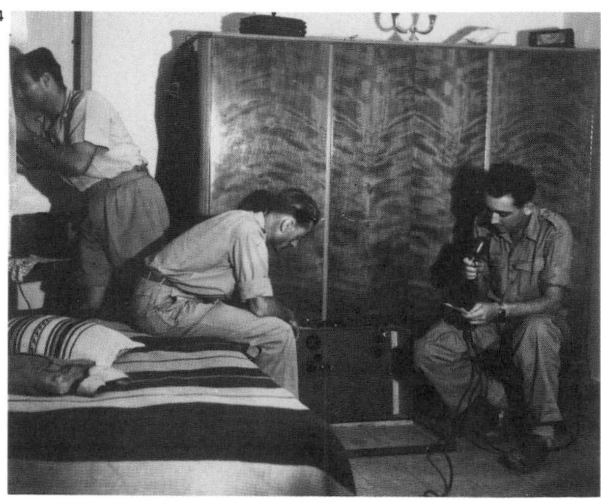

Freedom Fighters of Israel) in 1940. At the end of 1943, Menahem Begin was appointed *IZL* commander [6]. Attempts to influence Britain to adopt a policy favorable to Zionism were now dropped. The new aim was to drive the British out of the country and establish a Jewish state in Ereẓ Israel. In February 1944 *IZL* declared a revolt against British rule, and commenced sabotaging British installations. The British responded with a heavy hand, arresting many and expelling others to detention camps in East Africa. In July 1945 *IZL* reached a cooperation agreement with *Lehi*.

Lehi's revolutionary ideology supported the absolute sovereignty of the Jewish people in Ereẓ Israel, and the use of military force as a means to attain national goals. Britain was its main enemy, and for a short while it even looked to the Axis countries for support. To finance its activities it resorted to bank robberies and kidnappings. Terrorist operations against the British brought sharp reactions, and in February 1942 the police caught and murdered the *Lehi* commander, Avraham Stern, known as "Ya'ir" [5]. Most of *Lehi*'s plots against leaders of the British ruling establishment in the country failed or were aborted, apart from the assassination in Cairo of Lord Moyne, British Minister of State for the Middle East.

IZL's activities aroused the opposition of the Jewish Agency and the *Haganah* who, in a campaign nicknamed the "season" in November 1944 collaborated with the British by supplying them with *IZL* membership lists and even kidnapped *IZL* members. The morality and wisdom of the "season" aroused doubts in the *Yishuv* and among some of the perpetrators. At the end of World War II, with the extent of the Holocaust against the Jews now clear, and Britain firm in its decision to seek a non-Zionist solution in Ereẓ Israel, the three underground groups resolved to cooperate.

KEY

The Palmach organized hikes in order to get to know the land. The *Palmach* was an unusual military organization: neither rank-insignia nor army-type decorum separated commanders from the rank-and-file. In *Palmach* camps, a special style emerged: a manner of speech and dress, of songs and anecdotes. This, together with the bravery and dedication they revealed, created the special image of the *Palmach* man and woman. They played a key role in illegal immigration operations, the establishment of settlements and outposts and, above all, in the War of Independence.

5

5 Lehi reorganized after the death of "Ya'ir" under the joint leadership of I. Yezernizky-Shamir, N. Yellin-Mor and I. Eldad-Scheib. *Lehi* terrorist attacks sought to cause heavy losses to the British, thereby undermining their confidence. Many *Lehi* members were arrested and tried. They exploited the courts as a platform for proclaiming their views. *Lehi*'s operations [picture: a scene from a movie reconstructing the period] were particularly controversial due to the movement's refusal to cease its attacks on the British during World War II, and the deaths of innocent bystanders.

6

6 Menahem Begin (b. 1913) was commander of *IZL*. In the 1930s he headed Polish *Betar* and was a member of the Revisionist Zionist Federation. He came to Erez Israel as a Polish soldier (1942), and was appointed *IZL* commander a year later. In 1944, after he declared and organized the revolt against Britain, he was forced to go underground. He initiated the agreement with Israel's provisional government (1948) under which *IZL* soldiers joined the IDF. He founded the *Herut* movement and was a member of parliament from 1948. In 1977 he led the *Likud* party — a coalition in which *Herut* was the predominant partner — to victory in elections and became prime minister of Israel. He stepped down from the premiership in 1983.

7

7 Wanted! Sir Harold MacMichael, British High Commissioner in Palestine, was accused of the deaths of nearly 800 Jewish refugees after he refused them entry to the country, their ship *Struma* sank in the Black Sea. Britain's uncompromising attitude toward the refugees' plight united all sectors of the *Yishuv* in opposition.

8 Tolerance and self-restraint were urged on the Jewish community after *IZL*'s Shlomo Ben Yosef was sent to the gallows by the British. Sharp differences over methods of fighting Arab terror and, later, the British, resulted in great tensions among the underground movements. The terrorist operations of *IZL* and *Lehi* angered those who preached restraint.

8

מועצת פועלי תל־אביב ויפו

לכל פועלי תל־אביב!

כוחות בלתי אחראים משתדלים לנצל את
בל ניתן להם לבצע את זממם!

ולכן: כל אחד לעבודתו:
כל אחד למילוי תפקידו בהגנת הישוב:
אל תתנו יד להפגנות המסכנות את
שלום הצבור!
אל תתנו יד לכל נסיון של הפרעת סדר,
של גירוי יצרים, ע״י הפרת המשמעת
למוסדות הישוב וההסתדרות!

במלוא כוחו ימשיך צבור הפועלים לעמוד על
משמר כבודו ושלומו של הישוב והמפעל הציוני.

The Jews in the Trap of Nazi Rule

Toward the end of the 1930s the Nazi net began to tighten around the Jews living under the conquest of Germany and in its satellite countries. Nurtured by traditional anti-Semitic sentiments, attempts to separate the Jews from their gentile environment were made even before the decision was taken in principle, in the beginning of 1941, to exterminate all the Jews.

The first stage — isolation of the Jews — began in Germany in the 1930s. All Jews were dismissed from administrative positions, and were prevented from participating in education and in intellectual, public and cultural life. In Austria, which had a Jewish population of 185,000, a *Zentralstelle für jüdische Auswanderung* (Central Office for Jewish Emigration) had already forced more than 45,000 Jews to leave the country by 1938, and had plundered their property. Forced emigration was employed in Germany and Czechoslovakia as well. On the eve of World War II about 400,000 Jews remained under Nazi control, after an equal number had been forced to emigrate.

With the outbreak of the war and the conquest of western Poland another two million Jews came under German rule. Persecution in the conquered territories and in Germany's East European satellite states increased, and emigration ceased to be a feasible option. The Jews were forced to wear special identifying badges [Key], and in Eastern Europe were concentrated in special residential quarters — the ghettos [2]. The Jews were isolated in the conquered West European countries, as well [1].

Along with isolation and concentration went systematic plundering of Jews' property. Abandoned apartments were seized, together with any belongings left in them; bank accounts were expropriated. The movable valuables which the expellees took with them were seized, and in the camps even their clothing was confiscated. After a Jew had been murdered the Nazis even removed from the corpse anything which they deemed could possibly be of use [6].

The Trap

The prevalent notion that the Jews passively accepted the Nazi onslaught is not accurate. On the contrary, Jews did much to preserve the meaning of their lives and life itself, showed great resourcefulness under difficult conditions, and even engaged in underground activity. However, the balance of power tipped the scales from the outset. Dispersed over all of Europe, lacking unified leadership, with only paltry means of self-defense at its disposal, the Central and the East European Diaspora faced the most efficient governmental machine of the time, motivated by a resolute desire to "solve the Jewish question." That machine was backed by the German army, which in a short period of time had succeeded in defeating the armies of Poland, France, Belgium, Holland, the British forces stationed in Europe in 1939, and a large portion of the Russian army.

CONNECTIONS

146 Nazi Anti-Semitic Policy
164 The Holocaust

1 With the Nazi conquest of the Netherlands, the German authorities began to harass the Jews and restrict their movement. Yet, the Jews' condition at the beginning of the war generally was not as bad there as in Eastern Europe. The "Optical Ghetto" [illustration] which was established in Amsterdam was surrounded solely by signs, not by a fence or wall, as was the case in Eastern Europe. However, in the middle of 1942 the expulsion of the Jews of Holland eastward began; and within the year over 110,000 had been deported to death camps.

2 Concentration of Jews in the cities was ordered by Reinhard Heydrich, in September 1939. Thus the Jews were moved to urban ghettos [Illustration — *The Expulsion to the Ghetto*, a painting by Szymon Szerman, Lodz 1940]. The ghettos were fenced and walled in, and were guarded from within by Jewish guards, and from without by Germans. Exit from the ghetto was permitted only in order to work for Aryans. The Nazis encouraged the ghetto Jews to collaborate by holding out the hope of survival — until it was too late. By the time most of the ghettos were wiped out, in 1942, tens of thousands had died of overcrowding, hunger and disease.

3 The Jewish community of Greece, which numbered 75,000 at the eve of the war, lived primarily in Salonika, in territory conquered by Germany. In July 1941 all the Jewish males aged 18 to 45 were sent to hard labor paving roads and quarrying. In July 1942, 9,000 of these Jews were gathered in the town square, in sweltering heat, where they were abused and humiliated by the Germans [picture]. In February 1943 the persecutions became worse; the Jews were forced to wear yellow stars, their freedom of movement was restricted, and they were concentrated in a ghetto. In March 1943 the deportation of 65,000 Greek Jews to Auschwitz-Birkenau began.

4 Germany was "cleansed" of its Jews by November 1943. The community which had numbered some 500,000 in 1933, was reduced to about 10,000. Many had managed to flee. But many had remained in Germany due to misplaced trust, and worldwide immigration restrictions. When the war began, the gates closed. Now the Nazis did not even spare the elderly or the handicapped. The feeble and ill were killed cruelly on the way to the ghettos; those who managed to survive the conditions of the ghetto and to escape the "actions" which the Germans took at regular intervals ultimately found their end in the death camps. The illustration shows the residents of an old age home in Frankfurt, before being deported to Eastern Europe.

Aside from military force, the Nazi regime had at its disposal a tool of unprecedented efficiency — the SS (*Schutzstaffel*), which, shortly after the Nazis' rise to power, had taken control of the police force [5]. The long arm of Reich Security Main Office (RSHA) — established in 1939 within the framework of the SS and controlled by Reinhard Heydrich — reached every nook of society under Nazi domination. Adolf Eichmann's department, which was responsible for dealing with the "Jewish question," operated under this office. Not only Jews failed in their attempts to fight this apparatus; other Europeans, as well — politicians, partisans, and members of the underground — were no match for it.

Options Facing the Jews

It was not only Nazi power that trapped the Jews; ideology added the most decisive dimension. A non-Jewish European had three options open to him — to collaborate, to oppose the Nazis, or to bow his head and go on with life as usual (the option which the vast majority of the non-Jewish public chose). But a Jew was considered an enemy even if he chose the option of collaborating or submitting.

Under such circumstances, the surrounding population remained the only possible point of support. The Jews accepted help from their neighbors, both as individuals and as a community; but the possibilities of such aid were extremely limited. The tradition of hatred toward Jews, even in anti-Nazi movements, reduced willingness to help. Moreover the German government had made unequivocally clear what fate awaited anyone who assisted Jews.

The ideology of Nazism, the nature of the government, the geographical area controlled, and the historical relations between the Jews and their neighbors in Europe all combined to form a trap which closed, almost hermetically, around the Jews of Europe.

KEY

In November 1939 all the Jews of Poland, "from age ten and up, (were) compelled to wear... on the right sleeve of their garments, and on their coats, a white band, at least 10 cm. (4") wide, with a Star of David on it." In the center of the badge the word "Jew" was designated, either in the local dialect, or by the letter J. The most common badge in the countries conquered by the Nazis was the *Magen David* or "Jewish Star" [illustration — in Hungary]. The practice of degrading Jews by special identifying signs dates back to the Middle Ages, and was especially common in Central Europe. The Nazis' use of the "Jewish Star" was the first step in the extermination process.

5

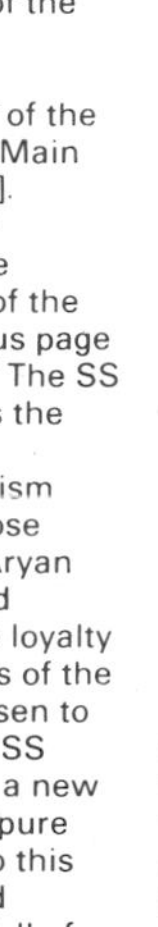

5 Heinrich Himmler, national chief of the SS [in center], and Reinhard Heydrich, chief of the Reich Security Main Office [on right]. It was Himmler who termed the extermination of the Jews "a glorious page in our history." The SS viewed itself as the avant-garde of National Socialism. Hence, only those individuals of Aryan appearance and unimpeachable loyalty to the principles of the party were chosen to serve in it. The SS sought to raise a new generation of "pure Aryans," and to this end established *Lebensborn* (Well of Life) — a chain of "breeding houses" for SS members and Aryan women.

6

6 The Nazis exploited the population of the territory they conquered, both in life and after death. In the ghettos and camps these populations were used to supply cheap labor to manufacture supplies for the German army, and for heavy labor. Even after death anything of use was taken from them. When the Auschwitz deathcamp was liberated by the Russians, in 1945, storerooms with heaps of eyeglasses, shoes, clothing, and false teeth were discovered there. Several dozen of the storerooms were destroyed by the Nazis shortly before the liberation; yet, even the few which remained sufficed to bear witness to the efficiency of the German extermination machine. A further, and horrifying, expression of German efficiency was the use of the bones of the murdered to make soap, and their skin to make lampshades.

7 A

7 B

7 C

7 Disparaging humiliation and abuse were the lot of the Jewish victims of Nazi rule, along with hunger, disease, and, for most, ultimate death. Tattooing a Star of David on a person's forehead [A], shearing the hair of a woman's head in public to amuse masses of onlookers [B], and humiliatingly searching a woman's clothes [C], were but some of the means employed. Nazi sadism was legendary, but it required a passive and often cooperative population to facilitate the Final Solution. The humiliation and tortures found expression in the diary (1941-1942), of Helena Kotorgina of Kovno (Kaunas, Lithuania): "July 29: a hot day, wonderful. Some sick people came and told how Jews were forced to scoop up refuse with their hands, to dig holes with spoons, to drink sewage water; how they were made to lie on the ground in rows and were stabbed indiscriminately, and had their skulls smashed with wooden poles...."

Life in the Ghetto

CONNECTIONS
160 The Jews in the Trap of Nazi Rule
164 The Holocaust

By imprisoning a group of people in a restricted area, and severing them almost completely from any contact with the surrounding population, the Nazi regime created a unique situation in the history of the modern world. While the Nazis denoted this area with a term from the Late Middle Ages — ghetto — the Nazi ghetto resembled the medieval ghetto only on the surface. The latter had been intended to restrict Jewish residence and social contact with the general populace, for religious reasons; but these limitations did not apply to commerce and freedom of movement. Now, however, the purpose was total isolation of the "Jewish microbe" from the rest of society. Historically, the ghettos were the transitional stage between the freedom enjoyed by East European Jews before World War II — and their extermination. They enabled the Nazis to assemble millions of Jews for orderly transport to the death camps.

The idea of incarcerating the Jews in ghettos first arose after *Kristallnacht* (1938), but Reinhard Heydrich, chief of the Security Police (RSHA) and the SD, opposed the idea. Less than one year later the Germans invaded Poland, where two million Jews lived in the territories they conquered; now a quick decision was made to move Jews living in towns and villages to ghettos in the larger cities: "concentrating the Jews in the cities will, it seems, necessitate issuing an order, for reasons of general governmental security, that entrance to certain quarters shall be altogether forbidden to Jews; likewise, and always in consideration of economic needs, they shall not be permitted to leave the ghetto or go out after a certain hour of the evening" (Heydrich, to the officers of the *Einsatzgruppen*, September 21, 1939) [2].

Ghettos were only established in Eastern Europe. In Germany itself, and in western, northern and southern Europe, isolation of the Jews was achieved by other means.

Inside the ghetto

Life in the ghetto was organized and run by the *Judenrat*, the Jewish Council [1]. The council's authority extended over municipal functions, including finance [4], sanitation, industry and crafts [3], etc. Some of these responsibilities were undertaken by the councils on their own initiative, in order to maintain the Jewish community as a whole.

Daily life was extremely hard. For its food supply the ghetto was officially dependent on the very limited rations allocated it by the German authorities. Hunger was a perennial condition, which affected the thoughts and deeds of every resident of the ghetto. Fruits and vegetables were grown in every possible corner; food was smuggled into the ghetto [7], and acquired on the black market and through bribery. In this struggle for survival the wealthy and the physically strong had the advantage, and personal probity became very important. Various economic classes emerged within the ghetto, and crimes

1 The Judenrat (Jewish Council) was viewed by the Nazis as an executive arm responsible for implementing their orders. The Jews viewed the *Judenrat* as a body which would defend their interests. Initially the *Judenrat* was comprised of former community leaders, but at a later stage these members were removed from office or murdered, and others more acceptable to the Nazis were appointed in their stead. In addition to its traditional duties, the *Judenrat* was delegated judicial and constabulary authority. The ghetto police force [here, in the streets of the Warsaw ghetto], comprised a number of criminals and underworld characters who collaborated with the *Gestapo* and turned Jews over to the Nazis.

2 A model of the Vilna ghetto, by Leib Sha'ar. In September 1941, some 40,000 Jewish residents of the city were locked in two ghettos, one for skilled workers and professionals, and another for those with no trade. Thousands died of hunger and disease, and thousands were executed by the Nazis at nearby Ponary. By December only about 17,000 Jews remained in the city. In the Vilna ghetto there were schools, a library, archives and a museum, an orchestra, choral groups, and a theater. The youth organized a fighting unit which attempted an armed resistance. In September 1943 the ghetto was surrounded and wiped out.

3 A workshop in the Theresienstadt ghetto [by Otto Krauss-Kaufmann, 1943]. The Nazis imposed forced labor on the Jews, for which they paid at most a trifling sum of money or a small ration of food. In several ghettos the Jews were forced to work in shops manufacturing uniforms for the German army, or for private German factories. Enterprising Jews managed to sell Jewish-made products on the Polish market, some of which were manufactured using scraps.

4 Special banknotes bearing the signatures of the *Ältestenrat* (the Council of Elders, a form of *Judenrat*) were issued in several ghettos, such as Lodz and Theresienstadt [illustration — a banknote from Theresienstadt]. The Germans sought to present Theresienstadt as an example of Jewish autonomy in the ghettos, resembling ghetto self-government of the Middle Ages. German publications spoke of the ghetto serving as "the best proof that we do not solve the Jewish question by means of pogroms." Some members of the *Judenrat* were indeed induced to think that "the form of the ghetto makes it possible for people... to work productively for the Jews, whose fate has decreed on them to dwell there" (Rumkowski, Jewish Elder, in the Lodz ghetto). Thus the Nazis induced a measure of Jewish submission prior to the extermination.

of an economic nature — such as black-marketing — became commonplace.

Another characteristic feature of the ghetto was extreme overcrowding. The Warsaw ghetto, for example, covered 2.4% of the area of the city, but held some 450,000 people, or 30% of the city's population. Overcrowding was evident everywhere: several families would live in a single apartment, and masses of people filled the street. Despite considerable efforts to preserve hygiene and elementary sanitation, disease and epidemics became routine. This led to high mortality. In 1941 alone, some 43,000 people died in the Warsaw ghetto — more than a tenth of its population at that time.

The Will to Live

The oppressive conditions led some people to commit suicide. But this was not characteristic of the atmosphere in the ghetto. The Jewish public evinced a strong will to live, and great creative powers [Key]. Every ghetto organized an extensive educational and cultural system [5, 6, 8]. Welfare and mutual aid were administered equitably by the *Judenrat* and through the "tenants' committees." In all spheres of activity, and among the vast majority of the residents of the ghetto, the desire to preserve their image as human beings in general, and as Jews in particular, was evident. Here the synagogues played an important role, both as a place for spiritual uplift, and as a meeting place which imparted a feeling of togetherness even to the non-religious.

Considering the Nazi oppression, life in the ghetto was a testimony to the struggle for survival, as expressed by R. Isaac Nissenbaum, of Warsaw: "This is an hour of sanctification of life, and not of sanctification of God through martyrdom and death. In the past our enemies demanded of us our soul, and the Jew gave his body to sanctify God; now our oppressor is demanding the Jewish body, and so it is the Jew's duty to defend it, to protect his life."

KEY

"Music in the ghetto? Songs in the cemetery? What sense is there in that?" Thus I. Gurewitz, from the Vilna ghetto, described the debate over establishing an orchestra in the ghetto. But there was a strong counter-argument: "Together with the sounds of the orchestra, the hearts of the Jews were filled with an underlying sound which said, 'The Jewish people is alive!'" "Even though we are condemned to death, we have not lost the aspect of human beings," wrote Dr. Emanuel Ringelblum, the historian of the Warsaw ghetto (1900-1944). The illustration shows the Warsaw ghetto children's chorus.

5

5 Itzhak Katzenelson (1886-1944), educator, writer, dramatist, and poet, bewailed the "Murdered Jewish People" in his great work bearing this title from the time of the Holocaust. He lived in the Warsaw ghetto, and died at Auschwitz.

6 Education in the ghetto was under the authority of the *Judenrat*. Many ghettos [illustration — Warsaw ghetto] contained nursery, elementary and trade schools which taught in Hebrew and Yiddish, as well as provisions for adult education. "Some Jews would go out on work brigades, and, instead of food, would bring with them in their sacks books which they had found in the ruins of houses" (Testimony of Aaron Perez of the Kovno ghetto).

6

7

8 "The Eternal Jew" was performed in the Vilna ghetto in 1943. Cultural and educational activities were maintained even under the most difficult of circumstances, and challenged the Nazis' attempt to deprive the Jews of their humanity. They were often initiated by the *Judenrat*, along with religious and welfare programs. The Warsaw ghetto had a cultural society, five regular theaters, an orchestra, and choral groups.

8

9 A

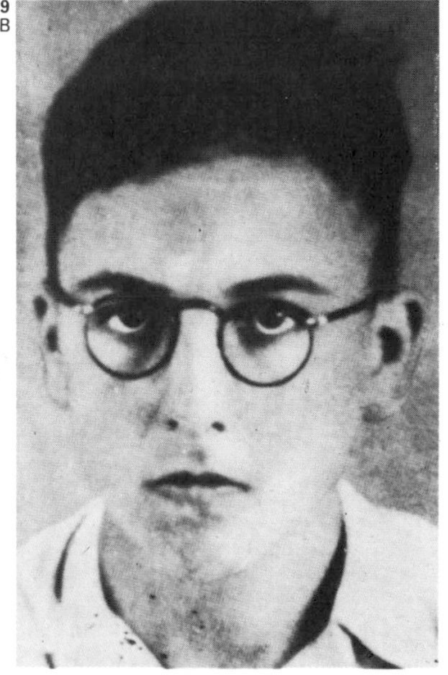

9 B

7 Smuggling food into the ghetto became a necessity, despite the consequent risk of life, since the rations supplied by the Germans were insufficient for survival. Much of the smuggling was done by children.

9 Diaries written in hiding, in ghettos, and in camps, are an important historical source on the period. The diaries written by children are particularly moving. *The Diary of Anne Frank*, written in hiding in Holland, attained wide publicity in book, play and movie form. In [A] we see an illustrated page from the diary of Carol Konitski, Buchenwald, 1944. Moshe Flinker [B] (1927-1944) also left a diary.

The Holocaust

In the first few years of Nazi rule the solution of the "Jewish question" had not yet been stated in terms of murder. The change came about in the wake of *Kristallnacht* (November 9-10, 1938) when the idea of a radical treatment of the Jews was mentioned for the first time in the same breath with the war. "Should the German Reich become involved in an international conflict in the foreseeable future, it goes without saying that we in Germany will have to think, first and foremost, about a thorough settling of accounts with the Jews within Germany," said Goering. A few weeks later Hitler threatened in public: "If the Jewry of international finance inside and outside of Europe should succeed once more in plunging nations into another world war, the consequences will... be... the annihilation of the Jewish race in Europe."

From Theory to Practice

With Germany's invasion of Poland the persecution of the Jews escalated. At this stage Jews were still allowed to leave the lands under German control. The decision in principle to exterminate the Jews was made in the course of planning the war against "Bolshevist-Jewish" Russia, some time in February-March, 1941. The Nazis used two main methods of killing Jews. The first employed mobile death units, the *Einsatzgruppen* (task forces), to kill victims not far from their places of residence. Beginning in June 1941, these groups operated in territories captured from the Soviet Union, and killed approximately 1.5 million Jews. The second method was to establish extermination camps — *Vernichtungslager* [Key] — to which victims would be brought from great distances. As part of the plan for the Final Solution, such camps were established in Chelmno, Auschwitz-Birkenau, Treblinka, Sobibor, Belzec, and Majdanek [1]. Special installations for mass murder were set up — gas chambers disguised as showers, firing squads and burial pits, and crematoria. About four million Jews were murdered in the camps.

In order to carry out murder on this unprecedented scale the Nazis formed a special administrative apparatus in the Reich Security Main Office, under which Adolf Eichmann's division operated [4]. The setting of quotas for deportation to the death camps, allocation of trains and manpower, and coordination of operations among various countries were all handled by a broad network of officials. The Nazis used bureaucratic code words: "deportation to the east" and "transferral of place of residence" (*Umsiedlung*) were codes for deportation to the extermination camps; "special treatment" meant extermination. The Nazis also deliberately gave captive Jewish populations the temporary feeling that there was a way out, by creating the concept of "groups protected against deportation" — workers of the Jewish Council, Jews who worked in munitions factories or important production plants, and the like.

CONNECTIONS

160 The Jews in the Trap of Nazi Rule
162 Life in the Ghetto
166 Rescue Operations During the Holocaust
168 Jewish Resistance in the Holocaust

1 **The crematoria in the extermination camp at Majdanek** worked day and night, and even then could not manage to cremate all the bodies of those killed in the gas chambers. A survivor of an extermination camp who worked in a *Sonder-kommando* (special commando) that cremated the corpses, testified: "Four hundred people entered the small gas chamber.... Thirty-five minutes later they were dead... When we opened the gas chambers, on the floor we saw children who had remained alive. The Germans shot them."

2 **The extermination** of Jews in Europe. In the beginning of 1939, Europe had approximately 9,400,000 Jews. Of those approximately 6,000,000 died in the Holocaust. In bold type — the number of Jews in 1939; below — the number of victims.

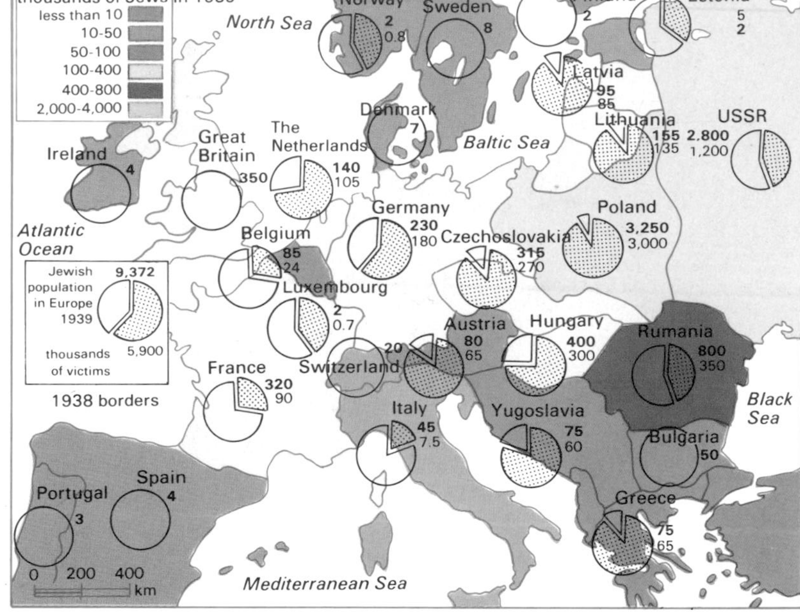

3 **"Death Dance"** (1943-44) by Felix Nussbaum, who hid in Brussels from 1941 to 1944, but was caught and deported to a death camp, where he died. "Should I perish," he told his friends, "do not allow my works to die; exhibit them to the public."

4 **Adolf Eichmann** took part in drafting the Final Solution, and was in charge of deporting the Jews to the extermination camps. He fled to Argentina. In 1960 he was captured by Israeli *Mossad* agents and tried in Israel. At his trial, from which this sketch by Edward Ishelbaum is taken, dozens of Holocaust survivors testified. Eichmann was convicted and executed.

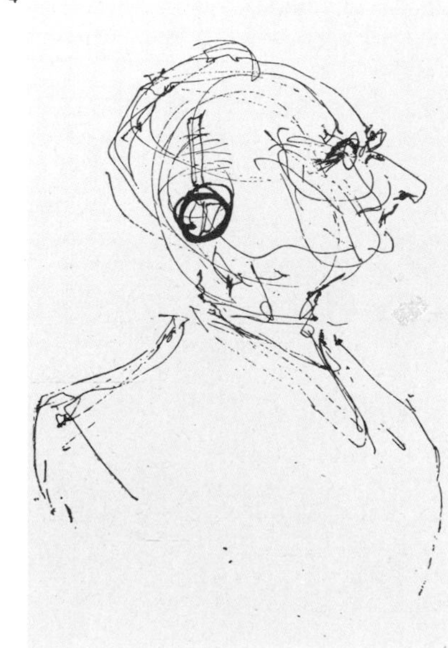

Jews destined for murder were by and large rounded up in surprise "actions" — by cordoning off a region and arresting the Jews there, or by sending "work" orders [6]. The Jews were then herded onto trains or trucks, and transferred to the extermination camps.

Atrocities

Every step of the way this campaign of murder was accompanied by cruelty and abuse. When the Jews were being gathered, they would be hit, humiliated, and attacked by dogs. Then the deportees would be crammed into cattle cars or trucks — sometimes up to a thousand people in a sealed car, with no ventilation. In the camps they suffered further indescribable acts of cruelty.

Two testimonies will suffice to give an intimation of these atrocities: "We reached Treblinka. Only when we arrived there did the blindfold come off our eyes. On the roofs of the huts stood Ukrainians with rifles and machine-guns. The ground was strewn with corpses, some in clothes, some naked. Their faces were distorted with horror and fear. They were black and swollen; their eyes frozen, their tongues hanging out, their brains shattered, the corpses twisted.... we stood helpless, feeling that there was no escaping our fate."

And the testimony of a Pole concerning the fate of the Jews of Kislovodsk, a town in the Soviet Union: "The train with the deported Jews arrived at the glass factory. The Germans accompanying the deportation ordered the Jews to get out of the train cars, to hand over any money and valuables they had, and then ordered them to get undressed. With heart-rending cries the women, children, and elderly took off their clothes and remained standing only in their undergarments. Then this mass of people, almost out of its mind from sheer terror... was led to anti-tank trenches. Whoever tried to flee along the way was shot dead. Next to the trenches were the Germans firing submachine and machine guns."

KEY

The death camps were described as "another planet." The inmate was stripped of his identity, his name, his social status, his family and friends. Human life had no value. Sadistic guards victimized the inmates and watched their every step. Starvation turned men into living-dead. They were forced to work in industrial plants until they dropped. In April 1945, the French artist P.C. Dabouis painted the inmates of Dachau after the camp had been liberated. Many had been force-marched by the Germans from extermination camps further to the east, as German SS units fled the approaching Red Army.

5

5 A child in a concentration camp. Thus the painter Isaac Feder (1943, Drancy Camp, France) imagined him. The children were inevitably the first to be transported from the ghettos to the camps, and then the first to be sent to the gas chambers. In his poem, "Of all the nations," Nathan Alterman wrote: "As our children march in the shadow of the gallows / Jewish children, bright children, / they know that their blood is taken to be of no account — / They only call to their mothers: Do not look... / Their eyes speak: Do not look, mother, / how in long rows we were laid. / Seasoned soldiers and of note are we, / only of low stature."

6

7

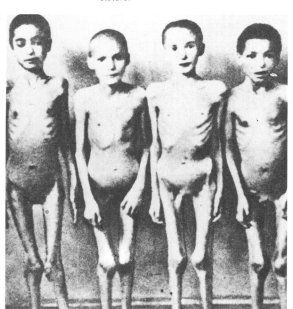

7 The Allied soldiers who liberated the camps stood dumbfounded at the horrors revealed before their eyes: "living skeletons, with no flesh and no color, and with no sign of vitality whatsoever, save for their eyes. Many could not even speak. They fell on food like vultures, after having been starved for years. What they could not eat they hid under mattresses or in secluded corners, lest the days of horror return." Many of those rescued from the camps died after the liberation from weakness and unsupervised food consumption. In addition to the camps designed specifically for mass extermination — multitudes of Jews were killed by improvised methods.

8

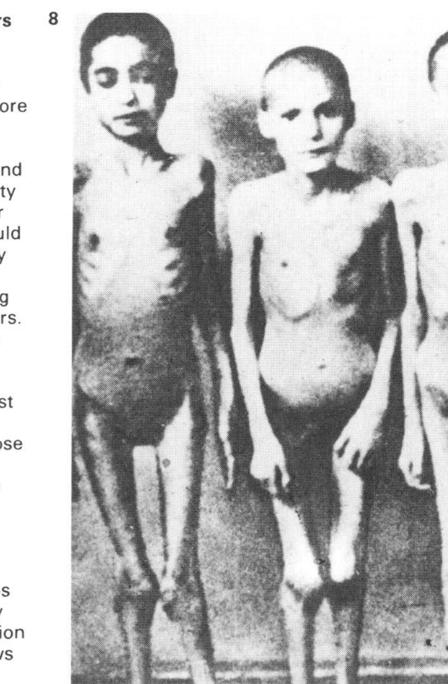

6 "Mass Deportation" (1944) by H. Valk. Special "commandos" would come to large concentrations of Jews and, with the aid of SS forces and the local police, send the Jews to the death camps.

8 "Medical" experiments were conducted on the inmates of several concentration and death camps. Joseph Mengele, an SS doctor at Auschwitz, designed cruel experiments which led to the death of many Jewish prisoners. Mengele was particularly interested in the genetic structure of twins and midgets, many of whom fell victim to his sadistic "studies." The illustration shows twins in Mengele's "experiments."

Rescue Operations During the Holocaust

Several factors determined the Jew's chances of rescue from the Nazis in Occupied Europe: anti-Semitic attitudes; the size of the Jewish community; the degree of dependence on the Nazis; and Nazi attitudes toward the conquered peoples. While there were many who collaborated with the murderers there were also those who could not accept what was being done, and risked their lives to save Jews. As for the free world, it could have tried to pressure the Nazis, and could have taken action to disrupt, at least partially, the slaughter of the Jews. But for the most part it remained passive.

The main stage in the rescue operations began once it became known that Germany was moving toward a Final Solution — the systematic murder of the Jews under Nazi control. Some 40,000 of Vilna's Jews were massacred in Ponary, only 10 km (6 miles) from the city; however, news of this began to spread only two months later. More weeks elapsed until the news reached Warsaw, months until it reached beyond the areas under Nazi control, and years until it reached endangered Jewish communities elsewhere. The directors of the Jewish Agency in Palestine published a report on the systematic murder of Jews by the Germans only in November 1942, and the Allies did not report it until December of that year. By that time more than 2.5 million Jews had been murdered. The Nazis maintained utter secrecy regarding the extermination, and few survivors remained to testify about it. Even after word of the extensive killings emerged, many people refused to believe the horrifying facts [2].

Organized Rescue Operations

Even before implementation of the Final Solution, attempts were made to extricate Jews from territories under Nazi control. One of the methods was to negotiate with the Germans to allow Jews to leave in exchange for ransom. The first agreement of this type — the "Transfer" agreement between the Jewish Agency and the German government, in August 1933 — allowed Jews to immigrate to Palestine in exchange for the purchase of German goods with their money. In the winter of 1938-1939 negotiations were conducted to take 250,000 Jews out of Germany on the basis of a similar agreement, but the free world did not manage to organize finances in time.

In 1942, Rabbi Michael Dov Weissmandel, of Slovakia, reached an agreement with Dieter Wisliceny, Eichmann's representative in charge of deportation of Jews there. In exchange for a ransom payment the deportation of several thousand Slovak Jews was postponed for two years. Rabbi Weissmandel tried to extend the "Slovakia Plan" to all of Europe, but without success.

In 1942-1944, about 800 Jews were rescued through an exchange of Germans living in Palestine for Palestinian Jews in Europe and Zionists holding immigration permits. After the con-

CONNECTIONS

164 The Holocaust
168 Jewish Resistance in the Holocaust
172 Palestine During World War II

דבר
עתון פועלי ארץ ישראל
הגרמנים מודים
המצב במבואי ויאזמה קשה
התקפה מוצלחת על האויב בבורמה

2 Reports of the extermination of Jews began to be published in January 1942 by Soviet spokesmen; however, the number of murdered appeared exaggerated. In March 1942, *Davar* published testimony of the murder of 240,000 Ukrainian Jews, but the writer commented: "There is no doubt that the Nazis shed blood like water in their mission of conquest, but all these large numbers, cited by 'soldiers returning from the front,' must be viewed with great reservation."

1 The Jews of Denmark were untouched until 1943, due to the Danes' insistence that the Germans respect their rights. In the fall of that year reports of the Germans' intention to apply the Final Solution to Denmark's 8,000 Jews began to filter in. Various groups in the population immediately began to organize and draw up plans for extensive rescue operations. First the Jews were warned of what lay in store for them, then temporary hiding places were prepared, and finally all the Jews were transferred in fishing boats to the shores of neutral Sweden. This rescue operation was feasible because the Danes viewed the protection of the Jews as a test of their own struggle for freedom. The success of this operation spurred the Danish resistance into action. No other country in Europe succeeded in saving its entire Jewish population from the Holocaust, although Bulgaria made considerable efforts.

5 Devout Christians concealed Jews out of religious motives, as well as out of genuine humane feelings. In Catholic monasteries, largely cut off from their surroundings, many Jews were hidden, especially children. In more than a few instances the Christians who were providing refuge attempted to persuade the Jews to convert, and after the liberation they were not always willing to return the rescued children to their own families.

3 Youth Aliyah brought about 10,000 children and teenagers to Palestine from conquered Europe. A thousand Polish children reached Palestine via Teheran in 1943 [illustration]. Jewish war orphans constituted one of the main problems in rehabilitating Jewish communities.

4 Gentiles who aided Jews were motivated by sympathy for the persecuted, and their deeds cast a ray of light into the darkness of the animosity and indifference shown by the general populace. In their honor a row of trees, the "Boulevard of the Righteous Gentiles," was planted on the Mount of Remembrance, in Jerusalem.

quest of Hungary (March 1944), on the instruction of Adolf Eichmann, Joel Brand was sent to the rescue delegation of Palestinian Jewry in Istanbul with a proposal for the liberation of about "one million" Jews, primarily from Hungary, in exchange for goods for the German army on the eastern front. Much time elapsed in deliberations and desperate attempts at persuasion, and in the meanwhile most of the Jews of Hungary were deported for extermination. Contacts were made in Sweden and Switzerland in an attempt to rescue Jews up to the last few weeks before the capitulation of Nazi Germany, but without any substantial success.

Righteous Gentiles

Escape, smuggling people out, and hiding became the primary method of rescue [1]. Most of the rescuers worked out of a deep sense of persuasion and sympathy for the persecuted. Those who provided secret shelter to Jews, at the risk of their lives and the lives of their families, were people of high moral values and concern for society [4]. Among these rescuers were socialists, communists, pacifists, dedicated liberals, and devout Christians [5]. In most hiding places conditions were extremely difficult. The fugitives lived in almost complete and prolonged isolation, had to maintain the utmost care and secrecy, and experienced continual fear, and unbearable tension, much of which was shared by their rescuers. Well over 100,000 Jews were saved in this manner.

Worthy of special note are the remarkable rescue endeavors of several non-Jewish individuals. The Consul of Portugal in Bordeaux, Aristides De Sousa Mendes, issued thousands of entry permits to his country in 1940, contrary to his government's directives. The German "race expert" in Holland, Dr. Hans Callmeyer, declared many Jews to be "not Jewish by race." Perhaps the greatest gentile to help the Jews was Raoul Wallenberg [7], who saved tens of thousands of Hungarian Jews.

KEY

In the summer of 1944 the extermination complex of Auschwitz-Birkenau was within bombing range of US and British aircraft, and the plan of the camp was clear from aerial photographs; yet repeated requests to bomb the camp or the railroads leading to it, thus saving thousands of lives, were rejected. Influential figures in the Allied administration claimed that to do so would be a waste of war resources, and that the problem of the Jews was not essentially different from that of other nations under Nazi yoke. This, despite documented evidence that by early 1943 the Americans and the British possessed accurate information on the nature and extent of the Holocaust.

6 A

7 A

7 Raoul Wallenberg [A] was a Swedish diplomat who, in July 1944, arrived in Budapest to work to save the Jews of Hungary, of whom 300,000 had already been deported to Auschwitz. The Swedish passes [B] which he distributed are credited with saving at least 30,000.

7 B

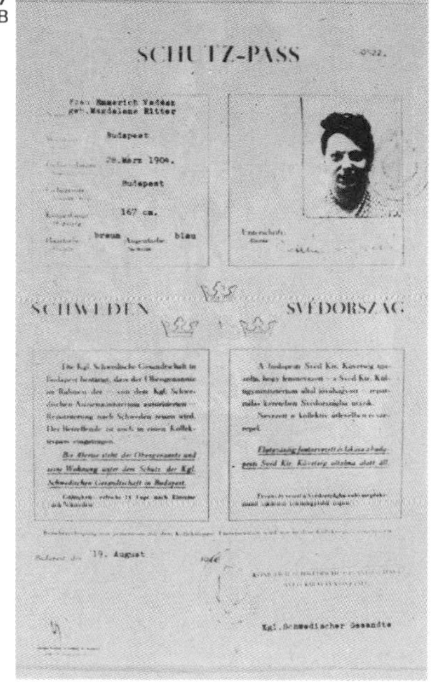

SCHUTZ-PASS

Frau Emmerich Vadász
geb. Magdalene Ritter

Budapest
28. März 1904.
Budapest
167 cm.
braun blau

SCHWEDEN SVÉDORSZÁG

19. August

Kgl. Schwedischer Gesandte

6 The Jewish community of Palestine was not able to extend much aid to the Jews of Europe, yet even those opportunities which it did have were not used to the fullest advantage. In 1944 Palestinian Jewish parachutists [A] were dropped into southeastern Europe in order to make contact with Jews and assist in smuggling them out. One of the prominent parachutists from Erez Israel was the Hungarian-born Hannah Szenes [B]; she was captured in Hungary, tortured, and executed. The small number of parachutists (only 34), and the restrictions placed on them by the British army, rendered their activities devoid of operational value.

6 B

8

8 Rescuing children was easier than rescuing adults, because of people's willingness to take in children and care for them. In the Netherlands, at the beginning of the period of deportations (summer 1942), a group of non-Jewish students organized a "Committee for Children" whose objective was to hide Jewish children. The "Committee for the Protection of Children," a Belgian underground organization, managed to save some 4,000 children. This child's drawing from Theresienstadt is one of a legacy of children's works from the death camps. The book *There are no Butterflies Here* contains a selection.

Jewish Resistance in the Holocaust

Unlike other peoples of conquered Europe, who could choose between cooperation or passive resistance, most of the Jews of Europe were deprived of the freedom of choice. Even those who collaborated willingly were ultimately destined for annihilation. Hence, the Jewish public had to fight for survival. Even though not all of the Jewish community withstood the persecution and humiliation which were its lot, nevertheless the power to survive evinced by the Jews in this era carried on a time-honored tradition of the Jewish people, which had suffered many adversities and discrimination, yet had managed to survive as an exile community for about 2,000 years.

Underground Activity

The Jews' reaction to Nazi policy was determined by their assessment of the Germans' objectives. In 1939 they assumed that the Germans' aim was to strike at their communal existence, to dehumanize the Jew and leave him to die of starvation and disease. Hence the extensive underground activity that developed was designed to perpetuate the Jewish identity. Despite prohibitions against doing so, prayers and public gatherings were held, extensive educational activities were organized, and Jewish books and newspapers were published [2]. The political youth movements, both Zionist and non-Zionist, which conducted these activities provided the nucleus for subsequent organized efforts during the period of deportations and mass murders.

Until 1942, the possibility of armed resistance was not considered. Indeed, it was clear that any armed action would bring on a swift and strong German reaction. The Jews could not expect substantial aid from any outside group, at a time when Germany was succeeding in conquest after conquest. Nor did anyone imagine that the Nazis were planning the systematic and total annihilation of the Jewish people. Only a few reports about what was happening leaked out beyond the conquered countries, and even these penetrated into the human consciousness only with the greatest of difficulty. When the nature of the new Nazi policy did become clear, calls for armed resistance were raised.

Uprisings

The chance of extricating oneself from the German trap by means of rebellion was nil. Locked in ghettos, and under strict supervision, the Jews faced more difficulties than others in obtaining weapons. The local, non-Jewish, underground in most places was only in the initial stages of organization, and even among the general populace only a small minority took part in anti-Nazi underground activity. Within a ghetto, or within a single Jewish community, one could not expect that everyone would join forces and succeed in an undertaking to rebel or to escape.

Responsibility for the well-being of the community weighed heavily on the shoulders of resistance leaders. Raising

CONNECTIONS

162 Life in the Ghetto
164 The Holocaust
166 Rescue Operations During the Holocaust

1

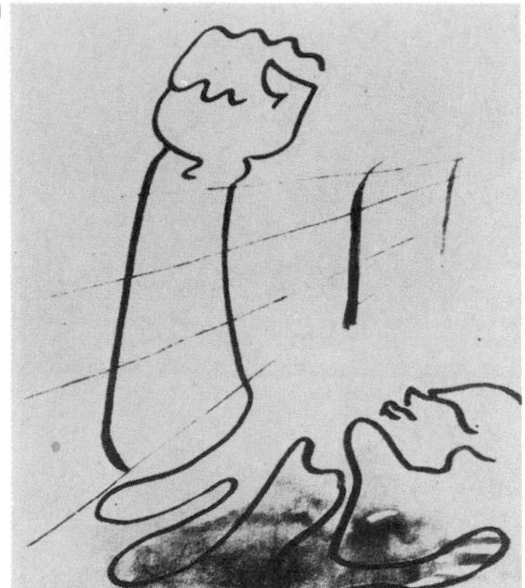

1 "Resistance behind barbed wire" [painting by Zdanek Elda, Buchenwald 1944]. Rebellion within the extermination camps was almost unfeasible. Nevertheless, an uprising broke out in the Treblinka death camp in August 1943. The inmates killed their commanders and guards, seized control of the arsenal, and set fire to the gas chambers. About 150 inmates escaped.

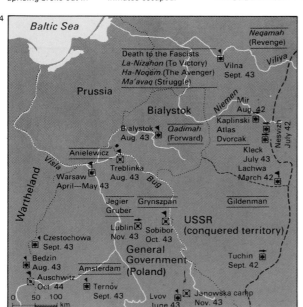

2 Underground newspapers of movements in France, Belgium, and Poland, some in camps and some in ghettos, served as an important source of information and means of maintaining contact. At the same time, the vast number of publications underscores the Jews' internal ideological and political differences. These did not cease to exist: even during the period of deportation and preparation for revolt these differences were not always overcome.

2

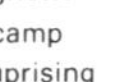

3 The French Resistance comprised a relatively high percentage of Jews — over 15% (as compared with their relative weight of 1% in the general population). Some Jews established separate Jewish groups, which worked primarily at rescuing Jews, by issuing forged papers or smuggling people across the border to Spain. Jews played an important part in the communist "National Council of the Revolt," and close collaboration developed between them and the *Maquis* guerrilla organizations. These organizations sabotaged the train lines and installations used by the Germans, especially after the allied invasion. The illustration shows a *Maquis* printing press operated by Jews.

3

4

ghetto
camp
uprising
uprising to flee to forests
armed resistance
Sept. 42 — date of uprising
Qadimah — key unit of Jewish partisans

4 Armed Jewish resistance took place in several ghettos and camps under Nazi conquest in Eastern Europe. In these uprisings German soldiers and collaborators were killed. In every instance only a few rebels managed to escape, and some of these were captured by the local population and turned in or murdered. A few who escaped joined general partisan groups, or established independent Jewish partisan units.

5

5 In the Vilna ghetto, in January 1942, a "United Partisans Organization" was established. Its deputy commander, Abba Kovner [center], issued a manifesto to the residents of the ghetto: "Hitler is plotting to annihilate all the Jews of Europe.... the only response to the murderers is self-defense." In September the organization issued a public call: "Jewish Masses! To the street! Whoever has no arms, let him.... take up a metal bar, a club, or a stick." However, the residents of the ghetto, believing Nazi promises that they would remain alive in the camps, decided to leave for the camps, and the fighters who remained became partisans in the forests.

the banner of revolt meant a lethal German reaction, essentially amounting to annihilation of the Jewish community; while relinquishing the idea of rebellion, even at the most difficult moments, left a faint hope that a few might be spared until such time as Germany were defeated. On the basis of such reasoning, the resistance leader of the Bialystok ghetto, Mordecai Tenenbaum-Tamaroff (1916-1943), decided to refrain from launching the rebellion in February 1943, on the eve of a large "action."

But the hope of rescue, too, was soon frustrated. The German stranglehold tightening around the Jews did not leave open many avenues of escape. The question of rebellion emerged again in the winter of 1942-1943, but this time took the form of a choice between death with honor — and going like sheep to the slaughter. As the fighters themselves put it: "Our fate has been sealed. We have only to choose between two ways of dying." The poet Abba Kovner, one of the commanders of the Vilna ghetto underground, said in 1945: "We wanted to remain alive in their memory."

The number of actual Jewish uprisings was considerable [4], especially in comparison to other nationalities. The more famous uprisings occurred in Warsaw [Key, 6, 8, 9], Bialystok, Kharkov and Bedzin. Many Jews also joined groups of partisans, or established partisan units of their own [7]. In 1943, uprisings even broke out in two of the extermination camps — Treblinka and Sobibor [1]: several hundred Jews who were forced to burn corpses and sort victims' clothing and belongings, succeeded in rebelling and even in escaping beyond the camp limits. There were also uprisings in several work camps. From the very outset these uprisings had virtually no chance of success. That they were executed by relatively few individuals only emphasizes the adverse conditions under which they were initiated. They expressed, above all, a heroic spirit against total adversity.

KEY

The Warsaw ghetto rebellion started on the eve of Passover, 1943, and was the largest and most comprehensive of the uprisings of that year. Groups of anti-Nazi fighters organized in July 1942 to form the "Jewish Fighting Organization," under the command of Mordechai Anielewicz. They obtained arms and manufactured sabotage materials in the ghetto, and with these they attacked the Germans. In reaction, the Germans attacked the ghetto and burned house after house. Twice the ghetto fighters forced them to retreat. The fighting continued until May 8, when the command bunker fell. By then, of the 55,000 Jews in the ghetto at the outbreak of the uprising, 50,000 had been killed. The illustration shows Jewish women fighters from the Warsaw ghetto falling into the hands of the Germans.

6 The Warsaw ghetto uprising became a symbol of Jewish resistance against the Nazis, and the last day of the main stage of the revolt has been proclaimed Holocaust Remembrance Day. Identical monuments by N. Rapaport, one in the city of Warsaw and one at the *Yad va-Shem* memorial in Jerusalem, commemorate the uprising. Two factors made the Warsaw ghetto uprising unique: the support provided by most of the remaining civilian population in the ghetto; and the ghetto fighters' readiness to fight to the finish. "This is a war for our freedom and yours! For your human, social, and national dignity and ours!" (quoted from a placard to the Polish population).

6

7

7 In April 1943 Jewish partisans in occupied Belgium attacked a train in which Jews were being deported to Auschwitz. Several hundreds managed to escape. The Jewish underground in Belgium received aid from the general and communist underground in the country. Elsewhere in Europe the poorly-armed Jews had to fight against the hostile local population as well as the Germans. Many partisan groups refused to accept Jews in their ranks.

8

8 Mordechai Anielewicz (1919-1943), a member of *Ha-Shomer ha-Za'ir*, was appointed commander of the "Jewish Fighting Organization" in Warsaw, and led the Warsaw ghetto uprising until his death, toward the end of the battle. Kibbutz Yad Mordechai is named after him, and has this monument in his honor. In a letter to his friend Itzhak Zuckerman, also a resistance commander, he said: "Something way above and beyond our boldest dreams has happened: the Germans have twice retreated from the ghetto.... The main thing is that the dream of my life has come true. I have had the fortune to set my eyes upon Jewish defense in the ghetto in all its greatness."

9

9 Photographs by German soldiers have preserved for posterity the extensive tortures and degradation which were inflicted upon the Jews in the ghettos and camps. Even as the Warsaw ghetto was falling, someone immortalized the surrender of the survivors — women and children who were forced out of gas and smoke-filled bunkers. "Many people... swelled forth from the bowels of the earth, laden with scraps of food, pots, sacks. Infants were carried in the arms of their mothers... their eyes wells of sadness and grief, confusion, and calls for deliverance" (from the testimony of Zivia Lubetkin, a member of the "Jewish Fighting Organization" general command).

Zionism and Aliyah from Muslim Countries

Throughout the generations, Jews in Muslim countries expressed their attachment to Erez Israel in prayers and customs, in poetry and song, through pilgrimage (the *Zi'ara*), by giving a regular tax such as "The Jerusalem Donation," and even by *aliyah*. More than thirty separate *aliyot* of individuals and groups were recorded during the 18th and 19th centuries, all based on messianic aspirations.

Early Zionist Movement

It was due to a combination of disappointment with the Emancipation, anti-Semitic manifestations, and a stirring of national feeling among the peoples of Europe, that the Zionist political movement arose there. No similar combination of circumstances existed in the Muslim countries, and the vast majority of Oriental Jewish communities were far removed from the activities of the World Zionist Organization. There was, nevertheless, limited Zionist activity between 1897 and 1917 [Key]: Hebrew was popularized, educational and fund-raising campaigns took place, the Zionist organization membership fee — the *shekel* — was purchased, and people came on *aliyah*, as well [2].

As the majority of the Muslim countries came under the European sphere of influence, and Arab nationalist feelings rose, the Zionist concept began to gain popularity among the educated Jewish youth. It was opposed, however, by the more traditional Jewish leadership, out of fear of reprisals by the anti-Zionist Arab nationalists. Thus Zionist activity was declared illegal in Turkey, Persia, Iraq, Syria, and Yemen [4].

During the 1920s and 1930s limits were placed on *aliyah*, and the Zionist movement focused its attention on the large European Jewish communities faced with annihilation. Nevertheless, *aliyah* from Muslim countries did continue: between the two world wars 50,000 Jews came to Erez Israel — one-tenth of all *olim* — mostly members of pioneering youth movements.

Ha'apala and Underground

It was during and after World War II that the illegal immigration organizations and Jewish underground movements in Muslim countries became most active [1, 3]. The Nazism rampant in Europe led to growing anti-Semitism in the Muslim countries. In June 1941, in a pogrom in Baghdad, 179 Jews were killed, over 2,000 injured, and Jewish property destroyed. This led to the establishment of *No'ar Ve'hatzala* — a Zionist self-defense organization. This and similar bodies provided the basis for the *He-Halutz* organization (the Babylonian Pioneer Movement) established in 1941 [7].

In March of 1942, Shaul Avigur, head of the *Mossad le'Aliyah Bet*, arrived in Iraq. He was followed by the emissaries Shemariah Guttman, Iraqi-born Ezra Kadoorie, and Hayyim Enzo Sereni. The Jewish defense organization gained strength, and in 1945 branches were set up in Basra and Kirkuk. Underground Zionist educational activities soon

1

COMITÉ CENTRAL SIONISTE d'EGYPTE
2, Boulevard EL-GOHARI

ועד מרכזי לציוני מצרים
קהיר

Le Caire, le 1. Juillet 1910

Zionistisches Centralbureau
24 JUIL 1910
№ 2611

Monsieur

1 Zionist activity in Egypt began with the founding of the *Bar Kokhba* Association in Cairo in 1897. Its aim was to achieve emancipation for Jews in Muslim countries, to popularize the study of Hebrew, and to encourage agricultural settlement in Erez Israel. Similar associations were established in other communities. World War I and the Balfour Declaration added momentum to Zionist activities in Egypt. On the eve of World War II Arab nationalist provocations grew more frequent. In late 1947, the leaders of the Zionist organizations were forced to go underground, and detention camps were even set up for suspected Zionists.

2

2 Associations to encourage the study of modern Hebrew were established in many Muslim and Balkan countries. One of these was *Hevrat Mahzikei Ivrit*, founded in Salonika in 1915 [pictured]. At its meetings the members spoke only Hebrew. The association published its own newspaper, *Noar Ivri* (Jewish Youth). Similar groups followed, such as *Dovrei Ivrit* (Hebrew Speakers), *Ohadi Sfat Zion* (Friends of the Language of Zion), and *Bar Kokhba*, which also provided sports activities. Other clubs operated in Casablanca, Tripoli, Alexandria, and Damascus. These cities had Jewish, Hebrew-speaking schools with teachers from Erez Israel.

4 Organization of Zionist associations was prohibited throughout the Ottoman Empire in the late 19th century. The hostile attitude toward Zionism increased after the Young Turks revolution of 1908, and Jewish economic and civil service activity was restricted. Nevertheless, official Zionist activities were carried on in Istanbul and in other centers in the empire, such as Salonika, Damascus, and of course Erez Israel. These activities were under the auspices of the World Zionist Organization. All Zionist activity was banned in Turkey after World War I. Pictured — The *Maccabi* gymnastic club anniversary, Istanbul.

3

3 In Syria, some Jewish activists began to organize into Zionist associations in 1903. Activity increased after World War I, but the opposition of the French regime and the rise of Arab nationalism curtailed it. World War II spurred Zionist activity again, because refugees from Europe came through Syria to Palestine. This work was interrupted altogether in 1946, due to the opposition of Syria's nationalist government. Consequently, Zionist activity in Syria in the years leading up to Israeli statehood consisted mainly of helping Jews reach Erez Israel. In the picture — the *He-Halutz* group, Damascus, 1929.

4

found their way into schools and synagogues. In 1948, *He-Halutz* had 48 branches in Iraq, with over 2,000 members organizing *Ha'apalah* (illegal immigration) to Ereẓ Israel. *Aliyah* routes were overland, through Transjordan, or via Iran to Turkey and Syria. In March of 1950 Jews were officially permitted to leave Iraq on condition that they relinquish their citizenship. Operation Ezra and Nehemiah was organized, and all 170,000 Iraqi Jews were brought to Israel.

In North Africa, too, the situation of the Jews during and after World War II was menaced. German forces in Libya and Tunisia, and the pro-German Vichy governments in Algeria and Morocco, endangered the survival of the Jewish communities. In the early 1940s anti-Semitic laws were enacted in all of North Africa, and the 1870 Crémieux Decree granting French citizenship and equal rights to the Jews of Algeria was revoked. On August 3, 1940 a brutal pogrom took place in Algeria, and most of the Jewish population of 130,000 were sent to concentration camps. In Tunisia and Libya, too, many were sent to camps [8]. In light of this situation, the Zionist movement grew stronger.

The Jewish underground movements in Algeria, Tunisia, and Libya came together for the first time at a training camp in Rovigo, in Algeria, and later in Lyon, France. The 1947 Rovigo convention paved the way for organization of the North African *Ha'apalah* Movement. On May 10, 1947, the first *Ma'apilim* ship, the Yehuda Halevi, set sail from Ténès, Algeria [6].

The North African underground, education for Zionism, and Jewish consciousness intensified when emissaries were sent from Israel. These factors, and the deep traditional attachment of North African Jews to Ereẓ Israel, all helped prepare the way for their mass *aliyah*, which took place upon the establishment of the State of Israel, and in successive waves thereafter, in the 1950s and 1960s.

KEY

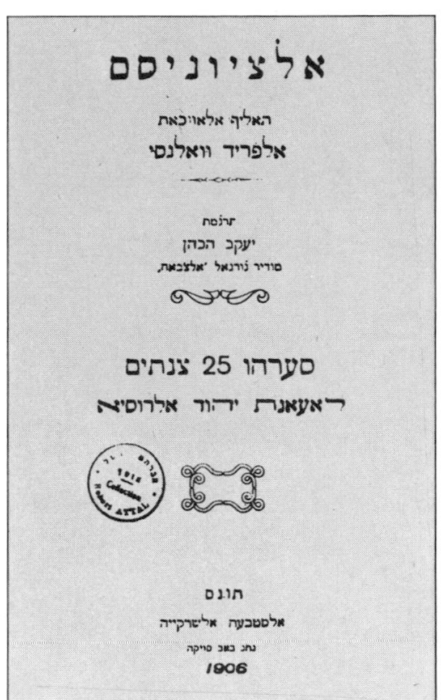
אלציוניסם
תאליף אלאוכאת
אלפריד ואלנסי
תרג'מת
יעקב הכהן
מדיר ג'ורנאל 'אלצבאח'
סערהו 25 צנתים
ראעאנת יהוד אלרוסיא
תונס
אלמטבעה אלשרקייה
נהג באב סויקה
1906

Conflicts like those between the European orthodox, and liberal or reform streams, did not evolve among North African Jewry, where most Zionist activists were rabbis and religious Jews, and nearly all Jews maintained traditional practices. Among the most prominent North African Jews was the attorney Alfred Valensi, active in Tunisia in the late 19th and early 20th centuries. His booklet "The Zionism" [pictured] was translated into Judeo-Arabic, and proceeds of its sale were sent to help refugees of the pogroms in Kishinev, Russia. Nevertheless at the First Zionist Congress (1897) there were only four delegates from the Balkan states, and one from Algeria.

5

6

5 In the Balkan states the Zionist Movement was received with great enthusiasm. One of the movement's earliest ideological spokesmen was Rabbi Judah Hai Alkalai (1798-1878) of Zemlin, Yugoslavia, who called for the development of industry and agriculture in Ereẓ Israel through a central organization, and with European assistance. This poster advertises the *Maccabi* movement's second convention, Bulgaria, 1930.

6 As in most Muslim and Balkan countries, Zionist activity in Morocco began with the founding of Zionist associations. In 1903, *Ahavat Zion* (Love of Zion) was established in Saphi. *Hibat Zion* groups were formed in Meknes, Mogador and Fez. All worked to raise money (the Zionist *shekel*) and sought to organize Jewish education within the traditional system. Pictured — members of a *Mizraha* group at Sali, Morocco.

7 Underground organization in Iraq was the Jews' response to pro-Nazi pogroms in 1941. Each of the branches was given a Hebrew code name [appearing on the map beneath the Arab names of the localities].

7

Turkey
Iran
Syria
Saudi Arabia
Jordan
Kuwait
Persian Gulf
To Damascus or Beirut
Arab Locality Arbil
He-Halutz Branch *Alonim*
Aliyah routes till 1946
Aliyah routes 1946-1948
Aliyah routes 1949-1950
0 100 200 km

8 Libyan Jews were exposed to attack by the Fascist Italian government as well as by fanatic Muslim mobs. In 1942 the government imposed a series of racist laws and all Jewish men were sent to forced labor camps. Anti-Jewish riots in 1941 and 1945 in Benghazi—under Italian, then British occupation — inspired the establishment of a Jewish defense organization and encouraged the Jews to evacuate Libya. Pictured — A Jewish Brigade soldier teaching Hebrew at a Benghazi school, 1944.

8

Palestine During World War II

During World War II, the battlefront approached Palestine's northern and southern borders [2]. Syria and Lebanon to the north were ruled by the Vichy government of France and in the south a German army under Rommel was advancing on Egypt. Within the *Yishuv*, it was feared that the Axis Powers might incite the Arab population to riot [1]. Twice — in April 1941 and in the summer of 1942 — invasion seemed imminent. In November 1942, however, Rommel's army was repulsed at El Alamein, and the danger of Nazi invasion passed.

The *Yishuv* joined in the war effort and flourished economically as the British military disposition developed [3]. An estimated 100,000 foreign servicemen were stationed there, and the increased demand for goods and services channeled a great deal of capital into factories, old and new alike. The citrus industry was badly hurt at the war's outset because of submarine activity in the Mediterranean, which curtailed shipping. The need to supply locally-based army markets, however, induced farmers to enlarge the range of their crops.

During the war, the number of Jews in Palestine increased; the total urban population grew from 337,000 in 1939 to 427,000 in 1944. In Haifa, factories and workshops established near the port helped turn that city into an industrial center [Key]. Most impressive, though, was the expansion of Tel Aviv, which continued to be the cultural and economic center of the *Yishuv*.

The Land Transfer Regulations published in 1940 by the British authorities as part of their White Paper policy limited Jewish settlement to within specific borders. Despite the law, land purchases continued, and during the course of the war 49 new settlements were established.

The Biltmore Conference

The war and news of the fate of European Jewry increased the need to find an immediate solution for the problem of Jewish national survival. The Zionist leaders came to the decision that after the war it was imperative to establish a Jewish State in Ereẓ Israel. In May of 1942 they gathered at the Biltmore Hotel in New York City, with Weizmann and Ben-Gurion in attendance. Here, a resolution was adopted, by unanimous vote, regarding the necessity to open the gates of the country for Jewish *aliyah*, and to establish Ereẓ Israel "as a Jewish Commonwealth integrated in the structure of the new democratic world." Despite objections of the Revisionists on the one hand, and the leftist Zionists, on the other, the Biltmore Plan was approved by the Zionist Executive Committee. It became the Zionist Federation's official political program.

The main effort was now the fight for *aliyah*. Underground organizations were active in arranging illegal immigration, but only a very few ships managed to leave European shores during World War II. The British were very hard on

CONNECTIONS

152 The Jewish Economy in Palestine until 1939
156 Britain Retreats from its Support for Zionism
164 The Holocaust
166 Rescue Operations During the Holocaust
176 The Yishuv Takes up the Struggle

1

1 Erez Israel came within the focus of the war when Italy joined the Axis Powers in June of 1940. Italian air force planes attacked strategic points in the region, including Palestine. Most of the bombing was aimed at the refineries and fleet installations at Haifa Port. Tel Aviv was also bombed. Loss of life and property in Haifa, which was protected by the British navy, was relatively low (70 killed). Tel Aviv, which was unprepared for aerial bombardment, suffered 128 killed and 150 wounded. The *Yishuv* began to organize for war; shelters and blast barriers [photo] were built, and gas masks distributed. Plans were made to concentrate the Jewish population in the north of the country for a last-ditch defense against invasion by Rommel's forces. The war, though, never reached Palestine. In 1941, when the Allies invaded Syria, Haifa and Tel Aviv were again bombed by French and German planes.

2

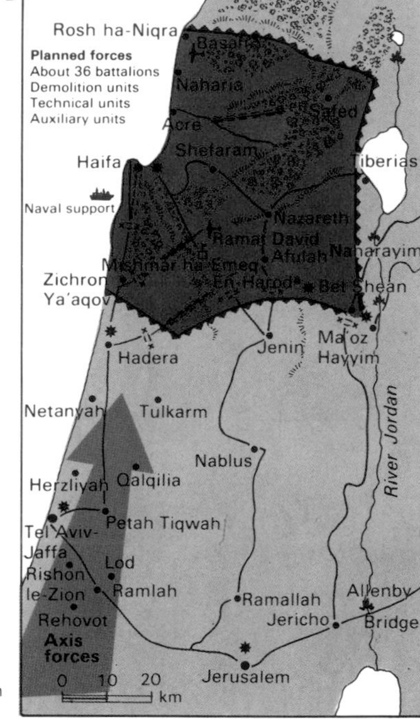

2 With the war front advancing closer to the Middle East in 1941, plans were made for defending the *Yishuv* in the event of a German invasion and a British withdrawal. When Rommel's forces neared El Alamein, *Palmach* units were moved south, and coastal dispositions were strengthened in case of invasion by sea. Plans were made to concentrate the *Yishuv*'s entire population in the north, where the rough seacoast would make landings difficult and the terrain would impede German tank movements.

3 A

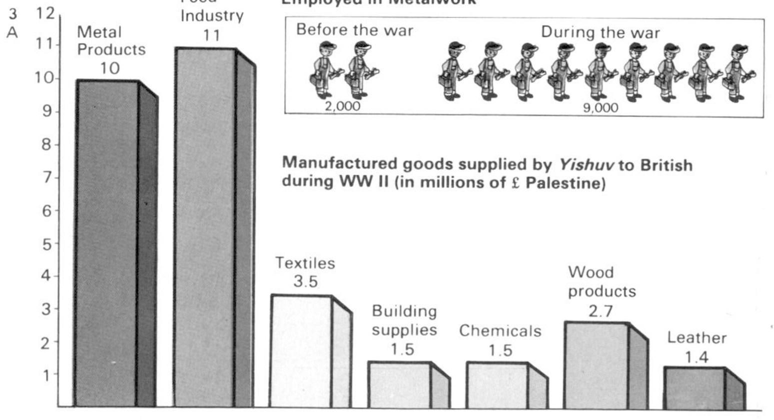

3 B

3 Industries in Erez Israel were enlisted to supply British armies in the Middle East after they were cut off from all their other sources of supply. The economic groundwork and technological know-how which had been amassed in the 1930s now found expression. *Yishuv* production [A] aided the war effort, spared the British vast import expenses, and strengthened the Jewish economy. Textile factories supplied clothing and tents, and food and tobacco plants provided cigarettes, canned fruits and vegetables, jams, etc. The chemical industry [B] and the Dead Sea potash plant provided vital war materials. *Solel Boneh* built airports and roads; and the metalworks supplied spare parts for machines and weapons and repaired instruments. After the war army requisitions dropped, and the economy again encountered difficulties.

those *ma'apilim* who managed to run the blockade successfully [6], and only about 15,000 succeeded in entering the country during the war. However, the *Yishuv* now organized the machinery for *aliyah* in anticipation of full-scale activities after the war; a network of *aliyah* agents (*shlichim*) was trained, and the *Palmach* established its own maritime division.

Volunteering for the British Army

When World War II broke out, Ben-Gurion proclaimed the Zionist motto: "We'll fight in Ereẓ Israel against the White Paper as if there were no world war, and we'll fight Hitler as if there were no White Paper." Cooperation with the British during the first half of the war was intended to fight the Nazi enemy and defend Ereẓ Israel; and during the second half, to be the first to meet the survivors. The *Yishuv* leadership was also hopeful that its cooperation could be advantageous in advancing Zionist political goals. Nevertheless, the issue of serving with the British Army aroused controversy within the *Yishuv* [8].

All through 1942 the *Yishuv* had received information about the annihilation of European Jewry, but it was only in the fall of that year that it actually accepted this as fact. A "United Relief Committee" began operating under the auspices of the Jewish Agency. Following incessant argument and pressure upon the British, a Jewish Brigade was finally formed and fought in Italy [4]. *Haganah* and *Palmach* parachutists were dropped into occupied Europe to carry out intelligence operations for the British Army and to make contact with the partisans and the Zionist underground.

All told, wartime developments in Palestine were beneficial in building the future state. After the war was over the *Yishuv* united in a struggle to abrogate "White Paper" policy, to open the country's gates [7], and to establish an independent Jewish state.

KEY

Haifa Port opened in 1933 and served as Erez Israel's main port for travelers, merchandise, and, from 1935 — for oil as well. After 1939 the British used it as an auxiliary base for their fleet in the eastern Mediterranean, stationed in Alexandria. The port's opening hastened Haifa's development — economically, commercially, and industrially — spurring the establishment of the *krayot* satellite towns to accommodate the growing population. Many factories were built near the port, including some of the largest plants in the country.

4

4 The Jewish Brigade Group was established in September of 1944, and was part of the British Army. Approximately 5,000 soldiers served in the Brigade and took part in fighting against the Germans in Italy. At war's end, the Brigade took care of Holocaust refugees and organized their illegal *aliyah*. Pictured: Chaim Laskov, one of the Brigade's commanders, and later IDF Commander-in-Chief (1958-61).

5

5 A "Jewish Soldiers Day" Poster. 30,000 members of the *Yishuv* enlisted in the British Army and were assigned to its various corps. The first group (enlisted 1939-40) was sent to dig trenches and to technical units. After 1940 the majority of enlistees went to the infantry and artillery corps.

6

6 Refugees from the Transnistria detention camp, still wearing their yellow badges, arrive in Palestine in 1944 aboard a Portuguese vessel. They were caught by the British and placed in detention camps at Atlit. In October 1945, in a daring operation, the *Palmach* broke into the Atlit camp, freed the prisoners, and concealed them in Jewish settlements. From August 1946 on, the *ma'apilim* were sent directly to detention camps on Cyprus.

7

8

7 The Berihah ("flight") organization was established in 1944 by Jewish partisans, surviving ghetto fighters, and graduates of pioneering youth movements, to prepare escape routes from Europe to Ereẓ Israel for Holocaust survivors. With the help of the *Haganah*'s *Mossad Le-Aliyah*, tens of thousands of Jews were smuggled out of Eastern Europe and housed in transit camps, then eventually transferred by ship to Palestine.

8 Approximately 4,000 Jewish women from Erez Israel volunteered to serve in the ATS — the British Army's Auxiliary Training Squad — from 1942 on as drivers, clerks, storekeepers, and nurses. In 1943, when British Air Force women's auxiliary began recruiting, 800 joined up. This aroused heated debate and controversy among some religious and ethnic elements within the *Yishuv*. But Jewish women were already serving in the *Haganah* and *Palmach*.

The National Institutions of the "State-in-the-Making"

In its endeavors to establish an independent Jewish state, the Zionist movement sought to create the foundations of a governmental system, despite the limitations imposed upon it by the mandatory government. Thus the *Yishuv* maintained an unofficial state of its own in Palestine, whose institutions were intended to take over the reins of government when the "State-in-the-Making" became a reality.

The Mandate, confirmed by the League of Nations on July 24, 1922, provided that the British would facilitate the establishment of institutions of self-government by the *Yishuv*. It also stated that a "Jewish Agency for Palestine" would represent the *Yishuv* before the British administration in all matters affecting the establishment of the Jewish National Home in Palestine. This lent legal validity, as it were, to the duality now created by organizing institutions for Jewish leadership in Palestine, on a parallel with the continued existence of the Zionist Movement.

Creating the Institutions

The bodies designated to serve the *Yishuv* in Palestine were given the general title "National Institutions." These were operated through the Zionist Organization, the Jewish Agency, and *Knesset Israel*. The Zionist Organization and the Jewish Agency were the organizational instruments of the Zionist Movement and the world Jewish community. *Knesset Israel* was the general organizational framework for the *Yishuv* in Palestine, responsible for choosing *Asefat ha-Nivharim* — the Elected Assembly. According to the constitution of *Knesset Israel* — authorized by the mandatory government on January 1, 1928 — any Jewish resident of Palestine was a member, unless he specifically chose otherwise (this was done, for example, by *Agudat Israel*, which opposed *Knesset Israel* on the grounds that it was based on secular law rather than on the *Torah*) [3].

The Elected Assembly — first chosen in 1920 — was the supreme legislative body of *Knesset Israel*; a *Va'ad Leumi* (National Council) and its Executive served as the administrative body which carried out decisions of the Elected Assembly [1]. This, then, was *Yishuv* leadership, and the right to participate in elections was granted to all those over 20 years of age. Elections were direct, secret, and proportional, and participants were either political parties or local ethnic groups.

Though the Elected Assembly and the *Va'ad Leumi* constituted the duly-elected representative bodies of the *Yishuv*, it was the Jewish Agency Executive with whom the British dealt and negotiated within the *Yishuv*. The other *Yishuv* institutions were weak because of insufficient funds, and, primarily, due to the very limited authority allowed them by the British.

The Jewish Agency for Palestine

Thus the Jewish Agency took on the role of the eventual government of the State of Israel. It was supported by

CONNECTIONS

138 The British Mandate and the Zionists
172 Palestine During World War II
180 Establishing the State of Israel

1

The Institutions from "State-in-the-Making" to the State of Israel

Knesset Israel		National Institutions		
Eligibility	**Legislative Authority**	**Executive Authority**		**Judicial Authority**
1922 Jewish residents of Palestine (membership not compulsory)	Elected Assembly elected by members of Knesset Israel	Va'ad Leumi (Asefat ha-Nivharim) chosen by Elected Assembly	The Va'ad Leumi Executive	Chief Rabbinate Ashkenazi Rabbi Sephardi Rabbi Recognized as supreme authority for Jewish religious and legal matters (1921)
1949 All citizens of the State of Israel	**The Knesset** Elected by all citizens of the State of Israel	**The Government**		**The Judicial System** Civil Courts Rabbinical Courts

1 The Va'ad Leumi, executive arm of the National Institutions, focused on education, health, and welfare. The educational system encompassed all stages — from nursery to university — and prepared curricula for study at all levels. Schools for the handicapped were established; welfare programs for the needy and undernourished were instituted; and there were night classes and *ulpanim* for adults. Health services were provided by *Kupat Holim*, by clinics and by hospitals sponsored by *Hadassah*. Centers to fight malaria and other contagious diseases were set up, and a broad network of public health institutions was established throughout the *Yishuv*.

2

2 The Zionist Commission was the British-approved delegation headed by Chaim Weizmann which arrived in Palestine after the British conquest (1918). It served as liaison between the British military authorities and the Jewish population toward implementation of the Balfour Declaration. For three years the Commission was active in welfare assistance and in establishing health and educational institutions. It was replaced in 1921 by the Zionist Executive, established in Jerusalem after the 12th Zionist Congress.

3

3 Rabbi Isaac Abraham Hacohen Kook (1865-1935) [1 in this photograph], served as Palestine's *Ashkenazi* Chief Rabbi between 1921 and 1935. Rabbi Kook sought to find a common meeting ground between *Agudat Israel* and the Zionist Movement and its concepts, and he viewed the settlement of Erez Israel as an important precept. He founded *Yeshivat Merkaz ha-Rav*, a Talmudical college, in 1924. Here studies were conducted in Hebrew, both secular and *Torah* subjects were required, and students were educated toward a love of the land and the concept of settlement. The Rabbi was active in public life and strenuously opposed the British Mandate's White Paper policy. He was also famous for his writings, which included works of philosophy, poetry, biblical commentary, and articles on *Halakhah* and *Kabbalah*.

4

4 The Emergency Tax was levied in 1939, when the *Yishuv* suffered a severe economic crisis, in order to alleviate the plight of the 26,000 unemployed. In 1941 a "Recruitment Fund" was established to finance security expenses and support the families of soldiers and constables. In 1946-7 another special fund was set up — "A Fighting People" — to finance preparations for the 1948 War of Independence.

Keren ha-Yesod (Palestine Foundation Fund) — the financial arm of the national institutions [6] — and *Ha-Keren ha-Kayemet* (Jewish National Fund), which was responsible for purchasing and reclaiming land for the *Yishuv*, for settlement, and for afforestation. The Agency's main efforts were centered on bringing Jews to Israel, and helping them to become economically, culturally, and socially acclimatized. In the realm of security, the Agency took upon itself the task of funding the *Haganah*.

During the 1930s, the national institutions gained strength, both politically and economically. *MAPAI* (acronym for *Mifleget Po'alei Ereẓ Israel* — The Palestine Workers' Party) assumed leadership of *Yishuv* institutions and of the Zionist Organization [5], and the focus of political activity shifted from London to Jerusalem.

In most areas, the national institutions worked in a spirit of cooperation and agreement with the British. However, the notable exception to Mandate policy was in the area of defense, where the *Haganah* steered a course between the legal and the clandestine [4, Key].

By the end of the 1930s, the leaders of the National Institutions had succeeded in establishing a governmental and organizational network which touched on all aspects of life in the *Yishuv*. When the British Mandate ended and the State of Israel was born, its governmental infrastructure was prepared for operation. Departments which had formerly belonged to the National Institutions now became government ministries [7]; many individuals who had been in key positions in the Institutions now became ministers. David Ben-Gurion, a central figure in *Yishuv* leadership — who represented it at congresses, on the Zionist Executive and in the Jewish Agency Directorate, and also served as chairman of the Jewish Agency in Jerusalem — became prime minister; and Chaim Weizmann was elected first president of the State of Israel.

KEY

Kofer ha-Yishuv was the name given to the fund-raising campaign initiated by the *Va'ad Leumi* on July 24, 1938. This campaign was, in effect, a tax. It was imposed on entertainment, public transportation, cigarettes, restaurants, and the like. The money was used to help pay for defense requirements — to fortify settlements, pave access roads, put up security fences, lighting and communication networks, and to purchase arms. In the first year, P£ 150,000 were raised. This sum paid for some 70% of *Haganah* expenses. Aside from its immediate importance, the very fact that it was collected as a tax served as yet another stepping stone toward statehood.

5 A

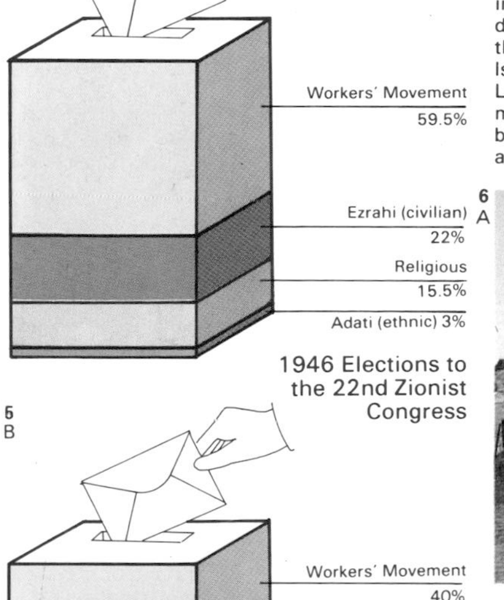

5 B

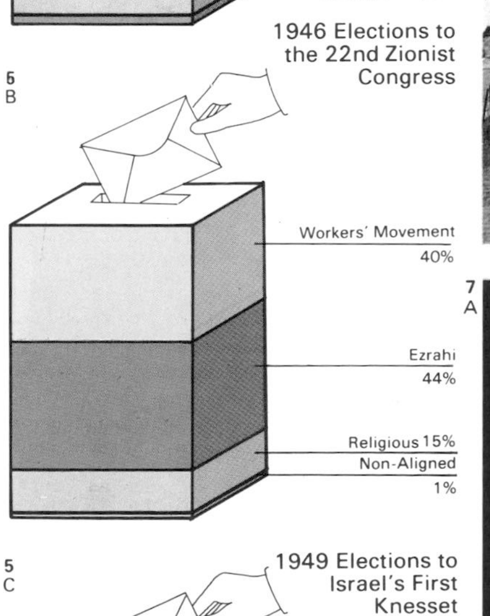

5 C

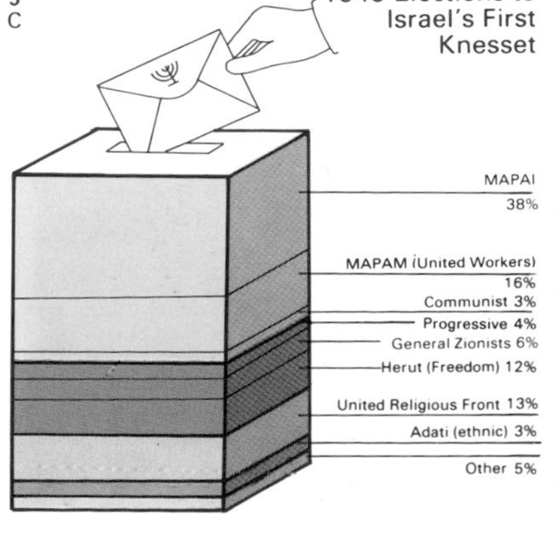

5 The political composition of the emerging Jewish state's official institutions was quite different from that of the first *Knesset* in Israel. In particular, the Labor Movement's majority was reduced between 1944 and 1948.

6 "Keren ha-Yesod" was founded by the 1920 Zionist Conference in London. Originally the financial instrument for the Zionist movement, it later encompassed the Jewish Agency as well. It supported *aliyah*, and established 257 settlements. It was responsible for building the Stockade and Tower settlements and the Negev outposts or *mitzpim* [A — Kibbutz Revivim]. It also financed defense and education, and helped found business enterprises [B — 25th anniversary poster].

6 A

6 B

7 A

7 B

7 National Institution departments became government ministries a short time before the British evacuation. Immediately following the UN decision of November 29, 1947, a committee was established to decide the structure of the future Jewish state's administration. The National Executive set up government ministries in areas which had formerly been the concern of the mandatory government, so that the absence of a civil administration would not be felt. Two outstanding examples were in finance and in communications. First, to insure that the country had a legal tender of its own, currency had been ordered several months before the end of the Mandate from an American firm [A]. In the absence of a sovereign governmental body to deal with financial matters, the order was submitted via the Anglo-Palestine Bank (the bank of the Zionist Organization), and therefore it was the bank's name that was printed on the bills. Secondly, the British Post Office was closed in late April 1948, and the Hebrew Post Office took its place. Its stamps were those of the Jewish National Fund for Palestine, which had earlier been used for domestic purposes [B]. Since the country's new name had not been decided upon, early stamps read *Doar Ivri* or "Hebrew Post."

The Yishuv Takes up the Struggle

In May 1939, the publication of the White Paper — a policy statement in which the British denied any kind of commitment to the Zionist movement — ended all cooperation that had existed between the British and the *Yishuv* during the Arab uprising (1936-1939). The *Yishuv* responded by embarking on a struggle for Jewish settlement and immigration. During 1939/40 fifteen stockade and tower settlements were established at strategic points, and small boats smuggled 10,000 illegal immigrants into Palestine.

While the *Haganah* command concentrated on settlement and immigration operations, the *IZL* came out in open revolt against British rule, attacking government offices and blowing up radar stations. The British responded with searches for ammunition, mass arrests and collective punishments.

The World War II Period

Britain's entry into World War II forced a reevaluation of the struggle against the British. But despite cooperation, no change was made in the White Paper. With the outbreak of war, Britain forbade entry to *olim* from zones under Nazi conquest. This order, aimed at preventing spies from entering Palestine, reduced the chances of rescue for Jews who had managed to flee the Nazis. In February 1940 the Lands Legislation was passed, introducing restrictions on the purchase of land in Palestine.

Meanwhile, the immigration network continued to bring illegal immigrants into Palestine. Refugees captured by the British were forced to put back to sea and others, caught on shore, were placed in detention camps. Several refugee ships sunk at sea on their way to Palestine, or after being expelled from the shores by the British. From 1942 a land operation for illegal immigrants was also organized, via Palestine's northern border; some 12,000 immigrants from Muslim countries came to Palestine in this way during the war. The British government responded by launching continued operations against illegal immigration activities, together with widespread weapons searches, mainly in *kibbutzim* and settlements with *Haganah* connections.

Intensive activity also continued in the matter of land acquisition and settlement. The Jewish National Fund took advantage of every loophole in the Lands Legislation, buying hundreds of thousands of acres, of which some 80% were in restricted or forbidden purchase zones. During 1941-1945, 37 new settlements were established, many in these zones. Remote areas like the Negev and Gush Etzion were settled.

The Hebrew Movement of Revolt

After the war, a change of government in Britain brought hopes for a change in mandatory government policy. Disappointment was not long in coming. The British government, particularly Foreign Minister Ernest Bevin (1881-1951), decided to maintain the White Paper

CONNECTIONS

156 Britain Retreats from its Support for Zionism
158 The Underground Movement
166 Rescue Operations During the Holocaust
170 Zionism and Aliyah from Muslim Countries
172 Palestine During World War II
180 Establishing the State of Israel

1 A

1 B

QUANTITY OF WEAPONS HELD BY HAGANAH (1936-1945)
(not including constabulary weaponry)

Type of weapon	Quantity late 1936	Spring 1939	October 1945
rifles	6,219	6,000	6,088
revolvers	3,316	?	2,456
medium machineguns	24	24	106
light machineguns	157	200	313
submachineguns	269	400	1,111
mortars	—	negligible	700

1 Haganah weapons [B] were acquired in various ways. Some were acquired and smuggled into the country, and some manufactured in underground factories. Initially, hand grenades were manufactured from plumbing materials. With time, production became more sophisticated [A]. With the approach of 1947, the factories were producing most types of arms and ammunition used by the *Haganah*.

2

3

4

2 Comprehensive settlement was carried out countrywide, especially after "Black Saturday," to demonstrate the *Yishuv*'s determination. In the Galilee, five settlements were established, among them Kibbutz Yehiam [here, on the day of settlement].

4 Searches for illegal weapons were discontinued in summer 1940 as the German front approached Palestine, and renewed in 1943. In November of that year, hundreds of British soldiers and police searched for weapons in Ramat ha-Kovesh. In the course of the violent search, buildings were destroyed [see picture], settlers were beaten and shots were fired, resulting in 15 casualties. Brutal weapons searches were conducted mainly in 1946, and the biggest cache was discovered at Kibbutz Yagur near Haifa.

3 On the Night of the Bridges (June 1947) 11 bridges on the country's border were attacked simultaneously, ten of them destroyed. In this operation the *Haganah* demonstrated superior planning, operational skills, and high moral standards in avoiding harm to Arab civilians and British policemen. In the picture — The *Memorial to the Fourteen* Bridge, at Achziv — a memorial park for 14 *Haganah* fighters who were killed while blowing up the railway bridge.

policy. The realization that "the war is over, but our war continues" brought the entire *Yishuv* into the struggle. Ben-Gurion ordered the *Haganah* to commence a struggle against British rule in Palestine [3].

The British reacted with mass searches [4] and arrests, culminating on Saturday, June 29, 1946 — "Black Saturday" — when some 2,700 *Yishuv* leaders and activists were arrested.

The disagreement over methods of struggle against the British grew sharper and, in July 1946, after the *IZL* blew up a wing of the King David Hotel where British government offices were housed, the *Haganah* decided to halt activities of the Hebrew Movement of Revolt. But the struggle for immigration and settlement continued [2]. In Europe the "Escape" (*Beriha*) organization was formed to care for Jewish refugees and arrange their transfer to Ereẓ Israel [8]. Despite mounting British attempts to foil the immigration activities at source, in Europe, more than 70,000 refugees managed to enter the country in 64 ships between May 1945 and late 1947.

The British sharpened their response to the Jewish struggle. British warships and scout planes began to track immigrant ships and, from mid-August 1946, almost every ship was captured and sent to Cyprus, where the refugees were held in detention camps. In summer 1947 the refugee ship *Exodus* was captured and returned to Europe in an act that attracted worldwide sympathy for the refugees' plight. The *Yishuv* retaliated by sending *Haganah* emissaries to penetrate the detention camps, where they began instructing the inmates and training them in the use of arms [6]. In preparation for a possible war, the *Haganah* changed organizational and training methods, with increased attention paid to the acquisition and manufacture of weapons [1]. The *IZL* and *Lehi* continued their armed struggle against the British, which reached a peak in the retaliatory hanging of two British sergeants in August 1947.

KEY

The arrest of the inhabitants of Biria and its occupation by British forces, on March 5, 1946, after the discovery of an arms cache, was the first case of the uprooting of a Jewish settlement by a military force. Ten days later, under the pretext of a pilgrimage to Tel Hai, thousands of youth reestablished the settlement. When British demands to disperse were refused, the settlement was surrounded. Its fence and tents were destroyed and resisters were beaten and arrested. When this became known, thousands of volunteers arrived and reoccupied the site. After three days of talks the British siege was lifted and Biria was once again a Jewish settlement.

5

5 Curfew in Tel Aviv in June 1947. The British curfew policy, enabled the British to assemble the population in streets and facilitated more efficient searches for weapons and fugitives.

6

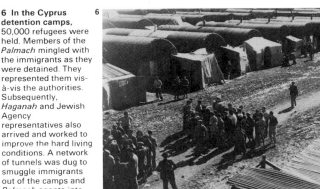

6 In the Cyprus detention camps, 50,000 refugees were held. Members of the *Palmach* mingled with the immigrants as they were detained. They represented them vis-à-vis the authorities. Subsequently, *Haganah* and Jewish Agency representatives also arrived and worked to improve the hard living conditions. A network of tunnels was dug to smuggle immigrants out of the camps and *Palmach* agents into them.

7

7 The railway track in Rehovot was blown up by *Lehi* in retaliation for the deaths of *Lehi* member Moshe Barazani and *IZL*'s Meir Feinstein, who blew themselves up before they could be executed. *IZL* and *Lehi* sabotage actions, which were carried out after the Revolt Movement was disbanded, were aimed at harassing the British army in the country and raising world awareness of events in Palestine.

8 A

8 B

8 Landing the illegal immigrants [A] and distributing them among settlements was one of the daring stages of the *Ha'apala* operation. After evading British patrols, the immigrants were deposited at various points along the shore, and then transferred to settlements. When it was clear that the British knew a "landing operation" was about to take place, a diversionary action would be mounted: hundreds of people would arrive on the beach and mingle with the new arrivals to prevent their being singled out and arrested. The British reacted by extending their struggle to Europe. Under pressure from the British government, the Italians delayed the departure of the ships from La Spezia. In response, the refugees declared a hunger strike which lasted for 75 hours, and published an appeal to the world demanding that survivors of the Nazi holocaust be allowed to reach safe shores [B].

American Jewry's Political Activities

American Jewry represents less than 3% of the population of the USA, but its political activities and influence greatly exceed its numbers. American Jews' involvement in many walks of life, their concentration in the densely populated states that are so important during presidential elections, and their active participation in politics — even financially supporting the desirable candidate — all strengthen the "Jewish vote." Their influence — exercised in the constitutional tradition of American interest groups and minority lobbies — is felt in the demand for a pro-Israel policy, in the use of America's political power to protect the rights of Jews in the Diaspora, and in the shaping of America's political power.

With respect to internal American issues, the Jews traditionally support liberal causes that they consider consonant with the spirit and essence of Judaism, such as protecting citizens' rights and perpetuating principles of cultural pluralism and inter-religious fraternity. To further such causes, "community relations committees" have been formed. Most American Jews also tend to promote welfare policies and to guard the principles of separation of church and state.

Anti-semitism in the United States in the mid-1980s was in no way as acute as in the 1920s and 1930s. Nevertheless in 1980 there were 974 deliberate attacks on Jewish property, and some 350 Jewish institutions and individuals were assaulted. Jewish organizations such as the Anti-Defamation League, the American Jewish Committee and the American Jewish Congress alert the public to these human rights violations.

Aiding World Jewry

Since 1881 American Jewry has tried to help Jews abroad. The "Joint" or the JDC (American Jewish Joint Distribution Committee) was founded in 1914 to centralize material aid for Jews in distress and help them to migrate and resettle. During World War II it mounted rescue operations and then helped rehabilitate the survivors. In Israel it helps resettle Jews from countries of oppression.

In the course of World War II the American Jewish leadership was torn between concern for European Jewry and its fear that attempts to help them would hurt the American war effort. Many feel guilty today because they did nothing to oppose the Holocaust, and this may explain later concern for Jews abroad. In the late 1960s American Jewry actively began to help Soviet Jews [9].

Attitude to Israel

Zionist leaders have always considered American Jewry more a source of economic and political support for Israel than of *aliyah*, although between the two world wars success in the former endeavor was also limited. A drastic change occurred as a result of the Holocaust in Europe. American Jewry had become the single largest Jewish

CONNECTIONS

130 Shaping the American Jewish Community
166 Rescue Operations During the Holocaust
172 Palestine During World War II
180 Establishing the State of Israel
212 American Jewry in the Mid-1980s

1 Mutual Aid was a guiding principle of American Jewry, which looked upon itself as the strong Jewish community capable of helping weaker ones. After the 1905 pogroms in Russia money was collected for welfare and self-defense. Judah Leib Magnes (1877-1948) headed the campaign for funds for Russian Jewry, and his name appears on this receipt for contributions. In 1905-1908 Magnes was Secretary of the Zionist Federation in the United States. He was also active in organizing the New York Jewish community. Magnes was among the founders of the Hebrew University and its chancellor (1925-35) and president (1935-48).

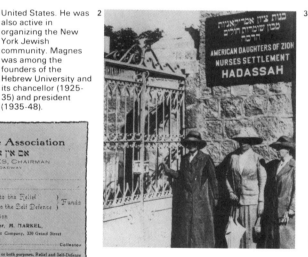

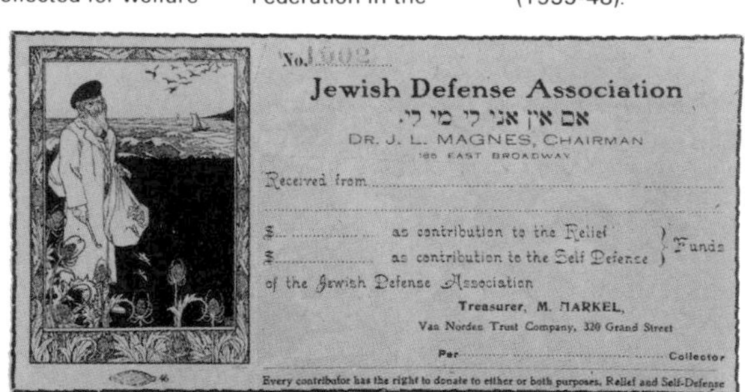

No.

Jewish Defense Association

אם אין אני לי מי לי.

DR. J. L. MAGNES, CHAIRMAN

Received from ....

$.............. as contribution to the Relief } Funds
$.............. as contribution to the Self Defence }
of the Jewish Defense Association

Treasurer, M. MARKEL,
Van Norden Trust Company, 320 Grand Street

Per .... Collector

Every contributor has the right to donate to either or both purposes, Relief and Self-Defense

2 Hadassah, the Women's Zionist Organization of America, was formed in 1912 as a voluntary national body deriving from the "Daughters of Zion," led by Henrietta Szold (1860-1945). The organization devoted itself to the "ideals of Judaism, Zionism and American Democracy." The *Hadassah* Medical Center on Mt. Scopus was inaugurated in 1938, and the new center in En Karem in 1960. In addition, *Hadassah* supports Youth *Aliyah*, operates vocational training schools and supports *Keren ha-Yesod*. In the picture: *Hadassah* members visiting Erez Israel in 1923.

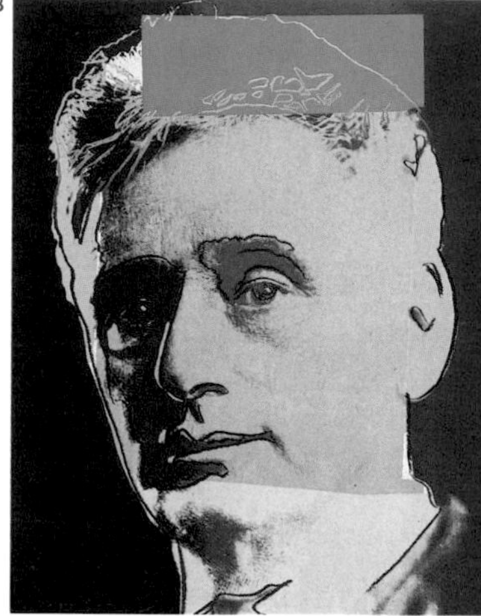

3 Louis Dembitz Brandeis (1856-1941), portrait by Andy Warhol. Brandeis the lawyer saw himself as the defender of the "little man" before gargantuan companies and property owners; he was known to the American public as the "peoples' attorney." In 1916 he was appointed to the US Supreme Court, the first Jew to hold this high office. He was also an active Zionist. During World War I he was made Chairman of the Provisional Committee for General Zionist Affairs. In 1918 he was made Honorary Chairman of the Zionist Organization of America. At the London Conference (1920), where he was chosen Honorary President of the Zionist Federation, he and Chaim Weizmann differed with respect to the path the Zionist movement should follow. Brandeis resigned, but continued to support Zionist aspirations.

4 The "Blue Box" in which donations were collected for the Jewish National Fund. Established by the Zionist Congress in 1901, the fund has been active ever since in purchasing and developing land in Israel.

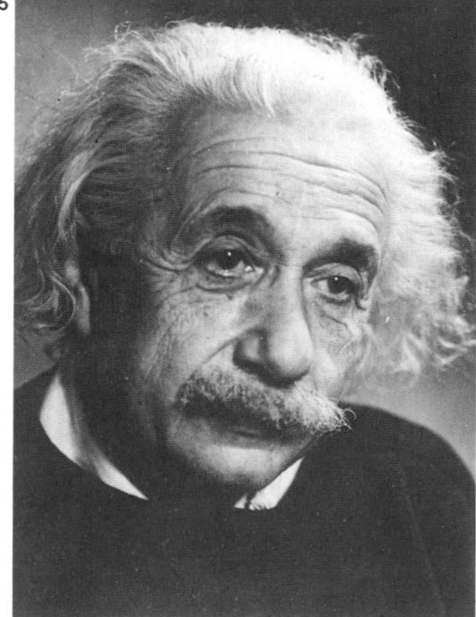

5 Albert Einstein (1879-1955), father of the Theory of Relativity that changed essential concepts of time and space. When Hitler rose to power Einstein left Germany for the United States. Einstein believed that it was his membership in the Jewish nation that evoked his urge to engage in research for its own sake, his fanatic love of justice and his striving for personal independence. He helped the Zionist movement, particularly the Hebrew University.

community in the free world, and in 1942 most US Jews united behind Zionist demands that Palestine be opened to Jewish immigration and become an independent Jewish entity (the Biltmore Program). Jewish leaders enlisted congressional support to counter State Department opposition, and in 1943 a congressional committee adopted a favorable resolution.

US Zionists directed the Jewish masses in four spheres of activity: politically, to influence the government to support the establishment of a Jewish state; in fund-raising, mainly through the United Jewish Appeal (UJA) [Key]; by recruiting volunteers (*Machal*) to help Israel during its War of Independence; and in identifying with Israel through publicity, mass meetings and other public manifestations of support [8]. The Jewish lobby, founded in 1954, has intensified activities. American Jewish leaders have convincingly argued that Israel's needs coincide with overall American interests.

During the Six-Day War Jews normally far from Zionism rallied to the cause of Israel. Since then, a mutual dependency between American and Israeli Jewry has become increasingly apparent: for many of the former, Israel is the criterion by which they — and possibly the general public — measure Jewish status and merit. There is also a growing conviction among the Jews of America that they have both the right and the obligation to take stands with respect to what happens in Israel. At the same time, Israel's Jews have learned that in times of crisis they can depend upon their fellow Jews abroad. During the Yom Kippur War the sense of partnership was reinforced when American Jews volunteered in unprecedented numbers. Since that war America's Jews and the Jewish lobby have mobilized behind the demand that the American government increase economic aid to Israel. In the early 1980s Israel received over 2 billion dollars annually from the United States.

KEY

we are all in the same boat

GIVE NOW TO THE JOINT ISRAEL APPEAL

The UJA is US Jewry's central fundraising organization. It supports both overseas Jewry and local needy Jews. In most communities the "Federation" conducts the campaign. Many American Jews consider successful fundraising to be evidence of their voluntary participation in determining the quality of Jewish life. In a few communities, 80% of the Jews contribute to the Federation. In New York some 25% of the Jewish public contributes; during emergencies peak sums have been collected — 240 million dollars during the Six-Day War (1967), and 260 million during the Yom Kippur War (1973).

6 Leonard Bernstein, pianist, conductor and composer, appearing before soldiers of the Negev Brigade during the Israel War of Independence (1948). Artists and public figures who came to Israel at this time reflected American Jewry's profound identification with the fate of the new-born state. American Jewish artists have continued to visit Israel, particularly at times of crisis, to express their support. The America-Israel Cultural Foundation supports young Israeli artists.

7 Edward Koch (born 1926), elected Mayor of New York in 1977, at the head of a pro-Israel parade. Koch succeeded Abraham David Beame (born 1906), also a Jew. The Jewish vote is particularly significant in greater New York, where there were some 2 million Jews in 1980. Despite the mobility that has characterized the young generation since the 1970s, some 36% of all American Jews still live in New York and its environs. Most Jewish organizations and institutions are located in New York.

8 Demonstrations in support of a Jewish state: a march by 1,000 rabbis in 1945 [A] and a protest against British policy and the expulsion of the "Exodus" passengers from the shores of Palestine in 1947 [B]. In its efforts to pressure the US government, the Zionist Emergency Council, founded in 1943 and headed by Abba Hillel Silver (1893-1963), mobilized political support. Pro-Zionist Christians also took part. Silver, a Reform rabbi, worked to convince members of the government and Congress, as well as United Nations delegates, to support Zionism. President Franklin D. Roosevelt (1882-1945), who took no initiative to rescue Holocaust survivors, felt obliged during the 1944 presidential race to make pro-Zionist declarations in order to win the Jewish vote. His successor, Harry Truman (1884-1972), decided in favor of the UN Partition Plan — against the wishes of the State Department — and worked to include the Negev within Israel. He was the first head of state to recognize Israel.

9 Supporting the State of Israel [photo: parade in honor of Israel's 35th anniversary] and Soviet Jewry's struggle are central aspects of American Jewry's public activities. The campaign to help the Russian Jews has the widespread support of the non-Jewish public as well. In 1973 the US Senate made the award of "most favored-nation status" to the USSR conditional upon its permitting emigration.

Establishing the State of Israel

When World War II ended, conditions became ripe for international recognition of the Jewish people's right to an independent state in Palestine. Several factors brought about this situation: the tens of thousands of displaced Jews in Europe desiring to immigrate to Palestine; the British government's stubborn insistence on immigration restrictions; world public opinion, particularly in the USA, that acknowledged a moral obligation to the survivors of the Holocaust; and the Soviet Union's desire to hasten what it perceived as the disintegration of colonial empires.

The Survivors

By the end of the war ten million refugees wended their way back to what was left of their homes. Displaced Jews, however, had no homes to return to. For the vast majority, families had perished, communities been destroyed and former means of livelihood cut off. Moreover, anti-Semitism had not disappeared with the fall of the Nazis.

The survivors gradually came to realize that the only way open for them was Palestine. Jews thus began heading toward French and Italian Mediterranean ports, hoping to book illegal passage to Palestine. Representatives of the *Yishuv* helped organize this migration, as did Jewish soldiers serving in the Occupation Forces, especially members of the British Army's Jewish Brigade.

The 1945 general elections in Britain brought the Labour Party to power. Although it had been pro-Zionist while in opposition, Labour now decided to continue the previous government's White Paper policy. Britain despatched land and sea forces, no longer needed for the war effort in Europe, to Palestine and the Mediterranean in order to intercept Holocaust survivors.

The general public in the United States, Britain and other countries was outraged to hear news reports of British Navy searches for illegal immigrant ships. When seized, these ships would be towed to Haifa port where all illegal immigrants were removed to detention camps on Cyprus. In November of 1945, British Foreign Minister Ernest Bevin [5] initiated the joint Anglo-American Committee of Inquiry to look into the question of Jewish immigration to Palestine. After visiting Palestine [2] and the various displaced persons camps in Europe [1], the Committee submitted ten recommendations, the second of which was that 100,000 certificates be authorized immediately for the admission into Palestine of Jews who had been the victims of Nazi and Fascist persecution; and that actual immigration be pushed forward as rapidly as possible. Bevin ignored these recommendations, but this only led to an even more vehement demand by world Jewry for the establishment of a Jewish state in Palestine.

The UN Resolution

The British government then decided to bring the question of Palestine before the United Nations. A special General

CONNECTIONS

164 The Holocaust
166 Rescue Operations During the Holocaust
174 The National Institutions of the "State-in-the-Making"
176 The Yishuv Takes Up the Struggle
178 American Jewry's Political Activities
182 The Israeli War of Independence (A)

1

1 More than 100,000 Jewish Holocaust survivors were eventually gathered in displaced persons camps throughout the American-occupied zones of Germany and Austria. Aid to the survivors came from the Joint and the Jewish Agency. Inside the camps *aliyah* groups were set up, Hebrew was taught and secret cells of the *Haganah* and *IZL* were organized. The American authorities did not prevent the entry of additional Jews smuggled by the *Berihah* organization from Eastern Europe. Nor did they attempt to stop Jews from leaving the ports of Italy and France with the intention of immigrating illegally to Palestine. Pictured are displaced persons at the Bergen-Belsen camp (in March 1946) holding a demonstration during the visit of the Anglo-American Committee of Inquiry in which they appealed for permission to immigrate to Palestine.

2

2 Appearing before the Anglo-American Committee of Inquiry, the Arabs presented an uncompromising position which called for the relocation of displaced Jews outside of Palestine so that Palestine's Arab majority might be preserved and its status as an Arab country fixed. In contrast, Jewish representatives set forward a broad spectrum of views. These ranged from establishing a Jewish state to some sort of binational solution — the proposal of *Brit Shalom* ("Covenant of Peace"). Pictured testifying before the Committee are Prof. J.L. Magnes and the renowned philosopher Martin Buber [on left].

3

3 Acre Prison, the central prison in Mandatory Palestine, also housed gallows where condemned prisoners were executed. Among these were members of *Lehi* and *IZL*. On May 4, 1947, in collaboration with the prisoners themselves, an *IZL* unit daringly broke through the prison walls, enabling 29 *IZL* and *Lehi* members to escape. Britain's decision to hang three *IZL* members in 1947 caused *IZL* to retaliate by hanging two British sergeants. The incident marked a new stage of escalation in the conflict.

4

4 It was Andrei Gromyko [on left, with M. Sharett] who forcefully articulated the sudden about-face in the Soviet Union's position. After having long opposed Zionism, the Soviets now expressed their support. In his speech to the UN General Assembly on May 14, 1947, Gromyko stated: "The fact that not a single Western European country was able to guarantee the protection of even the most elementary rights of the Jewish people, or to save them from their Fascist executioners, explains Jewish aspirations...."

5

5 Ernest Bevin (1884-1951), foreign minister in the Labour government from 1945 until 1951, was responsible for British policy in Palestine. He criticized the American Jewish community for pressuring the US administration to support Zionism, and cynically suggested that the American government supported immigration to Palestine in order to keep Jews from entering the US. However, Britain's critical dependency on American aid after the world war forced Bevin to show consideration for American opinion.

Assembly session held in New York on April 28th appointed the UN Special Committee on Palestine (UNSCOP, 1947) to prepare a report. It was during its visit to Palestine that UNSCOP witnessed three key episodes in the *Yishuv's* struggle: the execution by hanging of three members of *IZL* who had been caught when an *IZL* force broke into Acre Prison [3]; the reprisal hanging of two British sergeants whom the *IZL* had taken hostage when their captured fellow underground members were given death sentences; and the episode of *Exodus 1947* [Key].

In August 1947 UNSCOP recommended the termination of the Mandate and the partitioning of Palestine into a Jewish state and an Arab state, with an international regime for Jerusalem. But Palestinian Arabs and the governments of all the Arab countries declared that they would forcibly oppose any implementation of these recommendations.

When the General Assembly next convened in September 1947, the two-thirds majority required to approve the Commission's recommendations had not yet been mustered. The ten Arab and Muslim member states needed only to win nine other countries to their side in order to defeat the resolution. Representatives of the *Yishuv* therefore put most of their efforts into rallying support from Latin American countries. They were aided in this endeavor by the staunchly sympathetic position taken by two influential people: Jorge Garcia Granados of Guatemala, a member of UNSCOP, and the Chairman of the UN General Assembly, Osvaldo Aranha of Brazil.

The vote was finally held on November 29, 1947. With a majority of 33 in favor, 13 against, 10 abstaining and 1 absent, the Committee's recommendation to partition Palestine was adopted [8]. The next day the Arab High Committee of Palestine declared a general strike and a Jewish bus was attacked on its way to Jerusalem. The War of Independence had begun.

KEY

The ship "Exodus 1947" set sail from France on July 11, 1947, with 4,500 illegal immigrants on board. On July 18 British destroyers commandeered the ship to Haifa after a brief battle inside Palestinian territorial waters in which three immigrants were killed. From Haifa the immigrants were transferred by prison ship back to Europe. Refusing to disembark on the French coast, they were transported to Hamburg and returned to the displaced persons camps in Germany. The *Exodus* affair, widely publicized throughout the world, underscored Jewish aspirations to immigrate to Palestine.

6

For
Australia
Belgium
Bolivia
Brazil
Byelorussian SSR
Canada
Costa Rica
Czechoslovakia
Denmark
Dominican Republic
Ecuador
France
Guatemala
Haiti
Iceland
Liberia
Luxemburg
Netherlands
New Zealand
Nicaragua
Norway
Panama
Paraguay
Peru
Philippines
Poland
Sweden
Ukrainian SSR
Union of South Africa
USA
USSR
Uruguay
Venezuela

Against
Afghanistan
Cuba
Egypt
Greece
India
Iran
Iraq
Lebanon
Pakistan
Saudi Arabia
Syria
Turkey
Yemen

Abstain
Argentina
Chile
China
Colombia
El Salvador
Ethiopia
Honduras
Mexico
United Kingdom
Yugoslavia

Absent
Siam

6 The UN General Assembly decision on partition of Palestine: 33 voted for partition, 13 against, 10 abstained and one was absent.

9 After the results of the UN vote were broadcast on the night of November 29, 1947, jubilant crowds poured into the streets of all the Jewish cities in Palestine. Yet David Ben-Gurion wrote in his diary: "Only frivolous enthusiasm could lead one to believe that by the UN vote the problem has been solved and the Jewish state established.... Everything depends on being able to successfully raise a properly trained and equipped armed force which can withstand the onslaught of the troops that will no doubt be sent by the Arab rulers."

7

7 US President Harry S. Truman (1884-1972) instructed his country's UN delegate to vote in favor of the Partition Plan in spite of opposition from the US State Department. Earlier, Truman had supported measures to permit the *aliyah* of Holocaust survivors. Here, he is seen with Abba Eban and David Ben-Gurion.

8 According to the Partition Plan for Palestine, a Jewish state, an Arab state and an international zone would constitute a single economic entity. Most of the Jewish-owned land and settlements were part of the proposed Jewish state. The Jewish state was also supposed to encompass the Arab inhabitants of Haifa, Safed and other towns, while Jaffa was to remain an Arab enclave within it. The international legal status of the Arab state in Palestine became doubtful the moment the Arabs rejected the Partition Plan. Lands designated for this state were conquered by Jordan and Egypt in 1948.

9

8

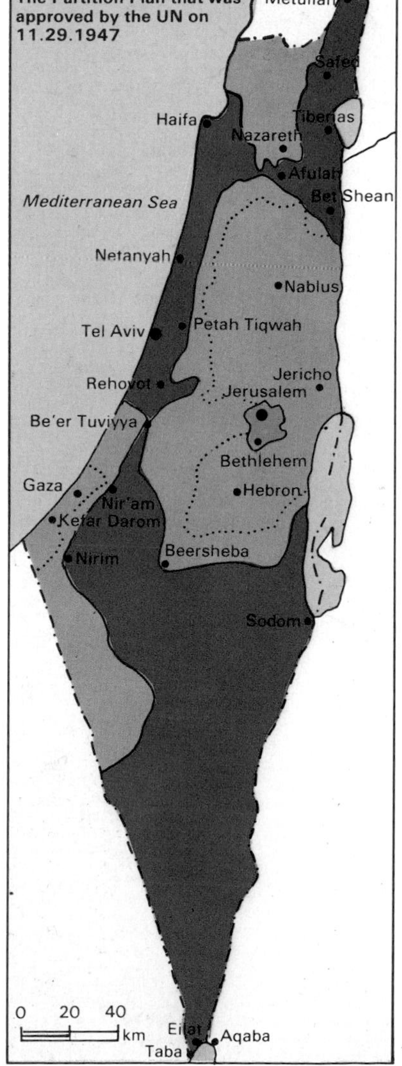

international zone
proposed Arab state
proposed Jewish state
international border
armistice line 1949

The Israeli War of Independence (A)

On November 30, 1947, the Palestinian Arabs launched their attack on the Jews. For the first part of the war, until the British Mandate ended on May 15, 1948, the *Yishuv* withstood the attack of local Arab irregulars. The end of the Mandate then led to the invasion of Israel by the combined armies of the neighboring Arab states; this phase lasted until Israel and the Arab states signed armistice agreements.

Arabs, Jews and British

Three fighting forces took part in the war's first phase: the Arabs, the Jews and the British. The approximately one million Palestinian Arabs constituted the majority of the local population, but they had no central military organization. Instead Arab military leadership was localized; its tactics consisted largely of inciting mobs of villagers, armed with rifles and light machineguns, to attack a Jewish settlement or convoy.

Among the 600,000 Jews of Palestine, the *Haganah, IZL* and *Lehi* together comprised some 60,000 fighting men and women. When the war began, they were joined by an additional 27,000 Palestinian Jews who had been serving in the British army, by 20,000 Holocaust survivors organized and trained in the *Gahal* (Overseas Enlistment) Program even before they arrived in Palestine, and by 3,000 Jews who had served with the US, South African and British forces during World War II and who volunteered their services to Israel through the *Mahal* (Volunteers from Abroad) Program. At first, the only arms available to the *Yishuv* were light weapons — barely enough to equip one quarter of the combat personnel [6].

In the first phase of the war, however, it was the British whose substantial influence was most felt. They had a sizable fighting force deployed in key positions, and large quantities of tanks, armored cars, planes and artillery. Great Britain, declaring that it would not cooperate in the implementation of the UN resolution, considered itself responsible only for the preservation of law and order until the Mandate ended. In theory, the British adopted a neutral position, but in their day-to-day operations they were aiding the Arab side.

The Arabs concentrated their attacks on mixed population cities [1, 2], on isolated communities and on the roads. Protecting the free movement of vehicles on roads that passed through Arab villages or through rural areas under Arab control was the most pressing task for the *Yishuv* [3, 4].

During the first months of the war, the Jewish defenders succeeded in repulsing Arab attempts to overrun Jewish settlements and neighborhoods. But once reinforcements started arriving from the neighboring Arab countries, the Arab war effort concentrated on attacking vehicular traffic, particularly on the all-important road from the coastal strip to Jerusalem. By the end of March 1948, the Arabs were on the verge of a decisive strategic achievement: they had practically cut off all

1

2 A

2 B

סכנה!
האויב רואה אותך
אם תתקדם-תירה

2 The boundary lines between Jewish and Arab neighborhoods in cities with mixed populations soon became battle lines. In Jerusalem an Arab mob tried to force its way into a Jewish neighborhood on the first day of the War of Independence, but was repulsed by the *Haganah*. From Jaffa, Arab snipers shot into the southern neighborhoods of Tel Aviv [A; B — a sign warns of snipers]. This struggle for urban positions continued until the Jews took over Jaffa and the Arab quarters of Tiberias, Haifa and Safed about two weeks before the invasion by the standing armies of the Arab countries. The battle lines that divided Jerusalem remained until the Six-Day War.

1 Jerusalem was a weak link in the Jewish defense. Surrounded by Arab towns and villages, Jerusalem's Jewish neighborhoods were interspersed with Arab sectors and British security zones. In a series of assault operations in the spring of 1948, a combined *Haganah-Palmach* and *IZL* force captured a number of Arab neighborhoods and created one continuous Jewish population area in the western half of the city. The Jewish Quarter in the Old City, however, was cut off; it was overrun by the Arabs just before the State of Israel was declared. Pictured is the Jewish outpost on Mount Scopus in East Jerusalem, which remained an Israeli enclave within Jordanian territory until the Six-Day War.

3

3 The Arabs enjoyed a series of victories in the battles for control of the roads. In March 1948, their successful blockade of the road to Jerusalem put the city under siege. Gush Etzion, a group of settlements south of Jerusalem, Atarot and Neve Ya'akov to the north of the city, as well as Bet ha-Arava and the potash plant at the Dead Sea east of the city were all cut off. Jewish settlements in the southwestern part of the country and in the Negev were isolated from the central areas; the roads to western Galilee were also blocked off. All over the country, settlements were in a virtual state of siege: Manara, Yehi'am, Ben Shemen, Hartuv, Gat, Gal'on, Bet Eshel and others. This desperate situation forced the *Haganah* to launch several assault operations to capture entire sectors of the country and create territorial continuity between Jewish population centers.

4 Jerusalem's Jews depended for their very survival on supplies coming in from the coastal plain. Prior to May 15, 1948, the armed convoy escorts were forced to hide their weapons from the British, who often stopped the trucks and confiscated whatever defensive firearms they found. When the War of Independence began, only a few trucks had armor-plated driver's cabs; thus the armed escorts were vulnerable to gunfire. As the "War for the Roads" progressed, however, special armored buses ("sandwich" buses) were built and covered with thin sheets of steel separated by a wooden board. Eventually, occupation of the key Latrun outpost by the Transjordanian Arab Legion forced the IDF to build a detour road to Jerusalem.

4

areas under Jewish control from one another, just as invasion by the neighboring Arab armies loomed on the horizon and the British maritime blockade prevented entry of men and equipment to aid the Jewish fighters.

The turning point came with the *Haganah*'s Operation Nachshon (April 3-15, 1948), which wrested control of key points along the Jerusalem road from the Arabs. Nachshon's greatest feat was to prove that the Jews could field a military force of no small consequence. It was in Operation Nachshon, too, that weapons from Czechoslovakia were first used. For the first time as well, the Arabs fielded a strong military force that included volunteers from Arab countries. This was the army under the command of Fawzi al-Kaukji; the failure of its attacks on Tirat Zvi and Mishmar ha-Emeq helped break the Arabs' fighting spirit.

The State Takes Form

Meanwhile, as the British mandatory authorities became increasingly concerned with protecting the evacuation of their military forces and administrative staff, the *Haganah* carried out Plan D, which created territorial continuity under Jewish control, in anticipation of a fullfledged Arab invasion [5].

As the Mandate drew to a close, it was necessary to prepare the groundwork for the governmental institutions of the future Jewish state. In April, the National Council was established; its 37 members included the executive committees of the Elected Assembly and the Jewish Agency, as well as representatives of other Jewish organizations. The National Council then selected 13 of its members to form the National Executive. Together, they quickly established government services of justice, police, post, taxes, sanitation and welfare. The National Council and National Executive also approved the final draft of the Declaration of Independence, which was prepared by Ben-Gurion, as well as the name of the new state — Israel.

KEY

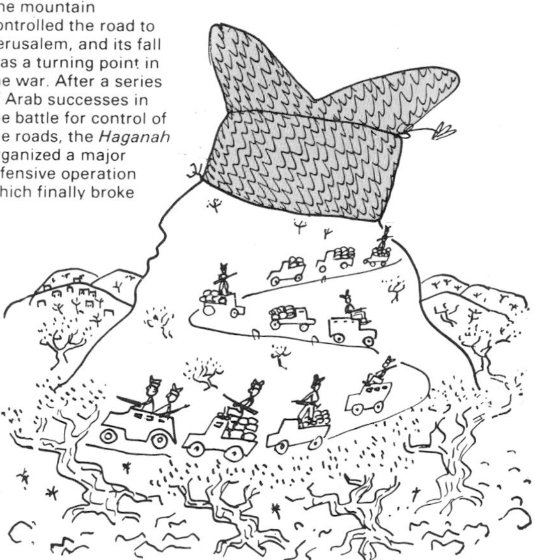

Mount Kastel was captured by the Jews early on April 3, 1948. The mountain controlled the road to Jerusalem, and its fall was a turning point in the war. After a series of Arab successes in the battle for control of the roads, the *Haganah* organized a major offensive operation which finally broke through the siege of Jerusalem. This cartoon sketch of the capture of the Kastel was drawn by Aryeh Navon.

5 Plan D created territorial continuity between Jewish population points. *Haganah* forces captured the Arab neighborhoods of Tiberias, Haifa and Safed. Jaffa, surrounded by the *Haganah*, surrendered after *IZL* launched an offensive. The Arab inhabitants of Bet Shean fled the town. Arab villages in the Sharon area were also abandoned and then occupied by the Jews just before the declaration of the State of Israel. But even when Plan D was completed, Jerusalem remained cut off. South of the city, Gush Etzion, also isolated, fell on May 13th. On May 17th Jewish forces captured Acre, thus ensuring a territorial link with the western Galilee.

5

Jewish settlement ●
Arab settlement ○
Isolated Jewish settlement ▲
Jewish Settlement captured or evacuated before May 15, 1948 △
Area under Israeli control on May 15, 1948
0 10 20 km

6

6 Haganah arms stores when the War of Independence began were meager indeed. Rifles, submachine guns, machine guns and mortars were either purchased or stolen from Arabs and British soldiers. Underground factories produced Sten submachine guns and mortars and their respective ammunition, as well as hand grenades and explosives. These *Haganah* members are training with a French light machinegun and a British rifle.

7

7 Fort 28 in the upper eastern Galilee was named for the 28 men who fell in the battle for its capture. In April 1948, the British evacuated this police fort and handed it over to the Arab forces. The fort commanded the only road that linked Rosh Pinnah to Metullah, a road that ran the length of the narrow strip between the Hula swamps and the Naftali Mountains. Its capture by Jewish forces was therefore deemed essential.

8

אל תושבי טבריה!

התושבים הערבים עזבו את העיר.
טבריה עברה כלה לידינו.

הנני מכריז על
משטר עברי עצמאי בעיר.

וזאת הודעתי הראשונה לתושבים:

א. הקימותי משמרה צבאית עברית. מתפקידה לשמור ולקיים את הסדר בעיר. על התושבים להשמע להוראותיה בקפדנות.
ב. הנני אוסר אסור מוחלט כל פגיעה שהיא ברכוש ממשלתי לשעבר, רכוש ערבי או כל רכוש אחר.
ג. על התושבים לשמור ולכבד את המקומות הקדושים של המוסלמים, הנוצרים ועדות אחרות בעיר.
ד. כל אדם שיפר את ההוראות הנ"ל יענש בכל חומר הדין.

מפקד ההגנה בטבריה.

8 This announcement to the residents of Tiberias of the establishment of an "independent Hebrew government in the town," was posted by the local *Haganah* command on April 19, 1948, two days after the Arab residents of the city had fled with British aid. As the date of the anticipated Arab invasion drew closer, there was a greater tendency for the Palestinian Arabs to flee the areas captured by Jews, since they anticipated a swift Arab victory.

The Israeli War of Independence (B)

On Friday afternoon, May 14, 1948, in the Tel Aviv Museum, David Ben-Gurion declared the establishment of the State of Israel [3]. The following day, May 15, the US granted Israel *de facto* recognition. Two days later, the USSR announced *de jure* recognition of the new state.

Repelling the Invasion

The Israeli forces, who until now had operated only in the underground, faced well-trained and equipped Arab troops. The Arab forces attacked immediately, and were only prevented from overrunning the country by the exemplary courage and devotion demonstrated by the Jewish defenders [2].

After ten days of fighting, the initial thrust of the invasion had been checked and the Arabs' objectives were clear. The newly-created (May 26) Israel Defense Forces (IDF) launched five major brigade-sized counterattacks: three against the Transjordanian Arab Legion in the Latrun area — aimed at opening the road to Jerusalem; one against the Iraqi army at Jenin; and one against Egyptian troops near Ashdod. Although the campaigns at Latrun and Jenin failed, they placed the Arab forces under unexpected pressure — one of the factors that led them to accede to the UN's call for a 28-day truce to begin on June 11.

Israel used the truce to refresh, equip and organize its troops. The IDF added three brigades to its existing nine. Four front commands were set up and arms and ammunition were acquired and distributed to frontline units.

As soon as the truce elapsed, fighting resumed and continued for ten days (July 9-18), during which the IDF scored major victories in the north and center of the country, and held its ground around Jerusalem and in the south. The Arab towns of Lydda, Ramlah and Nazareth were taken. A second truce, imposed on the sides by a UN Security Council resolution, took effect on July 18.

On May 21, the Security Council had appointed a Swede, Count Folke Bernadotte (1895-1948) as mediator. He began his mission by overseeing the first truce, aided by a team of observers. On July 28 he presented his proposals for a settlement to the governments of Israel and the Arab states: the Negev would be ceded to the Arabs; the Galilee would go to the Jews; Lydda and Ramlah would be returned to the Arabs; Jerusalem would be an international zone; both sides would have free access to the port at Haifa and airport at Lydda. Israel rejected these proposals and called for direct negotiations. The Arabs refused. On September 17, Bernadotte was assassinated in Jerusalem by Jews, former members of the underground organization *Lehi*. His proposals were now seen as a sort of political testament, and Israel's claim to the Negev was in jeopardy.

Decisive Battles

In Operation Yoav in October 1948,

CONNECTIONS

182 The Israeli War of Independence (A)
186 Building the New State

1 The central bus station of Tel Aviv was bombed by Egyptian aircraft, as the Arabs sent their air forces and navies into battle against Israel. The Egyptian Air Force bombed Tel Aviv several times and, together with the Syrian Air Force, supported Arab land forces in their offensives. Israeli aircraft bombed the invading troops, as well as Cairo, Damascus and Amman, and maintained contact with beleaguered settlements, including Jerusalem. The Egyptian Navy approached Tel Aviv before being routed by Israeli planes.

2 Arab forces invaded Israel the day after the State was declared. Some 30,000 soldiers of the armies of Egypt, Transjordan — most of whose troops were already in Palestine — Syria and Lebanon, were joined by additional forces from Iraq and Saudi Arabia and 10,000 Palestinian Arabs. Transjordan's army was halted near Jerusalem and Latrun; the Egyptians captured several settlements along the coast and were checked 32 kms from Tel Aviv; the Syrians were held off in the Jordan Valley and near Rosh Pinah; and the Lebanese at Malkia. This Syrian tank was halted at the entrance to Degania.

3 David Ben Gurion declared the establishment of the State of Israel on May 14, 1948, a decision taken by the National Executive despite the relative weakness of the Jewish forces and the certainty that the Arabs would attack as soon as the British Mandate terminated. The Declaration of Independence was signed by representatives of the Jewish community and the Zionist movement.

4 Shualei Shimshon (Samson's Foxes) fought in the south, first with machine guns mounted on jeeps and then with "Bren carriers" [shown here]. Initially, the IDF attacked with small mobile units; it hoped to throw the invading forces into disarray and compel them to halt and assume defensive positions. With no armor or artillery, the IDF relied on the courage and devotion of its soldiers and officers, who were undeterred despite heavy casualties. In effect, it was its weakness that forced the IDF to assume the offensive.

הוראות לשמוש יעיל במנות מים

5 Food and water were rationed in Jerusalem when some 100,000 Jewish residents were cut off from the coastal plain. Instructions for recycling of water [pictured] were issued to the public. Jerusalem was a major front in the War of Independence, as both sides held that the outcome of the entire war would be decided in the battle for the city. Ultimately, Israel was able to hold on to all Jewish neighborhoods except for the Jewish Quarter of the Old City. The extended siege by the Arab legion was broken only with the greatest of efforts.

the IDF opened the road to the Negev and captured Beersheba. In the western sector the Egyptians retreated nearly to Gaza and the Israeli forces gained control of Isdud (Ashdod) and Majdal (Ashkelon) and retook Nitzanim and Yad Mordechai from the Egyptians. The Israel navy attacked Egyptain vessels off Ashkelon and sank the flagship of the Egyptian fleet off the coast of Gaza.

Operation Hiram, launched in the last three days of October, brought all of the Galilee and a number of Lebanese villages in the region of Malkia-Manara under IDF control. In late November and early December, in several localized campaigns, the IDF expanded its hold on the South and opened the road to Sodom. Operation Horev, the largest offensive launched against the Egyptian forces, was mounted in December. The IDF broke through to Sinai and in a deep pincer movement cut off the Egyptian army and reached the outskirts of El-Arish and Rafah.

On January 7, a ceasefire was imposed under pressure from Britain and the US. Egypt agreed to begin negotiations to end the war. On February 24, 1949, representatives of Israel and Egypt signed an armistice agreement in Rhodes under UN auspices. The armistice was intended to settle outstanding military questions and pave the way for peace negotiations [6]. It promised each party the right to security and freedom from fear of attack. It forbade the use of military force, and both sides undertook to refrain from the use, plan, or threat of offensive action. It also stated that each country would prevent irregulars from leaving its territory in order to strike at the other. UN observers were to oversee implementation of the armistice, and the chief of the observers was to serve as head of the Armistice Commission. This document served as a model for armistice agreements with Israel's three other neighbors: Lebanon (on March 23, 1949), Transjordan (April 3), and Syria (July 20).

KEY

The "Inked Flag" was painted spontaneously and raised in Eilat at the end of Operation Uvda. It symbolized Israeli control of the entire Negev as well as the war's end. During the war some 6,000 Israeli soldiers and civilians were killed — one percent of all Jews in the country — and tens of thousands were wounded. The economy and administration suffered severely. Yet, as a result of the war, Israel's territory now extended from Metullah to Eilat. The armistice agreements afforded a certain degree of security, enabling the country to set to work to realize the Zionist vision — the ingathering of the exiles and establishment of a sovereign Jewish state in Erez Israel.

6

7

7 The Burma Road to Jerusalem, a makeshift route opened two days before the first truce took effect, was built in order to bypass the Arab Legion stronghold at Latrun. As a result, the siege of Jerusalem was broken. The Arab Legion's occupation of the eastern part of Jerusalem and the West Bank, like Egypt's capture of the Gaza Strip, denied the Palestinian Arabs self-determination in their part of Palestine.

8

6 Armistice agreements with Egypt, Transjordan, Lebanon and Syria brought the war to an end. Israel held all of the territory allocated to the Jewish State by the UN, as well as the Western Galilee, the Jewish sector of Jerusalem, and the Jerusalem corridor. Demilitarized zones were established along the borders.

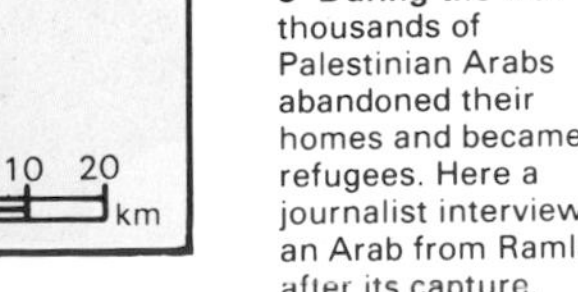

9 During the war thousands of Palestinian Arabs abandoned their homes and became refugees. Here a journalist interviews an Arab from Ramlah after its capture.

9

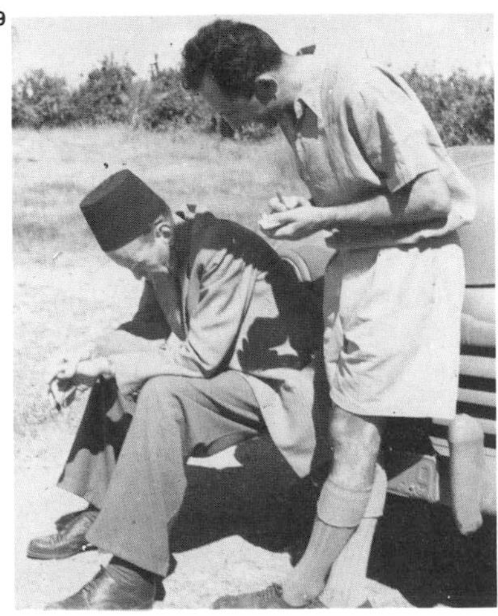

8 "Altalena", a landing craft carrying arms for the underground organization *IZL*, reached Israel on June 19, 1948, during the first truce. *IZL* had joined the IDF on June 1, but its soldiers fought in separate units for which it demanded these arms. The government claimed the weapons for itself and ordered the IDF to prevent their unloading. On the shore by Kefar Vitkin bloody fighting broke out between *IZL* and the IDF. The *Altalena* then sailed to Tel Aviv, where the battle continued until the ship was hit by a shell and went up in flames.

Building the New State

The establishment of the State of Israel represented a major turning point for the Jewish people: for the first time since losing their independence 1900 years before, Jews could now return to their homeland and live there as a free nation. The young country was faced with newfound possibilities and challenges [Key].

Mass Immigration

The first challenge was immigration. Thousands now flocked to Israel, some motivated by their distressed state as Jews, others urged on by a messianic vision. In just three years, from 1948 to 1951, 700,000 immigrants reached Israel — a number greater than the entire Jewish population when the State was declared [4].

Holocaust survivors arrived from German displaced-persons camps and British detention camps on Cyprus. Others came from Eastern Europe, particularly Poland and Rumania. Yemenite Jews were flown in by the *Magic Carpet* operation. Iraq allowed its Jews to leave. Almost all the Jews of Bulgaria arrived, having escaped the Nazi grasp. Many came from North Africa — Morocco, Algeria, Tunisia and Libya — and from Turkey and Afghanistan.

Israel welcomed every Jew, even those who were destitute, and with the aid of the Jewish Agency provided them with initial housing and basic necessities. They were housed in abandoned British army camps, in huts and in tents; some 150,000 in towns, quarters and villages abandoned by the Arabs during the war; and about 250,000 in specially built transit camps [2].

The immigrants' mass arrival and their dispersion into makeshift homes created widespread unemployment [1]. The war's ravages and the absorption of hundreds of thousands of people caused shortages of food and other items. In 1949, the Office of Supply and Rationing was established to assure the supply and equal distribution of basic commodities [8]. This system of rationing and control caused the government to play a major role in the economy. Additional factors influencing centralized control were the State's ownership of most of the land and sources of water, and the *Histadrut*. The latter played a major role in the government, and controlled most production and marketing of agricultural produce, a large part of construction and industry, public transportation, and medical services and facilities. The government controlled foreign currency transactions, set the import and agriculture quotas, imported essential goods, and decided on industrial priorities. Extensive government intervention in an economy in which both private and public sectors operate side by side is characteristic of the Israeli economy to this day.

After the War of Independence there was much land to be settled, and thousands of new immigrants required productive work. One result was a boom in settlement-building: 284 new settlements were established in the first five

CONNECTIONS

126 The Wandering Jew
136 Yemenite Jews and Erez Israel
166 Rescue Operations During the Holocaust
170 Zionism and Aliyah from Muslim Countries
174 The National Institutions of the "State-in-the-Making"
176 The Yishuv Takes up the Struggle
188 Israel's First Decade

1

1 Relief or "make-work" served as a temporary stopgap to immigrant unemployment. The primary aim of these jobs was to ensure the immigrant some sort of respectable work and wage so that he would not have to live on welfare. The transition to physical labor was often traumatic for *olim*. Most were employed in afforestation, land reclamation, and road works. Here immigrants work on an afforestation project in the Jerusalem corridor.

2

2 Some 100 transit camps, their small buildings first constructed from canvas and later from corrugated metal, were set up near urban centers throughout the country to house tens of thousands of new immigrants. In 1952 these camps housed approximately 250,000 immigrants. The last camps were dismantled only in the 1960s, and most immigrants spent 2-3 years at least in a camp before moving to permanent housing. This is the Farod (Fardia) camp.

4

4 About half of the new immigrants to Israel came from Islamic countries [these are from Kurdistan]. In bringing together Jews from all over the world within a society with a western cultural bias, traditional frameworks were sometimes unwittingly destroyed and eastern culture presented as inferior.

3 A

3 B

3 The Hula Lake, before it was drained, supplied fish to nearby settlements [B], but the mosquitoes infesting its swamps carried malaria. To eradicate this disease, and particularly to provide additional farmland and prevent Jordan River water from evaporating before it reached the Kinneret, the lake and swamp to its north were drained — a project begun in January, 1951 [A]. The Jordan outlet from the Hula was deepened and the Jordan River tributaries linked up to it by channels. A small portion of the lake was designated a nature preserve. This was the last of the swamp drainage projects that had begun in Hadera during the first *aliyah* and spread to the Jezreel and Zevulun valleys. Malaria, which had claimed the lives of many pioneers, was eliminated. Israel was now able to address the problem of transporting water from the north to the center and south in the National Water Carrier, a project which was completed in the early 1960s.

years of independence [5], compared with 227 throughout the 65 years before independence. In addition, towns and quarters abandoned by the Arabs were filled, and new quarters, and even new towns, established.

Forming a Government

On January 25, 1949, general elections for a Constituent Assembly were held [6]. The Assembly determined the parliamentary form of the Israeli government: the legislative body would be the *Knesset*; it would have 120 members and be chosen in direct general elections; the *Knesset* would confirm the cabinet or government and could dissolve it by a vote of no-confidence; the head of state would be the president, whose duties were largely ceremonial; the judiciary would be independent. To avoid an imminent second election, the Constituent Assembly invested itself as the first *Knesset*.

The first cabinet was confirmed on March 10, 1949. It was a coalition government of four of the ten parties represented in the *Knesset*, and enjoyed a majority of 71 members of *Knesset*. The coalition was formed by the social democratic Ereẓ Israel Workers Party (*Mapai*), the religious parties, and the moderate right. The extreme left and right remained in the opposition. This arrangement, with minor alterations, typified the Israeli political scene until 1977.

In order to avert dissension between the religious and non-religious public in Israel, the Constituent Assembly refrained from drafting a constitution, a policy later adopted by the *Knesset* as well. However the first *Knesset* did enact a number of Basic Laws that determine the nature of the daily life of the citizen, and the character of the country: the compulsory Military Service Act (September 1949); the Free Compulsory Education Act (September 1949); and the Law of Return, affording every Jew the right to settle in Israel and receive Israeli citizenship (July, 1950).

KEY

"If you will it, it is not a dream," Herzl's motto [here, in Hebrew on the wall] became a reality with the establishment of the State of Israel in 1948. Giving the vision actual form, however, entailed severe difficulties and hardship for those hundreds of thousands of *olim* who reached the country in its first years. Pictured: immigrants in the Beit Lid transit camp.

5

5 Many new Jewish immigrant settlements were founded in the early years of statehood. Immigrants from urban backgrounds now became farmers. Major water works were designed and constructed to expand the irrigated land and increase crop production. Small agricultural towns like Rehovot and Rishon le-Zion, Herzlia and Raanana, Kefar Sava and Hadera gradually became cities. Beersheba, too, grew into a large city. New quarters sprang up in Jerusalem, Haifa, Safed, Tiberias, Acre, Lydda and Ramlah. The towns in the Dan region around Tel Aviv expanded, and eventually merged. Here in a cartoon by Aryeh Navon, the Prophet Elijah has trouble finding his way around the rapidly growing young country on the eve of Passover, 1951.

6

6 Elections for the Constituent Assembly, which later became the first *Knesset*, were held even before the end of the War of Independence. All residents of Israel voted, including those groups not represented in the pre-state administration and those Arabs who had not left the country. The Constituent Assembly laid the foundations for democratic government in Israel. This picture shows a peddler against a backdrop of election posters.

7

7 Large-scale construction projects were undertaken to house new immigrants. Many of these were hastily erected in the urban centers [pictured: the new Beersheba, 1950]. Other housing solutions involved the occupation of abandoned Arab dwellings. All told, these measures often took a toll in building standards and the quality of tenants' lives, and by the 1970s extensive renovation and enlargement of dilapidated housing became necessary ("Project Renewal").

8 A

№ 239879

כרטיס ראש משפחה

8 B

8 The rationing of food and other items was accomplished by means of coupons [A] distributed to all Israeli citizens. No rationed commodity could be acquired without handing over the appropriate coupon. The government also set the prices of controlled products. Official inspectors searched travelers for produce smuggled from the countryside into the cities to prevent price gouging. Despite these measures, a black market developed, with smuggled goods sold at exorbitant prices. The government tried to mobilize public opinion against this [B — anti-black market poster].

Israel's First Decade

The waves of *olim* that streamed into Israel in its first years radically changed the world map of Jewish settlement [Key]. Most Jews were now concentrated in one of three main centers: Israel (about 20%), the Eastern Bloc countries, particularly the Soviet Union (about 20%), and the West, particularly the USA (some 56%). By the end of the decade, some 90% of the population of Israel was Jewish.

The map of Israel itself was drastically altered. New immigrants settled in abandoned Arab towns, in former Arab quarters of mixed cities, and in dozens of abandoned Arab villages. Numerous immigrant settlements, mostly *moshavim*, sprang up [2], along with a number of new *kibbutzim*. Many new settlements were founded along the border. Priority was given to settling the Jerusalem Corridor, and the entire area between Tel Aviv and Petah Tiqwah to the north and the Gaza Strip and Beersheba to the south was populated with new settlements.

Building a Modern Infrastructure

In order to expand regions capable of supporting agriculture, water had to be brought to potentially arable lands in the South. In July 1955, the Yarkon-Negev conduit was opened, channeling water to the South and the Negev from the Yarkon River sources at Rosh ha-Ayin. With cultivated and irrigated land thus extended [1], new settlements could be planned on a regional basis [6].

The industrial infrastructure was developed. The Dead Sea potash plant was expanded [5]. Oil was found [4], new roads were paved and the new Kishon port opened near Haifa. The electricity grid grew as power plants were built and additional lines laid.

The first decade also saw the growth of the Israeli Merchant Marine. The reparations paid by West Germany made it possible to purchase dozens of passenger and cargo ships. El Al Israel Airlines was founded, providing a secure air link to Europe and the US.

Unaided, the Israeli economy could not absorb the hundreds of thousands of *olim* and provide them with homes and jobs. Outside help came primarily from three sources: Jews outside Israel, West Germany, and the US.

The Diaspora, particularly American Jewry, sent aid to fellow Jews in Israel even before the State was declared. Along with the Jewish communities of South Africa, Argentina, England and France, they supplied most of the funds to organize illegal immigration and to acquire arms. By the late 1950s the UJA had collected some $520 million for Israel; through Israel Bonds another $360 million were raised, and immigrant capital and private donations contributed another $320 million.

West Germany agreed to compensate victims of the Holocaust personally, and to pay reparations to Israel as the representative of the Jewish people. Despite considerable public objection in Israel to the idea of dealing with the Germans, an agreement was signed on September 10, 1952 whereby West Ger-

CONNECTIONS

186 Building the New State
190 Defense in the First Decade
192 Economics and Society in Israel's Second Decade

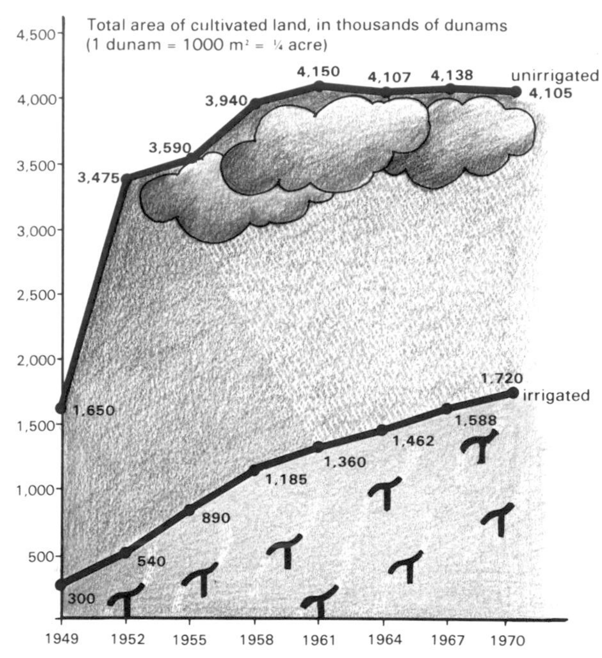

1 **Improved cultivation and irrigation techniques** doubled the total area of cultivated land between 1949 and 1952, with irrigated land tripling by 1955. The rate of growth slowed in later years, linked to the completion of new national water works. Recently, improved drip irrigation and greenhouse farming enhanced production while decreasing use of water.

2 **Moshavim** founded throughout the country became home for new immigrants and brought an end to the shortage of agricultural produce. The *moshav* was structured around cooperative marketing and purchasing arrangements, and family farming. It was hoped that this framework, which provided the opportunity for private enterprise together with the security of mutual aid — would ease the immigrants' adjustment to an alien way of life, since most had been craftsmen or tradesmen in the Diaspora. By spring 1952 the local crop of fruits and vegetables supplied the needs of the entire population. Here a Yemenite immigrant drives his tractor through Moshav Elyakim in the southern Carmel.

3 **Scientific research** is one of Israel's compensations for its lack of natural resources. The research institutes founded even before the establishment of the State (such as the Weizmann Institute of Science at Rehovot, shown here), were now expanded, and new ones opened.

4 **When oil was found at Heletz** in September 1955, hopes were high. Yet none of the many wells drilled in Israel since then has produced oil in any viable quantities, although they do supply natural gas.

5 **The building of the Beersheba-Sodom road** [shown here] and construction of the Dead Sea Works to extract potash and bromine from the Dead Sea, were two of the largest projects completed during Israel's first decade. The modern plant at Sodom, most of whose production was intended for export, made it possible to exploit Israel's largest natural resource — the Dead Sea — on a grand scale.

many undertook to pay Israel $829 million by 1965. The money was used to develop the infrastructure — water electricity, railroads, ships — and to purchase oil and industrial equipment.

In October 1951, Israel received the first of its annual foreign aid grants and loans from the US. By 1961, American loans reached $365 million, along with $159 million from the American Export-Import Bank.

"A Career or a Mission?"

Mass immigration and rapid development brought about changes in Israeli society. *Sephardi* Jews, who had constituted some 10% of the immigrants before 1948, accounted for 52% in the first decade of statehood. They encountered severe difficulties in assimilation and adjustment. As the transit camps were emptied and families moved to permanent housing, those left behind were largely *Sephardim*. The official establishment continued to reflect the largely *Ashkenazi* constellation in the country before independence, both politically and economically. Although this promoted stability and continuity, a socio-economic gap of an ethnic nature was slowly evolving and tension was building below the surface.

An Achilles' heel in Israel's massive development plans gradually became apparent: a widespread desire among the populace to enjoy their newfound peace and security — to look upon the establishment of the state as an end to the pioneering era. At a congress of youth in Tel Aviv in June 1954, Ben-Gurion presented the dilemma as the need for the new generation to choose between "a career or a mission." He appealed to Israeli youth to come to the aid of the immigrant settlements and to settle the arid and uninhabited Negev [9]. The response to this challenge was less than eager, and amply demonstrated that the effort required to realize the aims of the state would have to be equal to that invested in bringing about its establishment.

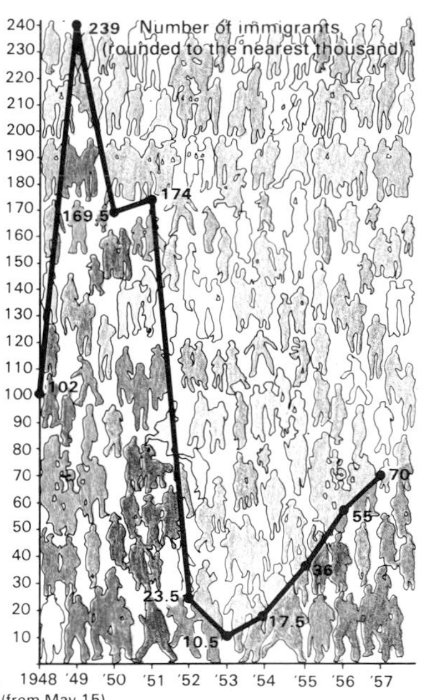

Between 1948 and 1957, some 900,000 immigrants reached Israel. About 700,000 arrived in the first wave of immigration (1948-1951), nearly half survivors of the Holocaust, and the rest from Iraq, Yemen and North African countries. More than any other factor, this mass immigration altered the face of Israel, establishing it as an undeniably Jewish country. However, by more than doubling its population in less than three years, Israel took on a burden of immigrant absorption that virtually ensured the eventual eruption of social strife. Particularly acute was the feeling of cultural alienation among the large body of *Sephardi olim* from Muslim countries.

6 A

6 B

6 Difficult early experience with the settling of untrained *olim* in agricultural villages caused Israeli planners to devise an improved settlement model that has been copied throughout the Third World. In the Ta'anach district in the southern Jezreel Valley, and in the Lachish district on the southeastern coastal plain, several settlements were established together in a regional network. The first Lachish settlements were founded in a region of barren hills in the mid-1950s [B] along with the opening of the Yarkon-Negev water conduit. Within six years, two rural centers surrounded by communal and cooperative *moshavim* were established in the district, whose urban center is Kiryat Gat. The centers housed educational and medical institutions, shops, supply depots, tractor service stations, agricultural services, and a community center [A].

7

7 Young writers and poets, known as the "1948" or *Palmach* Generation, recorded their impressions of the War of Independence in literature and drama. Their works display a variety of often conflicting viewpoints — from a depiction of heroism to severe criticism of unworthy aspects of the war or of the very fact of war itself. Y. Mossinsohn's play "On the Negev Plains," dramatizing the stand of Kibbutz Negba against the Egyptian army, was first staged in 1949 by *Habimah*.

8

8 Moshe Sharett (1894-1965), Israel's first foreign minister, was chosen prime minister after Ben-Gurion's retirement to Sede Boker. Before the declaration of the State he had served as head of the Political Department of the Jewish Agency, where he represented a more moderate line in the Zionist leadership than Ben-Gurion. He placed considerable stress on international public opinion and was especially concerned with Israel's standing in the UN. When Ben-Gurion resumed the post of prime minister, Sharett remained to serve as foreign minister until his resignation in 1956.

9

9 David Ben-Gurion shocked the nation in 1953 when he announced that he was retiring from politics to live and work on Kibbutz Sede Boker in the central Negev. In so doing he sought to encourage settlement of the Negev and the pioneering way of life. Even when he returned to politics (in February 1955, as minister of defense in Moshe Sharett's government, until he was again chosen prime minister in November 1955), Ben-Gurion continued to regard Sede Boker as his home. Today his grave and home at Sede Boker are national monuments.

Defense in the First Decade

The armistice agreements did not bring peace between Israel and its neighbors [Key]. Syria opposed Israel's attempts to widen the bed of the Jordan River and work lands in the demilitarized zones of the north, and took control of the area around El-Hama, along the Yarmuk River. Jordan refused to restore the water supply to Jerusalem via a pipeline which passed in part through its territory, and would not permit Jews access to the Western Wall. Shooting incidents erupted along the line dividing Jerusalem and along the border with Egypt. These and similar incidents were usually caused by conflicting interpretations of the armistice agreements.

Tens of thousands of Arab refugees had fled from their homes in the course of the War of Independence [3]. Most remained within the borders of Mandatory Palestine — 200,000 in the Gaza Strip, an equal number in the West Bank, and around 100,000 on the eastern bank of the Jordan. About 100,000 refugees left for Lebanon, and about 50,000 for Syria. Israel agreed to the return of 40,000 refugees cut off from their families, but would only discuss the overall fate of the refugees within the context of peace negotiations. The Arab states, who refused to enter peace negotiations, also refused to assimilate the refugees into their own lands, leaving them in camps built for them by the UN Relief and Works Agency. The governments of the "host" countries used the refugees as a weapon in their war against Israel.

With the end of hostilities, the refugees tried to infiltrate Israeli territory. Infiltration became worse after the Egyptians set up the *fedayeen* organization [2] in the Gaza Strip, with the aim of maintaining guerrilla warfare against Israel. Israel held the governments of Egypt and Jordan responsible for border violations, and to pressure them to fulfill their obligation initiated reprisal operations against Egyptian and Jordanian army bases and police stations [1].

Strengthening the IDF

At the end of the War of Independence, with budgetary priorities focusing on the economy, the IDF released tens of thousands of people. It was reformed as a small regular army, which at wartime could call up reserves and grow to a large force within a few hours. Thus a compulsory military service law was enacted, obliging every man and woman in Israel to serve in the armed forces for two or three years. Upon completion of his obligatory service a soldier was assigned to a reserve unit, which could be called up and equipped from emergency supply depots with great rapidity. The residents of border settlements were organized in regional defense units designed to absorb enemy attack while the IDF engaged in mobile warfare.

In the War of Independence and early 1950s the IDF comprised primarily infantry. Acquisition of tanks, APCs, artillery and aircraft was curbed due to a western arms embargo on Israel, while the Eastern Bloc refused to supply arms

CONNECTIONS

184 The Israeli War of Independence (B)

194 From the Sinai Campaign to the Six-Day War

1 **Reprisals** were the Israeli reaction to terrorist infiltration. The IDF carried out these actions against army bases and police stations in Egypt and Jordan. The raid on Qalqilia, on the night of October 11, 1956 [picture] developed into a large-scale battle between Israeli and Jordanian forces.

2 **The Fedayeen** ("Those who sacrifice their lives") infiltrated Israel to carry out terrorist activities and murder civilians. From August 1955 until October 1956 there were hundreds of incidents of bombing and sabotage, grenade-throwing and gunfire, and attacks on transportation, from the northern Negev up to the vicinity of Tel Aviv. This blood-stained prayer book remained after a *fedayeen* raid on pupils at Moshav Shafrir (October 3, 1956).

3 **Half a million Arabs** who fled from Israel during the War of Independence, lived in the refugee camps in the Gaza Strip, Jordan, Lebanon, and Syria. Their stay there was viewed as temporary, until the annihilation of Israel.

4 **Gamal Abdul Nasser,** leader of the "Free Officers" who seized power in Egypt in a military coup (1952), followed a policy of extreme enmity toward Israel. Under his leadership Egypt blocked the Suez Canal and Straits of Tiran to Israeli shipping. The picture shows Nasser [on the right] with Indian leader Jawaharlal Nehru [center] and Yugoslav leader Josip Broz Tito, at the Belgrade Conference (1961) of non-aligned states. In spite of Egypt's joining the non-aligned bloc, Nasser extensively equipped his army with the aid of Eastern Bloc countries.

5 **Chief of the IDF General Staff**, Major-General Moshe Dayan (1915-1981), fostered the paratrooper unit in the early and mid-1950s. It was this unit that executed most of the reprisal actions and set the pattern of combat for all of the IDF for years to come. The qualities of leadership, resourcefulness, physical courage and responsibility for the lives of soldiers which were developed by the paratroopers remained the IDF standard. Many early paratrooper commanders reached senior military posts over the years. In the picture, standing from right to left: Danny Mat, Dayan, Ariel Sharon, Meir Har-Zion. Seated right to left: Rafael Eitan, Ya'akov Ya'akov, Aharon Davidi.

once it became clear that Israel's political philosophy was inimical to its aims. The IDF was compelled to overhaul scrapped arms from World War II [8], or use the scant weaponry supplied by the Great Powers. A turning-point in the equipping of the IDF took place in the mid-1950s [7].

The Sinai Campaign

Gamal Abdul Nasser, president of Egypt from 1954, viewed himself as the leader of the Arab world against western imperialism and Israel [4]. An arms deal with Czechoslovakia in 1955 transformed Egypt into a first-rate military power. In July 1956, in response to a US refusal to finance construction of the Aswan Dam, Egypt nationalized the Suez Canal. This act roused Britain and France to plan a military operation to capture the Canal and bring about the collapse of Nasser's regime. Israel — fearful of Egypt's military intentions, continually harassed by *fedayeen* terror, and anxious to end Egypt's blockade of shipping to Eilat — joined the initiative and planned to take control of the Sinai Peninsula.

Meanwhile the Soviets completed a large arms deal with Syria, as well. Military pacts were signed between Egypt and Syria, and between Iraq and Jordan. Iraqi forces entered Jordan and finally, on October 25, 1956, Jordan joined the Egyptian-Syrian alliance.

On Monday, October 29, 1956, Israel embarked on the Sinai Campaign [6]. Concerted pressure by the Soviet Union and the US stopped the campaign and forced Israel to withdraw its forces from Sinai and Gaza — but only after the US guaranteed freedom of navigation through the Straits of Tiran, and after a UN force had been stationed in the Gaza Strip and Sinai, along the border with Israel, and at Sharm el-Sheikh. Despite Israel's military achievements, in the wake of the Sinai Campaign Soviet involvement in the region increased, Nasser's regime strengthened, and his enmity toward Israel grew.

KEY

Israel's geographical position in the heart of the Arab world presented a direct challenge to the pan-Arab political philosophy of Egyptian President Gamal Abdul Nasser. Moreover, the Arabs were still smarting from their 1948 defeat and incitement against Israel was a convenient tool for ensuring uncritical mass support for Arab leaders. Thus the Arabs initiated border incidents, infiltrated terrorists into Israel, waged economic and political warfare, and built up military forces toward the day when they would open a "second round" of the war. This Egyptian propaganda poster portrays all the Arab states stabbing bayonets into the "Zionist snake."

6

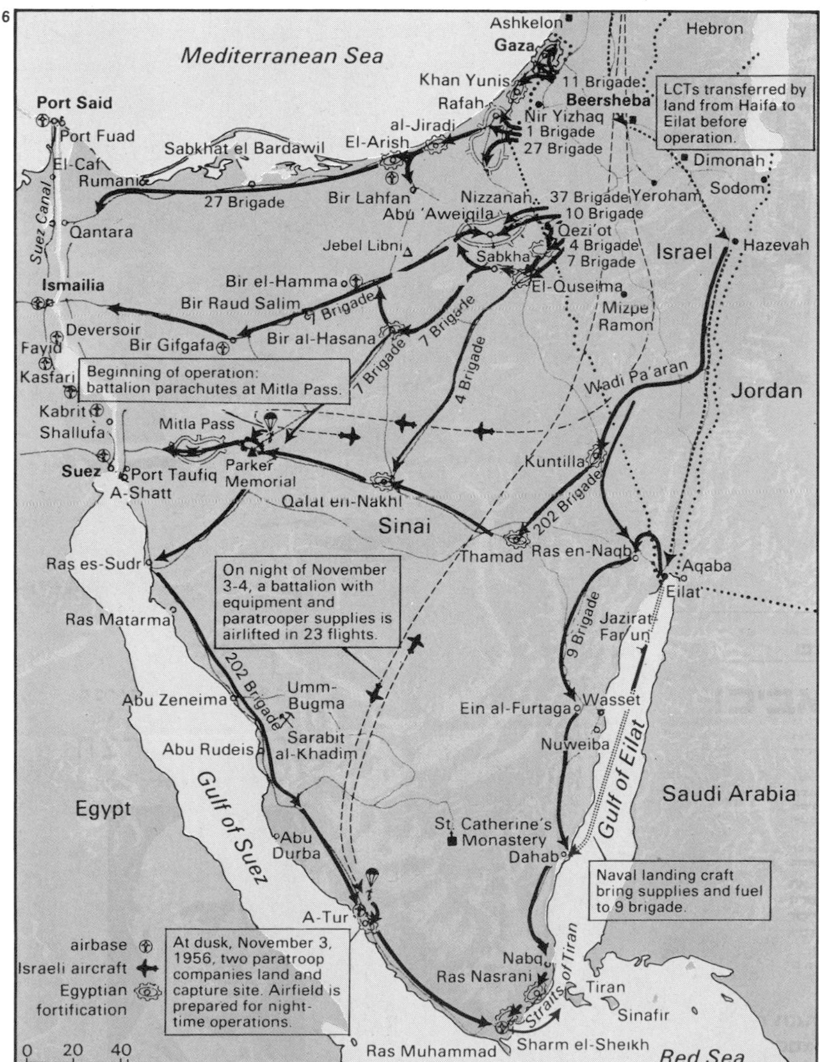

6 As the Sinai Campaign began, paratroopers dropped near the Mitla Pass in the Sinai Desert, some 50 km. (30 mi.) east of the Suez Canal. More paratroopers, the infantry, and the armor corps joined the attack over land. By November 5 the IDF had taken control of the entire Sinai Peninsula, assuming positions some 16 km. (10 mi.) from the Suez Canal. The air force took part in the paratroop landing, in attacking ground forces, in patrolling, and in evacuating the wounded; the navy landed supplies in the Red Sea and defended Israel's shores. An Egyptian destroyer which shelled the coast near Haifa was captured. While Israel was thus destroying the Egyptian army in Sinai, France and Britain attempted to retake the Suez Canal.

7

7 France was the first great power to begin supplying Israel with arms and munitions in any significant quantity and quality. French willingness to help Israel derived in part from the aid the Egyptian president gave the FLN rebels fighting French rule in Algeria. From 1955 on, France sold Israel tanks, half-tracks, artillery, and aircraft. Shortly before the Sinai Campaign (1956) French landing-craft arrived in Israel and secretly unloaded tanks and munitions. During the campaign itself French jets were stationed on an Israeli airfield, to defend Israeli airspace should that be necessary. The IDF's "French era" lasted for 11 years. [picture] A French-made *Mystère* jet in the Israel Air Force.

8 The main force of the IDF attack in the Sinai Campaign shifted from the infantry to the armor corps. At the beginning of the operation, armor was still thought of as a supporting force for the infantry, but this perception soon changed. Even though its tanks were outmoded models, the armor corps penetrated heavy fortifications and developed rapid mobile warfare through the ideal "tank country" of Sinai. After the Sinai Campaign there was an extensive move to strengthen the IDF, placing the focus on armor and the air force.

8

Economics and Society in Israel's Second Decade

In the years following the Sinai Campaign Israel's population stabilized and the momentum toward establishing new settlements slackened. In 1957 immigration was still about 70,000 per annum, but over the following three years total immigration came to 72,000. Only in 1961 did a new wave of *aliyah* begin, bringing 228,000 *olim* in four years. Economic difficulties then caused a drop in immigration, and in 1965 and 1966 only 46,000 immigrants came [7].

Development Towns

With the establishment of the state 97% of its Jewish inhabitants were concentrated in the central part of the country, in 22% of its total area. The Upper Galilee (8% of the area) held only some 2% of the country's Jews, and the Negev (70% of the area) was inhabited by less than 1% of the Jewish population. The new agricultural settlements were intended to prevent a close clustering of the population in a few coastal urban centers. However, by the late 1950s it was clear that agriculture alone was insufficient to support the arriving immigrants. In addition, many who had been settled in immigrant villages moved to the cities to find sources of livelihood familiar to them from their countries of origin, and to obtain a higher income. Residents of *ma'abarot* — immigrant camps — as well, settled on the outskirts of the cities.

Development towns were established with the objective of overcoming this trend. These were planned urban settlements, each designed to absorb up to 15,000 settlers. Some older settlements, too, were planned anew in accordance with these aims, or had new neighborhoods added to them [Key].

Only a few of the country's veteran inhabitants settled in these towns. Most veteran Israelis appointed to key posts in the town administration, in education, and in medicine, commuted daily from the older, established settlements. The two exceptions were Arad, in the Negev, and Karmiel, in the Galilee, both founded by youth from Israel's veteran community.

During the first half of the 1960s no new communities were established except a handful of *Nahal* settlements along the borders. In contrast, several large development projects were completed. The most important of these was the National Water Carrier [6]. The cornerstone of a deepwater port at Ashdod was laid in July 1961, and four years later the first ship docked there [4]. Phosphate mining and processing plants were developed near the Dead Sea and in Arad. The port of Eilat was expanded, and the laying of an oil pipeline from Eilat to Ashkelon was begun. A shipyard was built at the mouth of the Kishon River near Haifa.

In the 1960s Israel entered the nuclear age. An atomic research reactor built at Nahal Soreq, south of Tel Aviv, began operating in July 1960, and in December 1960 Israel announced the construction, with French assistance, of a large nuclear reactor in Dimona. The

CONNECTIONS

188 Israel's First Decade
190 Defense in the First Decade
194 From the Sinai Campaign to the Six-Day War
196 Economics and Society in Greater Israel (1967-1973)

1

1 Most olim who arrived in the early 1960s were settled in development towns. Several of these — Kiryat Shemonah, Hatzor ha-Glilit, Bet Shean, Migdal ha-Emeq, Kiryat Malachi, Sederot, Netivot — were populated largely by Moroccan Jews. Here *olim* from Morocco are seen arriving at their new settlement.

2

2 New immigrants settled in slums in the large cities. These, along with the still existing *ma'abarot*, also filled with immigrants who abandoned farming for urban life. Earning a living was difficult for all. Their plight first found violent expression in rioting at the Wadi Salib quarter in Haifa in July 1959, soon followed by similar demonstrations at Migdal ha-Emeq, Beersheba and Kiryat Shemonah.

3

3 The Nazi war criminal, Adolf Eichmann, who had been in charge of deporting Jews to the extermination camps, was discovered in Argentina in May 1960 by Israeli Intelligence. He was brought to Israel clandestinely, and tried under the 1950 law for bringing Nazis and their collaborators to justice. During his nine month trial the horrors of the Holocaust were revealed before the eyes of the entire world. Eichmann was sentenced to death, and was hanged in May 1962. His body was burned and his ashes cast over the Mediterranean Sea. Here Eichmann, enclosed in a bulletproof glass case, is seen listening to the chief prosecutor Gideon Hausner.

4

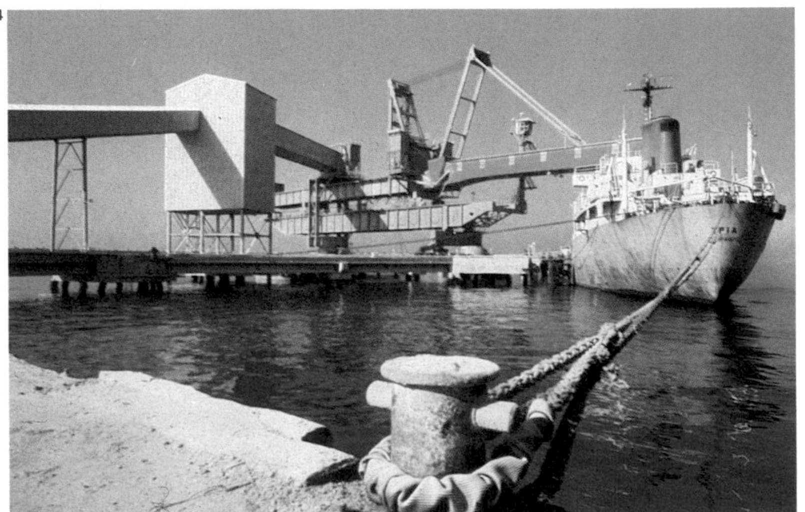

4 The Port of Ashdod was designed to serve the center and south of the country. Its construction made possible the closure of the obsolete ports of Jaffa and Tel Aviv. The port was built without the aid of a natural harbor. It was intentionally set far from the city to enable easy access by highway and train. The Tel Aviv-Ashdod highway, and a train link to the phosphate plants in the Negev, lent great impetus to the growth of Ashdod port and city. In addition, an oil pipeline was laid from Eilat to Ashkelon. Ashdod's population grew from 4,600 in 1961 to 25,000 in 1966.

Dimona nuclear research center was inaugurated in 1963. In July of the same year Israel joined the Moscow Accord, forbidding atmospheric nuclear tests, but in April 1964 Israel announced that it would not agree to international supervision of its nuclear research, which was intended for peaceful purposes. Even those experts who assume that Israel does not have nuclear arms hold that it has the necessary know-how, raw materials and equipment to manufacture such arms, if it so decides.

Boom and Recession

The extensive investment in infrastructure, particularly in agriculture, began to show results in production. The development of heavy industry and of the metal and electronics industries was accelerated, and industrial plants were directed to the development towns to provide employment. The construction sector was stimulated by home-building for new immigrants and for those leaving the *ma'abarot*.

The standard of living rose considerably. Many families improved their housing and acquired consumer goods which a few years earlier had been beyond their reach, such as refrigerators and washing machines. However, the weaker echelons of society fell behind in the race for affluence [2].

Inevitably this new affluence, along with a cut-back in the level of German reparations, led to a deterioration in the country's balance of payments, reaching a deficit of 572 million dollars in 1964. In September 1966 the government approved a two-year economic plan whose main objectives were to slacken the rate of increase in the standard of living and to direct additional resources toward investment and increased production. The government curtailed its spending, especially in building. Unemployment spread from the building industry to manufacturing; in March 1967 it reached 96,000 workers, even exceeding figures from the years of mass immigration.

KEY

The development towns [here, Sederot in the Negev] absorbed tens of thousands of immigrants. Eventually an undesirable sorting process occurred in these towns. Those residents, mostly of European origin, who could manage to move to the large cities, left; while those who were of lesser means, and who were by and large *Sephardim* from the Islamic countries, remained. This situation put a strain on local services, and as the level of these services dropped even more people left, thus breeding urban decay.

5

5 An incident associated with Pinhas Lavon (1905-1976) raised a storm in Israel in the early 1960s and led to the resignation of Prime Minister David Ben-Gurion in 1963. The controversy revolved around the question of whether or not Lavon, as minister of defense, ordered an Israeli espionage team to sabotage British and American installations in Egypt, in order to create the impression of Egyptian enmity against the West. The members of the team were captured (1954), two were executed and six imprisoned. Ben-Gurion resigned when his demands for a full investigation of Lavon's role were rejected by his own party.

6

6 The National Water Carrier, which began operating in June 1964, provided the foundation for a nationwide water system that unites regional waterworks and makes it possible to regulate the nation's water flow according to need. The carrier transports water from the Sea of Galilee to the center of the country and from there to the Negev. At its peak output, 365 million cubic meters of water flow through it annually.

8

8 Many African and Asian states that became independent in the 1960s received aid from Israel in agricultural development and education, and sent students and technicians to Israel for training. Here Golda Meir, foreign minister from 1956 to 1965, is seen with Kenyan President Jomo Kenyatta.

7

Rounded figures, in thousands

70 60 50 40 30 20 10

71 27 24 25.5 47.5 61 64.5 55 31 15.5

1957 1958 1959 1960 1961 1962 1963 1964 1965 1966

7 The second decade saw several years of slack immigration, between which there was a great wave of *aliyah* lasting from 1962 to 1964, mainly from Morocco. The difficulty associated with this *aliyah* was not a shortage of goods or housing, but rather the emergence of a socio-economic gap between the Jews from Muslim countries and the veteran Jews from Europe.

9

9 The Israel Museum exhibits archaeological findings from Erez Israel, Jewish art, and works of the world's great artists.

From the Sinai Campaign to the Six-Day War

After the Sinai Campaign emphasis was laid on a qualitative build-up of the IDF. The air force acquired jet combat aircraft and air-defense missiles [2]. The armor corps was enlarged and equipped with new tanks. Mobile artillery was introduced. and training came to emphasize combined operations involving armor, infantry, paratroops, artillery, and engineering corps, with air force support. In the early 1960s missile boats were ordered from Germany and France, and in Israel the *Gabriel* sea-to-sea missile was developed. The new Israel Aircraft Industry began to manufacture a jet trainer under license from France.

The Egyptian Threat

Egypt's defeat in the Sinai Campaign heightened Nasser's hostility toward Israel. In 1958 a military coup in Iraq ended the pro-western Hashemite dynasty there. The Hashemite regime of Jordan was also on the verge of collapse. Syria and Egypt agreed to unite into a single state — the United Arab Republic — under Nasser, while Yemen joined the UAR in a federation. In Lebanon, Nasserist elements threatened its pro-western regime. The western powers roused themselves to counter-action. In July 1958 American marines were landed in Beirut, and British paratroopers were flown into Jordan. Syria, in September 1961, underwent a coup aimed at freeing the country from Egyptian protectorship, and the UAR was dissolved.

Nasser still sought to achieve pan-Arab hegemony. In January 1964 an Arab summit conference in Cairo decided to divert the waters of two sources of the Jordan River which originate in Syria and Lebanon, and to channel them to the Jordanian irrigation system, in order to prevent operation of Israel's National Water Carrier [1]. A joint Arab military command was established to protect the Jordan-water diversion plan against Israeli attack. Also, the Palestine Liberation Organization (PLO) was established and introduced a new dimension to the conflict; *Fatah* (the Palestine Liberation Movement), backed by Syria, soon achieved control over it. *Fatah*'s first terrorist action, which took place on January 2, 1965, was planting a bomb in a National Water Carrier conduit. Other actions were launched from Jordan and Lebanon. The IDF took preventive and deterrent action against the states from whose territory terrorists operated [3].

Escalation

An incident on the Syrian border, in April 1967, began with the Syrians shooting at a tractor and shelling settlements. The Israel Air Force intervened, shooting down six Syrian jets in a dogfight. This led to increased Syrian pressure on Egypt to extend aid and support. On May 15 Nasser sent his armed forces into the Sinai, and the following day he demanded that UN forces be removed from the border. UN Secretary General U Thant reacted by with-

CONNECTIONS
190 Defense in the First Decade
192 Economics and Society in Israel's Second Decade
198 From the Six-Day War to the Yom Kippur War

1 A

1 B

1 Firing from across the Syrian border [A — plowing with an armored tractor] persisted after the Sinai Campaign. Israel reacted with punitive attacks on Syrian positions (Tawfiq, February 1960; Nuqeib, March 1962). When the Syrians began to divert the waters of the Banias and Hazbani rivers to the Jordanian irrigation project in the Yarmuk Valley [B], as decided at the 1964 Arab summit at Cairo, Israel responded by shelling the tractors. When the Syrians shifted their work beyond the range of Israeli tanks, the air force was called into action against them. In July 1966, work on the diversion project ceased. The diversion effort, shooting incidents involving disputed farmland, and *Fatah* terrorism backed by Syria all contributed to a general escalation in the region.

3 Palestinian terrorist organizations, especially *Fatah*, gathered strength during 1965-1966. Their avowed objective was to attack Israel and Israelis and create unabated tension along Israel's borders, in order to draw the Arab states into a total war against Israel. One Israeli reprisal action was undertaken by a large force of paratroops, tanks and aircraft on November 13, 1966, near Samua, in the southern Hebron Hills [illustration].

2

2 Hawk anti-aircraft missiles, transferred to Israel by the US in 1962, were the first US arms sold directly to Israel. Later the US agreed to Israel acquiring American Patton tanks from Germany, and in early 1966 it began selling Israel Skyhawk and Phantom jets. Over the course of time the United States has become Israel's main arms supplier, and a close defense relationship has developed between the two countries.

4

3

4 NAHAL — Noar Haluzi Lohem ("Fighting Pioneer Youth") played an important role in building settlements along Israel's extensive borders prior to the Six-Day War. *Nahal* units enable the youth movements to combine military service with preparation for founding agricultural settlements. Soldiers in *Nahal* do part of their military service on agricultural settlements [picture: a soldier shepherd], and part in regular army units. Many *Nahal* outposts have turned into permanent civilian settlements. The *Nahal* concept of army soldiers filling a pioneering role has been copied by many Third World countries.

drawing the UN force altogether from the Gaza Strip and Sharm el-Sheikh. On May 22 the Egyptians closed the Straits of Tiran, knowing that Israel would consider this act a *casus belli* under international law. On May 30 Jordan's King Hussein signed a defense agreement with Egypt, and Iraq joined in. In Israel IDF reserves had been called up, but the government decided to wait until all political possibilities had been exhausted. On June 1 a national unity government was established under the leadership of Levi Eshkol, with Moshe Dayan appointed minister of defense. On that same day the United States made clear to Israel that it had no intention of raising an international naval force to break the blockade of the straits. Israeli military and political circles reached consensus that any further delay merely heightened the impact of the Arabs' inevitable attack.

At dawn of June 5, 1967, the Israel Air Force launched a preventive attack on the airfields of Egypt [5]. Ground forces took the Gaza Strip and the Sinai Peninsula, all in four days. Meanwhile Jordan joined the war, enabling the IDF to capture Judea and Samaria, as far as the Jordan River [9]. Syria was shelling the northern settlements and had launched an attack in the Jordan Valley; hence on June 9 the IDF conquered the Golan Heights and took control of the slopes of Mount Hermon. On June 10 the war ended.

The Six-Day War brought about a drastic change in Israel's strategic position [8]. The military potential of three Arab states was convincingly destroyed. Water resources were safeguarded. The danger that Israel would be split in two at its "narrow waist," between Samaria and the sea, was dispelled. In the south Israel acquired hundreds of kilometers of room for maneuver and advance warning, with the Suez Canal separating the Egyptian army from the IDF. In the wake of the military victory, Israelis dared to hope that political activity would now bring peace.

KEY

The northern settlements were subject to every military whim of the Syrians, who enjoyed a topographical advantage since the War of Independence. From their positions on the Golan Heights they shot at Israeli farmers on the lands near the border, harassed sailing and fishing in the Sea of Galilee, and prevented expansion of the Jordan River channel for the National Water Carrier project. Due to Syrian shelling, for years the children in these communities had to sleep in underground shelters. She'ar-Yashuv and Dafna, two settlements in the northeastern Galilee, are seen here photographed from a Syrian position at Tel Azaziyat, on the Golan Heights.

5

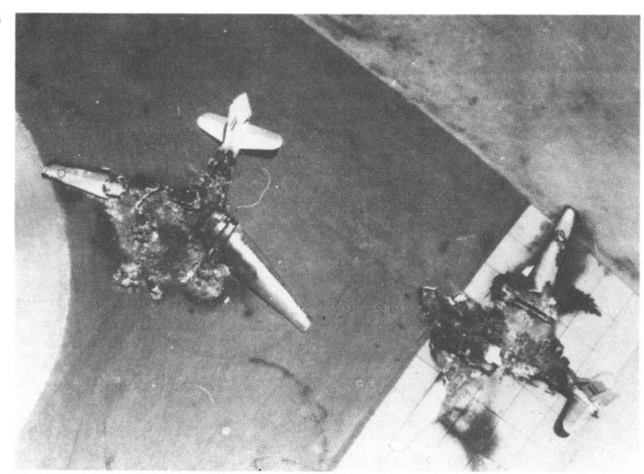

5 During the first few hours of the Six-Day War Israel's air force destroyed the bases of the Egyptian Air Force. That same day airfields in Jordan, Syria, and Iraq were also attacked [picture: Egyptian airfield after attack].

6

6 Three weeks passed between the time the Egyptian army moved a large force into the Sinai Peninsula, and June 5, when the war erupted. In Israel these were days of military preparedness and anticipation [picture: students digging defense trenches].

7 Educational and cultural activities are among the goals which the IDF set for itself, in addition to defense of the state. New immigrants learn Hebrew in the Israeli army, and are taught fundamental concepts in the history of the people and the land. Thousands of soldiers acquire a general education and professional training in the army. In the sphere of entertainment and morale, an important role is played by army entertainment troupes — which have given many young artists their first chance.

7

8

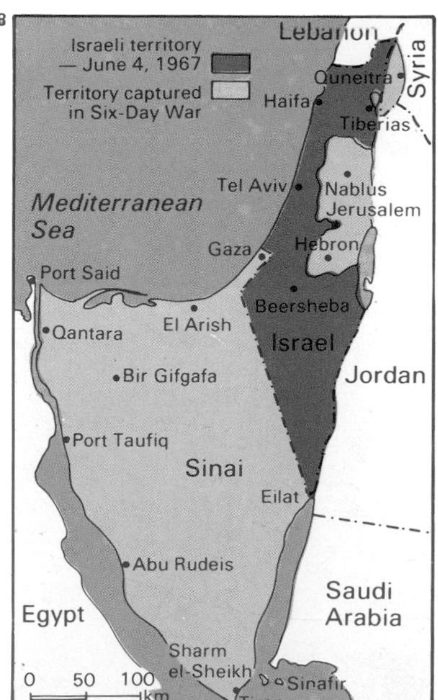

8 At the close of the Six-Day War the IDF was deployed in the Golan Heights, and along the Jordan River and the Suez Canal. The immediate threat to population centers along the coastal plain and to the capital, Jerusalem, had been removed. Maximum strategic depth had been achieved between Israel and its chief foe — Egypt.

9 After fierce battles to the north and south of Jerusalem, the Old City was surrounded by IDF forces. It then fell virtually without a battle. This was the climactic point of the Six-Day War. Israel found itself in control of sites associated with the dawn of Jewish history, and sacred to the Jewish people. The Israeli public was torn between a desire to retain the land which had been the inheritance of its forefathers, and an unwillingness to rule over the Arab population living there. The picture shows paratroopers near the Western Wall, on June 10, 1967.

9

Economics and Society in Greater Israel (1967-1973)

A wave of euphoria swept over Israel in the wake of the Six-Day War. Many people viewed it as the last battle of the War of Independence, reuniting all of western Ereẓ Israel under the rule of the State of Israel [Key].

Over one million Palestinian Arabs lived in the territory conquered by Israel — 670,000 in Judea and Samaria, including East Jerusalem, and about 350,000 in the Gaza Strip. Over 270,000 of these lived in refugee camps. The government of Israel brought East Jerusalem and the surrounding area under Israeli law and administration at the end of June 1967, and instituted military rule in the remaining territories.

Within Israel a sharp debate erupted over the future of the territories. A radical stand cited the Jewish people's historical tie to these lands, especially Judea and Samaria, as well as Israel's security needs, and called for annexation of these territories. The "Movement for a Unified Ereẓ Israel" and *Gush Emunim* emerged as the leading proponents of this stand. They began establishing settlements in the territories, without government sanction. An opposing stand viewed the one million inhabitants of the occupied territories as posing a threat to the Jewish character of the state, and called for withdrawal, even unilaterally. A third stand, advocated by most government ministers, asserted that Israel should continue to hold the territories as a temporary trust, with the view to reaching peace negotiations with the Arab states. Everyone, however, save for some fringe elements, agreed that there should be no return to the former state of affairs of vulnerable and insecure borders. In July 1967 cabinet minister Yigal Allon (1918-1980) submitted his plan for the future of Judea and Samaria to the government [4], which did not adopt his program officially but in practice began to establish settlements on that basis.

Recovery and Immigration

Immediately after the war, in the summer of 1967, the economy returned to a state of full employment, even absorbing into the labor force thousands of workers from the administered territories. The construction sector began to boom. New neighborhoods were built in reunited Jerusalem [6] and the Tel Aviv megalopolis expanded to comprise fully half the population of the state. Industry developed, and the standard of living rose [3].

But the gaps in Israeli society widened. In neighborhoods declared "hardship areas" a second generation of poverty-afflicted youth emerged, prevented by economic and social factors from functioning in the modern economy. Even the army refrained from drafting them, thus further increasing their alienation from society. From among this youth, the "Black Panthers" movement arose in mid-1971. Its protest actions included breaking into shops and distributing "expropriated" food products to needy families, and squatting in unoccupied apartments in public

CONNECTIONS

192 Economics and Society in Israel's Second Decade
194 From the Sinai Campaign to the Six-Day War
198 From the Six-Day War to the Yom Kippur War
202 A Decade of Change

1

1 Bridges over the Jordan River [here: the war-damaged Allenby Bridge] were restored and traffic across them renewed without any official arrangement between Israel and Jordan. Goods passed via these bridges to Judea, Samaria, and Jerusalem, and agricultural produce and other goods from the administered territories were exported in the reverse direction. Thousands of residents from neighboring countries come to Israel over these bridges in their summer travels. The open bridges underscore the special relationship between Israel and Jordan.

2

2 Golda Meir (1898-1979), a leader of the Labor Movement and former foreign minister, became prime minister in 1969. A central goal of her policy was to cultivate Israel's ties with the United States. Here she is seen during a visit to Washington, in 1969, with Ambassador Yitzhak Rabin.

3

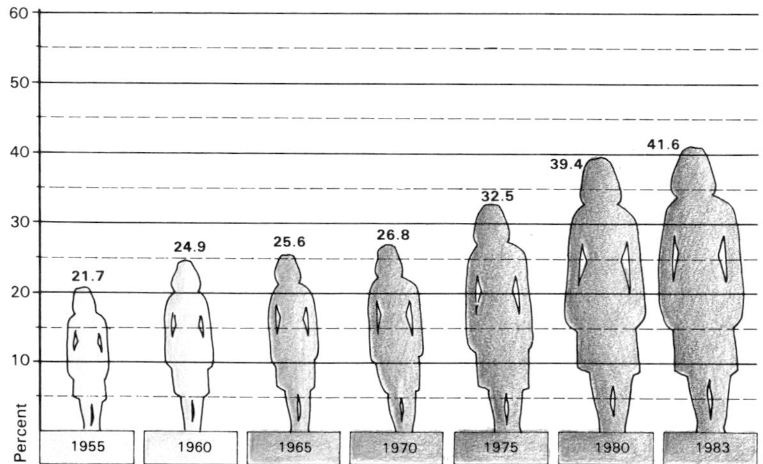

3 Post-1967 Israel became an affluent western society, as evidenced by indicators like modes of dress, popular music and purchasing habits. One index marking this development was the rise in the number of married women in the work force [see table].

4

4 The Allon Plan integrates two basic notions: turning the Jordan River into the eastern security boundary of Israel, while avoiding the necessity for controlling the Arab inhabitants of Judea and Samaria and granting them Israeli citizenship as a result of annexation. The plan proposed the establishment of army strongholds and civilian settlements along the river and on the western slopes of the Jordan Valley — regions in which Arab settlement was sparse. It also sought to broaden Israel's vulnerable narrow sections in the central coastal strip and the Jerusalem Corridor, through settlement in Samaria and Judea. By 1972, 44 settlements had been established throughout Judea, Samaria, Sinai and the Golan.

housing projects. Nevertheless, the general picture was one of affluence and prosperity, and this, coupled with the enthusiasm which gripped Jews throughout the world after the victory in the war, led to a rise in immigration [8].

Resolution 242 and the Rogers Plan

The Arabs' extremist position after the Six-Day War soon found expression at the Khartoum summit meeting where the "three no's" were declared: no recognition of Israel, no negotiations with Israel, and no peace. On November 22, 1967, the UN Security Council adopted a compromise formula — Resolution 242. It called for a just and lasting peace in the Middle East, based on the realization of two principles: withdrawal of Israeli armed forces from conquered territories; and termination of belligerency, as well as respect and recognition of the sovereignty, territorial integrity, and political independence of every state in the region, and of their right to live in peace within secure and recognized boundaries. The Security Council further affirmed the necessity for guaranteeing freedom of navigation on the international waterways of the region, and achieving a just settlement of the refugee problem.

Resolution 242 did not bear any real fruit. A plan advanced by American Secretary of State William Rogers [7] was accepted by a majority of the ministers of the Israeli government; those from *Gahal* (*Herut* and Liberal Party) who opposed the plan left the government, thus dissolving the national unity government formed on the eve of the Six-Day War. The American initiative was designed primarily to put an end to the War of Attrition along the Suez Canal. However, immediately after the ceasefire (August 1970) it became clear that the Egyptians had violated it by advancing anti-aircraft missiles to the canal. A political deadlock ensued, which eventually evolved into the Yom Kippur War, in October 1973.

KEY

Areas conquered by Israel in June 1967 are closely tied to the roots of Jewish history: the Western Wall, the Temple Mount, the Cave of the *Machpelah*, Rachel's Tomb, and Mount Sinai. Bulldozers demolished the cement anti-sniper walls which had been erected along the line dividing the city of Jerusalem. The engineer corps cleared the mines from the no-man's land between the two parts of the city. Israeli tourists flooded the West Bank, the Golan Heights, and the Sinai Peninsula. Jews thronged to the Old City of Jerusalem to pray at the Western Wall, to visit the Temple Mount, and to find bargains in the markets of the city. In the picture is Zion Gate of Old Jerusalem.

6

6 The eastern part of Jerusalem was extensively developed in the wake of the Six-Day War. On Mount Scopus a new campus was built for the Hebrew University. Jerusalem became the most populous city in Israel. Housing projects [picture: Ramot Eshkol, in the northeastern part] were planned with the purpose of making future partition unfeasible. The Arab neighborhoods developed as well, and services improved.

5 The public debate over the future of the administered territories, and the accusations directed against Golda Meir's government for rejecting opportunities to resolve the crisis with Egypt, left their mark in the realm of culture and art. Various artistic works conveyed the demand for increased efforts toward peace. The play "Queen of the Bath" by Hanokh Levine, which portrayed Israel as a territorial expansionist state, blind to peace, aroused a public storm. The sculptures of Igael Tumarkin portrayed the cruelty of war. The picture shows his sculpture "He walked in the fields."

5

7

7 William Rogers, the American secretary of state [here with President Nixon], played an active role in Middle Eastern affairs. The Rogers plan, based on Resolution 242, proposed establishment of a just and lasting peace in exchange for Israeli withdrawal from Sinai, Judea, and Samaria, save for minor border adjustments for security reasons. The plan, put forth in October 1969, was rejected by Egypt as being too pro-Israeli, and by Israel because it virtually called for a return to the 1967 boundaries and did not include suitable security provisions or a breakthrough which would bring about peace. After the Yom Kippur War Rogers' successor, Henry Kissinger, abandoned this comprehensive plan for a step-by-step approach that contributed to the Egypt-Israel peace treaty.

8 The Soviet Union generally prevents its citizens, including Jews, from leaving the country. Yet, as a result of protests by Soviet Jewry and pressure applied in the western world, the Soviets permitted immigration to Israel within the context of family reunification. In 1971 the Jewish Agency established a way station in Vienna for the Soviet Jews, and from there flew them to Israel. In 1972/3, 55,000 *olim* arrived from the USSR.

8

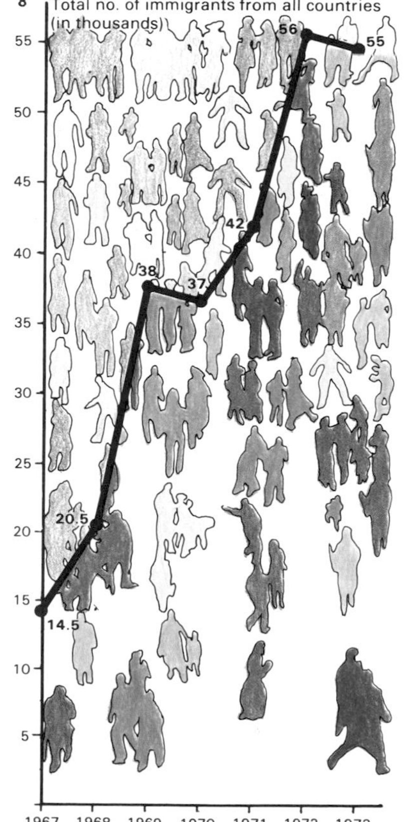

From the Six-Day War to the Yom Kippur War

At the close of the Six-Day War the IDF controlled large territories, with new and shorter ceasefire lines that followed easily defensible features: the Suez Canal, the Jordan River, and the basalt hills of the Golan Heights.

Attrition and Terrorism

Even though the Six-Day War terminated in a ceasefire, hostilities on the Egyptian front did not cease from July 1967 until August 1980. The War of Attrition was launched in full force in March 1969. The Egyptians sought to exploit their advantage in artillery to force the IDF to abandon the area adjacent to the canal. In response, the Israel Air Force bombed Egyptian emplacements. The Egyptians stepped up their shellings, and launched raids east of the canal. The IDF retaliated by raiding Egyptian territory [2].

When President Nasser realized how vulnerable Egypt was to air attack, he turned to the Soviet Union for aid. In 1970 Egypt received surface-to-air missiles, combat aircraft and Soviet personnel to operate them. By July 1970 there were 15,000 Soviet soldiers and advisors in Egypt. The Israel Air Force's penetration bombings into Egypt halted, although overflights in Egyptian airspace continued. On July 30 Israel Air Force jets downed four planes flown by Soviet pilots. Now the Soviets stepped up pressure on the Egyptians to cease the war. In late July Egypt and Israel agreed to the ceasefire initiative of US Secretary of State William Rogers.

Meanwhile, along the Jordanian front, PLO terrorists attempted to operate in the territories under Israeli control. By the end of 1967 they had been forced to shift their bases east of the Jordan River [3]. From there they penetrated westward from time to time, and Israeli settlements in the Bet Shean and Jordan valleys were shelled. The IDF retaliated across the Jordan: Jordanian settlements were destroyed, and the terrorists were forced to move further eastward. Finally, in September 1970 ("Black September"), Jordan's King Hussein averted a terrorist takeover by attacking the terrorists and expelling them. Syria backed the terrorists, but maintained its refusal to let them operate from its territory.

The PLO now moved its centers to Lebanon. It formed a sort of autonomous zone in southern Lebanon, dubbed "Fatah-land." Headquarters of the various organizations were established in Beirut, and training bases — in the neighboring refugee camps. From there the terrorists raided Israeli territory, and shelled the northern settlements. In May 1970 a band of terrorists attacked a schoolbus from Moshav Avivim, near the Lebanese border, killing 13 children and wounding 21. Thereafter the IDF patrolled inside Lebanese territory and launched deep raids to destroy terrorist camps. From Beirut the PLO planned attacks on Israeli targets in Europe and Israel, such as the May 1972 attack by Japanese terrorists allied to the PLO on passengers at Lod

CONNECTIONS

194 From the Sinai Campaign to the Six-Day War
202 A Decade of Change
204 Arabs and Other Minorities in Israel

1

2 A

1 IDF women soldiers learning to use small arms for self-defense. In the 1970s and 1980s many new areas of service were added for women: adjutancy, policing, education, welfare, communications, flight control, etc. Women also train male tank and artillery troops. Every young woman must serve at the age of 18 for two years, and is exempted only if she is married or opts out for religious reasons.

2 During the War of Attrition the Egyptians shelled Israeli defense lines. The IDF responded by shelling Egyptian cities along the Suez Canal, which were soon deserted, and by bombing targets deep inside Egypt: supply bases, arsenals, command posts and training bases, radar stations, and surface to-air missile batteries. A line of fortifications (the Bar-Lev Line) was constructed to withstand potential Egyptian attack and protect soldiers from bombardments and sniping. Illustration [A] shows the inside of a Bar-Lev Line bunker; [B] shows Egyptian refineries near the city of Suez, in flames following Israeli shelling in retaliation for the sinking of the Israeli destroyer *Eilat* in October 1967.

2 B

3 Bands of PLO terrorists made hundreds of attempts to penetrate the West Bank from Jordanian territory. The IDF constructed a network of defenses against infiltration along the Jordan River, until virtually all terrorist bands that penetrated Israeli-held territory were either killed or captured. The IDF also retaliated against Jordanian towns and outposts that harbored terrorists. One result of Israel's successes against the PLO was heightened Jordanian-PLO tension. The picture shows IDF soldiers preparing to blow up a cave west of the Jordan Valley, where infiltrating terrorists had taken shelter.

3

4

4 Missile boats (MFPBs) comprised the primary weapons system of the Israel Navy after the early 1970s. The boats and their *Gabriel* missiles were designed in Israel. The first 12 boats were built in France, but after seven were transferred to Israel, delivery of the remainder was held up by the French in accordance with their embargo on arms shipments to Israel after the Six-Day War. These were then smuggled out to Israel on Christmas Eve, 1969. Since then Israel has built its own MFPBs. Israel's missile boats were first used in the Yom Kippur War, against Egyptian and Syrian MFPBs of Soviet make, which the Israelis overcame in every naval engagement.

Airport, and the 1972 murder of the Israeli Olympic athletes at Munich.

The Yom Kippur War

The victories in the Six-Day War and the War of Attrition gave the IDF a sense of strength. It appeared as if the Arab states had been deterred from opening war, that Israel's primary security concern remained terrorism, and that time and a territorial advantage were on its side. The Arabs, however, were continuing preparations for war. By September 1973, Syria and Egypt had rehabilitated their armies. Egypt's new president, Anwar Sadat, viewed a broad-scale war as the only way out of the impasse. In order to break the "barrier of fear" of Israel, as he defined it, and to sustain an extended and damaging attack, he had to obtain the advantage of surprise. He recruited Syria to his aid, so that Israel would be forced to fight on an additional front.

On Yom Kippur, October 6, 1973, the armies of Egypt and Syria attacked. Israel was completely surprised [Key]. Its minimal regular forces at the fronts suffered heavy losses. The reserves were called up and entered battle in haste. By October 8 they were launching counter-offensives on both fronts, but the attack on the Egyptian front failed, and the IDF suffered heavy losses. In the Golan Heights the Syrians were repulsed by the morning of October 10. The following day the IDF launched an attack toward Damascus. On October 14 the IDF halted a new Egyptian armored attack, and destroyed hundreds of Egyptian tanks. On the night of October 15/16 IDF tank and paratroop forces launched a counter-attack, and crossed the Suez Canal [6].

The superpowers were involved in the Yom Kippur War on an unprecedented scale. The Soviets airlifted arms to Syria and Egypt, and the US to Israel. UN and superpower ceasefire attempts, initially rejected by an overconfident Egypt, were ultimately imposed on the advancing Israeli forces [5, 7].

KEY

The Yom Kippur War began with a surprise Egyptian-Syrian attack on Israel, and ended with IDF forces penetrating nearly to Cairo and Damascus. Here IDF reservists are seen recapturing the Golan Heights. The war exacted a high price from Israel in men and materials, and generated a sense of anger among the Israeli citizenry at the political and military leadership. The government and defense-intelligence establishment were blamed for allowing the IDF to sink into a sense of tranquility after its victory in the Six-Day War, and for being caught unawares. Ultimately the Golda Meir government resigned, and extensive changes were introduced in the military establishment.

5

5 American Secretary of State Henry Kissinger worked during the last stages of the Yom Kippur War to save Egypt from total defeat, and in 1974 and 1975 made several rounds of shuttle diplomacy between the Arab capitals and Israel, mediating separation of forces agreements. Kissinger maintained that by affording the Arabs some gains through negotiations, he could lay the groundwork for peace.

6 The crossing of the Suez Canal on the night of October 16 marked the turning point in the Yom Kippur War on the southern front. Within days the IDF's hold on territory west of the Canal was broadened, and three bridges were built, including the pontoon bridge in the picture. IDF tank forces encircled the Egyptian Third Army, east of the Canal, and reached within 101 km. (61 mi.) of Cairo. Egypt hastened to request a ceasefire.

6

7 The Yom Kippur War came to a close with the IDF deployed in most sectors beyond its pre-1973 lines. At war's start the Syrians captured the Israeli outposts on Mt. Hermon and advanced in the southern Golan Heights to points overlooking the Sea of Galilee and the Jordan River. The Israeli counter-offensive pushed them back toward Damascus. After the Egyptians crossed the Suez Canal they took control of a strip along its eastern bank, and maintained control of most of this area until the end of the war. In its counter-attack the IDF broke through this strip, captured territory west of the canal, and encircled the Egyptian force in the south of the eastern bank.

7A

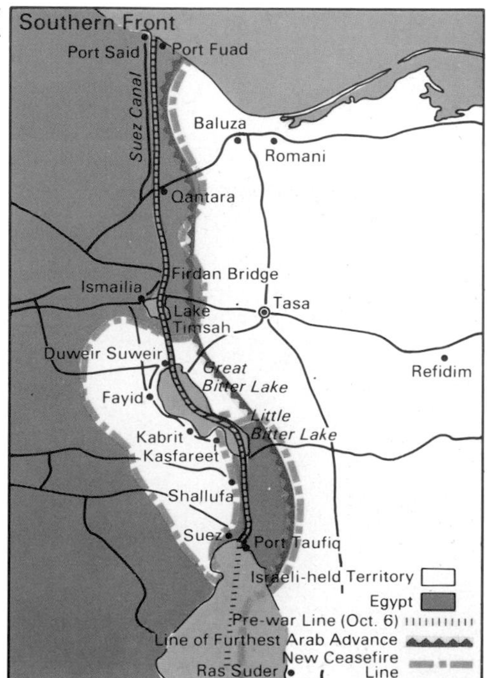

7B

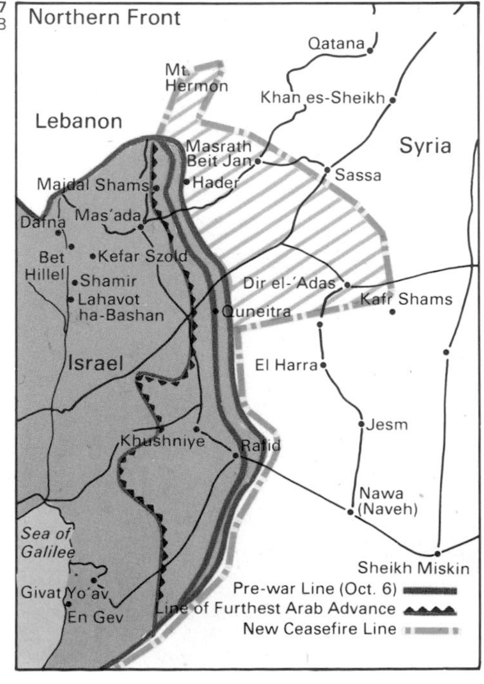

8

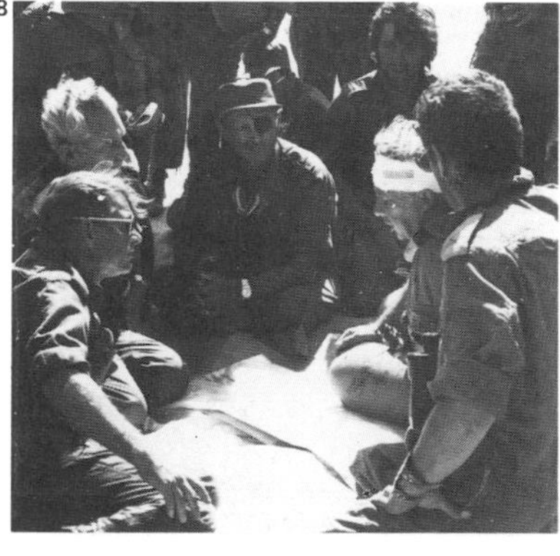

8 A meeting of commanders on the southern front, in the Yom Kippur War. From right to left: Maj. Gen. Ariel Sharon, Moshe Dayan, Lt. Gen. (res.) Chaim Bar-Lev, and Maj. Gen. Avraham Adan. One of the revelations about the war was the "war of the generals;" in some instances commanders had acted contrary to instructions, and the media were involved in discussions among IDF commanders over the way the war should have been fought. These developments, along with Israel's lack of preparedness and the war's heavy losses, left their mark on the Israel Defense Forces and the public in Israel for years to come.

Peace with Egypt; War in Lebanon

Speaking before the National Assembly in Cairo on November 9, 1977, President Anwar Sadat of Egypt declared his willingness to address the *Knesset* in Jerusalem in order to end the state of war between Egypt and Israel. Ten days later he proposed to the *Knesset* the establishment of peaceful relations. In exchange, Egypt demanded Israel's withdrawal from all of the Sinai, and an Israeli commitment to solve the Palestinian problem. Sadat apparently opted for this political approach when he realized, after the Yom Kippur War, that the Arabs would never achieve their final goals by force of arms. On the other hand, if considerable American pressure were brought to bear on Israel to withdraw to the 1967 borders, Israel might agree to do so in exchange for peace with its neighbors.

Following Sadat's visit to Jerusalem, Israel and Egypt commenced negotiations [Key] which led to a peace accord to be implemented in stages. In February 1980, the Israeli Embassy in Cairo and Egyptian Embassy in Tel Aviv were opened. In April 1982, Israel completed its withdrawal from Sinai [4].

Despite extreme Arab sanctions against Egypt — diplomatic relations were severed and Egypt expelled from the Arab League — Sadat remained firm in his support for peace. The peace agreement survived his assassination in 1981 [8] and, despite difficulties in Egyptian-Israeli relations, remained a landmark achievement.

War Against Terrorists

The regular Arab armies maintained the post-1973 ceasefire with Israel, but Palestinian terrorists based in Lebanon continued to carry out attacks and siege-hostage operations in Israel [7] and abroad [10]. Israel retaliated, but also opened border crossings at the Good Fence [5] to encourage neighborly relations. However, the civil war in Lebanon and the impotence of its central government enabled the PLO to establish an extensive infrastructure of camps and bases in the south.

In response to the hijacking of a bus on the coast road between Haifa and Tel Aviv (March 1978) in which 35 Israelis were killed, the IDF launched the Litani Operation, seizing control of South Lebanon. In its wake, the UN International Force In Lebanon (UNIFIL) was formed, and a militia led by Lebanese Major Sa'ad Hadad was recruited from the local citizenry to patrol a strip 5-10 kms wide along the border.

The "Hadad Strip" and UNIFIL-patrolled territory removed the terrorist strongholds to north of the Litani River. But actions against Israeli targets continued. Terrorist bombardment of Israel's northern settlements ended after the US helped mediate a ceasefire agreement with the PLO in the summer of 1981. With few violations, the ceasefire held until June 4, 1982, when the Israeli ambassador to London, Shlomo Argov, was critically wounded by Palestinian terrorists. This incident provided the catalyst for the IDF's Operation

CONNECTIONS

198 From the Six-Day War to the Yom Kippur War

202 A Decade of Change

1

1 The urgent need to coordinate infantry and paratroops with armor, artillery and engineering units was one of the major lessons learned from the Yom Kippur War. In the following years, the IDF acquired more sophisticated equipment, developed doctrinal concepts for combined operations, and practised new tactics. This process of self-improvement through analysis of errors was repeated after the 1982 Lebanon War.

2

2 Military aid to Israel from the US reflects the American view that since the Arab world relies on the Soviet Union to maintain a strike capability against Israel, the US must give Israel the military and economic aid necessary to ensure its security and power to withstand these armies. The Yom Kippur War lent support to this view. But American aid is not without conditions. For example, following Israel's destruction of the Iraqi nuclear reactor near Baghdad in June 1981, the US temporarily suspended delivery of F-16 combat aircraft [pictured]. Moreover, after making peace with Israel, Egypt was able to receive large-scale US military aid, as did Jordan and Saudi Arabia.

3

3 The situation in the administered territories from 1973 to 1982 was characterized by increased PLO influence, acts of terror against Jews, and stonethrowings at vehicles. However, normal daily life prevailed as a rule in most areas, even as settlement activity brought the Jewish population of the territories to some 30,000. Here Israeli soldiers patrol Hebron during a curfew.

4

4 The peace treaty required Israel to transfer all of the Sinai by April 25, 1982. This meant dismantling air force bases, as well as the Israeli settlements in Sinai — the town of Yamit and eleven *moshavim*. Some of the residents of Yamit resisted evacuation and had to be removed by force. The abortive effort to maintain an Israeli presence in the Sinai settlements was supported by settlers from Judea and Samaria, who feared the implications of the Yamit precedent.

5

5 The Good Fence along the Israel-Lebanon border expressed Israel's involvement in southern Lebanon after central rule in Beirut collapsed in 1976 and the Hadad militia was established. Lebanese were allowed to cross into Israel for medical care and supplies, and even to find employment. Lebanese merchants bought goods in Israel for sale in Lebanon. Following the 1982 Lebanon War, Israel's relations with southern Lebanon's Shi'ites initially improved; the Shi'ites welcomed the IDF for liberating them from the PLO's grip in the south. Soon, however, relations deteriorated; the Shi'ites became a hostile element and attacked IDF troops.

Peace for Galilee. Israel's immediate objective in its invasion of South Lebanon was to remove terrorist bases from within range of the Northern Galilee. Its long-range strategic goals included the destruction of the terrorist infrastructure, removal of Syrian forces from Beirut and the Beka'a Valley, and the establishment of a strong Maronite Christian-dominated regime that would make peace with Israel.

The war in Lebanon began on June 6 [9]. A ceasefire on June 11 left the IDF surrounding Beirut. Fighting then continued from one truce to the next, as the IDF besieged Beirut, bombed and shelled objectives in the city and took some of its suburbs. By late August the terrorists agreed to leave: 3,600 Syrian troops and 2,600 soldiers of the Palestine Liberation Army withdrew to Syria [6], while 8,000 left for other Arab countries.

Israel, however, did not achieve its long-term war goals. The Maronite leader, Bashir Jemayel, was indeed elected president (August 23, 1983), but he was assassinated three weeks later, before ever taking office. His brother Amin, elected to replace him, adopted a pro-Syrian policy. In May 1983, agreement was reached between Israel and Lebanon whereby Israel undertook to remove its forces from Lebanon simultaneously with withdrawal of the Syrian troops; Lebanon pledged to take steps to ensure that its south not serve as a staging area for raids against Israel, and to move toward peace with Israel. But strong Syrian opposition ensured the annulment of the agreement. Meanwhile, in Israel, agitation to withdraw from Lebanon increased as more and more Israeli soldiers were killed and wounded by a growing force of Shi'ite terrorists, or caught in the crossfire between rival Lebanese factions. In late 1983 the IDF began a gradual withdrawal from Lebanon, while endeavoring not to lose what had been gained by the war in terms of defeating terrorism. The withdrawal was completed in 1985.

KEY

The United States played an active role in the Camp David peace negotiations between Israel and Egypt in September 1978. Two framework agreements were drafted. In one, Israel undertook to transfer all of Sinai to Egypt, while Egypt pledged to establish full-scale relations with Israel. The second agreement stipulated that the Arab residents of the West Bank and the Gaza District be granted full autonomy for a 5-year transition period during which the ultimate status of these territories would be negotiated. The peace treaty was signed at the White House on March 26, 1979, with Menahem Begin and Anwar Sadat as signatories, and Jimmy Carter witnessing.

6

7

7 In siege-hostage operations in Kiryat Shmona, Nahariya, Ma'alot [picture: the rescue operation], Bet Shean and Tel Aviv, from April 1974 to March 1975, terrorists seized hostages and demanded the release of imprisoned comrades and immunity for the perpetrators. Working on the principle that acceding to these demands would encourage similar acts in the future, Israel used anti-terror squads to rescue the hostages.

6 Terrorist attacks against Israeli objectives [picture — an atrocity in Jerusalem] continued after 1982, despite the blow dealt the PLO in Lebanon. After their withdrawal from Beirut the terrorists dispersed in various Arab countries. A rift developed within the PLO, ostensibly over Yasir Arafat's selection of commanders, but in fact due to Syrian suspicions that Arafat, after his 1982 Beirut defeat, would now abandon terror and seek negotiations. It climaxed with a Syrian-inspired revolt against Arafat's leadership in North Lebanon in May 1983. Arafat's pro-Syrian opponents walked out of the Supreme Palestinian Council convened in Amman in November 1984.

9

8

8 After the assassination of Sadat in October 1981, Husni Mubarak, the new Egyptian president, adopted a policy of "cold peace" with Israel. When Israel occupied West Beirut and Palestinians there were massacred by Maronites allied to Israel, the Egyptian ambassador to Israel was recalled and no further progress in the peace process was registered. This policy suited Egypt's efforts to restore its status as leader of the pro-western Arab States opposing pro-Soviet Syria. Here Israel's President Yitzhak Navon (1978-1983) confers with President Mubarak after Sadat's assassination.

9 In the Peace for Galilee Operation the IDF fought in three sectors. In the west, Israeli forces captured all the populous coastal towns south of Beirut. In the mountainous central sector the IDF reached and cut the Beirut-Damascus highway. In the eastern sector, armored divisions engaged the Syrian Army, while the air force destroyed Syrian anti-aircraft missile batteries and the IDF took Mt. Barouq and the southern Beka'a.

10

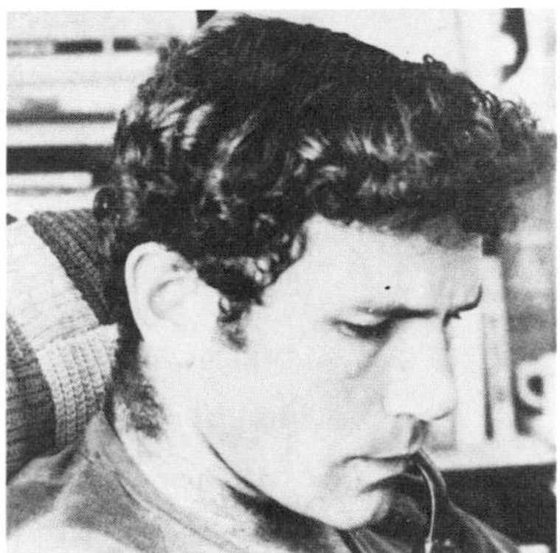

10 An Air France plane en route from Tel Aviv to Paris on June 27, 1976 was hijacked to the Ugandan airport at Entebbe. In exchange for the Israeli hostages, the terrorists demanded the release of 53 of their imprisoned comrades. On July 4 the hostages were rescued by IDF commandos who landed covertly in Entebbe. Pictured: Lt. Col. Jonathan Netanyahu their leader, who was killed during the operation.

A Decade of Change (1974-1984)

Far reaching changes took place in Israeli society in the wake of the Yom Kippur War. The major change was political, with the rise of the *Likud* to power after 50 years of Labor leadership. The Agranat Commission, appointed by the government to investigate events leading up to the Yom Kippur War and the early phases of the battle, laid the blame on army officers, first and foremost the Chief of Staff, Lieutenant General David Elazar. The Commission's exoneration of the political echelon only increased embitterment against the government. On April 10, 1974, Prime Minister Golda Meir announced her resignation and was replaced by Yitzhak Rabin.

The financial cost of the Yom Kippur War was equivalent to Israel's GNP for an entire year. The deficit in foreign currency worsened as defense imports increased, economic growth was halted, and inflation spiraled. The Arab states' "petroleum war" against the West also hurt Israel.

Switch of Government

In the elections to the ninth *Knesset*, in May 1977, the *Likud* emerged as the largest faction, and its leader Menahem Begin was called upon to form a government. This political upheaval brought with it a liberal economic revolution, as the government set out to reduce its economic involvement and encourage a free market economy [2]. But the country's economic problems were not solved. Foreign currency reserves dropped and inflation rose. A large proportion of the country's budget was devoted to social services — health, education, and welfare — and to subsidizing essential food products, electricity, and public transportation. This eased the burden on low-income groups, but the resultant deficit budget spending primed inflation.

In Israel, inflation assumed a special character. To protect the individual against the erosion of his purchasing power, a system of linkage encompassing wages, prices, savings, and other areas of the economy was created. Any rise in one of the components brought about a rise in others, bringing the system back to its starting point, but at a higher inflationary level. Even replacing the Israeli pound with the *shekel*, in October 1980, failed to halt the devaluation of the currency.

Despite these difficult conditions, the Israeli economy revealed an ability to continue functioning and developing. Development emphasis was placed on science-based industries, such as electronics and computers. Advanced agricultural techniques transformed Israel into the "hot-house of Europe" for fruits, vegetables, and flowers. The defense industry exported sophisticated weapons systems. Israel signed trade agreements with the EEC and the United States.

Societal Friction

The period following the Yom Kippur War was characterized by growing friction within Israeli society: between

CONNECTIONS

196 Economics and Society in Greater Israel (1967-1973)
198 From the Six-Day War to the Yom Kippur War
200 Peace with Egypt, War in Lebanon

1 The color televisions, loaded on trucks transporting them straight from the airport to the shops, are indicative of the way the country was flooded with imported consumer goods — some rushed by air freight to meet demand — during the early 1980s. By reducing taxes on imports, which increased purchases of televisions, videos, and automobiles, and allowing Israelis to purchase foreign currency in unlimited quantities, the government depleted foreign currency reserves and accelerated the rate of inflation.

2A

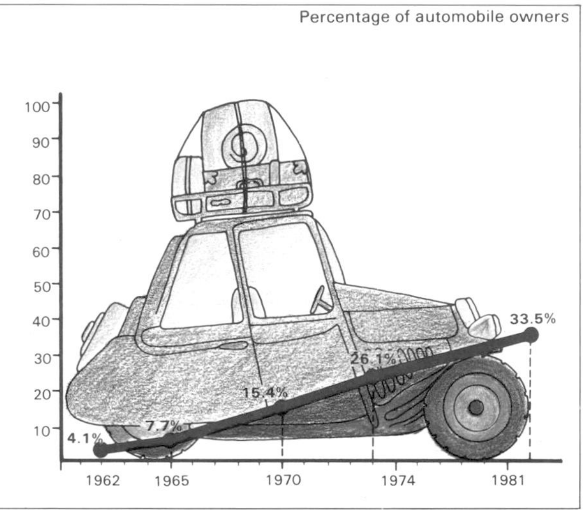

2B

Percentage of refrigerator owners

100 / 90 / 80 / 70 / 60 / 50 / 40 / 30 / 20 / 10

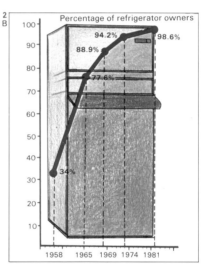

34% · 77.6% · 88.9% · 94.2% · 98.6%

1958 · 1965 · 1969 · 1974 · 1981

2 One manifestation of the rise in the standard of living was the increased demand for luxury goods, travel abroad, high fashion, and durable goods. The table shows the rate of increase in the number of automobiles [A] and refrigerators [B] per family. This development led to a considerable erosion in Israel's foreign currency reserves, and to an acceleration in the rate of inflation. The wage/price linkage system minimized the ravaging effect of inflation on the individual, but created a vicious cycle of price and wage hikes, which further fed the inflation.

1

3

5 Sephardi Jews increased their influence in the country, in both the political and the cultural sphere. Political parties having an ethnic character, such as *Tami* and the Sephardic *Torah* Party (*Shas*) succeeded in winning representation in the 10th and 11th *Knesset*. The cultural heritage of *Sephardi* Jewry also found greater expression. The illustration is from the play "A Moroccan King," by Gabriel ben Simhon, staged by *Habimah*.

5

4 The "Peace Now" movement appealed to public opinion, calling for peace agreements with the Arab countries in exchange for territorial concessions by Israel, and castigating settlement activities in the territories as an obstacle to peace.

4

3 Over 80,000 Arabs residing in the administered territories worked daily in Israel — in construction, agriculture, services, and industry. Many aspects of the economy in the territories themselves became linked to Israel.

Sephardi and *Ashkenazi* Jews [5], religious and secular [7], left and right [4, 6]. Controversy between Jews and Israeli Arabs also characterized this decade. The Arab public was split between nationalistic leanings and a willingness to coexist with the Jews. Extremism existed among the Jewish public, too.

The controversy between left and right became more pronounced during the war in Lebanon. The left wing opposition accused the *Likud* government of extending the scope of the war beyond what was necessary to protect the northern settlements. During the war demonstrations were held calling for its cessation. Under opposition pressure, the Kahn Commission was appointed to investigate possible indirect Israeli involvement in Lebanese Christian massacres in the Beirut refugee camps in September 1982. The commission found that Defense Minister Ariel Sharon and several army generals had not acted to prevent the massacre. As a result, Sharon was forced to resign. During a related demonstration held in Jerusalem a hand grenade was thrown at the demonstrators, killing one of them. This incident deeply shocked the public, and political leaders from left and right called for an end to polarization. The elections to the 11th Knesset, on July 23, 1984, were held in a calm atmosphere. The outcome was a political stalemate; and since neither the Labor Alignment nor the *Likud* could muster a majority in the *Knesset*, a National Unity government was established, on September 13, 1984 [9]. The new government moved to allay public controversy by withdrawing the IDF from Lebanon. Initial measures to revitalize the economy proved less promising, however.

All told, Israel's parliamentary democracy, an independent judicial authority and free press displayed considerable vitality in weathering a decade of change and controversy, and in channeling dissent to legitimate paths.

KEY

Accelerated Jewish settlement in Judea and Samaria was one of the more tangible changes that took place in Israel with the *Likud's* rise to power in May 1977. An extensive program was launched, and the public received attractive offers from public and private developers to settle a short distance from the center of the country. The settlers in these areas were motivated by historical, defense, and economic considerations. Some of the new settlements were situated in areas with a dense Arab population. By the end of 1984, 114 Jewish settlements had been established in Judea, Samaria, and the Gaza District. Their population reached 42,600, of whom some 30,000 lived in 15 of the larger settlements. This is Barkan, in Samaria.

6 The standard-bearers of the Movement for Greater Israel were primarily members of *Gush Emunim* from religious nationalist circles. They called for settling all areas of Judea, Samaria, and the Gaza District, and opposed restrictions which the Alignment government placed on settlement. The picture shows two *Gush Emunim* leaders, Rabbi Moshe Levinger [left] and Hannan Porat [right], together with settlers, after receiving government approval for settling Elon Moreh, in Samaria, December 1975.

6

7

7 The polarization between religious and secular Israelis during the 1970s and 1980s was most prominently manifested by the assault made by religious circles on the Israeli secular public and on public life in general. At times this polarization deteriorated into violence, with religious Jews stoning cars traveling on the Sabbath near religious neighborhoods [illustration: demonstration at Ramot road, Jerusalem]. Religious-inspired legislative initiatives related to Jewish identity, autopsies, abortions, and Sabbath observance.

8 Immigration from the Soviet Union continued to comprise the bulk of *aliyah* to Israel during the post Yom Kippur War years. However, it was overcast by a considerable drop-out rate, with many Soviet immigrants opting for the United States. The number of immigrants coming to Israel dropped steadily after 1979, with the efforts of Jewish organizations to pressure the Soviet Union proving largely ineffective. Since there was no large immigration to Israel from developed western countries during these years, the rate of immigration dropped in comparison to earlier years, with the total from 1973 to 1983 reaching only 275,000.

8

Figures in thousands

40
35
30
25
20
15
10
5

33.5
21.5
21.1
22.8
28.8
39.6
22.2
14.6
16.1
19.1

1974 1975 1976 1977 1978 1979 1980 1981 1982 1983

9

9 The National Unity government [here, with President Chaim Herzog] was established in September 1984. The *Likud* and the Alignment agreed to establish the unity government together with other parties, and to institute a rotation in the office of prime minister — two years for Shimon Peres from the Alignment, and two years for Yitzhak Shamir from the *Likud*. The cabinet consisted of 26 ministers, and had the coalition support of 93 *Knesset* members. Its primary objectives were to stabilize the economy, and to remove the IDF from Lebanon while assuring the security of the northern settlements. The government's early efforts to stabilize the economy took the form of "package deals" between the government, the *Histadrut* and the private sector, in which all sides pledged to maintain fixed prices and wages, and attempts were made to cut the budget and absorb surplus public purchasing potential. By mid-1985 these measures had proved largely ineffective.

Arabs and Other Minorities in Israel

In the mid-1980s approximately 17% of all Israeli citizens were non-Jewish. In early 1984 they numbered 720,000 — compared with 160,000 immediately after the War of Independence. The natural birth rate of this population was especially high, although it has fallen off slightly in recent years.

Almost half the non-Jewish population in Israel is located in the Galilee. Nazareth [2] is the heart of the Arab Galilee settlements. The "little triangle" — part of the pre-1948 "big triangle" of Nablus-Tulkarm-Jenin — extends from the end of the Jezreel Valley in the north down to Kefar Kassem in the south, and comprises the two largest Arab towns, Taiyiba and Umm el Fahm. In the mid-1980s over 100,000 Arabs lived in this area. Israel's extension of its sovereignty over East Jerusalem, in 1967, added another 100,000 people to the non-Jewish population.

Religious Sects

In Israel, as in most Middle Eastern countries that inherited Ottoman legal practices, all religious sects possess singular authority in matters of individual status and consecration. Each sect has its own set of institutions and religious services, which also receive government funding.

Sunni Arabs account for the vast majority of Israel's 552,000 Muslims. Although the Circassians, who originated in the Caucasus, are Muslim, they constitute a distinct group, and — unlike other Muslim Arabs — they volunteer to serve in the IDF. Members of the Druze sect have earned a unique position in Israeli society; their cooperation with Jewish settlements began before 1948 [3].

Israel's Christians are mainly Arabs, and live in the cities and towns; this population is composed of a large number of sects, each maintaining its own independent institutions [1].

Changing Life Style

The Arab population in Israel in the mid-1980s was a remnant of the larger Arab population which resided within the country's borders before the War of Independence. During that war, the Arab-Palestinian establishment was destroyed, and its leaders fled to other countries. Some cities — such as Jaffa, Ramlah, Lydda, and Haifa — emptied out, and those who left became refugees.

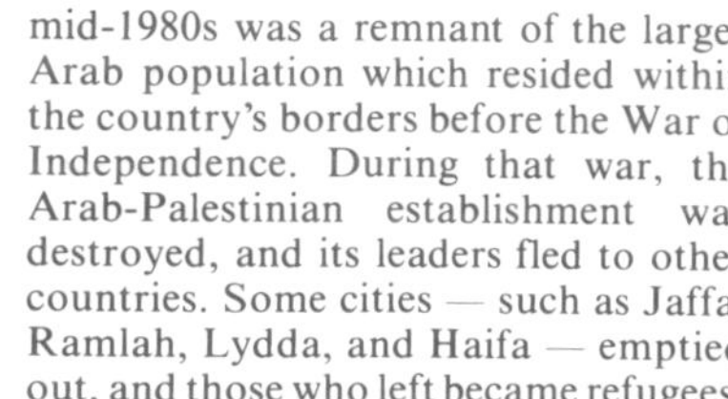

Since the establishment of the State of Israel, a "quiet revolution" has taken place in the economic, social, and political world of Israel's minorities. Arab society has developed new patterns of production and consumption, as well as different modes of thought. It has adopted modern political concepts, has adapted, in part, to new technological methods, and has even altered modes of dress. There has also been substantial progress at all educational levels.

One significant contributing factor to the development of greater contact with the Jewish population was the abolition of the military government (1966), imposed on the Arab sector during the

CONNECTIONS

198 From the Six-Day War to the Yom Kippur War
200 Peace with Egypt; War in Lebanon

1 A

2 Nazareth, the Christian holy city, has gone through many transformations throughout its long history. In 1985 the city had about 45,000 inhabitants, mainly Christian and Muslim Arabs. It contains Arab cultural and educational institutions, and is the hub of Arab political activity in Israel. In 1957, a development town — Nazareth Illit, where some 26,000 Jews lived by 1985 — was established near Nazareth. Many Arabs from Nazareth and the surrounding villages have found employment here, but neither neighborly proximity nor working together have managed to lessen tensions between residents of the two cities.

1 The Christian population of Israel in the mid-1980s was about 90,000, composed of some 35 sects and communities. Some of these maintain independent jurisdictional frameworks: the largest and most consolidated (approximately 40% of all Christians) is the Greek Orthodox Church, headed by the Bishop of Jerusalem. The Latin, or Roman Catholic Church, is second in size (15%), and is headed by the Patriarch of Jerusalem. In addition, there are the Maronite Christians (5%), the Armenians, who number 1,500, and several small Protestant sects. Pictured: [A] A Coptic nun in East Jerusalem; [B] Christmas in Bethlehem.

3 The Druze belong to the Arab/Islamic world linguistically and historically. In 1985 there were 65,000 Israeli Druze, living in 18 villages in the Galilee and on Mt. Carmel. Their position as a legally-recognized religious sect was defined in 1957. Several fragmenting trends affect the Druze: a tendency toward integration into Israeli society — expressed by their service in the IDF [A] and by their political involvement [B — MK Jabber Múaddi hosting Minister Shlomo Hillel at his home in Yirka]; a competing tendency to identify with Arab nationalism; and a sense of identification with the Druze of Syria and Lebanon.

War of Independence (1948). The Arab village has gradually begun to adopt modern work methods, which include new types of processing [Key], mechanization, and irrigation. Along with these agricultural developments, traditional village life has also been upset by the fact that over half the breadwinners commute each day to work in the Jewish sector. This process has altered the employment structure of the Arab village, moving the center of gravity from farming and country life into the cities. However during the late 1970s a limited trend toward industrialization began in the Arab villages, and their linkup to the national electric power grid contributed significantly to their augmented standard of living.

Increased contact with Israeli-Jewish society has gradually undermined the traditional foundations of the Arab village. The earlier social framework was based on blood ties (the *hamula*), and dictated a land-based economic structure; now the individual has taken on greater significance, although traditional frameworks still remained politically, socially, and economically strong in the mid-1980s.

Israeli democratic values have been absorbed by Arab society. Israeli Arabs' rate of participation in Knesset elections — an average of 80% — is higher than that of the Israeli population as a whole. However, they have had less representation in the *Knesset* than their numbers would indicate, mainly because many tend to support small, shortlived political parties which fail to reach the necessary minimum quotient.

After the Six-Day War, renewed contact between Israeli Arabs and their brethren in the West Bank and the Gaza Strip reawakened the national-political awareness of the Israeli Arabs [5]. Many experienced a heightened sense of affinity with the Palestinian Arab people, who were perceived as a consolidated political community with their own leadership, intelligentsia, and national political consciousness.

KEY

In Arab villages throughout Israel, a revolution in land cultivation and irrigation has taken place. Israel's unique agricultural achievements — drip irrigation, low plastic tunneling [pictured], and introduction of new varieties — have been adopted by the Arab farmer, thereby increasing crop yields significantly. Agriculture, however, is no longer the major source of employment for the young Arab. Industrialization has reached even the smallest village; this, combined with the Arab custom (dictated by Muslim law) of dividing up the cultivated lands equally among a man's sons, has caused a mass exodus to the cities in search of work.

4 A

4 The Bedouin are mostly Muslims. They are organized into tribes of different sizes, strengths, and nomadic routes. Each tribe is headed by a *sheikh* who is its representative to the authorities. The Bedouin are well-known for their customs of hospitality, family loyalty, and family honor (sometimes taking the form of vendettas). By the mid-1980s Israeli Bedouin were distancing themselves from the nomadic tradition [A] and seeking higher education. Land requirements in the Negev dictated a government policy of encouraging their settlement in permanent farming villages and adopting modern life styles [B].

4 B

5

5 Relations between Arabs and Jews changed dramatically after the Six-Day War and the Yom Kippur War. Israeli Arabs became troubled by questions of loyalty and identity. This resulted both from meetings with Arabs from the administered territories and neighboring countries, and from their encounter with PLO propaganda. Extremist nationalistic ideas became popular, especially with the younger generation. When Arab lands in the Galilee were expropriated by the Israeli government the Arabs voiced sharp criticism (as did many Jews); they held a demonstration on March 30, 1976. Since then, March 30 has become "Land Day," and is commemorated each year [picture]. The Galilee land question is particularly acute due to the demographic factor: with their higher birth rate the Arabs would in effect make this part of Israel an "Arab island" by the year 2000. Government land expropriations, then, were designed to facilitate Jewish settlement.

6

6 Bahai followers are scattered in approximately 80 countries — with only 200 living in Israel. Bahai has Islamic origins. Its founder, Mirza Ali Muhammad, known as the *Bab*, called for the unity of all mankind, and for goodwill between all religions. As a result, his followers were excluded from Islam. The *Bab* himself was murdered in Persia in 1850, and in 1899 his remains were brought to Acre for burial. In 1909 they were moved to Haifa, and an elaborate mausoleum was built around them [pictured]. An exact replica of this temple was built in Chicago, Illinois (where there is a large Bahai following). In 1971 the Bahais in Israel received legal status similar to other religions.

Education and Culture in Israel

With its establishment, the State of Israel had to deal with problems in education that derived from its varied ethnic and cultural composition. The *Knesset* enacted two Basic (i.e., quasi-constitutional) Laws, intended to bridge the differences and gaps among the various groups of society: the Compulsory Education Law of 1949, for all 5 to 14 year-olds; and the State Education Law of 1953. The latter abrogated the system of separate cultural currents in the educational system — general, labor movement, *Mizrahi*, and *Agudat Israel* — and replaced these with state schools and state-religious schools, in both of which the curriculum is set by the Ministry of Education and Culture. The school system of *Agudat Israel* remained independent, and *kibbutz* schools continued to maintain their special status within the framework of the state schools [2].

In 1978 a law extended compulsory education to the age of 16, and free education to 18. Since 1968 the educational system has been divided into six years of elementary neighborhood schools, and six of secondary comprehensive schools — three of intermediate level junior high school and three of upper level high school. One of the purposes of this reform was to achieve greater social integration by bringing together children from different classes of society, in order to reduce disparities.

Unique Educational Problems

The educational system has tried in varied ways to cope with discrepancies in academic achievement that stem from socio-economic gaps. During Israel's first decade, its leaders believed that the provision of equal education to everyone would solve the problem. During the second decade, when the great extent of the gap became clear, special educational projects were established to give equal educational opportunity and compensate underprivileged students for what they lacked in their primary environment [1]. During the third decade efforts focused on dealing with the causes of the gap, i.e., working with the families at an early stage, and involving the population in solving its own problems. Several principles took root: leniency in advancing weak students, supplementary lessons for the weak, and adjusting the structure and methods of education to the needs of various population groups [Key].

The educational system in Israel attempts to teach national, social, and religious values. The "Jewish consciousness" program for imbuing a sense of the Jewish people's historical heritage, was initiated in the late 1950s. In the 1970s institutes for Zionist education were established [9], and added emphasis was placed on Jewish studies in the state schools. Curricula which promote democratic values and greater understanding between ethnic groups and between Jews and Arabs were also introduced.

Israel's Arab minority, which wishes to preserve its culture, identity, and

CONNECTIONS

186 Building the New State
188 Israel's First Decade
192 Economics and Society in Israel's Second Decade
196 Economics and Society in Greater Israel (1967-1973)

1 Informal education in Israel has many settings: youth movements, school-sponsored extra-curricular activities, community centers, field schools, school citizenship programs, etc. Over 70% of the youth from ages 10 to 18 participate in these activities, and about one third of youth above 14 are members in one of Israel's 13 youth movements. The picture shows members of a youth movement sailing on rafts in the Sea of Galilee.

2 The kibbutz educational system created unique approaches to education. Collective education is based on the principle of equality championed by the *kibbutz*. It encompasses all the children of the *kibbutz* from infancy through the age of 18, and touches on all spheres of life, cultivating body and mind, and including work all year round.

3

FORMAL EDUCATION IN ISRAEL SINCE 1948

Year	Number of Schools	Number of teaching posts	Number of Pupils
1948-9	611	5,264	140,817
1959-60	2,000	22,890	580,202
1969-70	2,320	40,868	824,432
1979-80	2,367	72,840	1,203,836
1983-4	2,456	81,115	1,330,026

4

החברה להגנת הטבע
SOCIETY FOR PROTECTION OF NATURE
רשות שמורות הטבע
NATURE RESERVES AUTHORITY
פרחי-בר מוגנים
PROTECTED WILD FLOWERS
أزهار برية يجب حمايتها
צא לנוף אך אל תקטוף!

4 The Israeli public is becoming increasingly aware of the need to preserve the landscape and to cope with environmental problems. Organizations like the Society for the Protection of Nature, educational programs in the schools, and various laws enacted by the *Knesset*, contribute to environmental protection.

5 Israeli song and folk-dance groups attracted some 100,000 participants in 1985. Evenings of song are also popular.

rights, is itself not homogenous in terms of religion, culture, and ethnic composition. The education system takes this heterogeneity into account. It encompasses the entire Arab sector, and Arabic is the language of instruction.

There are a number of frameworks for adult education in Israel: *ulpanim* for teaching Hebrew to immigrants; programs in basic education for the underprivileged; an extensive system of instruction for IDF soldiers with deficient educational backgrounds; and regular educational programs for all soldiers, with lectures on a wide variety of subjects. An extensive selection of oral and written instruction is offered in religious studies.

Cultural Activities

The arts in Israel have been influenced by developments in the arts throughout the world, as well as by local conditions of life, with their particular problems and challenges [6, 10]. Extensive efforts to attract new audiences to cultural activity are made by such bodies as the Society for Promoting Art for the People, which focuses its endeavors on bringing artistic productions to development towns and poor neighborhoods. Greater cultural involvement is also cultivated by communal activities in the *Matnasim* (community centers).

Israel has about 250 cultural institutions, active in theater, music, dance, literature, film, visual arts, and folklore, as well as schools in all the arts. The government, in cooperation with the municipal councils, supports about 60% of these institutions' budgets. While there is a government council for reviewing films and plays, intervention in freedom of creativity and artistic content is in line with western democracies, and refers primarily to pornography.

Thus the educational system and cultural creativity in Israel contend with the unique needs of Israeli society, and with the tensions between an emerging national culture and the impact of a universal, technological culture.

KEY

Comprehensive secondary schools were established in Israel during the mid-1960s, primarily in the development towns. The curriculum of the comprehensive school encompasses both liberal arts and vocational training, with a view to satisfying the needs of a diverse population. In 1985 most of the secondary schools were comprehensive, in terms of both the composition of their student body and the subjects taught. Vocational and agricultural schools are gradually becoming comprehensive too. The range of subjects has also been extended by the introduction of a point system in matriculation exams, allowing students to select courses of instruction at the level and scope which they desire.

6

7

7 Vocational schools comprise about half of the secondary school student body in Israel. This large figure may be explained by the attitude of the state's founding fathers toward productive labor, and by the needs of the state's developing economy. These schools train students in technological vocations, the arts and crafts, maritime vocations, and electronics and computer studies.

6 A variety of musical activity in Israel reflects diverse socio-cultural influences. Attempts at developing a clear Israeli identity in music would appear to be premature, yet extremely promising in the long run. The high level of performance of the Israel Philharmonic Orchestra [illustration], the proportion of concert-goers, and the large number of visiting musical artists, have given Israel a name as a musical country.

8

8 Israel has seven recognized institutions of higher education: the Technion, Hebrew University of Jerusalem, Weizmann Institute of Science, Bar Ilan University, Tel Aviv University, University of Haifa, and Ben Gurion University of Beersheba [illustrated].

10 Theater in Israel is primarily a public institution. There are five public theaters, as well as a state children's theater which operates under the aegis of the Ministry of Education and Culture. Experimental and fringe activities center around the "Festival for a Different Theater," held every year in Acre. Israel has one of the highest rates of theater attendance in the world. Production of original Israeli plays has been expanding. Here playwright Hanokh Levine stages *The Great Harlot from Babylon* (1982).

9 The Museum of the Diaspora, built with money contributed by world Jewry, provides Jews from Israel and abroad an opportunity to become acquainted with the roots of their people, and to explore common elements in all the different Jewish communities. The museum features a permanent collection — which houses this model of the Florence Synagogue — as well as occasional exhibitions on a variety of subjects.

9

10

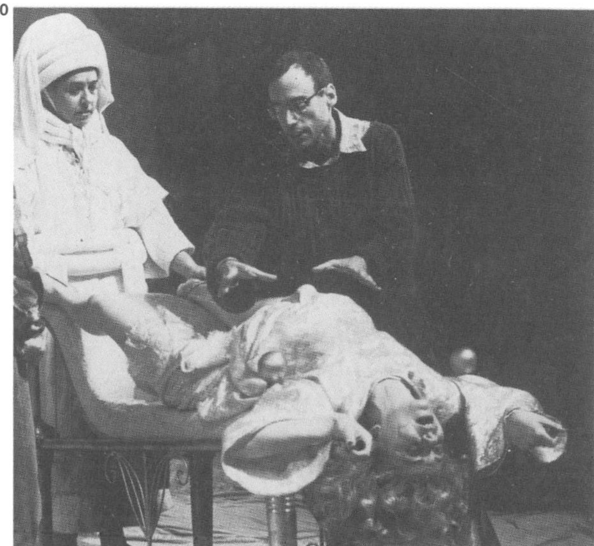

The Histadrut (General Federation of Labor)

The great majority of Jewish and Arab workers in Israel belong to the *Histadrut*: manual laborers and white collar workers, salaried workers and the self-employed. Like other labor unions throughout the world, the *Histadrut* ensures the fair wages, welfare and working conditions of all employees. But unlike other such organizations, it is also active in building an independent economy, in settlement, mutual aid, culture and education.

Principles and Structure

At its founding convention in Haifa in December 1920, the *Histadrut* declared as its aims to unite and unionize all workers who earn their living without exploiting the work of others, and to create a working society in Erez Israel.

The conditions that shaped the special nature of the *Histadrut* were those of Palestine under the British Mandate. The economy was primitive, agricultural settlements minimal, and unemployment rife. The pioneers arriving in Palestine needed help in adjusting to their new circumstances, finding work, acquiring a trade, learning the language, receiving medical care, and not a few even in obtaining a square meal. The *Histadrut* sought to fulfil these needs, and at the same time build an economy in the country based on public ownership on the socialist model.

The *Histadrut* congress, convened approximately once every four years, is elected in general proportional elections in which all members can participate. All of the political parties in the *Histadrut* are represented on the national council, which is elected by the congress and serves as the supreme legislative body. The *Histadrut* executive is chosen by the national council and deals with ongoing affairs throughout the year. The *Histadrut*'s "cabinet" — the central committee, headed by the general secretary — is responsible for overseeing the activities of all of the various branches.

The basic unit of the union, concerned with the wages, welfare and working conditions of *Histadrut* members, is the works committee elected directly in each place of employment. It is the official representative of all employees under its jurisdiction. Each worker also belongs to a national union of members of the same profession. The Union Department of the executive coordinates all these professional unions.

Hevrat ha-Ovdim is the supreme body in charge of all companies owned by the *Histadrut*. Every member of the *Histadrut* also belongs to *Hevrat ha-Ovdim*. Its independent enterprises include *moshav* and *kibbutz* enterprises and a large cooperative industry with production and service branches. Its directorships comprise the spheres of industry — *Koor* [8]; finance and insurance — *Bank ha-Poalim* [5], *Hassneh*; and contracting firms for construction and public works in Israel and abroad — *Solel Boneh* [3], *Shikun Ovdim*.

All of these concerns were founded both to create jobs for immigrants and

CONNECTIONS

140 Aliyah During the 1920s
148 Immigration and Settlement in the 1930s
152 The Jewish Economy in Palestine until 1939
210 The Kibbutz

1 The cultural and educational activities of the *Histadrut* are directed toward building a free workers' society in Israel. [In picture shown history lesson in one of the Histadrut factories during lunchbreak (1938)]. These efforts are administered by five departments: information — disseminating the labor movement's basic tenets; education — teaching Hebrew and organizing adult education; vocational training — through courses and lectures; art — promoting original work; and libraries and cultural centers.

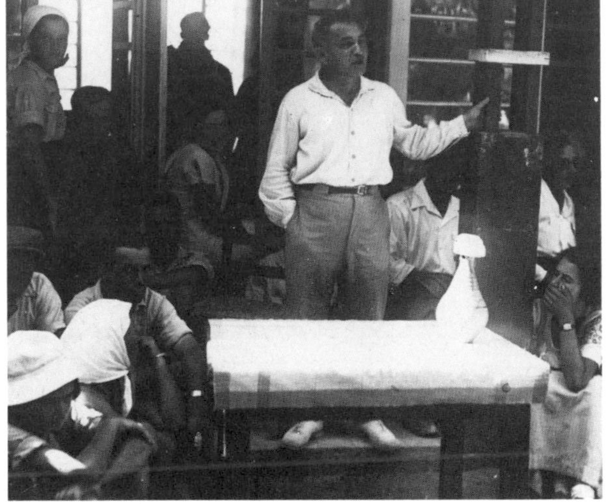

2 Berl Katznelson (1887-1944) was one of the founding fathers of the labor movement and the *Histadrut*. Believing that Zionism must be realized through cultural and ideological activities as well as political endeavors, he initiated the establishment of the *Histadrut*'s schools and educational facilities. He was zealous in preserving the link with Jewish tradition and religion, and fought to maintain kosher kitchens in *Histadrut* institutions and to ensure the status of its religious members.

3 Solel Boneh, like most *Hevrat ha-Ovdim* enterprises, was founded to ease immigrant absorption and vocational training as well as to further the development of the country. Its first projects were the building of roads contracted for by the British. During the riots of 1936, it participated in erecting the stockade and tower settlements, and in building the Tel Aviv port. During World War II, *Solel Boneh* built scores of police stations and army camps; its knowledge of the plans for these structures was shared with the *Haganah*, and facilitated their capture during the War of Independence. Today the enterprise carries out construction and development work in Israel and abroad, produces raw materials and construction equipment.

4 On May Day, the *Histadrut* displays its solidarity with workers the world over. The *Histadrut* is an active member of all international unions and of the International Labor Organization (ILO). A *Histadrut* delegate serves as vice president of the Confederation of Free Labor Unions and of the Asian Organization of Labor Unions. The *Histadrut* assists unions throughout the world, particularly in developing countries, by training foreign students at its Afro-Asian Institute in Tel Aviv, where they study social and labor models unique to Israel: the *kibbutz* and *moshav*, and *Histadrut*-owned industries.

to serve the central purpose of the *Histadrut* as a social movement: building and developing the country while creating a free Jewish working society that would itself own companies and have the resources to finance its productive operations.

Welfare, Education and Culture

The principle of mutual aid is realized in *Kupat Holim* — the system of health services established even before the *Histadrut* itself [7] — a strike fund to finance work disputes, and some ten insurance and pension funds.

The *Histadrut*'s educational arm is the *Amal* vocational school system. *Histadrut ha-Noar ha-Oved Ve-ha-Lomed* (The Organization of Working and Studying Youth) is Israel's largest youth movement. The *Histadrut* publishes a daily newspaper, *Davar*, owns a publishing house (*Am Oved*), and operates cultural centers throughout the country. For working women there is a parallel organization, *Na'amat*, whose activities include an extensive network of day-care centers, kindergartens and nursery schools, vocational training for young girls and women, and courses and centers for general education and cultural improvement [1].

With the establishment of the State, several of the *Histadrut*'s nationwide functions were transferred to government bodies. The first of these was defense. At its founding convention in December, 1920, the *Histadrut* had accepted the responsibility for guard and defense matters, i.e. for the *Haganah*, which later became the basic component of the Israel Defense Forces. The *Histadrut*'s many schools also became part of the national school system. As a result, the *Histadrut*'s function as a labor union is now a much more central feature of its activities than it was before statehood. On the other hand, the *Histadrut*'s successes have made it one of Israel's foremost social models to be emulated by developing countries [4].

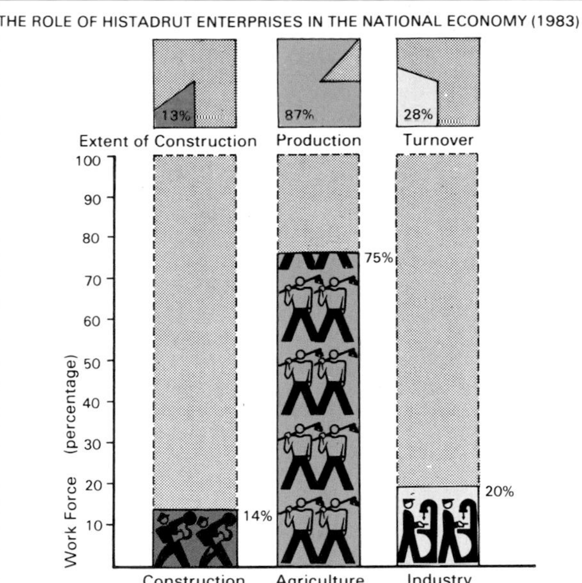

5

5 Bank ha-Poalim, one of the three largest in Israel, is the central fiscal institution financing *Histadrut* operations. In order to attract investment capital, an affiliate, *Ampal* (America-Palestine), was established during World War II. During Israel's first 35 years it invested some 100 million dollars in oil drilling, quarries, the merchant marine, and the aircraft industries.

7 Kupat Holim, the *Histadrut* network of health services, provides medical care and hospitalization for some 76% of the Israeli population, who are insured by it. [This is *Kupat Holim*'s Carmel Hospital.] Health insurance is one of a wide range of institutions and funds serving *Histadrut* members. *Mishan*, one of several large pension and provident funds, supports homes for the aged and for needy children, and supplies meal services, rest homes and summer camps.

6

6 The post of Histadrut general secretary has been held by such prominent figures as David Remez, Mordechai Namir, Yitzhak Ben-Aharon [shown here], and even David Ben-Gurion and Golda Meir who went on to become prime ministers of Israel.

7

8

8 Koor is the largest industrial concern in Israel, comprising 280 companies whose factories produce 20% of the total Israeli industrial output. It is unique in its combined financial, social and national objectives, and a pioneer in worker participation in management and profits and in promoting its workers' welfare and benefits. *Tiyus* is a conglomerate of 22 firms and factories that complements *Koor* by concentrating on industrializing development and border towns.

The Kibbutz

The *kibbutz* is one of Zionism's most original creations, evolving as part of the renewal of Jewish independence and settlement in Erez Israel. During the early days of the Second *Aliyah*, the most urgent needs were to build the country and redeem the land, and the *kibbutz* provided a solution. It was born in 1909 at Um Juni by the Sea of Galilee, when ten young men and two young women began a small farming operation based on cooperation, equality, and mutual aid. They thus laid the foundations for the first *kevutzah* [4] — Deganyah — and for the concept of communal settlement.

There was no grand design or idealism in this decision to establish a commune in which production and consumption were shared, all were equal, and all assisted each other. Rather, this way of life was imposed on the young pioneers by their circumstances. Alone, they simply could not cope with the arduous work or harsh conditions.

In the 1930s and 1940s, with the *Yishuv* fighting for independence, *kibbutzim* served as *Haganah* bases, particularly for *Palmach* recruits, as the home base for emissaries sent abroad to educate Jewish youth and organize illegal immigration, and as the first new home for illegal immigrants. The distribution of *kibbutzim* around the country helped determine Israel's borders and dispersed the population to uninhabited areas [2].

Structure and Ideology

The *kibbutz* ideology was first formulated by the pioneers of the Third *Aliyah*. With their revolutionary Marxist ideals, they saw each *kibbutz* as part of a countrywide movement aimed at bringing about a national revolution through Zionist immigration to, and settlement in, Erez Israel. The fundamental ethical principles of the *kibbutz* stemmed from these ideals: cooperation, equality, mutual aid, settlement, work, and a free and democratic society.

Kibbutz membership is voluntary. It operates as a direct democracy through the general meeting of all members [Key]. Committees are responsible for carrying out members' decisions in areas such as work, culture, and finance. Central coordination is in the hands of the secretary, treasurer, and work programer. These posts are rotated among the members.

Rotation as a principle is a feature which meets the growing need of many members to perform professional functions that demand expertise and afford them interest and satisfaction, as well as intensifying the identification of each individual with the social unit as a whole. Without such identification, it would be difficult to maintain the *kibbutz* principle of "to each according to his needs."

The unique structure of the *kibbutz* has engendered a characteristic lifestyle and original forms for the celebration of festive occasions, particularly seasonal and national holidays, which blend traditional Jewish values with distinctly

CONNECTIONS

134 Foundations of Zionism in Erez Israel
140 Aliyah During the 1920s
148 Immigration and Settlement in the 1930s
158 The Underground Movement
208 The Histadrut (General Federation of Labor).

1 A

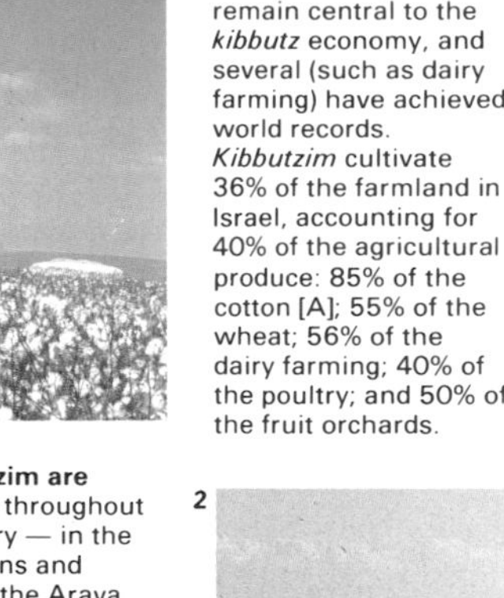

1 Agriculture was the major economic activity of the *kibbutz* in its early days [B]. Today too, certain branches of agriculture remain central to the *kibbutz* economy, and several (such as dairy farming) have achieved world records. *Kibbutzim* cultivate 36% of the farmland in Israel, accounting for 40% of the agricultural produce: 85% of the cotton [A]; 55% of the wheat; 56% of the dairy farming; 40% of the poultry; and 50% of the fruit orchards.

1 B

3 The "industrial revolution" in the *kibbutz* is almost complete; today there is no *kibbutz* without at least one industrial plant. *Kibbutz* industry is now undergoing another revolution — the transition to automation and robotization. Regional factories shared by a number of *kibbutzim* (as well as *moshavim*) process agricultural produce [pictured is the Granot processing plant, north of Hadera]. In some areas, these factories are a prime source of employment for the residents of nearby development towns, a trend which runs counter to the principle of not hiring laborers and which even tends to generate a certain tension between the *kibbutz* and the town. *Kibbutz* industries produce 6.5% of the industrial output in Israel. The value of *kibbutz* industrial exports in 1985 was 230 million dollars, 7.5% of the Israeli total.

2 Kibbutzim are scattered throughout the country — in the hilly regions and valleys in the Arava, the Jordan River Valley and along the Coastal Plain. Establishing settlements throughout Erez Israel, even in regions which economically are not viable and strategically are vulnerable, is a basic tenet of *kibbutz* ideology. The picture shows *Kibbutz* Farod, situated in the Upper Galilee, and founded in 1949.

2

3

4

4 Kibbutz En Harod was founded in 1921 by young members of the Work Battalions from the Third *Aliyah*. They envisioned a large, growing and open "*kibbutz*" in contrast to the smaller, already existing "*kevutzah*" — one that would combine agriculture, crafts and industry and be part of a national network of *kibbutzim*. Today there is no longer any distinction between the size, structure, economy and ideals of the *kevutzah* and the *kibbutz*.

Israeli elements. Thus, changes were made in the Passover *haggadah* at the *kibbutzim*, and in the festivals celebrating the early harvest, the first fruits, reaping and planting.

The Kibbutz Economy

The *kibbutz* economy combines a wide range of highly centralized and mechanized agricultural branches, with increasing emphasis on industrial agriculture [1], services and diversified light and heavy industry [3]. There is a growing trend toward high-technology, automation, and sophisticated industry.

Although only 3.5% of Israel's Jewish population live on *kibbutzim*, their contribution to the national economy in agricultural and industrial production and export is much higher.

All told, 271 *kibbutzim* comprise the *kibbutz* movement and belong to one of three affiliations: the United Kibbutz Movement — founded in 1980 by the merger of *ha-Kibbutz ha-Meuhad* and *Ihud ha-Kev'utzot Ve-ha-Kibbutzim* (170); *Ha-Kibbutz ha-Artzi ha-Shomer ha-Tzair* (85); and the Religious Kibbutz Movement (16). Each group is affiliated with a different political party, the two larger ones with Labor and *Mapam*, and the Religious Kibbutz Movement with the National Religious Party [5].

Many people in Israel and around the world view the *kibbutz* as a unique social experiment and study its structure and way of life. Some consider it a possible model for a future socialistic society. The real test of the *kibbutz* is the number of members who remain and the integration of the children of the founders into the community. A further test is its ability to continue to be an idealistic pioneering movement, fulfilling national and social needs in Israel in the second half of the 20th century. Many years ago the Jewish philosopher Martin Buber defined the *kibbutz* as "a distinct non-failure." In its eighth decade, many would now define it as "a distinct success."

KEY

The powers of the general members meeting have changed over the years. As *kibbutz* society grew and diversified, the issues before it became more complex. Many decisions are now made by professional committees or teams. Nevertheless, the *kibbutz* employs various means — including a newsletter, visual aids and, recently, closed-circuit television — to provide members with information. This ensures a high level of involvement in decisionmaking and enables members to consider pertinent issues intelligently.

5

5 Ideological and political tensions are part of *kibbutz* life. At times, extreme differences of opinion have resulted in deep and painful rifts. The most severe was the schism in *ha-Kibbutz ha-Meuhad* in 1951. Some members left their *kibbutz* because of ideological disputes, and several *kibbutzim* actually split in two. Eventually the differences in the economic and social structure of the *kibbutz* and the *kvutzah* became less discernible, and political factions moved closer together, generating a process of cooperation and unification.

6

6 The kibbutz artist is recognized as a producer of income no different from any other sector of the economy. The *kibbutz* movement supports dance groups, orchestras, choirs, singing troupes and a theater — *Bimat ha-Kibbutz* — and has two art galleries, in Tel Aviv and Jaffa. Many *kibbutzim* maintain their own local art galleries or museums, in which member artists exhibit their work. There are two *kibbutz* publishing houses, and various weekly and quarterly journals to which *kibbutz* members contribute. The work of some of Israel's most noted authors, poets and painters first appeared in *kibbutz* organs. Several highly acclaimed creative artists of the 1970s and 1980s were kibbutz members, including Amos Oz. *Kibbutz* was painted by the Israeli artist Naftali Bezem.

7

7 Communal education involves the entire *kibbutz* community. From birth to adolescence, the child belongs to a peer group and is cared for by members selected for their suitability and given professional training. The child spends most of its time in educational frameworks, while afternoon hours, Saturdays and holidays are reserved for its biological family. In recent years many *kibbutzim* have arranged for the young children to sleep at home rather than in the communal children's houses. Each *kibbutz* has its own primary school, while most secondary schools are regional. The *kibbutz* school system also accepts children from outside the community.

8

8 Communal consumption is a basic principle of the *kibbutz*, as are communal production and ownership of property. The *kibbutz* is responsible for supplying all of the needs of each of its individuals, and this is done through institutions like the central dining room, the clothing store [shown here], and the grocery and general store from which each member can choose what he needs according to his own taste, within the budgetary constraints of the *kibbutz*. In its early days the *kibbutz* was stricter in enforcing the principle of equality in consumption, and there was virtually no "private property" even in regard to clothes.

American Jewry in the Mid-1980s

American Jewry's identification and awareness is influenced both by its immediate surroundings and by its participation in world Jewry. The individual Jew expresses his identification in the fields of religion, welfare and education, by establishing Jewish institutions and organizations, and by his attitude to the State of Israel.

Religious Denominations

Few American Jews are traditionally observant, while another small minority attributes no significance at all to being Jewish. It is doubtful if more than 20% of US Jewry fall into these two extreme categories together. Rather, most of the Jewish public has some attachment, however tenuous, to a Jewish framework. Most blend into the society around them, while less than 50% belong to a synagogue. Religion, however, remains important, at least symbolically: data from 1970 show that some 85% of all American Jews consider themselves part of one of the Jewish denominations: Reform (about 33%), Conservative (42%), Orthodox (11%), and a small number of Reconstructionists. (Among American-born Jews, 40% are Reform and 30% Conservative.)

Reform Judaism was brought to the United States in the mid-19th century by Jews of Central Europe who did not accept the obligatory behavioral norms of the traditional *Halakhah*. Seeing Judaism only as a religion with no national connotation meant belief in one God and in Jewish ethical principles. The leaders of the Reform movement therefore opposed Zionism. These convictions facilitated their social adaptation to their new country. Since the 1930s, however, Reform Jewry has tended to move closer to traditional ritual, Jewish education is stressed more, and it supports the State of Israel [2].

The Conservative movement springs from the idea of "positive historical Judaism." Founded by Zacharias Frankel (1801-1875) in the middle of the 19th century and taught at the Jewish Theological Seminary at Breslau, Germany, its basic concept is the religious cross-fertilization of the sustaining positive element that is constant in Judaism, with the historical element that changes and develops. Solomon Schechter (1847-1915), who became president of the Jewish Theological Seminary of America after its reorganization in 1902, headed the movement when it began in the US. Conservative Judaism aims to adapt the *Halakhah* to modern society's everyday needs.

Reconstructionism, founded by Mordechai Kaplan, is another school of thought that developed into a movement. It negates the supernatural in Judaism, and perceives it solely as a civilization.

All Orthodox sects accept the traditional *Halakhah* as the obligatory norm. Some extreme groups (*Satmar Hasidim)* reject the State of Israel, and some, such as the *Lubavich Hasidim* [3], maintain a special way of life in

CONNECTIONS

130 Shaping the American Jewish Community

178 American Jewry's Political Activities

216 The Jewish People in the Contemporary Period

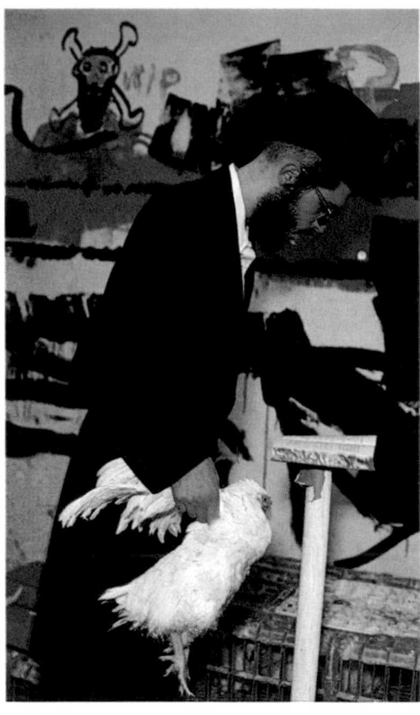

1 After the 1970s Jewish neighborhoods in America's large cities, above all in New York, were increasingly populated by other minorities. Jews moved to more affluent areas and their apartments were taken over mainly by Blacks and Hispanics. Old people, as well as some extreme Orthodox who preferred to remain near the local synagogue, stayed in the old areas. The mixed population occasionally causes tensions that have been expressed in stereotypical anti-Semitic outbursts. In 1981, revealing phrases were gleaned from compositions written by black children living in mixed neighborhoods, e.g., "It is the Jewish landlords who have made the neighborhood poor;" and "All the Jews are rich."

2 About a million of America's Jews at the beginning of the 1980s belonged to the Reform Movement. Reform Judaism does not dictate a single traditional approach to Judaism, but allows a certain freedom of choice. Research done in the early 1980s indicated that the third generation tended toward Reform rather than Conservative or Orthodox Judaism. The movement passed an important milestone in 1971 when it decided to transfer its international center from New York to Jerusalem. The move expressed a compromise between Zionist belief in national Jewish existence and Reform belief in universality — in the Jewish "mission" in the world. In the picture: The Isaac Mayer Wise Reform Synagogue in Cincinnati, Ohio.

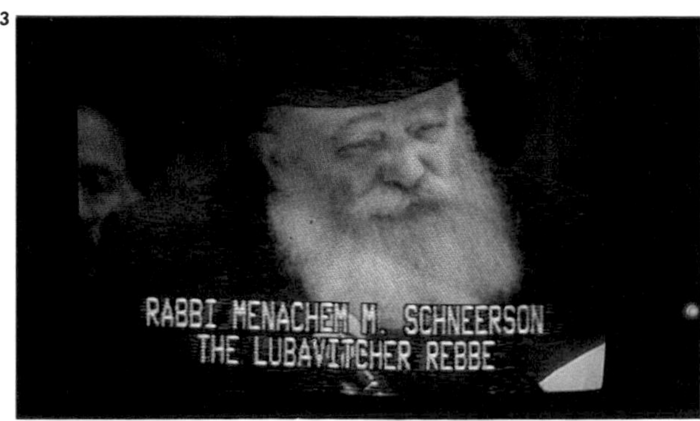

3 The Habad community in New York, with about a thousand permanent families, centers around its Rabbi [in the picture]. *Habad* — the acronym of the Hebrew words for wisdom, understanding and knowledge — uses communications media to perpetuate Jewish religion and bring Jewish groups back to the traditional fold. The center in New York maintains contact with Jews throughout the world and sends young people on missions to Russia, Europe and North Africa. The *Habad Yeshiva* in New York trains the youthful leadership, and Hasidic assemblies in the Rabbi's court are attended by thousands.

4 The American Jewish community's increasing resemblance to its surroundings — in language, education, occupations and way of life — threatens to blur Jewish particularity. Jews who are not traditionally observant celebrate the Jewish holidays in ways that blend the Jewish tradition with American customs. *Hanukkah*, for example, is often celebrated very much like Christmas, with abundant gifts for the children. Many Reform rabbis will conduct marriage ceremonies even if one of the couple is not Jewish. In the picture: Jewish children masquerading as movie heroes on *Purim*.

defined residential areas, but relate positively to Israel and to the rest of Jewry.

American Jewry is an extremely active, dynamic body. The roof organization covering most of its welfare activities is the Jewish Federation and Welfare Fund in every Jewish community. The Federations' National Council is the main welfare office of all of Jewry and the local federations are American Jewry's most powerful organizations.

Roof organizations have also been created to express Jewry's views to the government. The important ones are the "Presidents' Conference" (Conference of Presidents of Major American Jewish Organizations), now representing over 30 organizations, and the National Jewish Community Relations Advisory Council, comprising nine organizations.

Significant expansion in Jewish education took place after World War II, although the numbers attending Jewish educational institutions again declined in the 1960s. In 1983 all types of Jewish schools combined had only some 360,000 pupils, most of elementary school age, and only about a quarter of these were day schools. The proportion of Jews among university teachers and students, however, is much higher than their proportion in the population.

Uncertain Future

As part of the educated and economic elite, Jews have contributed greatly to America's scientific achievements and cultural strength. Second-generation Jews have left the large cities for the suburbs and the third generation exhibits the same high mobility as is manifested by American society in general. At the same time, however, the American Jewish community is shrinking due to a low birthrate and mixed marriages. There are fewer than two children on the average per Jewish family, and mixed marriages increase in direct relation to rising level of education and mobility. This raises troubling questions concerning Jewry's future in the United States.

KEY

Community centers were established even before World War II to serve as clubs for youth, on the model of Christian youth clubs. They were intended to offer amusement and social activities, and to help young Jewish immigrants integrate into surrounding society by encouraging them to engage in sports and hobbies. They also work to deepen Jewish identity. The centers generally include a place for worship, a Hebrew school, halls for concerts, lectures, exhibits and plays, a kindergarten, playing field and swimming pool. At the beginning of the 1980s there were some 300 centers catering to about 900,000 Jews. In the picture — the Hillcrest, New York Community Center.

5

6 Judaica became a focus of interest for American Jewry in the 1980s. This phenomenon found expression in the issue of a growing number of publications — studies, literature and criticism — written by local authors or translated from Hebrew and other languages, some of which became best sellers on the American market. This pamphlet cover advertizes the Jewish Publication Society (JPS), which disseminates books on Jewish history, tradition, and contemporary issues.

7 The United States continues to attract immigrants, Jews among them. As a rule, immigration to the United States is restricted. But when, in the 1970s and early 1980s, the Soviet Union allowed Jews to emigrate, the United States relaxed its immigration laws in order to receive them. Many Soviet Jews were absorbed in the United States with the aid of HIAS and their fellow countrymen. In the picture: immigrant children from Russia study English in Rome, Italy, before departing for the United States.

6

Join the Jewish Publication Society's Campus Program.

1984–1985

7

5 Mark Rothko (1903-1970), an outstanding expressionist and abstract painter of the New York School, exemplifies the role played by many Jews in shaping American art. Rothko, born Markos Rothkovitz, left Dvinsk, Russia in 1913 with his family and settled in the Jewish neighborhood of Portland, New Haven. In 1925 he moved to New York. He made his worldwide reputation beginning in 1948 by creating great expanses of color. In the picture — "Purple, Black, Orange, Yellow on White and Red," 1949.

8 A

8 Jewish writers, among them the Nobel prizewinner for literature (1976) Saul Bellow [A], Bernard Malamud and Philip Roth, are among modern America's important literary figures. Their writing reflects the experience of urban Jews and Jewish intellectuals. From time to time characters appear in their books that are based on the Eastern European *Shlemiel* type. The *Shlemiel* — who in his American metamorphosis is bedeviled by inferiority complexes — is also portrayed in the films of the actor-director Woody Allen [B].

8 B

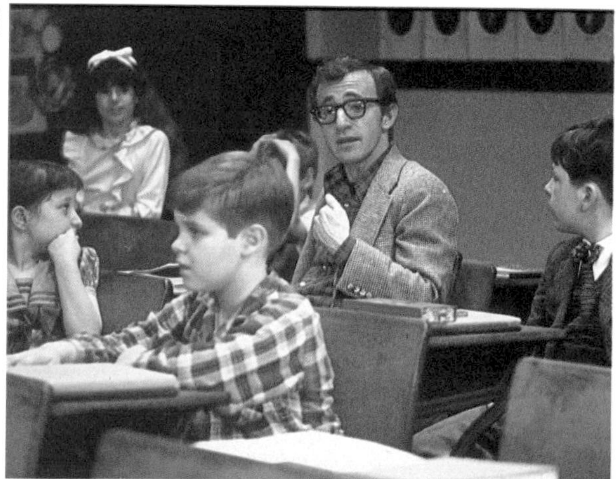

Jews in the Soviet Union and Eastern Europe

After World War II, two million Jews were left in the Soviet Union. This was the largest concentration of Jews in the world after the USA. Once the Soviet Union took over the countries of Eastern Europe following World War II, the number of Jews living under the Soviet regime reached three million. Since then the number has dwindled; in the early 1980s it was about two million.

Fluctuating Soviet Attitudes

During World War II Soviet authorities established the Jewish Anti-Fascist Committee. This was the only Jewish organization permitted, and was used to encourage Jews to join the anti-Nazi war effort and as a gesture to win the approval of western Jewry. In the first few years after the war, the committee continued to operate, and in 1947 the Soviet Union surprised the world by supporting — together with its satellites — the establishment of the State of Israel. This expression of support stemmed from Soviet expectations that Israel would ally itself with the Eastern Bloc against western influence in the Middle East. It was met with great enthusiasm by Soviet Jewry, but it signaled a turning point in the government's attitude toward the Jews there. The Jewish Anti-Fascist Committee was discontinued in late 1948, and a bitter propaganda campaign began against Jews, Zionism, and the State of Israel. During the last years of Stalin (1879-1953) the agitation and persecutions mounted. Many of the leading intelligentsia of Soviet Jewry were imprisoned and even executed [1]. Jewish culture came to a standstill, and the Jews of the Soviet Union were cut off from the rest of the world. After Stalin died, the Jews' position improved slightly. But in the late 1950s anti-Semitic propaganda began again: Zionism and Judaism were presented as reactionary, fascist phenomena [4].

This renewed anti-Semitism had one unanticipated result: from the mid-1960s a number of Soviet Jews began to experience feelings of Jewish nationalism. Many began studying Hebrew and visiting the few existing synagogues, and thousands openly expressed their desire to move to Israel. The authorities reacted by persecuting those who led the struggle to leave. However, beginning in the late 1960s pressure of world public opinion, combined with internal considerations, induced the Soviets to let Jews out. From 1970 to 1981, 246,000 Jews left the Soviet Union, of which 160,000 came to Israel. The remainder immigrated to other countries, especially the USA. The number of Jews who "dropped out" was constantly on the increase, sometimes reaching as high as 90%. Soviet authorities soon began to limit emigration. By 1984, only 800 Jews left the Soviet Union.

The Jewish communities in the Soviet Union and other Eastern European countries are concentrated mostly in the cities, and they usually have an above-average education. Social, economic and political pressures have accelerated

CONNECTIONS

122 Jewish Culture in Eastern Europe until World War II
126 The Wandering Jew
164 The Holocaust
216 The Jewish People in the Contemporary Period

1 The change in Stalin's attitude toward the Jews of the Soviet Union was evidenced by the liquidation of the actor, Shlomo Mikhoels [pictured — in the role of King Lear, 1935]. Though ostensibly killed in a car accident on January 13, 1948, Mikhoels — who was chairman of the Jewish Anti-Fascist Committee, Director of the Jewish State Theater in Moscow, and had been awarded the title "People's Actor," the Lenin Decoration and the Stalin Prize — was clearly murdered on Stalin's orders.

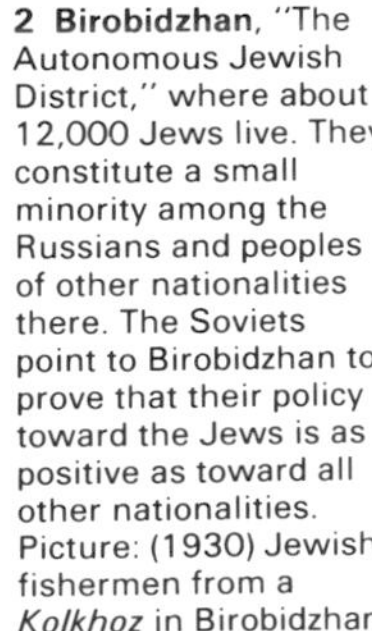

2 Birobidzhan, "The Autonomous Jewish District," where about 12,000 Jews live. They constitute a small minority among the Russians and peoples of other nationalities there. The Soviets point to Birobidzhan to prove that their policy toward the Jews is as positive as toward all other nationalities. Picture: (1930) Jewish fishermen from a *Kolkhoz* in Birobidzhan.

3 Soviet Jewry is concentrated mainly in the larger cities (mostly Moscow and Leningrad) while small numbers are scattered throughout the various republics. Unlike the European regions of the Soviet Union, there have been practically no mixed marriages among the Jews of the Caucasus and Central Asia. The latter continue to live within the traditional extended patriarchal framework. The government's policy of assimilation — by which it intends to nullify whatever special national characteristics remain among various Soviet peoples — has failed in these places, and the Jewish enclaves retain their unique character. In historic Bukhara there were about 45,000 Jews in the early 1970s. More than 10,000 of them came at that time to Israel. A number of Bukharan Jews had also settled in Erez Israel nearly a hundred years before. Pictured: — a synagogue in Tashkent, Bukhara, with characteristic tapestries.

4 The anti-Semitic caricature has figured prominently in Soviet propaganda directed at Zionism and Israel. Most obvious is the identification of the Zionist movement with Nazism. Jews are shown in distorted form, using negative-symbolic motifs: Jews as spiders, long hooked noses, etc. The message is clear: A Jewish-Zionist plot threatens world peace!

5 The Leningrad community is one of the two largest Jewish centers in the Soviet Union. In the mid-1980s Leningrad numbered about 165,000 Jews. Leningrad played a major role in the Jewish national revival movement, and came to stand for this cause during the "Leningrad Trial" in early 1971, when a group of Jews was accused of attempting to hijack a plane in order to leave the Soviet Union. Pictured: the Leningrad synagogue.

assimilation, threatening their existence. In the larger cities, religious life centers around the few remaining synagogues [5]. There is no official authorized body to coordinate Jewish religious activities. A newspaper and a periodical in Yiddish, which are mostly distributed for outside consumption, and two amateur acting troupes — one in Birobidzhan [2] and the other in Vilna — are the official representatives of Jewish culture [Key].

Eastern Europe

In the first few years after the war, Holocaust survivors in Eastern Europe were busy with their own social and economic rehabilitation. Public and political movements and organizations, including the different streams of the Zionist movement, began to be active again. Zionist emissaries organized the local communities in preparation for *aliyah*. But the communist takeover in these countries brought them into line with Soviet policy, and by the time Stalin died, the Zionist movement had been totally eliminated there. Nevertheless, the governments of Hungary, Bulgaria, Poland, and Rumania did allow Jews to emigrate later, in the 1950s, and the majority came to Israel.

Despite the presence of but a few Jews in the countries of Eastern Europe, anti-Semitism continues, and it is used most obviously as a political weapon. At the same time, though, Jewish citizens are allowed to maintain social and cultural activities. The Jews of Rumania [10], Hungary [9], Czechoslovakia, and Yugoslavia maintain contact with Jewish organizations in other countries and even receive outside aid.

The revival of Jewish nationalism among Soviet Jews has affected Eastern European Jewry as well. However, by the mid-1980s, the increased ageing of East Europe's Jewish population, combined with assimilation and emigration, all served to highlight the danger that Jews would eventually disappear from this part of the world.

KEY

The policy of merging diverse cultural elements, the high rate of intermarriage, and discrimination in employment and higher education, are endangering the future of the Jewish community in the Soviet Union. Jewish culture is being methodically strangled, and religious persecution has forced the Soviet Jew to face up to a most difficult dilemma: he is prohibited from leaving the country; he is persecuted as a Jew; yet even if he abandons his Jewish identity there will still be those who label him "Jew." Pictured — dais of the synagogue in the city of Tarnow, Galicia, destroyed during the Holocaust.

6 A

6 B

6 During riots in Poland after World War II, about 800 Jews were killed, including 41 slaughtered in a pogrom in the town of Kielce [pictured: [A] gravestones from the Kielce cemetery used for flooring and construction in 1960; [B] burial of pogrom victims]. Rabblerousers saw the Jews' active role in the higher echelons of the Polish Communist Party as proof of their plan to take over Poland.

7

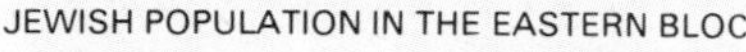

JEWISH POPULATION IN THE EASTERN BLOC

Year	Soviet Union	Bulgaria	East Germany	Hungary	Yugoslavia	Poland	Czecho-slovakia	Rumania
1939	3,000,000	49,000	—	725,000	75,000	3,500,000	360,000	757,000
1980	1,800,000	5,000	900	60,000	5,500	6,000	6,000	26,000

7 Statistics on the number of Jews in the Communist Bloc countries are based on census surveys conducted by the government. However many Jews probably fail to declare their Jewishness.

8

8 About 10,000 "refuseniks" were being persecuted by Soviet authorities in 1984-5. Despite many who "drop out" on their way to Israel, there remains a large Jewish public in Russia that is waiting for the gates of *aliyah* to open. In early 1985, when a new Soviet leadership took over, hopes again rose, and pressures were renewed by various international organizations. Pictured: Tel Aviv demonstration in support of Soviet "prisoners of Zion."

9

9 The bet midrash for rabbis in Budapest is the only one of its kind in the Eastern Bloc. It trains rabbis for all the countries in the area. Jewish subjects often appear in Hungarian literature and movies, as the Hungarians' attempt to come to grips with their role in the Holocaust. The Hungarian government is also making efforts to preserve and restore the main Jewish historical sites. Pictured — the Dohány Synagogue, Budapest.

10

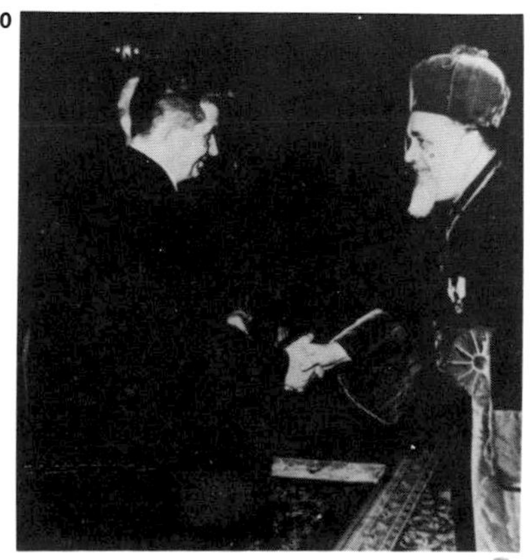

10 Rumanian Jews are allowed the freedom to develop extensive religious, cultural, and social activities. The Jews of Rumania have their own newspaper. They are also permitted contact with Israel and Diaspora Jews, including Eastern European Jews, and are allowed to immigrate to Israel. Their leader, Rabbi Emanuel Rosen [with Rumanian Premier Nicolae Ceausescu] is held in high esteem and is a member of the Rumanian National Assembly.

The Jewish People in the Contemporary Period

In all countries of the Diaspora the Jewish community has perforce to wage a struggle to maintain its Jewish identity. Intermarriage between Jews and non-Jews is constantly on the rise, and frequently the Jewish partner in such marriages is lost to the Jewish community. In the USSR, where Jews are denied the possibility of even the most elementary Jewish education, many Jews are estranged from their heritage. But even in the free countries forces are at work which weaken the Jewish identity.

A Jewish identity in its full compass is a blend of religious, traditional, historical and national components, inextricably interwoven. A weakening in one of these components undermines the Jewish identity as a whole. Secular Jewishness has severe limitations, and its durability over the generations is questionable. There are also limitations to a strictly religious Jewishness of the kind which endeavors to strip Judaism of its national component, and/or sees in it only a religious creed.

Jewish Identity in the Diaspora

The process of secularization has further contributed to the erosion of Jewish identity. The religiously observant Jew knows — and in the daily conduct of his life gives expression to — that which sets him off from others in the non-Jewish society surrounding him. But the secular Jew, constantly exposed to the pervasive influences of the majority culture, becomes engulfed by them unless specific Jewish content is introduced into his life.

If we look at the largest of the diasporas — that of the United States — it is precisely the content of its Jewishness which constitutes a problem for the third generation of American Jews, grandchildren of the immigrants who came in the mass migrations from Eastern Europe. There are indications that the third generation — unlike some of their second-generation parents — may quite readily accept their Jewish affiliation, but its content may have been considerably diluted. They look upon themselves as Jews, they are looked upon by others as such, their social contacts generally are with Jews, but their lives lack Jewish content. The problem is thus not so much one of identification with the Jewish group as of giving distinctiveness to their identity as Jews.

The Jewish cultural environment in which some of the communities in Eastern Europe once lived allowed for the development of an intensive Jewish identity. The American and other Diaspora milieus do not provide the conditions for the sort of Jewish living conducive to such identities. Language, for example, reflects a people's cultural cast of mind. In the great centers of Jewish culture in Europe before the Holocaust, one distinct and important expression of a Jewish identity was a specific Jewish language — Yiddish. The overwhelming majority of Jews in the Diaspora now know only the languages of the country in which they dwell. Although Hebrew is firmly entrenched in Israel, Jews in the Diaspora have not

CONNECTIONS

126 The Wandering Jew

212 American Jewry in the Mid-1980s

214 Jews in the Soviet Union and Eastern Europe

1 Assimilation and intense Jewish awareness exist side by side among the Jews of England. While about 20% intermarry, the Jewish educational system and Jewish cultural activities are quite extensive. Activity on behalf of Soviet Jewry is also intensive, and the rate of *aliyah* is rising. Pictured — a synagogue in St. Johns' Wood, London.

2 Maccabiada Pan Americana — poster for sports competition held in Buenos Aires, 1964. Argentina has a community of approximately 300,000 Jews. They maintain Zionist, social, and cultural organizations.

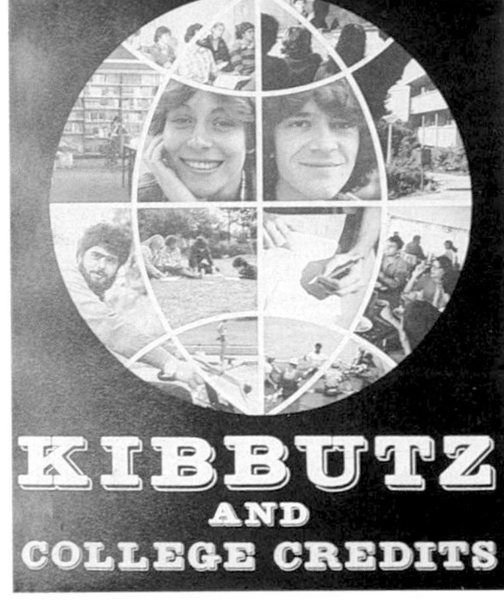

3 The kibbutz serves as a source of attraction to US college students. A work period at a kibbutz, together with studies at an Israeli university, earn college credits, and help acquaint American Jews with life in Israel. Such study visits generally result in an intensification of Jewish identity. But most Diaspora Jewish youth remain outside the circle of acquaintance with Israel.

4 Planting on Tu B'Shvat in Capetown, South Africa. The dayschool network, with its 8,000 pupils, is maintained by the community.

5 Lag ba-Omer festivities on the island of Djerba, off the Tunisian coast. According to tradition, the community was established by priests who were exiled after the destruction of the Second Temple. The priests are said to have brought with them one of the doors of the Holy Temple, which they then placed at the entrance to the synagogue in Djerba. Every year, at *Lag ba-Omer*, Jews gather here from all over the island.

been drawn to adopt it as a second language. The fact that these Jews no longer use a distinctive language and use only the language of the majority culture, constitutes a step on the road to assimilation.

Jewish leadership — and in particular the Zionist movement — is becoming increasingly aware that intensive Jewish education is necessary to develop a distinctive Jewish identity in the Diaspora and so to prevent assimilation. This can be best achieved in those communities which maintain a comprehensive network of Jewish schools and encourage and support informal supplemental education through Zionist youth movement and summer camp activities.

Activity in a variety of forms on behalf of Israel has become one of the most concrete demonstrations of Jewishness [9]. The number of Jews who visit Israel is considerable, and a study period in Israel has complemented the Jewish education of many students [3].

Jewish Identity in Israel

In Israel the problem is not one of distinctiveness, but rather a question of giving meaningful content to the Jewish identity. Israeli educators have increasingly recognized the importance of the Jewish dimension in the education of the young generation. In order to strengthen the Jewish consciousness Zionist institutes were established and the study of the Holocaust became obligatory in the school curriculum.

The existence of a Jewish state has helped give Jews a sense of pride in their Jewishness. As a Jewish majority society in the Jewish homeland, it has the possibility and obligation to serve as the spiritual and cultural powerhouse of the Jewish world, and to reflect Jewish social ideals. It participates — through the medium of the Zionist Organization — in Jewish education in the Diaspora, and renders special support to the smaller communities. Indeed, Israel is becoming the center for worldwide Jewish education.

KEY

The vital importance of maintaining a distinct Jewish identity is being recognized by ever-growing numbers of Reform Jewry in the Diaspora. This is most clearly shown by the increasing tendency of Reform Jews in the US and England to cultivate Jewish awareness by more closely observing religious traditions and by expanding the scope and content of Jewish and Zionist education. Pictured — Reform synagogue in New York City.

6

6 Anti-Semitism, rekindled worldwide in the 1970s and 1980s, has not spared France. In the heart of Paris, the *Rue Copernique* Reform Synagogue was attacked in the early 1980s, and a bomb was thrown at a kosher restaurant in the city's Jewish quarter. These acts, together with official expressions of anti-Zionism and anti-Israel attitudes, have strengthened national and religious feelings of identity among the Jews of France — in contrast to an overall process of assimilation in which French Jewry's identity has become increasingly compromised. This Paris bakery displays a *kashrut* certificate issued by a local *Bet Din*.

7

7 Jewish cultural activity is widespread among the Jews of Brazil. However, only one quarter of Brazil's youngsters are given any Jewish education. Brazil has more than 150,000 *Ashkenazi* and *Sephardi* Jews who are organized within the framework of a Jewish federation; interest in Israel appears to be on the increase. Pictured — elderly Jews meet in the park, in Bon Rateiro, Sao Paolo. Only the older people remain in this neighborhood, which was predominantly Jewish when waves of Jewish immigrants arrived in the early 20th century. The younger Jews have moved to more elegant neighborhoods.

8 The Ethiopian Jewish community was in dire straits after the military upheaval of 1974 and the subsequent introduction of a Marxist regime there. In early 1984 Ethiopia was plagued by a severe famine, and this induced Israel to bring Ethiopia's Jewish community on *aliyah* in a swift operation. Lessons learned from absorbing groups of Jews from underdeveloped regions in the 1950s, led to several changes in the immigrant absorption process: pride in a community's specific Jewish background and recognition of its innate values is encouraged; community institutions are retained intact, and young people remain with their families. Efforts are made to teach Hebrew to entire families from the start.

8

9

9 The distress of Soviet Jewry has stirred Jews in many countries to join the struggle on their behalf [Pictured — demonstration held in Paris, calling for the release of Joseph Begun, a Soviet "Prisoner of Zion"]. Although their Jewish education is often not well-developed, many Soviet Jews defy the suppression of Jewish cultural and national expression. During the 1970s, thousands of Jews left; 50,000 in 1979 alone. It is perhaps characteristic of the situation of contemporary Jewry that many Soviet Jewish emigrants — particularly those who chose to go to the United States rather than come to Israel — had very little Jewish consciousness.

Jerusalem Throughout the Ages

Jerusalem is the only city in the world that is sacred to half the world's population — Jews, Christians, and Muslims.

When the Israelites settled in the Land of Canaan, the Jebusites lived in Jerusalem, and constituted an enclave between the tribes of Judah and Benjamin. King David conquered Jerusalem (*c.* 1000 BCE), made it the capital of his kingdom, and had the Ark of the Covenant brought up to the city. Solomon, his son, built a Temple to house the Ark (*c.* 960 BCE). The people gravitated toward the Temple and it became their religious center, especially on the pilgrim festivals.

The destruction of the First Temple and of Jerusalem by Nebuchadnezzar (586 BCE) only enhanced the city's holiness in the people's eyes, and when they were permitted to return to their land (538 BCE), they turned to Jerusalem first of all; here they built the altar and the Second Temple, which stood for 600 years thereafter. During all of this period, Jerusalem and the Temple remained a pivotal focus for the entire Jewish people. In Ereẓ Israel as well as in the Diaspora, they would turn to face the city in prayer [Key], make pilgrimages, and send contributions.

During the greater part of this time, the land was ruled by foreign conquerors — Persians, Greeks, Romans. However, when the Holy Temple was pillaged during the reign of Antiochus IV Epiphanes, this sparked the Maccabean Revolt, and led once more to political freedom. Independence lasted for about 80 years (141-63 BCE), until abrogated by the Romans. The most elaborate and far-reaching improvements in the city were made during the reign of King Herod, under Roman patronage (37-4 BCE). The city's population at that time was approximately 100,000.

Yet it was the Romans who, in the end, burned the Holy Temple and destroyed Jerusalem, during the Great Revolt of 70 CE. Rumors that the Roman emperor intended to build a pagan city atop the city ruins helped spark the Bar Kokhba Revolt (132-135 CE). The rebels were defeated, Judea was laid waste, and, upon the ruins of Jerusalem, the Romans did indeed build a pagan city, *Aelia Capitolina.* From then on — for almost 1,800 years — the city was under foreign rule, and it became a source of longing for all Jews, who prayed daily for its redemption.

Christian and Muslim Links

The Christian bond to Jerusalem stems from the fact that Jesus was active — and later crucified and buried — there. When the city fell into the hands of the Byzantine Christians (324 CE), extensive construction was undertaken. The Church of the Sepulcher was built on the very spot where, according to Christian tradition, Jesus was buried [2]. As in the time of the Babylonian exile, Jews were once again forbidden to live in Jerusalem. Although the city was conquered by Muslim Arabs in 638, the Christian population nevertheless continued to treat Jerusalem as a holy city;

CONNECTIONS

28 The Kingdom: United and Divided
34 Destruction and Exile
36 The Return to Zion
42 The Hasmonean Revolt and Political Independence
50 The Great Revolt
74 Jews and Crusaders in Ereẓ Israel
88 16th Century Erez Israel
132 19th Century Erez Israel
154 The Emergence of Hebrew Culture in Erez Israel
182 The Israeli War of Independence (A)
198 From the Six-Day War to the Yom Kippur War

1

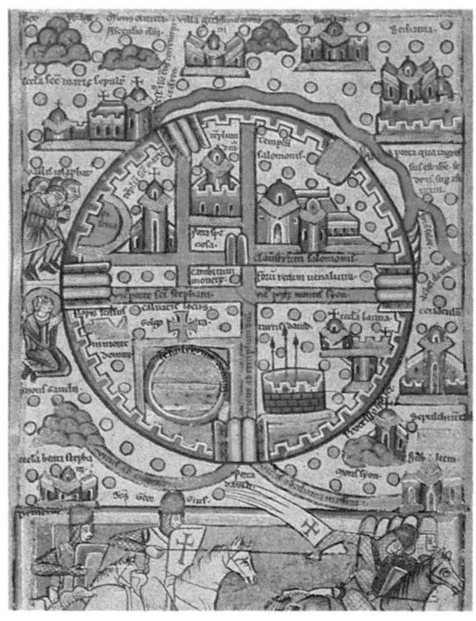

1 Jerusalem, the hub of the universe, on a map from the Crusader period. Crosses were erected over the Dome of the Rock — which became "The Lord's Temple," and on top of the el-Aqsa Mosque — which became "The Temple of Solomon." When the Crusaders set out to free the Holy Sepulcher from the Muslims, they were promised by the Pope that they would be rewarded with entry to the Kingdom of Heaven. Christian pilgrims believed that visiting the holy places provided absolution for one's sins, and that it helped the Christian to reach Paradise after death.

2

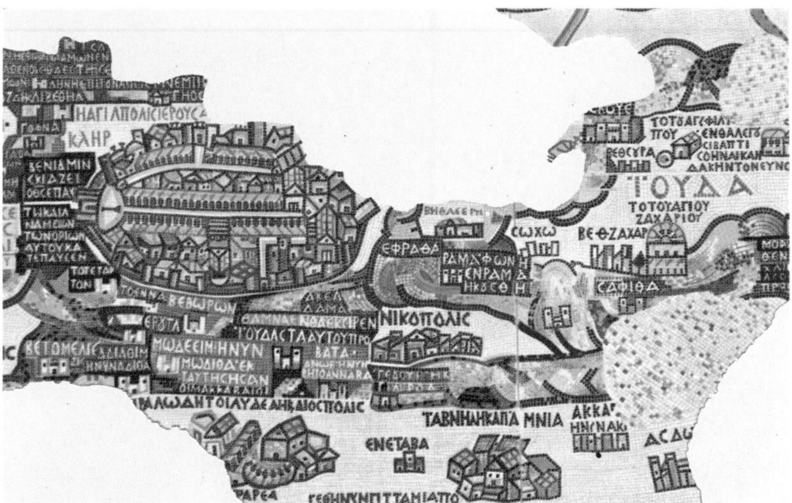

3

3 The Old City — in a drawing by Anna Ticho done in 1917. Until the mid-19th century, the Jewish population of Jerusalem lived entirely within the walls of the Old City, in the Jewish Quarter, which lies adjacent to Mount Zion and the Temple Mount. The present walls were constructed by Suleiman "the Magnificent."

4

4 The Dome of the Rock — the mosque built in 691 on top of the foundation stone which, according to Muslim tradition, is the hub of the universe. On this spot human souls are to be judged in the End of Days and sent to either Heaven or Hell. Tradition has it that Mohammed rose to heaven from the near-by el-Aqsa Mosque.

5

2 Erez Israel, with Jerusalem at its center, as seen by a Christian who arrived by sea. This mosaic map was discovered in 1884 on the floor of a 5th century Byzantine church in Medeba in Transjordan. The Church of the Sepulcher figures very prominently in the portrayal of the city. As early as the second century, Origen, a Christian scholar, claimed that the Jerusalem of the Hebrews had been destroyed as punishment for the Jews' failure to believe in Jesus, and that the Church constituted a "New Jerusalem."

5 Via Dolorosa in old Jerusalem. According to Christian tradition, this was the path along which Jesus was led to crucifixion. Churches and other Christian institutions have been built along this way, and pilgrims have walked along it in prayer.

pilgrimages continued, and a small Christian enclave was maintained.

The city became Christian once again when the Crusaders conquered it in 1099. They slaughtered all non-Christians and made Jerusalem their capital [1]. Pilgrimages increased [5] until 1187, when the Muslim Arabs once more took over the city; it remained under Muslim rule until 1917.

Jerusalem's sanctity to the Muslim peoples is signified by two monumental edifices, The Dome of the Rock and The el-Aqsa Mosque [4], both built on the Temple Mount during the Muslim's first period of rule. When Saladin reconquered the city from the Crusaders in 1187, Jews were allowed to stay. Saladin's successors neglected the city, and its population dwindled. In 1516, the Turks took over Ereẓ Israel. Suleiman "the Magnificent" built the walls around the Old City and repaired the water supply system (1537-1540). The city was again neglected, and had only 9,000 inhabitants in 1800.

A Jewish City Again

Early in the 19th century, the European powers developed an interest in Ereẓ Israel and Jerusalem. They helped support the Christians living in the city and built churches, monasteries, hospitals, and charitable institutions. The Jewish population of the city began expanding toward the middle of that century, and Jewish neighborhoods were first built outside the walls of the Old City beginning in 1860 [8].

On November 29, 1947, when the UN voted to partition Palestine, it decided that Jerusalem would come under UN Trusteeship to preserve its sanctity for all religions. However, following the 1948 War of Independence, Jerusalem was divided between Israel and Jordan. On December 15, 1949, Israel proclaimed the new part of the city capital of the State of Israel. In the Six-Day War (1967) East Jerusalem and the Old City were captured and on June 28, 1967, the Israeli government declared the unification of Jerusalem [9].

KEY

The "mizrah" — the eastern side — of houses and synagogues indicates to worshipers the direction of Jerusalem and the Holy Temple. Throughout the ages worshipers in the Diaspora have faced this direction in prayer, recalling "the city of God, desecrated to the depths of Hell," while other cities remain whole. Popular Jewish motifs are shown on this *mizrah* papercut from late 19th century Poland.

6

7

6 The Wall is the remnant of the western wall which supported the Temple Mount during the period of the Second Temple. After the destruction this site became sacred, and throughout the ages Jews have come here to mourn the Temple's destruction and to pray for Redemption; the Jews of Jerusalem also sought to build their homes with a view to the Wall.

7 The memory of the Temple has been preserved on coins, in mosaic floors and in book illustrations. The destruction of the Temple was recalled on fast days and even at celebrations. To this day, a glass is traditionally broken during the wedding ceremony in recollection of the Temple's destruction. Pictured — The Temple Mount in a *Ketubbah* from Padua (1735).

8 Mishkanot Sha'ananim ("dwellings of tranquility") was the first Jewish community built outside the Old City, in 1860. In 1917, when the British conquered Palestine, Jerusalem had a population of 55,000: 32,500 Jews, 12,000 Christians, and 10,500 Muslims. Before 1917 most of the new Jewish neighborhoods were built west and northwest of the Old City. During the British Mandate the Jewish population expanded greatly, and by 1939, 17 new neighborhoods were built; two agricultural settlements — Neve Ya'akov and Atarot — were established north of the city, but only the Hebrew University was built on the eastern side (1925). During the War of Independence the Arabs destroyed both agricultural settlements, and cut off the Hebrew University on Mt. Scopus from the other Jewish sections of the city. Many new suburbs were built after the Six-Day War [illustrated].

8

9

9 A church, a mosque, and a synagogue, drawn by a Jewish girl, from the worldwide exhibition "Children of the world paint Jerusalem." During the Jordanian occupation (1948-1967) the Arabs destroyed the synagogues in the Old City, desecrated Jewish cemeteries (they ran a road through the cemetery on the Mount of Olives, scattering gravestones heedlessly), and prevented Jews' access to the Wall. After the city was reunited under Israeli law (1967) equal services — utilities, sanitation, municipal development, etc. — were provided to all its residents, regardless of religion or nationality. Efforts to involve Jerusalem's Arabs in municipal affairs were less than successful, though the percentage of Arabs voting in municipal elections rose steadily.

"**Beauty of view,** joy of the earth, city for a great king," Jerusalem, the ancient capital of Israel and Judah and capital of the State of Israel.

Appendices

Ancient Hebrew Script

The alphabet is considered the most recent set of communicative signs invented by man. It contains a small number of characters which are easy to record, remember and pronounce, while a large variety of possible permutations allows for a myriad of meanings. The alphabet is commonly believed to be Semitic in origin and to have come into being in the Middle East toward the end of the second millenium BCE.

The Aramaic Alphabet

The ancient Hebrew alphabet belongs to the Canaanite family of writing, although the modern Hebrew script in use today derives from Aramaic, a different branch of the family of Semitic languages. The Hebrew alphabet is considered the most ancient still in use.

Aramaic writing was introduced into the land of the Israelites in the sixth to eighth centuries BCE by the Assyrians and Babylonians, who brought their alphabet with them as conquerors. Gradually, it replaced the ancient Hebrew alphabet known in traditional sources as *daatz*. The new Semitic letters were different in form: the characters were both more abstract and more uniform — giving rise to their later designation as "square writing" — and the pictographic origins of the shapes were less obvious. This Hebrew-Assyrian alphabet, and others closely related to it, such as the Phoenician, were also the source of the Greek and early Latin alphabets.

Aramaic script spread throughout the Kingdom of Israel in the early sixth century BCE. It was only in Judah, remote from the main spheres of foreign political influence, that the use of *daatz* writing continued. In time, however, its use declined too, and this ancient script was reserved primarily for recording the name of God in sacred texts written in Aramaic. It was also preferred by religious sects, such as the Samaritans, who had split with the mainstreams of tradition.

Samples of the Hebrew letter that survive from the late Second Temple period (1st century BCE to 1st century CE) reveal undeniable aesthetic qualities, and it seems clear that much care was taken to turn the letters into a series of clean and uniform geometric signs while preserving the graphic and meaningful individuality of each. The forms are economical and simple, and are drawn in parallel horizontal and vertical lines with a regularity of size that evidences stability even when seen from a distance. The desire to create a uniform and dense line of text led to the nearly horizontal shape of the letters, with the auxiliary marks connecting them serving as more than mere decoration. Yet the written text does not achieve perfect aesthetic uniformity or linear simplicity. The letters with their numerous serifs hang below the ruled lines (*shitin*) and are imperfectly balanced.

Few examples of writing survive from the period between the second century and the ninth or tenth. The little we have, mainly carved inscriptions, clearly indicates that Hebrew writing continued to follow the cursive rather than the monumental style of letters favored by the Greek and Latin alphabets at that time.

The Middle Ages

Between the 9th century and the invention of printing in Europe in the 15th — at a time when Hebrew ceased almost entirely to function as a spoken language — the Hebrew letter acquired its now traditional features, and specific uses for various forms of the letters were established. A wealth of examples of both written and carved letters from this period has survived: manuscripts, books, letters, and tombstones have been found wherever Jews lived.

During this period, the upper and lower horizontal strokes of the square Hebrew letter were straightened, principally because the addition of vowels and accents to the biblical texts required that space be left above and below the letters. Clear distinctions in the uses of the various types of Hebrew script were made: the square letters were reserved for sacred texts alone, while the other styles were used for secular texts, as well as exegesis and commentaries on biblical texts. Due to the strict rabbinical prohibition against the use of the sacred square letters together with any other type of script, their form remained unchanged. They became the exclusive province of highly skilled scribes known as *sofrei stam* who worked only on holy texts and were required to preserve every detail precisely lest it invalidate the entire manuscript.

Hebrew writing in the Middle Ages is generally classified geographically: Eastern script in Ereẓ Israel, Egypt, Syria, and Eastern Turkey; Yemenite script with its unique and uniform style; Persian script in Persia, Kurdistan, Bukhara, and Central Asia; Byzantine script in Greece, the Balkan countries, Western Turkey, Crete and Rhodes; Karaite script in Karaite communities in Egypt, Persia, Turkey, the Crimean Peninsula, and Eastern Europe; *Sephardi* script of three types — "square," intermediate and cursive — in Spain, Provence, and North Africa; *Ashkenazi* script in Germany, Northern France, England, and Eastern Europe; and Italian script.

In Spain, where Jews lived for a long time in a Muslim environment and employed a reed pen, the influence of Arabic writing can be seen in all three types of script. Thus, for example, there was practically no difference in the thickness of the horizontal and vertical strokes of the letters. In *Ashkenaz*, the Hebrew scribes were influenced mainly by the Latin alphabet, and from the 13th century by Gothic letters as well, written with a quill or bone pen. Here, a clear distinction between the horizontal and vertical strokes of the square letters evolved. Thus, at the dawn of the modern era — the age of printing — there were two distinct major forms of Hebrew writing: the *Ashkenazi* and the *Sephardi*.

1 **This inscription uncovered on the Temple Mount** is carved in the Hebrew letter still in use today. The Second Temple period letters read: "To the house of the *shofar* blast [to declare]."

5 **The Shiloh inscription**, written in *daatz* script, describes the excavation of a water-supply channel during the First Temple period.

6 **The Samaritan alphabet**, still used by this community, appears in the book *Arhuta Dekadishta* (Holy Ways) from Nablus (Shechem), 1215.

9 **Persian script** was used for this *Ketubbah* (marriage contract) for the wedding of *Anusim* from Meshed in 1901.

2

2 A 6th century CE mosaic from ancient En Gedi contains inscriptions in the ancient Hebrew alphabet.

3

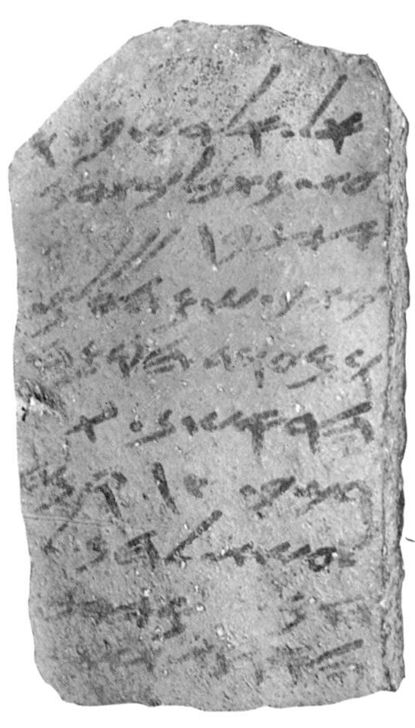

3 This ostrakon — potsherd — containing *daatz* writing comes from Arad, First Temple period.

4

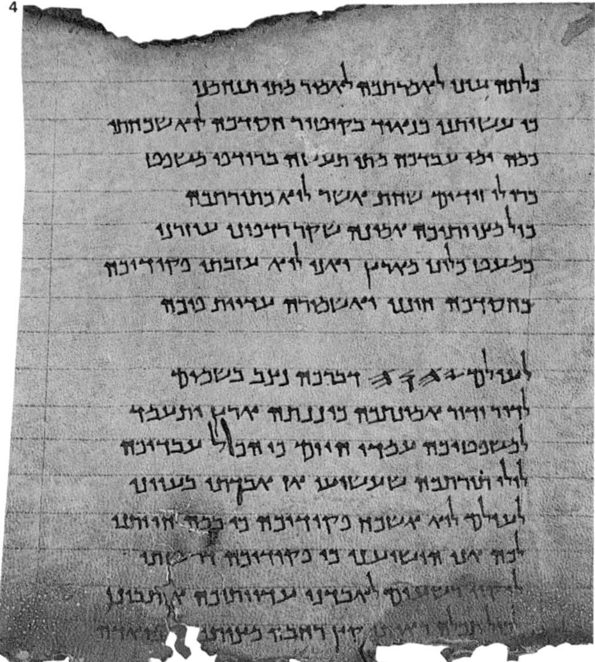

4 A scroll from the Qumran region by the Dead Sea, written by a member of the Essene cult in the 2nd century BCE. The name of the Lord appears in ancient *daatz* script to set it apart.

7

7 Yemenite script is used here in a *Pentateuch* from the 15th century.

8

8 Square and Cursive Ashkenazi Script, from a 14th century *Mahzor.*

10

10 This embellished initial letter comes from Rabbi Asher bar Yehiel's commentary on the *Talmud* from the 14th century.

11

11 Karaite Ketubbah from the Cairo *genizah.* The 11th century.

From Hebrew Manuscripts to Hebrew Printing

From the end of the 15th century, the Humanism that spread through central and western Europe, particularly Italy and Holland, brought in its wake an increasing interest in Hebrew writing and printing presses. The print shops which were established enabled the printing of many copies of a book.

The distinction between the *Ashkenazi* and *Sephardi* scripts remained intact even after the invention of the process of printing from movable type by Johannes Gutenberg. Now, however, a new factor restricted the natural development of letter design. The cutters of the new printed letters brought an end to the traditional method of writing Hebrew books. The purveyors of this new trade, most of whom were Christian, transferred the square Hebrew letter to lead type, thereby stifling the development of square and cursive styles. Halachic and rabbinical literature were no longer painstakingly written by hand, but reproduced in hundreds of copies from a single plate, often on the basis of inferior examples of the formal square script. Thus were perpetuated distortions and inaccuracies — in particular, the thick horizontal strokes were overly highlighted.

Italy, Cradle of Hebrew Printing

Most of the Hebrew books printed by both Jewish and Christian printers in the seventy years following the invention of the printing press were religious in nature: biblical texts, the *Talmud*, and major Halachic literature. It was the printers themselves who chose their texts. The first Hebrew printers worked mainly in Italy. In 1475 the Old Testament was printed in Reggio di Calabria using an elegant square letter based on the *Sephardi* script produced with a reed pen. The *Pentateuch* was accompanied by Rashi's commentaries printed in a different letter evolved from cursive handwriting, and this came to be known as Rashi script. Nevertheless, the *Ashkenazi* quill pen letter was the most commonly used for printing in Italy, as most of the printers of Hebrew texts were of *Ashkenazi* descent. The Italian Renaissance, however, rounded this script, distorting its form. Although the result served printers for many years, several successful attempts at improving the letters were made by two highly skilled letter cutters: Guillaume Le Bé, who had cut the letters for the multilingual Bible of Christopher Plantin of Antwerp (1569-1572), and Christopher van Dyck, who had worked for Jewish printers in Holland, among them the Athias family from Amsterdam who printed Maimonides' *Mishneh Torah* (1702-3). These two master craftsmen modeled their designs on the square *Sephardi* letters, correcting the distortions and eliminating the Gothic influence. Their work represents the one bright spot in this period of Hebrew typography. Others attempted to copy their style, but their pale and poorly executed results only emphasized the inferiority of the Hebrew letter at the time beside its younger Latin sister.

The Soncino Family of Jewish Printers

Samuel and Simon Soncino fled the persecutions in *Ashkenaz* in the 15th century and settled in Italy in the town of Soncino near Cremona. It was Samuel's son, Israel Nathan, a doctor and *Torah* scholar, who realized the potential of the printed book in spreading the word of the *Torah*, and at his urging his son, Joshua Solomon, established the first Hebrew press. Their first book was the Talmudic tractate *Berachot*, printed in 1484. Israel Nathan's grandson, Gershom Soncino (died 1534), was the most productive Hebrew printer in history. His printing presses operated in Italy in Soncino, Casalmaggiore, Brescia, Barco, Fano, Pesaro, Rimini, and elsewhere, as well as in Salonika and Constantinople. He was the first to print a Hebrew book illustrated with woodcuts, in 1491. The most famous books printed by the Soncino family include a fully voweled and accented Old Testament (1488) and a prayer book following the Roman ritual, *Mahzor Minhag Roma* (1486). The letters cut for them by the craftsman Francesco Griffo were designed in the spirit of the *Sephardi* script.

During this period Daniel Bomberg, a Christian humanist from Antwerp, founded a modern press in Venice on which he printed the magnificient Bomberg Bible. Craftsmen of many sorts — letter cutters, proofreaders, scribes and illustrators — worked together to produce this flawless creation, considered a milestone in the history of Hebrew printing. At the same time, printing presses were also operating in North Africa and the eastern part of the Mediterranean.

In 1831, Israel Bak established a press in Safed, moving it to Jerusalem in 1841. He is noteworthy for being the only independent Jewish printer of Hebrew in the Holy Land.

Prague Haggadah — the Acme of Ashkenazi Typography

Gershom Kohen, a member of a noted family of printers from Prague, produced the Prague *Haggadah* in 1526. It was printed in an elegant *Ashkenazi* letter cut in wood and embellished with woodcuts and majestic initial letters. These letters, copied and reduced in size, then served other printing houses throughout Europe. The Prague *Haggadah* represents the high point in the design of the printed *Ashkenazi* letter.

Over the next few centuries a wide variety of Hebrew texts, not necessarily of a religious nature, were printed for European intellectuals. With the rapidly growing demand for books, many printers were in need of a better and more durable Hebrew letter. Some of the attempts to "improve" the letters merely exaggerated the contrast between the thick and thin strokes, as they followed the example of the Frenchman Didot and the prolific Italian typographer Giambattista Bodoni. Basically, however, the form of the printed Hebrew letter remained unchanged until the early 19th century.

1 Manuscript of the Torah from the 10th century; vocalized with commentaries in the margin according to the Tiberian *Masorah*.

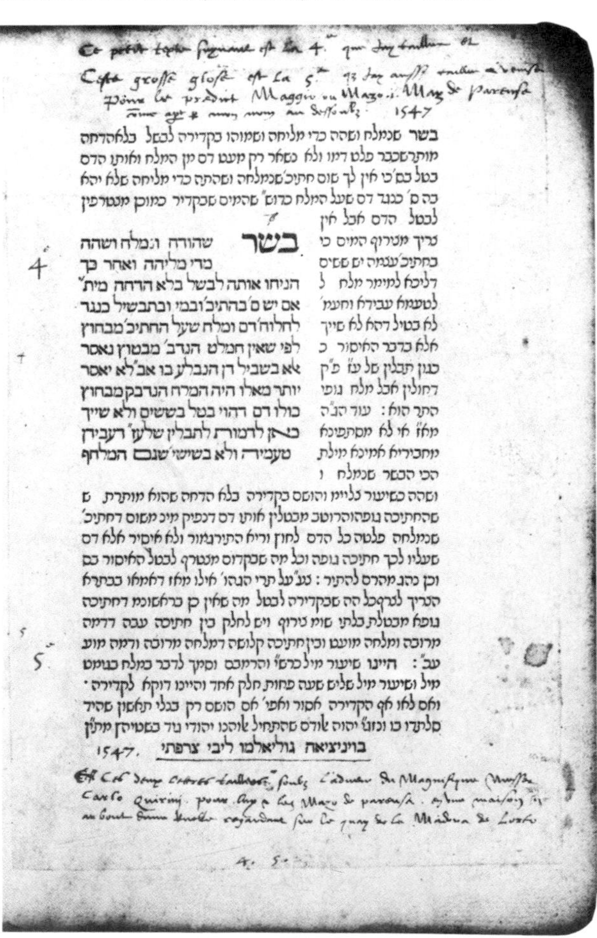

6 The fourth and fifth Hebrew letters designed and cut by Guillaume Le Bé (1525-1598). His most famous Hebrew typeface, the *Grosse Glose,* was later used to set Rashi's (R. Solomon Ben Isaac) Bible commentaries and subsequently became known as *Rashi* script.

2 **The Babylonian Talmud** was printed by Daniel Bomberg in the 16th century, using wooden and lead type.

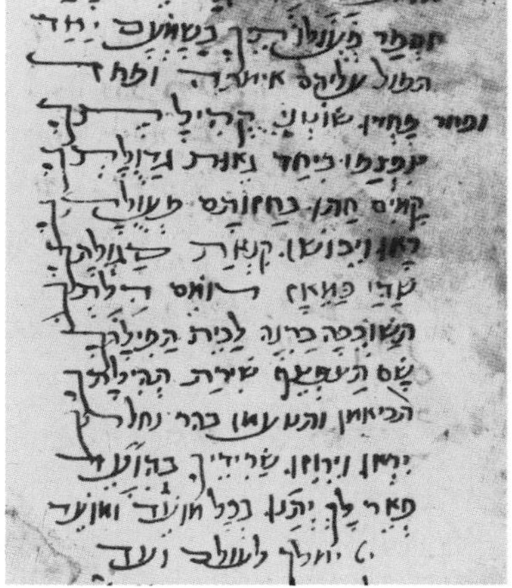

3 **Sephardic cursive letters** were used to record a liturgical poem by Joseph Ibn Avitur from the 10-11th centuries.

4 **The Prague Haggadah** was printed in 1526 using lead type with the initial words cut in wood. It employed an elegant *Ashkenazi* letter.

5 **Nearly every page of this Book of Esther,** produced in *Ashkenazi* script in the 19th century, begins with the word *melech* (king). Such scrolls are therefore known as Scrolls of the King.

7 **This book** was printed in the 19th century in Jerusalem by Israel Bak, who started the first Jewish printing press in Erez Israel.

8 **Liturgical poem** from the *Manuscript of the Wisdom of the Sages*, Crete, late 16th century.

55 GENESIS CAP. 44. 45. מד מה

22 עבדיך הורדהו אלי ואשימה עיני עליו: ויאמר אל־אדני לא־יוכל
23 הנער לעזב את־אביו ועזב את־אביו ומת: ותאמר אל־עבדיך אם־לא
24 ירד אחיכם הקטן אתכם לא תספון לראות פני: ויהי כי עלינו אל־
כה עבדך אבי ונגד־לו את דברי אדני: ויאמר אבינו שבו שברו־לנו
26 מעט־אכל: ונאמר לא נוכל לרדת אם־יש אחינו הקטן אתנו וירדנו
27 כי־לא נוכל לראות פני האיש ואחינו הקטן איננו אתנו: ויאמר
28 עבדך אבי אלינו אתם ידעתם כי שנים ילדה־לי אשתי: ויצא האחד
29 מאתי ואמר אך טרף טרף ולא ראיתיו עד־הנה: ולקחתם גם־את־
ל זה מעם פני וקרהו אסון והורדתם את־שיבתי ברעה שאלה: ועתה

9 **This Bible is voweled and accented** throughout and was printed in letters cut by Didot in the early 18th century.

אבדהוזחטיכךלמ
םנןסעפףצץקרשת

10 **These Hebrew letters** were cut by Guillaume Le Bé for the Plantin printing house of Antwerp.

Modern Hebrew Letter Printing

The development of the printed Hebrew letter in the twentieth century is linked to political, social and economic changes affecting the Jewish communities in Israel and abroad, to the revival of the Hebrew language, and to the renaissance of "youth" traditions in European art.

For more than 300 years, until the late 19th century, no significant changes were made in the form, use and rigid squareness of printed Hebrew letters. They continued to serve for sacred texts, halachic literature, and religious writing, as well as for secular literature and journalism. The appearance of printed letters from this period clearly reflects the printers' lack of interest in these antiquated and inaccurate copies of late medieval forms.

Hebrew Revival in Europe

The spirit of nationalism that spread throughout Europe from the mid-19th century, together with a stylistic fascination with the myths of the past, also had an impact on the revival of the Hebrew language. A new Hebrew letter was fashioned in Germany for the prominent type foundry, Berthold, by two designers, Raphael Frank, the son of the rabbi and cantor of Leipzig, and Rühl, a non-Jewish letter cutter. They based their design on the ancient *Sephardi* letter, rectifying distortions in the relative thickness of the horizontal and vertical strokes which were the hallmark of printed and written *Ashkenazi* letters. Their letter shows a certain affinity with *Art Nouveau*, popular in Europe at the time. The distinctive features of each letter were highlighted, eliminating the difficulty in differentiating between those of similar shape, such as ב (*beth*) and כ (*kaph*); ו (*vav*) and ז (*zayin*), and ד (*dalet*) and ר (*resh*). To this day the *Frank-Rühl* typeface is the most widely used for printing a variety of texts ranging from advertising, through literature and religious writing.

The late 19th century saw the publication of Hebrew newspapers, and the new Hebrew letters were printed on handbills, product labels, and newspaper advertisements. The language was no longer the sole province of religion and scanty Enlightenment literature, but was undergoing revolutionary changes. Indeed, most European designers of the Hebrew letter did not come from a traditional Jewish background. It was their professional interest as illustrators, designers and printers that was aroused. Some attempts to redesign the letters were commissioned by patrons who needed them for their own purposes, such as the *Schocken-Baruch* letter designed by Franzisca Baruch between 1930 and 1946 for the Schocken publishing house in Germany. Baruch began with *Ashkenazi* texts from the late Middle Ages (e.g., the Prague *Haggadah*, 1526), and preserved the splendor of the printed Gothic letter in her design.

Jan Le Witt returned from Palestine to his native Poland in 1928 and designed the *Haim* typeface which aroused the indignation of traditional typographers. It was fashioned in the spirit of the Bauhaus in lines of uniform thickness with no rounded corners, and was sharply angled and totally *sans serif*. It was thus not sufficiently legible for texts, but its solid and stable presence in large sizes made it such a perfect letter for display that even later versions, correcting most of its more grotesque features, could not surpass it.

New Israeli Designs

The revival of the Hebrew language in Ereẓ Israel was well under way by the end of the 19th century. In 1906, the Bezalel Academy of Art was founded in Jerusalem, with prominent artists, illustrators and designers as its teachers. Letters designed in the contemporary spirit by Bezalel artists Ya'acov Stark, Ze'ev Raban and Ephraim Moshe Lilien, display an exaggerated fondness for the curling arabesque-like line which was extremely popular at that time. In 1960, Ismar David designed the modern *David* typeface based on cursive script. One of its forms, the Slanted *David*, is the only genuine italic Hebrew letter.

A feature unique to Hebrew is the addition of vowels and accents — in use since the sixth century. These adjuncts present a problem in designing letters suitable for the needs of typesetters, since there are several hundred possible combinations. A modern and legible voweled and accented letter was designed by Eliahu Koren (Korngold) in 1963. The clean and precise lines of the *Koren* letter, along with its high degree of legibility and stately appearance, make it the preferred typeface for the voweled and accented religious texts for which it was indeed intended.

In 1958, the typographer Henri Friedlaender completed the design of the *Hadassah* letter: highly legible, simple, neat and elegant. Its square lines and the large white spaces within them are clearly distinguishable in most sizes.

Since the late 1950s, the typographer Zvi Narkiss has been responsible for a wide range of typefaces for printed, caption, manuscript and calligraphic letters. The latest are the *New Narkiss* group of letters and a new typeface, *Narkissim*. These designs are becoming ever more widely used in modern Hebrew printing. Their clarity and refined lines rank them among the leading contenders to replace the *Frank-Rühl* letter.

Dr. Moshe Spitzer (1900-1982), scholar, typographer, book and typeface designer, founder and director of the Tarshish publishing house and of the Jerusalem Type Foundry, was active in Ereẓ Israel from the 40s until his death in 1982, serving as collaborator and advisor to many of the country's type designers. Among them was Zevi Hausmann, the designer of the *Ha-Zevi* family of Hebrew typefaces. Spitzer's expert knowledge of the history of the Hebrew letter and his ability to translate the rigid tradition of Hebrew typography into modern forms made him a key figure in the revival of the Hebrew typeface in Israel.

1

יורם ברונובסקי

„נסיעה" לפנחס שדה

1 This excerpt from the newspaper Ha'aretz is printed in the *Frank-Rühl* typeface designed in the early 20th century — still the most popular letter for Hebrew printing.

4

פרק ראשון / ימים ראשונים

העיירה בין ביצות הפריפט / בני משפחתי / מורי הראשונים / תחום המושב / סבא / מסחר העצים / אבי / הרפסודות / האיכרים והיהודים / שני העולמות / חלומות-ציון הראשונים / אמי / משרתים / סטודנטים יהודים, ציונים מתבוללים, מהפכנים / תפקידה של אמי בחיינו / השפעת אבי.

עיירת מולדתי, מוטול, ישבה – ואולי עודנה יושבת – על שפת נחל בחבל־הביצות הגדול התופס חלק גדול של מחוז מינסק ומחוזות סמוכים שברוסיה הלבנה; ארץ מישור, פתוחה, עגומה וחדגונית, אבל כמות שהיא בנהרותיה, יעריה ואגמיה, אין היא נטולת ציוריות. האדמה בין הנהרות היתה אדמת-חול מצמיחה עצי-אורן ורותם עוקצני; סמוך יותר לגדות הנהר היתה האדמה שחורה, העצים עושי-עלים. באביב ובסתיו היה האזור ים של בוץ; בחורף – עולם של שלג וקרח; בקיץ – היה מעולף כעין אד של אבק. במרחב מסביב, במאות ערים ועיירות, חיו יהודים כדרך שחיו לפני דורות רבים, איים מפוזרים בים של גויים; ובתוכם היו בני משפחתי, מצד אבי ומצד אמי, שיעור לא בלתי-ניכר. לא הרחק מחוץ לעיירה מוטול נשפך הנחל לתוך אגם גדול, ובצאתו מן העבר השני אחז דרכו הלאה אל נהר פינה; וזה שוב יובל של הפריפט הוא, אף הוא יובל

4 The Schocken-Baruch letter was designed by Franzisca Baruch on the basis of *Ashkenazi* manuscripts and printed texts. The illustration is a page from Chaim Weizmann's autobiography set in this typeface.

6

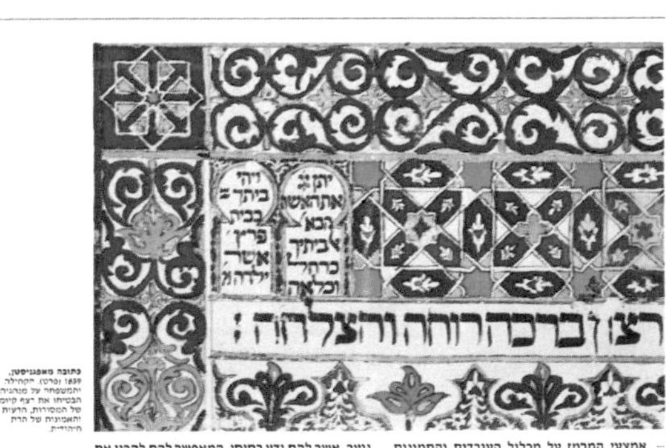

6 Narkissim typeface designed by Zvi Narkiss is from the Hebrew edition of this book published by Massada.

2

2 The Drogolin letter was designed in the early 20th century in Poland. Here it is used in a special edition of a book by S.Y. Agnon

5

באות זו ניתן בידי בעל המקצוע כלי חרש המעשיר את מערכת אותיות הדפוס

This new Hebrew type face is one of the last ripe achievements of the late Eric Gill,

העבריות בתוספת רבת־חן ועזת־אופי. יוצרו של הכתב, המפתיע בסגולותיו המיוחדות

the distinguished British sculptor and letter-artist. While living for some time

ובקוי־האופי החדשים שלו, הוא אֶרִיק גִיל, הפסל ואמן־האות הבריטי הנודע,

5 This flier announced the introduction of the new *Gill* typeface, inspired by the inscriptions carved on the marble walls of the Rockefeller Museum by the artist Eric Gill.

3

3 This calligraphic illumination by Ze'ev Raban (1890-1970) from the *Song of Songs* was published in 1923. In 1912, Raban was accepted as a teacher at the Bezalel School of Art and Crafts in Jerusalem.

7

מדינת ישראל

הממשלה הזמנית

הכרזה

אל כל תושבי מדינת ישראל

אזרחים,

בתקופת מבחן עליון, בימי התקפת־זדון של אויבים, נוטלת
הממשלה הזמנית את השלטון בישראל לידיה. מדינתנו נגלמת
בתוכה את מיטב החזון של דורות. על הגשמת חזון זה אנו מצווים
להגן בכל הכוח, בכל תוקף ההחלטה.

7 A poster from 1948. The large letters are in the *Haim* typeface and the smaller ones in *Aharoni*, more legible for texts.

8

8 Henri Friedlaender's Bold Hadassah letters, and a pomegranate printer's flower.

9

9 A page from the Koren Bible set in the *Koren* typeface with vowels and accents.

10

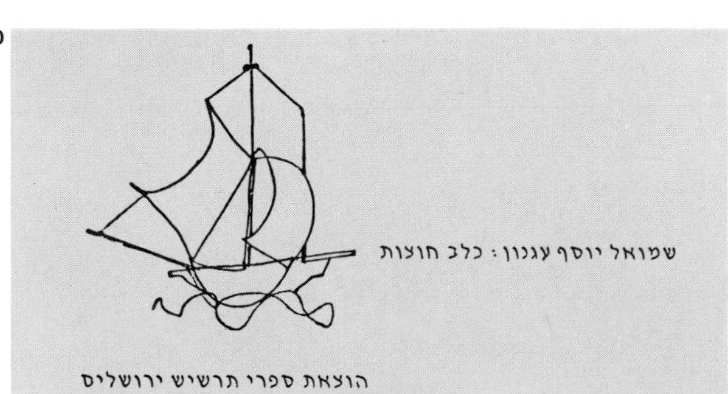

10 A book by S.Y. Agnon, published by Tarshish, using the Slanted *David* typeface.

11

11 An excerpt from the Koren Bible shows a voweled and accented passage from the *Book of Psalms.*

Symbols in Jewish Art: Myths of Creation

Man's relationship to nature and to society and his constant search for ways to explain the formation, indeed the existence, of the universe, have led him to develop the myth. Over the ages, the different faiths and religions have given expression to myth through art and symbolism. The Jewish religion forbade all corporeal description of divinity. Thus, while Jewish art was developing, the artist was obliged to reconcile his desire to express his beliefs through plastic means, with the limitations set by Jewish law (*Halakhah*) or externally imposed upon the Jewish community.

The work of Jewish artists was generally folkloristic, and employed simple motifs for decoration. Despite this simplicity, however, it symbolized and expressed abstract ideas.

Zodiac, Flora and Fauna Motifs

Jewish art absorbed formal motifs from the non-Jewish environment where these were deemed appropriate to the Jewish spirit and religion, and fit in with its symbolic systems. Since the Jewish artist sought to express the wonders of Creation and divine power without actually illustrating or embodying them, many works included motifs from the world of nature and the stars, as well as abstract geometric patterns woven into decorative systems.

The idea that to depict nature is to describe divine power — an idea which is also present in the Psalms, which are songs of praise to the Creator — explains the presence in Jewish art of many motifs that for the most part lacked any narrative content. These symbols were influenced considerably by neighboring cultures, and were absorbed into Jewish tradition after undergoing transformations in shape, form and, especially, meaning. One of these is the zodiac, which decorated the mosaic floors of ancient synagogues in Erez Israel. At Bet Alfa it is of unique design: the twelve signs of the zodiac are displayed in a square, in each corner of which are allegorical figures, representing the four seasons. In the center of the zodiac, the sun appears in the form of Helios and his chariot. While these mosaic floors were being designed (4th — 6th century CE), the influence of pagan religions was on the decline, thus apparently enabling the artists to use these decorative symbols with interpretations of their own. The abstract geometric pattern used in the synagogue decorations is based on the wheel and the square. It employs the numbers 4 and 12, which represent the seasons and months of the year, and the hours of the day and night — all of which, in turn, are symbols for the order of nature and the cyclical aspect of life.

As generations passed, and kabbalistic influences grew, the cosmic images — the stars and signs — were also interpreted as forces which mediated between divine and earthly powers. At times the artist added written indications that these superintended man's moral behavior. Indeed, in the 17th century, when mystic influences gained ground among Eastern European Jewry, the zodiac decorated many synagogues, and drawings of animals appeared once more. Some of these were familiar: lions, bears, deer, eagles; others legendary, such as the unicorn and the wild ox.

Flora and fauna motifs are an intrinsic element in Jewish art, and they may be found in mosaic floor designs and papercuttings, and on ceremonial objects and gravestones.

Crown, Eagle, Lion

In many decorations, a pair of animals — generally lions or griffins — is depicted wearing crowns. The crown also appears in the upper part of many ritual objects, and has become a popular central motif in Jewish art over recent centuries. We may assume that its popularity and key position in so many compositions were influenced by kabbalistic images. According to the *Kabbalah*, the uppermost *sefirah* in the tree of ten *sefirot* which represent the divine powers, is the crown. In the complex symbolic system of the *Kabbalah*, the *sefirah* of the crown, or *keter*, is closest to Infinity. Undoubtedly, it was this exalted and unique position which enhanced the popularity of the *keter* as a symbol in Jewish art. Therefore, interpretations which combine the myths of creation and of existence can also be related to the shape of the crown in Jewish art.

In many compositions, the crown decorates the head of a spreadwinged eagle, often very similar to the eagle in European royal crests. Carved eagles were also discovered at archaeological sites and in ancient synagogues. Throughout the centuries, the eagle has retained its symbolic importance, and perhaps, too, the symbolic association with high places, fire and sun, attributed to it in the ancient world. Allegorical descriptions in the Bible, likening God to the eagle watching over her young, undoubtedly contributed to the status of this symbol in Jewish art as well. The biblical and universal foundations were reinforced by Kabbalistic interpretation, some of which selected the eagle as the symbol of the Divine Presence.

The lion motif, also very popular in synagogue decoration, on gravestones, on ritual objects and decorated manuscripts, is used in the Bible to symbolize a supernatural power, capable of protection, salvation, and punishment. In later commentaries, the righteous individual is likened to the lion, for he is the basis upon which the world exists. The supernatural, symbolic power attributed to the lion in art is even more evident when it is depicted on either side of the Tree of Life. This universal mythical motif links the earthly and the organic with the infinite and the celestial.

The lion, the Tree of Life, the eagle, the crown, and the zodiac — all testify to the multiple values attributed to the symbol. In their simple forms, symbols relate to the myths surrounding creation and existence. In equal measure, they relate to the historical memory of the Jewish people and its messianic hopes.

1 The zodiac and the seasons, main portion of the mosaic floor at the 6th century synagogue, Bet Alfa, Erez Israel.

4 Detail from the painted ceiling of the Chodorov synagogue, 17th century, Poland; reconstructed at Beth Hatefutsoth.

7 Lions, a crown, and a set of pillars, decorating a *Torah* breastplate of silverplate and foil, Germany, 18th century.

2

2 A menorah, lions, and palm trees, in the mosaic floor at the Maon synagogue, 6th century, Erez Israel.

3

3 Zodiac, with an eagle at its center, surrounded by flora and fauna. Part of the painted ceiling at the Chodorov synagogue, 17th century, Poland; reconstructed at Beth Hatefutsoth Museum.

5

5 The Tree of Life and a pair of birds. Carved tombstone at a Jewish cemetery, the Ukraine.

6

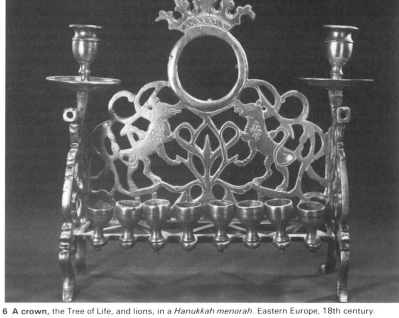

6 A crown, the Tree of Life, and lions, in a *Hanukkah menorah*. Eastern Europe, 18th century.

8

8 Eagle carved in stone, central motif on the facade of the Chorazin synagogue, 3rd century, Erez Israel.

9

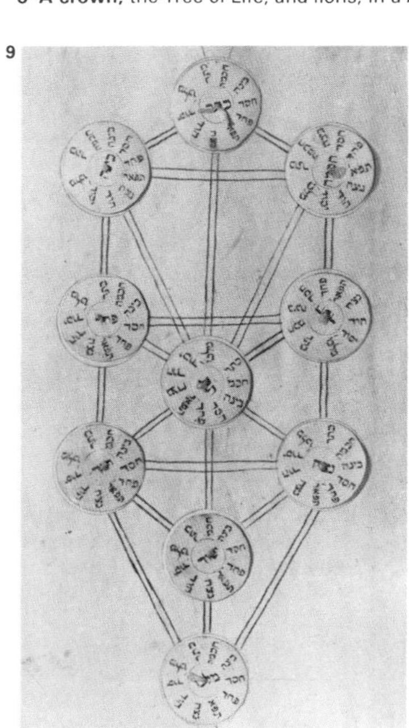

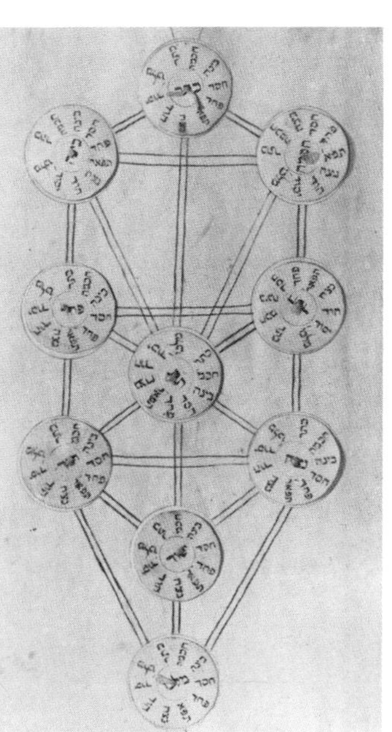

10

10 Hanukkah menorah from Morocco, early 20th century.

9 The Tree of Sefirot, illustration in *Pardes Rimmonim*, by Moses Cordovero, 16th century.

Symbols in Jewish Art: Exile and Redemption

In symbolic expression, it is not possible to differentiate between the universal and the mythical, on the one hand, and the mundane, on the other. Past and present — recalling the destruction of the Holy Temple alongside awareness of Diaspora realities — have been woven into a web of multi-faceted symbols.

Crowns: Torah, Priesthood, Royalty

The crown, a motif employed in Jewish art to symbolize the cosmic forces and divine inspiration, also represents historical values. In Jewish art, a triple-crown decoration is customary: the crown of *Torah*, the crown of priesthood, and the crown of royalty. The crown of royalty, representing the Kingdom of David, symbolizes anticipation of the Messiah's arrival, just as the crown of priesthood symbolizes reestablishment of the Holy Temple. Royalty also refers to the Kingdom of Heaven. Inclusion of the crown of *Torah* in the symbolic composition associates the *Torah*, an existential fundamental, with metaphysical and historical symbolism.

Over the years, the myths of exile and redemption have become intimately associated with the *Torah* in Jewish art. Thus, prayer halls and holy arks in synagogues all over the world are positioned to face Jerusalem. The decorations on the doors and curtains of the holy ark and on *Torah* mantels and breastplates include many symbols in use for generation upon generation: lions, the crown, the gate, pillars, and the Tree of Life.

The lion, in Jewish tradition, is the symbol for the Tribe of Judah, Bearer of the Redemption. The common practice of decorating ceremonial objects with two lions — symmetrically arranged on either side of a gate, crown, or the Tree of Life — may also be a symbolic link to the tribes of Dan and Judah, who participated in the erection of the Tabernacle, understood in Jewish tradition as the microcosm.

The gate and pillars are not only a decorative motif; very often they serve as the basis for the design of the holy ark itself, or for the alcove which holds the *Torah* scroll. In the ancient world, the gate had already been assigned the symbolism of abstract ideas. Many works of art created in the Mediterranean region and in the East employed motifs which strengthened the idea of transition: from material to spiritual, from mundane to heavenly, from darkness to light, and from the finite to the infinite. Descriptions of the gate in ancient Jewish art were also assigned spiritual significance, though neither figurative depictions nor the images of the pagan gods were included in them. Instead, the gate symbolized passage into the world of the *Torah*. And, as with all multi-faceted motifs, the gate expresses an additional symbolism as well — anchored in historical values and based on remembrance of the past and anticipation of future redemption. In Jewish tradition, this motif was used to perpetuate the memory of the Temple and also to represent the universal elements. The pillars, too, have dual meaning: they symbolize the two pillars, Jachin and Boaz, which are said to have stood in Solomon's Temple, and also the spiritual link between heaven and earth. In the Middle Ages, Jewish mystical tradition — influenced by the *Kabbalah* — enhanced the pillar motif by characterizing the pillars as upholders of the world and the worldly order.

The Menorah

A widely-used motif, steeped in symbolism, is the seven-branched *menorah*. Originally one of the ritual and ceremonial objects used in the Holy Temple, the *menorah* became a popular Jewish symbol after the Destruction; it was used to express national and religious longings. Generally, whenever a *menorah* was unearthed at an excavation, it indicated a Jewish site.

Menorot carved in wood decorated the entrances of ancient synagogues and constituted a central motif in floor mosaics of Jewish prayer halls. In many burial places, too, the *menorah* motif had been popular since ancient times. Its vitality as a symbol has never ebbed, and in the past several hundred years the *menorah* has continued to decorate synagogues and holy articles. When the State of Israel was established, the *menorah* served as a symbol of redemption become reality, and the model used by the new state was a replica of the *menorah* which decorates the Arch of Titus — a symbol of exile.

The *menorah* has been interpreted in non-historical ways, as well. It has been likened to the solar system and the sun, the Sabbath and the weekdays, the purity of the heavens, and the Tree of Life. The *menorah* is shown next to palm trees, which were already symbols for Paradise in ancient Jewish art. In later periods, artists occasionally drew or engraved the *menorah* metaphorically — as the Tree of Life, or the Sabbath candlesticks. Metaphoric designs of this kind were also found on gravestones, possibly to indicate the symbolism connecting life and death, exile and redemption.

Gravestones in Europe over the last several centuries were often adorned by an open bookcase, with the lion or crown motif carved above or beside it. These emphasized that the deceased had attached great importance to *Torah* learning. They also symbolized the connection between study — as a value in itself, not only as a reflection of one's adherence to the laws of the *Torah* — and the redemption idea. This motif was used on the gravestones of men, whereas the lighted Sabbath candles would decorate the women's gravestones, also evoking associations to the Tree of Life, and, occasionally, to the seven-branched *menorah*. Gold glass medallions, made by encasing decorations of thin gold foil between two layers of glass and dating from the 3rd and 4th centuries, were found in Jewish catacombs in Rome. These medallions had representations of the Ark of the Covenant flanked by lions or *menorot*.

1

1 Three crowns, an eagle, and pillars, in a varied arrangement of symbols decorating the upper portion of the Holy Ark at the Olkienniki Synagogue, Poland, 18th century.

4

4 Amulet to ward off evil eye, flanked by *menorot*, designed in the shape of a house. 5th century.

8

8 Gravestone. Rumania, 19th century. Note open bookcase, lion and crown motifs and the birds and trees on the doors of the bookcase.

2 **A typical arrangement** of symbols is used to decorate this embroidered curtain covering the Holy Ark, Germany, 1725. The motifs serve as a reminder of the original function of the curtain, to separate the Holy from the Holy of Holies in the Temple.

3 **Richly decorated motifs** of the Temple. Papercut, North Africa, 19th or 20th century.

5 **Mosaic floor** at the Bet Alfa Synagogue, Bet Shean Valley, Ereẓ Israel, 6th century.

6 **Tombstone** from Kosow, 19th century, symbolizing: seven-branched *menorah*, Tree of Life, Sabbath candlesticks, and woman's hands performing the Sabbath blessing.

7 **Niche, housing the Torah Scroll,** in the shape of a gate and pillars, and depicting the Holy Temple and the sacrifice of Isaac. Dura Europus (Syria), 3rd century.

9 **The bear and the Tree of Life** — drawing based on a tombstone carving, Rumania.

10 **Hamsa,** popular symbol in synagogues in Muslim countries. Morocco.

Symbols in Jewish Art: The Meeting of Cultures

Until the modern era, visual symbols were seldom used to represent Judaism to the non-Jewish world. Those motifs developed in the past which symbolized the Jews' collective longings, were understood largely within the community, by implication and association.

Magen David, Holy Tablets

As the Enlightenment and the Emancipation spread throughout the countries of Europe in the late 18th and early 19th centuries, the meeting of cultures became one of the principal objectives for emancipated Jewry. Jews chose symbols as one means of representing themselves before the non-Jewish public. Two of these gained widespread popularity — the *Magen David* (Star of David) and the Holy Tablets. The synagogues built in 19th century Europe were as large and elaborate as the Christian churches of the time, often reflecting the influence of Christian architectural styles of the Middle Ages. They were identified by the symbols over their gates or upon their roofs, sometimes positioned in the very same spot as the cross in the church. Another major form of identification was the Oriental style of architecture used in synagogues to indicate the Jews' Eastern origins.

The *Magen David* motif was very prominent in 19th century synagogues. It eventually evolved into a national symbol which, in the 20th century, represents the Jewish people to themselves and to the world. The Tablets of the Covenant motif had already become part of Jewish art prior to the Emancipation. However, beginning in the 19th century this symbol appeared not only on the holy ark and as a decoration on ritual objects, but also as the identifying emblem in the synagogue, alongside the *Magen David*. The Tablets were particularly prominent because they exemplified the mood of the times: this was a period when philosophers and men of letters extolled the virtues of morality and law, and these they found reflected in the *Torah* of Moses, as represented by the Tablets.

Modern Times

During the Enlightenment — whose adherents strove to shake off the mystical tradition of the *Kabbalah* — traditional symbols were used less, and even the seven-branched *menorah*, which had always been of paramount importance, was replaced. The *menorah* reappeared, however, in the early 20th century, when it was used to symbolize the new Jewish national awakening. The Zionist Movement adopted the *menorah* as its symbol alongside the *Magen David*; both are now official emblems of the State of Israel.

In the modern era, Jewish artists were able to develop under conditions which they had never before enjoyed. Many young Jews with artistic talent gathered at the cultural centers of Europe. Most had been educated in the traditional Jewish atmosphere of Eastern Europe, and their arrival at the big cities of Central and Western Europe and the USA produced a cultural confrontation between Jewish tradition and the myths and symbols of pagan and Christian cultures, which is reflected in their art. The work of the sculptor Jacques Lipchitz (1891-1973) includes motifs from the Bible as well as from Greek mythology, which have undergone the artist's own individual interpretation. His statues of Prometheus and Europa, although based on mythological origins, were the artist's reaction to immediate events, and he used them to symbolize the struggle of his people and the enlightened world against Nazism.

The painter Marc Chagall (1887-1985) expressed a confluence of motifs — taken from both the Jewish way of life and European culture. He sometimes substituted the *Star of David* for the cross, and vice versa, or the Jewish mother for the Christian madonna, or the suffering Jew enveloped in his *tallit* for the crucified Jesus.

The search for a meeting ground between the past and the new creativity was evident in the works of the early teachers and students at the Bezalel Art Academy in Jerusalem, at the turn of the century, when art in Ereẓ Israel was in its infancy.

The founders of Bezalel were motivated by nationalistic fervor. They tended to draw upon both the symbols of ancient Jewish art and those which had developed over the last several hundred years, such as the *Magen David* and the Holy Tablets. Landscapes of the Holy Land and Jerusalem, or Hebrew letters, were also interwoven into their painting and sculpture, and were especially prominent in the decorative arts: rugs, jewelry, or ritual objects.

The methods and styles of the Academy's instructors provoked criticism from the younger generation of artists. At a later stage some rebelled, seeking other means of self-expression, and a meeting with the world of modern art in Europe. One Bezalel student who did continue to draw on traditional Jewish symbolism — albeit with the influence of modernistic styles — was Naftali Bezem. His paintings include such motifs as the lion, *shofar*, fish, candles, and ladder — and they symbolize subjects related to the Holocaust, *aliyah*, and Jewish national regeneration.

Since the 1950s, several well-known Jewish artists have again begun to derive inspiration from Jewish mysticism, neglected over the past century. Israeli artist Mordecai Ardon, for example, focuses many of his works on the kabbalistic Tree of *Sefirot* — relating the earthly and the heavenly, the mundane and the universal. Hebrew letters, which were used in Jewish writings of the Middle Ages to express the myths of Creation and existence, are today a popular motif for many artists, including the Jewish American painter, Ben Shahn. The basic elements of the Creation — fire, water, and movement — all steeped in kabbalistic imagery, have been focused upon by Israel's Yaacov Agam, who has expressed them in new forms, styles, and techniques.

1

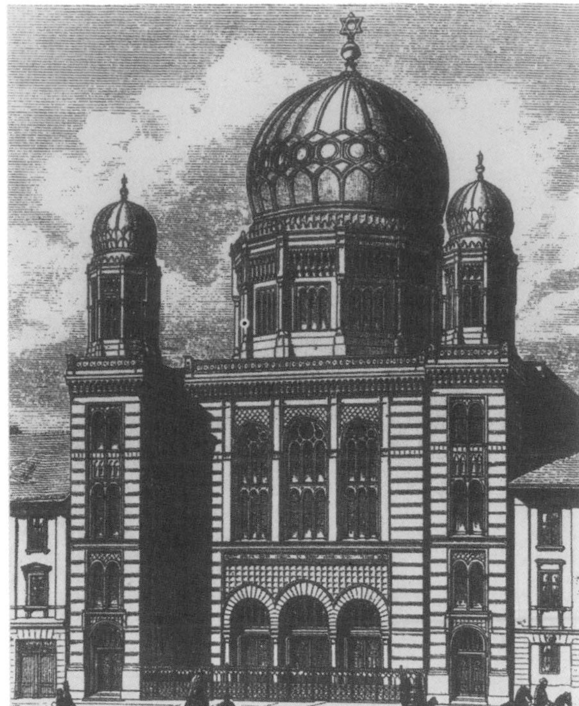

1 A synagogue built in the so-called Oriental style, with a *Magen David*. Berlin, 19th century.

5

5 Silver Torah breastplate, with colored stone decoration. Germany, 18th century.

9

9 A bronze sketch for the *Prometheus* sculpture by Jacques Lipchitz.

2

2 **Magen David** over synagogue entrance. Seged, Hungary, 19th century.

3

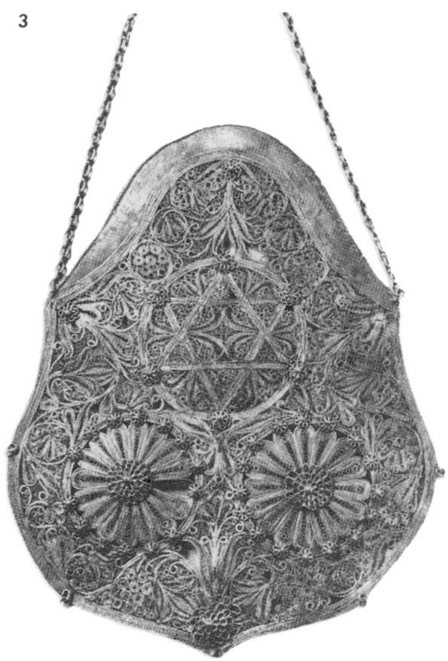

3 **Magen David** at center of filigree *Torah* breastplate, Turkey, 20th century.

4

4 **Bookplate** designed by G.M. Lilien (1874-1925), using the *Magen David* motif.

6

6 **Fire and Water**, Sculpture by Yaacov Agam. 1972.

7

7 **Sign**, Part of a triptych entitled "At the Gates of Jerusalem," by Mordecai Ardon.

8

8 **New Immigrant** kissing the Earth, oil painting by Naftali Bezem, Tel Aviv Museum.

10

10 **Motif** decorating the synagogue in Essen, Germany. Sketch, 1913.

11

11 **Grouping of symbols** in a rug made at the Bezalel Academy, Jerusalem.

12

12 **The Alphabet of Creation**. Silkscreen by Ben Shahn, 1957. Hebrew letters expressed creation and existence in the Middle Ages.

Distinctive Features of Jewish Costume

The attire of Jews all over the world generally followed the style of the costumes worn by their Christian or Muslim neighbors. In places and times when garments served to identify a person's social status or ethnic group, Jews also had a specific costume, or at least some distinctive element particular only to them. In days of intolerance, some imposed features — the bell-shaped hat in the Middle Ages, the yellow badge, revived by the Nazis in modern times — served as discriminatory signs of persecution. In time, some of these — e.g., the black color of mens' garments in Morocco or the rope-belt in Bukhara — were transformed in the eyes of their wearers into positive marks of traditionalism and even of honor. On the other hand, orthodox Jews everywhere still refrain from dressing like Gentiles, in compliance with the *Leviticus* (20:23) prohibition "Ye shall not walk in the manners of the nation...," or the *Shulkhan Arukh*, which is the basic Rabbinical code compiled in the 16th century.

Anachronism and Tradition

The only features surviving to this day from all the ancient Eastern peoples are the Jewish sidelocks, or *pe'oth*, and the fringes, *tzitzioth*, of the Jewish man's prayer shawl. Ritualized by scriptural decrees, these are still obligatory for orthodox Jews. But even without going so far back into history, Jewish garb is markedly traditional, often verging on the anachronistic. Jews tended to adhere to features discarded long before by their non-Jewish neighbors. In time, certain aspects of dress came to be considered distinctive features of Jewish costume. The typical Hassidic attire is the best known example of this process: it derives from the Polish nobleman's dress of the 16th century. Even the *yarmulke* — the undercap that is now the universal headgear of all religious Jews — was formerly part of a Gentile Polish costume. The distinctive "Great Dress" of Jewish women in the cities of Morocco must have evolved in a similar way, as it derives from Spanish ladies' costumes of the Exile period. The same applies to the specifically Jewish wrap of Baghdadi women, which clearly had its antecedents in Muslim dress.

Distinctive Features in Modern Times

The ingathering of the exiles brought to Israel a Babel of styles and modes of dress. Amidst this great wealth of costume types an attempt was made to identify features that could be regarded as distinctive to the Jewish community of a given area or locality — features that generally prevailed among the Jews of that community between the end of the 19th century and their immigration to Israel.

Jews were found to have worn specifically Jewish garments until the middle of the 20th century on the streets of San'a in Yemen, on the island of Djerba in Tunisia, and in the villages of the Atlas Mountains in Morocco. In Baghdad, Jewish women were recognized until the 1930s by a distinctive wrap which hid their European-fashioned dresses.

Even today in Israel and in the cities of Morocco, very distinctive garments are worn by Jewish women for weddings and for other festive occasions. In Salonika and many other Jewish centers in the Balkans and the Middle East prior to World War II, elderly ladies dressed in the traditional garments typical to the costume of Jews one or two generations ago.

Isolated elements were found even in the costumes of Bukharan Jews, such as the *pulaktshe*, a bespangled tulle veil. Again, in Morocco, in the town of Marrakesh and southward, rabbis and elderly men wrapped a blue, white-dotted kerchief around their heads.

From Eastern Europe, with its unique Jewish tradition and folklore, only a very few items, especially women's breastpieces, *brusttuch*, and head ornaments, *sterntichl*, survived the Holocaust. On the other hand, East European Jewish menswear was to a certain extent perpetuated by the Hassidic costume: Orthodox Jews actually flaunt their identity in the streets of New York or Antwerp, while each religious group or the followers of each rabbi are recognized by distinctive features in their Hassidic costume.

In modern times, with assimilation on the rise, these marks of exterior distinctiveness have been gradually abandoned. The total or piecemeal renunciation of traditional costume still can, in certain cases — as in the orthodox societies — provide an excellent indicator of the degree to which an individual or a community has assimilated.

10 Hassidic youth from Jerusalem. Everyday wear, after *Bar-Mitzvah*.

1 Shtraymel — Ashkenazi orthodox man's hat. Originally the formal hat for the Sabbath in Galicia. A man's wealth was measured by the number of fur-tails incorporated in his hat.

5 Jewish lady from Salonika, Greece. This is the most distinctive dress of all former Ottoman districts.

6 Detail of Salonika woman's headgear, kofia, a pearl-embroidered adornment at the end of the snood.

11 Detail of plastron to "Great Dress" (12A). The two-headed eagle was said to be specific to Jewish dress and ornamentation in Morocco.

2 **Jewish woman's festive bonnet with sterntichel** from Eastern Europe. Pictured in most Jewish costume representations of the 18th and 19th century.

3 **Brusttuch — Jewish woman's traditional plastron — Eastern Europe.** Mostly of *spanierarbeit*, used also for the ornamentation of the *talith*.

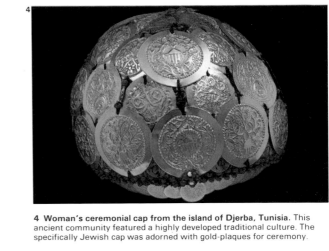

4 **Woman's ceremonial cap from the island of Djerba, Tunisia.** This ancient community featured a highly developed traditional culture. The specifically Jewish cap was adorned with gold-plaques for ceremony.

7 **Izar — Baghdadi Jewish ladies' distinctive ceremonial streetwear.** Precious gold and silver brocade on silk; face hidden by net-mask of horsehair.

8 **Honored elder from Marrakesh.** In the south of Morocco elderly Jewish men were recognized by the polka-dotted kerchiefs bound over their caps.

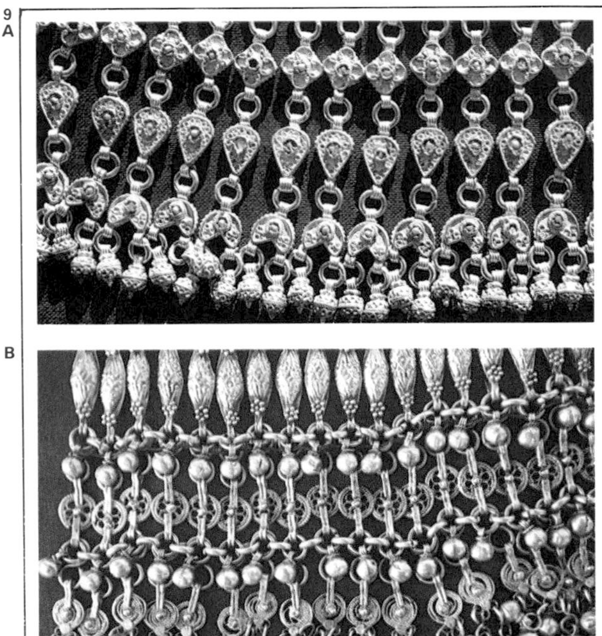

9 **Jewish pectoral necklace, lebbe** (A), compared to same type of Muslim necklace (B). The two are similar in general design, but differ in details of motifs and techniques. Both are from San'a, the capital of Yemen.

12 **The Jewish "Great Dress"** (A) from Tetouan, and a **qaftan** (B). The latter was formerly a distinctively Muslim garment.

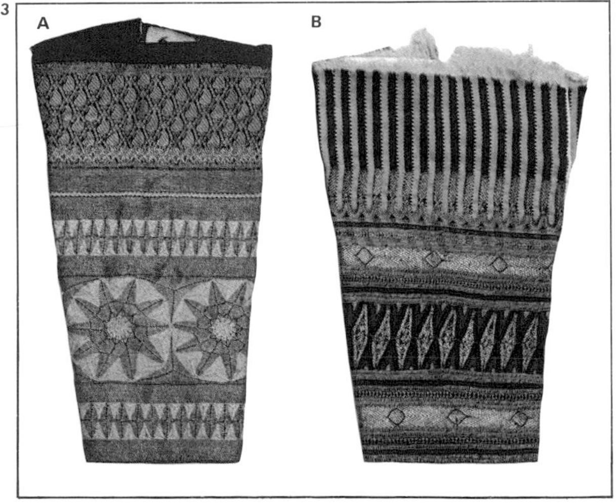

13 **Comparison of Jewish** (A) (*kebir* type) and Muslim (B) leggings from Yemen. Stitches were similar.

Ritual and Ceremonial Aspects of Jewish Dress

Religion has determined not only the ritual and ceremonial aspects of Jewish life, but has impregnated with its halakhik precepts the Jew's entire existence, including his material culture. *Halakhah* prescribes the type and form of dress to be worn by the godfearing man and woman. Moreover, rules of modesty have generated local sumptuary laws regarding ostentation and extravagance since antiquity. These are echoed today by rabbinical exhortations posted in the orthodox quarters of Jerusalem, summoning girls to dress modestly.

Only two of the halakhik precepts were anchored in the Scriptures: *Hukat ha-Goyim*, the admonition to Jews not to follow the ways and customs of their neighbors, and the law of *sha'tnez*, which forbids the mixture of wool and linen in the same garment and is still strictly observed by orthodox Jews, but has no stylistic implications whatsoever.

The Talith

The prayer shawl, bearing the four ritual, knotted fringes, *tzitzioth*, embodies, so to speak, the Jewish man's faith. Historically it probably derives from ancient, Middle Eastern wraps: it has the form either of a longitudinal shawl or, for the very pious, it is a poncho-like raiment called the *talith kattan*, worn permanently. In spite of its being the only element of dress common to the Jews of all the world, the proverbial white color of the *talith* is not universal: it prevailed only in Europe, while in the towns of Yemen it was of fine, black goat-hair or brown and white sheepwool. From other parts of Yemen we have fringed shawls with *tzitzioth*, woven with red, green and yellow stripes. In Italy the *talith* was silk, magnificently embroidered, while in the Tafilalet of Morocco it bore the typical local red embroidery. In Poland it was adorned with the *atara* — special silver and gold embellishments made of *spanierarbeit*, probably brought to Eastern Europe by the Spanish Exiles — while in Hungary, the same type of ornamentation was made up of very small hammered and chiseled silver plaques.

Head-covering

The stipulation that married women cover their hair has no definite Scriptural basis, but was, and still is, quite rigorously observed by traditionally-minded women. It is the source of an endless variation of headgear, some most probably original, as in the village-dress of Morocco, others related to local non-Jewish prototypes, as in most European countries.

Men's headcovering is even less rooted in the Bible or the *Talmud*. But the *Shulkhan Arukh* prescribes it, and in present times a kind of fashion has made the skull-cap, in its endless forms and types, an emblem of Jewish piety.

Ceremonial Costumes

With a few exceptions, such as the white color of *Yom Kippur* garments, there was no stylistic consistency in ceremonial or festive wear. The *Yom Kippur* distinction was most apparent in Bukhara, where men and women alike were usually dressed in resplendent, multicolored attire. Another exception was the great dark-blue, silver embroidered gown or *lului* of San'a women, which they wore at their childbirth ceremonies and on *Yom Kippur*, and in which they were buried. In other places as well Jews were not buried in the usual sheet-shrouds: in Greece an extremely wide gown made of white gauze silk was used, while in Tetouan the Jews had a shroud made as a tailored suit of several pieces, heavily embroidered, white on white.

As for rabbinical costumes, in general they had no distinctive features. From the gallery of rabbinical portraits published by Alfred Rubens, it would seem that their garments were modeled upon those of the Christian or Muslim clergy. Even the distinctive sidelocks, or *pe'oth*, are concealed by the rabbis' beards.

Bridal Outfits

Almost everywhere bridal outfits were used as ceremonial costumes in later life, again with several rare exceptions. One of these is the striking ensemble of the Yemenite Jewish bride from San'a, reconstructed in Israel, and still worn in traditional families by the bride on the *henna* evening preceding the official, white-clad nuptial ceremony. The San'a bridal dress is the most remarkable and exotic complete Jewish costume extant: it is a marvel of white pearls, gilt and silver filigree jewelry, heavy gold brocade and shining silver embroidery, crowned with natural leaves and flowers of magic potency.

The Afghan bride from Herat was also a glittering prodigy: her front was adorned with shiny, multi-colored spangles, golden tinsel paper was braided into her hair and gold jewels, studded with precious stones, were hung around her face.

The all-white, *Ashkenazi* bridal attire of the last century was, and still is, in line with European fashions. For the marriage ceremony, orthodox bridegrooms follow the tradition of wearing a *kittel*, the long white over-garment that also serves as *Yom Kippur* garment in the synagogue and even as shroud.

Hidden Signs and Implications

Certain features adopted by Jews were charged with religious implications, perceived only by the Jews themselves. One such concept preserved by Jews everywhere was mourning for the destruction of the Temple, conveyed in many and various ways. The dark-colored garments of Morocco were given this interpretation, as were the black beads in the white pearl ornamentation of the Jewish bride in San'a, or, in that same town, the two slits at the hem on the sides of a man's *kaftan*. While these slits were common in various oriental garments, the Jews of Yemen firmly believed them to be their specific sign of mourning. The same hidden sign of mourning was implied in Tunisia by a black band hemming men's trousers.

1

1 European talith — prayer shawl. The white and black striped type prevalent throughout the Jewish world. Silverwork *atara*.

5

5 Baby jacket for Brit Mila, circumcision ceremony, 18th century, Germany. Exceptionally rich example, gold-leaf and lace ornamented.

9

9 Tishbuq-lulu — the Jewish bridal attire from San'a. Reconstructed in 1960 for the Israel Museum; has served as model for ensembles still worn for *henna* ceremony.

2

2 Talith from Venice, 18th century. Very fine silk-embroidered ornamentation in the four corners bearing the ritual fringes (*tzitzioth*).

3

3 Talith kattan from rural Yemen. This type is worn constantly by pious Jews everywhere, but is color-striped only in Yemen.

4

4 Talith from the Tafilalet, Morocco. Unique example with red corners — *kanfot* — and the typical red embroidery of the region.

6

6 Yemenite rural bride from Ḣeidan, north Yemen. Wedded in Israel, 1960; her front-ornament is the *shams* pectoral necklace. *Futa* head veil is striped cotton-satin.

7

7 Bridegroom of the Heidan bride in Israel. Wearing the heavy color-striped, traditional *talith* with the recently acquired modern hat, and holding *shadab*, beneficial plant leaves.

8

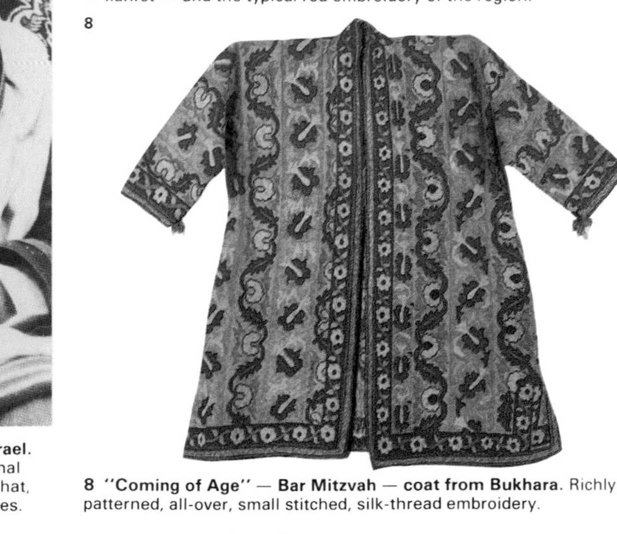

8 "Coming of Age" — Bar Mitzvah — coat from Bukhara. Richly patterned, all-over, small stitched, silk-thread embroidery.

10

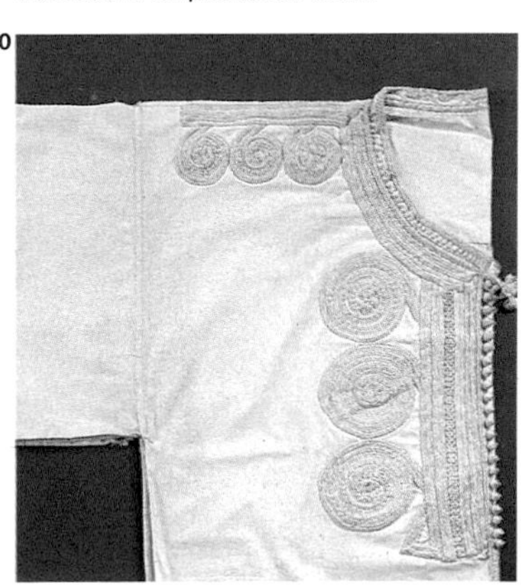

10 Coat from set of shrouds, or *takhrikhim*, Tetouan. Cut and ornaments similar to those of ceremonial dress, but white on white.

11

11 Lului — San'a woman's ceremonial gown and shroud. Indigo-dyed checked cotton; exceedingly wide sleeves.

12

12 Jewish bridal attire from Herat, Afghanistan. Specific, scintillant front-ornamentation — *zaraq* — reconstructed in Israel (1970s).

Costumes of Moroccan Jews

Of all North African communities, the Jews of Morocco have preserved the widest variety of styles in costume. Up to the middle of the 20th century, collectors and ethnographers could still buy and photograph a varied assortment of Jewish costumes, the most distinctive of which, the "Great Dress" of urban women, is worn at the *henna* pre-nuptial ceremony to this very day. Old men from Morocco wore their genuine *jellaba* on the streets of Israeli towns even in the 1970s. The styles of Moroccan clothing are also relatively well known due to the interest shown by French orientalists — both scientists and artists — in the rich and picturesque folk art of Morocco as early as the beginning of the 19th century.

Differences in Urban and Rural Styles
The basic difference between city and villagewear has a special historical background in Morocco.

The rural styles, with all their regional variety, stem from pre-Islamic times, and were common to Jews and Berbers. In towns, and to a certain extent in some villages of the Sous in the Anti-Atlas area, the costumes of Jewish women bore the distinctive marks of a more recent heritage — that of their Spanish ancestors who arrived in Morocco with the great Exile of the Jews from Spain in 1492. Distinctions between Muslim and Jewish costume were more prominent in towns, where Jews lived in the seclusion of their *mellah*, while in the villages they were much more an integral part of the local population.

The primary difference between urban and rural costumes was in the garment's form: in towns they were cut, fashioned and sewn, while in villages the main items of clothing were of the type known as "flat" — one-pieced wrapping sheets wound, draped and fastened in various ways according to local or regional fashions.

There were important differences in the materials employed for clothing: in the country, wool, goat-hair and cotton were used, while in the towns, by the mid-19th century, imported velvet, brocade and silk were popular. Jewels differed even more: in the far countryside, extraordinary heavy, silver, often nielloed or enameled pieces were piled upon the person. They had more than a trace of the Sahara and black Africa in their style. Jewels of the cities were exclusively made of gold, delicately wrought, mainly following the design of Hispano-Mauresque metalwork.

Urban Costume
Toward the end of the 19th century, Jewish men in the large towns of Morocco began to wear European-fashioned garments. By the time of the French occupation (1912) most of them, except in the remote mountain regions, dressed more or less in European style. Only rabbis and elderly men continued to wear the black, embroidered, distinctive *jokha* with the once obligatory *sheshiye*, toque-shaped cap, while young men began to flaunt their newly won liberty by donning bright-colored vests and adopting the once exclusively Muslim *jellaba* cloak.

Women's very distinctive, Spanish-inspired, sumptuous ceremonial "Great Dress" prevailed in several regional versions and colors, always gold-embroidered in a variety of techniques, most often with the characteristic ornamentation of parallel, arched bands applied to the front of the skirt. Other motifs of the gold-embroidery were found to be specific to Jewish ornamentation during the late 19th and early 20th centuries: the bird — often an eagle, sometimes double-headed, or a pair of ordinary birds face to face on the plastron — or a repeated motif of large, spiral circles on the front of the bodice and a kind of "whirling-star" — both particular to the resplendent Tetouan costume. Plastrons seem to have been the most important and the most lavishly ornamented piece of the outfit; they are still carefully preserved in many Moroccan families.

Rural Dress
Regionality was much more pronounced in rural areas than in the towns. Before European uniformity penetrated even the remotest villages, men of South Marrakesh were draped in the large *chayyik*, a finely woven, generally white, woolen sheet, kept in place only by the strap of their bag — the belt, holding a weapon, being forbidden to Jews. Among other restrictions, Jews were obliged to wear inside-out the beautifully adorned *akhnif* cape of the mountain shepherds.

Female costume was basically composed of some kind of shirt-blouse, over which the *izar* sheet-wrap was folded, draped and fastened at both shoulders in various ways, but always leaving enough cloth with which to throw over the head or to carry a baby. The *izar* was kept in place by a pair of silver, sometimes profusely decorated, fibula-pins — a reminder, as the *izar* wrap itself, of antique, Mediterranean forms of dress and adornment.

Women's Headdresses
Jewish women's headdresses were the most distinctive feature of their costume. Married women would hide their hair beneath intricate, ingenious arrangements of false-hair (silk or woolen threads, or horse or bovine hair tufts), often with gold-woven bands, kerchiefs and bonnets, and a great variety of ornaments. The Spanish-styled, urban dress was accompanied by a white-pearl-embroidered, gold-adorned headband and large, delicately wrought, stone-set, golden ear-hangings. In the southern Atlas valleys bordering the Sahara, intricate chain and nielloed silver-plaque ornaments were worn to keep the head-veil in place. The Tafilalet "horned" hair-do, fitted to the bride's head only after consummation of the marriage, was perhaps the most spectacular and probably the most charged with occult traditions, going far back into ancient history.

1

1 Urban "Great Dress" — Tetouan and other northern cities. Open, fan-shaped skirt, short-sleeved jacket, sumptuous plastron, separate, flaring sleeves and gold-lamé belt.

8

8 Front part of shirt-dress from the Tafilalet. The red color and the floss-silk embroidery were peculiar to this once-wealthy community.

2 **Plastron to the Tetouan "Great Dress."** Velvet, gold embroidered over cut-out patterns. Hispano-mauresque styled palmette design; central cone possibly a stylized pomegranate, symbolizing fertility.

3 **Traditional wear of urban notable — Mogador.** Several richly embroidered garments were worn superposed.

4 **Eagle pendant-medallion — Tangier or Tetouan.** Best example known of splendid jewel type, worn with the "Great Dress."

5 **Headdress from the Sous — mahdour** — Silver-wire and enameled ornaments on a foundation of horse or bovine-tail hair. A wig and elaborate head-ornament in one, often covered by a scarf or a pearled crown.

6 **Rural fibula-pins — bzim** or *khlala* from Tiznit. Ornate type of nielloed fibulahead; not definitely known to have been worn by Jewish women, though made by Jews.

7 **Rural wear Tamgrout near Zagora.** Similar to Muslim-Berber attire, except for the ostrich feather tufts, donned to replace the hair, which was traditionally kept hidden. Rural women went about their daily tasks adorned in their complete jewelry outfit.

9 **Bracelets, mainly from Tahala in the Sous.** Niello and enameled ornamentation, said to have been brought to Morocco by Spanish silversmiths. The design is specific to this southern region.

10 **Shepherd's akhnif from the High Atlas Mountains.** Very singular woven and loom-embroidered decoration on back.

11 A

11 B

11 **The tasfift crown from the Valley of Dades.** Jewish women were never tattooed, but did paint ornaments on their faces.

Costumes of Yemenite Jews

Jewish dress regulations and restrictions were more rigorous and more strictly observed in Yemen than in other Islamic countries. The general impression of austerity created by the costumes, however, probably derives also from the poverty prevailing in this land, once called *Arabia Felix*. Travelers' frequently distressing reports on Jewish dress were given the lie only in Israel when the Jews of Yemen unveiled the bright, colorful sides of their costume.

It emerged that in Yemen, even rich Jews were careful never to display their own and their wives' ceremonial, bejeweled costumes. They would appear in the obligatory dark, generally dark-blue, plain garments by which they could be unmistakably identified, as they could by their long, curled sidelocks called *simonim*, "signs." Women and children wore distinctive garments only in San'a, where they lived in the seclusion of the Jewish quarter, *Ga'el Yahud*, though recent Israeli research points to distinctive features of Jewish women's dress in the countryside as well.

Origins and Affinities

The distinctive features of Yemenite dress and jewelry were initially thought to have originated in ancient Roman-Hellenistic and Byzantine modes. While this theory still enjoys certain historical support, ethnographic and comparative stylistic material now available seems to point to more recent affinities. Since Yemen is that part of the Arab world which looks toward Africa and the Far East, several costume features, and especially ornamental elements, common to Yemen, India and Ethiopia can be clearly identified. These include the men's long shawls, folded and wound around their upper arm and shoulders, into the four corners of which Jews have strung their ritual fringes, and the general shapes and elements of the heavy silverwork of the Yemenite countryside, refined into the daintier gilt filigree jewelry of San'a, but basically similar in design to Ethiopian and Indian metalwork. Particularly telling resemblances have been found in embroidery stitches and motifs in silk as well as in metal thread embroideries.

San'a Costume

San'a Jews were a world apart, differing in many ways from their brethren in the countryside, as well as from their Muslim neighbors. They retained the traditional costumes described by 19th century travelers into the middle of the 20th century, when they all immigrated to Israel.

The men's underwear consisted of a unique loin-cloth, *maizar*, reaching the knees, which, like all South-Arabian men, they wore instead of trousers. Then came a long shirt-dress and the main garment, the *qaftan*, usually dark-blue, but white on the Sabbath, and worn only at home or in the synagogue. The long shawl bearing the ritual fringes, *tzitzioth*, was the black, woolen *shamla*, which was worn exactly in the manner described in the Bible (Exod. 12:34) and which is a feature of both Muslim and Indian costume as well, though in India the term *shamla* means "girdle." The prayershawl as known in Europe — white with black or blue stripes at the borders — was introduced into Yemen at a very late date.

San'a women's costume bore many features peculiar to Jews, and has come to be considered virtually a national costume in Israel. Its main pieces were the very characteristic hood, *gargush*, of black velvet for everyday use and of gold brocade for festive occasions. It hid the hair entirely, and was worn from the age of one year until menopause. It was covered in the street by the no less typical square kerchief, *lachfe*, imported from India or Italy, and made of shiny black cotton with strictly uniform white and red patterns. Jewish women were not hidden by veils like their Muslim counterparts, but they did lift the edge of their *lachfe* to hide their mouths at the sight of a stranger. Their dresses — whether the street dress, *antari*, of black satined cotton, or the ceremonial indigo-tinted gown, *lului* — were ornamented only along the front opening, either with silver and red silk-thread embroidery, or with silverwork bands, chains and buttons.

The most characteristic part of women's costume were the embroidered leggings of their trousers, which in many parts of the Muslim world were worn by women only. The ornamentation of the leggings — and, to a certain extent, also that of the *gargush* — was made to suit the social class of the wearer, her age and marital status, as well as the circumstances, whether everyday or festive. The *gargush* was never worn after menopause, while an eligible young girl wore it with a special ornamentation, mainly of red embroidery.

Rural Wear

In the countryside, where interdependence between the Jewish artisan and the Muslim farmer compelled them to live in close symbiosis, there were no marked differences in clothing, though a Jew could always be recognized by his long, curled sidelocks. The *maizar* loincloth, also named *futa*, or *magdab*, was here held in place by a belt into which Jews were permitted, in remote regions such as Heidan, to insert a *jambiya* (dagger), an inconceivable privilege in towns.

In women's dress, regionalism was established only recently. The only features all village costumes shared was again the fact that women wore trousers with more or less profusely embroidered leggings, and hid their hair under tightly wound black or dark-blue scarves or looser, more colorful veils.

Among the regional dresses recently found in Israel are the typical indigo-tinted and polished *messabaq*, a wide-sleeved gown from Heidan, and the richly embroidered dress from Sharaf, with an angular, asymmetric design which recalls the African affinities of these costumes.

1

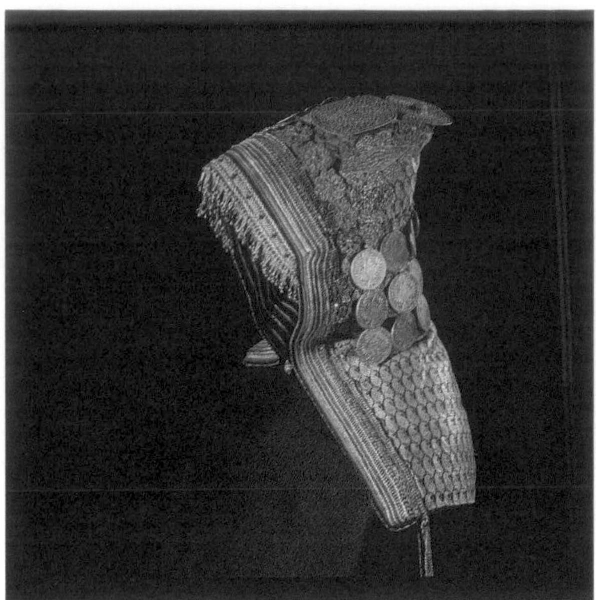

1 The "full-golden" gargush — San'a. Dowry item; gilt-silver filigree plaques and Maria-Theresa coins were an investment in case of penury.

5

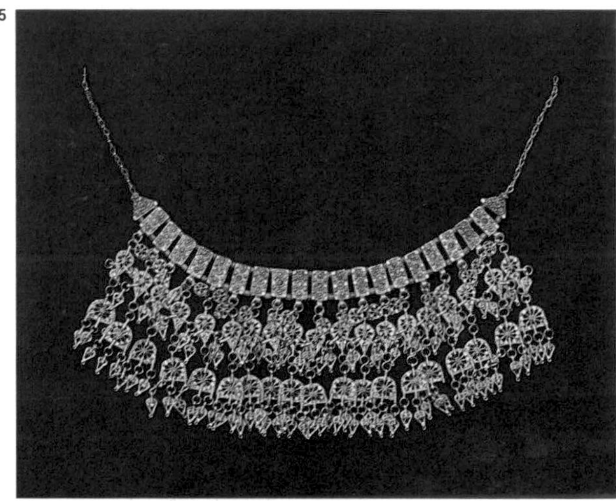

5 Shams, the rural formula of the San'a pectoral necklace (*lebbe*). Always made by Jews; worn also by Muslim women, even in San'a.

9

9 Basta type leggings of Jewish woman's trousers — San'a. Double silverthreads, couched on velvet with red silk in brick pattern, were a specifically Jewish type of embroidery.

2

2 Old man and women in San'a, the 1930s. Demonstration of how the black *shamla talith* and the *lachfe* scarf covering the *gargush* were worn.

3

3 Chief Rabbi's hat — ligge — San'a. Red roundels on this ancient type of hat are similar to certain Indian embroideries.

4

4 Young girl's festive gargush from San'a. The red embroidery on the *gargush* is only for children and young girls before marriage.

6

6 Detail of lului, Jewish woman's special ceremonial gown — San'a. The intricate rosace motif and the silver halfbeads are also to be found in Indian urban embroidery.

7

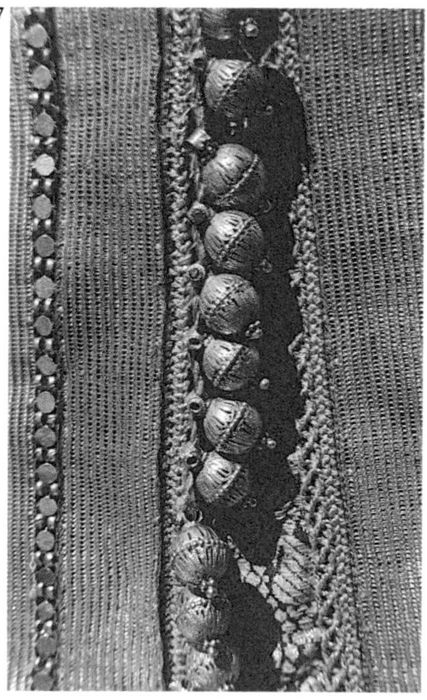

7 Detail of ornament on Jewish woman's dress — antari — San'a. Ribbons of knitted silverwire, gilt chains and filigree buttons, gold cord-embroidery.

8

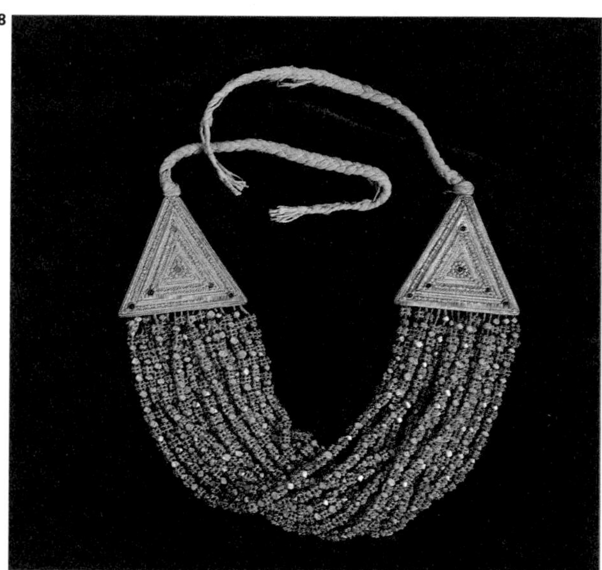

8 Ma'anaqe — Jewish necklace from San'a. Characteristic torsion of the strings; made of granulated and polygonal beads.

10

10 Mecharrar — silk embroidered everyday leggings of girls and young women in San'a. Red leggings were specific to Jewish women.

11

11 Woman from Sa'ada in Heidan, the northern region of Yemen. Typical indigo-dyed and polished (*messabaq*) dress.

12

12 Rural woman's dress from the Sharaf region. Singular asymmetric design, possibly of African (or Byzantine?) affiliation; talismanic motifs. Inside pocket hemmed with same ornamental band as front slit.

Costumes of Jews in the Middle East and Central Asia

Jewish communities in the Middle East and Central Asia can almost all be considered more or less direct descendants of the Babylonian exiles, banished from Jerusalem after the fall of the First Temple in the 6th century BCE. Only one of these communities, the Kurdish Jews, have retained the Aramaic language which was common to all Semitic peoples in the Fertile Crescent prior to the transition to Arabic in the 7th or 8th century CE. On the other hand, in Turkey and its Balkan dependencies, *Sephardi* Jews speaking their Ladino dialect were dominant.

The Jews of these regions were on the whole culturally integrated into the prevailing Islamic civilization, though each community had its specific traditions and patterns of life. Several distinctive elements of their costumes have already been mentioned, but a number of features, identical or similar to those worn by Muslims, have still to be considered, because they characterize the great diversity of the ethnic and cultural constituents making up the Jewish nation.

Turkey and the Fertile Crescent

The many and varied ethno-religious communities living under Ottoman rule until the 19th and 20th centuries were granted rights of self-administration and jurisdiction: thus Jews in Turkey, Greece, Egypt, Ereẓ Israel, Syria and Iraq, could lead their communal and religious life in relative freedom.

The richness and variety of the traditional costumes in most of these regions have often been illustrated and described. But the very few actual dress and ornamental items still extant are much more recent than the lithographs and other representations published by European travelers dazzled by the exotic variety of costumes worn in the Ottoman Empire. Extant garments and ornaments therefore mainly reflect the influence of European styles which reached Turkey and the entire region even before the 19th century. In fact, the only distinctive Jewish Ottoman attire from the early 20th century that has reached us, is the Salonika married woman's costume already mentioned.

In former times, in Turkey itself, where Jews as a rule lived in towns, their garments and jewelry were always patterned after the relatively wealthy, local, urban wear: Jewish women wore the typical Turkish *entari* — a long, fitted coat-dress with side-slits reaching up to the hips, and long sleeves, narrowly fitted at the shoulders and generally widening to the wrists, often with ample, richly trimmed flaps. The *entari* was sewn from a variety of fabrics, including cotton and wool; the ceremonial ones prevailing in museums are of precious, embroidered silks and brocades. Another typical Turkish garment adopted by Jewish women was the *bindal* — a wedding and ceremonial gown, always profusely gold-embroidered, mostly on velvet, less frequently on silk. It was still made and worn in Turkey in the 1940s; Jews ceased wearing it much earlier. Many *bindal* gowns have reached us in the form of *Torah* Ark curtains, into which they were altered in order to be dedicated to the synagogue.

Jewish costumes from Syria and Iraq were very rarely recorded, and almost no garments of these ancient and highly developed communities have reached us, with the exception of the Baghdadi women's *izar* mentioned earlier.

Kurdistan and Bukhara

The Kurds living in Iraq, Iran, Syria, Turkey and the USSR form a unique Middle Eastern community, and are the most thoroughly studied to date. They were almost exclusively part of agrarian society, and their colorful costumes bear the mark of true folk-art. The relatively comfortable economic status of Kurdish Jews was manifest in the quality and elaborate ornamentation of their dress. Outstanding were the men's suits, made of silky wool — *ma'araz* — and woven mainly by Jewish men from goat-hair, with multi-colored loom and needle embroidery. Women's dresses and dress-coats were of raw silk, most often in strong lilac and green hues. Typical also were the wide and very long scarves worn by both men and women, wound around the waist as a girdle or coiled around a cap as large, intricate turbans.

Until the USSR took control of the region in the 1920s, Bukharan Jews belonged to the urban, mercantile class of Uzbekistan society. It was said that the exceptional magnificence of their heavy, gold-embroidered velvet ceremonial gowns and *qaftans* echoed the splendor of the garb worn by the Emir and his courtiers. Their chatoyant silk garments were typical of *ikat* tinting derived from far eastern dyeing techniques. Jewelry was rich, gold, and stone-studded, often reflecting the lavish patterns of India.

Persia, Afghanistan and Georgia

In modes of dress and costume, Jews of Persia and Afghanistan can be clearly considered as one group. Traditional urban women's costume consisted of narrow, generally dark-colored trousers, over which a singular, very short, gathered ballerina skirt was worn. It was often made of wine-red or green silk, the borders of which were tinsel-embroidered in flowery patterns. In older times jackets typically had a narrow, tight-fitting cut and were made of various locally-woven silk or block-printed cotton materials. After the European cuts were introduced, jackets became broader and longer, and were made of velvet or taffeta-silk, heavily embroidered in gold tinsel. Women in the streets of Persian towns were shrouded from head to toe in the *choddar*, a printed-cotton or silk wrap, cut in the form of a large half-circle. In the house they wore a large square shawl of plain cotton or tulle, fastened under the chin, and embroidered with gold or silver flat-tinsel.

Jews from Georgia brought very few samples of traditional dress to Israel. The typical Caucasian men's outfit was worn, with arms, even to synagogue.

1

1 Jewish woman from Iraqi Kurdistan. Turban of square, fine silk scarf, block-printed in brownish, yellow and some red colors. Silk tassels in vivid hues.

5

5 Iran — detail of woman's scarf. Gold-tinsel two-faced embroidery, typical of Persian dress ornament.

9

9 Georgia (Gruzinia) — man's ceremonial jacket. Silk, trimmed with silver ribbons; worn at *Hatan Torah* ceremony.

2

2 **Boy's ceremonial vest — Iraqi Kurdistan.** Multi-colored silk embroidering was a homecraft widely plied by Jewish women. The motifs generally had talismanic protective implications.

3

3 **Kurdish woman's jacket.** Quilted and embroidered patchwork. Typical vivid colors.

4

4 **Man's trousers — Zacho, Iraqi Kurdistan.** Goat-hair weave (*ma'araz*), loom-embroidery, part of suit still worn by Kurdish Jews in Israel on festive occasions.

6

6 **Detail of Bukharan coat.** Gold and silver embroidery, enhanced with colored silk threads.

7

7 **Bukhara — man's great ceremonial jom'a.** Type of royal vestments still worn on festive occasions in Israel.

8

8 **Bukhara — parkhona front ornament;** *pulaktshe* veil. The bespangled tulle veil was the only distinctive Jewish item in the Bukharan costume.

10

10 **Afghanistan — ear-hangings.** Painted-enamel on gold, typical of Persian and Afghani goldsmith work.

11

11 **Ikat-tinted silk wear, Uzbekistan, Bukhara.** Bukhara was famous for its fine, resplendent-colored silks.

12
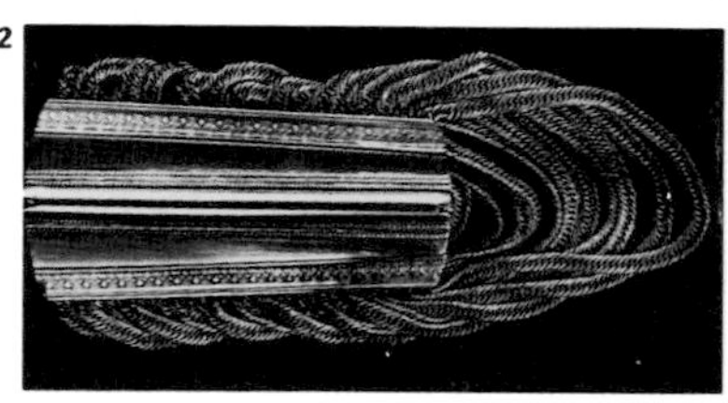
12 **Turkey — gold bracelet.** Urban traditional type; bride's dowry or given by in-laws.

13

13 **Balkans — bindal ceremonial gown.** Purple velvet, gold embroidered patterns.

Jewish Paper-Cuts

The art of the paper-cut is very ancient, and probably originated in the Far East. It is a folk art, fulfilling a well-defined function in the life of the individual and the community. We know of Jewish paper and parchment cut-outs from at least the 17th century onwards. They were common in communities in Eastern and Central Europe, as well as in the Middle East, until World War II. Jews in Islamic countries probably became familiar with the form before those in Christian Europe. In the late 19th century, this art was also practiced in the United States, brought by immigrants from Eastern Europe. Paper-cuts were produced exclusively by men, usually *yeshiva* students, religious scholars and their assistants. Although generally a leisure time activity, the art was treated with religious devotion.

Motifs and Symbols

Jewish cut-outs appeared in many different forms and several varieties of motifs, accompanied by inscriptions and verses from the Bible and other sources. The paper-cuts are almost totally lacking in human figures, landscapes or narrative motifs. The motifs and symbols that do appear are typical of all branches of Jewish art and ritual decoration, whether done in wood, metal or embroidery. The most common motifs are the seven-branched candelabrum (*menorah*), the Tablets of the Law, and the Scroll of the Law with a crown, Star of David or eagle above. The borders, and at times the entire background, are intricately worked in leaf patterns, geometrical shapes, or animal forms.

The most frequently depicted animals are the lion, deer, leopard and eagle, illustrating the maxim of Rabbi Yehuda ben Tema: "Be ardent as the leopard, swift as an eagle, fleet as the deer and brave as the lion to do the will of thy Father in Heaven" (*Pirkei Avot* 5:20). The lion, symbol of the tribe of Judah, is an ancient motif. It represents power and bravery, and appears in the precept: "Rise as a lion to the work of the Creator." The eagle, symbol of majesty and patronage, recalls the verse, "As an eagle stirreth up her nest, fluttereth over her young" (*Deut.* 32:11). At times a twin-headed eagle appears, a form also found in the ancient art of the Far East and on Arab coins from medieval times. Other popular animal motifs are birds — including mythological winged creatures such as griffins — hares, squirrels, pelicans, bears, elephants and camels. The ancient motif of the tree of life, depicted in any number of fashions, was frequently used to enhance the paper-cut, as were the signs of the zodiac, architectural details symbolizing Jerusalem and the Temple.

Types of Paper-Cuts

The different designs of the various types of paper-cuts were determined by their purpose. The *Mizrach* (east) was the most popular sort, as well as the most lavish from the point of view of composition and intricacy. These paper-cuts were affixed to the eastern wall of homes, synagogues and study houses to indicate the direction of Jerusalem and the Temple toward which one faces when praying. One type of *Mizrach* hung in the synagogue is known as *Shiviti* from the verse *Shiviti Adonai le-negdi tamid* ("I have set the Lord always before me", *Psalms* 16:8) which often appears in it. Another verse often found on the *Mizrach* is *Da lifnei mi ata omed* ("know before whom you stand", *Berakhot* 28:2). *Mizrach* paper-cuts were usually made of white paper, tinted with watercolors, and mounted on colored paper.

Many of the paper-cuts, and those of the *Mizrach* variety in particular, include texts praising Jerusalem and the Temple, stressing the importance of a life of piety and good deeds, or disdaining the vanity of this world. Mystical and kabbalistic phrases formed from the initial letters of the names of God or of Biblical verses appear as well.

Another type of Jewish paper-cut, the *Menorah*, comes from North Africa and the Near East. This motif is often repeated several times, with biblical verses, primarily from the Book of Psalms, curling about the branches of the candelabrum. Colorful tin-foil candy wrappings serve as the background for these paper-cuts. Those featuring large *menorot* fulfilled a function similar to that of the *Mizrach* in Eastern Europe, while those with smaller motifs were used as charms and often contain kabbalistic phrases. The *hamsa* — an open palm protecting and warding off danger — which also appears in Middle Eastern paper-cuts, was totally unknown in Eastern Europe.

A third type of paper-cut is the *Shevuosl* or *Roysele*, used to decorate the window panes during the holiday of *Shavuot*. The name *Roysele* derives from the round rosette-like shape of many of these paper-cuts, although some are also rectangular. They were made of white paper and rarely tinted. They are small in size and some include the phrase *Hag ha-Shavuot ha-zeh* ("This holiday of *Shavuot*"). An occasional *Shevuosl* will have a motif depicting soldiers and cavalrymen. The cut-outs of *Shavuot* were known only in certain parts of Poland and Russia.

Other types of paper-cuts popular in Europe were the *Kimpetbriefel* or *Shir ha-ma'alosl*, used as a charm for women giving birth; the *Ketubbah* (marriage agreement) which was often decorated, and parts of which were often made of cut-outs; calendars for counting the days of the *Omer* between Passover and *Shavuot; Ushpizin* which served as decorations for the *Sukkah; Mi-she-nikhnas Adar* calendars for the month of *Adar* when *Purim* is celebrated; flags for the holiday of *Simchat Torah*; memorial tablets and lanterns; and lanterns used for lighting outdoor festivities.

Few original Jewish paper-cuts have survived. Most of these are from Poland and Russia, with only a small number from North Africa, Turkey and Erez Israel.

1 Mizrach, Medzhibezh, Ukraine, 19th century, 60×76 cm.

4 Shevuosl, Poland, 19th century, 31×49 cm.

5 Mizrach, designed and executed by Chaim Katz Silbiger, Oswiencim (Auschwitz), Poland, 1891, 46×36.5 cm.

2 Mizrach, Poland, late 19th century, 51×32.5 cm.

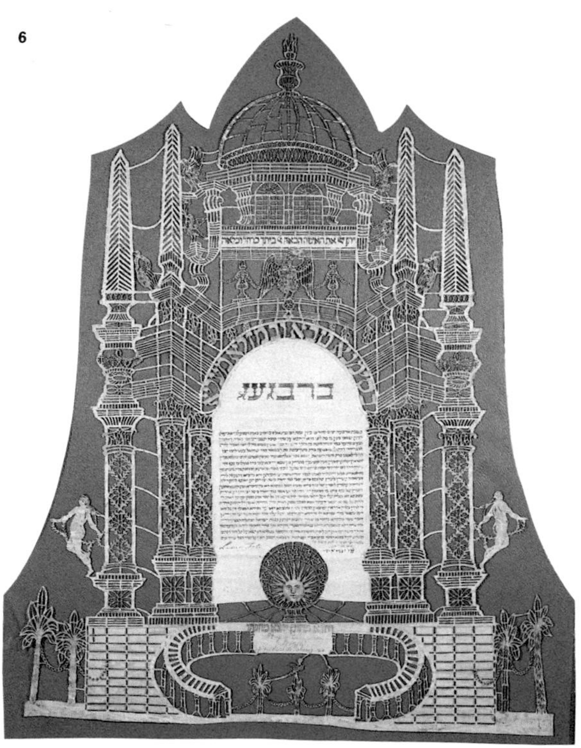

6 Ketubbah, Lugo, Italy, 1847. The text in the panel above the eagle blesses the groom that his bride be like the matriarchs. Parchment, 74×56 cm.

3 Shiviti, Galicia, Poland, 19th century, 44×56.5 cm.

7 Menorah, North Africa, 19th or early 20th century, 47×62 cm.

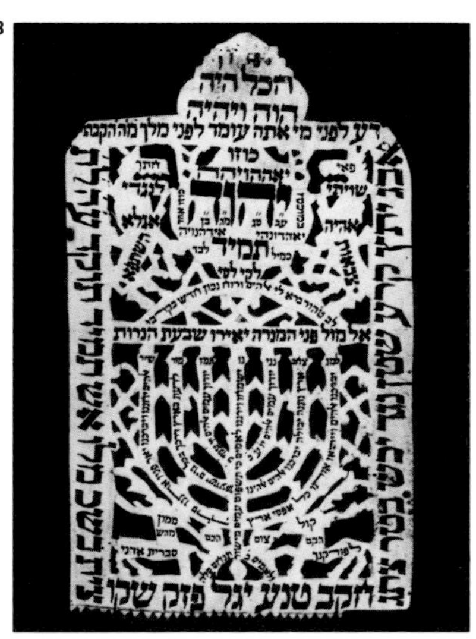

8 Menorah Amulet, Syria or Ereẓ Israel, 18th or 19th century, parchment, 14.7×8.8 cm.

9 Menorah Amulet, Persia (?), parchment, 18th century.

Traditional Tomb of Rachel at the entrance to Bethlehem. Photograph from 1922.

Chronological Chart of Jewish and World History

5000-700 BCE

Erez Israel		Egypt	Mesopotamia, Assyria		Crete, Greece, Rome
5000 Beginning of transition to sedentary settlement; Jericho; The alphabet		Pre-dynastic civilization	Jarmu civilization Cuneiform writing		
4000 Influx of Canaanites; Organized settlements			Urban development in Sumer		
3000 Influx of Phoenicians; Bet Yerah culture					
		1991 12th Dynasty	**1950** Assyria independent		
2000 Patriarchs Hyksos		**1786** Second interregnum	**1750-1700** Mari period		
		1720-1570 Rule of the Hyksos	**1728-1686** Hammurabi; Early Hittite Kingdom; Mitanni Kingdom; New Hittite Kingdom		**2000-1700** Cretan culture
		Israelites in Egypt **1550** The New Kingdom			
		1501-1447 Hatshepsut			**1600** Beginning of Mycenaean culture in Greece
		1450 Thutmose III			
		1440-1350 Tel el-Amarna period			**1450** Destruction of Minoan Crete
		1370-1353 Akhenaton			
		1309-1290 Seti I	**1300-587** Kingdom of Assyria		
	1280 Exodus from Egypt	**1290-1224** Ramses II			
1250 Conquest of Canaan; Philistines in Erez Israel		**1224-1216** Merneptah			
1200-1020 Period of the Judges			**1090** Tiglath Pileser		**1200** Trojan War
				Aram Damascus Rezin	
1020-1004 Saul					
1004-965 David					
965-928 Solomon		**935-914** Shishak			
Judah	**Israel**				
928-911 Rehoboam	**928-907** Jeroboam I	**918-917** Shishak invades Erez Israel			
911-908 Abijah	**907-906** Nadab				
908-867 Asa	**906-883** Baasha			Ben Hadad I	
	883-882 Elah **882** Zimri		**883-859** Ashurnasirpal II		
	882-871 Omri				
867-846 Jehoshaphat	**871-852** Ahab			Ben Hadad II	
	852-851 Ahaziah				
			858-824 Shalmaneser III	**853** Battle of Karkar	**850** Homer
846-843 Jehoram	**851-842** Jehoram				
843-842 Ahaziah	**842-814** Jehu			Hazael	**814** Founding of Carthage
842-836 Athaliah					
836-798 Jehoash	**814-800** Jehoahaz				
798-769 Amaziah	**800-784** Jehoash			Ben Hadad III	
769-733 Uzziah	**784-748** Jeroboam II		**820-780** Adadnirri II		**800-600** Founding of Rome; expansion of Greece
758-743 Jotham (regent)	**748** Zechariah **748** Shallum		**783-773** Shalmaneser IV		
743-733 Ahaz (regent)	**747-737** Menahem		**744-727** Tiglath Pileser III		
	737-735 Pekahiah				
733-727 Ahaz				Rezin	
	735-733 Pekah				
727-698 Hezekiah	**733-724** Hoshea **722** Samaria conquered		**727-722** Shalmaneser V		
	720 Exile to Assyria		**722-705** Sargon II	Rezin	

7TH CENTURY BCE — 2ND CENTURY CE

Erez Israel

701 Campaign of Sennacherib
698-642 Manasseh
641-640 Amon
639-609 Josiah
609 Battle of Megiddo
608-598 Jehoiakim
597 Jehoiachin
597 Deportation of Jehoiachin
595-586 Zedekiah
586 Destruction of Jerusalem and exile to Babylonia
585? Murder of Gedaliah
538 Cyrus' proclamation Return to Zion
520-515 Beginning of building of Second Temple
332 Conquest by Alexander the Great
301 Ptolemies begin rule over Erez Israel
198 Seleucids begin rule over Erez Israel
168 Hasmonean revolt
161 Defeat of Nicanor
160-142 Jonathan son of Mattathias
142-135 Simeon Thassis
135-104 John Hyrcanus I
103-76 Alexander Yannai
76-67 Salome Alexandra
67-63 Judah Aristobulus II
63 Pompey in Erez Israel
67, 63-40 John Hyrcanus II
40-37 Mattathias Antigonus
37-4 Herod
6-14 Judah, Samaria, and Edom become a Roman province
5-30 Wanderings of Jesus
26-36 Pontius Pilate *praefectus*
33 Crucifixion of Jesus
38-44 Agrippa I
44-66 Agrippa II
66 Beginning of revolt against Rome
67 Vespasian conquers the Galilee
70 Jerusalem falls
73 Masada falls; Judea made a Roman province
106 Roman conquest of Nabatea
132-135 Bar Kokhba revolt
135 Beitar falls; Aelia Capitolina founded

Egypt

663 Destruction of Thebes
525 Persian conquest
411 Destruction of the temple at Elephantine
404 Egypt regains independence
343 Persian conquest
333 Battle of Issus
323-285 Ptolemy I
285-246 Ptolemy II Philadelphus
246-221 Ptolemy III Euergetes
221-203 Ptolemy IV Philopator
203-181 Ptolemy V Epiphanes
181-146 Ptolemy VI Philometor
168 Antiochus IV invades Egypt
69-30 Cleopatra VII
38 Riots against Jews of Alexandria
115-117 Jews revolt against Trajan

Assyria

704-681 Sennacherib
681-669 Esar-Haddon
668-627 Asshurbanipal

Babylonia
625-605 Nabopalassar
612 Fall of Nineveh
605 Battle of Charchemish
605-562 Nebuchadnezzar

Persia
550-530 Nabonidus
539 Cyrus conquers Babylonia
529-522 Cambyses II
548-486 Darius I
486-465 Xerxes (Ahasverus?)
465-423 Artaxerxes I
423-404 Darius II
404-358 Artaxerxes II
358-335 Artaxerxes III
335-330 Darius III

Syria
175-164 Antiochus IV
162-152 Demetrius I
152-142 Alexander Balas
145-138 Demetrius II, Antiochus VI, Tryphon
138-129 Antiochus VII Sidetes
129-125 Demetrius III
75-55 Gabinius, Roman Procurator in Syria

Crete, Greece, Rome

621 Draconian code
594 Legal reforms of Solon
510 Beginning of Roman republic
490 Battle of Marathon
480 Battle of Thermopylea
461-429 Age of Pericles
431-404 Peloponnesian War
399 Death of Socrates
336 Alexander inherits the throne
323 Death of Alexander
300 Euclid
287-212 Archimedes
264-241 First Punic War
218-202 Second Punic War
146 Destruction of Carthage
133 Beginning of revolt in Rome
100-44 Julius Caesar
60 First Triumvirate
31 BCE-12 CE Augustus
14-37 Tiberius
37-41 Caius Caligula
41-54 Claudius
54-68 Nero
64 Persecution of Christians
69-79 Vespasian
79-81 Titus
81-96 Domitian
98-117 Trajan
117-138 Hadrian

138-1096

Erez Israel

140 *Sanhedrin* located at Usha

170 *Sanhedrin* at Beth Shearim

200 *Sanhedrin* at Sepphoris

210 Redaction of the *Mishnah*

235 *Sanhedrin* at Tiberias

320 Death of Judah II

324 Erez Israel under Byzantine rule

351 Sepphoris revolts against Gallus

359 Intercalation technique introduced

365 Death of Hillel II

385 Death of Gamaliel V

390 *Jerusalem Talmud* completed

400 Death of Judah IV

426 Death of Gamaliel VI

520 Mar Zutra heads *Sanhedrin* in Tiberius

614-618 Jerusalem conquered by Persians

632 Heraclius decrees forced baptism

638 Jerusalem conquered by Umayyad Muslims

750 Erez Israel conquered by Abbasids

825 Karaites in Jerusalem

878 Conquest of Erez Israel by Ahmad Ibn Tulun

922-946 Reign of Muhammad Ibn Tughj

1070-1078 Seljuks conquer Erez Israel

World History

138-161 Antoninus Pius

161-180 Marcus Aurelius

180-192 Commodus

193-211 Septimus Severus

211-217 Caracalla

224 Beginning of Sassanid dynasty in Persia

285-305 Diocletian

285-337 Constantine I

313 Edict of Milan

325 Council of Nicaea

337-361 Constantine II

340 Christianity made state religion in Roman Empire; Death of Eusebius

406 Vandals invade Spain and Gaul

410 Visigoths invade Italy

476 Last Roman Emperor in West deposed

486 Clovis founds Frankish kingdom

482-565 Justinian I

590-604 Pope Gregory I

622 *Hijra* to Medina

632 Beginning of Muslim conquests

640-642 Muslim conquest of Egypt

661 Rise of Umayyads

670 Muslim conquest of North Africa

711 Muslim conquest of Spain

750 Beginning of Muslim Empire

750-1258 Abbasid Caliphate

756-1031 Umayyads in Spain

768-814 Charlemagne

843 Treaty of Verdun; Carolingian Empire divided

966 King of Poland adopts Christianity

979 Unification of China under Sung dynasty

987 Rise of Capetians in France

968-1171 Fatimids in Egypt

1055 Seljuks conquer Baghdad

1066 William of Normandy conquers England

1077 Canossa — Emperor Henry IV submits to the Pope

1085 Toledo conquered by the Christians

Jews of Europe

321 Jews in Cologne

325 Christian Church formulates its policy toward the Jews: for the sake of Christianity they must continue to exist in isolation and humiliation

339 Constantine II prohibits marriage between Jews and Christians and possession of Christian slaves by Jews

553 Justinian interferes in Jewish worship

Bulls of Pope Gregory I — fix church attitude toward Jews of Europe

612, 633, 638 Persecutions of Jews in Visigothic Spain

628 Expulsion of Jews from the Frankish kingdom

8th-10th centuries Jewish Khazar Kingdom

955 Letter of Hisdai ibn Shaprut to Joseph, King of the Khazars

970 Death of Menahem ibn Saruq and of Hisdai ibn Shaprut

990 Death of Dunash b. Labrat

1012 Expulsion of Jews from Mainz

1028 Death of Rabbenu Gershom *Meor ha-Golah*

1056 Death of Samuel ha-Nagid and of Solomon ibn Gabirol

1073 Jews first settle in England

Jews of the East and North Africa

210-240 Mar Ukba exilarch

247 death of Rav (Abba Arikha)

320 Death of Rav Huna

330 Death of Rabbah b. Nahamani

338 Death of Abbaye

352 Death of Raba

427 Death of Rav Ashi

455 Jews forbidden to observe the Sabbath in Babylonia

470 **Persecutions by the authorities;** Huna the exilarch and others executed

495-502 Revolt of Mar Zutra the exilarch

500 *Babylonian Talmud* completed

500-540 *Savoraim*

589 Beginning of era of *Geonim*

623-629 Muhammad fights Jews of Arabian Peninsula

762-767 Beginning of Karaite movement

858 Death of R. Natronai Gaon

921-2 Calendar dispute between Babylonia and Erez Israel

935 Saadiah Gaon writes *Emunot ve-Deot*

942 Death of Saadiah Gaon

10th century Jewish center in Kairouan

998 Death of Sherira Gaon

1008 Persecutions of al-Hakim

1013 Death of Samuel b. Hophni

1038 Death of R. Hai Gaon

1038-1058 R. Hezekiah b. R. David *gaon* and exilarch in Babylonia

1083-1089 David b. Daniel heads Talmudic Academy in Fostat

1096-1492

Erez Israel

1099 Jerusalem conquered by Crusaders

1101-1118 Campaign of Baldwin I to consolidate Crusader Kingdom of Jerusalem

1160-1173 Travels of Benjamin of Tudela

1170 Beginning of Saladin's conquests

1175 R. Pethahiah of Regensburg visits Erez Israel

1187 Saladin conquers Jerusalem

1210-1211 *Aliyah* of 300 French and English rabbis

1250 Beginning of Mameluke rule

1260, 1299 Mongol invasions of Erez Israel

1260-1271 Conquest by Baybars, the Mameluke

1267-1270 Nahmanides in Erez Israel

1291 Acre conquered by Mameluke Muslims; Latin Kingdom of Jerusalem

1291-1516 Mameluke rule

End of 14th cent. First *aliyah* of Jews and *Anusim* from Spain and Portugal

1401-5 Tamerlane the Tatar in Erez Israel

World History

1096-1099 First Crusade

1122 Compromise reached between Emperor and Pope

1147-1149 Second Crusade

1179 Third Lateran Council

1187 Military dictatorship by Minamoto Shoguns in Japan

1198-1216 Innocent III

1204 Fourth Crusade: Byzantium conquered by Franks

1206 Genghis Khan conquers Asia

1215 Magna Carta; Fourth Lateran Council

1226-1274 Thomas Aquinas

1227-1241 Gregory IX

1258 Mongols conquer Baghdad

1260-1516 Mamelukes rule Egypt

1264 Kublai Khan founds Yuan Dynasty in China

1271-1293 Travels of Marco Polo

1309-1378 Popes in Avignon

1333 Civil war in Japan

1337 Beginning of Hundred Years' War between France and England

1348 Black Death

1378 Beginning of Great Schism in papacy

1380 Beginning of Tamerlane's conquests

1381, 1383 Peasants revolt in England

1394-1460 Henry the Navigator

1415 Portuguese expansion into Africa; John Huss burned at the stake

1419-1436 Hussite Wars in Europe

1431 Joan of Arc burned at the stake

1450 Invention of printing

1453 Constantinople falls to the Turks; End of Hundred Years' War

1479 Castile and Aragon united

1480 End of Tatar rule in Russia

1483 Torquemada appointed to head Inquisition

Jews of Spain and Portugal

1135 Death of Moses Ibn Ezra

1141 Death of Judah Ha-Levi

1164 Death of Abraham Ibn Ezra

1180 Death of Abraham Ibn Daud; First Maimonidean controversy

1230-32 Second Maimonidean controversy

1263 Disputation of Barcelona

1270 Death of Nahmanides

1286 Final form of *Zohar* completed

1291 Death of Abraham Abulafia

1300-1306 Third Maimonidean controversy

1310 Death of Solomon b. Abraham Adret (Rashba)

1327 Death of Asher b. Jehiel

1340 Death of Jacob b. Asher *Ba'al ha-Turim*

1348 Black Death massacres

1354 Council of Jewish communities of Aragon

1375 Death of Nissim b. Reuben Gerondi

1391 Massacres and conversions in Spanish Jewish communities

1408 Death of Isaac b. Sheshet Perfet

1412 Death of Hasdai Crescas

1413-14 Disputation of Tortosa

1435 Massacres and conversions of Jews of Majorca

1454 Death of Abraham Benveniste

1473 Marranos of Cordoba and Valladolid massacred

1474 Marranos of Segovia massacred

1490 Blood libel in La Guardia

Jews of England and Italy

1100 Freedom of movement for Jews of England

1144 Blood libel in Norwich

1189-1190 Edicts against Jews in England; Massacre of Jews of York

1222 Council of Oxford proclaims discriminatory measures

1241 "Parliament of Jews" meets in Worcester

1255 Blood libel in Lincoln

1275 Moneylending forbidden to Jews of England

1278 Imprisonment and execution of Jews in London

1290 Expulsion of Jews from England

1348 Jews of Italy granted charter by Clement VI

1415 Benedict XIII orders censorship of *Talmud*

1419 Martin V opposes forced conversion

1427 Papal edict prohibits transporting of Jews to Erez Israel in ships from Venice and Ancona

1475 Beginning of Hebrew printing; Blood libel in Trent

1475-1494 Preaching against Jews; Jews expelled from several towns in Italy

Jews of France and Germany	Jews of Poland and Lithuania	Jews of the East and North Africa
1096 Crusaders massacre Jews of the Rhineland		
1105 Death of Rashi		**1103** Death of Isaac Alfasi
		1121-1135 David Alroy leads messianic movement
		1140 R. Judah Ha-Levi to Egypt
		1160-1173 Travels of Benjamin of Tudela
1171 Blois community destroyed; Death of Rabbenu Tam		**1172** "Messiah" appears in Yemen
1182 Expulsion of Jews from France		
1195-96 Anti-Jewish riots in Speyer and Boppard		
1217 Death of R. Judah he-Hasid		
1235 Blood libel in Fulda; Death of David Kimhi		
1236 Persecutions in W. France; Frederick II introduces concept of *servi camerae*		
1238 Death of Eleazar b. Judah of Worms		
1242 Burning of *Talmud* in Paris		
1244 Frederick II, Duke of Austria, grants charter		
	1264 Charter of Boleslav V, the Pious	
1285 Munich community destroyed		
1288 Jews of Troyes burned at the stake		
1293 R. Meir of Rothenburg dies in prison		
1298-99 Rindfleisch persecutions in Germany		
1306 Expulsion of Jews from France		
1315 Jews recalled to France		
1320-21 Pastoureaux and lepers persecutions in southern France and Spain		
1322 Expulsion of Jews from France	**1334** Casimir III extends the charter of 1264	
1342 Louis IX introduces poll tax in Germany		
1348 Black Death massacres	**1348-9** Immigration from Germany	
1356 Charles IV of Germany allows Electors to tax Jews		
1359 Jews of France recalled		
1367 Expulsion of Jews from Hungary	**1364, 1367** Casimir III extends charter	**14th cent.** Few Jews in Byzantium
1389 Massacre of Jews of Prague	**1388** Witold of Lithuania grants charter to Jews of Brest-Litovsk	
1394 Expulsion of Jews from France	**1399** Blood libel in Poznan	
1420 Expulsion of Jews from Mainz		
1421 Expulsion of Jews from Austria		
1426 Expulsion of Jews from Cologne		
1439 Expulsion of Jews from Augsburg		
1453 Burning of Jews in Breslau, and expulsions	**1454** Privileges revoked; riots in Cracow	**1453** Jews of Ottoman Empire granted preferential status in commerce and crafts
	1483 Expulsion of Jews from Warsaw	

1492-1775

Erez Israel

1485-1515 Obadiah of Bertinoro in Jerusalem

1516 Conquest of Erez Israel by Ottoman Turks

1538 Ordination renewed in Safed

1553-1573 Radbaz (David ben Solomon ibn Abi Zimra) in Jerusalem and Safed

1561 Don Joseph Nasi leases Tiberias

1572 Death of Isaac Luria

1575 Death of Joseph Caro

1620 Death of Hayyim Vital

1630-1660 Center of Kabbalism in Jerusalem

1700 Judah Hasid and his group arrive in Erez Israel

1720 Destruction of the *Ashkenazi* community of Jerusalem

1740 R. Hayyim Abulafia renews Jewish community in Tiberias

1741 Hayyim Attar and his group arrive in Jerusalem

1746 Beginning of *aliyah* of *Hasidim*

1750 R. Shalom Sharabi immigrates to Jerusalem from Yemen

1756 R. Judah Ayash immigrates to Jerusalem from Algiers

1774 Gedaliah Hayyun immigrates to Jerusalem from Salonika; *Hasidim* arrive from Poland and Russia

World History

1492 Discovery of America

1483-1546 Martin Luther

1498 Vasco da Gama reaches India

1517 Luther's 95 theses; Reformation

1533-1584 Ivan the Terrible

1534 Anglican Church founded

1545-1563 Council of Trent; Counter-reformation

1555 Peace of Augsburg

1572 St. Bartholomew's Day massacre

1588 Spanish Armada defeated

1598 Edict of Nantes

1600 British East India Co.

1602 Dutch East India Co.

1609 Tokugawa shogunate rules Japan; Dutch independence

1613-1643 Louis XIII in France

1613 Romanov dynasty comes to power in Russia

1618 Beginning of Thirty Years' War

1620 *Mayflower* sails to America

1625-1649 Charles I in England

1643-1715 Louis XIV in France

1644 Manchu found Ch'ing dynasty in China

1648-49 Chmielnicki rebellion in Poland

1648 Peace of Westphalia

1649-1660 Cromwell and the Commonwealth in England

1654 Portuguese reconquer Brazil

1688-9 The Glorious Revolution in England

1689-1725 Peter the Great in Russia

1701-1714 War of the Spanish Succession

1707 Unification of England and Scotland

1714 Beginning of Hanover rule in England

1740-1786 Frederick the Great

1740-1748 War of the Austrian Succession

1756-1763 Seven Years' War

1772, 1793, 1795 Partitionings of Poland

1774-1792 Louis XVI in France

Jews of Central and Western Europe

1492 Expulsion of Jews from Castile and Aragon

1496-97 Expulsion from Portugal; mass forced conversion

1497 Expulsion from Nuremberg

1516 Venice ghetto

1519 Expulsion from Regensburg

1532 Solomon Molcho burned at the stake

1533 Burning of the *Talmud* in Rome

1541 Expulsion from Naples

1542 David Reuveni burned at the stake in Portugal

1556 *Anusim* burned in Ancona

1590 *Anusim* settle in Holland

1593 Expulsion from the Papal State

1597 Expulsion from Milan

since 1602 Jewish community and centers of *Torah* in Amsterdam

1603 *Takkanot* of the Synod of Frankfurt

1615 Expulsion from Worms

1616 Jews return to Frankfurt and Worms

1624 Uriel da Costa excommunicated

1649 Expulsion from Hamburg

1655 Manasseh Ben Israel in London

1656 Jews permitted to return to England; Baruch Spinoza excommunicated

1670 Blood libel in Metz; Expulsion from Vienna

1671 Jews permitted to settle in Brandenburg

1685 Jews of England granted religious freedom

1712 First public synagogue in Berlin

1723 General Council of Jews of Piedmont; Jews in France given official recognition

1729-1786 Moses Mendelssohn

1738 Joseph Suess Oppenheimer executed

1750 Legislation against Jews of Prussia

1760 Board of Deputies of British Jews established

1761 Cardinal Ganganelli's memorandum against blood libels in Italy

1764 Maria Theresa's *Judenordnung*

1769 Mendelssohn-Lavater controversy

Jews of Eastern Europe

1495 Expulsion from Cracow
Expulsion from Lithuania

1503 Jews return to Lithuania

1534 Sigismund I rescinds edict requiring Jews to wear badge

1563 Riots against Jews of Polotsk

1581 Beginning of Jewish autonomy in Poland;
Council of the Four Lands founded

1623 Separate council established for Lithuania

1648-49 Chmielnicki massacres

1655-6 Massacre of Jews of Poland

1664 Riots in Lvov (Lemberg)

1680 Riots in Brest-Litovsk

1682 Riots in Cracow

1687 Jews of Poznan attacked

1700-1760 The *Ba'al Shem Tov* and the beginning of *Hasidism*

1707-1747 R. Moses Hayyim Luzzatto

1720-1797 Vilna *Gaon*

1734-1736 Attacks by the Haidamacks

1759 Jacob Frank and his followers accept Christianity

1764 Council of the Four Lands abrogated

1768 Haidamack massacres

1772 First ban pronounced on *Hasidim*

Jews of the East and North Africa

1492 Gates of Ottoman Empire opened to Spanish exiles;
R. David ben Solomon ibn Abi Zimra (Radbaz) settles in Egypt

1555-1575 Activities of Don Joseph *Nasi*

1567-1625 R. Solomon Adani in Yemen

1619-1680 R. Shalom Shabazi in Yemen

1656-1661 Anti-Jewish decrees in Persia

1663 Shabbetai Zevi false messiah

1666 Shabbetai Zevi converts to Islam

1680 Jews of Yemen exiled to Mawza;
Death of Nathan of Gaza

1710 Leghorn community established in Tunisia

1723 Death of Abraham Mimran leader of Moroccan Jewry

1727 "Council of the Commissioners of Jerusalem" established in Istanbul

1740 Bible translated into Persian

1743 R. Zedakah Huzin in Baghdad

1762 Death of R. Shalom Iraqi, Courtier and *Nasi* of Yemenite Jewish community

1762-1792 San'a Synagogue closed

Jews of America

1642 Jews arrive in Brazil

1654 Jews arrive in New Amsterdam;
Refugees from Brazil to the West Indies

1695 First Jews arrive in Charleston, S.C.

1730 First public synagogue in New York City

1733 Jews settle in Georgia

1742 Jewish community founded in Philadelphia

1749 Jewish community in Charleston, S.C.

1775-1860

Erez Israel

1777 Menahem Mendel of Vitebsk settles in Galilee with his *Hasidim*

1799 Napoleon in Erez Israel

1808-1810 Disciples of Vilna *Gaon* settle

1812 First *olim* from Kurdistan

1815 Thirty Persian Jewish families arrive to settle

1829 R. Isaiah Adjiman, Jewish minister of finance from Turkey, establishes court of immigrants in Acre

1831 Erez Israel in hands of Muhammad Ali

1837 Earthquake in Safed and Tiberias

1840 Restoration of Turkish rule in Erez Israel;
Chelouche family immigrates from Algiers

1852 "Status Quo" confirmed in Holy Places

1856 *Mishkenot Sha'ananim*, first Jewish quarter outside city walls of Jerusalem

World History

1776 American Declaration of Independence

1776-1783 American War of Independence

1789 French Revolution

1792 French Republic declared

1799 Napoleon becomes First Consul

1804 Napoleon crowns himself Emperor

1805 Battles of Trafalgar and Austerlitz

1805-1848 Muhammad Ali in Egypt

1806 End of the Holy Roman Empire

1807 Emancipation of serfs in Prussia;
Peace of Tilsit;
Continental System blockade of England

1812 Napoleon invades Russia and is routed

1813 Beginning of independence of South American countries;
Battle of Leipzig

1814-1815 Congress of Vienna

1815 Battle of Waterloo; Napoleon exiled to St. Helena

1821 Greek War of Independence

1823 Monroe Doctrine

1825-1855 Reign of Czar Nicholas I

1825 Decembrist Conspiracy in Russia

1826 11 independent countries in South America

1827 Battle of Navarino

1830 French begin conquest of Algeria;
July Revolution in France;
Uprising in Poland

1831 Belgium independent

1833 Turkey recognizes independence of Egypt

1836 Chartist movement in England

1839 Turkey invades Syria;
Opium War between Great Britain and China

1845 Famine in Ireland and emigration to USA

1846 US-Mexican War

1848 Revolutions of 1848;
Second Republic declared in France

1852 Louis Napoleon become Emperor of France

1854 Japan opens door to trade with USA

1854-1856 Crimean War

1856 Treaty of Paris

1857 Sepoy Rebellion in India

1858 Treaty of Tientsin opens China to foreign trade

1859 Rumania independent

1860 Lincoln president of USA;
Garibaldi conquers Naples and Sicily

Jews of Central and Western Europe

1775 Anti-Jewish edict of Pius VI

1782 *Toleranzpatent* issued by Joseph II of Austria

1784-1885 Moses Montefiore

1784 Body tax (*péage*) abolished in France

1791 Full civil rights granted all Jews of France

1792 *Judenamt* opened in Vienna

1793 Attack on the ghetto of Rome

1796 Jews of the Batavian Republic (Holland) emancipated

1797-1799 Temporary emancipation of Jews of Italy by the French Army

1807 French *Sanhedrin*;
Napoleon's "Infamous Decree"

1808 Beginning of emancipation of German Jews

1818 Restoration of rights to Jews of France;
Beginning of *Wissenschaft des Judentums* in Germany;
Reform Movement

1824 Rabbinical seminary founded in Metz

1829 Rabbinical seminary opened in Padua

1831 Judaism granted equal status with other religions in France

1833 British Parliament deliberates Jewish emancipation

1837 Moses Montefiore knighted;
Jewish newspaper founded in Berlin

1841 *Jewish Chronicle* founded in London

1842 First Reform synagogue in London

1845 Reform congregation in Berlin

1846 "Jewish Oath" abolished in France

1848 Adolphe Crémieux minister of justice in France;
Emancipation for Jews of Germany

Beginning of emancipation of Italian Jews;
Anti-Jewish riots in Austria-Hungary

1855 Jewish Lord Mayor of London

1856 Jew's College founded in England

1859 Rabbinical seminary moves from Metz to Paris

1860 *Alliance Israélite Universelle* established in France; Austrian Jews permitted to own real estate

Jews of Eastern Europe	Jews of the East and North Africa	Jews of America
		1777 Jews of New York granted equality under the law
1783 Jews permitted to serve on city councils in Russia		**1786, 1792** Equal rights granted Jews of several American states
1791 Pale of Settlement established	**1790-92** Persecution of Moroccan Jews under al-Yazid	**1790** 2,500 Jews in census of North America
	1792 Death of R. David Hassin	
1797 *Tanya* published		
	1805 Death of Hayyim Joseph David Azulai (*Hida*)	
	1807 Special Jewish quarters established in Morocco	
		1817 Jews settle in Cincinnati
1824 Expulsions from Russian villages	**1822** Death of Raphael Birdoko of Morocco	**1824** Reform congregation in Charleston, S.C.
		1825 M.M. Noah proposes founding Jewish colony, Ararat, near Buffalo
1826-1835 Velizh blood libel		
1827 Beginning of Cantonist legislation		
1835 Anti-Jewish legislation in Russia		
	1839 Head tax abolished and citizenship given to Jews of Turkey; Entire Jewish community of Meshed (Persia) forced to convert to Islam	
1842 Jews conscripted into Russian army	**1840** Damascus blood libel; Montefiore intervenes on behalf of Persian Jewry	**1843** *B'nai Brith* founded
1846 Moses Montefiore visits Russia		
		1848 First influx of Jews from Germany
		1849 Jews settle in San Francisco and Los Angeles
1853 Saratov blood libel		**1854** First YMHA founded
1856 Cantonist legislation abrogated		
1859 Selected groups of "useful" Jews permitted to reside outside Pale of Settlement		**1859** "Council of Jewish Congressmen in America" founded

1860-1914

Erez Israel

1868 Templers found 7 colonies

1870 Mikveh Israel founded

1878 Petah Tikva founded

1881 Eliezer ben Yehuda in Erez Israel

1882 Immigration from Yemen; Beginning of First *Aliyah* (*Bilu*); Rishon le-Zion founded

1883 Beginning of Baron de Rothschild's assistance to Jewish settlements

1884 Gederah founded

1890-1 Immigration from Russia

1890 Rehovot and Hadera founded; *Va'ad ha-Lashon* founded

1893 Large immigration from Persia

1901 Yavne'el founded

1902 Sha'arei Zedek hospital founded in Jerusalem; Sejera founded

1903 Office of Anglo-Palestine Company (APC) Bank opened

1904 Beginning of Second *Aliyah*

1905 Vitkin's "Call to Youth" published; *Ha-Poel ha-Zair* founded

1906 Herzlia Gymnasium founded; Bezalel School founded; Strike by Jewish laborers in Rishon le-Zion

1907 *Bar Giora* founded

1908 Kinneret, Jewish training farm, established; Society for Training the *Yishuv* established; Founding of Erez Israeli Office

1909 *Ha-Shomer* founded; Hebrew Gymnasium founded; Ahuzat Bayit founded; Deganyah founded

1911 Merhavyah founded

1912 *Histadrut* Sick Fund founded

1913 Fight over official language; *Gidonim* group founded

1914 Rothschild visits Erez Israel

World History

1861-1865 American Civil War

1861 Emancipation of serfs in Russia

1863-1864 Polish revolution

1863 French protectorate in Indo-China

1866 Austro-Prussian War

1868 Meiji restoration in Japan

1869 Opening of the Suez Canal

1870-71 Franco-German War

1870 Unification of Italy

1871 Unification of Germany; Third Republic in France

1877-78 Russo-Turkish War

1878 Congress of Berlin

1881 Czar Alexander II assassinated; France conquers Tunisia

1882 Triple Alliance formed; Britain conquers Egypt; Italy takes control of Eritrea

1884-85 Berlin conference on Africa

1894 Franco-Russian alliance

1894-95 Chinese-Japanese war

1896 Ethiopia wins war of independence against Italy

1898 Fashoda incident; Spanish-American War

1899-1902 Boer War

1900 Boxer Rebellion in China

1903 Beginning of Bolshevism

1904 Franco-British Entente Cordiale; Triple Entente of France, Britain, and Russia

1904-5 Russo-Japanese War

1905 Abortive revolution in Russia; Separation of church and state in France

1908 Young Turk revolution; Austria-Hungary annexes Bosnia and Hercegovina

1909 British Parliament recognizes establishment of Union of South Africa

1910 Japan annexes Korea

1911 Moroccan crisis; Sun Yat-sen President of China

1912 France conquers Morocco

1912-1913 Balkan Wars

1913 Alliance between Germany and Turkey

1914 World War I begins

Zionism

1862 *Rome and Jerusalem* by Moses Hess

1874 Death of Z. H. Kalischer

1882 Leo Pinsker's *Autoemancipation*

1884 Kattowitz Conference

1885 National Jewish Congress

1887 Druzgenik Conference of *Hovevei Zion*

1889 Vilna Conference; *Benei Moshe* founded by Ahad ha-Am

1890 Odessa Conference

1896 Herzl's *Der Judenstaat*

1897 1st Zionist Congress in Basle

1898 Herzl confers with Wilhelm II

1900 4th Zionist Congress in London

1901 Herzl meets with Turkish Sultan; 5th Zionist Congress in Basle; Jewish National Fund established

1902 *Mizrachi* founded in Vilna; Herzl's *Altneuland*

1903 Uganda project; 6th Zionist Congress in Basle; *Po'alei Zion* founded

1904 Uganda crisis; Death of Herzl

1905 7th Zionist Congress in Basle

1906 Helsingfors Program

1907 8th Zionist Congress in the Hague

1909 9th Zionist Congress in Hamburg

1911 10th Zionist Congress in Basle

1912 *Agudat Israel* founded; *Hadassah* founded

1913 13th Zionist Congress in Basle

Jews of Central and Western Europe

1867 Austro-Hungarian Jews granted rights

1868 *Ha-Shahar* published in Vienna

1870 Ghetto of Rome abolished; United Synagogue founded in England

1871 German Jews granted rights

1872 *Israelitische Allianz* founded in Vienna

1873 Rabbinical seminary opened in Berlin

1877 Rabbinical seminary opened in Budapest

1878 Beginning of anti-Semitic political movement in Berlin

1879 Anti-Semitic articles by H. von Treitschke

1881 Death of Disraeli

1882 *Kadimah* society founded in Vienna; Death of Charles Netter

1885 Expulsion of Russian refugees from Germany; Death of Moses Montefiore

1891 Jewish Colonization Association (ICA) founded in England

1894 Dreyfus trial

1898 Emile Zola's *J'Accuse*

1899 Dreyfus retried and pardoned

1900 Blood libel in Konitz, Germany

1901 *Hilfsverein der Deutschen Juden* founded

1906 Dreyfus exonerated

1911 Organization of Jewish Italian Communities founded

1912 *Blau-Weiss*, Jewish youth movement, founded in Germany and Czechoslovakia

Jews of Eastern Europe

1861 Jews with academic degrees permitted to live outside the Pale

1863 Society for the Promotion of Culture among the Jews of Russia founded

1864 Jews admitted to the bar

1865 Jewish craftsmen permitted to live outside the Pale

1871 Pogrom in Odessa

1871-72 Attacks on Rumanian Jews

1879 Rumanian Jews granted equality

1881 Pogroms in Russia;

1882 "May Laws" in Russia; Tiszaeszlar blood libel in Hungary

1887 Small percentage of Jews admitted to high schools and universities

1891 Expulsion of Jews from Moscow

1895 Anti Semitic League founded in Rumania

1897 *Bund* founded in Russia

1903 Pogrom in Kishinev and Homel; Publication of *Protocols of the Elders of Zion*; Beginning of Jewish self-defense

1904 *Habimah* Theater founded

1905-6 Pogroms in Russia; mass emigration

1908 Yiddish proclaimed national language

1909-10 Polish boycott against Jews

1910 Expulsion from Kiev

1911-13 Beilis trial

Jews of the East and North Africa

1850-1932 R. Yihye Kafah of Yemen

1880 *Alliance* school opened in Damascus

1903 Zionist organizations established in Syria and Morocco

1906 Proclamation of the Imam Yahya in Yemen on status of the Jews, in the spirit of the Covenant of Omar

1911 Yavne'eli in Yemen

1913 *Alliance* school founded in Morocco

Jews of America

1869 Philadelphia Conference

1873 Union of American Hebrew Congregations founded; Hebrew Union College founded in Cincinnati

1881 Wave of immigration from Eastern Europe

1882 *Hovevei Zion* lodge founded in NY

1885 Pittsburgh Conference of Reform Jews

1886 Jewish Theological Seminary founded in NY

1891 Emigration to Argentina with help of Baron Hirsch

1895 Federation of Boston Community founded

1896 Jews settle in Miami

1897 Zionist Federation of America founded

1898 Union of Orthodox Synagogues founded

1906-1909 Peak of Jewish immigration to USA, 642,000

1906 American Jewish Committee founded

1909 HIAS founded; First Jewish organization founded in Chile

1914 American Jewish Joint Distribution Committee founded

Erez Israel and the Zionist Movement	World History	Jews of the Diaspora
1915 *Nili* spy ring established; Zion Mule Corps formed;	**1915** Italy joins the Allies; Battle of Gallipoli; Sinking of the Lusitania	
1916 Kefar Giladi founded	**1916** Battle of Jutland; Battles of Verdun; Sykes-Picot Agreement	
1917 British conquer Erez Israel; Balfour Declaration	**1917** Submarine warfare; US enters the war; October Revolution in Russia	**1917** Great fire in Salonika; Anti-Jewish legislation rescinded in Russia; Zionist Organization of America established
1918 Zionist Commission led by Weizmann, visits Erez Israel; Weizmann meets with Feisal; Cornerstone laid for Hebrew University in Jerusalem; Tel Hai founded; Temporary commission appointed for Jews of Erez Israel	**1918** Treaty of Brest-Litovsk; Germany defeated on western front; Russian Civil War; Bulgaria and Turkey surrender; Austria-Hungary disintegrates; Germany surrenders; Wilson's Fourteen Points	**1918** *Yevsektsiya* established; American Jewish Congress founded
1919 *Ahdut ha-Avodah* established; *He-Halutz* conference in Petersburg **1919-1923** Third *Aliyah*	**1919** Spartacist outbreak in Berlin; Treaty of Versailles; Decision to establish League of Nations; Weimar Republic proclaimed; Amritsar massacre; Revolt of Mustafa Pasha in Egypt; Fourth of May movement in China	**1919** Pogroms against Jews in Poland and the Ukraine; Pogroms in Hungary; Zionist institutions shut down in Russia
1920 Beginning of British Mandate: First High Commissioner a Jew, Sir Herbert Samuel; Tel Hai falls; Arab riots in Jerusalem; *Haganah* founded; *Keren ha-Yesod* established; National Council of Jews of Palestine established; *Histadrut* founded; *Gedud ha-Avodah* (Trumpeldor Labor Legion) founded	**1920** San Remo Conference; Kapp putsch in Germany; Treaty of Sèvres; Damascus conquered by France; Polish-Russian War	**1920** *Wizo* founded
1921 Arab riots in Jaffa; Brenner murdered; Nahalal founded; 12th Zionist Congress; Weizmann Pres. of Zionist Organization	**1921** Reza Shah in Iran; Treaty of Riga; New Economic Policy (NEP) in Russia; Beginning of Communist Party in China; US Immigration Act sets 3% quota	**1921** *Tarbut* schools opened in Poland
1922 Churchill White Paper	**1922** Conference of Lausanne; Partitioning of Ottoman Empire; Victory of Fascism in Italy; Walter Rathenau assassinated in Germany; Unrest in India	**1922** *Po'alei Emunei Israel* (*Po'alei Agudat Israel*) founded in Poland; Law passed against working on the Sabbath in Salonika
1923 League of Nations confirms British Mandate over Palestine; *Hevrat ha-Ovedim* (workers' cooperative) established; Erez Israel Opera founded	**1923** France and Belgium take Ruhr Basin; Soviet Russian cooperation with Kuomintang in China; Rampant inflation in Germany; Turkey becomes a republic under Kemal Ataturk; Hitler's "beer-hall putsch"	**1923** *Protocols of the Elders of Zion*
1924-1932 Fourth *Aliyah*; Palestine Jewish Colonization Assoc. (*PICA*) founded; Bialik immigrates	**1924** Death of Lenin	**1924** Economic restrictions on Jews in Poland; Attempt to settle Jews in the Crimea; Immigration restriction in USA
1925 Technion opened; Hebrew University opened; Zionist Revisionists' Congress; *Brit-Shalom* Peace Association founded	**1925** French withdraw from Ruhr; *Mein Kampf* published; Death of Sun Yat-sen; Druze revolt in Syria	
1926 *Ohel* theater founded; Schism in *Gedud ha-Avodah*		
1927 *Ha-Kibbutz ha-Arzi* founded	**1927** Chiang Kai-shek's expedition to northern China; General Tanaka Prime Minister of Japan	
1928 *Habimah* Theater moves to Erez Israel; First electric power plant established in Naharayim	**1928** Chiang Kai-shek completes conquest of China	**1928** Beginning of Jewish settlement in Birobidzhan

Erez Israel and the Zionist Movement	World History	Jews of the Diaspora
1929 Jewish Agency established; Arab massacres in Hebron and Safed, and riots in Jerusalem; Weizmann Institute of Science founded	**1929-1933** Crash of NY Stock Market, worldwide depression	
1930 Passfield White Paper; Dead Sea potash works established	**1930** London "Round Table" on India	**1930** *Yevsektsiya* abolished
1931 MacDonald letter; Schism in *Haganah*, *IZL* founded	**1931** Japanese invasion of Manchuria	
1932 Youth *Aliyah* founded	**1932** Franklin D. Roosevelt president of USA; Egypt becomes independent; Iraq becomes independent	**1932** Pogroms in Salonika
1933-1936 Fifth *Aliyah* **1933** Arlosoroff murdered; Haifa Port opened; Revisionists secede from World Zionist Organization	**1933** Hitler becomes Chancellor of Germany; New Deal policy in US; Japan secedes from League of Nations; *Reichstag* set on fire; Germany secedes from League of Nations	**1933** Economic boycott against German Jews; First concentration camps
1934 Levant Fair opens in Tel-Aviv; Beginning of *Aliyah Bet* ("illegal" immigration); Death of Chaim Naḥman Bialik	**1934** "Long March" of Chinese Communists	**1934** Massacre of Iraqi Jews; Constantine massacre in Algeria; Poland annuls Minorities Treaties
1935 Inauguration of Kirkuk-Haifa oil pipeline; Nuremberg Laws in Germany	**1935** Saarland becomes part of Germany; Italy invades Ethiopia; Great Purge in USSR	**1935** Nuremberg Laws
1936-39 Arab Revolt **1936** Massacres of 1936; Palestine Orchestra founded; Tel Aviv Port opened; Beginning of "Stockade and Watchtower" settlements; Kibbutz Movement Alliance founded	**1936** Germany enters the Rhineland; Anti-Comintern Pact between Germany and Japan; Farouk king of Egypt; Beginning of Spanish Civil War; Rome-Berlin Axis established	**1936** Leon Blum heads Popular Front government in France; Pogrom in Poland; World Jewish Congress established
1937 Peel Commission proposal for partition of Palestine; Split in *Irgun* establishes new *Irgun Zevai Le'umi* (*IZL*); *Pelugot ha-Sadeh* (field companies) founded	**1937** Japan attacks China	**1937** Anti-Jewish legislation in Rumania; Discrimination against Jews in Polish universities
1938 Wingate organizes Special Night Squads	**1938** Austria annexed to Germany; Munich Pact, partitioning of Czechoslovakia; Japan conquers Canton	**1938** Pogrom against Jews of Vienna; Evian Conference; Forced emigration from Austria and Czechoslovakia; Racist legislation in Italy; Anti-Jewish legislation in Hungary; *Kristallnacht*
1939 MacDonald White Paper; General strike	**1939** Stalin-Hitler Non-Aggression Pact, dual conquest of Poland, beginning of World War II; Soviet Union invades Finland	**1939** Central Office for Jewish Emigration from Germany established; Anti-Jewish legislation in the Protectorate (Czechoslovakia); Many Hungarian Jews deprived of citizenship; Pogroms in Poland; United Jewish Appeal established; 43,000 refugees from Germany to US; Yellow badge instituted in German-occupied regions of Poland
1940 Land Transfer Regulation; Italian air force bombs Tel-Aviv; *Shai* (intelligence service) established; *Patria* sabotaged; *Lehi* established	**1940** Italy enters war; Denmark surrenders; Norway, Holland, Belgium and France conquered; French-German ceasefire; Vichy government; Battle of Britain; USSR annexes Baltic States; Germany conquers Balkans; Japan signs pact with Germany and Italy; Ethiopia liberated by British	**1940** Ghettos in Poland; Madagascar Plan; Anti-Jewish laws in Vichy France and North Africa
1941 *Palmaḥ* established	**1941** Germany invades USSR; Lend-Lease Agreement between Britain and US; Japan and US enter war; Japan conquers Indo-China	**1941** "Final Solution" drafted; Jewish emigration from Germany prohibited; Pogroms in Jassy (Rumania); *Einsatzgruppen* massacres; Jews of the Reich deported to the East; First death camp — Chelmno; Massacre of Jews of Baghdad; Jewish underground established in Iraq
1942 Food rationing in Erez Israel; Avraham Stern killed; *Va'ad ha-Hazzalah ha-Meuḥad* (Rescue Committee) founded; Biltmore Program	**1942** Allies invade North Africa; Battle of Midway; Battle of el-Alamein; Indian National Congress demands British leave	**1942** Wannsee Conference; Massacres in Russia; Mass deportations to death camps; Sinking of the *Struma*; Biltmore Conference
1943 *IZL* operations; General strike to protest failure to save Jews of Europe	**1943** Battle of Stalingrad, Russians advance westward; Teheran Conference; Allied landing in Italy, Italy surrenders	**1943** Germany declared to be *Judenrein*; Uprising in the ghettos and in two death camps; Liquidation of most ghettos; Jews of Denmark smuggled to Sweden; Greek Jews deported to Auschwitz

	Erez Israel and the Zionist Movement	World History	Jews of the Diaspora
1944	*IZL* and *Lehi* fight the British; Jewish Brigade organized; *MAPAI* splits and *Ahdut ha-Avodah* is founded; Palestinian Jewish paratroopers in occupied Europe; The "Season" operation Lord Moyne murdered	Germany moves into Hungary; Allies capture Rome; Allied landing in Normandy; Liberation of Paris; Allied victories in Pacific; Roosevelt elected to 4th term	Extermination of Hungarian Jewry; *Beriha* movement organized by Jewish partisans
1945	"Illegal" immigration and struggle against British intensify; Cooperation between *Haganah* and *IZL*; Break into Atlit detention camp; Appointment of Anglo-American Committee of Enquiry regarding the problems of European Jewry and Palestine	Yalta Conference; Russians take over Warsaw, Budapest, Vienna and Berlin; Germany surrenders; Potsdam Conference; United Nations founded; Atom bombs dropped on Japan, Japan surrenders; Nuremberg trials; Civil war renewed in China; Syria and Lebanon become independent Roosevelt dies; Truman president	Death camps liberated, Jewish victims in Holocaust total 6 million; Massacre of Libyan Jews
1946	Anglo-American Committee publishes recommendations; *Histadrut ha-Zionim ha-Kelali'im* (General Zionists) established; "Night of the Bridges;" "Black Sabbath;" King David Hotel blown up; "Illegal" immigrants deported to Cyprus; March on Biriyyah and establishment of 11 settlements in Negev	Communist regimes established in Czechoslovakia, Hungary, Poland and Rumania; Trial of war criminals in Japan; Democratization of Japan; British Agreement with Transjordan; Indochina War	Pogroms against Jews of Poland; Brandeis University founded in USA
1947	Acre prison-break; *Exodus*; Dead Sea Scrolls discovered; Executions of *IZL* and *Lehi* men and hangings of British sergeants; UN Security Council adopts resolution for partition of Palestine; Beginning of Arab attacks	Paris Peace Conference; Marshall Plan; India and Pakistan become independent; *Cominform* established; Greek Civil War	Massacres of Jews in Iraq, Persia, and Pakistan; UJA fund-raising in USA for establishment of State of Israel; Jews flee from Syria and Lebanon
1948	Arab attacks on Jewish settlements; Siege of Jerusalem; Ratification of Partition Plan, End of British Mandate and Proclamation of the State of Israel; Invasion by Arab states, alternating fighting and ceasefires; *Herut* Movement founded; *Altalena* affair; *Palmah* disbanded, IDF founded	Mahatma Gandhi assassinated; Beginning of Cold War; Berlin blockade; Communists defeated in Greece; Communist coup in Czechoslovakia; Yugoslavia severs ties with *Cominform*	Suppression of Jewish culture in USSR; Jewish Anti-Fascist Committee disbanded in USSR; *GAHAL* (overseas volunteer Jewish fighting unit) founded

1949-1961

Israel	World History	Jews of the Diaspora
1949 Armistice agreements; 240,000 immigrants; Israel becomes member of UN; Elections to first *Knesset;* Chaim Weizmann first president of Israel, David Ben-Gurion prime minister	**1949** NATO established; East and West Germany become separate entities; China becomes communist republic, Chiang Kai-shek flees to Formosa; Ireland leaves the Commonwealth; Beginning of apartheid policy in South Africa; Russians develop atom bomb	**1949** Operation Magic Carpet brings Yemenite Jews to Israel; Persecution of Iraqi Jews
1950 Mass *aliyah;* Austerity period; Law of Return	**1950** Korean War; Sino-Soviet friendship agreement	**1950** Operation Ezra and Nehemiah brings Jews of Iraq to Israel
1951 Border tension; Elections to second *Knesset;* Seamen's strike; Split in *Ha-Kibbutz ha-Meuhad*	**1951** Jordan's King Abdullah assassinated; Churchill prime minister of Britain; End of state of belligerency between Germany and countries of the West; Communist leaders executed in Czechoslovakia; American bases in Japan; Libya becomes independent	
1952 Izhak Ben-Zvi president; *Knesset* deliberates German reparations	**1952** Military coup in Egypt; Mau-Mau revolt in Kenya; First hydrogen bomb exploded; Britain has atom bomb	**1952** Prominent Jews executed in USSR
1953 Attacks by Arab infiltrators; First reprisal action; Ben-Gurion retires to Sdeh Boker; Sharett prime minister; Kastner trial	**1953** Dag Hammarskjold UN secretary general; Eisenhower president of USA; Korean Armistice; Death of Stalin; Khrushchev first secretary of Soviet Communist Party; Anti-Soviet riots in East Berlin; Reconciliation between USSR and Yugoslavia	**1953** "Doctors' plot" in USSR
1954 Mass immigration from Morocco; Bus attacked at Ma'aleh-Akrabbim	**1954** French defeated in Indochina; McCarthyism in USA; West Germany joins NATO; Beginning of Algerian rebellion	**1954** Mass immigration of North African Jews to France; Mendes-France prime minister of France; Jewish lobby in Washington organized
1955 *Fedayeen* attacks and Israeli reprisals; Ben-Gurion prime minister; Oil discovered at Helez; Yarkon-Negev water pipeline opened	**1955** Diplomatic relations between USSR and West Germany; Churchill resigns; Eden prime minister; Signing of Warsaw Pact	**1955** Cairo trial, Moshe Marzouk and Samuel Azaar executed; Nahum Goldmann President of World Zionist Organization
1956 Sinai Campaign; Kafr Qasim massacre; Tel-Aviv, Haifa, and Bar Ilan universities opened	**1956** Revolts in Hungary and Poland; Beginning of de-Stalinization; *Cominform* dissolved; Suez crisis; Eisenhower elected to 2nd term; Sudan, Morocco and Algeria become independent	**1956** Jews of Egypt expelled
1957 Withdrawal from Sinai; UN observers posted along border with Egypt; Draining of Hula Valley completed; Druze granted legal status as religion	**1957** Egypt and Syria unite to form UAR; Ghana, Singapore, and Malaysia become independent; Vietnamese civil war; British army leaves Jordan; EEC established; Struggle of blacks in USA ecalates; Soviets launch 1st space satellite	**1957** Poland restricts exit of Jews "essential" to the state
1958 "Who is a Jew?" polemic; Hostilities along Syrian border	**1958** Fifth Republic in France, De Gaulle president; Coup in Iraq; Civil war in Lebanon	
1959 Wadi-Salib riots; Elections to fourth *Knesset*	**1959** Cuban Revolution; Khrushchev-Eisenhower summit in USA; Alaska and Hawaii become 49th and 50th states in USA	
1960 Ben-Gurion — Adenauer meeting; Beginning of Yosele Shuchmacher affair; Eichmann kidnapped and brought to Israel; Lavon affair	**1960** Sino-Soviet conflict; Independence and civil war in Congo; US-Cuban relations strained; Kennedy elected US president; France has atom bomb	**1960** Wave of anti-Semitism in Europe
1961 Ben-Gurion resigns; Eichmann trial; Elections to fifth *Knesset;* Cornerstone laid for Port of Ashdod	**1961** US heightens involvement in Vietnam; Berlin wall built; South Africa becomes independent republic; First man in space — Yuri Gagarin; Belgrade Conference of Non-Aligned States	**1961** Confrontations between Jews and Muslims in Algeria

1962-1976

Israel	World History	Jews of the Diaspora
1962 IDF operation in Syria	**1962** War between India and China; Algeria becomes independent; Cuban missile crisis	**1962** Pogroms in Jewish areas of Algeria
1963 Zalman Shazar president, Levi Eshkol prime minister; Ultra-orthodox riot against public transportation on the Sabbath	**1963** Coup in Iraq; Kennedy assassinated	**1963** Soviet Jews imprisoned for crime of baking *matzah*
1964 Construction of the National Water Carrier completed; Pope visits Israel; University of Beer Sheba opened; Beginning of *Fatah* actions in Israel	**1964** Khrushchev ousted; Cairo Conference of Non-Aligned States; First atomic test in China	**1964** Jewish self-defense in New York in wake of anti-Semitism
1965 Diplomatic relations established with West Germany; Eli Cohen executed in Damascus; IDF reprisals in Jordan; Elections to the 6th *Knesset*	**1965** War between India and Pakistan; White minority in Rhodesia declares independence; American offensive in Vietnam	
1966 Agnon awarded Nobel Prize for Literature; Recession in Israel; Reprisal raid on Samu'	**1966** Show trial of writers in USSR; Cultural Revolution in China; Rise of "Black Power" in USA	**1966** Vatican Council denounces anti-Semitism; Black anti-Semitism manifested in USA; Wave of anti-Semitism in France
1967 Six-Day War; French arms embargo; Sinking of the destroyer *Eilat*; UN Resolution 242	**1967** Civil war in Nigeria; Rightist military coup in Greece	
1968 Archaeological excavations in Jerusalem; IDF penetrates deep into Upper Egypt; Karame Operation; El-Al airliner hijacked to Algeria	**1968** Soviet invasion of Czechoslovakia; Student riots in Paris; Martin Luther King assassinated	**1968** Wave of anti-Semitism in Poland; most Jews emigrate
1969 Beginning of War of Attrition; Golda Meir prime minister; Cherbourg missile boats smuggled out of France	**1969** First man on the moon; Violence in Northern Ireland; Qaddafi ruler in Libya; Fall of Biafra	**1969** Jews executed in Iraq
1970 Pursuit of terrorists in Jordan Valley, incidents along the Suez Canal and Syrian border, massacre of children at Avivim	**1970** De facto recognition of Polish-German borders; Allende prime minister of Chile; Black September in Jordan; Death of Nasser, Sadat president of Egypt	**1970** Leningrad trials; Unrest among Soviet Jewry over right to emigrate to Israel; Jewish property confiscated in Libya
1971 Demonstrations by Israeli "Black Panthers"	**1971** Peoples Republic of China joins UN; Beginning of Detente; Bangladesh established	**1971** Reform Movement decides to move its center from NY to Jerusalem
1972 Mayoral elections in West Bank cities; Sabena airliner hijacked and freed; Massacre at Lod airport; Massacre of Israeli Olympic team in Munich; Confrontations with Syrian army on Golan Heights	**1972** Nixon visits Peking; Paris Peace Talks on Vietnam; Heavy shelling of Hanoi; Last American soldiers leave South Vietnam; Helsinki SALT talks; Nixon to Moscow; SALT I Agreement	**1972** First woman ordained to the Rabbinate by Reform Movement in USA; Soviet Union imposes heavy fines on Jewish academicians seeking to emigrate to Israel; Letter bombs sent to Jewish companies and organizations in London and Geneva
1973 Yom Kippur War; African states sever relations with Israel; Death of David Ben-Gurion; Elections to 8th *Knesset*	**1973** Britain, Ireland, and Denmark join EEC; Economic recession in USA; Watergate scandal; Algiers Conference of Non-Aligned States	**1973** New York City elects Jewish mayor — Abraham Beame
1974 Signing of Disengagement Agreements with Egypt; Mounting protests against government shortcomings in Yom Kippur War; Golda Meir resigns; Palestinian terrorist actions: Kiryat Shemonah, Ma'alot, Shamir, Naharia, Bet Shean, Tel Aviv; Death of Zalman Shazar, Ephraim Katzir president	**1974** Nixon resigns American presidency; End of dictatorship in Portugal; Death of Juan Peron in Argentina; Turkish invasion of Cyprus; Haile Selassie deposed; Yassir Arafat addresses UN General Assembly	**1974** Rape and murder of Jewish women in Damascus; Bombing in Buenos Aires synagogue; decline in immigration from USSR; 50 *aliyah* activists in Soviet Union arrested during Nixon visit
1975 Agranat Commission report; UN censures Zionism; Palestinian terrorist actions: Savoy Hotel, Kefar Yuval, Jerusalem; Kissinger's shuttle diplomacy, signing of Interim Agreements, withdrawal from Abu Rudeis	**1975** Civil war in Lebanon; End of Kurdish rebellion in Iraq; Khmer Rouge regime in Cambodia; End of Vietnamese War; Suez Canal reopened to navigation; Helsinki Accords; Death of Franco, Juan Carlos King of Spain	**1975** 100,000th immigrant to Israel arrives from USSR; Moscow police interrupt synagogue Passover services; Bombings in synagogue and Jewish center in Mendoza, Argentina
1976 "Land-Day;" *Gush Emunim* march; Operation Jonathan in Entebbe; Yadlin affair; Cabinet crisis over arrival of F15 jets on the Sabbath eve	**1976** Hua Guofeng premier of China; Army coup in Argentina; Race riots in South Africa; Death of Mao Zedong; Civil war in Lebanon; Jimmy Carter president of USA	**1976** Jewish organizations demonstrate outside UN Headquarters against PLO participation in UN Security Council deliberations; First worldwide congress on Yiddish language and culture held in Jerusalem; *Aliyah* protest march of Jews, wearing yellow badges, through streets of Moscow; Symposium on Jewish culture in Moscow, 45 participants arrested

1977-1984

Israel	World History	Jews of the Diaspora
1977 Rabin resigns; **Election reversal — Begin prime minister;** Extensive economic reforms; Sadat visits Jerusalem, Begin visits Ismailia	**1977** Mengistu head of state in Ethiopia; Deng Xiaoping strong man in China; Security Council opposes supply of arms to South Africa	**1977** Grenades thrown at Rome Synagogue on Jewish New Year; Drop-out rate among immigrants from USSR reaches 50%; Hundreds of thousands demonstrate in New York against persecution of Soviet Jewry; 12 young Jewish women allowed to leave Damascus for USA
1978 Meetings between Egyptian and Israeli military and political committees; Terrorist actions along Coastal Road; Operation Litani; Yitzhak Navon president; Camp David talks; Death of Golda Meir	**1978** Unrest in Iran; Treaty between Japan and China; Fighting between Vietnam and Cambodia escalates; Military coup in Afghanistan; Death of Kenya President Jomo Kenyatta	**1978** Sentences handed down in trial of Soviet Jewish activists, Ida Nudel and Vladimir Slepak; Trial of Anatoly Sharansky in USSR; Drop out rate among immigrants from USSR reaches 62%
1979 Carter visits Israel; Camp David Accords signed on White House lawn; Begin visits Cairo; Palestinian terrorist actions: Kiryat Shemonah, Naharia; Begin-Sadat meeting in El-Arish, and reciprocal visits in Egypt and Israel; Air battle between Israeli and Syrian jets over southern Lebanon; Foreign Minister Moshe Dayan resigns	**1979** Diplomatic relations established between USA and China; Islamic revolution in Iran, Shah leaves the country, hostages held in American Embassy in Teheran; Margaret Thatcher prime minister of UK; Sandanistas come to power in Nicaragua; SALT II Agreements signed; Beginning of Soviet intervention in Afghanistan	**1979** One thousand Jews flown out of Iran on eve of Islamic revolution
1980 Diplomatic relations established between Israel and Egypt; Security Council calls for halt to settlement in Administered Territories; Palestinian terrorist action: Misgav Am; IDF attacks in Lebanon; Cars of West Bank mayors blown up; Israeli law extended over all Jerusalem; *Shekel* introduced	**1980** Civil war in El-Salvador; US grain boycott of USSR; Zimbabwe (Rhodesia) becomes independent; Death of Tito; Phalangists take over rival Christian militias in Lebanon; Unrest in Poland: "Solidarity" trade union; Military coup in Turkey; Iraq-Iran War; Soviet Premier Kosygin resigns; Ronald Reagan president of USA	**1980** Bombing in Rue Copernic Synagogue in Paris, sympathy demonstration through the streets of city; Argentinian journalist Jacubo Timmerman freed from prison; Iranian Jews seeking to emigrate subject to severe punishment; Petition by Soviet Jews: Hunger strike threatened if exit permits not issued
1981 Iraqi atomic reactor bombed; Elections to 10th *Knesset*; War of attrition along Lebanese border; Memorandum of Understanding signed with USA; Israeli law extended over Golan Heights	**1981** Greece joins EEC; Violence in Lebanon; *Columbia* space-shuttle flight; Assassination attempt on Reagan; François Mitterand president of France; Women franchised in Switzerland; Underground movements in Iran; 1st conference of "Solidarity" in Poland; Violent confrontations in Gdansk, Poland; Sadat assassinated; Hosni Mubarak president of Egypt	**1981** Tombstones desecrated in Jewish cemetery near Paris; Lustiger, apostate, Archbishop of Paris; Rise in number of exit permits given Soviet Jews; Jewish Agency decides not to assist "drop-outs" in Vienna, HIAS undertakes to aid them; Attack on Vienna synagogue; Conference of European Rabbis in Bucharest; Bombing near synagogue in Antwerp; Emergency meeting for Soviet Jewry held in Paris
1982 Druze strike in the Golan; Unrest in the territories; Withdrawal from Yamit; Attempt on life of Israeli ambassador in London, beginning of Lebanon War; Reagan Plan for renewing autonomy talks; Kahan Commission investigates Sabra and Shatila massacres	**1982** Falkland War; Iran-Iraq War continues; "Solidarity" outlawed; Bashir Jemayel assassinated in Lebanon; Socialists win in Spain; Brezhnev, Secretary of USSR Communist Party, dies, Andropov succeeds him	**1982** Anti-Semitic campaign by Soviet authorities to account for riots in Poland; Explosives planted at Jewish sites in Vienna and Rome; World Jewish Congress calls for recognition of Palestinians' rights; Attack on Central Synagogue of Rome; World conference for Ethiopian Jewry
1983 Talks between Israel and Lebanon; Publication of Kahan Commission Report; Emil Greenzweig slain at "Peace Now" demonstration; Chaim Herzog president; Ultra-Orthodox riots at City of David archaeological excavations; IDF redeployment along Awali River; Begin resigns, Yitzhak Shamir prime minister; Bank-shares crash; Car bombing in Tyre	**1983** Hindus massacre Muslims in Assam, India; Demonstrations in Europe against stationing nuclear warheads there; Fighting between Arafat supporters and PLO rebels; US invasion of Grenada; End of dictatorship in Argentina; American cruise missiles stationed in Britain; Soviets walk out on SALT talks; New Delhi Conference of Non-Aligned States	**1983** Soviet Jews call on participants of Jerusalem conference to continue struggle on their behalf; March for Israel in NY; Hundreds of Jews arrested in Iran; Synagogue burned in southern Tunisia; Yosef Begun sentenced to prison for teaching Hebrew in USSR; Relatives of missing Argentinian Jews prepare for struggle; London Conference of Jews from Arab states closes with call to Arab states to cease persecuting Jews; Bombing in Jewish restaurant in Paris
1984 Lebanon abrogates agreement with Israel; Jewish terrorist organization uncovered; Palestinian terrorist actions: Jerusalem, bus to Ashkelon; Elections to 11th *Knesset*; Shimon Peres sets up National Unity Government; Beginning of IDF withdrawal from Lebanon	**1984** Iraqi and Iranian offensives in Persian Gulf; Indira Gandhi assassinated; Death of Andropov, election of Chernenko; Reagan reelected; Famine in Ethiopia	**1984** Most Ethiopian Jews brought to Israel; Israelis participate in Jewish conference in Rabat, Morocco

Mimuna celebrations, Jerusalem, 1984. The *Mimuna* is celebrated by North African Jewry on the last day of Pesach week when, according to tradition, Maimonides' father died.

Glossary

The terms which appear in this glossary refer largely to concepts related to Judaism or Zionism. The aim of the glossary is to provide more extensive information on topics treated in the Encyclopedia, or to define terms used in it. Unless otherwise noted, all terms defined here are from the Hebrew.

Agudat Israel
A Jewish religious movement which regards the *Torah* and traditional Judaism as the basis for the survival of the Jewish people. Its initial affiliation with the Jewish Agency was contingent on the removal of education and cultural affairs from the Agency's jurisdiction. With the establishment of the State of Israel, *Agudat Israel* joined with *Poalei Agudat Israel* to form the "religious front" that became the third largest faction in the *Knesset*.

Ahdut ha-Avodah
Literally "unity of labor." A Zionist, socialist association of Jewish workers in Ereẓ Israel. Established in 1919 by a majority of the members of the *Po'alei Zion* Party along with some members of *Ha-Po'el ha-Zair*. Its ambition was to unite all Jewish workers in Ereẓ Israel and all federations and parties in the Jewish labor movement and the Zionist movement abroad. *Ahdut ha-Avodah* joined the World Alliance of *Po'alei Zion*. It was active in *aliyah*, absorption, and public works. When the *Histadrut* was established it functioned like all other parties (albeit the largest) within that organization.

Aliyah
Literally "going up." The immigration of Jews to Ereẓ Israel.

Am ha-Aretz
Literally "People of the Land." A biblical designation for a sector of the population. At different times it referred to different groups. In *Genesis* 23:12 the term refers to the local residents: In II *Kings* 24:14 it refers to the peasant class. At the time of Ezra and Nehemiah, when the Jews were returning from exile in Babylonia, the foreign nations who had settled in Israel were designated in this way. From the Second Temple period to the present, the term has been used to denote those who are unfamiliar with the Law and do not properly observe rabbinical rulings.

Am Olam
Literally "Eternal Nation." A Jewish movement which originated in Russia following the pogroms of 1881-2. Its aim was to seek a solution to the economic and social problems of the Jews, by emigration from Russia and a return to physical work, particularly farming.

Amora, Amoraim
From the Aramaic *omer*, one who explains or lectures. The term was originally used to designate someone who presented, interpreted or translated the words of a sage for the public. In time it came to refer only to the Talmudic sages active from the time of the completion of the *Mishnah* to the completion of the *Talmud*. Their primary work was in interpreting the words of the *Tannaim* and resolving the differences between the *Mishnah* and the *Baraitha* (the writings of the *Tannaim* which Rabbi Yehudah ha-Nasi did not include in the *Mishnah*). The *Amoraim* in Israel were given the title Rabbi; in Babylonia they were known as *Rav* or *Mar*.

Antiquities of the Jews
A book by Josephus Flavius (c. 37-100 CE) comprising twenty sections that present a thorough survey of the history of Israel from the beginning of the biblical period to the generation before the destruction of the Temple. The book was written in Greek and its aim was to acquaint the Gentiles with the Jews and Judaism. The author claimed that hatred of the Jews stemmed from ignorance of them, and attempted to prove the antiquity, and therefore special status, of the Jewish people. See also Flavius' *The Jewish Wars*.

Aphebion
A stadium for horse races, from the ancient Greek.

Asefat ha-Nivharim
Literally "Assembly of Representatives." The supreme representative body of the *Yishuv* in Palestine during the British Mandate. It was first elected in 1920, and its functions and authority were transferred to the *Knesset* in 1949.

Ashkenazi, Ashkenazim
A term designating Jews of Eastern and Central European extraction.

Bakasha, Bakashot
Literally "request." Liturgical hymns.

Bar-Giora
An underground defense league established by a group of immigrants of the *Poalei Zion* movement in 1907. It propounded Jewish labor, guard duty, and defense in order to realize the Zionist-socialist vision. The league formed the nucleus for the establishment of *Ha-Shomer*, a national defense organization, during the Second *Aliyah*.

Beit Din, Batei Din
Any rabbinical court. According to the Bible (*Deut.* 16:18), the Children of Israel were commanded to appoint a court in each city. A panel of three judges sat in civil matters; a panel of five judges determined the intercalation of the month and heard criminal cases. The higher courts were the Great and Small *Sanhedrin*. Jewish courts existed in every generation throughout the Diaspora. In the Middle Ages they were elected by the community. The Jews preferred their own courts to those of the Gentiles, and appealed to them in matters in which only Jews were involved, and at times even in the case of a dispute with a non-Jew. Today rabbinical courts in Israel have jurisdiction only in matters of personal status.

Beit Midrash
A school for the study of the Bible, *Talmud* and *midrashim* (homiletics) which also served as a house of prayer. We know, for example, of the *Beit Midrash* of Shemaiah and Abtalion from the period of the *Mishnah*. The *Beit Midrash* existed throughout the Diaspora in every period.

BETAR
The Hebrew acronym for "Joseph Trumpeldor Hebrew Youth Society," the youth movement allied with the World *Herut* Movement (*Ha-Tsohar*). Its ideals — territorial integrity of the homeland, ingathering of the exiles, individual freedom, and social justice. The movement also supports a sports society of the same name. Prior to 1948 *BETAR* members were active in *IZL*.

BILU
The Hebrew acronym of the biblical verse, "House of Jacob, come ye and let us go" (*Isaiah* 2:5). A Zionist society whose members — from the non-religious, Jewish-Russian intelligentsia — advocated immigration to and settlement in Israel. The motivation for the founding of the society came from the pogroms of 1882. Its members were influenced by socialistic ideals and sought to establish a farming community based on the cooperative principle.

Brit-Shalom
A Jewish organization established in Jerusalem in 1925 by intellectuals and scholars, in order to improve relations between Jews and Arabs, and to seek a solution to the question of Palestine's future to which both sides could agree. Differences of opinion plagued the organization and brought about its disintegration.

Bund
A political-labor organization of Jewish workers founded in Vilna in 1897. The name is an abbreviation of the Yiddish for "The General Union of Jewish Workers in Russia, Lithuania, and Poland." The *Bund* opposed Zionism, rejecting immigration to Israel as a solution to the problem of the Jews, and regarded Yiddish as the only Jewish language. In czarist Russia it was active in political and labor causes and in self-defense leagues formed to combat pogroms. Following the communist revolution, many of its members joined the communist party. Between the two world wars, the organization was primarily active in Poland, and in 1947, following the Holocaust, the World *Bund* was founded.

Chalutz, Chalutzim
Literally "pioneer." The Jewish settlers in modern Erez Israel between 1882 and 1935.

Codex Sinaiticus
One of the manuscripts of the *Septuagint* (the translation of the Bible into Greek) found in the Saint Catherine monastery in Sinai. The manuscript dates from 200-300 CE.

Dayan, Dayyanim
Rabbinical court judge. The title *Dayan* is also given the assistant to the chief rabbi of a community who hears cases together with the rabbi.

Dinar
A monetary unit, a silver or gold coin used in Israel during Roman rule.

Donme
Turkish for "convert." A Shabbatean-Muslim cult that originated in 1683 when some 300 Shabbatean families from Salonika converted to Islam. Members of the cult lived like forced converts, leading a double life. Outwardly they were perfect Muslims, but in secret they maintained their belief in the messianism of Shabbetai Zevi. Until 1923 they lived as a separate community in two sections of Salonika. In 1923, the Turkish residents of Greece, including the 14,000 members of the cult, were deported to Turkey. The *Donme* dispersed, settling mainly in the cities of Istanbul, Izmir, Ankara, Bursa and Konya. Some assimilated and married outside the community.

Eber Hanahar
Literally "across the river." The designation of a geographical region which also acquired a political-administrative significance. The river is the Euphrates, and the area "across the river" depends on the point of view of the speaker. During Persian rule, *Abar-Nahara* was the official name of the province encompassing Israel and Syria.

Epistle to Yemen
A letter from Maimonides (Rabbi Moshe ben Maimon — Rambam) to the Jews in Yemen which dates from c. 1170 CE, when he was living in Egypt. During this time, growing religious fanaticism in Yemen caused repressive measures to be imposed on the Jews. These hardships aroused messianic yearnings that created fertile soil for the emergence of a false messiah. In their distress, the Jews appealed to Maimonides for advice and instruction. In his answer, known as the Epistle to Yemen, Maimonides advised them to flee their persecutors to distant lands until it was safe to return, and to meticulously observe all of the biblical commandments. He offered comfort and encouragement, and detailed the qualities of the prophet to come.

Essenes
See — Sects and Parties during the Second Temple Period.

Etrog
See — Four Species, The

Exodus from Egypt, The
The Exodus from Egypt is one of the major events of Jewish history. In the national memory it has become a symbol of freedom and release from bondage. The story of the slavery in Egypt, the Exodus, and the miracles that accompanied it is told in *Exodus* 12-15. The obligation to remember the Exodus and recount it is one of the biblical commandments.

Exodus 1947
An illegal immigrant ship which sailed to Palestine from a French port on July 11, 1947 with some 4,500 illegal immigrants. The British spotted the ship in the first stages of its journey, and took it by force as soon as it neared the Palestine coast. Three of the immigrants were killed in their attempts to resist the British. The passengers were sent back to France where the British forcibly removed them to shore. The incident generated worldwide publicity for the plight of Jewish Holocaust refugees in Europe who were prohibited by the British from coming to Palestine.

Ezra
Literally "aid." The *Ezra* Society of German Jews was established in Berlin in 1901 to improve the social and political conditions of the Jews in Eastern Europe and the Orient. The society assisted the victims of the Russian pogroms and financially supported self-defense leagues. In Erez Israel the society founded educational institutions and laid the foundations for the Institute of Technology in Haifa.

Fedayeen
Literally (Arabic) "those who risk their lives." Name given to Arab infiltrators in the early 1950s. Most belonged to a special Egyptian-officered unit of Palestinians recruited in the Gaza Strip who began operations in August 1955. The *fedayeen* carried out a series of terrorist assaults in Israel. They disbanded following the Sinai Campaign (1956).

Four Species, The
The four types of plants blessed on *Sukkot* (the Feast of Tabernacles) in accordance with the instruction: "And ye shall take you on the first day the fruit of goodly trees, branches of palm trees, and the boughs of thick trees, and willows of the brook; and ye shall rejoice before the Lord your God seven days" (*Lev.* 23:40). The sages ruled that the "fruit of goodly trees" was the *etrog* (i.e., citron); the "branches of palm trees" were the *lulav* (palm branch); the "boughs of thick trees," the *hadas* (myrtle); and the "willows of the brook," the *arava* (willow).

GAHAL
Acronym for *Giyus Huz la-Arez*. Jewish *oleh* volunteers who came to Israel from North Africa and Eastern Europe, to help the *Yishuv* during the War of Independence. Many came directly from the Cyprus detention camps and refugee camps in Europe. The volunteers were organized and trained abroad by *Haganah* representatives. Some had fought in World War II in armies and partisan units.

GAHAL
Political movement; see *Herut*.

Gaon, Geonim
A title given the heads of two *yeshivoth* in Babylonia, Sura and Pumbedita, between the sixth and eleventh centuries. The heads of *yeshivoth* in Erez Israel, Baghdad and Damascus similarly held this title, as did the great *Torah* scholars and sages such as the Vilna Gaon, Rabbi Eliahu Ben Shlomo Zalman (1720-1797). The *Geonim* of Babylonia (and of Erez Israel at a certain period) were regarded as supreme authorities by Jews throughout the world. To this day, the responsa of the *Geonim* constitute a highly valuable source both for knowledge of the practises common at the time they lived and taught, and for an understanding of Talmudic exegesis.

Gedud ha-Avodah
Literally "the work battalion." An organization founded by Joseph Trumpeldor's followers in the *He-Halutz* movement, six months after he fell at Tel-Hai (1920). Its aims were work, defense and communal settlement. Its members, from the Third *Aliyah*, worked throughout the country paving roads, draining swamps, and in public sector jobs for the Mandatory government, the British army, and the Zionist Organization. Together with the veterans from the Second *Aliyah*, they

founded the *kibbutzim* Tel Yosef, En Harod, and Kefar Giladi.

Geniza
Literally "hiding place." Usually a room in a synagogue in which tattered sacred books or flawed ritual objects are kept. The best known is the Cairo *Geniza*, unearthed in the Ezra Synagogue in Fostat, ancient Cairo.

Guide to the Perplexed
A complex and recondite book, both in content and form, written by Rabbi Moshe ben Maimon (Maimonides) in the 12th century, in which he presents his philosophy. The intended audience for the book are the perplexed — those who studied and understood the truth of the written and oral law, and then turned to the sciences, where they reached the outer limits of physics and mathematics, and were disquieted by the discrepancies they found between the words of the prophets and the conclusions to which their studies had led them.

Gush Emunim
Literally "band of the faithful." A social movement, founded after the Six-Day War (1967) by Israelis who were graduates of *yeshiva*-type high schools. They settle on the lands occupied by Israel after the Six-Day War. Their resolute bond with the land is based on God's Promise to the Jewish People. It therefore corresponds with religious requirements, but is likewise in line with the Zionist, pioneering tradition.

HABAD
Acronym for *Hokhmah, Binah, Da'at* (wisdom, comprehension, knowledge). A central stream of *Hasidut*, its founder was Rabbi Shneur Zalman of Lyady. It began in Belorussia, in a town called Lubavitch (therefore these *Hasidim* are called *Lubavitchers* and their rabbi is the Rabbi of Lubavitch), and spread from there to Latvia, Poland, and the US. *HABAD* differs from other methods of *Hasidism* in the way it imparts Hasidic ideas and in the organizational forms it has developed.

Habimah
Literally "the stage." Israel's national theater. Beginning as a small repertory company in Moscow in 1914, it took the name of *Habimah* in 1917. The troupe left Moscow in 1926, and, after a two-year world tour, settled in Ereẓ Israel.

Hadassah
The federation of Zionist women in America, founded in 1912 at the instigation of Henrietta Szold. Its activities in Ereẓ Israel were limited at first to health and medical care, and then extended to include social and educational projects. *Hadassah* played a significant role in the development of medical institutions in Ereẓ Israel. The organization is one of the major supporters of Youth *Aliyah*.

Haganah
Literally "defense." The security force of the Jewish community in Palestine. Founded during the Third *Aliyah* at the *Ahdut ha-Avodah* convention (1920), it was linked with the *Histadrut*. The original aim was to turn it into a people's organization for the entire community, but dissension, particularly in regard to ways of fighting the Arabs and the British, led several groups to break away. The *Haganah* laid the foundations for the establishment of the IDF — the Israel Defense Forces — with regard to personnel, tactics, and fighting spirit.

Haggadah
Literally "telling" or "tale." An anthology of blessings, prayers, commentaries, and hymns from the Bible and the *Midrash*, which tell the story of the Exodus of the Israelites from Egypt. The *Haggadah* explains the different steps of the Passover Eve *Seder*. During the *Seder*, the *Haggadah* is read, and participants are encouraged to discuss the story of the Exodus.

Hakham, Hakhamim
A wise man, well-versed in the Bible. An honorary title, given to rabbis and Jewish community leaders.

Hakham Bashi
In the early 19th century, the supreme religious authority for Jews of the Ottoman Empire, and their representative before the authorities.

Ha-Kibbutz ha-Arzi — Ha-Shomer ha-Za'ir
The federation of *Ha-Shomer ha-Za'ir* (The Young Guard) *kibbutzim* in Ereẓ Israel. This movement began with the arrival during the Third *Aliyah* (1919-1923) of veterans of *Ha-Shomer ha-Za'ir* who banded into groups and worked in road construction and other public works. *Ha-Shomer ha-Za'ir* is part of the *kibbutz* movement and its ideological principles are Zionism, socialism, and a combination of *kibbutz* settlement enterprise and class struggle. The movement emphasizes the social and economic independence of each *kibbutz*, but requires collective ideology. Politically, it is associated with *Mapam* — the United Workers' Party.

Ha-kibbutz ha-Me'uhad
Literally "the united *kibbutz*." The national *kibbutz* movement founded in 1927 by the association of *Kibbutz* En Harod — which developed as a result of the first rift in the *Gedud ha-Avodah* ("labor legion") when it split off from *Ha-Kibbutz ha-Arzi* ("national *kibbutz*") — along with other *kibbutz* settlements. Their goal was "To build large, open, collective settlements based on combining self-labor and hired labor, agriculture, trade, and industry, and a blend of settlers coming from many countries." Due to differences of opinion on ideological and political party matters, *Ha-Kibbutz ha-Meu'had* split into two factions in 1951, and the *Ihud ha-Kevuzot ve-ha-Kibbutzim* was formed. Today both are reunited in *Takam* (United Kibbutz Movement).

Halakhah
Literally "walking" (poetic allusion to walking along the path of righteousness). The part of the *Talmud* containing a system of laws and regulations determined by the Sages. A product of many centuries of negotiation and discussion, of explanation and commentary on the Bible, often using the techniques of analogy and inference for interpretation.

Halukah
Literally "distribution." Financial aid donated to the early Jewish community in Ereẓ Israel by Diaspora Jews. The beneficiaries were divided into groups known as *kolelim* according to the donor countries from which they had come, with each country supporting its own *kolel*. In time, strong opposition to the *halukah* was voiced, particularly by members of the First and the Second *Aliyot*, who claimed that it was habituating the Jews in Ereẓ Israel to a life of idleness and dependency.

Ha-Nodedet
Literally "the wanderer." A unit of the *Haganah* founded by Yitzhak Sadeh (later head of the *Palmach*) to undertake active security operations. Its aim was to transfer the battlefield to Arab sectors where concentrations of Arab irregulars would be identified and attacked, rather than to wait for them to attack the Jews.

Ha-Mossad
Literally "the institution," short for "Institution for Intelligence and for Special Missions." Responsible for clandestine state activities outside the country. Founded in 1951.

Hamula
Arabic for extended family, clan.

Hanukkah
Literally "dedication." An eight-day holiday celebrated from the 25th of *Kislev* (Jewish month coinciding with December), commemorating the rededication of the altar at the Holy Temple, after it was purified by Judah the Maccabee. Another reason for the holiday is given in the *Sabbath* Tractate (21) of the *Talmud*: the Greeks, who ruled the country in 164 BCE, entered the Temple and contaminated all the oil there. After the Hasmoneans' victory, a search for oil was made, but only one jar was found, and this jar miraculously lasted for eight days. Therefore the holiday is celebrated by lighting candles, and each day another is added until eight are reached.

Ha-Shomer
Literally "the guard." An organization of Jewish guards in Ereẓ Israel established in 1909. Its aim — to preserve life, dignity and property. Its members replaced Arab and Circassian guards. They linked the idea of Jewish defense to Jewish labor, and sought to found villages of guardsmen. They also took part in "occupation groups" which

settled on land immediately after its acquisition in order to establish *de facto* Jewish ownership. During the Second *Aliyah, Ha-Shomer* operated as a closed and tightly knit underground movement, developing special customs and a way of life.

Ha-Shomer ha-Zair
Literally "the young guard." The oldest of the Jewish youth movements in Israel and abroad. The movement strives to instill in its members national values, Zionist awareness, and socialist ideals, as well as to prepare them for *kibbutz* life. Its affiliate, *Ha-Kibbutz ha-Arzi*, is part of the *kibbutz* movement. It propounds conceptual collectivism along with the economic and social autonomy of each *kibbutz*.

Hasidim — Hasidut
The fundamental meaning of *Hasid* is: a God-fearing person who follows the precepts. Today the term *Hasidim* has come to denote those who belong to the movement called *Hasidut*. A popular religious and social movement, it was founded by Rabbi Israel Baal Shem Tov, of Podolia, in Eastern Europe, in the 18th century. The movement stresses the importance of *devekut* (devoutness) in prayer; of serving God in ecstasy while dealing with the banalities of everyday life; and of happiness and absolute belief in the *ẓadik* or wise man. The movement continues to be active to this day.

Haskamot
See — *Takkanot*.

Havlagah
Literally "restraint." The response determined by the *Yishuv* institutions in Palestine to the violence perpetrated by bands of Arab irregulars between 1936 and 1939. The principle underlying this policy was to refrain from any violent actions which might cause injury to innocent people.

Hazarah Be-teshuvah
Abandoning the secular way of life, and returning to religion.

Heder
Literally "room." A school for young children, where they were taught Hebrew reading, writing, and prayers.

He-Halutz
The World Federation of Zionist Youth, who trained abroad for *aliyah* to Ereẓ Israel. Initiated in Russia in 1917. Its guidelines were personal fulfillment, physical and spiritual fitness, Hebrew culture, and a commitment to the *Histadrut*. For its members still living in the Diaspora, *He-Halutz* established *kibbutzim* for agricultural training there. The movement spread throughout Europe, to the Muslim countries, North and South America, and even to Australia. It numbered 100,000 before World War II. During the war, members took part in rescue operations and illegal immigration to Ereẓ Israel. In the 1980s, various pioneering youth movements continued in the *He-Halutz* tradition.

Herut
Literally "freedom." An Israeli political party, founded by *IZL*, and headed by former *IZL* members and veteran Revisionists. Its policy centered on nationalism — stating that Israel must expand to its full "historical" borders and adopt an aggressive attitude toward the Arab countries. In 1965 *Herut* combined with the Liberal Party, and the two became *GAHAL* (acronym for *Gush Herut Liberalim*). In 1973 several other small parties joined them, and they have since been known as the *Likud*.

Hever Ha-Yehudim
Literally "the company of Jews." A sovereign institution begun during Hasmonean times, represented by the people's assembly and perceived as the embodiment of the will of the people. According to several opinions, this body was the forerunner of the *Sanhedrin* or the *Knesset Hagdolah*.

Hevrat ha-Ovdim
The cooperative association of all members of the *Histadrut*, organized in 1923. Serves as the ultimate authority — legislative, supervisory, and managerial — for all of the *Histadrut*'s economic enterprises, as well as their official legal framework. These enterprises are independent, with *Hevrat ha-Ovdim* supervising management, authorizing plans, and overseeing operations.

Hibbat Zion — Hovevei Zion
Literally "Love of Zion" and "Lovers of Zion." An ideological movement and a social and nationalist organization. It had its beginnings after the Odessa pogrom of 1881. After witnessing how the masses and their governments treated the Jews the founders concluded that there was no other way to save the Jewish people but to return to Zion and rebuild the land. After Herzl founded the Zionist Organization, the great majority of *Hovevei Zion* groups joined; most of them favored "Practical Zionism," which advocated settlement in Ereẓ Israel.

Histadrut
The General Federation of Labor in Israel. A trade union associating all the salaried and independent workers in Israel — Jews and Arabs alike.

Ihud ha-Kevutzot ve-ha-Kibbutzim
A *kibbutz* movement in Israel, established in 1951 after a rift in *Ha-Kibbutz ha-Meuhad*. Today both are part of *Takam* (United Kibbutz Movement).

Irgun Bet
Literally "Organization B." A group of activists, who resigned from the *Haganah* and formed their own defense framework. The antecedent to *IZL*.

IZL
The initials of the *Irgun Zvai Leumi*, or National Military Organization (pronounced *etzel* as an acronym of its Hebrew name; in English also known as the *Irgun*). A Jewish underground organization active during the time of the British Mandate. It was created from *Irgun Bet*. *IZL* preached unrelenting armed resistance to the British authorities in Palestine. Between 1945 and 1947 it launched attacks on British police and military installations.

Jewish Agency
The executive arm of the World Zionist Organization. During the period of the British Mandate, it was recognized by international law as representative of the Jewish people on all matters relating to the establishment of the Jewish National Home in Palestine. In 1929, the Reconstituted Jewish Agency was established in conjunction with non-Zionist public bodies. Today, Jewish Agency and World Zionist institutions are one and the same. Major Agency activities now include *aliyah* (bringing Jews to Israel), *klitah* (absorption), and *hityashvut* (settlement).

Kabbalah
The theory of Jewish mysticism and hidden wisdom. Its roots go back to early Jewish history, and there are hints of its existence in the Babylonian *Talmud* and the Jerusalem *Talmud*, as well as in the literature of the Essenes. During the Second Temple period, *Kabbalah* was influenced by several schools of thought: Greek philosophy, Persian dualism, and Pythagorean and Gnostic ideas. These, combined with man's natural inclination to ponder the phenomenal and to investigate the supernatural and the infinite, and with the effects of formidable external events such as destruction and exile, resulted in the development and dissemination of the *Kabbalah*. Its influence spread from East to West, and kabbalistic centers developed in Italy, Ashkenaz, Spain, and Provence, in the south of France. *Kabbalah* reached its height in the 13th and 14th centuries, when the *Book of the Zohar*, the fundamental work on Jewish mysticism, first became known.

Only a chosen few were permitted to study these esoteric theories. A well-known legend concerns the four sages who entered a *pardes* (a grove; an acronym for *peshat* — the literal; *remez* — the allegorical, *derash* — the homiletical, and *sod* — the mystical; i.e., the whole of Kabbalistic theory). One "looked and died," one "looked and was smitten" (went out of his mind), one became an apostate, and only one — Rabbi Akiva — left the *pardes* unharmed. Kabbalistic theory is based on a recognition of the Divinity and the striving of the human soul to attain it. The path to God is through fasting and self-inflicted suffering. God is the "infinite" — the *Ein-Sof*. The Ten *Sefirot* are the stages of emanation of the Divine Entity. They are: *Keter* (supreme crown), *Hokhmah* (wisdom), *Binah* (intelligence), *Gedullah* (greatness), *Gevurah* (power), *Tiferet* (beauty), *Neẓah* (lasting endurance), *Hod* (majesty), *Yesod* (foundation of the world), and *Malkhut* (kingdom). The *Sefirot* affect the world; however man, too, can have an affect upon the *Sefirot*, and this is his role. Man and the Divinity were sent into exile because of Adam's original sin, and therefore the Israelite must strive to redeem them both. This cannot be done simply by performing the *mitzvot* (commands or precepts). There must also be *kavvanot* — man's prayers and *Torah* study must be instilled with special devotional, religious meaning, achieved by contemplation of the hidden secrets of the Hebrew words and letters.

Kashrut
The laws that refer to the types of food and drink which Jews are permitted to eat, or to the manner of preparation required to render foods *kasher* and thus suitable to eat.

Kavvanot
See — *Kabbalah* and Lurianic *Kabbalah.*

Kehilla, kehillot
Literally "community." The organizational framework in which Diaspora Jews lived and within which they enjoyed internal autonomy; *kehillot* of Jews existed even in Erez Israel when the land was under foreign domination. The *kehilla*'s internal government was authorized to decide rules and arrangements covering all aspects of everyday life — religion, religious law, education, welfare, charity, trade, health, decorum, and traditions. In time, the heads of the *kehilla* were assigned to represent it before the government, especially to serve as agents for tax collection and payment of ransoms, and to mediate when the community was threatened with edicts or libels. The *kehilla* had judicial power over marital and interpersonal relations.

Keren Hayesod
Literally "Foundation Fund." The central fiscal institution of the World Zionist Organization, that financed its activities in Palestine. It was founded in 1920 following the Balfour Declaration. Its funds, coming from contributions, financed activities in the fields of immigration, absorption, settlement, development of water resources, and investment in economic projects.

Keren Kayemet
The Jewish National Fund. The central body appointed by the Zionist Organization to acquire and develop land in Erez Israel. It began acquiring land in Erez Israel in 1905, and by 1948 had purchased some one million dunams (approx. 250,000 acres). With the establishment of the State of Israel, the Fund's activities turned largely to forestation and land reclamation, as well as the development of parks and picnic and camping grounds in nature preserves and national parks. In 1960 the *Knesset* enacted the Israel Land Administration Act, transferring ownership of all land not privately owned, including that of *Keren Kayemet*, to the State of Israel.

Klezmerim
Literally "musical instruments." Bands of musicians who played Jewish folk music at celebrations such as weddings, *benei mitzva*, and parties given by the Polish nobility.

Knesset
The legislature of the State of Israel, comprising 120 elected members. Its functions and authority include legislation, election of the president of Israel, confirmation of the government, recommending the appointment of a state controller, overseeing administration, and, in certain instances, judicial powers such as the suspension of immunity of a *Knesset* member, and appeal of election results.

Knesset ha-Gedollah
Literally "The Great Assembly." The supreme Jewish council during the early period following the return from the Babylonian exile (from c. 538 BCE). The sages of the *Talmud* interpreted the council's activity in the area of religious matters, making no mention of any political enterprise. The council has been chiefly associated with the composition of the benedictions and prayers, canonization of the Scriptures and development of *Halakhah* and *Aggadah.*

Ketubbah
The written contract which a man gives his wife at the wedding ceremony. In the *ketubbah*, the man undertakes to support his wife honorably and to provide her with all her needs so long as she is his wife, and to give or leave her a specific sum of money if he should divorce her or if she is widowed.

Kofer ha-Yishuv
Literally "community indemnity." A donation imposed on the Jews in Palestine in 1938 by the National Council.

Kol Yisrael Haverim
Literally "All Israel are comrades." A Jewish organization in France, *Alliance Israelite Universelle*, founded in Paris in 1860 following anti-Semitic events in several parts of the Diaspora. Its founders wished to help Jews all over the world to defend themselves against anti-Semitism, to improve their civil status, and to fight for equal rights, by disseminating knowledge and education and providing training in useful occupations. *Alliance* was extremely helpful, both materially and spiritually, to the Jews of Eastern Europe, the Balkan States, Asia, and North Africa. It gave assistance to refugees fleeing pogroms and anti-Jewish edicts, and set up French-speaking schools, mainly in Muslim countries. In Erez Israel, *Alliance* was the first to establish a Jewish agricultural school and rural community — *Mikveh Israel* (1870). The *Alliance* schools in Erez Israel were incorporated into the comprehensive educational system.

Kupat Holim
Literally "sick fund." The health care institution of the *Histadrut.* Its members and their families pay a monthly fee, calculated as a percentage of their income, and receive total medical coverage. Some two-thirds of the population of Israel belong to the *Histadrut Kupat Holim.*

Kvutza/Kibbutz
Literally "group/grouping." A type of settlement unique to Israel. Its members believe in cooperative living and equality in all aspects of production, consumption, and education. Their guiding principle: "Each according to his abilities, and to each according to his needs."

Landsmannschaften
A German/Yiddish term denoting groups of Jewish émigrés from various parts of Eastern Europe, originating from the same city or province. Initially their purpose was to provide assistance to immigrants. Over the years they became places of social gathering.

LEHI
Hebrew acronym for *Lohamei Herut Israel* — "Fighters for the Freedom of Israel." An underground movement active during the time of the British Mandate over Palestine. It was founded in 1939, as a result of a split in the *IZL.*

Likud
See — *Herut.*

Lulav
See — Four Species, The

Lurianic Kabbalah
Developed in Safed in the 16th century. Created and named for *Ha-Ari* ("the lion," a kabbalist name given to Rabbi Isaac Luria, 1534-1572). Lurianic *Kabbalah* imposed the task of redemption of the Divinity upon the individual, and it led to the propagation of a movement of penitence and intense anticipation of the Messiah's coming. Luria described the process of Creation, the impairment of the Divinity, and its redemption, by means of three concepts: *zimzum* (contraction), *shvirat ha-kelim* (breaking of the vessels), and *tikkun* (restoration). *Zimzum* — the *Ein-Sof* (the "infinite") first undertook contracting, concealed activities, instead of revelation and emanation. The Act of Creation marred Divine Infinity, and was therefore carried out by "the entry of God into Himself." At the *Sof*, the end, the world was created. *Shvirat ha-kelim* — the vessels are the *Sefirot* which were to contain the supernal light. The lower six *Sefirot* were unable to contain all the light of the *Ein-Sof*, and it was then that the catastrophe of the Divinity took place — the breaking of the vessels. The broken pieces scattered, but held sparks of light which nourished and vitalized the *kelippot* (husks) — the sources of evil. Finally, *tikkun* — it was man's job to repair the broken vessels. He must rescue the sparks from the husks

through *mitzvot* (commandments, precepts), good deeds and *kavvanot*. Some tried to do this by self-inflicted suffering or through the powers of mystical combinations of holy names, especially the Tetragammaton (the secret, unpronounceable name of God, *YHVH*).

Ma'apilim
The illegal immigrants who entered Palestine despite the strict immigration quotas imposed by the British mandatory government. The beginning of such immigration, called *ha'apalah*, dates to 1934. It peaked in the post World War II period, with the aim of providing refuge for Holocaust survivors.

Maccabees, Books of
Four books of the *Apocrypha* (i.e., books written during the Second Temple period which are not included in the Old Testament but which are considered holy and are included in the Catholic and Greek Orthodox Testaments). The first of the four was probably written in Hebrew (but is extant only in Greek), during the rule of Johanan Hyrcanus. It recounts the history of the Jewish people over thirty-two years (167-135 BCE).

The second book is an abridgement of a five-volume work by Jason of Cyrene, written in Greek. Its aim is to glorify Judaism in the eyes of Greek-speaking Jews and so to strengthen their faith.

The third book, in Greek, recounts the persecutions of the Jews in Egypt at the time of Ptolemy IV.

The fourth book is a religious-moral homily in praise of the wisdom and awesomeness of God who rules all creatures. The book was written in Greek, probably in the first century CE.

Magen David
Literally "shield of David." The Star of David, the religious and national symbol of the Jewish people. In 1897 the First Zionist Congress chose the *Magen David* as the symbol for the World Zionist Organization. In 1934, the Nazis made the *Magen David* the identification badge which the Jews were forced to wear on their clothing. Upon the establishment of the State of Israel (1948), the *Magen David* became a national emblem.

Magic Carpet
The airlift operation to bring the Jews of Yemen to Israel, in 1949-1950. Over 30,000 Jews reached Israel during this period, in 378 flights.

MAHAL
Acronym for *Mitnadvei Huẓ la-Areẓ* (foreign volunteers). A group of approximately 3,000 soldiers — Jews and non-Jews — who came to Palestine to fight in the War of Independence.

MAPAI
The acronym for *Mifleget Po'alei Ereẓ Israel* — "Ereẓ Israel Workers' Party." A Zionist-Socialist political party founded in the early 1930s through the union of the labor parties *Ahdut ha-Avodah* and *Ha-Poel ha-Za'ir*. The party enjoyed a decisive working majority in the *Histadrut*. After 1948, *MAPAI* headed the Israeli government continuously until 1977. In 1965 the *Ma'arakh* ("Alignment") was established with *Ahdut ha-Avodah — Po'alei Zion*. As a result of this decision and of dissension in the party, a minority group led by David Ben-Gurion split off and formed *RAFI* (*Reshimat Po'alei Israel* — "Israel Labor List"). After the Six-Day War (1967) the two factions reunited. In 1968 *MAPAI, Ahdut ha-Avodah*, and *RAFI* united to form *Mifleget ha-Avodah ha-Israelit*, the Israel Labor Party.

Masorah
From *massar*, "passed on." The compilation of notes and instructions which guide the Bible reader to read correctly and precisely, in keeping with the holiness of the Book. The purpose of the *Masorah* was to create a uniform version of the Bible, by setting down rules on how it should be read, written, vocalized, and accented.

Menorah
Literally "lamp." A holy vessel of the *mishkan* and the Holy Temple, cast in the desert, in accordance with the explicit instructions given in the Bible. The *menorah* had seven branches of gold, and was decorated with cups, knobs, and flowers. The *menorah* has become a representative symbol of the Jewish people.

Midrash, Midrashim
From *darash*, "to expound or interpret." Anthology of sermons and expositions by the sages on matters of law and legend, divided into weekly portions. The earlier *midrashim* were essentially halakhic — interpretations of laws based on verses of the Bible, interspersed with proverbs or legends. Later *midrashim* were legendary or sermonic.

Minyan
Literally "number." The group of ten Jewish men over age 13 who together constitute an *eder* (flock) or *kahal* (congregation). A *minyan* is needed in order to recite prayers in public or for religious ceremonies.

Mish'an
Literally "support." An institution of the *Histadrut* established in 1931 to help the unemployed by providing support and financial loans, medical aid, professional retraining, child welfare, rehabilitation, nutrition, rest and recreation.

Mishkan
The portable sanctuary (tabernacle) which the Israelites constructed when they wandered through the desert after their Exodus from Egypt. The *mishkan* went with them into Ereẓ Israel, and served until the permanent Temple was built. The *mishkan* was tentlike (hence the term *ohel moed*, or "tent of congregation"); it housed the Ark of the Testimony, the Tablets of the Covenant, the *menorah*, table for the shewbread, and the incense altar.

Mishnah
From the word *shinun* meaning "teaching" or "repetition." The system of Jewish law which developed and evolved until finally arranged and organized by Yehuda Ha-Nasi at the beginning of the 3rd century. This editor collected anthologies of *Mishnayot* that were already in existence. By himself or in discussion with his students, he ruled on phraseology and text. The *Mishnayot* are divided into six parts, called *sedarim*, or orders, according to topic: *Zera'im* (seeds): agricultural laws, such as *trumot* (offerings), *ma'asrot* (tithes), *shemittah* (the fallow, sabbatical year), *orlah* (fruit of tree in first three years after planting), and *bikurrim* (the first fruits); *Mo'ed* (festival): laws of the Sabbath and holidays; *Nashim* (women): laws of marriage, divorce, vows, and abstinence; *Nezikin* (damages): civil and criminal law; *Kodashim* (sacred things): laws concerning sacrifices and offerings; and *Tohorot* (purification): laws about uncleanness and purification. The *sedarim* are divided into *massekhtot* or tractates, and the tractates are divided into *perakim* (chapters). The *Mishnah* was written in Hebrew, interspersed with many Aramaic, Greek, and Latin expressions.

Mishneh Torah
Literally "repetition of the law." Book by Maimonides (Rabbi Moses ben Maimon, the Rambam). Also called *Yad ha-Hazakah* (The Strong Hand). The largest single Jewish literary achievement of one individual, since completion of the *Mishnah*. In logical sequence, using clear, explicit, unequivocal language, the Rambam presented a compilation of the Oral Laws and philosophical thinking. The book reflects the author's extraordinary erudition in sources of the *halakhah*. The book was first published in Rome in 1480 and has since appeared in many editions and with numerous commentaries.

Miẓpeh-Miẓpim
Literally "observation post." Jewish agricultural pioneer settlements established to gain a foothold in the Negev (and later also in other regions), in response to British proposals for partitioning Palestine between Jews and Arabs, and to British land decrees published in the White Paper.

Mizrachi
Literally "eastern." Part of the religious Zionist movement. Together with *Ha-Po'el ha-Mizrachi*, constitutes The World Mizrachi Federation. Founded in 1902 under the slogan "Ereẓ Israel — For the People of Israel — By the *Torah* of Israel."

Moshav-Moshavim
An agricultural settlement built on nationally owned land and based on individual labor, mutual assistance, and cooperative marketing and purchasing

of supplies. The lands of the *moshav* are divided equally among the members. Farmsteads are privately owned by each family. The *moshav* provides many public as well as professional services, such as supplying water and agricultural machinery, and also provides credit to its members. Nahalal, the first *moshav*, was founded in 1919.

Moshavah-Moshavot
Literally "colony." The first form of settlement established by the *Yishuv* in Ereẓ Israel. An agricultural settlement, based on private farming. The *moshavot* established cooperative societies for the benefit of their settlers.

Musta'rabs
Originally, Arabs of Spanish descent who were apparently not of Arab origin, but had been assimilated in Arab families. Since the 15th century, ancient Jewish, Arab-speaking communities.

NA'AMAT
Acronym: *Nashim Ovdot U-Mitnadvot* (working and volunteering women). The women's organization of the General Federation of Labor in Israel (*Histadrut*). Its principal activities center on assistance to working women in the form of day-care centers, as well as defending women's rights through legal counsel and assistance.

Nagid-Negidim
A title given to the head of the Jewish community in the Muslim countries, and during the Middle Ages even in Christian countries.

NAHAL
Acronym for *Noar Haluẓi Lohem*. A corps of the IDF which combines military training and agricultural settlement. *Nahal* is composed of groups of male and female soldiers, whose main task is to populate settlements, especially in the outlying areas.

Nasi-Nesi'im
Literally "prince," "patriarch," "president." In Scripture, the title of the head of the people or the tribe. During the Second Temple period this title was conferred, by a large assembly of the people, upon Simeon, son of Mattathias the Hasmonean, giving him rights to declare war and make peace, to appoint officials and dismiss them, and to oversee the Temple. The office of *Nasi* passed by inheritance to Simeon's sons. Also known by the title of *Nasi* were the first of the pairs of sages (the *zuggot*) who presided over the *Sanhedrin*. Also called *Nesi'im* (Patriarchs) were the descendants of Hillel ha-Nasi: Rabban Gamaliel the Elder, Rabban Gamaliel of Jabneh, Rabban Simeon ben Gamaliel, Rabbi Judah ha-Nasi, and others. In modern times this title has been given to the Israeli head of state, who is elected by the *Knesset*.

NILI
Acronym for *Neẓaḥ Israel Lo Yeshakker*, "The Everlasting of Israel will not lie." An underground espionage organization which operated in Ereẓ Israel during World War I. Members sought to assist the British army which was then fighting near Ereẓ Israel, in the hope that the latter would reciprocate after taking control of the country by enabling the *Yishuv* to establish a national home in the land. Led by Aharon Aaronson, an agronomist.

Notrim (Ghafirs)
Jewish auxiliary police or constables who operated within the framework of the Mandate police force in Palestine. The *notrim* were essentially drafted by the *Haganah*, acted on its orders, and received their salaries from the Jewish Agency or the local authorities. Their arms, however, were supplied by the British police, to whom they were disciplinarily subordinated. Their conscription and training began in 1936, following the outbreak of the Arab riots.

Olim
Literally "those who ascend." Immigrants to Ereẓ Israel.

PALMAH
Acronym for *Peluggot ha-Maḥaẓ* — "assault companies." The mobilized force of the *Haganah*, which operated from 1941 through Israel's War of Independence (1948). Its bases were the *kibbutzim*, and its time was divided between training and work.

Initially the *PALMAH* worked in cooperation with the British, and even received training from British officers in combat techniques and sabotage. During World War II the *PALMAH* participated in assaults into Syria, in order to drive out Vichy French forces who were cooperating with Nazi Germany, and sent paratroopers to Europe to fight the Germans. After Rommel's defeat in the Western Desert, the British were less solicitous, and the *PALMAH* went underground. Now the organization's main objective became the struggle for immigration and independence. In Israel's War of Independence the *PALMAH* was a key fighting force. After the war it was disbanded and its units made directly subordinate to the IDF General Staff.

Paytanim, Piyyut
Piyyutim are liturgical poems — songs of thanksgiving and praise, of supplication and entreaty, and of poetic effusion — written in ornate language and added to the liturgy after the completion of the *Talmud*. *Piyyutim* were generally written for the Jewish holidays, and many have come to be included in prayer books. There are several known categories of *piyyutim*, such as: *azharot* ("warnings"), which are *piyyutim* for the Feast of Weeks (Pentecost); *havdalot* ("distinctions"), to mark the end of the Sabbath, distinguishing it from ordinary weekdays; *viduyim* ("confessions"), for the Day of Atonement; *hoshanot* (after *hoshana* — "Save, I pray"), for the Feast of Tabernacles; and others.

Pesah (Passover)
Literally "passing over." A holiday celebrated from the 15th day of the month of *Nisan* (the Jewish month coinciding with April-May), lasting seven days in Israel, and eight days in the Diaspora, to commemorate the Exodus (specifically, God's "passing over" the Jewish first born and slaying only those of the Egyptians). This is the first of the three Pilgrim Festivals (the others are *Shavuot* and *Sukkot*), on which the Israelites were commanded to "go up" to the Holy Temple. It is also called the Feast of *Mazzot* (unleavened bread) and the Time of Liberation. Among the traditions of the holiday: A *seder* is held on the first night of the festival, during which the *Haggadah* is read. *Mazzot* are eaten, and it is forbidden to keep *hameẓ* (leaven) in the home.

Pharisees
See — Sects and Parties in the Second Temple period.

Po'alei Zion
Literally "workers of Zion." A Zionist socialist workers' party, which began in Russia, Austria, and the USA in the late 19th and early 20th centuries. Influenced by Dov Ber Borochov (1881-1919), *Poalei Zion*'s platform was based on Marxist principles developed along nationalist lines. The party's worldwide movement was continually involved in arguments on such fundamental issues as cooperative settlement activity in Ereẓ Israel initiated by the labor class, membership in the Zionist Movement (which included members of the bourgeoisie), and the party's relationship to the Communist International.

Purim
A Jewish holiday, on the 14th of *Adar* (the Jewish month coinciding with March). Traditionally celebrated in commemoration of the miracle by which the Jews were saved from the wicked devices of Haman, who had cast a lot (*pur*) to determine the day on which the Jews throughout the Persian kingdom of Ahasuerus were all to be annihilated. The customs of the holiday include reading the *Scroll of Esther*, sending gifts (*mishloah manot*), a festive Purim meal, and masquerading.

Qorban
An animal or plant offering to God. The custom of bringing offerings dates back to the period of ancient Israel. With the construction of the Temple, sacrifical worship became centered around Jerusalem. After the destruction of the Second Temple sacrificial worship was replaced by prayer.

Romaniots
Ancient Jewish communities, living in the Ottoman Empire, and dating back to the time of the Roman Empire and its heir, Byzantium.

Sanhedrin
(Greek — Council of Elders or the Great Assembly). The religious, judicial, and

legislative institution of the Second Temple period. Historically, its growth and development is linked to the decline of the *Knesset ha-Gedolla.* Headed by a pair (*zug*) of officials: the *Nasi* and the High Priest. The Great *Sanhedrin*, consisting of 71 people, sat in Jerusalem, in the "Chamber of Hewn Stone" in the Temple courtyard. The *Sanhedrin* served as a supreme court of justice, deliberating on capital offenses affecting the general community, laws of the priesthood, and questions of uncertainty in *halakhah.* Most of its work involved interpreting the *Torah*, which often led it to enact *takkanot*, or regulations, binding upon the entire people. Its members came from among the scholars, priests, judges, and notables. A small *Sanhedrin*, consisting of 23 men, sat in every city, and had jurisdiction over criminal cases involving individuals, questions of property boundaries and inheritance, fines and lashings.

After the destruction of the Second Temple the *Sanhedrin* became the supreme institution for religious study. During this period the *Sanhedrin* focused on maintaining the ties between Ereẓ Israel and the Diaspora, by proclaiming the new month and intercalating the year, and by publicizing its rulings in the Diaspora by means of emissaries. Its status gradually declined, until it finally ceased functioning altogether in 429.

Sects and Parties in the Second Temple Period
During the Second Temple period there were several politico-religious sects and parties in Ereẓ Israel. The most prominent of these were the Pharisees, the Sadducees, and the Essenes.
Pharisees (Heb. *Perushim*) — The most influential party during the Second Temple period, it was based primarily on the lower-middle class of farmers and artisans. Its members adhered strictly to the laws of ritual purity, and observed the Oral Law and the written *Torah.* The Pharisees had sharp disagreements with the Sadducees regarding the Oral Law, with the former insisting that the people's good required the rule of the *Torah* as the basis for extending the regulations of the Oral Law.
Sadducees (Heb. *Zedukim*) — The Sadducean party was composed of the wealthy classes, close to the governing circles and favorably inclined toward Hellenism. The Sadducees, who held high positions in the Hasmonean regime, and from whose ranks the high priests were appointed during the period of Roman rule, believed only in the written *Torah.* They disagreed with the Pharisees in matters of *halakhah*, and in philosophical questions such as resurrection of the dead, predestination, and free will.
Essenes — A Jewish sect which sought to live a life of holiness and purity, in segregation from the general community. The Essenes lived together in groups, primarily around the Dead Sea. Most lived in villages, and only a few in cities. Various sources, especially the Dead Sea Scrolls, discovered in the Judean Desert and attributed to this sect, indicate that they led a communal life: they had jointly held funds and property, lived in communal houses, and ate in communal dining halls. New members were accepted only after a trial period of several years. Members were sworn not to reveal the secrets of the sect or its books. The group lived in messianic expectation, and sought to hasten the coming of the day of Redemption.

Seder
The Passover Feast, held on the eve of the first day of Passover. The details of the rite are explicity laid forth in the *Haggadah*, and are the same throughout all the Jewish communities of the Diaspora, save for specific customs which have arisen in individual communities. Some of the practices characterizing the *seder* are: drinking four cups of wine; telling the story of the Exodus from Egypt; reciting the "Four Questions;" eating the *afikoman* (the middle of three *matzot* on the *seder* plate, required for concluding the feast); the presence on the table of *mazzah* (unleavened bread), bitter herbs, *haroset* (a food made to resemble the mortar used by the Children of Israel to make bricks in Egypt), and *karpas* (vegetables for dipping in salt-water); and pouring a glass of wine for Elijah the Prophet.

Sefirot
See — *Kabbalah* and Lurianic *Kabbalah.*

Sephardi, Sepharadim
The name given to Jews descended from the exiles from Spain (*Sepharad*) and Portugal, who settled primarily in countries of the Mediterranean basin: North Africa, the Balkans, Ereẓ Israel, and other parts of the Ottoman Empire. Centers of *Sephardi* Jews emerged in Europe, too — in Holland, England, and several cities of Germany. They spoke Ladino, a Jewish dialect based on Castilian Spanish. In Israel the term is generally used to encompass all the non-*Ashkenazi* Jewish communities, including those from the Muslim countries of Asia and Africa.

Shabbat ha-Gadol
Literally "the great Sabbath." The Sabbath preceding the festival of Passover. A day on which it was customary for rabbis to deliver sermons to their congregants regarding the festival.

SHAI
Acronym for *Sherut Yediot* — "information service." The intelligence service of the *Haganah*, established in 1940. *SHAI* contributed greatly to the *Yishuv* in its struggle for *aliyah*, arms acquisition, and sabotage of British army and police installations during the War of Independence, until the establishment of the intelligence branch of the IDF.

Shavuot
Literally the "Feast of Weeks." The second of the three Pilgrim Festivals, celebrated on the 6th day of *Sivan* (the Jewish month coinciding with June), ending a period of seven weeks (hence its name) counted from the first day of Passover. Also called *Hag ha-Kazir* (Harvest Festival) because in biblical times crops were harvested at this season, and *Hag ha-Bikkurim* (Festival of First-fruits) because the first fruits of the land were brought at this time to the Holy Temple. According to tradition, the *Torah* was given on this day, and therefore the holiday is also called *Yom Mattan Torah* (Day of the Giving of the Law). Holiday traditions include reading the *Book of Ruth*, decoration of synagogues and homes with greenery, and eating dairy products.

Shekel, Shkalim
The official Hebrew name for Israel's currency. Also, traditional contribution to Zionist movement, purchasing right to vote.

Shelihim
Literally "emissaries." Members of the organized Jewish community in Ereẓ Israel during the Mandate period, who were sent by the *Yishuv* to countries of the Diaspora in order to assist Jews in immigrating to Ereẓ Israel.

Shema Yisrael
"Hear, O, Israel." One of three passages in the *Torah* which Jews are obliged to read in *shaharit* (morning prayers) and *'arvit* (evening prayers) before the *shemoneh esreh* (Eighteen Benedictions): "Hear, O, Israel: the Lord our God, the Lord is One" (*Deut.* 6:3) and before retiring to bed. These words were the last utterance of Jewish martyrs before their death, and have become a hallowed watchword of the Jewish people.

Shemittah
The Sabbatical Year. In practice, an ordinance in the *Torah*, forbidding one to work the soil on the last year in a cycle of seven years. On this year there is also a remission of debts.

Shephelah
A low, mildly hilly region in central Ereẓ Israel, separating the highlands from the coastal plain. The *Shephelah* has some plain areas suitable for agriculture. Since time immemorial the *Shephelah* has been a place of strategic importance, situated on the crossroads between north and south and between east and west.

Shevirah
See — Lurianic *Kabbalah.*

Shofar
The horn of a ram or an ibex, formerly blown on holy days and festivals, and today blown in the synagogue. During the time of the Temple the *shofar* was blown as part of the sacrificial service and on various festive occasions. It was also used for summoning the people or terrifying an enemy. In modern times the *shofar* is blown throughout the Jewish month of *Elul* (the Jewish month coinciding with August), on the days of

selihot — special services preceeding the Jewish New Year and Day of Atonement, on the Jewish New Year, and at the closing service — *ne'ilah* — on the Day of Atonement. The sound of the *shofar* is intended to rouse the people to penance, and to open the gates of Heaven to prayer and mercy.

Shtetl
The Yiddish term for a small-town Jewish community in Eastern Europe.

Shulhan Arukh
A standard Jewish halakhic code, comprising laws and customs applicable to the individual and to the community, based on the written *Torah* and the Oral Law, and the responsa of *geonim* and *posekim* (rabbis who ruled on questions of *halakhah*). The author of the book was Joseph Caro (1488-1575), born in Toledo, Spain. After the expulsion of the Jews from Spain he migrated to Istanbul, and from there to Safed in Erez Israel. The book was written in Erez Israel, and first printed in Venice in 1565. The *Shulhan Arukh* was accepted by all the communities of Spain and the East as a binding legislative work; but all the Jewish communities of *Ashkenaz* opposed it because, according to them, it ignored the rulings of rabbis from *Ashkenaz*. However, after R. Moses Isserles (*Rema*) added his glosses to the book in his own works, *Darkhei Moshe* and the *Mappah*, the *Shulhan Arukh* also became accepted by the Jews of *Ashkenaz* as an authoritative codification of Jewish practice.

Solel Boneh
Literally "paves and builds." A road-building and construction company belonging to the *Histadrut*. During the riots of 1936-39, *Solel Boneh* helped build farm settlements, pave security roads, construct airfields and erect fortifications. During World War II it helped the British army pave roads and construct airfields, bridges, and army camps. *Solel Boneh* subsidiaries supply almost the entire Israeli national demand for stone, gravel, marble and cement, as well as most of its plumbing and bathroom fittings. The company employs a great many factory workers in its various enterprises. Its activities have even become international; since the 1960s considerable contract work has been carried out in Africa.

Sukkot
Literally "Feast of Tabernacles." A holiday celebrated in remembrance of the *sukkot* (booths or tabernacles) in which the Israelites dwelled after their Exodus from Egypt. The third of the three Pilgrim Festivals, it is celebrated for seven days, beginning on the 15th day of the month of *Tishri* (the Jewish month coinciding with September). In Erez Israel the eighth and last day is *Shemini Azeret*, a separate festival and *Simhat Torah* ("rejoicing in the Torah"). In the Diaspora, *Simhat Torah* is added as the ninth day. The most important *mitzvot* of the *Sukkot* festival are dwelling in the *sukkah*, and performing the blessing over the *lulav*. On *Simhat Torah* the cycle of the reading of the *Torah* in weekly portions is completed. The festival is also called the Feast of Ingathering, because at this time the last of the summer fruits are picked.

Ta'as — Ta'asiya Tzvait
Literally "military industry." An enterprise devoted to development and manufacture of weapons and munitions for the IDF and the defense establishment. Initiated in the aftermath of the anti-Jewish riots of 1921, when the need arose for guns and ammunition to arm the *Haganah*.

Takkanah — Takkanot
Laws, decisions, and temporary provisions, legislated by the great religious leaders of the Jewish people, such as Moses and the prophets, Ezra and the *Knesset ha-Gedollah*, the *Sanhedrin*, the *Tannaim*, and in later periods by Rabbenu Gershom *Me'or ha-Golah* and other rabbis. *Takkanot* for the Jewish community were established by Jewish communal institutions from the 10th century, when the Jewish community was an autonomous institution. These *takkanot* were made to regulate problems of life, in accordance with the needs of the hour. Best known are the *takkanot* of Speier, Worms, and Mayence, and the *takkanot* of the Council of the Four Lands.

Talmud
A body of teaching comprising the commentary and discussions of the *amoraim* on the *Mishnah*. It is a collection of the ordinances and laws, the beliefs and philosophy of Judaism, and is the product of more than 3,000 sages from various countries, over the first five hundred years of the Common Era. The *Talmud*, or the *Gemara* (Aramaic, "completion"), comprises religious laws, legislative proposals and material from the realms of law, medicine, health, and agriculture, as well as ethical affairs and philosophical treatises on the nature of God and the human soul. The rulings are presented in the form of the deliberations which took place among the sages until they reached a decision.

Until the redaction of the *Mishnah*, the center of talmudic work was Erez Israel where the Jerusalem *Talmud* was composed. After some time the center moved to Babylonia, where the Babylonian *Talmud*, larger in scope than the Jerusalem *Talmud*, was compiled.

Talmud-Torah
An educational institution, at the level of an elementary school. In such schools children were taught prayers, *Torah*, Prophets, and some *Gemara*. Unlike the *heder*, which was private, the *Talmud-Torah* was a public institution, financed by the Jewish community, and intended primarily for the poor.

Tanna-Tannaim
A term applied to the sages who took part in the creation of the *Mishnah*. Some scholars draw a distinction between early and later *tannaim*. The early *tannaim* were active from the time of Simeon the Just (2nd century BCE) until the time of Shammai and Hillel (a period of around 300 years), and the later *tannaim* from the time of the schools of Hillel and of Shammai until the redaction of the *Mishnah* by Rabbi Judah ha-Nasi. These *tannaim* are divided into pairs, five in all. Other scholars apply the name *tannaim* only to the latter group, which is divided into five generations. The sixth generation (approx. 200-220 CE) was the generation of transition between the *tannaim* and the *amoraim*, who lived and worked after them and whose opinions are recorded in the *Talmud*.

Tarbut
Literally "culture." An organization for the promotion of Hebrew culture, language, and literature, and its dissemination among the Jews of the Diaspora. The organization was active in Poland, Lithuania, Estonia, Rumania, Czechoslovakia, Bulgaria and elsewhere, during the period between the two world wars. It established a network of educational institutions for all ages and published books, periodicals, and newspapers. The Hebrew education (in Lithuania Hebrew was the language of instruction) and the Erez Israel atmosphere inspired many graduates of *Tarbut* schools to join pioneering Zionist youth movements.

Tell
An archaeological term denoting a man-made hill, built by successive levels of habitation, one over the other. Formed through the years by alternating eras of construction and destruction.

The Jewish Wars
A book written by Josephus Flavius (c. 37-100 CE). Virtually the only source of information on the history of the Jewish people during the late Second Temple period, and up to the Temple's destruction. Published between 75-79 CE. It was written in Greek in deference to the wishes of Emperor Vespasian, whose policies Flavius wished to support in repayment for the favors the Emperor had bestowed upon him.

Tikkunim — See Lurianic *Kabbalah*.

Torah (Pentateuch)
The first of the three groups of books of the *Tanach* (The Holy Scriptures), comprising five books: *Genesis, Exodus, Leviticus, Numbers, Deuteronomy*. (The other groups are Prophets and Writings.) According to Jewish belief, the *Torah* was given in writing to Moses at the Revelation on Mount Sinai; hence these books are called the Written, as opposed to the Oral Law.

Torah she-be-al Peh
Literally "Oral Law." Commentaries on the *Torah*, arranged in books called the *Mishnah* Anthology, the *Tosefta*, the *Talmud*, and the *Midrashic* litera-

ture. The Oral Law holds a very special, vital position in Jewish life, and was of crucial importance over the past generations in establishing the character of Jews and of Judaism. The origin of Oral Law derives from the fact that many laws and rules in the Written Law are either implicit or contradictory; since it was impossible to fulfill these laws according to their simple, literary meaning, commentaries were required.

Ulpan, Ulpanim
Total immersion adult immigrant schools for teaching the Hebrew language and fundamentals about Israeli culture.

Va'ad Leumi
Literally "National Committee." The administrative and executive body of the organized *Yishuv* in Ereẓ Israel during the time of the British Mandate. The *Va'ad* saw to internal affairs and security, and supplied services in the fields of education, culture, health, welfare, and religion. It also represented the *Yishuv* before the British authorities, dealt with recruiting volunteers for the British army during World War II, cared for the families of the conscripted, and helped rehabilitate discharged soldiers.

Via Maris
Latin; literally "The Way of the Sea" or the Coast Road. A section of an important ancient road traversing the Near East. The southern part of this road, the *Via Maris*, crossed Ereẓ Israel.

White Papers
Official reports issued by government commissions in Britain or British colonies. Six such documents were issued in Palestine between the years 1922 and 1939. The 1939 White Paper recommended to limit the sale of land to Jews, to limit *aliyah* to 75,000 people in five years, and within ten years to establish an independent Palestinian state where the essential interests of both Arabs and Jews would be safeguarded.

Yad va-Shem
Israel Martyrs' and Heroes' Remembrance Authority. A commemorative authority for the Jews of Europe slaughtered in the Nazi Holocaust, established on a hill in western Jerusalem, near Mt. Herzl. It serves as a center for Holocaust research and a repository for pictures, documents, and other testimony which provide an everlasting remembrance of the atrocities perpetrated by the Nazis.

Yeshiva — Yeshivot
Talmudic academies for advanced study in *Torah, Mishnah*, and *Talmud*. They date back to Ereẓ Israel during the time of the *Talmud*. The *Yeshiva* of Ereẓ Israel was established after the destruction of the Second Temple. It was the supreme institution in matters of Jewish law, and determined the *Halakhah* for Jews throughout the Diaspora. The *Yeshiva* inherited the place of the *Sanhedrin*. During the time of the *amoraim* the *Yeshiva* was located in Tiberias, where the Jerusalem *Talmud* was completed and the *masorah* redacted. Under the rule of the Christian emperors over Ereẓ Israel the status of the *Yeshiva* of Ereẓ Israel declined, until in 429 CE it ceased to exist, and the center of leadership passed to Babylonia.

In Babylonia, *yeshivot* existed from the 3rd until the 11th century. These *yeshivot* dominated the scene until the fifth century CE, at which time new centers of talmudic study emerged in North Africa and Europe.

Yeshivot also exist in modern days in various Jewish communities, primarily in Israel and in the United States.

Yihudim — See Lurianic *Kabbalah*.

Yishuv
Literally "settlement." The body of Jews settled in Ereẓ Israel, from the era of renewed Jewish settlement in the land in the days of the First *Aliyah* (1882), until the establishment of the State of Israel in 1948.

Yom Kippur
The Day of Atonement. A festival from the *Torah*, falling on the tenth day of *Tishri* (the Jewish month coinciding with September). On this day man is judged before God, and hence it is customary to observe it as a day of repentance, confession, abstinence, fasting, and prayer for forgiveness and pardon.

Ẓadik, Zadikkim
Literally, "a righteous one," a just and kind person, benevolent to mankind and fearing of God. In Jewish tradition the image of the righteous person has acquired a halo of mysticism. Jewish legend tells of the existence of 36 undisclosed *ẓadikkim*, whose righteousness is not known at large and generally is revealed by chance. These *ẓadikkim* have a place assured them in the Garden of Eden, where they will enjoy special rights and privileges which had not always been their lot in this world.

In Hasidism the *ẓadik* enjoys a special status. He is the channel through which the Divine abundance descends to earth. He serves as the mediator between the individual and the community, before God, and brings their prayers before Him. The hasidic *ẓadik* is considered to be a holy man, and is treated with honor, admiration, and self-denial on the part of his followers. Some *ẓadikkim* have also been considered miracle workers. It was customary for the *Hasidim* to visit the *ẓadik* at regular intervals, bringing "presents" with them for the support of the *ẓadik* and his household, and also to ask his advice in various matters.

Ẓe'irei Ẓion
Literally "The Young of Zion." A Zionist party, whose origins lay in Zionist youth organizations in cities of Russia, Galicia, and Rumania. The members of the party came to Ereẓ Israel in the Second *Aliyah*, and were among those who prepared the Third *Aliyah* and the *He-Halutz* movement. The party received great impetus during the Russian Revolution (1917), its membership reaching several tens of thousands in Eastern Europe alone. A faction of the party established *Ha-Poel ha-Zair* (1905) in Ereẓ Israel, which later united with *Ahdut ha-Avodah*, forming *Mifleget Poalei Ereẓ Israel (MAPAI)*, now the Labor Party.

Zerubavel
A Zionist organization founded in Odessa in 1883. It is named after the leader of the repatriates from Babylonia, who was also one of the rebuilders of the Second Temple. The organization essentially constituted the nucleus from which the broader popular movement of *Hovevei Zion* later emerged.

Zohar
Literally "splendor." The central work in the *Kabbalah*, constituting a mystical commentary on the Bible. It is attributed to R. Simeon bar Yohai, although a prevalent theory holds that the kabbalist Moses de Leon, who lived in 13th century Spain and who revealed the book, was also its author. The book is written in a unique Aramaic idiom which synthesizes the language of the *Talmudim* and the *Targumim* (Aramaic translations of the Bible). The work is comprised of several parts: the main *Zohar; Ha-Midrash ha-Ne'lam* ("The Concealed Midrash"); *Ra'ya Meheimna* ("The Faithful Shepherd") in which Moses converses with R. Simeon in Heaven; *Tikkunei ha-Zohar; Sefer ha-Zeni'ut* ("The Book of Concealment") which is attributed to the Patriarch, Jacob; *Idra Rabba* ("The Greater Assembly") in which R. Simeon b. Yohai revealed to his followers mysteries about the revelation of the Divine in the form of Primordial Man, and *Idra Zuta* ("The Lesser Assembly") describing the death of R. Simeon b. Yohai; passages of *Torah; Sava de Mishpatim* ("Discourse of the Old Man") in which R. Yeiva, an old man and great kabbalist, discourses on the theory of the soul; and *Raza de Razin* ("The Secret of Secrets") on physiognomy and chiromancy.

Zug — Zuggot
Literally "pairs." The term, from the Greek, denoting the two sages who headed the *Sanhedrin* and the *Beit ha-Din ha-Gadol* (High Court of Justice). One served as the *Nasi* of the *Sanhedrin*, and the other as the *Av Bet ha-Din*, or presiding judge.

Index

Page numbers in Roman type are references to text; bold numbers refer to illustrations or captions to illustrations.
Index Editor: Shefi Paz

Picture Credits

Special thanks to Ruth Porter of Beth Hatefutsoth, Irene Lewitt and Genya Markon of the Israel Museum, and Andrea Stern of Keter Publishing House.

Israel Museum, Jerusalem [photographers: D. Harris, N. Slepak, H. Sadeh, H. Burger, R. Milon, Z. Radovan, B. Rimon]: 10; 11; 15; 19; 22-1; 23-6, 8; 27-5; 28-1; 29-8; 31-8B; 32-3; 36-2, 3, 4A, B, D; 38-2, 3; 40-3; 41-6; 43-6; 44-2, 3; 46-2; 47-9; 49-key; 50-3; 51-key; 52-4; 53-key; 54-1, 2; 55-key, 6; 58-1; 59-7; 62-4; 75-7; 82-1, 2; 83-key, 5, 6; 87-6; 91-5, 8; 92-1, 3; 100-3; 102-3, 4; 103-8; 105-5, key; 108-3; 110-1, 4, 5; 111-6; 112-2; 113-key, 7, 9, 10; 116-4; 117-7; 123-key, 6, 8; 124-1A, 2, 3; 125-key, 6; 126-1B; 132-4; 133-key, 5A, 6, 8; 136-1; 137-8; 138-2 (photo Narinsky); 139-6 (photo Ben-Dov); 143-7 (photo Ben-Dov); 155-5; 176-2 (photo Rosner); 183-6 (photo Rosner); 193-9; 210-4 (photo Ben-Dov); 218-3; 219-6 (photo Ben-Dov), 7, 9; 225-8; 227-3; 228-7; 229-6, 10; 230-4; 231-2; 232-3, 5, 9, 10; 233-11, 12; 234-243 (photo D. Harris, Y. Hayibi, F. Brenner, A. Muller-Lancet)

Israel Department of Antiquities and Museums, Jerusalem (Photography, Israel Museum): 20-4, 5; 21-key, 6, 7, 8; 22-3, 5; 23-7, key; 25-5; 27-4, 7; 30-1, 3; 31-6, 7, 8A, key; 32-4; 33-7, 8; 34-1,3; 35-4; 37-5, 6, 7; 39-9; 41-7; 43-5B; 44-5; 46-4; 47-8; 48-2; 49-6, 7, 9; 54-3, 4; 90-3A

Beth Hatefutsoth, The Nahum Goldmann Museum of the Jewish Diaspora, Tel-Aviv: 58-3; 60-4; 61-key; 67-key, 6; 81-4, 7, 9; 86-2; 90-2; 98-2, 3; 100-2; 101-6; 103-6; 109-4, 8; 110-2 (photo: Jan Parik); 111-key; 116-1; 117-key; 122-3; 171-8; 173-4; 207-9; 214-2, 3, 5; 215-key, (photo: Natan Birk); 9, 10; 216-4, 5 (photo: Jan Parik); 217-7, 8 (photo: D. Bachar); 228-4; 229-3, 5; 231-6, 7; 232-1, 2, 10

By courtesy of Mary Black, N.Y and the Diaspora Museum (from the exhibition — Beyond the Golden Gate): Hadassah N.Y — 178-2; New York Historical Society — 128-1; Jewish Museum, N.Y — 131-8; Museum City of N.Y — 129-4; 130-4

"Ghetto Fighters" House in Memory of Yizhak Katznelson, Kibbutz Lohamei Haghetaot: 146-2; 147-key, 6; 160-2, 4; 161-7; 166-1; 215-6

Islam Museum, Jerusalem (photo: Y. Gal): 75-6

Maritime Museum, Haifa: 28-3; 39-8; 84-3

Mishkan le-Omanut, Ein Harod: 219-key

Reuven Rubin House, Tel Aviv: 2; 134-3

Tel Aviv Museum (photo: A. Hay): 96-4; 102-2; 107-6; 114-2; 178-3

Museum of Theater, Haaretz Museum, Tel Aviv: 154-1

Central Zionist Archives, Jerusalem: 116-2; 117-9; 120-1, 2, 3, 4 (photo Ben-Dov), 5; 121-key, 8, 9; 126-3; 133-5B; 134-4; 135-5, 6B, 7, 8; 138-4; 139-5, 7; 140-4 (photo S.J. Schweig), 5; 141-7, 8, 9 (photo Ben-Dov); 142-1A, 2, 3; 143-key, 6; 145-9; 148-3; 149-6; 151-key; 152-2, 4; 155-key, 9; 156-3; 171-6; 177-8; 179-8; 180-1, 2; 182-2

Central Archives for the History of the Jewish People, Jerusalem: 115-key; 178-1; 214-1

Haganah Archives, Tel Aviv: 144-1, 3; 145-key, 8; 150-3B; 157-key; 176-4; 182-3

Hamaccabi World Union Archives, Kefar Hamaccabia: 170-4; 171-5; 216-2

IZL Archives, Tel Aviv: 158-3; 159-7; 180-3

IDF Archives, Givatayim: 190-1, 5; 191-7; 194-3; 197-key; 198-3

The Jewish National and University Library, Jerusalem: 14; 65-7; 76-2; 83-8; 85-4 (photo: D. Harris); 86-4; 87-key; 89-key, 6, 8 (Jan Johnson, from Eran Laor collection); 95-4; 98-4; 106-1; 108-2; 109-key, 5, 7; 112-4; 113-8; 116-3; 123-5; 135-6A; 136-4; 137-key, 6; 143-8; 153-6, 8; 154-2; 174-3; 225-5; 228-4

Jewish National Fund Archives, Jerusalem: 135-9; 149-key (photo Dr. Tim Gidal); 178-4; 186-1

JDC Israel, Jerusalem: 213-7

Keren Hayesod Archives (U.J.A), Jerusalem: 112-1; 156-4

Institute for Labor Research in Memory of Pinhas Lavon, Tel Aviv: 140-3; 141-key; 144-2; 151-5; 154-3; 159-8

Yad Vashem Archives, Jerusalem: 146-3, 4; 160-1, 3; 161-5, 6, key; 166-5; 167-key, 6, 7, 8; 168-1, 3, 4; 169-key, 6, 7, 9

Bank Hapoalim: 209-5

Ben Gurion University, Beersheba: 207-8 (photo: E. Fefer); Archeology department 25-4 (courtesy: E. Oren)

Cameri Theater, Tel Aviv: 207-10

Dvir Publishing House: 115-5

Granot, Central Agriculture Cooperative Society: 210-3

Habimah National Theater: 155-8; 189-7

Hebrew Union College: 131-5, 217-key

Hebrew University, Jerusalem, Institute of Archaeology: 20-1 (courtesy: O. Bar-Yosef); 33-6 (courtesy: Y. Shilo); 45-key (courtesy: Y. Zafrir)

Holyland Hotel, Jerusalem: 46-1

Israel Exploration Society, Jerusalem: 46-5; 48-3; 51-6

Israel Philharmonic Orchestra, Tel Aviv: 207-6

Kibbutz Meffalsim Archives: 115-7

Kupat Holim, Department of Public Relations: 209-7

Massada Press Ltd.: 45-7A; 52-2

Menorah Club, Jerusalem (photo: Eyal Itzhar): 138-3

Schoken Institute, Jerusalem: 126-1A

Solel Boneh: 208-3

Tel Aviv University — Archeology department: 33-5A (courtesy: D. Ussishkin)

Yad Izhak Ben Zvi Institute, Jerusalem: 83-7, 170-3

Yavneh Publishing House: 24-3; 27-6

British Museum, London: 31-5, 33-5B (photo: A. Hay); 35-6; 36-4C; 37-key; 64-3; 223-7, 8; 224-1

The Brooklyn Museum, N.Y: 39-7; 58-2

Musée de Cluny, Paris: 88-3; 93-9

Musej Czrada, Sarajevo: 97-7

Guggenheim Museum, N.Y: © Estate of Mark Rothko, 1984: 213-5

Historisch Museum, Amsterdam: 87-5

Museé Lambinet, Versailles 235-8

Musée Nationale du Louvre, Paris: 22-4

Mansion House, City of York: 78-2

New Jersey State Museum, Trenton: 129-5

Museo del Prado, Madrid: 84-1

Jewish Museum, Prague: 95-6

Rijksmuseum, Amsterdam: 34-2

Semitic Museum, Massachusetts: 60-1

Städelsches Kunstinstitut, Frankfurt am Main: 86-3; 99-8

Stadtmuseum, Kassel (Courtesy: Beth Hatefutsoth): 103-key

Statens Museum fur Kunst, Kobenhavn: 99-6

Civici Musei Veneziani d'Arte e di Storia: 109-6

Victoria and Albert Museum, London (photo: Eileen Tweedy): 132-2

Yale University Art Gallery, New Haven: 58-4

Wallraf-Richartz Museums, Köln: 102-1

American Jewish Historical Society, Massachusetts: 128-2A

Atlas van Stolk, Rotterdam: 77-5

Basilica Concattedrale di S. Andrea Ap. Mantova: 79-5

Bezirkspital an der Drau, Kärnter, Austria: 71-5

Dargaud Editeur, Paris 217-6

Heinrich Heine Institut, Düsseldorf: 99-key

Patrimonio Nacional, Madrid: 71-8

Penguin Books, London: 118-4

Society of Friends of Touro Synagogue, Newport: 86-1

Bibliotheque et Archives de l'Alliance Israelite Universelle, Paris: 114-1

Bibliotheque Municipale, Amiens: 70-1c

Bibliotheca Ambrosiana, Milano: 73-7

Bayerische Staatsbibliothek, München: 94-2

Bodleian Library, Oxford: 68-1 (224-3); 81-8

Bibliotheque Nationale, Paris: 53-6; 61-8; 68-4; 70-1B; 74-1; 76-3; 90-4; 97-5; 223-10

Bibliotheca Rosenthaliana, Amsterdam: 87-7, 8

Biblioteca Apostolica Citta del Vaticano: 94-1, 3
Bibliotheque Royale, Bruxelles: 72-1; 79-key
British Library, London: 64-3 (224-1); 90-1; 95-5; 136-2; 223-7
Cambridge University Library: 64-1; 66-1
Hessische Landes- und Hochschulbibliothek, Darmstadt: 71-key
Library of Congress, Washington: 91-key; 212-2
Det Kongelige Bibliothek, Kobenhavn: 77-6
Universität Bremen Bibliothek: 59-8
National Library, Leningrad: 65-5
Österreichische Nationalbibliothek: 71-7
Staats- und Universitätsbibliothek, Hamburg: 41-5; 72-5; 73-6; 79-7
Universität Bibliotheque, Leipzig: 72-4; 73-key, 9
Staatsbibliothek Preussischer Kulturbesitz, Berlin: 124-4
Zentralbibliothek, Zürich: 93-key

American Jewish Archives, Cincinnati: 128-3
Archivo Historica Provincial, Avila: 79-6a
Archivo Historico Nacional, Madrid: 85-key
Archivo general de Simancas, Valladolid: 85-5
Yivo Institute for Jewish Research, NY: 122-2, 4

The publisher wishes to thank the collectors and artists who have so kindly allowed their work to appear in this book.

Hanah Amram, Rehovot: 137-7
Max Berger, Vienna: 105-3; 115-6
Gabi Dabara, Herzliyyah: 150-1; 152-3
Yitzchak Einhorn, Tel Aviv: 81-key (photo: R. Erda), 6; 93-8; 104-2; 107-5; 124-1B; 139-8; 240-4; 241-2, 3, 9
Zussia Efron: 107-key; 230-8
Isaar Feder: 165-5
Israel Finkelstein: 26-3; 27-key
By Courtesy of Yona Fischer, Jerusalem: 141-6; 149-5
Samuel Givon, Tel Aviv: 148-1; 211-6
Avraham Hatal: 171-key
Isaac Meir Heschel, The Zaddik of Medzibezh, Haifa: 240-1
Ida Huberman: 96-1
Edward Ishellaum: 164-4
Shmuel Katz, kibbutz Ga'aton: 158-2
Franz Krausz, Tel Aviv: 145-7 (courtesy of A. Shamir); 149-7 (courtesy D. Tartakover); 153-5 (courtesy of Yona Fischer); 174-4, 7; 175-key
Daniel Levinson, Nahariya: 130-1
Rina Nehar-Berenheim: 118-3
Avi Nesher and Yitzhak Zhaeik, Tel Aviv: 157-8; 159-5
Zeev Raban: 152-3
Edgar F. Rebner, N.Y (photo: Israel Museum): 101-5A
Alfred Rubens, London: 101-key
Gabriel Secal, Spain: 76-1
Gerard Silvan, Paris: 98-1; 105-6; 107-3; 112-6; 127-key; 129-key
Zionah Tadjar, 148-1; 155-7
David Tartakover, Tel Aviv: 202-4
Courtesy of D. Tartakover: 175-6B (R. Sidner); 179-key (Paul Kor); 187-8B; 208-4 (Shamir Brothers)
Nahum Yuda-Levi "Ginzei Yemen", Rishon Le-Zion: 93-6
Samuel Zilbiger, Benei Brak: 240-6

Photographers:

Bar-David Photo Agency: 213-8; 217-9
Werner Braun, Jerusalem: 20-2; 22-2; 30-4; 33-key; 37-8A; 40-4; 44-4; 45-6B; 46-1; 47-key, 6; 48-4, 5; 50-1; 51-5, 8; 54-5; 55-7B; 56-2; 57-key, 6, 7; 63-5, 7; 64-4; 65-6; 88-1, 2; 89-7
Theodor Cohen, N.Y: 130-3; 131-7; 179-7, 9; 213-key
Government Press Office, Jerusalem: 41-key; 55-7A; 90-3B; 132-1; 133-7; 142-1B; 144-4; 147-7; 172-1, 3B (photo Kluger); 173-key, 5 (photo Pin, poster: F. Krausz), 8 (photo Kluger); 179-6; 180-4; 181-key, 9 (photo H. Pin); 184-1, 2, 4; 185-key, 7, 9; 186-2, 3, 4; 187-key, 6, 7; 188-2, 3, 4, 5; 189-6B, 8, 9; 190-2; 191-key, 8; 192-3, 4; 193-key, 5, 8; 194-1A; 195-5, 6, 9 (photo D. Rubinger); 196-1, 2; 197-7; 198-2, 4; 199-key, 5, 6, 8; 200; 201; 202-1, 5; 203-key, 6, 7, 9; 204-1A (photo Kluger), 1B, 3; 205-4B, 5, 6; 206-1, 5; 207-key; 208-1, 2 (photo H. Pin); 209-6, 8; 210-1B; 211-7; 215-8
Alex Gal, Tel Aviv: 194-4; 195-7; 198-1
Devorah Gruda, Tel Aviv: 189-6A; 206-2; 211-8
Abraham Hay: 16; 24-1; 25-6, key; 31-5; 33-5B; 6; 62-3; 142-4; 158-1; 176-3; 177-key; 183-7; 205-key, 4A; 206-4; 210-2; 211-5; 228-1; 230-5
Eyal Itzhar, Jerusalem: 157-5; 190-3; 197-6; 202-3; 218-4; 219-8; 220, 264
Ruth Kalusky, Kibbutz Revivim: 175-6A
David Katzir, Kibbutz Dafna: 195-key
Garo Nalbandian: 38-1, 4; 45-6A; 47-7; 74-3
Palphot: 42-3; 75-key; 88-5; 204-2
Ze'ev Radovan, Jerusalem: 45-7B; 62-2; 132-3; 223-2
Riki Rosen, N.Y: 212-1, 3, 4
Ami Shamir, Rehovot: 69-key, 5; 77-key, 4; 194-1B, 2
Oskar Tauber, Haifa: 192-2

Maps, Diagrams and Illustrations

Carta, Jerusalem: 24-2; 26-2; 29-5; 32-2; 35-5; 36-1; 39-6; 40-1; 42-1; 44-1; 53-5; 59-6; 66-3; 69-6; 71-6; 75-5; 78-3; 80-3; 82-3; 104-1; 106-2; 111-7; 127-6; 137-5; 148-2; 164-2; 168-4; 191-6
Dalia and Menahem Egozi: 143-5; 156-1; 171-7; 172-2; 181-8; 183-5; 185-6; 195-8; 196-4; 199-7
Roma Annenburg: 28-4; 29-8
Ehud Oren: 21-9; 25-4; 26-1; 29-key, 6; 30-2; 32-1; 38-5; 43-7; 48-1; 60-2A; 61-5, 6; 63-key, 6; 66-2; 67-4; 74-2; 83-4; 89-9; 91-6; 95-key; 99-7; 107-4; 114-3; 121-6; 125-5; 126-2; 127-4; 129-6; 131-key; 147-6; 149-4; 150-2; 172-3A; 175-5; 188-1; 189-key; 193-7; 196-3; 197-8; 202-2; 203-8; 209-key